CONTEMPORARY BLACK DRAMA

CONTEMPORARY BLACK DRAMA

From **A RAISIN IN THE SUN**

to *NO PLACE TO BE SOMEBODY*

Selected and Edited with Introductions by

Clinton F. Oliver
Queens College

Stephanie Sills
Co-editor

CHARLES SCRIBNER'S SONS   NEW YORK

5 7 9 11 13 15 17 19 H/C 20 18 16 14 12 10 8 6 4

Printed in the United States of America
SBN684-41432-5
Library of Congress Catalog Card Number 77-132574

ACKNOWLEDGMENTS

On this and the following page, which constitutes an extension of the copyright
page, acknowledgment is gratefully made to the following publishers, agents,
and individuals who have permitted the use of their materials in copyright:

The Bobbs-Merrill Company, Inc. for *No Place to Be Somebody* by Charles
Gordone. Copyright © 1969 by Charles Gordone. Reprinted by permission of
the publishers, The Bobbs-Merrill Company, Inc.

Ed Bullins—Resident Playwright at The New Lafayette Theatre for *The Gentleman Caller* by Ed Bullins. Copyright 1968 by Ed Bullins.

The Dial Press, Inc. for *Blues for Mister Charlie* by James Baldwin. Copyright
© 1964 by James Baldwin. Used by permission of the publisher, The Dial
Press, Inc.

Dramatists Play Service, Inc. for *Happy Ending* and *Day of Absence* by Douglas
Turner Ward. Copyright © 1966 by Douglas Turner Ward. Reprinted by permission of the author and of Dramatists Play Service, Inc.

Caution: *Happy Ending* and *Day of Absence* being duly copyrighted, are subject
to a royalty. The amateur acting rights in both plays are controlled exclusively

This book is for
Phyllis R. Oliver
Carroll Phyllis Oliver
and for William Penn Mc Donald—
scholar, mentor, friend

PERSONAL ACKNOWLEDGMENTS

It is a pleasure to acknowledge my indebtedness and appreciation to those who in the progress of this book afforded sustenance and aid. Mr. James Harmon and Miss Susan Kornit of Charles Scribner's Sons were always helpful and faithful. I am deeply indebted to a number of my colleagues at Queens College of the City University of New York but especially to Professors Helene Brewer, Malcolm Goldstein, Myron Matlaw, William Green, Michael Timko, Stanley Friedman, and to Mr. Thomas Kotarski. I am also indebted to my students at Queens College, The State University of Iowa, and the University of Chicago who helped me to clarify and strengthen my ideas on black thought and literature in the United States as a subject for serious appraisal, and as a subject of fundamental significance to the urgencies of our day.

C.F.O.
FLUSHING, N.Y., 1971

CONTENTS

Introduction   3

A RAISIN IN THE SUN
Lorraine Hansberry   27

Purlie Victorious
Ossie Davis   121

FUNNYHOUSE OF A NEGRO
Adrienne Kennedy   187

DUTCHMAN
LeRoi Jones   207

xi

Blues for Mister Charlie
James Baldwin   233

Happy Ending
and Day of Absence
Douglas Turner Ward   315

The Gentleman Caller
Ed Bullins   365

NO PLACE TO BE SOMEBODY
Charles Gordone   381

CONTEMPORARY BLACK DRAMA

AN INTRODUCTORY ESSAY
THE NEGRO AND THE AMERICAN THEATER
by Clinton F. Oliver[1]

"The blacks enter, prepared to honor the wonder of their lives; they are cocksure (and strong) and speak to what has been salvaged in a continuing struggle . . . address a people's survival, encourage the demise of dead forms and actions . . . shouting a new life into choked channels of expression . . . celebrating the end of useless disciplines, blowing hard riffs of renaissance with strong lungs filling legend and fable-bound horns. Black hands caress the bass that thumps the rich/warm issues of the heart, Blood reigns . . . and Black hands bring showers out of golden cymbals—to-ta-ting, to-ta-ting. . . . Black pianos screaming crazy in the middle of all the shadows, tickled ivories awaken sleepy hearts, finger tips trip lightly toward melody and remembrance. Such things as may serve us, move us away from dying (there is no death we have not experienced), such as Langston Hughes must have known: '*I am the singer and the song.*' Right on."[1]

Thus Clayton Riley, a young black critic, writing recently on *A Black Quartet,* a program of plays by Ben Caldwell, Ron Milner, Ed Bullins, and Le-Roi Jones, could sing of the aims and aspirations of the new black theater, and by inference present a statement of significance on the entire new Black Arts Movement. One notes at once the rhapsodic quality basic to this statement. There is something apocalyptic in the quintessential ecstasy of its belief

---

1. Clayton Riley, *Theater Review,* "A Black Quartet," *Liberator* (September, 1969), 21.

3

and in the celebration of its vision. There is an unmistakable fire derived from a glimmering realization of a dream deferred. The expression is bardic: the expression of the poet-critic-seer, looking into the deep recesses of a national experience with wariness and hope. Also there is something peculiarly black in the cadenced prose as it combines in a single texture the rhythms and fervor of the old Negro sermon with its typical repetition and incremental shout and current idioms dug out of the jazz experience as they contribute to the shaping of the black man's daily parlance. And for the purpose of this introduction, I could think of no better way to open a discussion of the new black theater and some of its playwrights than by invoking, out of a number of possibilities, the words of a particular young writer deeply engaged in its progress and in its basic concerns.

Immediately, however, there come to mind two generalizations which, in order to arrive at a proper perspective on our subject, have to be superimposed upon this initial statement. The first is that the black American, as in other aspects of our national life, was in the American theater long before he was a genuine part of it. The second is that the notion of a black theater with black playwrights, actors, composers, musicians, and technicians, founded primarily to serve the cultural needs of the black community and to express its life, was an idea with a traceable history long before it became anything approaching a verifiable reality.

Where the rise of an autochthonous American theater is concerned, it has been generally recognized that, in addition to such native types as the Indian aborigines (see James Nelson Barker's *The Indian Princess,* 1808) and the virtuous Yankee as opposed to Europeanized "gentleman" (see Royal Tyler's *The Contrast,* 1787), and the new world city tough, "the B'hoy" (see Benjamin A. Baker's *A Glance at New York,* 1848), the most indigenous American stage type was the American Negro.

"Negro minstrelsy," writes Myron Matlaw, summarizing the situation of the Negro stage type in the early American theater, "probably began in the 1820's with T. D. Rice and his 'Jim Crow' song and shuffle routine in which the infant Joseph Jefferson III made one of his first stage appearances. By the 1840's such black face troupes as those of Dan Emmett and E. P. Christy offered full evening entertainments in major theaters. Later in the century came such famous minstrels as McIntyre and Heath and Lew Dockstader in whose troupe Al Jolson began his career."[2] Minstrelsy and its aftermath are succinctly described in the following terms: "In the first part of the minstrel show the entertainers, grouped in a semicircular lineup, featured singing and a comic repartee among the two end men (Tambo and Bones) and the Interlocutor; the second part, the olio, was somewhat like the old vaudeville finales, and concluded with a travesty (called 'burlesque') of one of the currently popular plays, including the Shakespearean and other prenineteenth-century drama that provided most of the theatrical staple. Scripts of such burlesques are still extant, and they furnish an interesting glimpse

2. Myron Matlaw, *The Black Crook and Other Nineteenth-Century American Plays* (New York: E. P. Dutton and Co., 1967), p. 14.

into the theatre of the age. The minstrel, played by white actors in blackface, was a native stage character as romantically (or unrealistically) conceived as other type characters—shiftless but jolly and good-natured. He is the only native nineteenth-century stage character, however, who remained theatrically intact well into our century. He found his way into much nineteenth-century drama, including [Dion Boucicault's] *The Octoroon* [1859] and the . . . most popular of all American plays, George L. Aiken's 1852 dramatization of *Uncle Tom's Cabin*."[3]

There can be no question that minstrels, once the blacks had themselves engaged in them, provided the first professional training ground for the black man in the American theater. James A. Bland, the composer whose most famous song is "Carry Me Back to Old Virginny," was a minstrel man for years before he became a star, singing his songs without the aid of blackface on the concert and recital stage in England and in the United States. Years later, W. C. Handy, "the father of the blues," composer of "St. Louis Blues," began his career as the head of the band for Mahara's Minstrels.

The minstrel tradition, long a-dying, was carried from the stage to the motion pictures, with Al Jolson in the first talking picture playing *The Jazz Singer,* and more ostentatiously in roles given not only to Stepin Fetchit, Willie Best, and Mantan Moreland, but those also assigned to Louise Beavers, to Clarence Muse, to Bill "Bojangles" Robinson, Ethel Waters, Hattie McDaniel, Butterfly McQueen, and even up to a point to Lena Horne. As Langston Hughes puts it, there was a gradual decline in minstrelsy after the advent of motion pictures: "Large groups of performers in blackface ceased to exist. However, individual entertainers, both colored and white, continued to work under cork in vaudeville for many years. Bert Williams, the great Negro comic, performed in blackface until his death in 1922. With white comedians the tradition continued until Eddie Cantor died in 1964. Among the whites who continued to entertain in blackface long after the death of the minstrels were Al Jolson, Frank Tinney, Lou Holtz, George Jessel, Moran and Mack as the Two Black Crows, Tess Gardella as Aunt Jemima, and Amos and Andy in radio and television for some forty years."[4]

With an eye to the main chance, making a smart profit on Negro materials, white minstrels in blackface were on the scene for a quarter of a century before the first Negro minstrels made their appearance. Lew Johnson's Plantation Minstrel Company entered the field in 1852. Despite their color, black minstrels followed the custom of the whites, blackening their faces and circling their lips with blazing red or white. With the black minstrels, however, something new also came into the theatrical arena—a richly authentic quality of imitation and caricature, a riotous freedom in the movement of the dances, a new beat in the songs, and new materials, hitherto unappropriated by the whites. Wallace King, Charles Cruso, and the Bohee Brothers were among the early stars of Negro minstrelsy.

3. *Ibid.*
4. Langston Hughes and Milton Metzer, *Black Magic* (Englewood Cliffs, New Jersey: Prentice Hall, 1967), p. 28.

Billy Kersand and Sam Lucas were the stars of Charles Hicks' Georgia Minstrels, a black company organized in 1865. So successful was this company that it was put under the management of Charles Callender, a white manager, and for a number of years it enjoyed a highly successful tour of the United States. An equally successful tour of Europe followed when the company assumed the name of Haverly's European Minstrels. Sam Lucas, it should be noted, played the title role in the first motion picture version of *Uncle Tom's Cabin,* in 1915.

Other successful Negro minstrel companies were formed by Richards and Pringle, Hicks and Sawyer, and McCabe and Young. In 1893, an innovation appeared when Primrose and West organized the first mixed minstrel company in this country, The Forty Whites and the Thirty Blacks.

American minstrelsy, based originally on the plantation entertainments of the slaves—with their rhythmic music, dancing, song, and badinage—first for their own diversion and then frequently full of satire for the amusement of their masters, and upon the performances of free Negroes in the northern and southern cities, was as Edith J. R. Isaacs says "our first authentic American theatre form."[5] Soon broadened into gross caricature, it was nonetheless discovered, upon serious study, to be a highly ritualistic form of art. (The subterranean African remnants in its rites still need to be explored.) On the social level, the widespread popularity among whites suggests that it somehow satisfied some deep-seated fantasy of white audiences which gave sanction to certain aspects of their past, including the enslavement of the African in all of its ramifications, and settling notions on the relations between blacks and whites in the modern world. It was, can we say, a form of assuagement and catharsis for unrecognized, and possibly recognized, feelings of guilt. The fact, however, that blacks, once they were admitted to theaters where black minstrels performed, showed an equal enthusiasm for the form asserts something of the validity of the minstrels in saying important things to black men on the black experience in this country. And this is worth more than passing notice.

There are those, however, who regard the minstrel tradition in the American theater as a negative genre. Sterling Brown, the eminent Negro critic, for instance, could say: "Though black-face minstrelsy started out with rudimentary realism, it soon degenerated into fantastic artificiality. It must be remembered that Ethiopian minstrelsy was white masquerade; Negro performers were not allowed to appear in it until after the Civil War; it was composed by whites, acted and sung by whites in burnt cork for white audiences. It succeeded in fixing one stereotype deeply in the American consciousness: the shiftless, lazy, improvident, loud-mouthed, flashily dressed Negro, with kinky hair and large lips, overaddicted to the eating of watermelon and chicken (almost always purloined), the drinking of gin, the shooting of dice and the twisting of language into ludicrous malformations. Life was a perennial joke or 'breakdown.' Black-face minstrelsy underestimated

5. Edith J. R. Isaacs, *The Negro in the American Theatre* (New York: Theatre Arts, Inc., 1947), p. 27.

and misrepresented the American Negro in much the same way that the English drama treated the stage Irishman."[6]

But the cultural historian, Constance Rourke, in her important *The Roots of American Culture* could take a deeper and more functional view of the minstrel shows. Maintaining—as a basic aspect of her anthropological approach to cultural history—that no art could speak a world language without an inheritance of local expression behind it, she accepted the views of the German romantic, Herder, who held that the folk forms were essential in any communal group since they formed the texture of communal experience and expression. The fine arts she maintained grew out of the folk arts and one had to study them in order to discover the source of any culture.[7] So in a short piece on the minstrel shows, "Traditions for a Negro Literature," she could hold that "This improbable medium provides the outlines of a Negro tradition, broken though it often was by alien elements."[8] She could note that minstrelsy has long been considered a white man's travesty in which the black man was burlesqued. She goes on to remark, "To the primitive comic sense to be black is to be funny, and many minstrels made the most of the simple appeal. This exploitation was resented by the anti-slavery leaders of an early period; in the end they went far in creating the idea that the Negro lacked humor. After the Civil War it would still have been possible to reveal the many-sided Negro of the old plantations, but minstrelsy with its air of irreverence seems to have blocked the way. Because the minstrels had sported with the Negro and had sentimentalized his lot in a few songs, because of his tragic fate and a wish to prove that he possessed moral worth, dignity, and capacity, for the time at least his friends collected and discussed and displayed only his religious pieces. None the less, early minstrelsy offered a rounded portraiture which is only now coming into a genuine completion."[9]

Against the partisan conclusion of writers like S. Foster Damon that no Negro materials exist in the minstrel tradition, Constance Rourke demonstrated, as Stanley Edgar Hyman points out, that all classic white minstrel compositions were borrowings: that Dan Emmet's "Old Dan Tucker," for instance, was either Negro-derived or wholly of Negro origin, with a Negro-type tune, a Negro shout choral effect, and a content of cryptic Negro animal fables about the jay bird and the bulldog. Similarly "Turkey in the Straw" is certainly a Negro dance song, and Dan Rice's "Clar de Kitchen" is an animal fable in which the Negro triumphs. She also demonstrated that "the ritual forms and conventions of the minstrel, its dance routines, its cries added to its musical and anecdotal material, were all of Negro origin or Negro-derived." Miss Rourke concluded that "much of the Negro material preserved in a distorted and offensive form in the minstrel shows had been preserved

6. Sterling Brown, "The Negro in the American Theatre," *The Oxford Companion to the Theatre,* 2nd ed. (London: The Oxford University Press, 1957), p. 566.
7. Constance Rourke, *The Roots of American Culture.* Edited with a Preface by Van Wyck Brooks (New York: Harcourt, Brace and Co., 1942), pp. 263-264.
8. *Ibid.,* p. 264.
9. *Ibid.*

nowhere else, and it could be lifted from the minstrel setting, cleansed and refurbished, to form a vital tradition for American Negro literature."[10]

In regard to Miss Rourke's prognosis it is interesting to note that the minstrel tradition has been richly refurbished in the new black theater of the 1960's. In 1965 the San Francisco Mime Troupe with an interracial cast presented a new kind of minstrel show entitled *Civil Rights in a Cracker Barrel,* based upon original, traditional, and improvised material, thus converting an old art form into a vehicle for anger and satire. Douglas Turner Ward's *Day of Absence* presents blacks in white make-up and is designated as a minstrel show in reverse, and Ossie Davis's *Purlie Victorious* can be read in the same light. A redemption of the old form to new meanings is clearly the intent of LeRoi Jones's *Great Goodness of Life* which he parenthetically calls *A Coon Show.* And there are unquestionably elements of the minstrel underlying Ed Bullins's strangely moving *Gentleman Caller.*

II

That the black man showed an interest in the activities of what we have come to call the legitimate theater—hybrid as it was in its emergence in the United States—is illustrated by the careers of James Hewlett and Ira Aldridge. Both of these men were inspired by performances and productions of Shakespeare and other classic plays that they saw from their segregated seats in the balcony of the Park Theatre. As early as 1821, antedating the rise of Negro minstrels by some forty years, the semi-professional African Company, of which Hewlett was a leading figure, presented *Othello, Richard III,* and other classics interspersed with comic acts, at the African Grove Theater, on the corner of Bleecker and Mercer Streets in lower New York. Later, having enjoyed a certain prosperity, the company hired the *hotel* next door to the Grove for its performance. James Hewlett was highly popular as the first Negro Othello, setting a precedent for Ira Aldridge, Paul Robeson, William Marshall, James Earle Jones, Moses Gunn, and other black actors who were to essay the role. The African Company played mainly to black audiences, but as a contemporary newspaper notice reads, "They . . . graciously made a partition at the back of the house for whites." This paper also states that the attendance of whites who came to deride the performers and to throw bottles eventually forced the theater to close. But there is evidence that the theater reopened and continued to give performances until 1823.[11]

Ira Frederick Aldridge, who was to become one of the world's great tragedians, and the first international Afro-American star, saw Hewlett's Othello and was inspired by the African Company as well as by what he had seen at the Park Theatre. Born in New York City, July 24, 1807, Aldridge began his education at the African Free School not far from the African Grove Theater. While yet a boy he made his first appearance on the stage as the hero of Sheridan's *Pizarro,* presented in a private theater with an all-Negro

10. Stanley Edgar Hyman, *The Armed Vision* (New York: Alfred A. Knopf, 1948), p. 131-132.

11. See James Weldon Johnson, *Black Manhattan* (New York: Alfred Knopf, 1930), pp. 78-80.

cast. He worked for a while, possibly as a call boy, at the Chatham Theater, where behind the scenes he could see and hear the actors perform their roles. His father, the prominent Presbyterian minister of the Greene Street Chapel, frowned, of course, upon the theater, and in due course sent his son to the school he had attended, Schenectady College, and then to the University of Glasgow to pursue studies in theology. At Glasgow he made a notable record as a scholar, winning several prizes and the medal for Latin composition. After a year and a half, he abandoned his studies and went to London where he managed, after considerable difficulty, to appear as Othello at the Royalty, an East End theater. At the Coburg he was to be seen in *Oroonoko* and other plays. From the Coburg he went to Sadler's Wells. Determined to improve his acting technique and his stature as an artist, he set out upon a tour of the provinces playing a variety of roles in such places as Brighton, Chichester, Leicester, Liverpool, Manchester, Glasgow, Edinburgh, and Exeter. In 1833 he made a highly successful appearance at Covent Garden in *Othello,* with Ellen Tree playing Desdemona.

Edmund Kean, one of the greatest actors of his day, saw Aldridge's Othello in Dublin and engaged him to play the Moor to his Iago. In this vehicle they toured England and the continent for two years. Othello was Aldridge's favorite and most applauded role, but he also delighted in the role of Aaron, the Moor, in *Titus Andronicus,* and in Macbeth, Shylock, and Lear, played in white make-up. His success in the British Isles was indisputably great, but it was on the continent that he gained his widest recognition. He became an intimate friend of Alexander Dumas. Showered with honors, he was admitted to a number of learned societies and among other distinctions, the Order of Chevalier was conferred upon him by the King of Prussia, the Cross of Leopold by the Czar of Russia, the Golden Order of Service from the royal house of Saxony. In 1865 Aldridge made his final appearance in London, at the Haymarket Theater, once more as Othello, with the brilliant Mrs. Kendal, at the threshold of her career, as his Desdemona. Aldridge died in Lodz, Poland, while on his way to St. Petersburg, on the seventh of August, 1867, and was given a civic funeral. Just prior to his death he had completed plans for an American tour. It is interesting to conjecture what kind of reception this serious black actor would have received in his native land.

In the fourth row of stalls of the Shakespearean Memorial Theatre at Stratford on Avon, there stands the Ira Aldridge Memorial Chair established through the auspices of James Weldon Johnson and other Afro-American admirers of Aldridge's accomplishments. Johnson, however, in *Black Manhattan,* maintains that Aldridge "was a sport; his career was in no degree a factor in the Negro's theatrical development."[12] And he goes on to comment, "In a less degree did the efforts made at the African Grove Theater have any consequent effects."[13] His point is, of course, that an abidingly original and innovating theatrical force was to come with the rise of Negro minstrels.

12. *Ibid.,* p. 87.
13. *Ibid.*

This cannot be gainsaid. The fact remains, however, that many theater groups and societies have been named in Aldridge's honor, and that the Ira Aldridge Society in the United States was founded "to advance the cultural cooperation of people of all colors and creeds." Aldridge functions, as does the African Grove Theater, as a lege .dary force serving the devotees of the new black theater in terms of their aspirations and their realities, their struggles and their hopes.

III

Where the black theater in the United States is concerned, a new era was ushered in when black artists, not altogether freed of the minstrel tradition, set out consciously to alter what they considered to be its deleterious effects. This gave rise to the production of early Negro musicals, the first of which was Bob Cole's *A Trip to Coontown* (1898) starring Sam Lucas who had been a popular stage figure in *Uncle Tom's Cabin*. This play was probably the first all-Negro musical comedy, the first musical show in America to be entirely produced, directed, and managed by blacks. The early Negro musicals such as Sam T. Jack's *Creole Show* (1890), John W. Isham's *The Octoroons* (1895), and *Oriental America* (1896), made innovations in the Negro theater, the major aspect of which was the introduction of a chorus of beautiful colored girls, replacing the older male minstrel chorus. They used trained musicians such as the young composer, J. Rosamond Johnson, whose original compositions were used alongside classical materials and operatic arias. J. Rosamond Johnson composed, sang, and acted in a number of musicals, including *Shoofly Regiment* (1906) and *Red Moon* (1908).

In the summer of 1898 Will Marion Cook composed the music for *Clorindy—The Origin of the Cake Walk*—with lyrics by Paul Laurence Dunbar. *Clorindy* starred the great minstrel, Ernest Hogan, and Belle Davis, and soon became the talk of the town. Its choruses and finales were brilliant. It was the first musical to reveal the possibilities of Negro syncopated music, ragtime, for dramatic use in the musical theater.

When *In Dahomey* opened in 1902 in the heart of Broadway at the New York Theater in Times Square, George Walker and Bert Williams emerged as the top stars of the Negro theatrical world. In the spring of 1903 *In Dahomey* was taken to London where it ran successfully for seven months at the Shaftesbury Theatre, and went on to tour the provinces. A command performance was given at Buckingham Palace, on June 23. *In Dahomey* made the cakewalk the social rage, not only in the United States but also in England and France. Other successful Williams and Walker musicals were *Abyssinia* (1906) and *Bandana Days* (1907).

The Williams and Walker company has been described as "all in all, the strongest Negro theatrical combination that had yet been assembled."[14] It included, in addition to Williams and Walker, Jesse Shipp, Alex Rogers, Will Marion Cook, and Ada Overton (Mrs. George Walker). Ada Overton has been described as the "brightest star among women on the Negro stage

14. *Ibid.,* p. 107.

of the period." George Walker was "the sleek, smiling, prancing dandy," Bert Williams "the slow-witted, good-natured, shuffling darky."[15] Bert Williams, according to all accounts, was one of America's great comedians, with few equals in the art of pantomime. After the failure of his one-man show, *Lode of Kole* (1909), Williams became lost to the Negro theater when he was signed to star in the *Ziegfeld Follies,* where he was to remain as a central attraction for some ten seasons. Williams died March 11, 1922. He was not yet forty-seven years old.

In 1921 a highwater mark was reached in the development of the Negro musical theater with the appearance of *Shuffle Along* at the 63rd Street Theater. *Shuffle Along* seemed to mark a culmination of the Williams and Walker, Cole and Johnson tradition. Written, produced and performed by Negroes—Flourney E. Miller, Aubrey Lyles, Eubie Blake and Noble Sissle— it played first before Negro audiences at the Howard Theater in Washington and at the Dunbar Theater in Philadelphia. *Shuffle Along* eventually took New York by storm. The show was full of future stars, Caterina Jarboro, Josephine Baker, Gertrude Saunders, Florence Mills. William Grant Still and Hall Johnson were in the orchestra. No Negro musical had so many hits— "Bandana Days," "Love Will Find a Way," "I'm Just Wild About Harry," and "He May Be Your Man but He Comes to See Me Sometimes"—which were heard around the world. *Shuffle Along* set a vogue for Negro musicals that continued to the retrenchment that followed the Great Depression. In 1923, Irving C. Miller's *Liza* and Miller and Lyles' *Runnin' Wild,* both appeared. *Runnin' Wild* introduced a Negro dance, the Charleston, to America and to the world, and helped to define "The Jazz Age." That same year Sissle and Blake's *Chocolate Dandies* started Josephine Baker on her way to international stardom. In 1924, Florence Mills became a star in *From Dixie to Broadway* and went on to ever-mounting success in Lew Leslie's *Blackbirds* in New York, Paris, and London. Florence Mills died in November of 1927, at the height of her career, presaging, as it were, the end of an era.

IV

After the demise of the African Grove Theater, as Langston Hughes points out, it was over half a century before black actors and technicians had command of theaters in which they could develop their craft. In several Southern cities because of laws separating the races, there grew up theaters and places of amusement for blacks. The success of Robert Mott's Pekin Theatre in Chicago in 1906 led many show houses to open their doors to Negro entertainers covering a wide range of presentations from burlesque to Broadway drama. Soon the Negro theaters had as tenants stock companies which produced plays with all black casts. Such a company was headed by Bob Cole at Worth's Museum at Sixth Avenue and Thirtieth Street. This was one of the first places where a group of black performers could gain anything approaching dramatic training and experience on the strictly professional stage. Two Harlem theaters, the Lafayette and the Lincoln, developed outstanding stock companies.

15. *Ibid.,* pp. 107-108.

Their repertories consisted of classics, Shakespeare, and adaptations of downtown hits sometimes modified to suit the needs and tastes of black audiences. The Lafayette Players, founded by Lester Walton in 1914, developed an especially proficient company. From Harlem productions like *Othello, Madame X, The Servant in the House, The Count of Monte Cristo, The Love of Choo Chin, Within the Law, Dr. Jekyll and Mr. Hyde,* and *On Trial* a number of talented players emerged. Charles Gilpin, Inez Clough, Abbie Mitchell, Laura Bowman, Cleo Desmond, Jack Carter, Evelyn Ellis, Frank Wilson, Andrew Bishop, Edna Thomas, and Clarence Muse were favorites with Harlem audiences.

April 5, 1917, saw the beginning of serious drama in the Broadway theater for Negro artists with the performance of three dramatic plays given by the Colored Players at the Garden Theater in Madison Square Garden. The plays by the white dramatist, Ridgely Torrence, *The Rider of Dreams, Granny Maumee,* and *Simon the Cyrenian* were produced by Mrs. Emily Hapgood while the settings and costumes were designed by Robert Edmond Jones who was also the director. A rustic comedy, a voodoo tragedy, and a passion play, these works made a high demand on the artistry of the company. The cast, many of whom had been members of the Lafayette Players, was excellent. George Jean Nathan commended the performances and judged the actors, Opal Cooper and Inez Clough, among the top ten theatrical entertainers of the year. As James Weldon Johnson says—"the stereotyped traditions regarding the Negro's histrionic limitations were smashed. It was the first time anywhere in the United States for Negro actors in the dramatic theater to command the serious attention of the critics and of the general press and public."[16]

In 1920, Eugene O'Neill's *The Emperor Jones* was produced at the Provincetown Playhouse in Greenwich Village with Charles Gilpin playing the title role. The play was an enormous success and proved once more that blacks could perform as movingly in the legitimate theater as they had done on the musical stage. With *The Emperor Jones* O'Neill began his ascent to fame as America's foremost dramatist. Charles Gilpin received the Spingarn Medal and the vote of the Drama League as one of the ten persons who had done most for the American theater during this season. Although O'Neill had Negro characters in other plays such as *The Moon of the Caribbees* and *The Iceman Cometh,* he wrote two other plays centered in Negro life. One was *The Dreamy Kid,* a one act play produced in 1919. The other and more important work was *All God's Chillun Got Wings* (1924), treating the theme of miscegenation. The play, co-starring Paul Robeson and Mary Blair, a white actress, created a sensation.

In February of 1926, David Belasco presented Edward Sheldon and Charles MacArthur's sensational melodrama, *Lulu Belle,* with Evelyn Preer and Edna Thomas among the many Negroes who supported Leonore Ulric and Henry Hull, the stars, who essayed roles in dark paint as mulattoes.[17] The

16. *Ibid.,* p. 175.
17. In this connection and in terms of this production, see David Belasco,

same year Paul Robeson appeared in James Tully and Frank Dazey's *Black Boy*, a play dealing with the rise and fall of a black prizefighter. The same season saw Lawrence Stallings and Frank Harling's *Deep River* with Charlotte Murray, Jules Bledsoe, and Rose McClendon. Paul Green, of the University of North Carolina, who had written a number of one-act plays on Southern Negro life, had his *In Abraham's Bosom* produced at the Provincetown Playhouse in 1926 with a cast that included Rose McClendon, Abbie Mitchell, Frank Wilson, and Jules Bledsoe. *In Abraham's Bosom* won the Pulitzer Prize in 1927 as the original American play best representing the educational value and power of the stage. In 1927 also came the New Playwrights production of Em Jo Bashee's *Earth* with Inez Clough and Daniel Haynes as its stars. This year also saw the Theater Guild's production of *Porgy*, Dorothy and DuBose Heyward's dramatization of Mr. Heyward's famous novel. Directed by Reuben Mamoulian, with a cast that included Rose McClendon, Frank Wilson, Georgette Harvey, Leigh Whipper and Jack Carter, *Porgy* was the great hit of the season and proved as successful in London as it had been in New York. Ziegfeld's *Show Boat*, starring Jules Bledsoe, came in 1928 as did *Goin' Home*.

A lively decade of Negro participation in the American legitimate and musical theater was crowned with the appearance, in 1930, of Marc Connelly's *The Green Pastures*, based upon Roark Bradford's southern folk sketches, *Old Man Adam and His Chillun*. *The Green Pastures* opened at the Mansfield Theater on February 26, 1930, with Richard B. Harrison as "De Lawd" and an all-Negro cast, including Wesley Hill, Daniel Haynes, Josephine Byrd, Florence Fields, Tutt Whitney, and Charles Moore. The play was accompanied by a singing orchestra headed by Hall Johnson, and was brilliantly staged against expressive settings by Robert Edmond Jones. *The Green Pastures* was an epoch-making work. Appearing at the end of the decade that had seen the beginnings of the Negro Renaissance in Harlem, it won the Pulitzer Prize, and achieved one of the longest runs in Negro theatrical history. Of this play John Gassner could say: "*The Green Pastures* is unique: it cannot be placed in any existing classification without some reservations. . . . Yet one cannot overlook the tremendous fascination the play exerted for years after it opened on Broadway. It seemed everything we considered a movement toward folk drama for at least a decade, and it was also the only religious drama anyone had succeeded in making tolerable to the American public since the vogue of Charles Rann Kennedy's old-fashioned morality play, *The Servant in the House*." [18]

V

According to the chronicle given above the most successful plays, commercially and quantitatively, concerned with American Negro life on the professional stage, represent a major collaboration between white playwrights and

"Tomorrow's Stage and the Negro," subtitled "The Producer of the Sensational 'Lulu Belle' makes a Discovery and a Prophecy," *Liberty*, August 7, 1926, pp. 17-23.

18. John Gassner, ed., *Treasury of the Theater* (New York: Simon and Schuster, 1964), II, 896.

producers and black actors and musicians. But written, as we would say, from the outside and reflecting consciously and unconsciously deep-seated racial attitudes that frequently portrayed deep-seated stereotypes and primitive anthropological attitudes, these plays did not always win unequivocal approval of black spectators and critics. Meantime the black playwright was working against great odds to make his voice heard and to interpret the life and aspirations of his people in terms of an intimate inside vision. As Langston Hughes has put it, "with little chance to even see plays in many parts of the country because of Jim Crow, and with almost no chance even to gain any technical knowledge of theater craft, the black playwright had a hard row to hoe. In the old days his scripts seldom got from the typed page to even the amateur stage, but perhaps a church might sponsor a reading."[19]

The first known American Negro playwright was William Wells Brown (1816-1884). An ex-slave, abolitionist, and early man of letters, Brown wrote a *Narrative* of his life under slavery (1842). As an anti-slavery agent he delivered well over a thousand speeches in America and Great Britain and described his travels in *Three Years in Europe: or, Places I Have Seen and People I Have Met* (1852). He is also the author of the first published Negro novel, *Clotele: or The Colored Heroine* (1867). Brown wrote two plays, *Experience, or How to Give a Northern Man a Backbone* (1856) and *Escape, or A Leap for Freedom* (1858). Written in the vein of the protest poetry of James Whitfield and abolitionist polemics of the day, Brown's plays were not produced even by amateurs. He gave one-man readings of them, in churches and other assemblies, which enjoyed considerable popularity.

The first serious drama from a black writer to be published was Joseph Seamon Cotter, Sr.'s *Caleb, the Degenerate, or A Study of the Types, Customs, and Needs of the American Negro* (1903). Cotter was a school teacher and principal of the Colored Ward School in Louisville, Kentucky, when *Caleb, the Degenerate* was published. He seems, however, to have known little of the theater and its needs. What he managed to write was a pretentious four-act play in blank verse, based upon an acceptance of Booker T. Washington's philosophy on racial matters, and on the relative merits of industrial versus liberal education. It has been assessed as "even less actable than William Wells Brown's *The Escape*."

In 1913, Dr. W. E. B. DuBois' *Star of Ethiopia* was presented in New York at Madison Square Garden Theater and proved to be the first successful undertaking in pageantry produced by Negroes. Angelina Grimke's three-act play, *Rachel*, produced by the drama committee of the Washington, D.C., branch of the National Association for the Advancement of Colored People in March, 1916, was received with high praise as the first successful play by a Negro playwright. In addition to the Washington production, *Rachel* was presented in New York at the Neighborhood Playhouse and in Cambridge, Massachusetts.

Interest in plays of black life with Negro actors grew as an important

19. Langston Hughes, "The Negro in American Entertainment," in *The American Negro Reference Book*, John P. Davis, ed. (Englewood Cliffs, New Jersey: Prentice Hall, Inc., 1966), p. 834.

aspect of the little theater movement initiated by George Cram Cook, Susan Glaspell, Eugene O'Neill, and Edna St. Vincent Millay. The Provincetown Players, the Howard University Players, and the Ethiopian Art Theater sponsored a series of productions dealing with Negro life. O'Neill's one-act play, *The Dreamy Kid,* and his *The Emperor Jones,* and *All God's Chillun Got Wings,* as we have seen, grew out of this movement to revitalize the American theater through the artistic use of native themes and contemporary materials.

At Washington, D. C., Alain Locke and Montgomery Gregory organized the Howard University Players as an experimental laboratory of Negro drama. Like the Provincetown Players in the American theater, they sought to develop a national Negro theater. The Howard Players produced *Simon the Cyrenian* and *The Emperor Jones* in March, 1921. Charles Gilpin and Jasper Deeter played the leading roles in the O'Neill play, while students composed the supporting cast. Other plays produced by the Howard group were *Genifrede* and the *Yellow Tree,* written by students of the Howard University drama department; *Dance Calinda,* a pantomime by Ridgely Torrence, in June, 1922; *The Death Dance,* a one-act play of African life by Thelma Duncan, in April, 1923; and Willis Richardson's one-act play, *Mortgaged,* in March, 1924.

The Ethiopian Art Theater was founded in Chicago early in 1923 by Raymond O'Neill and Mrs. Sherwood Anderson. The group had its New York premiere on May 7 of that year, at the Frazee Theatre. The initial presentations included only one Negro play, Willis Richardson's *The Chip Woman's Fortune.* This play and others of the series, Oscar Wilde's *Salome* and a jazz rendition of Shakespeare's *Comedy of Errors,* won generous applause from the critics, and fine performances of Evelyn Preer, Sidney Kirkpatrick, Charles Olden, and Laura Bowman led to a demand for more Negro plays. Nan Bagby Stephen's *Roseanne* was presented by the Ethiopian Art Theater, in 1923, at the Greenwich Village Theater. This was followed by *Taboo,* a fine study of voodooism by Mary Hoyt Wilborg, which brought Paul Robeson forward as the successor to Charles Gilpin as America's outstanding black actor.

But the largest accolades and financial rewards were to be felt on the professional Broadway stage. Here black playwrights for a number of reasons achieved few spectacular successes. Aside from serving as sketch writers and occasional librettists for musical shows black writers exerted little effort in the writing of plays for the Broadway Colossus. When they did, there seemed to be a sense that their efforts would find no market if, in their treatment of Negro life, they were attended by serious intentions. From 1917 to 1930, for instance, no less than fifteen white playwrights, with various degrees of merit, presented works on the Broadway stage, dealing with Negro themes and characters, while only five plays on Negro life by black playwrights managed Broadway production. Garland Anderson's *Appearances* (1925), the most successful of these plays, although played by a mixed cast of fourteen whites and three blacks, with a Negro as the principal character, was not really what we would call a Negro play. It was, according to Anderson's basic intention a highly didactic dramatization of Christian Science doctrines. In the second act, however, a courtroom scene, in which the hero through conspiracy is almost convicted of assaulting a white woman, had dramatic power and gave momentum to the play. *Appearances,* sponsored by a number of important theatrical and literary personages, got good notices, but had, at first, a relatively short run. It was successfully revived in 1929. Willis Richardson's one-act play, *The Chip Woman's Fortune* (1923), referred to above, produced by Mrs. Sherwood Anderson, and Frank Wilson's *Meek Mose* (1928), produced by Lester A. Walton, were failures. Wallace Thurman's *Harlem* (1929), written in collaboration with a white writer, William Jordan Rapp, a sensational, melodramatic, and at the same time, realistic treatment of Harlem life in a railroad flat, with such actors as Inez Clough, Isabell Washington, Ernest Clough, and Billy Andrews, enjoyed a short run.

According to Langston Hughes, "In the thirty-five years since Wallace Thurman's *Harlem* there have been ten Negro playwrights—only ten—produced on Broadway."[20] His list includes: the revival of Anderson's *Appearances* (1929); Frank Wilson's *Brother Mose* (the retitled *Meek Mose*); Langston Hughes' *Mulatto* (1938); Richard Wright's *Native Son,* written with Paul Green (1947); Theodore Ward's *Our Lan'* (1947); Louis Petersen's *Take a Giant Step* (1953); Charles Sebree's *Mrs. Patterson* (1954); Hughes' *Simply Heavenly* (1958); Lorainne Hansberry's *A Raisin in the Sun* (1959); Ossie Davis's *Purlie Victorious* (1961); Hughes' *Tambourines to Glory* (1963); James Baldwin's *Blues for Mister Charlie,* and Hansberry's *The Sign in Sidney Brustein's Window* (1964). And Hughes goes on to note that "Only Lorraine Hansberry and Langston Hughes have had more than one production on Broadway . . . *Mulatto* . . . and *A Raisin in the Sun* enjoyed the longest runs of any vehicles by Negro authors, each playing for over a year in New York followed by extensive cross country tours. Both plays have been translated and played abroad, and *A Raisin in the Sun* became a Hollywood picture."[21]

VI

After 1929 a period in the professional American theater that had shown considerable interest in the black man as artist and entertainer—but only incidental and superficial concern for his basic problems and fundamental human needs—came to a waning. But a new era of social consciousness and significance for the blacks in the theater was soon to be ushered in. As the Great Depression settled over the land, the black man—"the last to be hired and the first to be fired"—felt the fullest brunt of the deprivations of this dismal era. There were lean days in the theater, as in other aspects of the economy, and hundreds of Negro actors, entertainers, technicians, and musicians were hard pressed to earn a livelihood. In 1935, the Federal Theater was founded as part of the Works Progress Administration of Franklin Delano Roosevelt's New Deal, with Hallie Flanagan, a former Professor of Drama at Vassar, as its national director. The Federal Theater put actors, directors, technicians, and writers to work and brought theater to metropolitan

20. Langston Hughes and Milton Meltzer, *op. cit.,* p. 834.
21. *Ibid.,* pp. 834-835.

centers all over the country. For the first time in the United States there was something approaching a national theater.

In the larger cities Negro units of the Federal Theater were soon established which proved to be not only an economic boon but also an important training ground for Negroes in all aspects of theater. In places like Chicago the Negro division of the Federal Theater first revived old time minstrels for presentation in parks, hospitals, and schools, but later at Igoe Hall presented full length plays such as *Did Adam Sin?, Every Man in His Humor, Romy and July. Romy and July* was a curtain raiser for the *Swing Mikado* that proved so successful that it finally reached Broadway as *The Hot Mikado* under the auspices of the producer, Mike Todd, with Bill Robinson as its star. Based upon Shakespeare's *Romeo and Juliet, Romy and July* became a Negro version of the plight of the "star-crossed lovers," caught up in a feud between West Indian and American Negro families. The Chicago Negro unit also produced, with notable success, *Big White Fog* by the black playwright Theodore Ward, at the Great Northern Theater.

New York, with its resources, as was to be expected, developed a fine Negro unit of the Federal Theater at the Lafayette Theater, with Orson Welles and John Houseman, then at the beginning of their careers, at the helm. Among its productions were William Du Bois' *Haiti,* dealing with the Black Revolution against Napoleon and the French led by Henri Christophe played by Rex Ingram and Toussaint L'Ouverture played by Louis Sharp; Hall Johnson's *Run, Little Chillun*; Frank Wilson's *Brother Mose* and *Walk Together Chillun*; Rudolph Fisher's *Conjur Man Dies*; George McEntee's *The Case of Phillip Lawrence;* and classics like Shaw's *Androcles and the Lion;* and André Obey's *Noah.* But the most spectacular and most successful of the Federal Theater productions at the Lafayette was the Orson Welles-John Houseman production of Shakespeare's *Macbeth* with a Haitian setting and an all Negro cast. Jack Carter played Macbeth, with Edna Thomas as Lady Macbeth, and Canada Lee as Banquo. The overture was James P. Johnson's "Yamekraw," the voodoo chants and dances were by Asadata Dafora Horton, while Leonard De Paur conducted the chorus.

The Federal Theater Project was brought to an untimely end in 1939 by a Congressional Act that reflected suspicions of left-of-center social and political implications in some of its productions. There can be no question, however, that the Federal Theater was the source of many talents and invaluable theatrical experiments such as *The Living Newspaper,* and that it had greatly enriched the American cultural scene. Most certainly it performed a distinct and original service for many black urban communities and for innumerable black artists in the American theater. Indeed, Edith Isaacs could say, "No part of the Federal Theater brought more ample returns to the project itself than did the Negro units and, conversely, no American theater project (except perhaps the Lafayette Theater during its long history) has meant more to Negro players and other theater artists than the Federal Theater did."[22]

22. Edith J. R. Isaacs, *op. cit.,* p. 106.

Bridging the past and the present, reflecting past influences upon the present, it is interesting to note the remarks of Robert Macbeth, who as artistic director of the New Lafayette Theater, is an important force in the new black theater of the 1960's. Speaking in an interview on the backgrounds of The New Lafayette Theater, Macbeth could say: "The idea for the creation of a New Lafayette Theater as far as it relates to the old Lafayette Theater came to me once while I was reading a biography of Orson Welles. The Lafayette Theater as a total entity is perhaps not as attractive a historical piece as we might like it to be because it was a vaudeville house in lots of ways, and a lot of things done there were done not necessarily for the audience of the black community but done during that time when Harlem was the exotic place for others to come to visit. But during the WPA theater period when Welles was there, they did a production of *Macbeth*. . . . That production was oriented around trying to do that play in a way that related to black people who made up both the acting company and the audience for the play. It wasn't the time of tripping up to Harlem to visit; it was a time when most of the people who were there lived there, and that theater was there for them. What Welles and Housman did was to reset the play in a black environment in Haiti and then look at all the elements of the play from Haitian history. Luckily, Shakespeare being a great poet, the values of the play were not tied to its location or its heritage. The values of the play were human ambition, etc. That production turned out to be very representative of a black theater by a black company even though the director happened to be white."[23] And he goes on to say, "that's what the New Lafayette Theater creation really stems from: the idea of a theater in the Black community by those artists who are a part of that Black community, and with that as the total theme. It has some historical validity, because it has the name and because we are in the same spot."[24]

But an earlier source for the aspirations of the new black theatre of the '60's is unquestionably to be discovered in the cultural program espoused by W. E. B. DuBois in the literary and editorial policies of the *Crisis*, the official organ of the National Association for the Advancement of Colored People, both founded in 1910. W. E. B. DuBois' consistent advocacy of black cultural nationalism, his encouragement and publication of young writers and artists such as Countee Cullen, and Langston Hughes, Aaron Douglass, and Claude McKay led to the first flowering of black expression known as the Negro Renaissance of the twenties. In 1920, one of DuBois's editorials was to say: "We have today all too few writers, for the reason that there is small market for their ideas among whites, and their energies are being called to other more lucrative ways of earning a living. Nevertheless we have literary ability and the race needs it. A renaissance of Negro literature is due; the material about us in the strange, heart-rending race tangle is rich beyond dream and only we can tell the tale and the song from the heart."[25]

23. "the electronic nigger meets the gold dust twins, Clifford Mason Talks With Robert Macbeth And Ed Bullins," *Black Theater 1*, New York, 1968, p. 25.
24. *Ibid.*
25. See "To Encourage Negro Art," *Crisis*, Vol. 29, No. 1 (November, 1929), 11.

In this connection, Mark Seyboldt's short and pointed essay in *Crisis* on playwriting is of specific interest. He gives the prospective dramatist eight basic references including William Archer's *Playmaking*, George P. Baker's *Dramatic Technique*, Brander Matthews, *A Study of Drama*, and Percival Wilde's *Craftsmanship of the One Act Play*. He quotes Professor Baker as saying that most attempts at writing plays fall into two classes, "the well written but trite; the fresh and interesting but badly written" and expresses the interest of *Crisis* in fresh, experimental, and possibly inexpert writing. Seyboldt's concentrated suggestions on problems of audience, actors, and story are of particular point to our analysis. He writes in part: "Our writers may have two different audiences in mind. A. White Americans used to theatre going. B. Colored folk. While we set no limitations, we are mainly interested in the second audience; we want colored folk to add the new diversion of drama to their lives. We want the dramatic instinct of the masses to find outlet in the seen and spoken drama. It will stimulate and broaden cramped lives; it will bring inspiration, ambition, satisfaction. Hitherto, they have had almost nothing but caricature and broad farce. . . . The actors need not bother our playwright as actual staging is a matter of the future, and good colored and white actors are procurable. The chief thing is the story. . . . There are lynchings in the United States; there is sorrow among black folk; there is poverty, misfortune and sometimes despair; but do not confine yourself to these themes. There are also sunshine and kindness and hope."[26]

The Krigwa Players' Little Negro Theatre in Harlem, organized by W. E. B. DuBois in 1926 as part of the literary and artistic program of *Crisis*, has to be regarded as part of the Little Theatre Movement in America started by George Cram Cook, Susan Glaspel, and Eugene O'Neill.[27] But again there were claims to cultural individuality and distinction of purpose and function. In a *Crisis* article published in the year of the founding of this group, its program is described in what might be called a kind of manifesto for a Negro theatre.[28] Extending his call to "a new birth" in the theatre, as an important part of the "renaissance of art among American Negroes," this article discusses some of the social and cultural forces that have stood in the way of progress toward a Negro theatre. "In America the road to freedom of the Negro lay through religious organization long before physical emancipation came. The Negro church gave the slave almost his only freedom of spirit and of the churches that came to proselytize among the slaves, only those were permanently successful which were strongly tinged with Puritanism: the Baptist and the Methodist. These churches frowned upon the drama and the play, upon the theatre and the dance.

---

26. "Play-writing," *Crisis*, Vol. 30 (February, 1925), 165-166.

27. See James Weldon Johnson, *op. cit.*, pp. 180-181. See also Sterling Brown, *Negro Poetry and Drama* (Washington, D.C.: Associates in Negro Folk Education, 1938), pp. 124-142.

28. "Krigwa Players' Little Theatre Movement," an unsigned article, written, I have learned, by W. E. B. DuBois, *Crisis*, Vol. 32, No. 3 (July, 1926), 134-136.

. . ."[29] A contemporary difficulty towards the realization of a Negro theatre lay, this article asserts, in the failure of most people to see wherein "the novelty" must come. "The Negro has already been in the theatre and has been there a long time; but his presence there is not yet thoroughly normal. His audience is mainly a white audience and the Negro actor has for a long time been asked to entertain this more or less alien group and their conceptions of Negroes have set the norm for the black actor. He has been a minstrel, comedian, singer and lay figures of all sorts. Only recently has he begun tentatively to emerge as an ordinary human being with every day reactions. And here he is handicapped and put forth with much hesitation as in the case of 'Nigger' and 'Lulu Belle' and 'The Emperor Jones.' "[30]

Under these circumstances, in the words of the Krigwa statement, "the best Negro actor and the poignant Negro drama have not been called for. This could be evolved only by a Negro audience desiring to see its own life depicted by its own writers and actors."[31] Amateur groups bringing the theater to Negro audiences in places like Cleveland and Philadelphia are given praise but are seriously criticized for "playing Shakespeare or Synge or . . . resetting a successful Broadway play with colored principles."[32] The Krigwa Players, seeking a more autochthonous theatre, laid down four principles as fundamental to their work, and to the way in which "a real folk-play movement of American Negroes [could] be built. . . . The plays of a real Negro theatre must be: 1. *About us*. That is, they must have plots that reveal Negro life as it is. 2. *By us*. That is they must be written by Negro authors who understand from birth and continued association just what it means to be a Negro today. 3. *For us*. That is the Negro theatre must cater primarily to Negro audiences and be supported by their entertainment and approval. 4. *Near us*. The theatre must be in a neighborhood near the mass of Negro people."[33]

The impulses set forth by the *Crisis* pronouncements of the 1920's on the need for a Negro theater as part of a Negro Renaissance in literature and the arts had proliferations that come down into the present and are readily recognizable in some of the assertions of the new black arts and theater movement of the 1960's. In its own time the Krigwa Players served as a model for other black little theater groups throughout the country. The group won a place in the Little Theater Tournament and competed, although unsuccessfully, for the David Belasco Trophy; however its production of Eulalie Spence's *The Fool's Errand* won the Samuel French Prize for the best unpublished manuscripts in the contest. In the course of its career, the Krigwa Players produced such other works by black playwrights as Willis Richardson's *Compromise* and *Broken Banjo*, Georgia Douglas Johnson's *Blue Blood*, and Eulalie Spence's *Brothers and Sisters of the Church Council*. Other groups that followed the Krigwa Players in New York, for instance, were the Harlem

29. *Ibid.*, p. 134.
30. *Ibid.*
31. *Ibid.*
32. *Ibid.*
33. *Ibid.*

Experimental Theatre (1928), the Negro Art Theater (1929), the Dunbar Gardens Players (1929).

The thirties saw a continuation of the movement to found a black community theater with the Negro People's Theatre organized by Dick Campbell and Rose McClendon in 1935. Because of Miss McClendon's untimely death, and because many of its members soon joined the Negro unit of the Federal Theatre this group presented only one work, a black version of Clifford Odets' *Waiting for Lefty*. This production and Langston Hughes' *Don't You Want to Be Free?* (1936), which had a long run at his improvised Suitcase Theatre in a Harlem loft, showed the influence of the social-problem drama of the leftist agit-prop theatre as seen in such works as John Wexley's *They Shall Not Die* (1934), based upon the Scottsboro case, and Paul Peters and George Sklar's *Stevedore* (1934), produced by the Theatre Union, at the old Civic Repertory Theatre on 14th Street.

In the late thirties the Rose McClendon Players was founded by the actor-director, Dick Campbell, and his wife, the late singer-actress, Muriel Rahn. Highly serious in its purposes, the McClendon Players engaged Theodore Komisarevsky, formerly of the Moscow Art Theatre, to train them in the art of ensemble playing, and sought to develop a community theater which would provide a strong base for black actors, playwrights, directors, and technicians. Out of this group came such future notables of the drama world as Frederick O'Neal, Ossie Davis, Ruby Dee, and Jane White. Giving revivals, at first, of Broadway successes like *Goodbye Again* and *Having Wonderful Time*, the group met some criticism for devoting themselves merely to entertainment rather than to the presentation of works centered in the problems and aspirations of Negro life. To redress this grievance the McClendon Players went on to give admirable productions of Abram Hill's *On Striver's Row* and William Ashley's *Booker T. Washington*. The latter, with Dooley Wilson in the title role, had successful runs in Harlem and at the 1939 World's Fair. The McClendon Players disbanded with the advent of World War II, and were never reassembled; nevertheless, the group was an important force, and left a memorable mark in the traditional history of the attempts to create a black community theater in New York.

Another landmark in this history was the establishment in 1939 of the American Negro Theatre, organized by the playwright-director, Abram Hill, Austin Briggs-Hall, Frederick O'Neal, Hattie King-Reeves and a number of persons formerly associated with the Rose McClendon Players. This group produced a revival of Abram Hill's *On Strivers' Row;* the young Chicago playwright, Theodore Browne's *Natural Man* (a play on John Brown); Owen Dodson's *The Garden of Time;* Abram Hill's *Walk Hard;* and Hill's adaptation of Phillip Yordan's *Anna Lucasta*.

The Negro Playwrights' Company organized by Powell Lindsay, George Norford, Theodore Browne, and Owen Dodson gave, as their only production, a new presentation of Theodore Ward's *Big White Fog* in 1940. The forties also saw Canada Lee on Broadway as Bigger Thomas in the Richard Wright-Paul Green-Orson Welles production of *Native Son;* Paul Robeson's fascinating revival of *Othello*, directed by Margaret Webster for the Theatre

Guild, with Jose Ferrer and Uta Hagen as co-stars; and the long running downtown production of *Anna Lucasta*, directed by Harry Wagstaff Gribble, with a cast including Hilda Simms, Frederick O'Neal, Alice Childress, Alvin Childress, Earle Hyman, and Herbert Henry. Such productions furthered discussion of the Negro in the American theatre and discussions on a more substantially black-oriented theater. Organizations like the Harlem Writers Club encouraged writing for a black theater; the *Committee for the Negro in the Arts* (1947) and the Harlem Council on the Theatre (1950) were prominent in the production of a number of plays, such as William Branch's *A Medal for Willie;* Alice Childress' *Just a Little Simple* (based upon Langston Hughes' *Simple Speaks His Mind), Florence,* and *Gold Through the Trees.* The late forties also saw the production of D'Usseau and Gow's *Deep Are the Roots* with Gordon Heath, and Maxine Woods' *On Whitman Avenue* with Canada Lee; and Theodore Ward's *Our Lan';* while there were notable productions in the fifties and sixties of Alice Childress' *Trouble in Mind;* William Branch's *In Splendid Error* (a play dealing with John Brown and Frederick Douglass); Loften Mitchell's *A Land Beyond the River;* Langston Hughes' *Simply Heavenly* and *Tambourines to Glory;* and, among others, fine Broadway and off-Broadway productions of the works of Miss Hansberry, Ossie Davis, LeRoi Jones, James Baldwin and the other playwrights presented in this anthology.

VII

When we come to look at the plays presented in this anthology covering as they do the time span of a decade—1959 to 1969—we are confronted with an experience that ventures from what, in terms of dramaturgy or playmaking, is fairly familiar to what is excitingly and strangely new. Realism and naturalism, for instance, within the framework of the traditional well-made play make Lorraine Hansberry's *A Raisin in the Sun* an indisputably old-fashioned work, while the works of Adrienne Kennedy, LeRoi Jones and certain of his followers such as Ed Bullins, coming in the wake of Samuel Beckett's *Waiting for Godot* (1953) and *Endgame* (1957), Edward Albee's *The Zoo Story* (1958) and *The Death of Bessie Smith* (1959), and Jean Genet's *The Blacks* (1961-1964), form among other things an arresting part of what is best in the innovative European and American avant-garde theater. But the basic fact that all the plays in this textbook are representative of a new mood—though *new* must always be regarded as a fairly relative term—and are part of a *new* black theater that is still in the process of shaping and defining itself, needs to be underscored.

And when we come to speak of the ambience of the new black drama, under consideration here, as certainly the primary aspect of the new black theater, and come to ask why this, whether presented on Broadway or off-Broadway, forms such an exciting, dynamic, and artful genre in today's American theater, immediate answers are ascertainable in the fact that this drama is saying some of the most important things that need to be said today, at the same time that, in their search to entertain as well as to instruct, they aspire to artistic finality. What it has to say, of course, is concretely centered in the contemporary urgencies rendered in the black drama's alliance to the civil rights movement of the present and recent past, and to the black revolution in all of its recognizable manifestations. As an ally of the black revolution recent black drama is also deeply involved in what we have come to call an identity crisis, and this adds to its significance. Here the novelty lies in point of view or the vantage point of interpretation, wherein black writers, totally disenchanted with outside interpretations and appraisals, insist upon sizing up themselves, "doing their own thing"—black writers presenting black materials, played and directed by black artists mainly for black audiences with the unmistakably important purpose of defining and redefining the meaning of black lives historically and in terms of the twentieth-century American and modern worlds. Particularly is this true of the revolutionary black community theaters which as part of the Black Arts Movement consciously regard themselves as the cultural wing of the social and political assertions of the black revolution. But point of view, and identity crisis—audience notwithstanding—are as important to the validity of plays like *A Raisin in the Sun, Purlie Victorious,* or *Blues for Mr. Charlie,* which as Broadway productions were largely supported by white audiences, as they are to off-Broadway and black community theater productions— also supported by blacks and whites—of say, *Dutchman* or *Gentleman Caller* or *No Place to be Somebody.*

The imaginative appeal of the new black theater and its growing corpus of plays not only to blacks but also to white theater-goers and readers of dramatic literature has, in an introduction of this kind, to be accounted for. LeRoi Jones's *Dutchman,* for example, is widely acclaimed as one of the most important plays of the contemporary American theater. Considering its success we are reminded that all art, though nationalistic in origin, is also an act of interrelationship that aspires toward the universal. Look simply at Shakespeare, Ibsen, Victor Hugo, Pirandello, Synge, O'Casey, and O'Neill. It is a truism that the particular gains permanence and stature to the degree that in terms of its formal aesthetic and image-making qualities it makes its particular assertions at the same time that it transcends particularity and comes to illuminate the universal. Hence Jean Genet gains a universal audience with *The Blacks* as did Jean Paul Sartre with *The Respectful Prostitute,* based upon the American Scottsboro case. In this connection, Richard Wright's salient observation that the Negro is America's metaphor speaks volumes. And it perhaps is for this simple but very profound reason that modern Afro-American literature in general and black drama in particular take on their major significance for students of American civilization and culture. For basically it must be recognized that black literature, of which the new black drama is an important part, does not speak exclusively to the contemporary and historical condition of blacks in America. There is an important sense in which it speaks to the fundamental nature of America's psychic, spiritual, moral and social condition: and then moving beyond this, translating the particular into the universal, manages—consciously and unconsciously—to make important statements on what in broad existentialist terms we have come to call the human condition.

But while we can and must talk about universality and particularity in the theater, and of the demands of art as art, regardless of its origins, before concluding this introduction some distinction must be made, in terms of contemporary black thought, between bourgeois or middle class drama and art, and the aims of black revolutionary drama, and the criticism surrounding the ideas of a black aesthetic, as it informs and enlivens the new Black Arts Movement. In a word, middle class drama, written by blacks is essentially integrationist. This statement, however, must immediately be seen as an over-simplification. The segregation of the Negro from the mainstream of American life has made his art necessarily a reflection of this fact, and is therefore in its profoundest aspects, separatist. We have only, in this instance, to look back to the ideas of DuBois and Mark Seybolt, earlier referred to here, to find confirmation of this fact. As a consequence of this, it is also worth noting that, on one level, Miss Hansberry's *A Raisin in the Sun* is decidedly bourgeois in tendency. But being black, in the genuinely modern sense of this term, it also reflects, consciously and unconsciously, and quite necessarily, in its arguments, aspects of the concerns of the new revolutionary black dramatists.

The new black revolutionary theater evolves largely from the example, in specific dramatic works, and the critical theories of LeRoi Jones. A young critic, Larry Neal, however, gives an excellent synthesis of its major proposals in the *Black Theater* issue of *The Drama Review* (1968), under the special editorship of the young playwright and critic, Ed Bullins. Here we find Mr. Neal saying that the Black Arts Movement is radically opposed to the idea of the artist as one who is alienated from his community. And he notes that: "Black Art is the aesthetic and spiritual sister of the Black Power concept," envisioning "an art that speaks directly to the needs of Black America."[34] The black arts, he contends, are engaged in a radical reordering of the western cultural aesthetic and this necessarily involves "a separate symbolism, myth-ology, critique, and iconology."[35] And all of this is basically related to the Afro-American's will for self-determination and nationhood. Both concepts, he contends, are nationalistic. One relates to the connection between art and politics—the other with the art of politics. He sees the dual movements as beginning to merge. On this point he says: "the political values inherent in the Black Power concept are now finding concrete expression in the aesthetics of Afro-American dramatists, poets, choreographers, musicians, and novelists. A main tenet of Black Power is the necessity for Black people to define the world in their own terms. . . . The two movements postulate that there are in fact and in spirit two Americas—one black, one white. The Black artist takes this to mean that his primary duty is to speak to the spiritual and cultural needs of Black people."[36]

Currently, the new breed of writers are engaged in a critical reexam-ination of western aesthetics, the traditional role of the writer, and the social

34. Larry Neal, "The Black Arts Movement," *The Drama Review*, Vol. 12, No. 4, Summer, 1968, p. 29.
35. *Ibid.*
36. *Ibid.*

function of art in the interest of constructing a "black aesthetic." Generally, according to Neal, they conclude that western aesthetics have run their course and that it is impossible to construct anything meaningful in its decaying structure. They are the advocates of a cultural revolution in art and ideas. "The cultural values inherent in western history must either be radicalized or destroyed, and we will probably find that even radicalization is impossible."[37] Within this framework the Black Arts Movement finds little room for "protest" literature for the simple reason that "protest" implicitly involves an appeal to white morality. Ethridge Knight is quoted as saying: "any Black man who masters the technique of his particular art form, who adheres to the white aesthetic, and directs his work toward a white audience is, in one sense, protesting. And implicit in the act of protest is the belief that a change will be forthcoming once the masters are aware of the protester's 'grievance' (the very word connotes begging, supplication to the gods.) Only when that belief has faded and protestings end, will Black Art begin." In this connection, the poet Don L. Lee says: "We must destroy Faulkner, dick, jane, and other perpetuators of evil. It's time for DuBois, Nat Turner, and Kwame Nkrumah."[38] As Frantz Fanon points out: 'destroy the culture and you destroy the people. This must not happen. Black artists are culture stabilizers; bringing back old values, and introducing new ones. Black Art will talk to the people and with the will of the people stop impending 'protective custody.' "[39]

37. *Ibid.*
38. *Ibid.*, p. 30.
39. *Ibid.*, pp. 29-30.

A DRAMA IN THREE ACTS

A RAISIN IN THE SUN

by Lorraine Hansberry

Lorraine Hansberry *(1930-1965)*

Lorraine Hansberry was born in Chicago of prosperous upper middle class parents. Pride in family was one of Miss Hansberry's leading characteristics. Her father, a prominent real estate investor and banker, spent a private fortune, she tells us, in fighting restrictive covenants in Chicago. Several times the family withstood threats of violence and riot while their right to live in a hitherto all white neighborhood was carried to the courts. Ironically enough, in terms of this background and in terms of the theme of her most notable play, *A Raisin in the Sun,* a minor scandal broke out after the initial success of her play, when in the summer of 1959 it was revealed that the Hansberry Enterprises, of which Miss Hansberry was a corporate member, had invoked the wrath of the city fathers for innumerable infractions of the housing code and that the Hansberrys were, indeed, prominent slumlords on Chicago's Southside.

Educated first in the public schools of Chicago's Southside, Miss Hansberry sought initially to make a name for herself, not as a writer, but as a painter. She studied painting at The Chicago Art Institute, the University of Wisconsin, and the University of Guadalajara, in Mexico. Deciding that art was not her metier, Miss Hansberry left Chicago in 1950 to become a New Yorker, where she studied at the New School, worked at odd jobs as a department store clerk, a producer's helper, and as a waitress in a Greenwich Village restaurant run by the family of Robert Nemiroff, a composer and writer, whom she later married.

Turning from painting to writing, Miss Hansberry in New York joined the staff of Paul Robeson's *Freedom,* a left-wing Harlem journal, in 1951. She wrote articles and reviews, and tried her hand at poetry and the writing of plays. Her first complete play, *A Raisin in the Sun* opened in New York in 1959 after successful tryouts in Boston, Chicago, and Philadelphia and won the Critics Circle Award for that year. Dealing with the aspirations,

29

dreams, and frustrations of the Younger family, *A Raisin in the Sun* was the first play on the American stage to portray a black family in a natural and human manner. Miss Hansberry's second play, *The Sign in Sidney Brustein's Window* (1964) deals mainly with white characters. A posthumous compilation of unproduced works was presented in New York (1969), under the title *To Be Young, Beautiful and Black.*

INTRODUCTION

Important notice should be given to the fact that in the examination of the plays in this book the reader should not be unduly misled by all the things that our writers themselves have had to say about their work. In a period of shifting definitions and attitudes towards race, caste, nationality, and shifting considerations on the relation of art to society, nomenclature can sometimes be murky. Thus the intentional fallacy has frequently to be warned against as we give witness to what some of our writers have had to say about their efforts. Our first playwright, Lorraine Hansberry, is a particular case in point. *A Raisin in the Sun* opened at the Ethel Barrymore Theater, March 11, 1959 and ran well into 1960. Produced by Philip Rose and Daniel J. Cogan, it had the longest run on Broadway of any work by a Negro playwright. It won the Critics Circle Award over Tennessee Williams' *Sweet Bird of Youth* and Archibald MacLeish's *J. B.,* and Eugene O'Neill's *A Touch of the Poet.* It was a play of firsts. Miss Hansberry, at the age of 28, was the first Negro woman to have a play produced on Broadway. Its director, Lloyd Richards, was the first Negro to direct a play for the Broadway stage. And the play made stage stars of Sidney Poitier and Claudia McNeil. But as to the nature and intention of the play critics and playwrights demonstrated an interesting and to a degree understandable ambivalence.

"I wrote the play," Miss Hansberry was to say, "between my 26th and 27th birthdays. One night after seeing a play, I won't mention, I suddenly became disgusted with the whole body of material about Negroes—cardboard characters, cute dialect bits and hi-swing musicals from exotic scores."[1] *A Raisin in the Sun,* dealing with the aspirations and dreams of the Younger family, was likened by one critic to Chekhov's *Cherry Orchard* in that "the knowledge of how character is controlled by environment and the alteration of humor pathos is similar."[2] Others saw in it resemblance to Sean O'Casey's *Juno and the Paycock* and to Clifford Odets' *Awake and Sing!* In a *New York Times* interview, Miss Hansberry is reported as telling her husband before writing *A Raisin in the Sun,* "I'm going to write a social drama about Negroes that will be good art."[3] At this point the author seems

1. Interview in New York *Times,* March 8, 1959.
2. Brooks Atkinson, New York *Times,* March 8, 1959.
3. Interview in New York *Times,* March 8, 1959.

to have made it quite clear that she was writing as much for and of the Negro as she was for the American theater. And this is underscored when we find Miss Hansberry saying of her play, "The thing I tried to show was the many gradations of even one Negro family, the clash of the old and the new, but most of all, the unbelievable courage of the Negro people."[4]

But in time as part of the controversy that surrounded the true mean- ing of A Raisin in the Sun, involving the question as to whether the play was a work of social protest or not, Miss Hansberry could assert that her play was not a Negro play, but one about people who happened to be Negro, and she could insist that she was not a Negro playwright but a writer who hap- pened to be a Negro. And in 1964 when her second play, dealing with Bohemian life in Greenwich Village, The Sign in Sidney Brustein's Window, opened with Diana Sands and a largely white cast, Miss Hansberry had this to say: "Some persons ask how it is that I have 'left the Negro question' in the writing of this latest play. I hardly know how to answer as it seems to me that I have never written about 'the Negro question.' A Raisin in the Sun, for instance, was a play about an American family's conflict with certain of the mercenary values of its society, and its characters were Negroes. . . . I write plays about various matters which have both Negro and White charac- ters in them and there is really nothing else that I can think to say about the matter."[5]

The content of the play itself and the fact that the title comes from Langston Hughes' black poem, "Dream Deferred," finally say more about Miss Hansberry's accomplishment in A Raisin in the Sun than do her ambivalent and contradictory statements on her intentions.

The plot of A Raisin in the Sun is fairly well known. In brief outline it deals with the impact on the Younger family when it receives an insurance policy check for $10,000 after the death of the father, and what happens to the son, Walter, when he tries to use it in a business scheme—the buying of a liquor store—that he insists will free him from the limitations of his job as a chauffeur and make the family rich. The tension in the play centers in the differing views of Walter and his mother on the liberation of one black family from poverty and the cramped diminution of spirit bred by racial discrimination and the limited opportunities of life in the ghetto. The play is in turn melodramatic, comic, pathetic, realistic, idealistic, and triumphant. It abounds in stock characters; Lena Younger, Mama, is the tyrannical, good- natured, matriarchal head of the household; Walter Lee, her son, is a frus- trated and trapped young man, surrounded by too many women; Ruth is his exasperated and long-suffering wife; Beneatha is a self-consciously liberated, free-thinking college student; the African Asagai is an ambitious poetic revolu- tionary; the one white man in the cast is a tremulous, cliché-ridden suburban- ite. Certain critics severely impatient with the plot and characterization dubbed the play a black soap opera. But Harold Clurman, in his review of

4. Ibid.
5. New York Times, October 11, 1964, Section II, p. 3.

the Broadway production said: "The play is organic theatre: cast, text, direction are homogenous in social orientation and in sentiment, in technique and in quality of talent."[6]

The play concludes with Walter Lee Younger's coming into his manhood and with the Youngers, after many reversals, moving from their crowded Chicago Southside tenement to their new house in the suburbs. But it has to be remembered that the play does not have what is traditionally called a happy ending. It moves rather, as Robert Nemiroff points out, towards "a commitment to new levels of struggle."[7] This comment is important in a consideration of the social content of A Raisin in the Sun, as is John Davis' comment that a basic problem confronting the black writer is the fact that "he must write for a non-Negro market which often is also the object of his protest." And he could describe the social protest in A Raisin in the Sun as presented with such consummate art "that audiences were constrained to applaud the very protest directed against them."[8]

But Harold Cruse, in an interesting but somewhat partisan interpretation, has this to say: "The phenomenal success of A Raisin in the Sun has to be seen against the background of the temper of the radical situation in America and its cultural implications for American art forms. Broadway and the rest of the theatre has not been at all kind to the Negro playwright and performer. Miss Hansberry's play provided the perfect opportunity to make it all up, or at least assuage the commercial theater's liberal guilt. . . . What obviously elated the drama critics was the very relieving discovery that, what the publicity buildup actually heralded was not the arrival of belligerent forces across the color line to settle some long-standing racial accounts on stage, but a good old-fashioned, homespun saga of some good working-class folk in pursuit of the American dream . . . in their fashion."[9] It may be that the soundest analysis of this play will lie somewhere between the assessments of Atkinson, Clurman, Davis, Cruse and Nemiroff. But there can be little doubt that, in the words of Loften Mitchell, A Raisin in the Sun did crystallize an era that Negro playwrights began to call the nots. "The critics said In Splendid Error was not a message play. Trouble in Mind was not vindictive, Take a Giant Step was not just about Negroes. Simply Heavenly was not an angry play, A Land Beyond the River was not a propaganda play, and A Raisin in the Sun was not a Negro play. In other words, black playwrights were being praised for not making white people uncomfortable in the theatre. Black playwrights began to worry about their work."[10]

6. Harold Clurman, "Theatre," The Nation (April 4, 1959), 302.

7. Robert Nemiroff, "Introduction," The Sign in Sidney Brustein's Window (New York: Alfred A. Knopf, 1964), p. xxi.

. 8. John A. Davis, "Preface," The Negro Writer and His Roots (New York: The American Society of African Culture), pp. iii-iv.

9. Harold Cruse, The Crisis of the Negro Intellectual (New York: William Morrow, 1967), pp. 277-78.

10. Loften Mitchell, Black Drama, The Story of the American-Negro in the Theatre (New York: Hawthorn Books, 1967), p. 182.

A Raisin in the Sun

> To Mama:
> in gratitude for the dream

What happens to a dream deferred?
Does it dry up
Like a raisin in the sun?
And fester like a sore—
And then run?
Does it stink like rotten meat?
Or crust and sugar over—
Like a syrupy sweet?

Maybe it just sags
Like a heavy load.

Or does it explode?
                    —Langston Hughes

CHARACTERS

Ruth Younger
Travis Younger
Walter Lee Younger (Brother)
Beneatha Younger
Lena Younger (Mama)
Joseph Asagai
George Murchison
Bobo
Karl Lindner
Two Moving Men

The action takes place in the Younger's apartment in Chicago's South-side, sometime between World War II and the present. The production is in three acts and six scenes.

PRODUCTION NOTES
The Younger living room would be a comfortable and well-ordered room, if it were not for a number of indestructible contradictions to

this state of being. Its furnishings are typical and undistinguished and their primary feature now is that they have clearly had to accommodate the living of too many people for too many years—and they are tired. Still, we can see, at some time, a time probably no longer remembered by the family (except perhaps for Mama), the furnishings of this room were actually selected with care and love and even hope —and brought to this apartment and arranged with taste and pride.

That was a long time ago. Now the once loved pattern of the couch upholstery has to fight to show itself from under acres of crocheted doilies and couch covers which have themselves finally come to be more important than the upholstery. And here a table or a chair has been moved to disguise the worn places in the carpet; but the carpet has fought back by showing its weariness, with depressing uniformity, elsewhere on its surface.

Weariness has, in fact, won in this room. Everything has been polished, washed, sat on, used, scrubbed too often. All pretenses but Living itself have long since vanished from the very atmosphere of this room.

Moreover, a section of this room, for it is not really a room unto itself, though the landlord's lease would make it seem so, slopes backward to provide a small kitchen area where the family prepares the meals which are eaten in the living room proper which must also serve as dining room. The single window which has been provided for these "two" rooms is located in this kitchen area. The sole natural light which the family may enjoy in the course of a day is only that which fights its way through this little window.

At left, a door leads to a bedroom which is shared by Mama and her daughter, Beneatha. At right opposite, is a second room (which in the beginning of life for this apartment was probably a breakfast room or something) which serves as a bedroom for Brother and his wife, Ruth.

Act One

SCENE 1

Time: *Sometime between World War II and The Present.*
Place: *Chicago's Southside.* .
At Rise: At Curtain *it is morning dark in the living room.* **Travis** *is asleep on the makedown bed at C. An* ALARM CLOCK *sounds from within the bedroom at R.* **Ruth** *and* **Walter** *are in the bedroom.* **Ruth** *rises from the bed; shuts off the* ALARM; *crosses U.C.; raises the window shade; closes the window; shivers; puts on robe, slippers; grabs* **Travis'** *shirt, towel, toothbrush, glass and clock. She opens the door to the living room, crosses in to sofa, shakes* **Travis,** *places his towel and shirt on the back of the sofa, clock and glass on kitchen*

*table. She crosses in to kitchen, raises window-shade, closes window, washes face. She calls to **Travis** in a slightly muffled voice between yawns: Ad lib.: "Wake up, Travis!" "Come on, boy!" **Ruth** is about thirty. We can see that she was a pretty girl, even exceptionally so, but now it is apparent that life has been little that she expected and disappointment has already begun to hang in her face. In a few years, before thirty-five even, she will be known among her people as a "settled woman." She dries her face and hands, crosses to C. door, gets milk and newspaper, notes bathroom, and crosses to her son and gives him a good, final, rousing shake.*

Ruth: Come on now, boy, it's seven-thirty!

(*Travis sits up at last in a stupor of sleepiness.*)

I say hurry up, Travis! You ain't the only person in the world got to use a bathroom!

(*Travis drags himself out of the bed. **Ruth** gives him his shirt, towel, toothbrush and glass and pushes him out the door to the bathroom which is in an outside hall and which is shared by another family or families on the same floor. **Ruth** picks up newspaper, notes **Walter** is still asleep, crosses to the bedroom door at R., opens it and calls in to her husband.*)

WALTER LEE—its after seven-thirty! Lemme see you do some waking up in there now!

(*She crosses to kitchen, puts water on to boil, heats coffeepot. She waits.*)

You better get up from there, man! It's after seven-thirty, I tell you.

(*She sets table. She waits again.*)

All right, you just go ahead and lay there and next thing you know Travis be finished and Mr. Johnson'll be in there and you'll be fussing and cussing round here like a mad man! And be late, too—!

(*She waits. At the end of her patience she crosses R. to the bedroom.*)

WALTER LEE—it's time for you to get up!

(*She waits another second and then starts to go into the room but is apparently satisfied that her husband has started to get up. She stops, pulls the door to and crosses back to kitchen. She puts mixing bowl and fork on sink edge, gets eggs from icebox. The bedroom door at R. opens and her husband stands in the doorway in his pajamas, which are rumpled and mismated. He holds his clothes and toilet articles. He is a lean, intense young man in his middle thirties, inclined to quick movements and erratic speech habits—and always in his voice, indictment. As he enters **Ruth** runs her fingers through her sleep-disheveled hair in a vain effort and ties an apron around her housecoat.*)

Walter:

(*Enters and crosses in to C.*)

Is he out yet—?

Ruth: What you mean, out? He ain't hardly got in there good yet.

Walter:

(*Still more oriented to sleep than to a new day.*)

Well, what was you doing all that yelling for if I can't even get in there yet?

(*Crosses R. back of sofa to bedroom door R., stops and thinks.*)

Check coming today?

Ruth:

(*Gets eggs from the icebox and breaks them into bowl.*)

They *said* Saturday and this is just Friday and I hopes to God you ain't going to get up here first thing this morning and start talking to me 'bout no money —'cause I 'bout don't want to hear it.

Walter:

(*Crosses in to C.*)

Something the matter with you this morning?

Ruth: No—I'm just sleepy as the devil. What kind of eggs you want?

Walter: Not scrambled.

(**Ruth** *beats eggs.* **Walter** *notes her action, then puts his clothes on L. end of sofa, crosses to above table. Reading the news absently again.*)

Say, Colonel McCormick is sick.

Ruth:

(*Puts egg bowl back in icebox. Affecting tea-party interest.*)

Is he now? Po' thing.

Walter:

(*Sighing and looking at alarm clock.*)

Oh me.

(*He waits.*)

Now what is that boy doing in that bathroom all this time? He is just going to have to start getting up earlier. I can't be being late to work on account of him fooling around in there.

(*He rises, crosses up to door.*)

Ruth:

(*Pours and stirs oats in hot water.*)

Oh, no, he ain't going to be getting up no earlier no such thing! It ain't his fault that he can't get to bed no earlier nights 'cause he got a bunch of crazy good-for-nothing clowns sitting up running their mouths in what is supposed to be his bedroom after ten o'clock at night—

Walter:

(*Crosses back of kitchen table, gets a cigarette from* **Ruth**'s *handbag hanging on the back of the chair L.*)

That's what you're mad about, ain't it?

(*Topping her.*)

The things I want to talk about with my friends just couldn't be important in your mind, could they?

(*He crosses to kitchen window and looks out, smoking and enjoying this first one deeply.*)

Ruth:

(*Crosses to table for milk. Almost matter-of-factly, a complaint too automatic to deserve emphasis.*)

Why you always got to smoke before you eat in the morning?

Walter:

(At the window.)

Just look at 'em down there—running and racing to work—

(He turns and faces his wife and watchs her a moment at the stove. **Ruth** mixes milk in the eggs. **Walter** says suddenly.)

You look young this morning, Baby.

(He crosses D.L. to stove, L. of **Ruth**.)

Ruth:

(Indifferently.)

Yeah?

Walter: Just for a second—stirring them eggs.

(**Ruth** looks at him.)

Just for a second it was—you looked real young again.

(**Ruth** takes milk to the table, pours a glass for **Travis**. **Walter** says drily.)

It's gone now—you look like yourself again.

Ruth:

(Scrapes cereal into bowl.)

Man, if you don't shut up and leave me alone.

(Looking out to the street again.)

Walter:

First thing a man ought to learn in life is not to make love to no colored woman first thing in the morning. Y'all some evil people at eight o'clock in the morning.

(**Travis** appears in the hall doorway almost fully dressed and quite wide-awake now, his towel and pajamas across his shoulders. He is a sturdy, handsome little boy of ten or eleven. He opens the door and signals for his father to make the bathroom in a hurry. **Walter** starts to sit; springs up as **Travis** enters with his speech. **Ruth** puts cereal bowl on the table, pours milk on the cereal.)

Travis:

(Watching the bathroom.)

Daddy, come on!

(**Walter** gets his bathroom utensils and flies out to the bathroom.)

Ruth: Sit down and have your breakfast, Travis.

(She gets butter from icebox.)

Travis:

(Puts slippers L. end of sofa, toothbrush, glass on table. Then he gets his chair from L. wall and places it R. of table.)

Mama, this is Friday.

(Gleefully.)

Check coming tomorrow, huh?

Ruth:

(Puts butter on his cereal.)

You get your mind off money and eat your breakfast.

(Takes butter to stove, puts some in frying pan.)

A RAISIN IN THE SUN   37

Travis:
> *(Eating.)*

This is the morning we supposed to bring the fifty cents to school.

Ruth: Well, I ain't got no fifty cents this morning.

Travis: Teacher say we have to.

Ruth: I don't care what teacher say. I ain't got it. Eat your breakfast, Travis.

Travis: I *am* eating.

Ruth: Hush up now and just eat!

Travis:
> *(He gives her an exasperated look for her lack of understanding and eats grudgingly.)*

You think Grandmama would have it?

Ruth: No! And I want you to stop asking your grandmother for money, you hear me?

Travis:
> *(Outraged.)*

Gaaaleee! I don't ask her, she just gimme it sometimes!

Ruth:
> *(Under breath almost.)*

TRAVIS WILLARD YOUNGER—I got too much on me this morning to be—

Travis: Maybe Daddy—

Ruth: TRAVIS!
> *(**Travis** hushes abruptly. They are both qiuet and tense for several seconds. **Ruth** puts the butter in the icebox.)*

Travis:
> *(Presently.)*

Could I maybe go carry some groceries in front of the supermarket for a little while after school, then?

Ruth: Just hush, I said.
> *(**Travis** jabs his spoon into his cereal bowl viciously and rests his head in anger upon his fists.)*

If you're through eating you can get over there and make up your bed.

Travis:
> *(Obeys stiffly and rises from the table, crosses the room almost mechanically to the bed and more or less carefully folds the bed-clothes. He gets school books and cap from the buffet. He crosses to C. door. Sulking and standing apart from her unnaturally.)*

I'm gone.

Ruth:
> *(Looking up from the stove to inspect him automatically. She crosses to her handbag on chair L. of table.)*

Come here.
> *(He crosses to her and she studies his head.)*

If you don't take this comb and fix this here head you better!
> *(**Travis** puts down his books with a great sigh of oppression and returns D.R. to the mirror. His mother mutters under her breath about his "slubbornness.")*

'Bout to march out of here with that head looking just like chickens slept in it! I just don't know where you get your slubborn ways.
Travis:
> (With conspicuously brushed hair he gets his jacket and crosses to C. door.)

I'm gone.
Ruth:
> (Pours eggs into pan, puts egg bowl in the sink.)

And get your jacket, too. Looks chilly out this morning.
> (Finding her purse and fishing in it as she regards him again.)

Get your carfare and milk money—
> (Waving one finger.)

And not a single penny for no caps, you hear me?
Travis:
> (Crosses down above table to Ruth's handbag. With sullen politeness.)

Yes'm.
> (He turns in outrage to leave, crosses U.C. again to door. **Ruth** watches him as he approaches the door almost comically in his frustration. When she speaks to him her voice has become a very gentle tease.)

Ruth:
> (At R. end of sink. Mocking as she thinks **Travis** would say it.)

Oh, Mama makes me so mad sometimes I don't know what to do!
> (**Travis** stands at the door and **Ruth** waits and continues to his back as he stands stock still in front of the door.)

I wouldn't kiss that woman good-bye this morning not for nothing in this world!
> (**Travis** finally turns around and rolls his eyes at her knowing the mood has changed and he is vindicated; he does not, however, move toward her yet.)

Not for nothing in this world!
> (She finally laughs aloud at him and holds out her arms to him and we see that it is a way between them very old and practiced. **Travis** crosses D.C. and allows her to embrace him warmly but keeps his face fixed with masculine rigidity. She holds him back from her presently, and looks at him and runs her fingers over the features of his face. With utter gentleness.)

Now—whose little old angry man are you?
Travis:
> (The masculinity and gruffness start to fade at last.)

Aw Gaalee—Mama—
Ruth:
> (Mimicking.)

Aw—Gaaaalleeeeee, Mama!
> (She pushes him with rough playfulness and finality toward the door.)

Get on out of here or you going to be late.
Travis:
> (Crosses to C. door. In the face of love, new aggressiveness.)

Mama, could I please go carry groceries?
Ruth:
>*(Stirs eggs in pan.)*

Honey, it's starting to get so cold evenings.
Walter:
>*(Coming in from the bathroom, crosses R. into his bedroom with his pajamas, towel, toothbrush and glass.)*

What is it he wants to do?
Ruth: Go carry groceries after school at the supermarket.
Walter: Well, let him go—
Travis:
>*(Quickly to the ally. Crosses R. to bedroom door.)*

I *have* to—she won't gimme the fifty cents—
Walter:
>*(Re-enters from bedroom. To his wife only.)*

Why not—?
Ruth:
>*(Simply and with flavor.)*

'Cause we don't have it.
Walter:
>*(To **Ruth** only as he crosses to C.)*

What you tell the boy things like that for?
>*(Reaching down on the line into his pants' pocket with a rather important gesture. Turns, crosses down in front of sofa.)*

Here, son—
>*(He hands the boy the coin, but his eyes are only on his wife. **Travis** takes the money happily.)*

Travis: Thanks, Daddy.
>*(He starts out.)*
>*(**Ruth** watches both of them with murder in her eyes. **Walter** stands and stares back at her with defiance and suddenly reaches into his pocket again on an afterthought.)*

Walter:
>*(C.L. of sofa. Without even looking at his son, still staring hard at his wife.)*

In fact, here's another fifty cents— Buy yourself some fruit today—or take a taxi-cab to school or something!
Travis: Whoopee—
>*(**Ruth** starts serving eggs. **Travis** leaps up and clasps his father around the middle with his legs and they face each other in mutual appreciation; slowly **Walter** peeks around the boy to catch the ultra violent rays from his wife's eyes and draws his head back as if shot.)*

Walter: You better get down now—and get to school, man.
Travis:
>*(At the door.)*

O.K. Good-bye.
>*(He exits.)*

Walter:

(After him, pointing with pride. Crosses D.R. to mirror.)

That's *my* boy.

(**Ruth** looks at him in disgust and turns back to her work.)

You know what I was thinking 'bout in the bathroom this morning—?

Ruth: No.

Walter: How come you always try to be so pleasant!

Ruth: What is there to be pleasant 'bout!

(She serves eggs at the table.)

Walter: You want to know what I was thinking 'bout in the bathroom or not!

Ruth: I know what you was thinking 'bout.

Walter:

(Ignoring her.)

'Bout what me and Willy Harris was talking about last night.

Ruth:

(Pours two cups of coffee. Immediately—a refrain.)

Willy Harris a good for nothing loud mouth.

Walter:

(Crosses C. to front of sofa.)

Anybody who talks to me has got to be a good for nothing loud mouth, ain't he? And what you know about who is just a good for nothing loud mouth? Charlie Atkins was just a "good for nothing loud mouth" too, wasn't he! When he wanted me to go in the dry-cleaning business with him. And now— he's grossing $100,000 a year. $100,000 a year! You still call *him* a loud mouth?!

Ruth:

(Sits L. of table. Bitterly.)

Oh, Walter Lee—

(She folds her head over on the table on her arms.)

Walter:

(Rising and coming to her and standing over her.)

You tired, ain't you? Tired of everything. Me, the boy, the way we live—this beat up hole—everything. Ain't you?

(She doesn't look up, doesn't answer.)

So tired—moaning and groaning all the time but you wouldn't do nothing to help, would you. You couldn't be on my side that long for nothing, could you?

Ruth: Walter, please leave me alone.

Walter: A man needs for a woman to back him up—

Ruth: Walter—

Walter:

(Crosses to above table.)

Mama would listen to you. You know she listen to you more than she do me and Bennie. She think more of you. All you have to do is just sit down with her when she was drinking your coffee one morning and talking 'bout things like you do and—

(He sits down beside her and demonstrates graphically what he thinks her methods and tone should be.)

You just sip your coffee, see, and say easy like that you been thinking 'bout that deal Walter Lee is so interested in, 'bout the store and all, and sip some more coffee, like what you saying ain't really that important to you— And the next thing you know she listening good and asking you questions and when I come home—I can tell her the details. This ain't no fly-by-night proposition, Baby. I mean we figured it out, me and Willy and Bobo.

Ruth:

(With a frown.)

Bobo—?

Walter:

(Sits at chair above table.)

Yeah. You see, this little liquor store we got in mind cost $75,000 and we figured the initial investment on the place be 'bout $30,000, see. That be ten thousand each. Course, there's a couple of hundred you got to pay so's you don't spend your life just waiting for them clowns to let your license get approved—

Ruth: You mean graft?

Walter:

(Frowning impatiently.)

Don't call it that. See there, that just goes to show you what women understand about the world. Baby, don't *nothing* happen for you in this world 'less you pay *somebody* off!

Ruth: Walter, leave me alone!

(She raises her head on the line, and stares at him vigorously—then says more quietly.)

Eat your eggs, they gonna be cold.

Walter:

(Straightening up from her and looking off.)

You see that? Man says to his woman: I got me a dream. His woman say: Eat your eggs.

(Sadly, but gaining in power.)

Man say: I got to take hold of this here world, Baby! And a woman will say: Eat your eggs and go to work. Man say—

(Passionately now.)

I got to change my life, I'm choking to death, Baby! And his woman say—

(In utter anguish as he brings his fists down on his thighs.)

Your eggs is getting cold!—

Ruth:

(Softly.)

Walter, that ain't none of our money.

Walter:

(Not listening at all or even looking at her.)

This morning, I was lookin' in the mirror and thinking about it—I'm thirty-five years old; I been married eleven years and I got a boy who sleeps in the living-room—

(Very, very quietly.)
and all I got nothing to give him, nothing but stories about how rich white people live—
Ruth: Eat your eggs, Walter.
Walter:
(Rises, crosses R. to C.)
DAMN MY EGGS—DAMN ALL THE EGGS THAT EVER WAS!
Ruth: Then go to work.
Walter:
(Looking up at her, crosses L. to above table.)
See—I'm trying to talk to you 'bout me—
(Shaking his head with the repetition.)
And all you can say is eat them eggs and go to work.
Ruth:
(Wearily.)
Honey, you never say nothing new. I listen to you every day—every night and every morning and you never say nothing new.
(Shrugging.)
So you would rather *be* Mr. Arnold than be his chauffeur. So—I would *rather* be living in Buckingham Palace.
Walter: That is just what is wrong with the colored women in this world— don't understand about building their men up and making 'em feel like they somebody. Like they can do something.
Ruth:
(Drily, but to hurt.)
There are colored men who do things.
Walter: No thanks to the colored woman.
Ruth: Well, being a colored woman I guess I can't help myself none.
(She rises, crosses U.L. to closet for the ironing board, sets it up behind the sofa, attacks a huge pile of rough dried clothes, sprinkling them in preparation for the ironing and then rolling them into right fat balls.)
Walter:
(Sits above table. Mumbling.)
We one group of men tied to a race of women with small minds.
*(His sister **Beneatha** enters L. on the line. She is about twenty, as slim and intense as her brother. She is not as pretty as her sister-in-law, but her lean, almost intellectual face has a handsomeness of its own. She wears a pair of well-worn pajamas and her long thick hair stands wildly about her head. She appears and passes through the room without looking at either of them and goes to the outside door and looks, a little blindly, out to the bathroom. She sees that it has been lost to the Johnsons. She closes the door with a sleepy vengeance and crosses to the table and sits down a little defeated.)*
Beneatha:
(Her speech is a mixture of many things; it is different from the rest of the family's insofar as education has permeated her sense of English

—and perhaps the midwest rather than the south has finally—at last —won out in her inflection; but not altogether because over all of it is a soft slurring and transformed use of vowels which is the decided influence of the south side. She rises and crosses to place towel and socks on sofa L.)

I am going to start timing those people.

Walter: You should get up earlier.

Beneatha:

(Her face is in her hands—she is still fighting the urge to go back to bed. Sits R. of table.)

Really—would you suggest dawn? Where's the paper?

Walter:

(Senselessly.)

How is school coming?

Beneatha:

(In the same spirit.)

Lovely. Lovely. And you know, Biology is the greatest.

(Looking up at him.)

I dissected something that looked just like you yesterday.

Walter: I just wondered if you've made up your mind and everything.

Beneatha:

(Gaining in sharpness and impatience prematurely.)

And what did I answer yesterday morning—and the day before that—?

Ruth:

(Crossing back to ironing board R., like someone disinterested and old.)

Don't be so nasty, Bennie.

Beneatha:

(Still to her brother.)

And the day before that and the day before that!

Walter:

(Defensively.)

I'm interested in you. Something wrong with that? Ain't many girls who decide—

Walter *and* **Beneatha:**

(In unison.)

—"to be a doctor."

(Silence.)

Walter: Have we figured out yet just exactly how much medical school is going to cost?

Beneatha:

(Rises, exits to bathroom. Knocks on the door.)

Come on out of there, please!

(Re-enters.)

Ruth: Walter Lee, why don't you leave that girl alone and get out of here to work?

Walter:

(Looking at his sister intently.)

You know the check is coming tomorrow.

Beneatha:

>*(Turning on him with a sharpness all her own. She crosses D.R. and sprawls on sofa.)*

That money belongs to Mama, Walter, and it's for her to decide how she wants to use it. I don't care if she wants to buy a house or a rocket ship or just nail it up somewhere and look at it—it's hers. Not ours—*hers.*

Walter:

>*(Bitterly.)*

Now ain't that fine! You just got your mother's interests at heart, ain't you, girl? You such a nice girl—but if Mama got that money she can always take a few thousand and help you through school too—can't she?

Beneatha: I have never asked anyone around here to do anything for me!

Walter: No! But the line between asking and just accepting when the time comes is big and wide—ain't it!

Beneatha:

>*(With fury.)*

What do you want from me, Brother—that I quit school or just drop dead, which!

Walter:

>*(Rises, crosses down back of sofa.)*

I don't want nothing but for you to stop acting holy around here—me and Ruth done made some sacrifices for you—why can't you do something for the family?

Ruth: Walter, don't be dragging me in it.

Walter: You are in it—Don't you get up and go work in somebody's kitchen for the last three years to help put clothes on her back—?

>*(**Beneatha** rises, crosses, sits armchair D.R.)*

Ruth: Oh, Walter—that's not fair—

Walter: It ain't that nobody expects you to get on your knees and say thank you, Brother; thank you, Ruth; thank you, Mama—and thank you, Travis, for wearing the same pair of shoes for two semesters—

Beneatha:

>*(In front of sofa, falls on her knees.)*

WELL—I DO—ALL RIGHT?—THANK EVERYBODY—AND FORGIVE ME FOR EVER WANTING TO BE ANYTHING AT ALL—FORGIVE ME, FORGIVE ME!

>*(She rises, crosses D.R. to armchair.)*

Ruth: Please stop it! Your Mama'll hear you.

Walter:

>*(Crosses U.C. to kitchen table. Ties shoes at chair R. of table.)*

—Who the hell told you you had to be a doctor? If you so crazy 'bout messing round with sick people—then go be a nurse like other women—or just get married and be quiet—

Beneatha:

>*(Crossing toward L. end of sofa.)*

Well—you finally got it said— It took you three years but you finally got it said. Walter, give up; leave me alone—it's Mama's money.

Walter: HE WAS MY FATHER, TOO!

Beneatha: So what? He was mine, too—and Travis' grandfather—BUT the insurance money belongs to Mama. Picking on me is not going to make her give it to you to invest in any liquor stores—

(Sits armchair D.R. Under her breath.)

And I for one say, God bless Mama for that!

(On Beneatha's line Ruth crosses U.L. to closet.)

Walter:

(To Ruth.)

See—did you hear?—Did you hear!

Ruth:

(Crosses D.C. to Walter with Walter's jacket from the closet.)

Honey, please go to work.

Walter:

(Back of sofa, crosses U.C. to door.)

Nobody in this house is ever going to understand me.

Beneatha: Because you're a nut.

Walter:

(Stops, turns D.C.)

Who's a nut?

Beneatha: You—you are a nut. Thee is mad, boy.

Walter:

(Looking at his wife and sister from the door, very sadly.)

The world's most backward race of people and that's a fact.

(Exits C.)

Beneatha:

(Turning slowly in her chair.)

And then there are all those prophets who would lead us out of the wilderness—

(Rises, crosses U.C. to chair R. of kitchen table, sits. Walter slams out of the house.)

Into the swamps!

Ruth: Bennie, why you always gotta be pickin' on your brother? Can't you be a little sweeter sometimes?

(Door opens. Walter walks in.)

Walter:

(To Ruth.)

I need some money for carfare.

Ruth:

(Looks at him, then warms, teasing, but tenderly.)

Fifty cents?

(She crosses D.L. front of table, gets her purse from handbag.)

Here, take a taxi.

(Walter starts to leave, Ruth pecks his cheek affectionately. Walter exits. Mama enters L. She is a woman in her early sixties, full-bodied and strong. She is one of those women of certain grace and beauty

who wear it so unobtrusively that it takes a while to notice. Her dark brown face is surrounded by the total whiteness of her hair—and—being a woman who has adjusted to many things in life and over-come many more, her face is full of strength. She has, we can see, wit and faith of a kind that keep her eyes lit and full of interest and expectancy. She is, in a word, a beautiful woman. Her bearing is per-haps most like that of the Herero women—rather as if she imagines that as she walks she bears a basket or a vessel upon her head. Her speech on the other hand is as careless as her carriage is precise—she is inclined to slur everything—but the voice is perhaps not so much quiet as simply—soft.

Mama: Who that round here slamming doors at this hour?

(She crosses through the room, fixing a bandana on her head in honor of the forthcoming labors of the day. She goes to the window, opens it and brings in a feeble little plant growing doggedly in a small pot on the window sill. She feels the dirt.)

Ruth: That was Walter Lee. He and Bennie was at it again.

Mama:

(Takes the plant to the sink, waters it.)

My children and they tempers. Lord, if this little old plant don't get more sun than it's been getting it ain't never going to see Spring again. What's the matter with you this morning, Ruth, you looks right peaked. You aiming to iron all them things—leave some for me. I'll get to 'em this afternoon. Bennie honey, it's too drafty for you to be sitting round half dressed. Where's your robe?

Beneatha: In the cleaners.

Mama: Well, go get mine and put it on.

Beneatha: I'm not cold, Mama, honest.

Mama: I know—but you so thin—

Beneatha:

(Irritably.)

Mama, I'm not cold.

Mama:

*(Seeing the makedown bed as **Travis** has sloppily left it. Crosses R. to sofa.)*

Lord have mercy, look at that poor bed. Bless his heart—he tries, don't he?

Ruth:

(Crosses L. to sink above table with piece of laundry, tries rubbing out a spot under the faucet.)

No—he don't half try at all 'cause he knows you going to come along behind him and fix everything. That's just how come he don't know how to do nothing right now—you done spoiled that boy so.

Mama:

(Business with bedclothes.)

Well—he's a little boy. Ain't supposed to know 'bout housekeeping. My baby, that's what he is. What you fix for his breakfast this morning?

Ruth:

>   (*Angrily.*)

I feed my son, Lena!

Mama: I ain't meddling—

>   (*Kind of underbreath and busybodyish.*)

I just noticed all last week he had cold cereal. When it starts getting this chilly in the fall a child ought to have some hot grits or something when he goes out in the cold—

Ruth:

>   (*Crosses above table to ironing board. Furious.*)

I gave him hot oats—is that all right?

Mama: I ain't meddling.

>   (*Pause from working the bed. Crosses R. into bedroom R.*)

Put a lot of nice butter on it?

>   (**Ruth** *shoots her an angry look and does not reply.*)

He likes lots of butter.

>   (*She re-enters living room*).

Ruth:

>   (*Exasperated.*)

Lena—

Mama:

>   (*To* **Beneatha**. *She is inclined to wander sometimes conversationally.*)

What was you and your brother fussing 'bout—

>   (*The bathroom door slams.*)

This morning?

Beneatha: It's not important, Mama.

>   (*She gets up and goes to look out at the bathroom which is apparently free, and she picks up her towels and rushes out.*)

Mama:

>   (*U.C. back of L. end of sofa.*)

What was they fighting about?

Ruth: Now you know as well as I do.

Mama:

>   (*Shaking her head.*)

Brother still worrying hisself sick about that money?

Ruth: You know he is.

Mama: You had breakfast?

Ruth: Some coffee.

Mama:

>   (*Crosses to* **Ruth**.)

Girl, you better start eating and looking after yourself better. You almost thin as Travis.

>   (*Crosses into kitchen area to the sink L. with some dishes.*)

Ruth: Lena—

Mama: Un-hunh?

Ruth: What are you going to do with it?

Mama: Now don't you start, child. Its too early in the morning to be talking about money. Besides, it ain't Christian.

Ruth: It's just that he got his heart set on that store—

Mama: You mean that liquor store that Willy Harris want him to invest in?

    (She crosses above table, sits R. of table with coffee cup.)

Ruth: Yes—

Mama: We ain't no business people, Ruth. We just plain working folks.

Ruth:

    (Still at ironing board behind sofa.)

Ain't nobody business people till they go into business. Walter Lee say colored people ain't never going to start getting ahead till they start gambling on some different kinds of things in the world—investments and things.

Mama: What done got into you, girl? Walter Lee done finally sold you on investing.

Ruth: No Mama, something is happening between Walter and me. I don't know what it is—but he needs something—something I can't give him any more. He needs this chance, Lena.

Mama:

    (Frowning deeply.)

But liquor, honey—

Ruth:

    (Above sofa, sprinkling laundry.)

Well—like Walter say—I 'spec' people going to always be drinking themselves some liquor.

Mama:

    (Still sitting R. of kitchen table.)

Well—whether they drinks it or not ain't none of my business. But whether I sells it to 'em is, and I don't want that on my ledger this late in life.

    (Stopping suddenly and studying her daughter-in-law.)

Ruth Younger, what's the matter with you today? You look like you could fall over right there.

Ruth: I'm tired.

Mama: Then you better stay home from work today.

Ruth: I can't stay home. She be calling up the agency and screaming at them—"My girl didn't come in today—send me somebody! My girl didn't come in!" Oh, she just have a fit—

Mama: Well, let her have it. I'll just call her up and say you get the flu—

Ruth:

    (Laughing.)

Why the flu?

Mama: Cause it sounds respectable to 'em. Something white people get, too. They know 'bout the flu. Otherwise they think you been cut up or something when you tell 'em you sick.

Ruth: I got to go in. We need the money.

Mama:

    *(Rises, crosses D.L. to sink with **Travis's** milk glass.)*

Lord, have mercy! Somebody would of thought my children done all but starved to death the way they talk about money here late. Child, we got a great big old check coming tomorrow.

Ruth:

> *(Crosses L. to C. Sincerely—but also self-righteously.)*

Now that's your money. It ain't got nothing to do with me. We all feel like that—Walter and Bennie and me—even Travis.

Mama:

> *(Gets toast from oven. Thoughtfully and suddenly very far away.)*

Ten thousand dollars—

> *(She fingers her plant on R. edge of sink.)*

Ruth: Sure is wonderful.

Mama:

> *(Crosses R. to table and sits.)*

Ten thousand dollars.

Ruth:

> *(Crosses in to **Mama** to L. of kitchen table.)*

You know what you should do, Miss Lena? You should take yourself a trip somewhere. To Europe or South America or someplace—

Mama:

> *(Throwing up her hands at the thought.)*

Oh, child!

Ruth: I'm serious. Just pack up and leave! Go on away and enjoy yourself some. Forget about the family and have yourself a ball for once in your life—

Mama:

> *(Still sitting R. of kitchen table. Drily.)*

You sound like I'm just about ready to die. Who'd go with me? What I look like wandering 'round Europe by myself?

Ruth:

> *(Crossing to ironing board back of sofa.)*

Shoot—these here rich white women do it all the time. They don't think nothing of packing up they suitcases and piling on one of them big steamships and—swoosh!—they gone, child.

Mama: Something always told me I wasn't no rich white woman.

Ruth: Well—what are you going to do with it, then?

Mama: I ain't rightly decided.

> *(Thinking, and she says this with emphasis.)*

Course, some of it got to be put away for Beneatha and her medical schoolin' —and ain't nothing going to touch that part of it. Nothing.

> *(She waits several seconds trying to make up her mind about something and looks at **Ruth** a little tentatively before going on. Looking at **Ruth** askance.)*

Been thinking that we maybe could meet the notes on a little old two-story somewhere with a yard where Travis could play in the summertime—if we use part of the insurance for a down payment and everybody kind of pitch in. I could maybe take on a little day work again, few days a week—

Ruth:

> (*Studying her mother-in-law furtively and concentrating on her ironing, anxious to encourage without seeming to.*)

Well, lord knows, we've put enough rent into this here rat trap to pay for four houses by now—

> (*Crosses L. front of table to sink.*)

Mama:

> (*Still sitting R. of kitchen table. Looking up at the words "rat trap" and then looking around and leaning back and sighing—in a sudden reflective mood—*)

"Rat trap"—yes, that's all it is.

> (*Smiling.*)

I remember just as well the day me and Big Walter moved in here. Hadn't been married but two weeks and wasn't planning on living here no more than a year.

> (*She shakes her head at the dissolved dream.*)

We was going to set away, little by little, don't you know, and buy a little place out in Morgan Park. We had even picked out the house.

> (*Chuckling a little.* **Ruth** *holds at sink.*)

Looks right dumpy today. But lord, child, you should know all the dreams I had 'bout buying that house and fixing it up and making me a little garden in the back—

> (*She waits and stops smiling.*)

And didn't none of it happen.

Ruth:

> (*Sits in chair L. of table.*)

Yes, life can be a barrel of disappointments, sometimes.

Mama: Honey, Big Walter would come in here some nights back then and slump down on that couch there and just look at the rug, and look at me and look at the rug and then back at me—And I'd know he was down then—really down.

> (*After a second very long and thoughtful pause; she is seeing back to times that only she can see.*)

And then, lord, when I lost that baby—little Claude—I almost thought I was going to lose Big Walter, too. Oh that man grieved hisself! He was one man to love his children.

Ruth:

> (*Rises, crosses in front of table and goes U.R. to ironing board.*)

Ain't nothin' can tear at you like losin' your baby.

Mama: I guess that's how come that man finally worked hisself to death like he done. Like he was fighting his own war with this here world that took his baby from him.

Ruth:

> (*At ironing board.*)

He sure was a fine man, all right. I always liked Mr. Younger.

> (*She crosses L. side of couch with socks from basket.*)

Mama: Crazy 'bout his children! God knows there was plenty wrong with

Walter Younger—hard-headed, mean, kind of wild with women—plenty wrong with him. But he sure loved his children. Always wanted them to have something—be something. That's where Brother gets all these notions, I reckon. Big Walter used to say, he'd get right wet in the eyes sometimes, lean his head back with the water standing in his eyes and say "Seem like God didn't see fit to give the black man nothing but dreams— but He did give us children to make them dreams seem worthwhile."

(She smiles.)

He could talk like that, don't you know.

Ruth:

(Leaves sock on L. end of sofa.)

Yes, he sure could. He was a good man, Mr. Younger.

Mama: Yes, a fine man—just couldn't never catch up with his dreams, that's all.

Beneatha:

(She comes in brushing her hair and looking up to the ceiling where a vacuum cleaner has started up. Crosses to D.R. mirror.)

What could be so dirty on that woman's rugs that she has to vacuum them every single day?

Ruth: I wish a certain young woman 'round here who I could name would take inspiration about certain rugs in a certain apartment I could also mention.

Beneatha:

(Shrugging.)

How much cleaning can a house need, for Christ's sake?

Mama:

(Not liking the Lord's name used thus.)

Bennie!

Ruth: Just listen to her—just listen!

Beneatha: Oh God!

Mama: If you use the Lord's name just one more time—

Beneatha:

(A bit of a whine.)

Oh, Mama—

Ruth: Fresh—just fresh as salt, this girl!

Beneatha:

(Drily.)

Well—if the salt loses its savor—

Mama:

(Rises, partly clears table, crosses to sink.)

Now that will do. I just ain't going to have you 'round here reciting the scriptures in vain—you hear me?

Beneatha: How did I manage to get on everybody's wrong side by just walking into a room?

Ruth: If you weren't so fresh—

Beneatha: Ruth, I'm twenty years old.

Mama:

(Crosses back to table, clearing it and crosses D.L. to sink again.)

What time you be home from school today?

Beneatha: Kind of late. Madeline is going to start my guitar lessons today.

(Crosses U.C. to L. bedroom.)

(Mama and **Ruth** *look up with the same expression.)*

Mama:

(Gets cup and saucer from shelf.)

Your what kind of lessons?

Beneatha: Guitar.

Ruth: Oh Father!

Mama: How come you done taken it in your mind to learn to play the guitar?

Beneatha: I just want to, that's all.

Mama:

(Crosses to table, wipes it. Smiling.)

Lord, child, don't you know what to do with yourself? How long it going to be before you get tired of this now—

(Crosses R. to above table.)

Like you got tired of that little play-acting group you joined last year?

(Looking at **Ruth***)*

And what was it the year before that—?

Ruth: The horse-back riding club for which she bought that fifty-five dollar riding habit that's been hanging in the closet ever since!

Mama:

(Crosses to sink. To **Beneatha***.)*

Why you got to flit so from one thing to another, baby?

Beneatha:

(Entering from L. bedroom, dressed. Sharply.)

I just want to learn to play the guitar. Is there anything wrong with that!

Mama:

(Pours cup of coffee at stove.)

Ain't nobody trying to stop you.

*(***Beneatha** *exits L. again.)*

I just wonders sometimes why you has to flit so from one thing to another. You ain't never done nothing with all that camera equipment you brought home—

(Still D.L. at sink.)

Beneatha: I don't flit! I—I experiment with different forms of expression—

Ruth: Like riding a horse?

Beneatha: People have to express themselves one way or another.

Mama: What is it you want to express?

Beneatha:

(Entering from L. bedroom wearing sweater. Angrily.)

Me!

(Mama and **Ruth** *look at each other.)*

Don't worry—I don't expect you to understand.

(Sits L. of kitchen table.)

Mama:

(Brings cup of coffee to table. To change the subject.)

Who you going out with tomorrow night?
Beneatha:
> *(Pours milk in coffee. With displeasure.)*

George Murchison again.
Mama:
> *(Pleased.)*

Oh—you getting a little sweet on him?
Ruth: You ask me this child ain't sweet on nobody but herself—
> *(Underbreath.)*

Express herself!
> *(**Mama** picks up socks from sofa, sits chair R. of table.)*

Beneatha: Oh—I like George all right, Mama. I mean I like him enough to go out with him and stuff but—
Ruth:
> *(For devilment.)*

What does *and stuff* mean?
Beneatha: Mind your own business.
Mama: Stop picking at her now, Ruth.
> *(Thoughtful pause and then a suspicious sudden look at her daughter as she turns in her chair for emphasis.)*

What *does* it mean—?
Beneatha:
> *(Wearily.)*

Oh, I just mean I couldn't ever really be serious about George. He's—he's so shallow.
Ruth: Shallow? What do you mean he's shallow? He's RICH!
> *(**Mama** gets sewing basket from bureau, sits R. of table again.)*

Beneatha: I know he's rich. He knows he's rich, too.
Ruth: You mean you wouldn't marry George Murchison even if he asked you some day? That pretty, rich thing? Honey, I knew you was odd—
Beneatha: What are you talking about, Ruth? Listen, I'm going to be a doctor. I'm not worried about who I'm going to marry yet—if I ever get married.
> *(Rises, crosses U.L. and gets coat and bag from closet.)*

Mama *and* **Ruth:** IF!
Mama: Now, Bennie—
Beneatha:
> *(Crosses R. above sofa, puts coat on sofa.)*

Oh, I probably will—but first I'm going to be a doctor, and George, for one, still thinks that's pretty funny. I couldn't be bothered with that. I am going to be a doctor and everybody around here better understand that!
Mama:
> *(Crosses D.R. of sofa, puts rag on sofa, picks up books from floor, puts them on coffee table. Kindly.)*

'Course you going to be a doctor, honey, God willing.
Beneatha:
> *(Drily.)*

God hasn't got a thing to do with it.

Mama: Beneatha—that just wasn't necessary.

Beneatha:

(Gets her coat.)

Well—neither is God. I get sick of hearing about God.

Mama: Beneatha!

Beneatha: I mean it! I'm just tired of hearing about God all the time. What has He got to do with anything—? Does He pay tuition?

Mama: You 'bout to get your fresh little jaw slapped!

Ruth: That's just what she needs!

Beneatha: Why? Why can't I say what I want to around here like everybody else?

Mama: It don't sound nice for a young girl to say things like that—you wasn't brought up that way. Me and your father went to trouble to get you and Brother to church every Sunday.

Beneatha:

(D.R.)

Mama, you don't understand. It's all a matter of ideas and God is just one idea I don't accept. It's not important. I am not going out and be immoral or commit crimes because I don't believe in God. I don't even think about it. It's just that I get tired of Him getting credit for all the things the human race achieves through its own stubborn effort. There simply is no blasted God— there is only man, and it is he who makes miracles!

(Starts L.C. with books, etc.)

Mama:

(Absorbs this speech, studies her daughter and rises slowly from the kitchen table, crosses D.R.C. to where **Beneatha** is standing and slaps her powerfully across the face. After, there is only silence and the daughter drops her eyes from her mother's face and **Mama** is very tall before her.)

Now—you say after me, in my mother's house there is still God.

(There is a long pause and **Beneatha** stares at the floor wordlessly. **Mama** repeats with precision and cool emotion.)

In my mother's house there is still God.

Beneatha: In my mother's house there is still God.

(A long pause, then.)

Mama:

(Walking away from her, too disturbed for triumphant posture, crosses U.L., pauses, turns to her daughter.)

There are some ideas we ain't going to have in this house. Not long as I am still head of this family.

Beneatha: Yes, ma'am.

(**Mama** exists L.)

Ruth:

(Almost gently, with profound understanding.)

Bennie, you think you a woman—but you still a little girl. What you did was childish—so you got treated like a child.

Beneatha: I see.

(Quietly.)

I also see that everybody thinks it's all right for Mama to be a tyrant.

(She picks up her books and exits U.C.)

Ruth:

(Goes to Mama's door, then crosses R. to ironing board.)

She said she was sorry.

Mama:

(Coming out, crosses to C.)

They frightens me, Ruth. My children.

Ruth:

*(Crosses to **Mama**.)*

You got good children, Lena. They just a little off sometimes—but they're good.

Mama: No—there's something come down between me and them that don't let us understand each other and I don't know what it is. One done almost lost his mind thinking 'bout money all the time and the other done commence to talk about things I can't seem to understand in no form or fashion. What is it that's changing, Ruth?

Ruth:

(Soothingly, older than her years.)

Now—you taking it all too seriously. You just got strong-willed children and it takes a strong woman like you to keep 'em in hand.

Mama:

(Crosses D.C. then in front of table to sink. Bringing her plant in from sill and sprinkling a little water on it.)

They spirited all right, my children. Got to admit they got spirit—Bennie and Walter. Like this little old plant that ain't never had enough sunshine or nothing—and look at it.

*(She has her back to **Ruth**, who has had to stop ironing and lean against something and put the back of her hand to her forehead.)*

Ruth:

*(Crosses to R. kitchen chair. Trying to keep **Mama** from noticing.)*

You—sure—loves that little old thing, don't you—

Mama: Well, I always wanted me a garden like I used to see sometimes at the back of the houses down home. This plant is close as I ever got to having one.

(She looks out of the window as she replaces the plant.)

Lord, ain't nothing as dreary as the view from this window on a dreary day, is there. Why ain't you singing this morning, Ruth? Sing that *No Ways Tired.* That song always lifts me up so—

*(She turns at last to see that **Ruth** has slipped quietly into a chair, in a state of semi-consciousness.)*

Ruth! Ruth honey—what's the matter with you—Ruth!

Curtain

SCENE 2

It is the following morning; a Saturday morning and house-cleaning is in progress at the Youngers. Furniture has been shoved hither and yon, and **Mama** *at icebox is giving the kitchen area walls a washing down.* **Beneatha**, *in shorts or dungarees, is D.R. spraying insecticide into the cracks in the walls, with a handkerchief tied around her face.* **Travis**, *the sole idle one, is leaning on his arms looking out of the window. He crosses R. above table to C. door, then crosses D.C.*

Travis: Grandmama, that stuff Bennie is using smells awful. Can I go downstairs, please?

Mama: Did you get all them chores done already? I ain't seen you doing much.

Travis: Yes'm—finished early. Where did Mama go this morning?

Mama:
> *(Looking at* **Beneatha**.*)*
She had to go on a little errand.
> *(The PHONE rings.* **Beneatha** *runs to answer it and reaches it before* **Walter**, *who has entered R.)*

Travis: Where?

Mama: To tend to her business.

Beneatha: Haylo. Yes, he is.
> *(She hands the phone to* **Walter**.*)*
It's Willie Harris again.

Walter:
> *(Into phone.)*
Hello, Willy. Did you get the papers from the lawyer?—No, not yet. I told you the mailman doesn't get here till 10:30— No, I'll come over to your place— Yeah! Right away.
> *(He hangs up and goes U.L. for his coat.)*

Beneatha: Brother, where did Ruth go?

Walter:
> *(As he exits.)*
How should I know!

Travis: Aw come on, Grandma. Can I go outside?

Mama: Oh, I guess so. You better stay right in front of the house, though, and keep a good lookout for the postman.

Travis:
> *(Crosses into R. bedroom, gets ball and stick, re-enters.)*
Yes'm.
> *(He starts out and decides to give his* **Aunt Beneatha** *a good swat on the legs as he passes her.)*
Leave them poor little old cockroaches alone, they ain't bothering you none.
> *(He runs as she swings the spray gun at him both viciously and play-*

fully. **Mama** *picks up milk, chocolate milk, ritz crackers and sugar bowl.)*

Mama: Look out there, girl, before you be spilling some of that stuff on that child!

Travis:

(Teasing.)

That's right—look out, now!

(He exits.)

Beneatha:

(Sprawls on sofa. Drily.)

I can't imagine that it would hurt him—it has never hurt the roaches.

Mama: Well, little boys' hides ain't as tough as Southside roaches. You better get over there behind the bureau. I seen one marching out of there like Napoleon yesterday.

Beneatha:

(Crosses U.R. to bureau, following instructions and then sitting down.)

There's really only one way to get rid of them, Mama—

Mama: How?

Beneatha: Set fire to this building. Mama, where did Ruth go?

Mama:

(Looking at her with meaning.)

To the doctor, I think.

Beneatha: The doctor?—What's the matter?

(They exchange glances.)

You don't think—

Mama:

(With her sense of drama.)

Now I ain't saying what I think. But I ain't never been wrong 'bout a woman, neither.

(The PHONE rings.)

Beneatha:

(At the phone.)

Hay-lo— Oh!

(Pause and moment of recognition.)

Well—when did you get back!— And how was it— Of course I've missed you—in my way— This morning? No—housecleaning and all that, and Mama hates it if I let people come over when the house is like this— You *have?*— Well, that's different— What is it— Oh, what the hell, come on over— Right, see you then. Arrividerci.

(She hangs up.)

Mama:

(Who has listened vigorously, as is her habit.)

Who is that you inviting over here with this house looking like this? You ain't got the pride you was born with!

Beneatha: Asagai doesn't care how houses look, Mama—he's an intellectual.

(She crosses D.R. to mirror, snaps on FLOOR LAMP.)

Mama: Who—?

Beneatha: Asagai—Joseph Asagai. He's an African boy I met on campus—he's been studying in Canada all summer.

Mama: What's his name?

Beneatha: Asagai, Joseph AH-SAH-GUY—He's from Nigeria.

Mama: Oh, that's the little country that was founded by slaves way back—

Beneatha: No, Mama—that's Liberia.

Mama:

> *(Crosses D.L. At icebox.)*

I don't think I never met no African before.

Beneatha:

> *(D.R. front of sofa.)*

Well, do me a favor and don't ask him a whole lot of ignorant questions about Africans. I mean do they wear clothes and all that—

Mama:

> *(Crosses to above table with sponge.)*

Well, now, I guess if you think we so ignorant 'round here, maybe you shouldn't bring your friends here—

Beneatha: It's just that people ask such crazy things. All anyone seems to know about when it comes to Africa is Tarzan—

Mama:

> *(At table, wiping table. Indignantly.)*

Why should I know anything about Africa?

Beneatha: Why do you give money at church for the missionary work?

Mama: Well, that's to help save people.

Beneatha: You mean save them from *heathenism.*—

Mama:

> *(Innocently.)*

Yes.

Beneatha: I'm afraid they need more salvation from the British and the French.

> **(Ruth** *enters forlornly and pulls off her coat with dejection. They both turn to look at her.)*

Ruth:

> *(Dispiritedly.)*

Well, I guess from all the happy faces—everybody knows.

Beneatha:

> *(Crosses U.R. and above sofa.)*

Ruth. You pregnant!

Mama:

> *(Takes* **Ruth***'s coat, hangs it up in the closet.)*

Lord have mercy, I sure hope it's a little old girl. Travis ought to have a sister.

> **(Beneatha** and **Ruth** *give her a hopeless look for this grandmotherly enthusiasm.* **Ruth** *sits in chair R. of table, puts her handbag on the table.)*

Beneatha:

> *(Crosses to R. of* **Ruth***.)*

How far along are you?

Ruth: Two months.
Beneatha: Did you mean to? I mean did you plan it or was it an accident?
Mama: What do you know about planning or not planning?
Ruth:
> *(Wearily.)*

She's twenty years old, Lena.
Beneatha: Well, I mean it. Did you plan it, Ruth?
Ruth: Mind your own business.
Beneatha: It is my business—where is he going to sleep, on the *roof*?
> *(There is silence behind the remark as the three Women react to the sense of it.)*

Gee—I didn't mean that, Ruth, honest. Gee, I don't feel like that at all. I—I think it is wonderful.
Ruth:
> *(Dully.)*

Wonderful.
Beneatha: Yes—really.
Mama:
> *(Looking at **Ruth**, worried.)*

Doctor say everything going to be all right?
Ruth:
> *(Far away.)*

Yes—she says everything is going to be fine—
Mama:
> *(Immediately suspicious.)*

"She"? What doctor you went to?
> *(**Beneatha** sits on sofa. **Mama** worriedly hovers over **Ruth**.)*

Ruth honey—what's the matter with you—you sick?
> *(**Ruth** has her fists clenched on her thighs and is fighting hard to suppress a scream that seems to be rising in her.)*

Beneatha:
> *(Rises.)*

What's the matter with her, Mama?
Mama:
> *(Working her fingers in **Ruth's** shoulder to relax her.)*

She be all right. Women gets right depressed sometimes when they get her way.
> *(Speaking softly, expertly, rapidly.)*

Now you just relax, that's right—just lean back, don't think 'bout nothing at all—nothing at all—
Ruth: I'm all right—
> *(The glassy-eyed look melts and then she collapses into a fit of heavy sobbing.)*

Mama:
> *(Helps **Ruth** off R. above sofa. To **Ruth**.)*

Come on now, honey. You need to lie down and rest a while—then have some nice hot food.

(They exit, **Ruth's** *weight on her* mother-in-law *as the* DOORBELL *rings.)*

Beneatha: Oh, my God—that must be Asagai.

(Profoundly disturbed, she opens the door to admit a rather dramatic-looking young man with a large package.)

Asagai: Hello, Alaiyo—

Beneatha:

(Holding the door open and regarding him with pleasure.)

Hello—

(Long pause. She crosses L. to above the table, folds towel.)

Well—come in. And please excuse everything. My mother was very upset about my letting any one come here with the place like this.

Asagai:

(Coming into the room. U.C.)

You look disturbed—Is something wrong?

Beneatha:

(Continues to fold and "neats" up the towel **Mama** *had left on chair L. of table.)*

Yes—we've all got acute ghetto-itus.

(She smiles and comes toward him, finding a cigarette and sitting on sofa.)

So—sit down! No! Wait!

(Business straightening sofa cushions.)

So, how was Canada?

(She crosses D.C.)

Asagai:

(A sophisticate.)

Canadian.

Beneatha:

(Looking at him as they sit: she on the chair R. of sofa, he on the L. of the sofa.)

Asagai, I'm very glad you are back.

Asagai:

(Places the gift box on the coffee table. Looking at her.)

Are you really?

Beneatha: Yes—very.

Asagai: Why—you were quite glad when I went away. What happened?

Beneatha: You went away.

Asagai: Ahhhhhhhh.

Beneatha: Before—you wanted to be so serious before there was time.

Asagai: How much time must there be before one knows what one feels?

Beneatha:

(Stalling this particular conversation. Her hands pressed together deliberately childish.)

What did you bring me—?

Asagai:

(Indicating the package.)

Open it and see.
Beneatha:
> (*Rises from the chair D.R., gets package, crouches on sofa with* **Asagai,**
> *and eagerly opens the package. Drawing out some records and the
> colorful robes of a Nigerian woman.*)

Oh, Asagai! You got them for me! How beautiful— And the records, too!
> (*She lifts out the cloth and runs D.R. to mirror with it and holds the
> drapery up in front of herself.*)

Asagai:
> (*Rising from the sofa and coming D.R. to her at the mirror.*)

Wait! I shall have to teach you how to drape it properly.
> (*He drapes the material about her for the moment and stands back to
> look at her.*)

Ah—Oh-pay-gay-day! Oh-bah-mu-shay! ("*Opegede! Ogbamushe!*") You wear
it well—very well—mutilated hair and all.
Beneatha:
> (*Turning suddenly.*)

My hair—what's wrong with my hair?
Asagai:
> (*In front of sofa. Shrugging.*)

Were you born with it like that?
Beneatha:
> (*Reaching up to touch it.*)

No—of course not.
> (*She looks back to the mirror, disturbed.*)

Asagai:
> (*Smiling.*)

How then?
Beneatha:
> (*Embarrassed and a little demure to discuss the Great Hair question.*)

You know perfectly well how—as crinkly as yours—that's how.
Asagai: And it is ugly to you that way?
Beneatha:
> (*Quickly.*)

Oh, no—not *ugly*—
> (*More slowly, apologetically.*)

But it's so hard to manage when it's well—*raw.*
Asagai: And so to accommodate that—you mutilate it every week?
Beneatha: It's not mutilation!
Asagai:
> (*Laughing aloud at her seriousness.*)

Oh—please I am only teasing you because you are so very serious about
these things.
> (*He stands back from her and folds his arms across his chest as he
> watches her pulling her hair and frowning in the mirror.*)

Do you remember the first time you met me at school—?
> (*He laughs. Takes stage slightly R.C.*)

You came up to me and you said, and I thought you were the most serious little thing I had ever seen— You said,
(He imitates her.)
"Mr. Asagai—I want very much to talk with you. About Africa. You see, Mr. Asagai, I am looking for my *identity!*"
(Crossing to her, he folds over and roars.)
Beneatha:
(Turning to him, not laughing.)
Yes—
(Her face is quizzical, profoundly disturbed.)
Asagai:
(Still teasing, he crosses R. to her and, reaching out, takes her face in his hands and turns her profile to him.)
Well—it is true that this is not so much a profile of a Hollywood queen as perhaps a Queen of the Nile—
(A mock dismissal of the importance of the question. He crosses L. to C.)
But what does it matter? Assimilationism is so popular in your country.
Beneatha:
(Wheeling, passionately, sharply.)
I am not an assimilationist!
Asagai:
(The protest hangs in the room for a moment and **Asagai** studies her, his laughter fading.)
Such a serious one.
(There is a pause between them, then.)
So—you like the robes? You must take excellent care of them—they are from my sister's personal wardrobe.
Beneatha:
(With incredulity.)
You—you sent all the way home—for me?
Asagai:
(With charm.)
For you—I would do much more— Well, that is what I came for. I must go.
(He crosses to C. door.)
Beneatha:
(Crosses U.R. and above sofa to C.)
Will you call me Monday?
Asagai: Yes— We have a great deal to talk·about, you and I. I mean about identity and time and all that.
Beneatha: Time?
Asagai: Yes—about how much time one needs to know what one feels.
Beneatha:
(Crosses D.L. of sofa to front of sofa.)
You see! You never understood that there is more than one kind of feeling which can exist between a man and a woman—or at least—there should be.

Asagai:

> (Shaking his head negatively but gently, crosses D.C. to meet her in front of the sofa.)

No—between a man and a woman there need be only one kind of feeling. I have that for you— Now even—right this moment—

Beneatha: I know—and by itself—it won't do. I can find that anywhere.

Asagai: For a woman it should be enough.

Beneatha: I know— That's because that's what it says in all the novels that men write. But it isn't. Go ahead and laugh—but I'm not interested in being someone's little episode in America or—

> (With feminine vengeance.)

—one of them!

> (She removes the robe and folds it. **Asagai** has burst into laughter again.)

That's funny as hell, huh!

Asagai: It's just that every American girl I have known has said that to me. White—black—in this you are all the same. And that same speech, too!

Beneatha:

> (Angrily.)

Yuk, yuk, yuk!

> (Places folded robe in box.)

Asagai: It's how you can be sure that the world's most liberated women are not liberated at all. You all talk about it too much!

> (**Mama** enters and is immediately all social charm because of the presence of a guest.)

Beneatha:

> (Crosses U.R. and escorts **Mama** down to **Asagai**.)

Mama: How do you do?

Asagai:

> (Total politeness to an elder.)

How do you do, Mrs. Younger? Please forgive me for coming at such an outrageous hour on a Saturday.

Mama:

> (Crosses D.R. and then L. to middle front of sofa. **Beneatha** follows her and stands to **Mama's** R. **Asagai** is on **Mama's** L.)

Well, you are quite welcome. I just hope you understand that our house don't always look like this.

> (Chatterish.)

You must come again. I would love to hear all about—

> (Not sure of the name.)

your country. I think it's so sad the way our American Negroes don't know nothing about Africa 'cept Tarzan and all that. And all that money they pour into these churches when they ought to be helping you people over there drive out them French and Englishmen done taken away your land.

> (Flashes a slightly superior look at her daughter upon completion of the recitation.)

Asagai:
> *(Taken aback by this sudden and acutely unrelated expression of sympathy.)*

Yes—yes—

Mama: How many miles is it from here to where you come from?

Asagai: Many thousands.

Mama:
> *(Looking at him as she would **Walter**.)*

I bet you don't half look after yourself, being away from your mama so far. I 'spec' you better come 'round here from time to time and get yourself some home-cooked meals—

Asagai:
> *(Moved.)*

Thank you. Thank you very much.
> *(They are all quiet, then.)*

Asagai:
> *(Crosses U.C.)*

Well—I must go. I will call you Monday, Alaiyo.
> *(**Beneatha** crosses below coffee table to L.C.)*

Mama: What's that he call you?

Asagai: Oh—"Alaiyo"—I hope you don't mind. It is what you call a "nickname," I think. It is a Yoruba word. I am a Yoruba.
> *(He crosses D.C. between **Mama** and **Beneatha**.)*

Mama:
> *(Looking at **Beneatha**.)*

I—I thought he was from—
> *(**Beneatha** crosses D.L.)*

Asagai:
> *(Understanding.)*

Nigeria is my country. Yoruba is my tribal origin—

Beneatha:
> *(Crossing more D.L.)*

You didn't tell us what Alaiyo means—for all I know, you might be calling me *Little Idiot* or something—

Asagai: Well—let me see— I do not know how just to explain it— The sense of a thing can be so different when it changes languages.

Beneatha: You're evading.

Asagai: No—really it is difficult—
> *(Thinking.)*

It means—it means One For Whom Bread—Food—Is Not Enough.
> *(He looks at her.)*

Is that all right?

Beneatha:
> *(Understanding, softly.)*

Thank you.

Mama:

> (*Looking from one to the other and not understanding any of it.*)

Well—that's nice— You must come see us again—Mr.—

Asagai: AS-SA-GAI—

Mama: Yes— Do come again.

Asagai: Good-bye.

> (*He exits.*)

Mama:

> (*Crosses to sink L. for glass of water.*)

Lord, that's a pretty thing just went out of here!

> (*Insinuating to her daughter.*)

Yes, I guess I see why we done commence to get so interested in Africa 'round here. Missionaries my Aunt Jenny!

> (*She crosses U.R. to R. bedroom and exits.*)

Beneatha: Oh, Mama—!

> (*She sits on sofa, rises, picks up the Nigerian robe and holds it up to her in front of the mirror again. At first she sets the head-dress on haphazardly and then notices her hair again and clutches at it and then replaces the head-dress and frowns at herself. Then she starts to wriggle in front of the mirror as she thinks a Nigerian woman might.*)

Travis:

> (*He enters and regards her.*)

What's the matter, girl, you cracking up?

> (*She pulls the head-dress off and regards herself in the mirror and clutches at her hair again and squinches her eyes as if trying to imagine something. Then, suddenly, she gets her raincoat and kerchief and hurriedly prepares for going out.*)

Mama:

> (*Enters. She looks at her daughter and crosses L. above sofa and table to sink.*)

Where you going?

> (**Travis** *sprawls on couch with a comic book.*)

Beneatha:

> (*Halting at the door.*)

To become a queen of the Nile!

> (*She exits in a breathless blaze of glory.*)

Ruth:

> (*She appears in the bedroom doorway.*)

Where did Bennie go?

Mama:

> (*Drumming her fingers.*)

Far as I could make out—to Egypt. Who told you to get up?

Ruth: Ain't nothing wrong with me to be lying in no bed for.

Mama: What time is it getting to?

Ruth: Ten-twenty. And the mailman going to ring that bell this morning just like he done every morning for the last umpteen years.

> (*The BELL sounds suddenly and sharply, and all three people are*

stunned serious and silent in mid-speech. In spite of all other conversations and distractions of the morning, this is what they have been waiting for—even **Travis**, *who looks helplessly from his mother to grandmother.* **Ruth** *is the first to come to life again. To* **Travis**.)

GET DOWN THEM STEPS, BOY!

> *(She crosses U.R. and above sofa.* **Travis** *snaps to life and flies out to get the mail.)*

Mama:

> *(Crosses front of table in kitchen to C.)*

You mean it done really come?

Ruth:

> *(Excited.)*

Oh, Miss Lena!

Mama:

> *(Collecting herself.)*

Well— I don't know what we all so excited about 'round here for. We known it was coming for months.

> *(Sits R. of table.)*

Ruth: That's a whole lot different from having it come and being able to hold it in your hands—a piece of paper worth ten thousand dollars—

> *(**Travis** bursts back into the room, he holds the envelope high above his head like a little dancer. His face is radiant and he is breathless. The other mail is tossed carelessly on the kitchen table and he pirouettes with the envelope and deposits it with sudden slow ceremony in his grandmother's lap. She accepts it—and then—merely holds it and looks at it.* **Ruth** *crosses to behind kitchen table, L. of* **Mama**.)

Come on! Open it—Lord have mercy, I wish Walter Lee was here!

Travis:

> *(At* **Mama's** *R.)*

Open it, Grandmama!

Mama:

> *(Staring at it.)*

Now you all be quiet. It's just a check.

Ruth: Open it—

Mama:

> *(Still staring at it.)*

Now, don't act silly— We ain't never been no people to act silly 'bout no money—

Ruth:

> *(Swiftly.)*

We ain't never had none before—OPEN IT!

Mama:

> *(She finally makes a good strong tear and pulls out the thin blue slice of paper and inspects it closely. The boy and his mother study it raptly over her shoulders.)*

TRAVIS!

> *(She is counting off with doubt.)*

A RAISIN IN THE SUN   67

Is them the right amount of zeros?

Travis: Yes'm—ten thousand dollars. Gaa-lee, Grandmama, you rich.

Mama:

> (She holds out the check from her, still looking at it. Slowly her face sobers into a mask of unhappiness.)

Ten thousand dollars.

> (She hands it to **Ruth**.)

Put it away somewhere, Ruth.

> (She does not look at **Ruth** and her eyes seem to be seeing somewhere very far off. She rises and crosses D.L. to sink.)

Ten thousand dollars they give you. Ten thousand dollars.

Travis:

> (To his mother, sincerely.)

What's the matter with Grandmama—don't she want to be rich?

Ruth:

> (Distractedly.)

You go on out and play now, baby.

> (**Travis** exits C. **Mama** has gone back to wiping plates, humming to herself. With kind exasperation.)

You've gone and got yourself upset.

> (She crosses D.L. above table to **Mama** at sink.)

Mama:

> (Not looking at her.)

I 'spec' if it wasn't for you all—I would just put that money away or give it to the church or something.

Ruth: Now what kind of talk is that? Mr. Younger would just be plain mad if he could hear you talking foolish like that.

Mama:

> (Stopping and staring off.)

Yes—he sure would.

> (Sighing.)

We got enough to do with that money all right.

> (She halts then and turns and looks at her daughter-in-law hard; **Ruth** avoids her eyes and crosses far R. **Mama** wipes her hands with finality and starts to speak firmly to **Ruth**.)

Where did you go today, girl?

Ruth: To the doctor.

Mama:

> (Impatiently.)

Now, Ruth—you know better than that. Old Doctor Jones is strange enough in his way but there ain't nothing 'bout him make somebody slip and call him—she—like you done this morning.

> (Crosses R. to **Ruth**.)

Ruth: Well, that's what happened—my tongue slipped.

Mama: You went to see that woman, didn't you?

Ruth:

> (Defensively, giving herself away.)

What woman you talking about?
Mama:
(Angrily.)
That woman who—
Walter:
(He enters in great excitement.)
Mailman come!
*(To **Ruth** as he crosses D.C. to her at R. front of sofa.)*
Did it come?
*(**Ruth** unfolds the check and lays it quietly before him; watching him intently with thoughts of her own. **Mama** crosses L. to sink. **Walter** sits down and grasps the check close and counts off the zeros. He turns suddenly, frantically to his mother and draws some papers out of his breast pocket.)*
Mama—look, old Willy Harris put everything on paper—the lawyer just looked it over.
(He crosses to kitchen table and lays out the legal papers.)
Mama: Son—I think you ought to talk to your wife—I'll go on out and leave you alone if you want—
(Crosses up to L. bedroom door.)
Walter:
(Brings her the legal papers above table.)
Mama, look— Please! Please!
Mama: Son—
Walter: WILL SOMEBODY PLEASE LISTEN TO ME TODAY!
Mama:
(Quietly.)
I don't 'low no yellin' in this house, Walter Lee, and you know it—
*(**Walter** stares at them in frustration and starts to speak several times.)*
And there ain't going to be no investing in no liquor stores.
(She crushes one of the papers.)
Walter: But, Mama, you ain't even looked at it.
Mama: I don't aim to have to speak on that again.
(Long pause.)
Walter: You ain't looked at it and you don't aim to have to speak on that again? You ain't even looked at and *you* decided—
(Crumpling his papers.)
Well, *you* tell that to my boy tonight when you put him to sleep on the living-room couch—
*(This is to **Ruth** and **Mama** alike. **Mama** crosses up L. of kitchen table. He picks up his coat from the sofa, crosses U.C. and starts out.)*
Ruth: Where are you going?
Walter: Out!
Ruth: Where?
Walter: Just out of this house somewhere—
Ruth:
(Rises, crosses U.C.)

A RAISIN IN THE SUN   69

I'll come, too.

Walter: I don't want you to come!

Ruth:

>(Crosses U.L. to closet for her coat.)

I got something to talk to you about, Walter.

Walter: That's too bad.

>(He crosses to C. door.)

Mama:

>(Quietly still.)

Walter Lee—

>(She waits and he finally turns and looks at her.)

Sit down.

Walter:

>(Slams door shut and crosses D.L. to **Mama**.)

I'm a grown man, Mama.

Mama: Ain't nobody said you wasn't grown. But you still in my house and my presence. And as long as you are—you'll talk to your wife civil. Now sit down.

Ruth:

>(Hurls coat at **Walter**, crossing above sofa to exit R. Suddenly.)

Oh, let him go on out and drink himself to death! He makes me sick to my stomach!

Walter:

>(Crosses R. after her. Violently.)

And you turn mine too, Baby—!

>(**Ruth** goes into their bedroom and slams the door behind her.)

Mama:

>(Crosses to front of sofa. Still quietly.)

Walter, what is the matter with you?

Walter:

>(Crosses D.R. of sofa.)

Matter with me? Ain't nothing the matter with ME!

Mama:

>(Sits on sofa.)

Yes, there is. Something eating you up like a crazy man. Something more than me not giving you this money. The past few years I been watching it happen to you. You get all nervous acting and kind of wild in the eyes—

>(**Walter** jumps up impatiently at her words, crosses U.R. and back of sofa.)

I said sit there now, I'm talking to you!

Walter:

>(Circles D.C. around front of sofa, front of coffee table, front of arm-chair D.R.)

Mama—I don't need no nagging at me today.

Mama: Seem like you getting to a place where you always tied up in some kind of knot about something. But if anybody ask you 'bout it you just yell at 'em and bust out the house and go out and drink somewheres. Walter

Lee, people can't live with that. Ruth's a good, patient girl in her way—but you getting to be too much. Boy, don't make the mistake of driving that girl away from you.

Walter: Why—what she ever do for me?

Mama: She loves you.

Walter: Mama—I'm going out. I want to go off somewhere and be by myself for a while.

Mama: I'm sorry 'bout your liquor store, son. It just wasn't the thing for us to do. That's what I want to tell you about—

Walter: I got to go out, Mama—

(He rises, crosses back of sofa to C. door.)

Mama: It's dangerous, son.

Walter: What's dangerous?

Mama: When a man goes outside his home to look for peace.

Walter:

(Beseechingly. Crosses D.C.)

Then why can't there never be no peace in this house, then?

Mama: You done found it in some other house?

Walter:

(Crosses L., slams coat down on chair L. of kitchen table.)

No—there ain't no woman! Why do you always think there's a woman somewhere when a man gets restless?

(Coming to her.)

Do you know what this money means to me? Do you know what this money can do for us? Mama—Mama—I want so many things—

(He picks up check from table.)

Mama: Yes, son—

Walter: I want so many things that they are driving me kind of crazy. Mama —look at me.

Mama: I'm looking at you. You are a good-looking boy. You got a job, a nice wife, a fine boy and—

Walter: A job.

(Looks at her.)

Mama, a job? I open and close car doors all day long. I drive a man around in his limousine and say, "Yes, sir," "No, sir," "Very good, sir," "Shall I take the drive, sir?" Mama, that ain't no kind of job—that ain't nothin' at all.

(Very quietly.)

Mama, I don't know if I can make you understand.

*(Crosses D.R.C. to **Mama** on sofa.)*

Mama: Understand what, baby?

Walter:

(Quietly.)

Sometimes it's like I can see the future stretched out in front of me—just plain as day. The future, Mama. Hanging over there at the edge of my days. Just waiting for me—a big, looming blank space—full of *nothing*. Just waiting for *me*. But it don't have to be.

*(Big pause. **Walter** waits—crosses to **Mama**.)*

Mama—sometimes when I'm downtown driving that man around and I pass them cool, quiet-looking restaurants where them white boys are sitting back and talking 'bout things—

> (He kneels L. end of sofa near **Mama** on the sofa.)

Sitting there turning deals worth millions of dollars—sometimes I see guys don't look much older than me—

Mama: Son—how come you talk so much 'bout money?

Walter:

> (With immense passion.)

Because it is life, Mama!

Mama:

> (Quietly.)

Oh—

> (Very quietly.)

So now money is life. Once upon a time freedom used to be life—now it's money.

Walter: No—it was always money, Mama. We just didn't know about it.

Mama: No—something has changed.

> (She looks at him.)

You something new, boy. In my time we was worried about not being lynched and getting to the North if we could and how to stay alive and still have a pinch of dignity too— Now here come you and Beneatha—talking about things we ain't never even thought about hardly, me and your daddy. You ain't satisfied or proud of nothing we done. I mean that you had a home; that we kept you out of trouble till you was grown; that you don't have to ride to work on the back of nobody's street car— You my children —but how different we done become.

Walter:

> (Rises, crosses L., puts check on the kitchen table, picks up topcoat and starts to C. door.)

You don't understand, Mama, you just don't understand.

Mama: Son—do you know your wife is expecting another baby?

> (Pause. **Walter** crosses D.L. above table, circles in front of table, sinking down into chair R. of kitchen table.)

That's what she wanted to talk to you about. This ain't for me to be telling— but you ought to know.

> (She waits.)

I think Ruth is thinking 'bout getting rid of that child.

Walter:

> (Slowly understanding.)

No—no—Ruth wouldn't do that.

Mama:

> (Crossing L. to sink.)

When the world gets ugly enough—a woman will do anything for her family. *The part that's already living.*

Walter: You don't know Ruth, Mama, if you think she would do that.

Ruth:

> (*She opens the R. bedroom door and stands there a little limp. Beaten, she enters, crosses to R. end of sofa.*)

Yes, I would, too, Walter.

> (*Pause.*)

I gave her a five-dollar down-payment.

> (*There is total silence as the man stares at his wife and the mother stares at her son.*)

Mama:

> (*Presently. Crosses R. above table to* **Walter's** *L.*)

Well—

> (*Tightly.*)

Well—son, I'm waiting to hear you say something—I'm waiting to hear how you be your father's son. Be the man he was—

> (*Pause.*)

Your wife say she going to destroy your child. And I'm waiting to hear you talk like him and say we a people who give children life, not who destroys them—I'm waiting to see you stand up and look like your daddy and say we done give up one baby to poverty and that we ain't going to give up nary another one—I'm waiting. If you a son of mine, tell her.

> (**Walter** *turns, looks at her and starts to exit.*)

You—you are a disgrace to your father's memory.

> (**Walter** *completely exits C.*)

Somebody get me my hat.

> (*She exits L. bedroom.*)

Curtain

Act Two

SCENE 1

Time: *Later—same day.*

At Rise: **Ruth** is ironing again. She has the RADIO going. Presently the bedroom door opposite opens, and her mouth falls and she puts down the iron in fascination.

Ruth: What have we got on tonight!

Beneatha:

> (*Emerging, grandly, from the door L. so that we can see her thorough-ly robed in the costume which* **Asagai** *brought. She parades for* **Ruth** *by crossing C., then D.C., then R. in front of sofa.*)

You are looking at what a well-dressed Nigerian woman wears—

> (*With her hair completely hidden by the head-dress, she crosses L. to C.*)

Isn't it beautiful?

(She promenades R. in front of the sofa to the RADIO and turns off the good loud blues which is playing with an arrogant flourish.)

Enough of this assimilationist junk!

*(**Ruth** follows her with her eyes as she goes to the phonograph and puts on a record and turns and waits ceremoniously for the MUSIC to come up; then, with a shout.)*

OCOMOGOSIAY!

*(**Ruth** jumps. The MUSIC comes up, a lovely Nigerian melody, **Beneatha** listens, enraptured, her eyes far away—"back to the past." She begins to move, vaguely, genuinely and—as it gets good to her—exaggeratedly and comically. **Ruth** is dumbfounded.)*

Ruth: What kind of dance is that?

Beneatha: A folk dance.

Ruth:

("Pearl Bailey")

What kind of folks do that, honey?

Beneatha: It's from Nigeria. It's a dance of welcome.

Ruth: Who you welcoming?

Beneatha: The men back to the village.

Ruth: Where they been?

Beneatha: How should I know—out hunting or something—anyway, they are coming back now—

*(**Walter** enters.)*

Ruth: Well, that's good.

Beneatha:

(With the record.)

Alundi, alundi
Alundi alunya
Jop pu a jeepua
Ang gu soooooooooo

Ai yai yae—
Ayehaye—alundi

*(**Walter** has obviously been drinking. He leans against the door heavily and watches his sister. First with distaste. then—his eyes look off—"back to the past"—as he lifts both his fists to the roof, screaming.)*

Walter: YEAH—AND ETHIOPIA STRETCH FORTH HER ARMS AGAIN!

Ruth:

(Drily, looking at him.)

Yes—and Africa sure is claiming her own tonight.

(She starts ironing again, giving them both up.)

Walter:

(All is a drunken, dramatic shout.)

Shut up!—I'm digging them drums—them drums move me!

(He makes his weaving way to his wife's face and leans in close to her.)

In my heart of hearts.

(He thumps his chest.)

I am much warrior!

Ruth:

> (Without even looking up.)

In your heart of hearts you are much drunkard.

Walter:

> (Coming away from her and starting to wander around the room, shouting.)

Me and Jomo—

> (Intently, in his sister's face who has stopped dancing to watch him in this unknown mood.)

That's my man, Kenyatta.

> (Shouting and thumping his chest.)

FLAMING SPEAR! HOT DAMN!

> (He is suddenly in possession of an imaginary spear and actively spearing enemies all over the room.)

OCOMOGOSIAY—THE LION IS WAKING—OWIMOWEH!

> (He pulls his shirt open and leaps up on a table and gestures with his spear.)

Beneatha:

> (To encourage **Walter**, thoroughly caught up with this side of him.)

OCOMOGOSIAY, FLAMING SPEAR!

Walter:

> (On the table, very far gone, his eyes pure glass sheets, his posture that of Belafonte singing "Matilda" mixed with Paul Robeson at fever pitch. He sees what we cannot, that he is a leader of his people, a great chief, a descendant of Chaka, and that the hour to march has come.)

Listen, my black brothers—

Beneatha: OCOMOGOSIAY!

Walter: Do you hear the waters rushing against the shores of the coastlands—?

Beneatha: OCOMOGOSIAY!

Walter: Do you hear the screeching of the cocks in yonder hills beyond where the chiefs meet in council for the coming of the mighty war—?

Beneatha: OCOMOGOSIAY!

Walter: Do you hear the beating of the wings of the birds flying low over the mountains and the low places of our land—?

Beneatha: OCOMOGOSIAY!

Walter: Do you hear the singing of the women, singing the war songs of our fathers to the babies in the great houses—

> (The DOORBELL rings. **Ruth** goes to answer it.)

Singing the sweet war songs—OH, DO YOU HEAR, BLACK BROTHERS!

> (**Ruth** opens door, admits **George Murchison**, crosses quickly D.R., cuts off MUSIC.)

Beneatha:

> (Completely gone.)

We hear you, Flaming Spear—

Walter: Telling us to prepare for the greatness of the time—
>*(To **George**.)*

Black Brother—!
>*(He extends his hand for the fraternal clasp.)*

George: BLACK Brother, hell!

Ruth:
>*(Having had enough and embarrassed for the family, crosses U.R.C.)*

Beneatha, you got company—what's the matter with you? Walter Lee Younger, get down off that table and stop acting like a fool—
>**(Walter** *gets down from the table and makes a quick exit U.C. to the bathroom.)*

He's had a little to drink—I don't know what her excuse is.
>*(She crosses U.C., then L. above table, snaps on LIGHT SWITCH L.)*

George:
>*(To **Beneatha**.)*

Look, honey, we're going *to* the theatre—we're not going to be *in* it—so go change, huh?

Ruth:
>*(Crosses D.L. to front of table.)*

You expect this boy to go out with you looking like that?

Beneatha:
>*(Looking at **George**.)*

That's up to George. If he's ashamed of his heritage—

George: Oh, don't be so proud of yourself, Bennie—just 'cause you look eccentric.

Beneatha: How can something that's natural be eccentric?

George: That's what being eccentric means—being natural. Get dressed.

Beneatha: I don't like that, George.

Ruth:
>*(Crosses into C. between **George** and **Beneatha**.)*

Why must you and your brother make an argument out of everything people say?

Beneatha: Because I hate assimilationist Negroes!

Ruth: Will somebody please tell me what assimila-whoever means!

George:
>*(D.R. front of sofa.)*

Oh, it's just a college girl's way of calling people Uncle Toms—but that isn't what it means at all.

Ruth: Well, what does it mean?

Beneatha:
>*(Cutting **George** off and staring at him as she replies to **Ruth**, crossing R. into C.)*

It means someone who is willing to give up—his own culture—and submerge himself completely in the dominant and—in this case—*oppressive* culture!

George: Oh dear, dear, dear! Here we go! A lecture on the African past! On our great West African Heritage! In one second we will hear all about the

great Ashanti empires; the great Songhay civilizations; and the great sculpture of Benin—and then some poetry in the Bantu—and the whole monologue will end with the word *heritage!* Let's face it, baby, your heritage is nothing but a bunch of raggedyassed spirituals and some grass huts!
Beneatha: GRASS HUTS!
    *(**Ruth** manhandles **Beneatha** U.L. to L. bedroom.)*
See there—you are standing there in your splendid ignorance talking about people who were the first to smelt iron on the face of the earth!
    *(**Ruth** is pushing her into the door like a noisy jack-in-the-box.)*
The Ashanti were performing surgical operations when the English—
    *(**Ruth** pulls the door to with **Beneatha** on the other side and smiles graciously to **George**. **Beneatha** re-enters, then exits again.)*
Were still tatooing themselves with blue dragons—
Ruth: Have a seat, George.
    *(Crosses R., removes ironing board to upstage. **George** sits on sofa.)*
Warm, ain't it? I mean for September.
    (Crosses D.R., sits in armchair, folds her hands rather primly on her lap, determined to demonstrate the civilization of the family. Pause.)
Just like they always say about Chicago weather. If it's too hot or cold for you—just wait a minute and it'll change.
    (She smiles happily at this cliché of clichés.)
Everybody says it's got to do with them bombs and things they keep setting off.
    (Pause)
Would you like a nice cold beer?
    (Rises tentatively, sits again.)
George: No, thank you. I don't care for beer.
    (He looks at his watch.)
I hope she hurries up.
    (Rises, crosses C.)
Ruth: What time is the show?
George:
    *(Turns back to **Ruth** D.R., sits on sofa again.)*
It's an eight-thirty curtain. That's just Chicago, though. In New York standard curtain time is eight-forty.
    (He is rather proud of this knowledge.)
    *(**Walter** starts from bathroom.)*
Ruth:
    (Properly appreciating it.)
You get to New York a lot?
George:
    (Offhand.)
Few times a year.
Ruth: Oh—that's nice. I've never been to New York.
Walter:
    (He enters. We feel he has relieved himself but the edge of unreality is still with him. Crosses D.L. front of table to the kitchen.)

New York ain't got nothing Chicago ain't, except a bunch of hustling people all squeezed up together—being "Eastern."

(He turns his face into a screw of displeasure.)

George: Oh—you've been?

Walter: *Plenty* of times.

Ruth:

(Shocked at the lie.)

Walter Lee Younger!

Walter:

(Staring her down.)

Plenty!

(**Ruth** crosses U.R. of sofa to laundry on bureau. Pause.)

What we got to drink in this house? Why don't you offer this man some refreshment?

(He crosses L., front of kitchen table to icebox. To **George**.)

They don't know how to entertain in this house, man.

George: Thank you—I don't really care for anything.

Walter:

(Feeling his head, sobriety coming.)

Where's Mama?

(Crosses U.C. above table.)

Ruth: She ain't come back yet.

Walter:

(Looking **George** over from head to toe, scrutinizing his carefully casual tweed sports jacket, over cashmere V-neck sweater, over soft eyelet shirt and tie, and soft slacks below, finished off with white buckskin shoes.)

Why all you college boys wear them fairyish-looking white shoes?

(Crosses L. front of table.)

Ruth: Walter Lee!

(**George** ignores the remark.)

Walter:

(Crossing L. front of table gets beer from icebox. To **Ruth**.)

White shoes, cold as it is.

Ruth:

(Crushed.)

You have to excuse him—

Walter:

(At icebox.)

No, he don't! What you always excusing me for! I'll excuse myself when I needs to be excused!

(A pause.)

They look funny as hell—bad as them black knee socks Beneatha wears out of here all the time.

Ruth: It's the college *style*.

Walter:

(Crosses to sink, gets can opener.)

Style, hell, she looks like she got burnt legs or something!

Ruth: Oh, Walter—

Walter:

> *(Opening beer can at sink. To* **George***.)*

How's your old man making out? I understand you all going to buy that big hotel on the Drive?

> *(Crosses R. to back of kitchen table, crosses C., puts L. foot on chair R. of table.)*

Shrewd move. Your old man is all right, man.

> *(Tapping his head and half winking for emphasis.)*

I mean he knows how to operate. I mean he thinks *big,* you know what I mean. But I think he's kind of running out of ideas now. I'd like to talk to him. Listen, man, I got some plans that could turn this city upside down. I mean, I think like he does. *Big.* Invest big, gamble big, hell, lose—

> *(He picks up chair, straddles it L. of sofa.)*

big if you have to, you know what I mean. It's hard to find a man on this whole Southside who understands my kind of thinking—you dig?

> *(He scrutinizes* **George** *again, drinks from his beer, squints his eyes and leans in close, confidential, man-to-man.)*

Me and you ought to sit down and talk sometimes, man—Man, I got some ideas—

George:

> *(With disinterest.)*

Yeah—sometimes we'll have to do that, Walter.

Walter:

> *(Understanding the indifference and, offended, rises, replaces chair.)*

Yeah—well, when you get the time, man. I know you a busy little boy.

Ruth: Walter, please—

Walter:

> *(Bitterly, hurt.)*

I know ain't nothing in this world as busy as you colored college boys with your fraternity pins and white shoes—

Ruth:

> *(Covering her face with humiliation.)*

Oh, Walter Lee—

Walter:

> *(C.L. of sofa.)*

I see y'all all the time—with the books tucked under your arms—going to your "classes"—

> *(British "A"—a mimic.)*

And for what! What the hell you learning over there? Filling up your heads—

> *(On his fingers.)*

With the sociology and the psychology—

> *(Crosses L. front of table.)*

But they teaching you how to be a man? How to take over and run the world? They teaching you how to run a rubber plantation or a steel mill?

Naw—just to talk proper and read books and wear them fairyish-looking white shoes.

George:

(*Looking at him with distaste, a little above it all. Rises, crosses D.R.*)
You're all wacked up with bitterness, man.

Walter:

(*At kitchen window. Starts drive R. to* **George** *R. Intently, almost quietly, between the teeth, glaring at the boy.*)
And you—ain't you bitter, man? Ain't you just about had it yet? Don't you see no stars gleaming that you can't reach out and grab? You happy?—you contented son of a bitch—you happy? You got it made? Bitter? Man, I'm a volcano. Bitter? Here I am a giant—surrounded by ants! Ants who can't even understand what it is the giant is talking about.

Ruth:

(*Passionately and suddenly.*)
Oh, Walter—Ain't you with nobody!

Walter:

(*Violently.*)
No! 'Cause ain't nobody with me!
(*Opens C. door, looks out, returns, crosses D.L. to sink.*)
Not even my own mother!

Ruth: Walter, that's a terrible thing to say!

(**Beneatha** *enters, dressed for the evening in a soft dress and earrings.*)

George: Well—hey, you-look-great.

(*Crosses C. to* **Beneatha**. *Thoughtful, with emphasis, since this is a reversal. Looking at her.*)
I mean it—you really look sharp.
(*Helps her with her wrap.*)

Beneatha: See you all later.

Ruth: Have a nice time.

George: Thanks. Good night.

(*To* **Walter**.)
Good night. Prometheus.
(*Sarcastically.*)
(*They exit.* **Ruth** *sits on sofa.*)

Walter:

(*To* **Ruth**.)
Who is Promeetheeius—?
(*At sink with beer.*)

Ruth: I don't know, honey. Don't worry about it.

Walter:

(*Crosses above kitchen table. In a fury, pointing after* **George**.)
See there—they get to a point where they can't insult you man to man—they got to go talk about something ain't nobody never heard of!
(*Crosses to sink.*)

Ruth: How you know it was an insult?
(*To humor him.*)

Maybe Promeetheeius is a nice fellow.

Walter:

> (*Crosses below kitchen table.*)

Promeetheeius!—I bet there ain't even no such thing! I bet that simple-minded clown—

Ruth:

> (*Rises, starts to* **Walter L.**)

Walter—

Walter:

> (*Yelling.*)

Don't start!

Ruth: Start what?

Walter: Your nagging! Where was I? Who was I with—How much money did I spend?

Ruth:

> (*Plaintively.*)

Walter Lee—why don't we just try to talk about it—

Walter:

> (*Not listening.*)

I been out talking with people who understand me. People who care about the things I got on my mind.

Ruth:

> (*Wearily.*)

I guess that means people like Willy Harris.

> (*Crosses U.C., then above sofa.*)

Walter: Yes, people like Willy Harris.

Ruth:

> (*Crosses R., back of sofa to laundry. With a sudden flash of impatience.*)

Why don't y'all just hurry up and go into the banking business and stop talking about it!

Walter:

> (*Crosses U.L. above table.*)

Why?—You want to know why? 'Cause we all tied up in a race of people that don't know how to do nothing but moan, pray and have babies!

> (*The line is too bitter even for him and he looks at her and sits down.*)

Ruth: Oh, Walter—

> (*Softly.*)

Honey, why can't you stop fighting me?

Walter:

> (*Crosses D.L. to sink. Without thinking.*)

Who's fighting you? Who even cares about you—

> (*This line begins the retardation of this mood.*)

Ruth: Well—

> (*She waits a long time and then with resignation starts to put away the laundry.*)

I guess I might as well go on to bed—

(More or less to herself.)

I don't know where we lost it—but we have—

(Then to him as she crosses above sofa to C.)

I—I'm sorry about this new baby, Walter—I guess maybe I better go on and do what I started—I guess I just didn't realize how bad things was with us—

(Crosses R. front of sofa.)

I guess I just didn't realize—

(She picks up laundry basket and starts for R. bedroom, exits.)

Walter:

(He lifts his head and watches her going away from him in a new mood which began to emerge when he asked her "Who cares about you?" Crosses R. above table to C.)

Baby, it's been rough, ain't it?

(She hears and stops but does not turn around and he goes on to her back.)

I guess between two people there ain't never as much understanding as folks generally thinks there is. I mean like between me and you—

*(**Ruth** enters. She turns to face him.)*

How we gets to the place where we scared to talk softness to each other.

(He waits, thinking hard himself.)

Why you think it got to be like that?

(He is thoughtful, almost as a child would be.)

Ruth, what is it gets into people ought to be close?

Ruth:

(Above sofa.)

I don't know, honey. I think about it a lot.

Walter: On account of you and me, you mean. The way things are with us. The way something's come down between us.

Ruth: There ain't so much between us, Walter—Not when you come to me and try to talk to me. Try to be with me—a little, even.

Walter:

(Standing front of chair L. of table. Total honesty.)

Sometimes—sometimes—I don't even know how to try.

Ruth:

*(Crossing slowly L. toward **Walter**.)*

Walter—

Walter: Yes—?

Ruth:

(Coming to him, gently and with misgiving, but coming to him.)

Honey—Life don't have to be like this. I mean sometimes people can do things so that things are better—

(She crosses to him slowly and they embrace. She gropes for what she wants to tell him.)

You remember how we used to talk when Travis was born—about the way we were going to live—the kind of house—

(She is stroking his head.)

Well, it's all starting to slip away from us.

(Mama enters C. door and Walter crosses to her.)

Walter: Mama, where have you been?

Mama:

(Puts hat and handbag on bureau.)

My—them steps is getting longer and longer. Whew!

(She ignores Walter.)

How you feeling this evening, Ruth?

(She crosses L. to closet, hangs up coat, gets slippers.)

(Ruth shrugs, disturbed some at having been prematurely interrupted and watching her husband knowingly.)

Walter: Mama, where have you been all day?

Mama:

(Still ignoring him and crossing to C. with slippers from closet.)

Where's Travis?

Ruth:

(Crosses R. to bedroom with folded clothes, exits.)

I let him go out earlier and he ain't come back yet. Boy, is he going to get it!

Walter: Mama—!

Mama:

(As if she has heard him for the first time.)

Yes, son?

(Crosses, sits chair R. of kitchen table.)

Walter: Where did you go this afternoon?

Mama:

(Putting on slippers.)

I went downtown to tend to some business that I had to tend to.

Walter: What kind of business?

Mama: You know better than to question me like a—

(The front door opens slowly and Travis peeks his head in less than hopefully. Crosses R. to bedroom.)

child, Brother.

Walter:

(Bending over the table.)

Where were you, Mama!

(Bringing his fists down and shouting.)

Mama, you didn't go do something with that insurance money, something crazy.

(Ruth re-enters from bedroom R., confronts Travis in bedroom door-way.)

Travis:

(To his mother.)

Mama, I—

Ruth: "Mama, I," nothing! You're going to get it, boy! Get on in that bedroom and get yourself ready!

Travis: But I—

Mama: Why don't you never let the child explain hisself?

Ruth: Keep out of it now, Lena.

> *(**Mama** clamps her lips together and **Ruth** advances toward her son menacingly.)*

A thousand times I have told you not to go off like that—

Mama:

> *(Holding out her hand to her grandson.)*

Well—at least let me tell him something. I want him to be the first one to hear— Come here, Travis.

> *(**Travis** obeys, gladly, crosses L. front of sofa to **Mama**.)*

Travis—

> *(She takes him by the shoulders and looks into his face.)*

You know that money we got in the mail this morning?

Travis: Yes'm—

Mama: Well—what do you think your grandmama gone and done with that money?

> *(**Walter** crosses in to behind the kitchen table.)*

Travis: I don't know, Grandmama.

Mama:

> *(Putting her finger on his nose for emphasis.)*

She went and she bought you a house!

> *(The explosion comes from **Walter** at the end of the revelation and he crosses L. to kitchen, crushes beer glass in his hand, hurls it into the wastebasket by stove.)*

You glad about the house? It's going to be yours when you get to be a man.

Travis: Yes'm. I always wanted to live in a house.

Mama: All right, gimme some sugar, then—

> *(**Travis** puts his arms around her neck as she watches her son over his shoulder. Then, to **Travis**, after the embrace.)*

Now when you say your prayers tonight, you thank God and your grand-father—'cause it was him who give you the house—in his way.

Ruth:

> *(Crosses L. to **Travis** and **Mama**. Taking the boy from her and pushing him toward the bedroom.)*

Now you get out of here and get ready for your beating.

Travis: Aw, Mama— Aw—gee—

> *(Exits bedroom R. front of sofa. He changes to pajamas off R.)*

Ruth: Get on in there—

> *(Closing the door behind him and turning, radiant, to her mother-in-law.)*

So you went and did it!

> *(At L. end of sofa.)*

Mama:

> *(Quietly, looking at her son with pain.)*

Yes, I did.

Ruth:
> *(Raising both arms classically.)*

PRAISE GOD!
> *(Looks at **Walter** for a moment, who says nothing. Crosses D.L. above table to **Walter** in kitchen.)*

Please, honey—let me be glad—you be glad, too.
> *(She has laid her hands on his shoulders and he shakes himself free of her roughly without turning to face her.)*

Oh, Walter—a home—a home.
> *(She crosses back to **Mama** at table.)*

Well—where is it? How big is it? How much it going to cost—?

Mama: Well—

Ruth: When we moving?

Mama:
> *(Smiling at her.)*

First of the month.

Ruth:
> *(Crosses C. above **Mama**. Throwing back her head with jubilance.)*

PRAISE GOD!

Mama:
> *(Tentatively, still looking at her son's back turned against both of them.)*

It's—it's a nice house, too—
> *(**Walter** is L. of kitchen. **Mama** cannot help speaking directly to him; she is almost like a girl now in the imploring quality she uses to him.)*

Three bedrooms—nice big one for you and Ruth— Me and Beneatha still have to share our room but Travis have one of his own—and—
> *(With difficulty.)*

I figures if the—new baby—is a boy we could get one of them double-decker outfits— And there's a yard with a little patch of dirt where I could maybe get to grow me a few flowers— And a nice big basement—

Ruth: Walter, honey, be glad—
> *(Crosses L. to **Walter** front of table.)*

Mama:
> *(Still sitting R. of kitchen table. Still to **Walter's** back, fingering things on the table.)*

'Course I don't want to make it sound fancier than it is— It's just a plain little old house—but it's built good and solid and it will be *ours*. Walter Lee —it makes a difference in a man when he can walk on floors that belong to *him*—

Ruth:
> *(Crossing in R. toward **Mama** above table.)*

Where is it?

Mama:
> *(Frightened at this telling.)*

Well—well—it's out there in Clybourne Park—

(**Ruth's** *radiance fades abruptly and* **Walter** *finally turns slowly to face his mother with incredulity and hostility.*)

Ruth:

(*Between* **Mama** *and* **Walter.**)

Where?

Mama:

(*Matter-of-factly.*)

406 Clybourne Street, Clybourne Park.

Ruth:

(*Back of kitchen table.*)

Clybourne Park? Mama, there ain't no colored people living in Clybourne Park.

Mama:

(*Almost idiotically.*)

Well, there's going to be some now.

Walter:

(*Bitterly.*)

So that's the peace and comfort you went out and spent that money for today!

Mama:

(*Raising her eyes to meet his finally.*)

Son—I just tried to find the nicest place for the least amount of money for my family.

(**Walter** *crosses L. to kitchen.*)

Ruth:

(*Sits chair L. of table; trying to recover from the shock.*)

Well—well—'course I ain't one never been 'fraid of no crackers, mind you —but—well, wasn't there no other houses nowhere?

Mama: Them houses they put up for colored in them areas way out all seem to cost twice as much money as other houses. I did the best I could.

Ruth:

(*Who has been rather struck senseless with the news in its various degrees of goodness and trouble, sits a moment, her fists propping her chin in thought, and then she starts to rise, bringing her fists down with vigor and the radiation spreading from cheek to cheek again.*)

Well— WELL— All I can say is—if this is my time in life—MY TIME—to say good-bye—

(*And she builds with momentum as she starts to circle the room with an exuberant, almost tearfully happy release.*)

to these God-damned cracking walls!—

(*She pounds the walls.*)

and these marching roaches!—

(*She wipes at an imaginary army of marching roaches.*)

and this cramped little closet which ain't now or never was no kitchen!— then I say it loud and good, HALLELUYAH! AND GOOD-BYE, MISERY—I DON'T NEVER WANT TO SEE YOUR UGLY FACE AGAIN!

*(Crosses U.C. above kitchen table. She laughs joyously, having prac-
tically destroyed the apartment, and flings her arms up and lets them
come down happily, slowly, reflectively over her abdomen, aware for
the first time perhaps that the life therein pulses with happiness and
not despair.)*

Lena—?

Mama:

(Moved, watching her happiness.)

Yes, honey—?

Ruth:

(Looking off.)

Is there—is there a whole lot of sunlight?

Mama:

(Understanding.)

Yes, child, there's a whole lot of sunlight.

(Long pause.)

Ruth:

*(Collecting herself and crossing above sofa to the bedroom where
Travis is.)*

Well—I guess I better see 'bout Travis.

*(To **Mama**.)*

Lord, I sure don't feel like whipping nobody today!

(She exits.)

Mama:

*(The mother and son are left alone now and **Mama** waits a long time,
considering deeply, before she speaks.)*

Son—you—you understand what I done, don't you?

*(**Walter** crosses R. front of sofa. He is silent and sullen. **Mama** pauses.)*

I—I just seen my family falling apart today—just falling to pieces in front of
my eyes— We couldn't of gone on like we was today. We was going back-
wards 'stead of forwards—talking 'bout killing babies and wishing each other
was dead— When it gets like that in life—you just got to do something
different, push on out and do something bigger—

(She waits.)

I wish you say something, son—I wish you'd say how deep inside you you
think I done the right thing—

Walter:

*(Turning and crossing slowly to his bedroom door and finally turning
there and speaking measuredly.)*

What you need me to say you done right for? You the head of this family.
You run our lives like you want to. It was your money and you did what you
wanted with it. So what you need for me to say it was all right for?

(Bitterly, to hurt her as deeply as he knows is possible.)

So you butchered up a dream of mine—you—

(He turns to exit.)

who always talking 'bout your children's *dreams*—

A RAISIN IN THE SUN   87

Mama: Walter Lee—

(*He just closes the door behind him.* **Mama** *sits on alone thinking heavily.*)

Curtain

SCENE 2

Time: *Friday night. A few weeks later.*

At Rise: *Packing crates mark the intention of the family to move.* **Beneatha** *and* **George** *come in, presumably from an evening out again. Business in hallway.* **George** *opens door;* **Beneatha** *slips by him, crosses D.R., snaps on FLOOR LAMP, sits on sofa.*

George: O.K.—O.K., whatever you say—
> (*He tries to embrace her.*)

Beneatha: George! Please!

George: Look, we've had a nice evening; let's not spoil it, huh?
> (*He turns her head and tries to nuzzle in and she again turns away from him, not with distaste but momentary disinterest, in a mood to pursue what they were talking about.*)

Beneatha: I'm trying to talk to you.

George:
> (*Crosses U.R. of sofa.*)

We always talk.

Beneatha: Yes—and I love to talk.

George:
> (*Exasperated.*)

I know it and I don't mind it sometimes—you just listen to me—I want you to cut it out, see—the moody stuff, I mean. I don't like it. You're a nice-looking girl—all over. That's all you need, honey, forget the atmosphere. Guys aren't going to go for the atmosphere—they're going to go for what they see. Be glad for that. Beneatha, please drop the Garbo routine. It doesn't go with you.
> (*He sits.*)

As for myself, I want a nice—
> (*Groping.*)

simple—
> (*Thoughtfully.*)

sophisticated girl— Not a poet—O.K.?
> (*Rises, crosses U.C.*)

Beneatha: George, why are you angry?

George:
> (*Stops at C. door, turns, crosses D.C.*)

Because this is stupid! I don't go out with you to discuss the nature of quiet desperation or to hear all your thoughts—because the world will go on thinking what it thinks regardless—

Beneatha: Then why read books? Why go to school?

George:

> *(Crosses D.C. to L. end of sofa, sits. Patiently, with artificial patience, on his fingers.)*

It's simple. You read books—to learn facts—to get grades—to pass the course —to get a degree. That's all—it has nothing to do with thoughts.

Beneatha:

> *(A long pause.)*

I see.

> *(A longer pause as she looks at him.)*

Good night, George.

> *(**George** starts to sit, rises, looks at her a little oddly and crosses U.C. to door. He meets **Mama** coming in.)*

Mama: Hello, George, how are you feeling?

George: Fine—fine; how are you?

Mama: Oh, a little tired. You know them steps can get you after a day's work. You all have a nice time tonight?

George: Yes—a fine time. A fine time.

Mama: Well, good night.

> *(She closes the door after **George** exits.)*

Hello, honey— What you sitting like that for?

> *(Crosses to L.)*

Beneatha: I'm just sitting.

Mama: Well, now that your company's gone, why don't you make up Travis' bed for him?

> *(**Beneatha** rises, gets bedclothes from U.R. armchair, starts making **Travis'** bed.)*

Didn't you have a nice time *tonight?*

> *(She puts on LIGHT D.L.)*

Beneatha: No.

Mama:

> *(Crosses D.L. above table to kitchen with string bag of groceries.)*

No? What's the matter?

Beneatha: Mama, George is a fool—honest.

> *(Crosses in to C.)*

Mama:

> *(Hustling around unloading her packages, she stops.)*

Is he, baby?

Beneatha: Yes.

> *(Crosses R. for coat.)*

Mama: You sure?

Beneatha:

> *(Crosses U.C.)*

Yes.

Mama: Well—I guess you better not waste your time with no fools.

Beneatha:

> *(She looks up at her mother, watching her put groceries in the icebox.*

Finally she gathers up her things and starts to go into the L. bedroom. At the door she stops and looks back at her mother.)

Mama—

Mama: Yes, baby—

Beneatha: Thank you.

Mama: For what?

Beneatha: For understanding me this time.

*(As she exits quickly, the PHONE rings. **Mama** stands looking at the place where **Beneatha** just stood, smiling a little perhaps. **Ruth** enters and picks up the phone.)*

Ruth: Now don't you fool with any of that stuff, Lena—

Mama: Oh, I just thought I'd sort a few things out.

Ruth:
(At the phone.)
Hello—Just a minute.
(Crosses to R. door.)
Walter, it's Mrs. Arnold.
(Waits. Crosses back to phone. Then tense.)
Hello— Yes, this is his wife speaking— He's lying down now— Yes—well, he'll be in tomorrow. He's been very sick— Yes— I know we should have called, but we were so sure he'd be able to come in today— Yes—yes, I'm sorry— Yes— Thank you very much.
*(She hangs up and **Walter** enters and is standing in the doorway from the bedroom behind her.)*
That was Mrs. Arnold.

Walter:
(Indifferently.)
Was it?

Ruth: She said if you don't come in tomorrow that they are getting a new man—

Walter:
(Crosses D.R. to radio.)
Ain't that sad—ain't that crying sad?
(Turns on RADIO.)

Ruth: She said Mr. Arnold has had to take a cab for three days— Walter, you ain't been to work for three days!
(This is a revelation to her.)
Where you been, Walter Lee Younger?
*(**Walter** looks at her and starts to laugh.)*
You're going to lose your job.

Walter: That's right—
(Sits Downstage arm of chair D.R.)

Ruth: Oh, Walter, and with your mother working like a dog every day—

Walter: That's sad, too— Everything is sad.

Mama:
(Crosses in R.)
What you been doing these three days, son?

Walter: Mama—you don't know all the things a man what got leisure can find to do in this city— What's this—Friday night? Well—Wednesday I borrowed Willy Harris' car and I went for a drive—just me and myself, and I drove and drove—way out—way past South Chicago, and I parked the car and I sat and looked at the steel mills all day long. I just sat and looked at them big black chimnies for hours. Then I drove back and I went to the Green Hat.

(Rises, crosses C.)

And Thursday—Thursday I borrowed the car again and I got in it and I pointed it the other way and I drove the other way—

*(**Mama** sits.)*

for hours—way, way up to Wisconsin, and I looked at the farms. I just drove and looked at the farms. Then I drove back and I went to the Green Hat.

(Crosses U.L. to closet for coat.)

And today—today I didn't get the car. Today I just walked all over the Southside. And I looked at the Negroes and they looked at me, and finally I just sat down on the curb at 39th—

(Crosses to C.)

and South Parkway and I just sat there and watched the Negroes go by. And then I went to the Green Hat. Y'all sad? Y'all depressed? And you know where I am going right now—?

*(**Ruth** goes out quietly. He crosses after her to door R.)*

Mama:

(Sitting L. of kitchen table.)

Big Walter, is this the harvest of our days?

Walter: You know what I like about the Green Hat—?

(Crosses D.R. to radio.)

I like this little cat they got there who blows a sax. He blows. He talks to me. He ain't but 'bout five feet tall and he's got a conked head and his eyes is always closed and he's all music—

Mama: Walter—

Walter: And there's another fellow who plays the piano—and they got a sound. I mean they can work on some music— They got the best little combo in the world in the Green Hat— You can just sit there and drink and listen to them three men play and you realize that don't nothing count worth a damn, but being there—

Mama:

(Rises, crosses D.L.C.)

I've helped do it to you, haven't I, son? Walter, I been wrong.

Walter:

(Sits armchair D.R.)

Naw—you ain't never been wrong about nothing, Mama.

Mama:

*(Crosses R. to **Walter**.)*

Listen to me now. I say I been wrong, son. That I been doing to you what the rest of the world been doing to you.

(She turns off RADIO.)

Walter—

> (*She stops and he looks up slowly at her and she meets his eyes evenly.*)

what you ain't never understood is that I ain't got nothing, don't own nothing, ain't never really wanted nothing that wasn't for you. There ain't nothing as precious to me—there ain't nothing worth holding on to, money, dreams, nothing else—if it means—if it means it's going to destroy my boy.

> (*Crosses U.R.C. to buffet for her pocketbook and money. He watches her without speaking or moving.*)

I paid the man thirty-five hundred dollars down on the house. That leaves sixty-five hundred dollars. Monday morning I want you to take this money and take three thousand dollars and put it in a savings account for Beneatha's medical schooling.

> (**Walter** *rises, crosses U.C.*)

The rest you put in a checking account—with your name on it. And from now on any penny that comes out of it or that go in it is for you to look after. For you to decide.

> (*Puts money on coffee table and drops her hands a little helplessly.*)

It ain't much, but it's all I got in the world and I'm putting it in your hands. I'm telling you to be the head of this family from now on like you supposed to be.

> (*Crosses L. front of table.*)

Walter:

> (*Stares at money.*)

You trust me like that, Mama?

Mama: I ain't never stop trusting you. Like I ain't never stop loving you.

> (*She exits L. bedroom and* **Walter** *sits looking at the money on the table. He rises, crosses softly toward* **Mama's** *room, stands thinking at her door, crosses back to his son's made-up bed, picks up pillow, examines it, throws it down, turns toward his own bedroom, as* **Travis** *enters from it.* **Travis** *climbs into bed, pulls the covers up around him, looks up at his father.*)

Travis: Good night, Daddy.

> (**Walter** *looks at him for a moment, turns and rapidly exits through the C. door as Lights black out, and Curtain falls.*)

Curtain

SCENE 3

Time: *Saturday, one week later.*
Before the Curtain, **Ruth's** *voice, a strident, dramatic church alto, cuts through the silence. It is, in the darkness, a triumphant surge, a penetrating statement of expectation:* "Oh Lord, I don't feel no ways tired! Children, Oh Glory Halleluyah!"

At Rise: *As the Curtain rises we see that* **Ruth** *is alone in the living room, packing brac-a-brac in carton on chair against Upstage wall. Crosses L., stands on chair L., removes ornament from L. wall, crosses R. and packs it in box above sofa. She is finishing up the family's packing. It is moving day. She is tying cartons.* **Beneatha** *enters and watches her exuberant sister-in-law.*

Ruth: Hey!
Beneatha:
>   *(Putting guitar case and coat in closet.)*

Hi.
Ruth:
>   *(Crosses D.C. to coffee table. Pointing at a package.)*

Honey—look in that package there and see what I found on sale this morning at the South Center.
>   *(She goes to the package herself and draws out the curtains.)*

Lookahere—hand-turned hems!
Beneatha: How do you know the window size out there—?
Ruth:
>   *(Who hadn't thought of that.)*

Oh— Well, they bound to fit something in the whole house. Anyhow, they was too good a bargain to pass up.
>   (**Ruth** *slaps her head suddenly remembering something.*)

Oh, Bennie—I meant to put a special note on that carton over there. That's your mama's good china and she wants 'em to be very careful with it.
Beneatha: I'll do it.
>   *(She finds a piece of paper and starts to draw large letters on it.)*

Ruth:
>   *(Crosses U.R. of sofa.)*

You know what I'm going to do soon as I get in that new house?
Beneatha: What?
Ruth:
>   *(Crosses to trunk U.L., stands on lid, removes object from above closet, crosses R., packs it.)*

Honey—I'm going to run me a tub of water up to here—
>   *(With her fingers practically up to her nostrils.)*

and I'm going to get in it—and I am going to sit—and sit—
>   *(Noticing how large* **Beneatha** *is absent-mindedly making the note.)*

Honey, they ain't going to read that from no airplane.
Beneatha:
>   *(Laughing herself.)*

I guess I always think things have more emphasis if they are big, somehow.
Ruth:
>   *(Looking up at her and smiling.)*

You and your brother seem to have that as a philosophy of life. Lord, that man—done changed so 'round here. You know—you know what we **did** last night? Me and Walter Lee?

Beneatha:
> *(Sitting with her coffee.)*

What—?

Ruth:
> *(Smiling to herself.)*

We went to the movies.
> *(Looking at **Beneatha** to see if she understands.)*

We went to the movies. You know the last time me and Walter went to the movies together?

Beneatha: No.

Ruth: Me, neither. That's how long it been.
> *(Smiling again.)*

But we went last night. The picture wasn't much good, but that didn't seem to matter. We went—and we held hands.

Beneatha: Oh lord!

Ruth: We held hands—and you know what?

Beneatha: What?

Ruth: When we come out of the show it was late and dark and all the stores and things was closed up—and it was kind of chilly and there wasn't many people on the streets—and we was still holding hands, me and Walter.

Beneatha: You're killing me.
> *(**Walter** enters with a large package. His happiness is deep in him, he cannot keep still with his new found exuberance. He is singing and wiggling and snapping his fingers. He puts his package in a corner and puts a phonograph record, which he has brought in with him, on the record player. As the MUSIC comes up he dances over to **Ruth** and tries to get her to dance with him. She gives in at last to his raunchiness, and in a fit of giggling allows herself to be drawn into his mood and together they deliberately burlesque the old Warwick style social dance of their youth—cheek to cheek; torsos poked out behind. **Beneatha** regards them a long time as they dance, then drawing in her breath, with a deeply exaggerated comment which she does not particularly mean.)*

Talk about—olddddddddd—fashionedddddd—Negroes!

Walter:
> *(Stopping momentarily.)*

What kind of Negroes?
> *(For fun; he is not angry with her today, nor with anyone. He starts to dance with his wife again.)*

Beneatha: Old-fashioned.

Walter:
> *(As he dances with **Ruth**.)*

You know when all the professional New Negroes have their convention—
> *(Pointing at his sister.)*

that is going to be the chairman of the committee on ending agitation.
> *(He goes on dancing, then stops.)*

Race, race, race— Girl, I do believe you are the first person in the history of the entire human race to successfully brainwash your own self.

(**Beneatha** breaks up and he goes on dancing. He stops again, enjoying his tease.)

Damn, even the N DOUBLE A C P takes a holiday sometimes!

(**Beneatha** and **Ruth** laugh. He dances with **Ruth** some more and starts to laugh and stops and pantomimes slightly over someone on operating table.)

I—can just see that chick some day looking down at some poor cat on an operating table before she starts to slice him, saying—

(Pulling his sleeves back maliciously.)

now what did you say your views on Civil Rights were—?

(He laughs at her again and starts to dance happily. The BELL sounds.)

Beneatha:

(Crossing to the door.)

Sticks and stones may break my bones but—

(She sticks out her tongue at him for punctuation through the remark so that she ends up at the door and opens it.)

words will never hurt me!

(And looks directly in the face of the stranger—embarrassment as before for herself and brother and **Ruth** who are still dancing crazily in the corner, R. **Beneatha** is somewhat surprised to see a quiet-looking middle-aged white man in a business suit holding his hat and a brief case in his hand and consulting a small piece of paper.)

Man: Uh—How do you do, Miss? I am looking for a Mrs.—

(He looks at the slip of paper.)

Mrs. Lena Younger—?

Beneatha:

(Smoothing her hair with very slight embarrassment. **Walter** and **Ruth** stop dancing.)

Oh—yes, that's my mother. Ruth! Brother!

(**Ruth** crosses D.R. to RADIO, cuts it off. **Walter** crosses U.R. and above sofa.)

Uh—come in, please.

Man: Thank you.

Beneatha: My mother isn't here just now. Is it business?

Man: Yes—well, of a sort.

Walter:

(Freely, the Man of the House. Crosses L. above sofa to L.C.)

Have a seat.

(**Beneatha** crosses D.L. to front of table.)

Man: Thank you.

Walter: I'm Mrs. Younger's son. I look after most of her business matters.

(**Ruth** and **Beneatha** exchange glances.)

Man:

(Regarding **Walter** and sitting L. on sofa.)

Well— My name is Karl Lindner—
Walter:
> *(Stretching out his hand.)*

Walter Younger. This is my wife—
> (**Ruth** *nods politely; still brushing at her hair from the former activity.*)

and my sister.
Lindner: How do you do?
Walter:
> *(Crosses R. below coffee table to Upstage of armchair, D.R. Amiably, leaning with loose interest forward, looking expectantly into the newcomer's face.)*

What can we do for you, Mr. Lindner!
Lindner:
> *(Some minor shuffling of the hat and brief case on his knees.)*

Well—I am a representative of the Clybourne Park Improvement Association—
Walter:
> *(Indicating with remark.)*

Why don't you sit your things on the couch?
Lindner: Oh—yes. Thank you.
> *(He slides brief case and hat onto couch.)*

And as I was saying—I am from the Clybourne Park Improvement Association and we have had it brought to our attention at the last meeting that you people—or at least your mother has bought a piece of residential property at—
> *(He digs for the little slip of paper again.)*

406 Clybourne Street—
Walter: That's right. Care for something to drink? Ruth, get Mr. Lindner a beer.
Lindner:
> *(Upset for some reason.)*

Oh—no, really. I mean thank you very much, but no, thank you.
Ruth:
> *(Crosses L. above sofa, sits chair R. of table. Innocently.)*

Some coffee?
Lindner: Thank you, nothing at all. Well, I don't know how much you folks know about our organization.
> *(He is a gentle man; thoughtful and somewhat labored in his manner.* **Walter** *sits Downstage arm of chair D.R.)*

It is one of these community organizations set up to look after—oh, you know things like block upkeep and special projects and we also have what we call our New Neighbors Orientation Committee—
Beneatha:
> *(Drily.)*

Yes—and what do they do?
Lindner:
> *(Turning a little to her and then returning the main force to* **Walter.***)*

Well—it's what you might call a sort of Welcoming Committee I guess. I mean they, we, I'm the chairman of the committee—go around and see the new people who move into the neighborhood and sort of give 'em the lowdown on the way we do things out in Clybourne Park.

Beneatha:
 (With false appreciation, the two meanings of which escape all.)
Uh-huh.

Lindner: And we also have the category of what the Association calls uh—special community problems—

Beneatha: Yes—and what are some of those?

Walter: Girl, let the man talk.
 *(**Beneatha** crosses L. and above table, picks up an orange from table.)*

Lindner:
 (With understated relief.)
Thank you. I would sort of like to explain this thing in my own way. I mean I want to explain to you in a certain way.

Walter: Go ahead.

Lindner: Yes. Well. I'm going to try to get right to the point. I'm sure we'll all appreciate that in the long run.

Beneatha: Yes.

Walter: Be still now!
 *(**Beneatha** crosses R. above sofa, tossing the orange up and down in the air.)*

Lindner: Well—

Ruth:
 (Innocently still.)
Would you like another chair—you don't look comfortable.

Lindner:
 (More frustrated than annoyed.)
No, thank you very much. Please. Well—to get right to the point I—
 (A great breath and he is off at last.)
I am sure you people must be aware of some of the incidents which have happened in various parts of the city when colored people have moved into certain areas— Well—because we have what I think is going to be a unique type of organization in American community life—not only do we deplore that kind of thing—but we are trying to do something about it.
 *(**Walter** slides off arm into the chair. **Beneatha** halts with the tossing and turns with a new and quizzical interest to **Lindner**. She crosses D.R. of sofa to U.L. of **Walter's** chair.)*
We feel—
 (Gaining in confidence in his mission due to the interest in the faces of the people he is talking to.)
We feel that most of the trouble in this world, when you come right down to it—
 (He pounds his fist just a little for emphasis on his knee.)
Most of the trouble exists because people just don't sit down and talk to each other.

Ruth:

   (Nodding as she might in church, pleased with the remark.)
You can say that again, Mister.
   (The same.)
Now that's right.
   (**Beneatha** and **Walter** merely watch and listen with genuine interest.)
Lindner:

   (Also more encouraged by such affirmation.)
That we don't try hard enough in this world to understand the other fellow's problem. The other guy's point of view. Yes—that's the way we feel out in Clybourne Park. And that's why I was elected to come here this afternoon and talk to you people and see if we couldn't find some way to work this thing out. Anybody can see that you are a nice family of folks, hard working and honest, I'm sure. Today everybody knows what it means to be an outsider. Well—you see our community is made up of people who've worked hard as the dickens for years to build up that little community. We're not rich and fancy people; just hard working honest people who don't really have much but those little homes and a dream of the kind of community we want to raise our children in. Now I don't say we are perfect and there is a lot wrong in some of the things we want. But you've got to admit that man, right or wrong, has the right to want to have the neighborhood he lives in a certain kind of way. And at the moment the overwhelming majority of our people out there feel that people get along better; take more of a common interest in the life of the community when they share a common background. I want you to believe me when I tell you that race prejudice simply doesn't enter into it. It is a matter of the people of Clybourne Park believing, rightly or wrongly, as I say, that for the happiness of all concerned that our Negro families are happier when they live in their *own* communities.
Beneatha:

   (With a grand and bitter gesture.)
This, friends, is the Welcoming Committee.
Walter:

   . *(Dumbfounded, looking at* **Lindner***.)*
Is this what you came marching all the way over here to tell us?
Lindner: Well now we've been having a fine conversation I hope you'll hear me all the way through.
Walter:

   (Tightly.)
Go ahead, man.
Lindner: You see—in the face of all things I have said, we are prepared to make your family a very generous offer—
Beneatha: Thirty pieces and not a coin less!
Walter: Yeah—?
Lindner:

   (Putting on his glasses and drawing out a form from the brief case.)
Our association is prepared through the collective effort of our people to buy the house from you at a financial gain to your family.

Ruth:
> *(Rises, crosses L. front of table.)*

Lord have mercy, ain't this the living gall!

Walter: All right, you through?
> *(Rises.)*

Lindner: Well, I want to give you the exact terms of the financial arrangement—

Walter: We don't want to hear no exact terms of no arrangements. I want to know if you got any more to tell 'bout getting together.

Lindner:
> *(Taking off his glasses.)*

Well—I don't suppose that you feel—
> *(Rises.)*

Walter: Never mind how I feel—you got any more to say 'bout how people ought to sit down and talk to each other— Get out of my house, man.
> *(He turns his back and walks to the door.)*

Lindner:
> *(Looking around at the hostile faces and reaching and assembling his hat and brief case. Crosses L. to U.C.)*

I don't understand why you people are reacting this way. What do you think you are going to gain by moving into a neighborhood where you—
> (**Walter** *crosses front of sofa U.C. to door, opens it.*)

aren't wanted and where some elements—well—people can get awful worked up when they feel that their whole way of life and everything they've ever worked for is threatened.

Walter: Get out.

Lindner:
> *(At the door, holding a small card.)*

Well, I'm sorry it went like this.

Walter: Get out.
> *(Crosses to back of table, picks up newspaper.)*

Lindner:
> *(To* **Walter** *as he approaches the door with deep passion.)*

You just can't force people to change their hearts, son.
> *(He turns and puts his card on a table and exits.)*
> *(After the exit* **Walter** *pushes the door to with stinging hatred; and stands looking at it.* **Ruth** *sits L. of kitchen table.* **Beneatha** *sits on arm of chair D.R. They say nothing for several seconds.* **Mama** *and* **Travis** *enter C. door.* **Travis** *goes into bedroom R. with boxes.)*

Mama:
> *(Puts hat, bag, stringbag and broom on crate back of sofa; crosses D.L., front of table, putting sticks and string on table; gets plant from window, crosses R. above table, sits.)*

Well—this all the packing got done since I left out of here this morning? I testify before God that my children got all the energy of the dead. What time the moving men due—

Beneatha: Four o'clock. You had a caller, Mama.

(She is smiling, teasingly. She crosses L. front of sofa to **Mama**.*)*
Mama: Sure enough—who?
Beneatha:
> *(Her arms folded saucily.)*

The Welcoming Committee.
> **(Walter** and **Ruth** *giggle.)*

Mama:
> *(Innocently.)*

Who?
Beneatha: The Welcoming Committee They said they're sure going to be glad to see you when you get there.
Walter:
> *(Devilishly.)*

Yeah, they said they can't hardly wait to see your face.
> *(Laughter.)*
> **(Beneatha** *crosses R. above sofa.)*

Mama:
> *(Sensing their facetiousness and looking up and putting her hands on her hips.)*

What's the matter with you all?
Walter: Ain't nothing the matter with us. We just telling you 'bout the gentleman who came to see you this afternoon. From the Clybourne Park Improvement Association.
Mama: What he want?
Ruth:
> *(The same as* **Beneatha** *and* **Walter**.*)*

To welcome you, honey.
Walter: He said— He said it's one thing they don't have that they just dying to have out there and that's a fine family of fine colored people!
Ruth: Yeah! He left his card—
Beneatha:
> *(Taking card from table and handing it to* **Mama**.*)*

In case.
Mama:
> *(Throws it on the floor—understanding and looking off as she draws her chair to the table where she has put her plant and some sticks and some cord.* **Walter** *sprawls on sofa.)*

Father, give us strength.
> *(Knowingly and without fun.)*

Did he threaten us?
Beneatha: Oh—Mama—they don't do it like that any more. He talked Brotherhood. He said everybody ought to learn how to sit down and hate each other with good Christian fellowship.
Mama:
> *(Sadly.)*

Lord, protect us—

Ruth:

(Still in chair L. of kitchen table.)

You should hear the money those folks raised to buy the house back from us. All we paid and then some.

Beneatha:

(Crosses L. to above table.)

What they think we going to do—eat 'em?

Ruth: No, honey, marry 'em.

Mama:

(Shaking her head.)

Lord, Lord, Lord—

Ruth:

(Rises, takes wrapped bowl of fruit to barrel.)

Well—that's the way the crackers crumble. Joke.

Beneatha:

(Laughingly, noticing what her mother is doing.)

Mama, what are you doing?

Mama: Fixing my plant so it won't get hurt none on the way—

Beneatha: Mama, you going to take that to the new house?

Mama: Uh huh—

Beneatha: That raggedy-looking old thing?

Mama:

(Stopping and looking at her.)

It expresses me.

(**Beneatha** crosses D.L. to sink.)

Ruth:

(With delight, to **Beneatha**.)

So there! Miss Thing!

(**Walter** suddenly rises, crosses U.R. above sofa, crosses L. to **Mama** and bends down behind her and squeezes her in his arms with all his strength. She is overwhelmed by the suddenness of it and her manner is like that of **Ruth** with **Travis**.)

Mama: Look out now, boy! You make me mess up my thing here!

Walter:

(His face lit, he slips down on his knees beside her, his arms still about her.)

Mama—you know what it means to climb up in the chariot?

Mama:

(Gruffly, very happy.)

Get on away from me now—

Ruth:

(Near the gift-wrapped package, trying to catch **Walter's** eye.)

Psst—

Walter: What the old song say, Mama—?

Ruth: Walter—Now?

(She is pointing at the package.)

(**Travis** *enters R. with box and hockey stick which he puts on bureau.*)
Walter:
*(Sweetly, playfully in **Mama's** face.)*
I got wings— You got wings— All God's children got wings—
Mama: Boy—get out of my face and do some work—
Walter:
(Crosses R. front of sofa, gets package D.R., crosses back to R.C.)
When I get to heaven gonna put on them wings. I'm gonna fly all over God's heaven—
Beneatha:
(Teasingly from across the room.)
Everybody talking 'bout heaven ain't going there!
Walter:
*(Crosses to C. to **Ruth**.)*
I don't know. You think we ought to give her that— Seems to me she ain't been very co-operative around here.
*(**Travis** crosses L. to above table.)*
Mama:
(Eyeing the box which is obviously a gift.)
What is it?
Walter:
*(Lifting it up on the table in front of **Mama** and standing D.R. of her.)*
Well—what y'all think? Should we give it to her?
Ruth:
*(Crosses L. to **Mama** and stands U.L. of her above the kitchen table.)*
Oh—she was pretty good today.
Mama: I'll good you—
(She turns her eyes to the box again.)
*(**Travis** crosses down and stands in front of the table between **Mama's** chair on the R. and **Beneatha** on the L.)*
Beneatha: Open it, Mama.
*(**Mama** stands up, looks at it—turns and looks at all of them and then presses her hands together and does not open it.)*
Walter:
(Placing the package on the chair. Sweetly.)
Open it, Mama. It's for you.
*(**Mama** looks in his eyes—it is the first present without Christmas in her life. Slowly she opens her package and lifts out, one by one, a brand new sparkling set of gardening tools. Prodding.)*
Read the note, Mama. Ruth wrote the note.
Mama:
(Picking up the card and adjusting her glasses.)
"To our own Mrs. Miniver—Love from Brother, Ruth and Beneatha." Ain't that lovely—
Travis:
(Crosses to C. Tugging at his fathers sleeve.)
Daddy, can I give her mine now?

Walter: All right, son.

> (**Travis** *flies to bedroom R.*)

Mama: Now I don't have to use my knives and forks any more.

Walter: Travis didn't want to go in with the rest of us, Mama. He got his own.

> (*Somewhat amused.*)

We don't know what it is—

Travis:

> (*Racing back into the room with a large hatbox, crossing D.R. front of sofa and putting it in front of his grandmother.*)

Here!

Mama: Lord have mercy, Baby. You done bought your grandmother a hat?

Travis:

> (*Very proud.*)

Open it!

> (**Mama** *does, and lifts out an elaborate, but very elaborate wide, gardening hat and all adults break up at the sight of it.*)

Ruth: Travis, honey, what is that?

Travis:

> (*Who thinks it is beautiful and appropriate.*)

It's a gardening hat! Like the ladies always have on in the magazines when they work in their gardens.

Beneatha:

> (*Giggling fiercely.*)

Travis—we were trying to make Mama "Mrs. Miniver"—not Scarlet O'Hara!

Mama:

> (*Indignantly.*)

What's the matter with y'all! This here is a beautiful hat!

> (*Absurdly.*)

I always wanted me one just like it!

> (*She pops it on her head to prove it to her grandson and it is as ludicrous as everything and considerably oversize.*)

Ruth: Hot dog; Go, Mama!

Walter:

> (*Doubled up with laughter.*)

I'm sorry, Mama—but you look like you ready to go out and chop cotton, sure enough!

> (*All laugh except* **Mama,** *out of deference to* **Travis'** *feelings.*)

Mama:

> (*Gathering* **Travis** *up to her.*)

Bless your heart—this is the prettiest hat I ever owned—

> (**Walter, Ruth** *and* **Beneatha** *chime in on congratulations to* **Travis** *on his gift noisily, festively and insincerely.*)

What are we all standing around here for? We ain't finished packin' yet. Bennie, you ain't packed one book.

> (**Walter** *starts to cross R. to bedroom. When he reaches the sofa, the DOORBELL rings.*)

Beneatha: That couldn't be the movers—it's not hardly two good yet—

(She goes L. into her room. **Mama** *starts for the C. door.)*

Walter:

(Turning, stiffening.)

Wait—wait—I'll get it.

(He stands and looks at the door.)

Mama: You expecting company, son?

Walter:

(Just looking at the door.)

Yeah—yeah—

*(***Mama*** *looks at* **Ruth** *and they exchange innocent and unfrightened glances.)*

Mama:

(Not understanding.)

Well, let them in, son.

Beneatha:

(From room.)

We need more string.

Mama: Travis—you run to the hardware and get me some string cord.

*(***Mama*** *goes out to L. bedroom.* **Walter** *turns and looks at* **Ruth.** **Travis** *goes to dish for money.)*

Ruth: Why don't you answer the door, man?

Walter:

(Suddenly bounding across the floor to her.)

'Cause sometimes it hard to let the future begin!

(The DOORBELL rings a second time. He crosses to the door and throws it open. **Travis** *exits; and there stands a very slight little man in a not too prosperous business suit and with hat pulled down tightly, brim up, around his forehead.* **Walter** *leans deep in face, still in his jubilance. The little man just stares at him.)*

Heaven—

(Suddenly he stops singing and looks past the little man into the empty hallway.)

Where's Willy, man?

Bobo: He ain't with me.

Walter:

(Not disturbed.)

Oh—come on in. You know my wife.

Bobo:

(Dumbly.)

Yes—h'you, Miss Ruth.

(Crosses D.C.)

Ruth:

(Quietly, a mood apart from her husband already, seeing **Bobo**.*)*

Hello, Bobo.

Walter: You right on time today—right on time. That's the way!

(He slaps **Bobo** *on his back.)*

Sit down—lemme hear.

(He sits in chair R. of kitchen table.)
*(**Ruth** at D.L. corner of kitchen table stands stiffly, quietly as though somehow she senses death, her eyes fixed on her husband.)*

Bobo:
(His frightened eyes on the floor, his hat in his hands, crosses in front of kitchen table and stands L.C. of the table.)
Could I please get a drink a water, before I tell you about it, Walter Lee?
*(**Walter** does not take his eyes off **Bobo**. **Ruth** goes blindly to the tap and gets a glass of water and brings it dumbly to **Bobo**.)*

Walter: There ain't nothing wrong, is there—

Bobo: Lemme tell you—

Walter: Man—didn't nothing go wrong—?

Bobo: Lemme tell you—Walter Lee.
*(Looking at **Ruth** and talking to her more than **Walter**.)*
You know how it was. I got to tell you how it was. I mean first I got to tell you how it was all the way—I mean about the money I put in, Walter Lee—

Walter:
(With taut agitation now.)
What about the money you put in?

Bobo: Well—it wasn't much as we told you—me and Willy—
(He stops.)
I'm sorry, Walter. I got a bad feeling about it. I got a real bad feeling about it—

Walter: Man, what you telling me about all this for— Tell me what happened in Springfield—

Bobo: Springfield.

Ruth:
(Like a dead woman.)
What was supposed to happen in Springfield?

Bobo:
(To her.)
This deal that me and Walter went into with Willy— Me and Willy was going to go down to Springfield and spread some money round so's we wouldn't have to wait so long for the liquor license— That's what we were going to do. Everybody said that was the way you had to do, you understand, Miss Ruth?

Walter: Man—what happened down there?

Bobo:
(A pitiful man, near tears.)
I'm trying to tell you, Walter.

Walter:
*(Grabs **Bobo**, swings him to C. facing L. Screaming at him suddenly.)*
THEN TELL ME, GODDAMNIT— WHAT'S THE MATTER WITH YOU?

Bobo: Man—I didn't go to no Springfield, yesterday.

Walter:
(Halted, life hanging in the moment.)
Why not?

Bobo:

> *(The long way, the hard way to tell.)*

'Cause I didn't have no reasons to—

Walter:

> *(C.)*

Man, what are you talking about!

Bobo:

> *(**Walter** backs him across D.R. front of sofa.)*

I'm talking about the fact that when I got to the train station yesterday morning—eight o'clock like we planned— Man—*Willy didn't never show up.*

Walter: Why—where was he—where is he?

Bobo: That's what I'm trying to tell you— I don't know— I waited six hours— I called his house—and I waited—six hours— I waited in that train station six hour—

> *(Breaking into tears. Looking up at **Walter** with the tears running down his face.)*

Man, *Willy is gone.*

Walter: Gone, what you mean Willy is gone? Gone where? You mean he went off to Springfield by himself—to take care of getting the license—

> *(He turns and looks anxiously at **Ruth** and paces L. around kitchen table then R. back to **Bobo**.)*

You mean maybe he didn't want too many people in on the business down there.

> *(Looks at **Ruth** again, as before.)*

You know Willy got his own ways.

> *(Looks back to **Bobo**.)*

Maybe you was late yesterday and he just went on down there without you. Maybe—maybe—he's been callin' you at home tryin' to tell you what happened or something. Maybe—maybe—he just got sick. He's somewhere—he's got to be somewhere. We just got to find him—me and you got to find him.

> *(Grabs **Bobo** senselessly by the collar and starts to shake him.)*

WE GOT TO!

> *(Turning, madly, as though he is looking for Willy in the very room.)*

WILLY!—WILLY—DON'T DO IT—

> *(**Mama** opens the L. bedroom door and enters with **Beneatha** behind her.)*

PLEASE DON'T DO IT—MAN, NOT WITH THAT MONEY—MAN, PLEASE, NOT WITH THAT MONEY— OH! GOD—DON'T LET IT BE TRUE—

> *(He is wandering around crying out for Willy and looking for him or perhaps help from God.)*

MAN— I TRUSTED YOU— MAN, I PUT MY LIFE IN YOUR HANDS—

> *(He starts to crumple down on the floor as **Ruth** just covers her face in horror.)*

MAN—

> *(He starts to pound the floor with his fists, sobbing wildly.)*

THAT MONEY IS MADE OUT OF MY FATHER'S FLESH—

Bobo:
>   *(Standing over him helplessly.)*

I'm sorry, Walter—
>   *(Only **Walter's** sobs reply. **Bobo** puts on his hat dumbly.)*

I had my life staked on this deal, too—
>   *(He exits C.)*

Mama:
>   *(To **Walter**.)*

Son—
>   *(She goes D.C. to him, bends down to him, talks to his bent head.)*

Son— Is it gone? Son, I gave you sixty-five hundred dollars. Is it gone? All of it? Beneatha's money, too?

Walter:
>   *(Lifting his head slowly.)*

Mama—I never—went to the bank at all—

Mama:
>   *(Stops and looks at both of her children and rises slowly and wanders vaguely, aimlessly away from them.)*

I seen—him—night after night—come in—and look at that rug—and then look at me—the red showing in his eyes—the veins moving in his head— I seen him grow thin and old before he was forty—working and working and working like somebody's old horse—killing himself. And you—you give it all away in one day—

Beneatha: Mama—

Mama: Oh, God—
>   *(She looks up to Him.)*

look down here—and show me the strength.

Beneatha: Mama—

Mama:
>   *(Folding over.)*

Father—strength—

Beneatha:
>   *(Plaintively.)*

Mama—

Mama: Strength!

>   *CURTAIN*

Act Three

Time: *An hour later.*

At Rise: *There is a sullen Light of gloom in the living room, grey light not unlike that which began the first scene of Act I. At R. we can see* **Walter** *within his room, alone with himself. He is stretched out on the bed, his shirt out and open, his arms under his head. He does not smoke; he does not cry out; he merely lies there, looking up at the ceiling, much as if he were alone in the world. In the living room*

Beneatha *sits at the kitchen table still surrounded by the now almost ominous packing crates. She sits looking off. We feel that this is a mood struck perhaps an hour before, and it lingers now, full of the empty sound of profound disappointment. We see on a line from her brother's bedroom the sameness of their attitudes. Presently the DOORBELL rings and* **Beneatha** *rises without ambition or interest to answer. It is* **Asagai,** *smiling broadly, striding into the room with energy and happy expectation and conversation.*

Asagai:

> *(Crosses R. above sofa, D.R., crosses L. front of sofa to barrel, crosses R. to* **Beneatha.***)*

I came over—I had some free time. I thought I might help with the packing. Ah, I like the look of packing crates! A household in preparation for a journey! It depresses some people—but for me—it is another feeling. Something full of the flow of life, do you understand— Movement, progress—it makes me think of Africa.

Beneatha: He gave away the money, Asagai—

Asagai: Who gave away what money?

Beneatha: The insurance money. My brother gave it away.

Asagai: Gave it away?

Beneatha: He made an investment! With a man even Travis wouldn't have trusted.

Asagai: And it's gone?

Beneatha:

> *(Sits on sofa.)*

Gone!

Asagai:

> *(Sits next to* **Beneatha** *on sofa.* **Beneatha** *rises, crosses U.R. of sofa, sits R. arm of sofa.)*

I'm very sorry— And you now?

Beneatha: Me?—Me? Me, I'm nothing— Me. When I was very small—we used to take our sleds out in the winter time and the only hills we had were the ice covered stone steps of some houses down the street. And we used to fill them in with snow and make them smooth and slide down them all day— and it was very dangerous, you know—far too steep—and sure enough one day a kid named Rufus came down too fast and hit the sidewalk—and we saw his face just split open right there in front of us— And I remember standing there looking at his bloody open face thinking that was the end of Rufus. But the ambulance came and they took him to the hospital and they fixed the broken bones and they sewed it all up—and the next time I saw Rufus he just had a little line down the middle of his face— I never got over that—

Asagai: What?

Beneatha: That that was what one human being could do for another, fix him up—sew up the problem, make him all right again. That was the most marvelous thing in the world— I wanted to do that. I always thought it was the one concrete thing in the world that a human being could do. Fix up the sick, you know—and make them whole again. This was truly being God—

Asagai: You wanted to be God—?

Beneatha: No—I wanted to cure. It used to be so important to me. I wanted to cure. It used to matter. I used to care. I mean about people and how their bodies hurt—

Asagai: And you've stopped caring—?

Beneatha: Yes—I think so.

Asagai:

> *(Rises.)*

Why?

Beneatha: Because it doesn't seem deep enough, close enough to what ails the world.

Asagai:

> *(Crosses L. to C.)*

I never thought to see *you* like this. You! Your brother made a mistake— and you are grateful to him. So that now you can give up the ailing human race on account of it. Now you can talk about what good is struggle; what good is anything? Where are we all going? And why are we bothering?

Beneatha:

> *(Rises, crosses L. to him.)*

AND YOU CANNOT ANSWER IT! All your talk and dreams about Africa and independence. Independence and then what? What about all the crooks and petty thieves and just plain idiots who will come into power to steal and plunder the same as before—only now they will be black and do it in the name of the new independence— You cannot answer that.

> *(Turns, crosses R. to armchair and sits.)*

Asagai:

> *(Shouting over her.)*

I LIVE THE ANSWER!

> *(Pause.)*

In my village at home it is the exceptional man who can even read a newspaper—or who ever *sees* a book at all.

> *(Crosses R. in to her, sits on sofa.)*

I will go home and much of what I will have to say will seem strange to the people of my village— But I will teach and work and things will happen, slowly and swiftly. At times it will seem that nothing changes at all—and then again—the sudden dramatic events which make history leap into the future. And then quiet again. Retrogression, even. Guns, murder, revolution. And I even will have moments when I wonder if the quiet was not better than all that death and hatred. But I will look about my village at the illiteracy and disease and ignorance and I will not wonder long. And perhaps— perhaps I will be a great man—I mean perhaps I will hold onto the substance of truth and find my way always with the right course—and perhaps for it I will be butchered in my bed some night by the servants of empire—

Beneatha: THE MARTYR!

Asagai: Or perhaps I shall live to be a very old man, respected and esteemed in my new nation— And perhaps I shall hold office and this *is* what I'm trying to tell you, Alaiyo, perhaps the things I believe now for my country will be wrong and outmoded, and I will not understand and do terrible things to have things my way or merely to keep my power. Don't you see that there will be young men and women, not British soldiers then, but my own black countrymen—to step out of the shadows some evening and slit my then useless throat? Don't you see, they have always been there—that they always will be? And that such a thing as my own death will be an advance? They who might kill me even—actually replenish all that I *was*.

Beneatha: Oh, Asagai, I know all that.

Asagai: Good! Then stop moaning and groaning and tell me what you plan to do.

Beneatha: Do?

Asagai: I have a bit of a suggestion.

Beneatha: What?

Asagai:
> *(Rather quietly for him.)*

That when it is all over—that you come home with me—
> *(Rises, crosses L. to kitchen.)*

Beneatha:
> *(Slapping herself on the forehead with exasperation out of misunderstanding.)*

Oh—Asagai—at this moment you decide to be romantic!

Asagai:
> *(Crosses to L. end of sofa. Quickly understanding the misunderstanding.)*

My dear, young, creature of the New World—I do not mean across the city—I mean across the ocean; home—to Africa.

Beneatha:
> *(Slowly understanding and turning to him with murmured amazement.)*

To—to Nigeria—?
> *(Rises, turns, crosses R. to front of kitchen table.)*

Asagai: Nigeria. Home.
> *(Crosses L. to her with genuine romantic flippancy.)*

I will show you our mountains and our stars; and give you cool drinks from gourds and teach you the old songs and the ways of our people—and in time—we will pretend that—
> *(Very softly.)*

you have only been away for a day— Say that you'll come.
> *(They nearly embrace.)*

Beneatha:
> *(Pulling away, crosses up back of kitchen table.)*

You're getting me all mixed up—

Asagai: Why—?

Beneatha: Too many things—too many things have happened here today.

I don't know what I feel about anything right this minute. I'm just going to sit down and think.

> (*Crosses D.C., sits on sofa and props her head on her hand.*)

Asagai: All right, I shall leave you.

> (*Crosses to C. above table.* **Beneatha** *starts to rise.*)

No—don't get up. Just sit a while and think— Never be afraid to sit a while and think.

> (*Goes to the C. door and turns.*)

How often I have looked at you and said, "Ah—so this is what the New World hath finally wrought—"

> (*He exits.*)

> (**Beneatha** *sits on alone. Presently* **Walter** *enters from his room and starts to rummage through things, feverishly looking for something. She looks up and turns in her seat.*)

Beneatha:

> (*Hissingly.*)

Yes—just look at what the New World hath wrought! Just look!

> (*She gestures with bitter disgust. Business of* **Walter** *searching for* **Lindner's** *card.*)

There he is! *Monsieur le petit bourgeois noir*—himself! There he is—Symbol of a Rising Class! Entrepreneur! Titan of the system!

> (**Walter** *ignores her completely and picks up his coat from chair D.R., frantically looking and hurling things to the floor and tearing things out of their place in his search.* **Beneatha** *ignores the eccentricity of his actions and goes on with the monologue of insult. Rises, crosses U.C., attacks him back of sofa.*)

Did you dream of yachts on Lake Michigan, Brother? Did you see yourself on that Great Day sitting down at the Conference—

> (**Walter** *finds it back of sofa by crate. Pushes it in his pocket and puts on his coat and rushes out without ever having looked at her. As he exits, she shouts after him the end of the following speech.*)

table, surrounded by all the mighty bald-headed men in America? All halted, waiting, breathless, waiting for your pronouncements on industry? Waiting for you—Chairman of the Board?

> (**Walter** *slams the door.* **Ruth** *comes out quickly from* **Mama's** *room L.*)

Ruth: Who was that?

Beneatha: Your husband.

> (*Crosses R. above sofa.*)

Ruth: Where did he go—?

Beneatha:

> (*Crosses D.R.*)

How do I know— Maybe he had an appointment at U. S. Steel.

> (*Sits on sofa.*)

Ruth:

> (*Anxiously, with frightened eyes.*)

You didn't say nothing bad to him, did you?

Beneatha:

(In anger.)

Bad—? Say anything bad to him. No— I told him he was a sweet boy and full of dreams and everything is strictly peachy keen.

(**Ruth** crosses U.L. to closet, pauses as **Mama** enters L. from her bedroom. **Mama** is lost, vague, trying to catch hold—to make some sense of her former command of the world, but it still eludes her. A sense of waste overwhelms her gait; a measure of apology rides on her shoulders.)

Mama:

(Goes to her plant which has remained on the table, looks at it; picks it up and takes it to the window sill and sets it outside and stands and looks at it a long moment. Then she closes the window, straightens her body with effort and turns around to her children.)

Well—ain't it a mess in here, though?

(**Ruth** crosses D.L. to icebox. **Mama** starts unpacking barrel R. of sink. A false cheerfulness, a beginning of something.)

I guess we all better stop moping around and get some work done. All this unpacking and everything—we got to do.

(**Ruth** raises her head slowly in response to the sense of the line; and **Beneatha** in similar manner turns very slowly to look at her mother.)

One of you all better call the moving people and tell 'em not to come.

Ruth: Tell 'em not to come?

(Crosses to **Mama**.)

Mama: Of course, baby. Ain't no need in 'em coming all the way here and having to go back. They charges for that, too.

Ruth: Lena—no. We got to go. Bennie—tell her—

She crosses to **Beneatha** with her arms outstretched. **Beneatha** doesn't respond.)

Tell her we can still move—

(Crosses to C.)

The notes ain't but a hundred and twenty-five a month.

(Crosses R. above sofa, packs marachas in box U.R.)

We got four grown people in this house—we can work—

(Crosses D.R. of sofa, gets lampshade, packs it U.R.)

Mama: This just ain't our time to be trying to take on something like that.

Ruth:

(Turning and going to **Mama** fast—the words pouring out with urgency and desperation.)

Lena—I'll work— I'll work twenty hours a day in all the kitchens in Chicago — I'll strap my baby on my back if I have to and scrub all the floors in America and wash all the sheets in America if I have to—but we got to move— We got to get out of here—

(Crosses D.L. above table to barrel again.)

Mama:

(Reaches out absently and pats **Ruth's** head.)

No— I sees things differently now. Been thinking 'bout some of the things we could do to fix this place up some. I seen a second hand bureau over on Maxwell Street just the other day that could fit right there.

(She points to back of the sofa and **Ruth** *wanders away from her.)*
Would need some new handles on it and then a little varnish and then it looks like something brand new. And—we can put up them new curtains in the kitchen— Why this place be looking fine. Cheer us all up so that we forget trouble ever came—

*(***Ruth** *crosses U.L. above table. To* **Ruth.**)*
And you could get some nice screens to put up in your room round the baby's bassinet—

(She looks at them both, pleadingly. Crosses D.R., sits armchair D.R.)
Sometimes you just got to know when to give up some things—and hold on to what you got.

> *(***Walter** *enters from the outside looking spent and leaning against the*
> *door with coat hanging from him.)*

Where you been, son?

Walter:

> *(At C., leaning against the door, breathing hard.)*

Made a call.

Mama: To who, son?

Walter: To The Man.

Mama: What man, baby?

Walter: The Man, Mama. Don't you know who The Man is?

Ruth: Walter Lee?

Walter: THE MAN. Like the guys in the streets say—The Man. Captain Boss—Mistuh Charley—Old Captain Please. Mr. Bossman.

Beneatha:

> *(Suddenly.)*

Lindner!

Walter: That's right. That's good. I told him to come right over.

Beneatha:

> *(Fiercely understanding.)*

For what? What do you want to see him for?

Walter:

> *(Looking at his sister.)*

We going to do business with him.

Mama: What you talking 'bout, son?

Walter: Talking 'bout life, Mama. You all always telling me to see life like it is. Well—I laid in there on my back today—and I figured it out. Life just like it is. Who gets and who don't get.

> *(He sits down in his coat and laughs.)*

Mama, you know it's all divided up. Life is. Sure enough. Between the takers and the "tooken."

> *(He laughs.)*

I've figured it out finally.

> *(He looks around at them.)*

Yeah. Some of us always getting "tooken."

(He laughs.)

People like Willy Harris, they don't never get "tooken." And you know why the rest of us do? 'Cause we all mixed up. Mixed up bad. We get to looking round for the right and the wrong; and we worry about it and cry about it and stay up nights trying to figure out 'bout the wrong and the right of things all the time— And all the time, man, them takers is out there operating, just taking and taking. Willy Harris? Shoot—Willy Harris don't even count. He don't even count in the big scheme of things. But I'll say one thing for old Willy Harris—he's taught me something. He's taught me to keep my eye on what does count in this world. Yeah.

(Shouting out a little.)

Thanks, Willy!

(Crosses R. above sofa to door R.)

Ruth:

(Step C.)

What did you call that man for, Walter Lee?

Walter:

(Crosses L. to C.)

Called him to tell him to come on over to the show. Gone to put on a show for the man. Just what he wants to see. You see, Mama? The man came before today and he told us that them people out there where you want us to move—well, they so upset they willing to pay us not to move out there.

(He laughs again.)

And—and oh, Mama—you would have been proud of the way me and Ruth and Bennie acted. We told him to get out— Lord have mercy! We told the man to get out. Oh, we was some proud folks this afternoon, yeah.

(Crosses D.L. above table to icebox.)

We were full of that old-time stuff—

Ruth:

(Crossing D.L. to him at icebox; slowly.)

You talking 'bout taking them people's money to keep us from moving in that house?

Walter: I ain't just talking 'bout it, baby—I'm telling you that's what's going to happen.

Beneatha: Oh God! Where is the bottom!

Walter:

(Crosses R. above table to above sofa.)

Where is the bottom? Where is the bottom? You and that boy that was here today. You all want everybody to carry a flag and a spear and sing some marching songs, huh? You wanna spend your life looking into things and trying to find the right and the wrong part, huh? Yeah. You know what's going to happen to that boy some day—he'll find himself sitting in a dungeon, locked in forever—and the takers will have the key! Forget it, baby! There ain't no causes—there ain't nothing but taking in this world and he who takes most is smartest—and it don't make a damn bit of difference *how*.

Mama: You making something inside me cry, son. Some awful pain inside me.

Ruth:
>(*Crosses R. to C.*)

Walter—

Walter: Don't cry, Mama. Understand. That white man is going to walk in that door able to write checks for more money than we ever had. It's important to him and I'm going to help him—I'm going to put on the show, Mama.

Mama: Son—I come from five generations of people who was slaves and share croppers—but ain't nobody in my family never let nobody pay 'em no money that was a way of telling us we wasn't fit to walk the earth. We ain't never been that poor.

>(*Raising her eyes and looking at him.*)

We ain't never been that dead inside.

Beneatha: Well—we are dead now. All the talk about dreams and sunlight that goes on in this house. It's all dead now.

Walter: What's the matter with you all! I didn't make this world!

>(**Ruth** *crosses L. front of table.*)

It was given to me this way! Hell yes, I want me some yachts some day! Yes, I want to hang some real pearls round my wife's neck. Ain't she supposed to wear no pearls? Somebody tell me—tell who it is that decides which woman is supposed to wear pearls in this world. I tell you I am a MAN— and I think my wife should wear some pearls in this world.

>(*This last line hangs a good while and* **Walter** *crosses L. front of sofa to C., the word "Man" has penetrated his own consciousness perhaps more than anyone else's and he mumbles it to himself repeatedly with strange agitated pauses between as he moves about.*)

Mama: Baby, how you going to feel on the inside?

Walter: Fine!—Going to feel fine—a man—

Mama: You won't have nothing left then, Walter Lee.

Walter:
>(*Coming to her.*)

I'm going to feel fine, Mama. I'm going to look that son-of-a-bitch in the eyes and say—

>(*He falters even more.*)

that's your neighborhood out there. You got the right to keep it like you want. You got the right to have it like you want. Just write the check and— the house is yours. And, and I am going to say—

>(*His voice almost breaks.*)

and you—you people just put the money in my hand and you won't have to live next to this bunch of stinking niggers!

>(*He straightens up from his mother and moves around the room.*)

Maybe—maybe I'll just get down on my black knees—

>(*He does so;* **Ruth** *and* **Beneatha** *and* **Mama** *watch him in frozen horror.*)

Captain, Mistuh, Bossman—

>(*He starts crying.*)

A-hee-hee-hee!

(Wringing his hands in profound anguished imitation.)

Yassssssuh! Great White Father, just gi' ussen de money fo' God's sake and we's aint gwine come out deh and dirty up yo' white folks' neighborhood—

(Exits bedroom R. **Note:** *On his exit into bedroom R.,* **Walter** *plants the car-coat he was wearing on bed off R.)*

Beneatha: That is not a man. That is nothing but a toothless rat.

*(***Ruth*** *remains far L. in kitchen.)*

Mama: Yes—death done come in this here house.

(She is nodding, slowly, reflectively.)

Done come walking in my house. On the lips of my children. You what supposed to be my beginning again. You—what supposed to be my harvest. How did we get to this here place? You mournin' your brother?

Beneatha: He's no brother of mine.

(Rises, crosses to C.)

Mama: What you say?

Beneatha:

(Halts L. of sofa.)

I said that that individual in that room is no brother of mine.

Mama: That's what I thought you said. You feeling like you better than he is today?

*(***Beneatha*** *does not answer. Crosses U.L., halts at door L.)*

Yeah? What you tell him a minute ago? That he wasn't a man? Yeah? You give him up for me? You done wrote his epitaph, too—like the rest of the world? Who give you that privilege?

Beneatha:

(Crosses D.C. to **Mama,** *sits coffee table.)*

Will you be on my side for once! You saw what he just did, Mama! You saw him—down on his knees. Wasn't it you who taught me to despise any man who would do that? Do what he's going to do?

Mama: Yes—I taught you that. Me and your daddy. But I thought I taught you something else, too—I thought I taught you to love him.

Beneatha: Love him? There is nothing left to love.

Mama:

(Sitting armchair R.)

There is always something left to love. And if you ain't learned that you ain't learned nothing.

(Looking at her.)

Have you cried for that boy today? I don't mean for yourself and for the family 'cause we lost the money. I mean for him; what he been through and what it done to him. Child, when do you think is the time to love somebody the most; when they done good and made things easy for everybody? That ain't the time at all. It's when he's at his lowest and can't believe in hisself 'cause the world done whipped him so.

(Rises.)

When you starts measuring somebody—measure him right, child. Measure him right. Make sure you done taken into account what hills and valleys he come through before he got to wherever he is.

Travis:

> (He bursts into the room at the end of the speech, leaving the door open. Crosses D.C. to L. end of sofa.)

Grandmama—the moving men are downstairs! The truck just pulled up.

Mama:

> (Turning and looking at him.)

Are they, baby? They downstairs?

> (She sighs and sits on sofa.)
>
> (**Lindner** appears in the doorway. He peers in and knocks lightly, superficially, to gain attention, and comes in. All turn to look at him.)

Lindner:

> (Hat and brief case in hand.)

Uh—hello—

> (**Ruth** crosses R. to bedroom mechanically and opens the door and lets it swing open freely and slowly as the LIGHTS come up on **Walter** within, sitting at the far corner of the room. He looks out through the room to **Lindner**.)

Ruth: He's here.

> (A long minute passes and **Walter** slowly gets up. **Beneatha** rises from coffee table, crosses extreme L. to kitchen sink.)

Lindner:

> (Crossing to L. end of kitchen table with efficiency; putting his brief case on the table and starting to unfold papers and unscrew fountain pens.)

Well, I certainly was glad to hear from you people.

> (**Walter** has begun the trek out of the room R., slowly, awkwardly— rather like a small boy, passing the back of his sleeve from time to time across his mouth.)

Life can really be so much simpler than people let it be most of the time. Well—with whom do I negotiate— You, Mrs. Younger, or your son here?

> (**Mama** sits with her hands folded on her lap and her eyes closed as **Walter** crosses slowly L. to U.C. **Travis** goes close to **Lindner** and looks at the papers curiously.)

Just some official papers, sonny.

Ruth:

> (Crosses D.R. of sofa.)

Travis, you go downstairs.

Mama:

> (Opening her eyes and looking into **Walter's**.)

No. Travis, you stay right here. And you make him understand what you doing, Walter Lee. You teach him good. Like Willy Harris taught you. You show where our five generations done come to. Go ahead, son.

> (**Ruth** sits D.R. in armchair.)

Walter:

> (Looks down in his boy's eyes. **Travis** grins at him merrily and **Walter** draws him beside him with his arm lightly around his shoulder.)

Well, Mr. Lindner.

(**Beneatha** *turns away.*)
We called you—
> (**Walter** *is U.R. of kitchen table with* **Travis** *at his right side. There is a profound simple groping quality in* **Walter's** *speech.*)

because, well, me and my family—
> (*He looks around and shifts from one foot to the other.*)

well—we are very plain people—
Lindner: Yes—
Walter: I mean—I have worked as a chauffeur most of my life—and my wife here, she does domestic work in people's kitchens. So does my mother. I mean—we are plain people—
Lindner: Yes. Mr. Younger—
Walter:
> (*Really like a small boy, looking down at his shoes and then up at the* **Man**.)

And—uh—well, my father, well, he was a laborer most of his life.
Lindner:
> (*Absolutely confused.*)

Uh, yes—
Walter:
> (*Looking down at his toes once again.*)

My father almost beat a man to death once because this man called him a bad name or something, you know what I mean?
Lindner: No, I'm afraid I don't.
Walter:
> (*Finally straightening up.*)

Well, what I mean is that we come from people who had a lot of pride. I mean—we are very proud people. And that's my sister over there and she's going to be a doctor—and we are very proud.
Lindner: Well—I am sure that is very nice, but—
Walter: What I am telling you is that we called you over here to tell you that we are very proud and that this is—this is my son and he makes the sixth generation of our family in this country and that we have all thought about your offer and we have decided to move into our house because my father earned it for us, brick by brick.
> (**Mama** *has her eyes closed and is rocking back and forth as though she were in church with her head nodding the amen yes.*)

We don't want to make no trouble for nobody or fight no causes—but we will try to be good neighbors. That's all we got to say.
> (*He looks the man absolutely in the eyes.*)

We don't want your money.
> (*He turns and walks away from the man.*)

Lindner:
> (*Looking around at all of them.*)

I take it, then, that you have decided to occupy.
Beneatha: That's what the man said.

Lindner:
>   (To **Mama** in her reverie; crossing to her.)

Then I would like to appeal to you, Mrs. Younger. You are older and wiser and understand things better, I am sure—

Mama:
>   (Rising.)

I am afraid you don't understand. My son said we was going to move and there ain't nothing left for me to say.
>   (Shaking her head with double meaning.)

You know how these young folks is nowadays, Mister. Can't do a thing with 'em. Good-bye.

Lindner:
>   (Folding up his materials.)

Well—if you are that final about it. There is nothing left for me to say.
>   (He finishes almost ignored by the family, who are concentrating on **Walter Lee**. At the door he halts and looks around.)

I sure hope you people know what you're doing.
>   (He shakes his head and exits.)

Ruth:
>   (Looking around and coming to life.)

Well for God's sake—if the moving men are here—LET'S GET THE HELL OUT OF HERE!

Mama:
>   (Rises, crosses L. to kitchen.)

Ain't it the truth. Look at all this here mess. Ruth, put Travis' good jacket on him— Walter Lee, fix your tie and tuck your shirt in—you look just like somebody's hoodlum. Lord, have mercy, where is my plant?
>   (She flies L. to kitchen window to get it amongst general bustling among the family, which is deliberately trying to ignore the nobility of the past moment.)

Y'all start on down— Travis, child, don't go empty-handed— Ruth, where did I put that box with my skillets in it? I want to be in charge of it myself— I'm going to make us the biggest dinner we ever ate tonight— Beneatha, what's the matter with them stockings? Pull them things up, girl—
>   (The family starts to file out as **Moving Men** appear and start bumping into them carying out the heavier pieces.)

Beneatha: Mama, Asagai—asked me to marry him today and go to Africa—

Mama:
>   (In the middle of her getting-ready activity.)

He did? You ain't old enough to marry nobody—
>   (Seeing one **Moving Man** lifting one of her chairs precariously.)

Darling, that ain't no bale of cotton; please handle it so we can sit in it again. I had that chair twenty-five years—
>   (The **Movers** sigh with exasperation and go on with their work.)

Beneatha:
>   (Girlishly and unreasonably trying to pursue the conversation.)

To go to Africa, Mama—be a doctor in Africa—
Mama:
>(Distracted.)

Yes, baby—
Walter: Africa! What he want you to go to Africa for?
Beneatha: To practice there—
Walter: Girl, if you don't get all them silly ideas out your head. You better marry yourself a man with some loot—
Beneatha:
>(Angrily, precisely as in the first scene of the play.)

What have you got to do with who I marry!
Walter: Plenty. Now I think George Murchison—
>(He and **Beneatha** go out yelling at one another vigorously; **Beneatha** is heard saying "George Murchison can go fly a kite"—and the anger is loud and real as their voices diminish. **Ruth** stands at the door and turns to **Mama** and smiles knowingly.)

Mama:
>(Fixing her hat at last.)

Yeah—they something, all right, my children.
Ruth: Yeah—they're something. Let's go, Lena.
Mama:
>(Stalling, starting to look around at the house.)

Yes—I'm coming. Ruth—
Ruth: Yes?
Mama:
>(Quietly, woman to woman.)

He finally come to manhood today, didn't he? Kind of like a rainbow after the rain—
Ruth:
>(Biting her lip lest her own pride explode in front of **Mama**.)

Yes, Lena.
>(**Walter's** voice calls for them raucously.)

Mama:
>(Waving **Ruth** out vaguely.)

All right, honey—go on down. I be down directly.
>(**Ruth** hesitates, then exits. **Mama** stands at last, alone in the living room, her plant on the table before her as the LIGHTS start to come down. She looks around at all the walls and ceilings and suddenly, despite her, the children calling below, a great heaving thing rises in her and she puts her fist to her mouth, takes a final desperate look, pulls her coat about her, pats her hat and starts out—the LIGHTS come down even more—and she comes back in, grabs her plant, and goes out for the last time. LIGHTS down and out.)

Final Curtain

A COMEDY IN THREE ACTS

Purlie Victorious

by Ossie Davis

Ossie Davis *(1917-   )*

Ossie Davis, who has been correctly described as one of the most talented men in the American theater, was born in Cogdell, Georgia, 23 miles from Waycross, which is the general locale for *Purlie Victorious.* His father was a railroad construction engineer. "My father's job was to keep the railroad between Cogdell and Waycross in good repair and to extend it—and to fight off the white folks who thought a Negro should not hold down the job," Davis says. "Some of the sweetest memories I have are of my father telling us stories. It gave us a chance to laugh at the world. I'm sorry he didn't live to see the play. It's his life."

Davis graduated from the local high school, attended Howard University in Washington, D.C., for three years, when upon deciding that he wanted to become a playwright and an actor, he turned to New York. In 1939 he joined the Rose McClendon Players in Harlem and his career in the theater was on its way. During World War II he was stationed in Liberia where he wrote and produced several army shows. Returning to civilian life, he made his Broadway debut in 1946 in *Jeb.* He was featured in *Anna Lucasta* and in *No Way Out.* His future wife, Ruby Dee, was also a member of the cast of *Jeb.* Miss Dee and Mr. Davis were married in 1948 and have often appeared together. They co-starred in *Purlie Victorious,* and previously appeared in *A Raisin in the Sun* when Ossie Davis replaced Sidney Poitier in the starring role.

Ossie Davis' interest in the development and encouragement of black theater has always been deep; since his earliest days on Broadway he has been a source of encouragement and funds in support of plays by black writers. The Davises are deeply involved in the aspirations of the contemporary black revolution in the United States. He notably delivered the stirring eulogy at the funeral of Malcolm X, and the assassination of Martin Luther

King, Jr. has led him to take an even more energetic daily role in the movement. "People have been trying to get me to run for office," he says, "but that would really end my writing." He is now working on his second play.

INTRODUCTION

Warmly received by the New York critics, Ossie Davis' *Purlie Victorious* opened at the Cort Theater on September 29, 1961, with the author in the title role, his wife, Ruby Dee, as Lutiebelle Gussiemae Jenkins, and Godfrey C. Cambridge as a memorable Gitlow Judson. The play was seen as falling somewhere between folk comedy and a social document, a gleeful satire of all the popular stereotypes of Negro-white relations in the South in particular and in the United States as a whole. It is indeed a farcical comedy done frankly and mockingly, satirizing every cliché of Southern life: the white pro-Confederate Colonel, the Uncle Tom, the Jim Crow system, the colored mammy and her white ward; the plantation store, the county sheriff, and the local cops, as well as the Supreme Court, the NAACP, the church, Constitutional rights and integration. But, like many great comic works, say, Moliere's *Tartuffe* or Ben Jonson's *Volpone*, or Gogol's *The Inspector General*, *Purlie Victorious* is an angry play, rooted in the basic indignation of its author. Anger rages through the scintillating comedy and the romp through the cotton-patch becomes a caper with the severest overtones.

Talking about his play, Ossie Davis once said, "The whole point of *Purlie Victorious* . . . is to prove that though the hour is late, there is still time for one more laugh—from the belly as well as the heart. Segregation— one of our most honored industries is no laughing matter. It is an abomination to the human spirit and a shame upon the face of the earth. I hate it! In all of its aspects North and South, I hate it! It is an evil thing and I cannot rest until mankind is done with it. And yet, looking at the world through Negro-colored glasses as I am forced to do every day of my life by segregation—what else can I do but laugh? It's absurd. The play is an attempt, a final attempt to hold that which is ridiculous up to ridicule—to round up all the indignities I have experienced in my own country and to laugh them out of existence." Again he was to say that his play was trying to do with laughter what Martin Luther King was trying to do with love.

Davis began working on *Purlie Victorious* in 1956 when he was stage manager for the Broadway production of *The World of Sholem Aleichem*, a play about Jews who found their principal salvation in an absurd and oppressive world in laughter. "I felt right at home," Davis was to say, "Sholem Aleichem's people were my people. They thought they had problems? Well, I wanted them to look inside *my* closet."

Davis' play tells the story of Purlie Victorious Judson, "a man consumed with that divine impatience without which nothing truly good, or truly bad, or even truly ridiculous, is ever accomplished in this world—with rhetoric and flourish to match." Purlie, bursting with the joy of life, is an unlicensed preacher (in an earlier stage he had been a professor of Negro philosophy) with the gift of tongues that echoes Ecclesiastes and Jeremiah, at the same time that it resounds in ethnic wit. Poetic in his vision of freedom, Purlie is a dreamer, a trickster, and a braggart, a self-appointed messiah of his race, "Who else is they got?" Shall we call him a black Quixote?

At the opening of the play he has come back to his old plantation village in south Georgia, bent upon acquiring Big Bethel, turned into a barn by the plantation owner, with the purpose of reconverting it into a symbol of freedom as an integrated church. To accomplish this he must claim a $500 inheritance left to the descendants of one of the family servants which is held "in trust" by Ol' Cap'n Stonewall Jackson Cotchipee. Ol' Cap'n Cotchipee, Purlie's antagonist, is the archetypal southern Colonel, a symbol of the unreconstructed South, replete with white suit, white hair and bull whip, confident that his "nigras" love him and that he is motivated by their best interests. The plot centers in Purlie's attempts to claim his inheritance, which in turn symbolizes the black man's heritage—his freedom and the recognition of his manhood.

Ol' Cap'n's son, Charlie Cotchipee, still awkward and adolescent at 25 or 30 is, to his father's unending consternation, sympathetic to the Supreme Court and the only white integrationist in Cotchipee County. This is largely the result of the subtle indoctrination of Idella Landy, his black mammy, the family's ancient woman of all work, who is the only mother Charlie has ever known and who has taught him all of his basic attitudes. In the course of the play, after being beaten at the local bar for speaking in favor of the Supreme Court's decision on desegregation in the local schools, he refuses to argue with his father who grabs him by the throat crying, "You tryin' to get non-violent with *me,* boy!"

Gitlow Judson, Purlie's brother, is Ol' Cap'n's "Uncle Tom," his "Deputy-for-the-Colored," whose job, in addition to being the "cotton-pickinist" cotton picker in the county, is to support his master's claims that his "nigras" are endeared to the Southern way of life and to sustain him against the assertions of the NAACP and the Supreme Court. Gitlow—"How low can you git, Gitlow?"—characteristically answers the Cap'n's diatribes with the refrain, "You is the boss, Boss!" and joins him in singing "Gone are the days," from "Old Black Joe" to console him in his moments of anger and frustration. It is important to note, however, that each of these motifs become increasingly ironic as the play progresses. Gitlow seems to grovel before the Southern white man, or the feudal South, if you will, but the humorous contempt beneath his feigned obsequiousness is one of the marvels of the play. He is a kind of Sancho Panza to Purlie's Quixote. Indeed, Gitlow's servility grows not so much out of cowardice as out of a sense of certain social realities. In trying, for instance, to dissuade Purlie from his intention to rush up to the big house to "stomp" Ol' Cap'n for pawing Lutiebelle, Gitlow says, "Now looka here, Purlie—don't you be no fool, boy—you still in Georgia. If you just got to defend the honor of the woman you love, do it somewhere else." And later he explains to Missy and Lutiebelle that against the hopelessly lone Purlie, Ol' Cap'n has on his side: the president, the governor, the courthouse, and both houses of Congress as well as the army, the navy, the marines, the sheriff, the judge, the jury, the police, the F.B.I., to say nothing of "a pair of brass knuckles and the hungriest dogs this side of hell!"

Purlie insists upon carrying out his assault upon Ol' Cap'n. And in the third act, the Captain's bull whip in hand, he proceeds to describe—in a passage that contains all of the eloquence and fervor of a hellfire and brimstone sermon—his siege of the big house and his monumental destruction of the old man. When his story is shown to be pure fantasy, he is only momentarily abashed. "While it's true," he says, "that, maybe, I did not go up that hill just word for word, and call that ol' man out, and beat him to death so much on the dotted line—!" And when Lutiebelle asks: "Why'd you have to preach all them wonderful things that wasn't so?" he replies, "I didn't mean for them not to be so: it was a parable! A prophecy! Believe me! I ain't ever in all my life told a lie I didn't mean to make come true some day!" His story, then, is a projection of his deepest feelings, at the same time that it must be seen as an emblem of the black man's rejection of white America's racial order. As a consequence of this he will remain to the end for Lutiebelle and his followers, "the hero of Cotchipee Hill." In short, the projection of his *will to be*, even if it involves the destruction of his enemy, takes on the force of a ritualistic miracle ending the drought in his wasteland. Purlie's dream action provides a strong catharsis and achieves his release and the release of the Negro people from Ol' Cap'n, or from the racism of the South and the country as a whole. "But one thing, Ol' Cap'n, I am released of you—the entire Negro people is released of you! No more shouting hallelujah! every time you sneeze, nor jumping jackass every time you whistle 'Dixie'! We gonna love you if you let us and laugh as we leave if you don't. We want our cut of the Constitution, and we want it now: and not with no teaspoon, white folks—throw it at us with a shovel!"

The Epilogue shows Purlie Vicorious inheriting his birthright as he stands in the pulpit of Big Bethel Church of the New Freedom For All Mankind, prepared to preach freedom in the cotton patch. But the immediate occasion also involves the integrated funeral of Ol' Cap'n Cotchipee, who died standing up and is to be buried in an upright position. "Take up his bones. For he who was my skin's enemy, was brave enough to die standing for what he believed. . . . Gently, gently. Put kindness in your fingers. He was a man—despite his own example. Take up his bones." And of the blacks: "Tonight, my friends—I find, in being black a thing of beauty: a joy; a strength; a secret cup of gladness; a native land in neither time or place— a native land in every Negro face." Purlie's Big Bethel sermon is not without its humor, but is notable for its basic humanity. As such it is a fitting conclusion to this comedy of anger and indignation. Its special fitness lies in its self-affirmative awareness of black dignity and the fundamental notion that the freedom of the black man involves the freedom of all men in America.

Purlie Victorious

"Our churches will say segregation is immoral because it makes perfectly wonderful people, white and black, do immoral things; . . .

Our courts will say segregation is illegal because it makes perfectly wonderful people, white and black, do illegal things; . . .

And finally our Theatre will say segregation is ridiculous because it makes perfectly wonderful people, white and black, do ridiculous things!"

— From "Purlie's I.O.U.."

CHARACTERS

Purlie Victorious Judson
Lutiebelle Gussiemae Jenkins
Missy Judson
Gitlow Judson
Charlie Cotchipee
Idella Landy
Ol' Cap'n Cotchipee
The Sheriff
The Deputy

Place: *The cotton plantation country of the Old South.*
Time: *The recent past.*

Act One
SCENE 1

Scene: *The setting is the plain and simple interior of an antiquated, run-down farmhouse such as Negro sharecroppers still live in, in South Georgia. Threadbare but warm-hearted, shabby but clean. In the Center is a large, rough-hewn table with three home-made chairs and a small bench. This table is the center of all family activities. The main entrance is a door in the Upstage Right corner, which leads in from a rickety porch which we cannot see. There is a small archway in the opposite corner, with some long strips of gunny-sacking hanging down to serve as a door, which leads off to the kitchen. In the center of the Right wall is a window that is wooden, which opens* outward on hinges. Downstage Right is a small door leading off to a bedroom, and opposite, Downstage Left, another door leads out into backyard, and on into the cotton fields beyond. There is also a smaller table and a cupboard against the wall. An old dresser stands against the Right wall, between the window and the Downstage door. There is a shelf on the Left wall with a pail of drinking water, and a large tin dipper. Various cooking utensils, and items like salt and pepper are scattered about in appropriate places.

At Rise: The Curtain rises on a stage in semi-darkness. After a moment, when the Lights have come up, the door in the Up Right corner bursts open: Enter **Purlie Judson. Purlie Judson** is tall, restless, and commanding. In his middle or late thirties, he wears a wide-brim, ministerial black hat, a string tie, and a claw hammer coat, which, though far from new, does not fit him too badly. His arms are loaded with large boxes and parcels, which must have come fresh from a department store. **Purlie** is a man consumed with that divine impatience, without which nothing truly good, or truly bad, or even truly ridiculous, is ever accomplished in this world—with rhetoric and flourish to match.

Purlie:

(Calling out loudly.)

Missy!

(No answer.)

Gitlow!—It's me—Purlie Victorious!

(Still no answer. **Purlie** empties his overloaded arms, with obvious relief, on top of the big Center table. He stands, mops his brow, and blows.)

Nobody home it seems.

(This last he says to someone he assumes has come in with him. When there is no answer he hurries to the door through which he entered.)

Come on—come on in!

(Enter **Lutiebelle Jenkins,** slowly, as if bemused. Young, eager, well-built: though we cannot tell it at the moment. Clearly a girl from the backwoods, she carries a suitcase tied up with a rope in one hand, and a greasy shoebox with what's left of her lunch, together with an out-moded, out-sized handbag, in the other. Obviously she has traveled a great distance, but she still manages to look fresh and healthy. Her hat is a horror with feathers, but she wears it like a banner. Her shoes are flat-heeled and plain white, such as a good servant girl in the white folks' kitchen who knows her place absolutely is bound to wear. Her fall coat is dowdy, but well-intentioned with a stingy strip of rabbit fur around the neck. **Lutiebelle** is like thousands of Negro girls you might know. Eager, desirous—even anxious, keenly in search for life and for love, trembling on the brink of self-confident and vigorous young womanhood—but afraid to take the final leap: because no one has ever told her it is no longer necessary to be white in order to be virtuous, charming, or beautiful.)

Lutiebelle:
> (*Looking round as if at a museum of great importance.*)

Nobody home it seems.

Purlie:
> (*Annoyed to find himself so exactly echoed, looks at her sharply. He takes his watch from his vest pocket, where he wears it on a chain.*)

Cotton-picking time in Georgia it's against the law to be home. Come in—unload yourself.
> (*Crosses and looks out into the kitchen.* **Lutiebelle** *is so enthralled, she still stands with all her bags and parcels in her arm.*)

Set your suitcase down.

Lutiebelle: What?

Purlie: It makes you lopsided.

Lutiebelle:
> (*Snapping out of it.*)

It is? I didn't even notice.
> (*Sets suitcase, lunch box, and parcels down.*)

Purlie:
> (*Studies her for a moment; goes and gently takes off her hat.*)

Tired?

Lutiebelle: Not stepping high as I am!

Purlie:
> (*Takes the rest of her things and sets them on the table.*)

Hungry?

Lutiebelle: No, sir. But there's still some of my lunch left if you—

Purlie:
> (*Quickly.*)

No, thank you. Two ham-hock sandwiches in one day is my limit.
> (*Sits down and fans himself with his hat.*)

Sorry I had to walk you so far so fast.

Lutiebelle:
> (*Dreamily.*)

Oh, I didn't mind, sir. Walking's good for you, Miz Emmylou sez—

Purlie: Miz Emmylou can afford to say that: Miz Emmylou got a car. While all the transportation we got in the world is tied up in second-hand shoe leather. But never mind, my sister, never-you-mind!
> (*Rises, almost as if to dance, exaltation glowing in his eyes.*)

And toll the bell, Big Bethel—toll that big, black, fat and sassy liberty bell! Tell Freedom the bridegroom cometh; the day of her deliverance is now at hand!
> (**Purlie** *catches sight of* **Missy** *through door Down Left.*)

Oh, there she is.
> (*Crosses to door and calls out.*)

Missy!—Oh, Missy!

Missy:
> (*From a distance.*)

Yes-s-s-s-!

Purlie: It's me!—Purlie!

Missy: Purlie Victorious?

Purlie: Yes. Put that battling stick down and come on in here!

Missy: All right!

Purlie:

> *(Crosses hurriedly back to above table at Center.)*

That's Missy, my sister-in-law I was telling you about.

> *(Clears the table of everything but one of the large cartons, which he proceeds to open.)*

Lutiebelle:

> *(Not hearing him. Still awe-struck to be in the very house, in perhaps the very same room that* **Purlie** *might have been born in.)*

So this is the house where you was born and bred at.

Purlie: Yep! Better'n being born outdoors.

Lutiebelle: What a lovely background for your homelife.

Purlie: I wouldn't give it to my dog to raise fleas in!

Lutiebelle: So clean—and nice—and warm-hearted!

Purlie: The first chance I get I'ma burn the damn thing down!

Lutiebelle: But—Reb'n Purlie!—It's yours, and that's what counts. Like Miz Emmylou sez—

Purlie: Come here!

> *(Pulls her across to the window, flings it open.)*

You see that big white house, perched on top of that hill with them two windows looking right down at us like two eyeballs: that's where Ol' Cap'n lives.

Lutiebelle: Ol' Cap'n?

Purlie: Stonewall Jackson Cotchipee. He owns this dump, not me.

Lutiebelle: Oh—

Purlie: And that ain't all: hill and dale, field and farm, truck and tractor, horse and mule, bird and bee and bush and tree—and cotton!—cotton by bole and by bale—every bit o' cotton you see in this county!—Everything and everybody he owns!

Lutiebelle: Everybody? You mean he owns people?

Purlie:

> *(Bridling his impatience.)*

Well—look!—ain't a man, woman or child working in this valley that ain't in debt to that ol' bastard!—

> *(Catches himself.)*

bustard!—

> *(This still won't do.)*

buzzard!—And that includes Gitlow and Missy—everybody—except me.—

Lutiebelle: But folks can't own people no more, Reb'n Purlie. Miz Emmylou sez that—

Purlie:

> *(Verging on explosion.)*

You ain't working for Miz Emmylou no more, you're working for me—Purlie Victorious. Freedom is my business, and I say that ol' man runs this plantation on debt: the longer you work for Ol Cap'n Cotchipee, the more you owe at the commissary; and if you don't pay up, you can't leave. And I don't give a damn what Miz Emmylou nor nobody else sez—that's slavery!

Lutiebelle: I'm sorry, Reb'n Purlie—

Purlie: Don't apologize, wait!—Just wait!—til I get my church;—wait til I buy Big Bethel back—

> (Crosses to window and looks out.)

Wait til I stand once again in the pulpit of Grandpaw Kinkaid, and call upon my people—and talk to my people— About Ol' Cap'n, that miserable son-of-a—

Lutiebelle:

> (Just in time to save him.)

Wait—

Purlie: Wait, I say! And we'll see who's gonna dominize this valley!—him or me!

> (Turns and sees **Missy** through door Down Left.)

Missy—!

> (Enter **Missy**, ageless, benign, and smiling. She wears a ragged old straw hat, a big house apron over her faded gingham, and low-cut, dragged-out tennis shoes on her feet. She is strong and of good cheer —of a certain shrewdness, yet full of the desire to believe. Her eyes light on **Lutiebelle**, and her arms go up and outward automatically.)

Missy: Purlie!

Purlie:

> (Thinks she is reaching for him.)

Missy!

Missy:

> (Ignoring him, clutching **Lutiebelle**, laughing and crying.)

Well—well—well!

Purlie:

> (Breaking the stranglehold.)

For God's sake, Missy, don't choke her to death!

Missy: All my life—all my life I been praying for me a daughter just like you. My prayers is been answered at last. Welcome to our home, whoever you is!

Lutiebelle:

> (Deeply moved.)

Thank you, ma'am.

Missy: "M'am—m'am." Listen to the child, Purlie. Everybody down here calls me Aunt Missy, and I'd be much obliged if you would, too.

Lutiebelle: It would make me very glad to do so—Aunt Missy.

Missy: Uhmmmmmm! Pretty as a pan of buttermilk biscuits. Where on earth did you find her, Purlie?

> (**Purlie** starts to answer.)

Let me take your things—now, you just make yourself at home— Are you hungry?

Lutiebelle: No, ma'am, but cheap as water is, I sure ain't got no business being this thirsty!

Missy:
> *(Starts forward.)*

I'll get some for you—

Purlie:
> *(Intercepts her; directs **Lutiebelle**.)*

There's the dipper. And right out yonder by the fence just this side of that great big live oak tree you'll find the well—sweetest water in Cotchipee county.

Lutiebelle: Thank you, Reb'n Purlie. I'm very much obliged.
> *(Takes dipper from water pail and exits Down Left.)*

Missy: Reb'n who?

Purlie:
> *(Looking off after **Lutiebelle**.)*

Perfection—absolute Ethiopian perfect. Hah, Missy?

Missy:
> *(Looking off after **Lutiebelle**.)*

Oh, I don't know about that.

Purlie: What you mean you don't know? This girl looks more like Cousin Bee than Cousin Bee ever did.

Missy: No resemblance to me.

Purlie: Don't be ridiculous; she's the spitting image—

Missy: No resemblance whatsoever!

Purlie: I ought to know how my own cousin looked—

Missy: But I was the last one to see her alive—

Purlie: Twins, if not closer!

Missy: Are you crazy? Bee was more lean, loose, and leggy—

Purlie: Maybe so, but this girl makes it up in—

Missy: With no chin to speak of—her eyes: sort of fickle one to another—

Purlie: I know, but even so—

Missy:
> *(Pointing off in **Lutibelle's** direction.)*

Look at her head—it ain't nearly as built like a rutabaga as Bee's own was!

Purlie:
> *(Exasperated.)*

What's the difference! White folks can't tell one of us from another by the head!

Missy: Twenty years ago it was, Purlie, Ol' Cap'n laid bull whip to your natural behind—

Purlie: Twenty years ago I swore I'd see his soul in hell!

Missy: And I don't think you come full back to your senses yet— That ol' man ain't no fool!

Purlie: That makes it one "no fool" against another.

Missy: He's dangerous, Purlie. We could get killed if that old man was to find out what we was trying to do to get that church back.

Purlie: How can he find out? Missy, how many times must I tell you, if it's one thing I am foolproof in it's white folks' psychology.

Missy: That's exactly what I'm afraid of.

Purlie: Freedom, Missy, that's what Big Bethel means. For you, me and Gitlow. And we can buy it for five hundred dollars, Missy. Freedom!—You want it, or don't you?

Missy: Of course I want it, but— After all, Purlie, that rich ol' lady didn't exactly leave that $500 to us—

Purlie: She left it to Aunt Henrietta—

Missy: Aunt Henrietta is dead—

Purlie: Exactly—

Missy: And Henrietta's daughter Cousin Bee is dead, too.

Purlie: Which makes us next in line to inherit the money by law!

Missy: All right, then, why don't we just go on up that hill man-to-man and tell Ol' Cap'n we want our money?

Purlie: Missy! You have been black as long as I have—

Missy:
> (Not above having her own little joke.)

Hell, boy, we could make him give it to us.

Purlie: Make him—how? He's a white man, Missy. What you plan to do, sue him?

Missy:
> (Drops her teasing; thinks seriously for a moment.)

After all, it is our money. And it was our church.

Purlie: And can you think of a better way to get it back than that girl out there?

Missy: But you think it'll work, Purlie? You really think she can fool Ol' Cap'n?

Purlie: He'll never know what hit him.

Missy: Maybe—but there's still the question of Gitlow.

Purlie: What about Gitlow?

Missy: Gitlow has changed his mind.

Purlie: Then you'll have to change it back.

Gitlow:
> (Offstage.)

Help, Missy; help, Missy; help, Missy; help, Missy!

> (**Gitlow** runs on.)

Missy: What the devil's the matter this time?

Gitlow: There I was, Missy, picking in the high cotton, twice as fast as the human eye could see. All of a sudden I missed a bole and it fell—it fell on the ground, Missy! I stooped as fast as I could to pick it up and—

> (He stoops to illustrate. There is a loud tearing of cloth.)

ripped the seat of my britches. There I was, Missy, exposed from stem to stern.

Missy: What's so awful about that? It's only cotton.

Gitlow: But cotton is white, Missy. We must maintain respect. Bring me my Sunday School britches.

Missy: What!

Gitlow: Ol' Cap'n is coming down into the cotton patch today, and I know you want your Gitlow to look his level best.

> (**Missy** starts to answer.)

Hurry, Missy, hurry!

>   (**Gitlow** *hurries her off.*)

Purlie: Gitlow—have I got the girl!

Gitlow: Is that so—what girl?

Purlie:

>   (*Taking him to the door.*)

See? There she is! Well?

Gitlow: Well what?

Purlie: What do you think?

Gitlow: Nope; she'll never do.

Purlie: What you mean, she'll never do?

Gitlow: My advice to you is to take that girl back to Florida as fast as you can!

Purlie: I can't take her back to Florida.

Gitlow: Why can't you take her back to Florida?

Purlie: 'Cause she comes from Alabama. Gitlow, look at her: she's just the size—just the type—just the style.

Gitlow: And just the girl to get us all in jail. The answer is no!

>   (*Crosses to kitchen door.*)

MISSY!

>   (*Back to* **Purlie**.)

Girl or no girl, I ain't getting mixed up in no more of your nightmares—I got my own. Dammit, Missy, I said let's go!

Missy:

>   (*Entering with trousers.*)

You want me to take a bat to you again?

Gitlow: No, Missy, control yourself. It's just that every second Gitlow's off the firing line-up, seven pounds of Ol' Cap'n's cotton don't git gotten.

>   (*Snatches pants from* **Missy**, *but is in too much of a hurry to put them on—starts off.*)

Purlie: Wait a minute, Gitlow. . . . Wait!

>   (**Gitlow** *is off in a flash.*)

Missy! Stop him!

Missy: He ain't as easy to stop as he used to be. Especially now Ol' Cap'n's made him Deputy-For-The-Colored.

Purlie: Deputy-For-The-Colored? What the devil is that?

Missy: Who knows? All I know is Gitlow's changed his mind.

Purlie: But Gitlow can't change his mind?

Missy: Oh, it's easy enough when you ain't got much to start with. I warned you. You don't know how shifty ol' Git can git. He's the hardest man to convince and keep convinced I ever seen in my life.

Purlie: Missy, you've got to make him go up that hill, he's got to identify this girl—Ol' Cap'n won't believe nobody else.

Missy: I know—

Purlie: He's got to swear before Ol' Cap'n that this girl is the real Cousin Bee—

Missy: I know.

Purlie: Missy, you're the only person in this world ol' Git'll really listen to.

Missy: I know.

Purlie: And what if you do have to hit him a time or two—it's for his own good!

Missy: I know.

Purlie: He'll recover from it, Missy. He always does—

Missy: I know.

Purlie: Freedom, Missy—Big Bethel; for you; me; and Gitlow—!

Missy: Freedom—and a little something left over—that's all I ever wanted all my life.

> *(Looks out into the yard.)*

She do look a little somewhat like Cousin Bee—about the feet!

Purlie: Of course she does—

Missy: I won't guarantee nothing, Purlie—but I'll try.

Purlie:

> *(Grabbing her and dancing her around.)*

Everytime I see you, Missy, you get prettier by the pound!

> *(**Lutiebelle** enters. **Missy** sees her.)*

Missy: Stop it, Purlie, stop it! Stop it. Quit cutting the fool in front of company!

Purlie:

> *(Sees **Lutiebelle**, crosses to her, grabs her about the waist and swings her around too.)*

How wondrous are the daughters of my people,
Yet knoweth not the glories of themselves!

> *(Spins her around for **Missy's** inspection. She does look better with her coat off, in her immaculate blue and white maid's uniform.)*

Where do you suppose I found her, Missy—
This Ibo prize—this Zulu Pearl—
This long lost lily of the black Mandingo—
Kikuyu maid, beneath whose brown embrace
Hot suns of Africa are burning still: where—where?
A drudge; a serving wench; a feudal fetch-pot:
A common scullion in the white man's kitchen.
Drowned is her youth in thankless Southern dishpans;
Her beauty split for Dixiecratic pigs!
This brown-skinned grape! this wine of Negro vintage—

Missy:

> *(Interrupting.)*

I know all that, Purlie, but what's her name?

> *(**Purlie** looks at **Lutiebelle** and turns abruptly away.)*

Lutiebelle: I don't think he likes my name so much—it's Lutiebelle, ma'am—Lutiebelle Gussiemae Jenkins!

Missy:

> *(Gushing with motherly reassurance.)*

Lutiebelle Gussiemae Jenkins! My, that's nice.

Purlie: Nice! It's an insult to the Negro people!

PURLIE VICTORIOUS   135

Missy: Purlie, behave yourself!

Purlie: A previous condition of servitude, a badge of inferiority, and I refuse to have it in my organization—change it!

Missy: You want me to box your mouth for you!

Purlie: Lutiebelle Gussiemae Jenkins! What does it mean in Swahili? Cheap labor!

Lutiebelle: Swahili?

Purlie: One of the thirteen silver tongues of Africa: Swahili, Bushengo, Ashanti, Baganda, Herero, Yoruba, Bambora, Mpongwe, Swahili: a language of moons, of velvet drums; hot days of rivers, red-splashed, and bird-song bright!, black fingers in rice white at sunset red!—ten thousand Queens of Sheba—

Missy:

> *(Having to interrupt.)*

Just where did Purlie find you, honey?

Lutiebelle: It was in Dothan, Alabama, last Sunday, Aunt Missy, right in the junior choir!

Missy: The junior choir—my, my, my!

Purlie:

> *(Still carried away.)*

Behold! I said, this dark and holy vessel
In whom should burn that golden nut-brown joy
Which Negro womanhood was meant to be.
Ten thousand queens, ten thousand Queens of Sheba:

> *(Pointing at **Lutiebelle**.)*

Ethiopia herself—in all her beauteous wonder,
Come to restore the ancient thrones of Cush!

Missy: Great Gawdamighty, Purlie, I can't hear myself think—!

Lutiebelle: That's just what I said last Sunday, Aunt Missy, when Reb'n Purlie started preaching that thing in the pulpit.

Missy: Preaching it!?

Lutiebelle: Lord, Aunt Missy, I shouted clear down to the Mourners' Bench.

Missy:

> *(To **Purlie**.)*

But last time you was a professor of Negro Philosophy.

Purlie: I told you, Missy: my intention is to buy Big Bethel back; to reclaim the ancient pulpit of Grandpaw Kincaid, and preach freedom in the cotton patch—I told you!

Missy: Maybe you did, Purlie, maybe you did. You got yourself a license?

Purlie: Naw!—but—

Missy:

> *(Looking him over.)*

Purlie Victorious Judson: Self-made minister of the gospel-claw-hammer coat-tail, shoe-string tie and all.

Purlie:

> *(Quietly but firmly holding his ground.)*

How else can you lead the Negro people?

Missy: Is that what you got in your mind: leading the Negro people?

Purlie: Who else is they got?

Missy: God help the race.

Lutiebelle: It was a sermon, I mean, Aunt Missy, the likes of which has never been heard before.

Missy: Oh, I bet that. Tell me about it, son. What did you preach?

Purlie: I preached the New Baptism of Freedom for all mankind, according to the Declaration of Independence, taking as my text the Constitution of the United States of America, Amendments First through Fifteenth, which readeth as follows: "Congress shall make no law—"

Missy: Enough—that's enough, son—I'm converted. But it is confusing, all the changes you keep going through.

> *(To* **Lutiebelle***.)*

Honey, every time I see Purlie he's somebody else.

Purlie: Not any more, Missy; and if I'm lying may the good Lord put me down in the book of bad names: Purlie is put forever!

Missy: Yes. But will he stay put forever?

Purlie: There is in every man a finger of iron that points him what he must and must not do—

Missy: And your finger points up the hill to that five hundred dollars with which you'll buy Big Bethel back, preach freedom in the cotton patch, and live happily ever after!

Purlie: The soul-consuming passion of my life!

> *(Draws out watch.)*

It's 2:15, Missy, and Gitlow's waiting. Missy, I suggest you get a move on.

Missy: I already got a move on. Had it since four o'clock this morning!

Purlie: Time, Missy—exactly what the colored man in this country ain't got and you're wasting it!

Missy:

> *(Looks at* **Purlie** *and decides not to strike him dead.)*

Purlie, would you mind stepping out into the cotton patch and telling your brother Gitlow I'd like a few words with him?

> *(***Purlie***, overjoyed, leaps at* **Missy** *as if to hug and dance her around again, but she is too fast.)*

Do like I tell you now—go on!

> *(***Purlie*** *exits singing.* **Missy** *turns to* **Lutiebelle** *to begin the important task of sizing her up.)*

Besides, it wouldn't be hospitable not to set and visit a spell with our distinguished guest over from Dothan, Alabama.

Lutiebelle:

> *(This is the first time she has been called anything of importance by anybody.)*

Thank you, ma'am.

Missy: Now. Let's you and me just set back and enjoy a piece of my potato pie. You like potato pie, don't you?

Lutiebelle: Oh, yes, ma'am, I like it very much.

Missy: And get real acquainted.

(Offers her a saucer with a slice of pie on it.)

Lutiebelle: I'm ever so much obliged. My, this looks nice! Uhm, uhn, uhn!

Missy:

(Takes a slice for herself and sits down.)

You know—ever since that ol' man—

(Indicates up the hill.)

took after Purlie so unmerciful with that bull whip twenty years ago—he fidgets! Always on the go; rattling around from place to place all over the country: one step ahead of the white folks—something about Purlie always did irritate the white folks.

Lutiebelle: Is that the truth!

Missy: Oh, my yes. Finally wound up being locked up a time or two for safekeeping—

*(**Lutiebelle** parts with a loud, sympathetic grunt. Changing her tack a bit.)*

Always kept up his schooling, though. In fact that boy's got one of the best second-hand educations in this country.

Lutiebelle:

(Brightening considerably.)

Is that a fact!

Missy: Used to read everything he could get his hands on.

Lutiebelle: He did? Ain't that wonderful!

Missy: Till one day he finally got tired, and throwed all his books to the hogs—not enough "Negro" in them, he said. After that he puttered around with first one thing then another. Remember that big bus boycott they had in Montgomery? Well, we don't travel by bus in the cotton patch, so Purlie boycotted mules!

Lutiebelle: You don't say so?

Missy: Another time he invented a secret language, that Negroes could understand but white folks couldn't.

Lutiebelle: Oh, my goodness gracious!

Missy: He sent it C.O.D. to the NAACP but they never answered his letter.

Lutiebelle: Oh, they will, Aunt Missy; you can just bet your life they will.

Missy: I don't mind it so much. Great leaders are bound to pop up from time to time 'mongst our people—in fact we sort of look forward to it. But Purlie's in such a hurry I'm afraid he'll lose his mind.

Lutiebelle: Lose his mind—no! Oh, no!

Missy: That is unless you and me can do something about it.

Lutiebelle: You and me? Do what, Aunt Missy? You tell me—I'll do anything!

Missy:

(Having found all she needs to know.)

Well, now; ain't nothing ever all that peculiar about a man a good wife— and a family—and some steady home cooking won't cure. Don't you think so?

Lutiebelle:

(Immensely relieved.)

Oh, yes, Aunt Missy, yes.

*(But still not getting **Missy's** intent.)*

You'd be surprised how many tall, good-looking, great big, ol' handsome looking mens—just like Reb'n Purlie—walking around, starving theyselves to death! Oh, I just wish I had one to aim my pot at!

Missy: Well, Purlie Judson is the uncrowned appetite of the age.

Lutiebelle: He is! What's his favorite?

Missy: Anything! Anything a fine-looking, strong and healthy—girl like you could put on the table.

Lutiebelle: Like me? Like ME! Oh, Aunt Missy—!

Missy:
> (**Purlie's** future is settled.)

Honey, I mind once at the Sunday School picnic Purlie et a whole sack o' pullets!

Lutiebelle: Oh, I just knowed there was something—something—just reeks about that man. He puts me in the mind of all the good things I ever had in my life. Picnics, fish-fries, corn-shuckings, and love-feasts, and gospel-singings—picking huckleberries, roasting groundpeas, quilting-bee parties and barbecues; that certain kind of—welcome—you can't get nowhere else in all this world. Aunt Missy, life is so good to us—sometimes!

Missy: Oh, child, being colored can be a lotta fun when ain't nobody looking.

Lutiebelle: Ain't it the truth! I always said I'd never pass for white, no matter how much they offered me, unless the things I love could pass, too.

Missy: Ain't it the beautiful truth!
> (**Purlie** enters again; agitated.)

Purlie: Missy—Gitlow says if you want him come and get him!

Missy:
> (Rises, crosses to door Down Left; looks out.)

Lawd, that man do take his cotton picking seriously.
> (Comes back to **Lutiebelle** and takes her saucer.)

Did you get enough to eat, honey?

Lutiebelle: Indeed I did. And Aunt Missy, I haven't had potato pie like that since the senior choir give—

Missy:
> (Still ignoring him.)

That's where I met Gitlow, you know. On the senior choir.

Lutiebelle: Aunt Missy! I didn't know you could sing!

Missy: Like a brown-skin nightingale. Well, it was a Sunday afternoon—Big Bethel had just been—

Purlie: Dammit, Missy! The white man is five hundred years ahead of us in this country, and we ain't gonna ever gonna catch up with him sitting around on our non-Caucasian rumps talking about the senior choir!

Missy:
> (Starts to bridle at this sudden display of passion, but changes her mind.)

Right this way, honey.
> (Heads for door Down Right.)

Where Cousin Bee used to sleep at.

Lutiebelle: Yes, ma'am.

PURLIE VICTORIOUS   139

(Starts to follow Missy.)
Purlie:
(Stopping her.)
Wait a minute—don't forget your clothes!
(Gives her a large carton.)
Missy: It ain't much, the roof leaks, and you can get as much September inside as you can outside any time; but I try to keep it clean.
Purlie: Cousin Bee was known for her clothes!
Missy: Stop nagging, Purlie—
(To Lutiebelle.)
There's plenty to eat in the kitchen.
Lutiebelle: Thank you, Aunt Missy.
(Exits Down Right.)
Purlie:
(Following after her.)
And hurry! We want to leave as soon as Missy gets Gitlow in from the cotton patch!
Missy:
(Blocking his path.)
Mr. Preacher—
(She pulls him out of earshot.)
If we do pull this thing off—
(Studying him a moment.)
what do you plan to do with her after that—send her back where she came from?
Purlie: Dothan, Alabama? Never! Missy, there a million things I can do with a girl like that, right here in Big Bethel!
Missy: Yeah! Just make sure they're all legitimate. Anyway, marriage is still cheap, and we can always use another cook in the family!
*(**Purlie** hasn't the slightest idea what **Missy** is talking about.)*
Lutiebelle:
(From Offstage.)
Aunt Missy.
Missy: Yes, honey.
Lutiebelle:
(Offstage.)
Whose picture is this on the dresser?
Missy: Why, that's Cousin Bee.
Lutiebelle:
(A moment's silence. Then she enters hastily, carrying a large photograph in her hand.)
Cousin Bee!
Missy: Yes, poor thing. She's the one the whole thing is all about.
Lutiebelle:
(The edge of panic.)
Cousin Bee— Oh, my!—Oh, my goodness! My goodness gracious!
Missy: What's the matter?

Lutiebelle: But she's pretty—she's so pretty!

Missy:

> *(Takes photograph; looks at it tenderly.)*

Yes—she was pretty. I guess they took this shortly before she died.

Lutiebelle: And you mean—you want me to look like her?

Purlie: That's the idea. Now go and get into your clothes.

> *(Starts to push her off.)*

Missy: They sent it down to us from the college. Don't she look smart? I'll bet she was a good student when she was living.

Lutiebelle:

> *(Evading* **Purlie***.)*

Good student!

Missy: Yes. One more year and she'd have finished.

Lutiebelle: Oh, my gracious Lord have mercy upon my poor soul!

Purlie:

> *(Not appreciating her distress or its causes.)*

Awake, awake! Put on thy strength, O, Zion—put on thy beautiful garments.

> *(Hurries her Offstage.)*

And hurry!

> *(Turning to* **Missy***.)*

Missy, Big Bethel and Gitlow is waiting. Grandpaw Kincaid gave his life.

> *(Gently places the bat into her hand.)*

It is a far greater thing you do now, than you've ever done before—and Gitlow ain't never got his head knocked off in a better cause.

> *(***Missy** *nods her head in sad agreement, and accepts the bat.* **Purlie** *helps her to the door Down Left, where she exits, a most reluctant executioner.* **Purlie** *stands and watches her off from the depth of his satisfaction. The door Down Right eases open, and* **Lutiebelle***, her suitcase, handbag, fall coat and lunch box firmly in hand, tries to sneak out the front door.* **Purlie** *hears her, and turns just in time.)*

Where do you think you're going?

Lutiebelle: Did you see that, Reb'n Purlie?

> *(Indicating bedroom from which she just came.)*

Did you see all them beautiful clothes—slips, hats, shoes, stockings? I mean nylon stockings like Miz Emmylou wears—and a dress, like even Miz Emmylou don't wear. Did you look at what was in that big box?

Purlie: Of course I looked at what was in that big box—I bought it—all of it —for you.

Lutiebelle: For me!

Purlie: Of course! I told you! And as soon as we finish you can have it!

Lutiebelle: Reb'n Purlie, I'm a good girl. I ain't never done nothing in all this world, white, colored or otherwise, to hurt nobody!

Purlie: I know that.

Lutiebelle: I work hard; I mop, I scrub, I iron; I'm clean and polite, and I know how to get along with white folks' children better'n they do. I pay my church dues every second and fourth Sunday the Lord sends; and I can cook catfish—and hushpuppies— You like hushpuppies, don't you, Reb'n Purlie?

Purlie: I love hushpuppies!

Lutiebelle: Hushpuppies—and corn dodgers; I can cook you a corn dodger would give you the swimming in the head!

Purlie: I'm sure you can, but—

Lutiebelle: But I ain't never been in a mess like this in all my life!

Purlie: Mess—what mess?

Lutibelle: You mean go up that hill, in all them pretty clothes, and pretend—in front of white folks—that—that I'm your Cousin Bee—somebody I ain't never seen or heard of before in my whole life!

Purlie: Why not? Some of the best pretending in the world is done in front of white folks.

Lutiebelle: But Reb'n Purlie, I didn't know your Cousin Bee was a student at the college; I thought she worked there!

Purlie: But I told you on the train—

Lutiebelle: Don't do no good to tell ME nothing, Reb'n Purlie! I never listen. Ask Miz Emmylou and 'em, they'll tell you I never listen. I didn't know it was a college lady you wanted me to make like. I thought it was for a sleep-in like me. I thought all that stuff you bought in them boxes was stuff for maids and cooks and— Why, I ain't never even been near a college!

Purlie: So what? College ain't so much where you been as how you talk when you get back. Anybody can do it; look at me.

Lutiebelle: Nawsir, I think you better look at me like Miz Emmylou sez—

Purlie:

>   *(Taking her by the shoulders, tenderly.)*

Calm down—just take it easy, and calm down.

>   *(She subsides a little, her chills banished by the warmth of him.)*

Now—don't tell me, after all that big talking you done on the train about white folks, you're scared.

Lutiebelle: Talking big is easy—from the proper distance.

Purlie: Why—don't you believe in yourself?

Lutiebelle: Some.

Purlie: Don't you believe in your own race of people?

Lutiebelle: Oh, yessir—a little.

Purlie: Don't you believe the black man is coming to power some day?

Lutiebelle: Almost.

Purlie: Ten thousand Queens of Sheba! What kind of a Negro are you! Where's your race pride?

Lutiebelle: Oh, I'm a great one for race pride, sir, believe me—it's just that I don't need it much in my line of work! Miz Emmylou sez—

Purlie: Damn Miz Emmylou! Does her blond hair and blue eyes make her any more of a woman in the sight of her men folks than your black hair and brown eyes in mine?

Lutiebelle: No, sir!

Purlie: Is her lily-white skin any more money-under-the-mattress than your fine fair brown? And if so, why does she spend half her life at the beach trying to get a sun tan?

Lutiebelle: I never thought of that!

Purlie: There's a whole lotta things about the Negro question you ain't thought of! The South is split like a fat man's underwear; and somebody beside the Supreme Court has got to make a stand for the everlasting glory of our people!

Lutiebelle: Yessir.

Purlie: Snatch Freedom from the jaws of force and filibuster!

Lutiebelle: Amen to that!

Purlie: Put thunder in the Senate—!

Lutiebelle: Yes, Lord!

Purlie: And righteous indignation back in the halls of Congress!

Lutiebelle: Ain't it the truth!

Purlie: Make Civil Rights from Civil Wrongs; and bring that ol' Civil War to a fair and a just conclusion!

Lutiebelle: Help him, Lord!

Purlie: Remind this white and wicked world there ain't been more'n a dime's worth of difference twixt one man and another'n, irregardless of race, gender, creed, or color—since God Himself Almighty set the first batch out to dry before the chimneys of Zion got hot! The eyes and ears of the world is on Big Bethel!

Lutiebelle: Amen and hallelujah!

Purlie: And whose side are you fighting on this evening, sister?

Lutiebelle: Great Gawdamighty, Reb'n Purlie, on the Lord's side! But Miss Emmylou sez—

Purlie:

> *(Blowing up.)*

This is outrageous—this is a catastrophe! You're a disgrace to the Negro profession!

Lutiebelle: That's just what she said all right—her exactly words.

Purlie: Who's responsible for this? Where's your Maw and Paw at?

Lutiebelle: I reckon I ain't rightly got no Maw and Paw, wherever they at.

Purlie: What!

Lutiebelle: And nobody else that I knows of. You see, sir—I been on the go from one white folks' kitchen to another since before I can remember. How I got there in the first place—whatever became of my Maw and Paw, and my kinfolks—even what my real name is—nobody is ever rightly said.

Purlie:

> *(Genuinely touched.)*

Oh. A motherless child—

Lutiebelle: That's what Miz Emmylou always sez—

Purlie: But—who cared for you—like a mother? Who brung you up—who raised you?

Lutiebelle: Nobody in particular—just whoever happened to be in charge of the kitchen that day.

Purlie: That explains the whole thing—no wonder; you've missed the most important part of being somebody.

Lutiebelle: I have? What part is that?

Purlie: Love—being appreciated, and sought out, and looked after; being fought to the bitter end over even.

Lutiebelle: Oh, I have missed that, Reb'n Purlie, I really have. Take mens—all my life they never looked at me the way other girls get looked at!

Purlie: That's not so. The very first time I saw you—right up there in the junior choir—I give you that look!

Lutiebelle:

(Turning to him in absolute ecstasy.)

You did; Oh, I thought so!—I prayed so. All through your sermon I thought I would faint from hoping so hard so. Oh, Reb'n Purlie—I think that's the finest look a person could ever give a person— Oh, Reb'n Purlie!

(She closes her eyes and points her lips at him.)

Purlie:

(Starts to kiss her, but draws back shyly.)

Lutiebelle—

Lutiebelle:

(Dreamily, her eyes still closed.)

Yes, Reb'n Purlie—

Purlie: There's something I want to ask you—something I never—in all my life—thought I'd be asking a woman— Would you—I don't know exactly how to say it—would you—

Lutiebelle: Yes, Reb'n Purlie?

Purlie: Would you be my disciple?

Lutiebelle:

(Rushing into his arms.)

Oh, yes, Reb'n Purlie, yes!

(They start to kiss, but are interrupted by a NOISE coming from Offstage.)

Gitlow:

(Offstage; in the extremity of death.)

No, Missy. No—no!—NO!—

(This last plea is choked off by the sound of some solid object brought smartly into contact with sudden flesh. "CLUNK!" **Purlie** *and* **Lutiebelle** *stand looking off Left, frozen for the moment.)*

Lutiebelle:

(Finally daring to speak.)

Oh, my Lord, Reb'n Purlie, what happened?

Purlie: Gitlow has changed his mind.

(Grabs her and swings her around bodily.)

Toll the bell, Big Bethel!—toll that big, fat, black and sassy liberty bell. Tell Freedom—

*(**Lutiebelle** suddenly leaps from the floor into his arms and plants her lips squarely on his. When finally he can come up for air.)*

Tell Freedom—tell Freedom—WOW!

Curtain

SCENE 2

Time: *It is a little later the same afternoon.*
Scene: *We are now in the little business office off from the commissary, where all the inhabitants of Cotchipee Valley buy food, clothing, and supplies. In the back a traveler has been drawn with just enough of an opening left to serve as the door to the main part of the store. On Stage Left and on Stage Right are simulated shelves where various items of reserve stock are kept: A wash tub, an axe, sacks of peas, and flour; bolts of gingham and calico, etc. Downstage Right is a small desk, on which an ancient typewriter, and an adding machine, with various papers and necessary books and records of commerce are placed. There is a small chair at this desk. Downstage Left is a table, with a large cash register, that has a functioning drawer. Below this is an entrance from the street.*
At Rise: *As the Curtain rises, a young white man of 25 or 30, but still gawky, awkward, and adolescent in outlook and behavior, is sitting on a high stool Downstage Right Center. His face is held in the hands of* **Idella**, *a Negro cook and woman of all work, who has been in the family since time immemorial. She is the only mother* **Charlie**, *who is very much oversized even for his age, has ever known.* **Idella** *is as little as she is old and as tough as she is tiny, and is busily applying medication to* **Charlie's** *black eye.*

Charlie: Ow, Idella, ow!—Ow!
Idella: Hold still, boy.
Charlie: But it hurts, Idella.
Idella: I know it hurts. Whoever done this to you musta meant to knock your natural brains out.
Charlie: I already told you who done it— OW!
Idella: Charlie Cotchipee, if you don't hold still and let me put this hot poultice on your eye, you better!
 (**Charlie** *subsides and meekly accepts her ministrations.*)
First the milking, then the breakfast, then the dishes, then the washing, then the scrubbing, then the lunch time, next the dishes, then the ironing—and now; just where the picking and plucking for supper ought to be—you!
Charlie: You didn't tell Paw?
Idella: Of course I didn't—but the sheriff did.
Charlie:
 (*Leaping up.*)
The sheriff!
Idella:
 (*Pushing him back down.*)
Him and the deputy come to the house less than a hour ago.

Charlie:
>*(Leaping up again.)*

Are they coming over here!

Idella: Of course they're coming over here—sooner or later.

Charlie: But what will I do, Idella, what will I say?

Idella:
>*(Pushing him down. **Charlie** subsides.)*

"He that keepeth his mouth keepeth his life—"

Charlie: Did they ask for me?

Idella: Of course they asked for you.

Charlie: What did they say?

Idella: I couldn't hear too well; your father took them into the study and locked the door behind them.

Charlie: Maybe it was about something else.

Idella: It was about YOU: that much I could hear! Charlie—you want to get us both killed!

Charlie: I'm sorry, Idella, but—

Idella:
>*(Overriding; finishing proverb she had begun.)*

"But he that openeth wide his lips shall have destruction!"

Charlie: But it was you who said it was the law of the land—

Idella: I know I did—

Charlie: It was you who said it's got to be obeyed—

Idella: I know it was me, but—

Charlie: It was you who said everybody had to stand up and take a stand against—

Idella: I know it was me, dammit! But I didn't say take a stand in no barroom!

Charlie: Ben started it, not me. And you always said never to take low from the likes of him!

Idella: Not so loud; they may be out there in the commissary!
>*(Goes quickly to door Up Center and peers out; satisfied no one has overheard them she crosses back down to **Charlie**.)*

Look, boy, everybody down here don't feel as friendly towards the Supreme Court as you and me do—you big enough to know that! And don't you ever go outta here and pull a fool trick like you done last night again and not let me know about it in advance. You hear me!

Charlie: I'm sorry.

Idella: When you didn't come to breakfast this morning, and I went upstairs looking for you, and you just setting there, looking at me with your big eyes, and I seen that they had done hurt you—my, my, my! Whatever happens to you happens to me—you big enough to know that!

Charlie: I didn't mean to make trouble, Idella.

Idella: I know that, son, I know it.
>*(Makes final adjustments to the poultice.)*

Now. No matter what happens when they do come I'll be right behind you. Keep your nerves calm and your mouth shut. Understand?

Charlie: Yes.

Idella: And as soon as you get a free minute come over to the house and let me put another hot poultice on that eye.

Charlie: Thank you, I'm very much obliged to you. Idella—

Idella: What is it, son?

Charlie: Sometimes I think I ought to run away from home.

Idella: I know, but you already tried that, honey.

Charlie: Sometimes I think I ought to run away from home—again!

> (**Ol' Cap'n** has entered from the Commissary just in time to hear this last remark.)

Ol' Cap'n: Why don't you, boy—why don't you?

> **Ol' Cap'n Cotchipee** is aged and withered a bit, but by no means infirm. Dressed in traditional southern linen, the wide hat, the shoe-string tie, the long coat, the twirling moustache of the Ol' Southern Colonel. In his left hand he carries a cane, and in his right a coiled bull whip: his last line of defense. He stops long enough to establish the fact that he means business, threatens them both with a mean cantankerous eye, then hangs his whip—the definitive answer to all who might foolishly question his Confederate power and glory—upon a peg. **Charlie** freezes at the sound of his voice. **Ol' Cap'n** crosses down, rudely pushes her hand aside, lifts up **Charlie's** chin so that he may examine the damage, shakes his head in disgust.)

You don't know, boy, what a strong stomach it takes to stomach you. Just look at you, sitting there—all slopped over like something the horses dropped; steam, stink and all!

Idella: Don't you dare talk like that to this child!

Ol' Cap'n:

> (This stops him—momentarily.)

When I think of his grandpaw, God rest his Confederate soul, hero of the battle of Chicamauga—

> (It's too much.)

Get outta my sight!

> (**Charlie** gets up to leave.)

Not you—you!

> (Indicates **Idella**. She gathers up her things in silence and starts to leave.)

Wait a minute—

> (**Idella** stops.)

You been closer to this boy than I have, even before his ma died—ain't a thought ever entered his head you didn't know 'bout it first. You got anything to do with what my boy's been thinking lately?

Idella: I didn't know he had been thinking lately.

Ol' Cap'n: Don't play with me, Idella—and you know what I mean! Who's been putting these integrationary ideas in my boy's head? Was it you—I'm asking you a question, dammit! Was it you?

Idella: Why don't you ask him?

Ol' Cap'n:
> (*Snorts.*)

Ask him! ASK HIM! He ain't gonna say a word unless you tell him to, and you know it. I'm asking you again, Idella Landy, have you been talking integration to my boy!?

Idella: I can't rightly answer you any more on that than he did.

Ol' Cap'n: By God, you will answer me. I'll make you stand right there—right there!—all day and all night long, till you do answer me!

Idella: That's just fine.

Ol' Cap'n: What's that! What's that you say?

Idella: I mean I ain't got nothing else to do—supper's on the stove; rice is ready, okra's fried, turnip's simmered, biscuits' baked, and stew is stewed. In fact them lemon pies you wanted special for supper are in the oven right now, just getting ready to burn—

Ol' Cap'n: Get outta here!

Idella: Oh—no hurry, Ol' Cap'n—

Ol' Cap'n: Get the hell out of here!
> (**Idella** *deliberately takes all the time in the world to pick up her*
> *things. Following her around trying to make his point.*)

I'm warning both of you; that little lick over the eye is a small skimption compared to what I'm gonna do.
> (**Idella** *pretends not to listen.*)

I won't stop till I get to the bottom of this!
> (**Idella** *still ignores him.*)

Get outta here, Idella Landy, before I take my cane and—
> (*He raises his cane but* **Idella** *insists on moving at her own pace to*
> *exit Down Left.*)

And save me some buttermilk to go with them lemon pies, you hear me!
> (*Turns to* **Charlie**; *not knowing how to approach him.*)

The sheriff was here this morning.

Charlie: Yessir.

Ol' Cap'n: Is that all you got to say to me: "Yessir"?

Charlie: Yessir.

Ol' Cap'n: You are a disgrace to the southland!

Charlie: Yessir.

Ol' Cap'n: Shut up! I could kill you, boy, you understand that? Kill you with my own two hands!

Charlie: Yessir.

Ol' Cap'n: Shut up! I could beat you to death with that bull whip—put my pistol to your good-for-nothing head—my own flesh and blood—and blow your blasted brains all over this valley!
> (*Fighting to retain his control.*)

If—if you wasn't the last living drop of Cotchipee blood in Cotchipee County, I'd—I'd—

Charlie: Yessir.
> (*This is too much.* **Ol' Cap'n** *snatches* **Charlie** *to his feet. But* **Charlie**
> *does not resist.*)

Ol' Cap'n: You trying to get non-violent with me, boy?

> (**Charlie** *does not answer, just dangles there.*)

Charlie:

> (*Finally.*)

I'm ready with the books, sir—that is—whenever you're ready.

Ol' Cap'n:

> (*Flinging* **Charlie** *into a chair.*)

Thank you—thank you! What with your Yankee propaganda, your barroom brawls, and all your other non-Confederate activities, I didn't think you had the time.

Charlie:

> (*Picks up account book; reads.*)

"Cotton report. Fifteen bales picked yesterday and sent to the cotton gin; bringing our total to 357 bales to date."

Ol' Cap'n:

> (*Impressed.*)

357—boy, that's some picking. Who's ahead?

Charlie: Gitlow Judson, with seventeen bales up to now.

Ol' Cap'n: Gitlow Judson; well I'll be damned; did you ever see a cotton-pickinger darky in your whole life?!

Charlie: Commissary report—

Ol' Cap'n: Did you ever look down into the valley and watch ol' Git a-picking his way through that cotton patch? Holy Saint Mother's Day! I'll bet you—

Charlie: Commissary report!

Ol' Cap'n: All right!—commissary report.

Charlie: Yessir—well, first, sir, there's been some complaints: the flour is spoiled, the beans are rotten, and the meat is tainted.

Ol' Cap'n: Cut the price on it.

Charlie: But it's also a little wormy—

Ol' Cap'n: Then sell it to the Negras— Is something wrong?

Charlie: No, sir—I mean, sir . . . , we can't go on doing that, sir.

Ol' Cap'n: Why not? It's traditional.

Charlie: Yessir, but times are changing—all this debt—

> (*Indicates book.*)

According to this book every family in this valley owes money they'll never be able to pay back.

Ol' Cap'n: Of course—it's the only way to keep 'em working. Didn't they teach you nothin' at school?

Charlie: We're cheating them—and they know we're cheating them. How long do you expect them to stand for it?

Ol' Cap'n: As long as they're Negras—

Charlie: How long before they start a-rearing up on their hind legs, and saying: "Enough, white folks—now that's enough! Either you start treating me like I'm somebody in this world, or I'll blow your brains out"?

Ol Cap'n:

> (*Shaken to the core.*)

Stop it—stop it! You're tampering with the economic foundation of the southland! Are you trying to ruin me? One more word like that and I'll kill—I'll shoot—

(Charlie attempts to answer.)

Shut up! One more word and I'll—I'll fling myself on your Maw's grave and die of apoplexy. I'll—I'll—! Shut up, do you hear me? Shut up!

(Enter Gitlow, hat in hand, grin on face, more obsequious today than ever.)

Now what the hell *you* want?

Gitlow:

(Taken aback.)

Nothing, sir, nothing!—That is—Missy, my ol' 'oman—well, suh, to git to the truth of the matter, I got a little business—

Ol' Cap'n: Negras ain't got no business. And if you don't get the hell back into that cotton patch you better. Git, I said!

(Gitlow starts to beat a hasty retreat.)

Oh, no—don't go. Uncle Gitlow—good ol' faithful o' Gitlow. Don't go—don't go.

Gitlow:

(Not quite sure.)

Well—you're the boss, boss.

Ol' Cap'n:

(Shoving a cigar into Gitlow's mouth.)

Just the other day, I was talking to the Senator about you— What's that great big knot on your head?

Gitlow: Missy—I mean, a mosquito!

Ol' Cap'n:

(In all seriousness, examining the bump.)

Uh! Musta been wearin' brass knuck— And he was telling me, the Senator was, how hard it was—impossible, he said, to find the old-fashioned, solid, hard-earned, Uncle Tom type Negra nowadays. I laughed in his face.

Gitlow: Yassuh. By the grace of God, there's still a few of us left.

Ol' Cap'n: I told him how you and me growed up together. Had the same mammy—my mammy was your mother.

Gitlow: Yessir! Bosom buddies!

Ol' Cap'n: And how you used to sing that favorite ol' speritual of mine:

(Sings.)

"I'm a-coming . . . I'm a-coming, For my head is bending low,"

(Gitlow joins in on harmony.)

"I hear the gentle voices calling, Ol' Black Joe. . . ."

(This proves too much for Charlie; he starts out.)

Where you going?

Charlie: Maybe they need me in the front of the store.

Ol' Cap'n: Come back here!

(Charlie returns.)

Turn around—show Gitlow that eye.

(Charlie reluctantly exposes black eye to view.)

Gitlow: Gret Gawdamighty, somebody done cold cocked this child! Who hit Mr. Charlie, tell Uncle Gitlow who hit you?

*(**Charlie** does not answer.)*

Ol' Cap'n: Would you believe it? All of a sudden he can't say a word. And last night, the boys was telling me, this son of mine made hisself a full-fledged speech.

Gitlow: You don't say.

Ol' Cap'n: All about Negras—NeGROES he called 'em—four years of college, and he still can't say the word right—seems he's quite a specialist on the subject.

Gitlow: Well, shut my hard-luck mouth!

Ol' Cap'n: Yessireebob. Told the boys over at Ben's bar in town, that he was all for mixing the races together.

Gitlow: You go 'way from hyeah!

Ol' Cap'n: Said white children and darky children ought to go to the same schoolhouse together!

Gitlow: Tell me the truth, Ol' Cap'n!

Ol' Cap'n: Got hisself so worked up some of 'em had to cool him down with a co-cola bottle!

Gitlow: Tell me the truth—again!

Charlie: That wasn't what I said!

Ol' Cap'n: You calling me a liar, boy!

Charlie: No, sir, but I just said, that since it was the law of the land—

Ol' Cap'n: It is not the law of the land no sucha thing!

Charlie: I didn't think it would do any harm if they went to school together —that's all.

Ol' Cap'n: That's all—that's enough!

Charlie: They do it up North—

Ol' Cap'n: This is down South. Down here they'll go to school together over me and Gitlow's dead body. Right, Git?!

Gitlow: Er, you the boss, boss!

Charlie: But this is the law of the—

Ol' Cap'n: Never mind the law! Boy—look! You like Gitlow, you trust him, you always did—didn't you?

Charlie: Yessir.

Ol' Cap'n: And Gitlow here, would cut off his right arm for you if you was to ask him. Wouldn't you, Git?

Gitlow:
(Gulping.)
You the boss, boss.

Ol' Cap'n: Now Gitlow ain't nothing if he ain't a Negra!—Ain't you, Git?

Gitlow: Oh—two-three hundred percent, I calculate.

Ol' Cap'n: Now, if you really want to know what the Negra thinks about this here integration and all lackathat, don't ask the Supreme Court—ask Gitlow. Go ahead—ask him!

Charlie: I don't need to ask him.

Ol' Cap'n: Then I'll ask him. Raise your right hand, Git. You solemnly swear to tell the truth, whole truth, nothing else but, so help you God?

Gitlow:

(Raising hand.)

I do.

Ol' Cap'n: Gitlow Judson, as God is your judge and maker, do you believe in your heart that God intended white folks and Negra children to go to school together?

Gitlow: Nawsuh, I do not!

Ol' Cap'n: Do you, so help you God, think that white folks and black should mix and 'sociate in street cars, buses, and railroad stations, in any way, shape, form, or fashion?

Gitlow: Absolutely not!

Ol' Cap'n: And is it not your considered opinion, God strike you dead if you lie, that all my Negras are happy with things in the southland just the way they are?

Gitlow: Indeed I do!

Ol' Cap'n: Do you think any single darky on my place would ever think of changing a single thing about the South, and to hell with the Supreme Court as God is your judge and maker?

Gitlow: As God is my judge and maker and you are my boss, I do not!

Ol' Cap'n:

(Turning in triumph to **Charlie**.*)*

The voice of the Negra himself! What more proof do you want!

Charlie: I don't care whose voice it is—it's still the law of the land, and I intend to obey it!

Ol' Cap'n:

(Losing control.)

Get outta my face, boy—get outta my face, before I kill you! Before I—

*(**Charlie** escapes into the commissary. **Ol' Cap'n** collapses.)*

Gitlow: Easy, Ol' Cap'n, easy, suh, easy!

*(**Ol' Cap'n** gives out a groan. **Gitlow** goes to shelf and comes back with a small bottle and a small box.)*

Some aspirins, suh . . . , some asaphoetida?

*(**Purlie** and **Lutiebelle** appear at door Left.)*

Not now—later—later!

*(Holds bottle to **Ol' Cap'n's** nose.)*

Ol' Cap'n: Gitlow—Gitlow!

Gitlow: Yassuh, Ol' Cap'n—Gitlow is here, suh; right here!

Ol' Cap'n: Quick, ol' friend—my heart. It's—quick! A few passels, if you please—of that ol' speritual.

Gitlow:

(Sings most tenderly.)

"Gone are the days, when my heart was young and gay . . ."

Ol' Cap'n: I can't tell you, Gitlow—how much it eases the pain—

*(**Gitlow** and **Ol' Cap'n** sing a phrase together.)*

Why can't he see what they're doing to the southland, Gitlow? Why can't he see it, like you and me? If there's one responsibility you got, boy, above all others, I said to him, it's these Negras—your Negras, boy. Good, honest, hard-working cotton choppers. If you keep after 'em.

Gitlow: Yes, Lawd.

(*Continues to sing.*)

Ol' Cap'n: Something between you and them no Supreme Court in the world can understand—and wasn't for me they'd starve to death. What's gonna become of 'em, boy, after I'm gone—?

Gitlow: Dass a good question, Lawd—you answer him.

(*Continues to sing.*)

Ol' Cap'n: They belong to you, boy—to you, evah one of 'em! My ol' Confederate father told me on his deathbed: feed the Negras first—after the horses and cattle—and I've done it evah time!

(*By now* **Ol' Cap'n** *is sheltered in* **Gitlow's** *arms. The LIGHTS begin slowly to fade away.* **Gitlow** *sings a little more.*)

Ah, Gitlow ol' friend—something, absolutely sacred 'bout that speritual—I live for the day you'll sing that thing over my grave.

Gitlow: Me, too, Ol' Cap'n, me, too!

(**Gitlow's** *voice rises to a slow, gentle, yet triumphant crescendo, as our LIGHTS fade away.*)

Blackout
Curtain

Act Two

SCENE 1

Time: *A short while later.*
Scene: *The scene is the same: the little commissary office.*
At Rise: *The Stage is empty. After a moment* **Gitlow** *hurries in from the commissary proper, crosses down to the little back door and opens it.*

Purlie:

(*Entering hurriedly.*)

What took you so long?

Gitlow: S-sh! Not so loud! He's right out there in the commissary!

(**Purlie** *crosses over and looks out into the commissary, then crosses back to the little back door and holds out his hands.* **Lutiebelle** *enters. She is dressed in what would be collegiate style. She is still full of awe and wonder, and—this time—of fear, which she is struggling to keep under cover.*)

Ain't she gonna carry no school books?

Purlie: What are they doing out there?

Gitlow: The watermelon books don't balance.

Purlie: What!

Gitlow: One of our melons is in shortage!

Purlie: You tell him about Lutiebelle—I mean, about Cousin Bee?

Gitlow: I didn't have time. Besides, I wanted you to have one more chance to get out of here alive!

Purlie: What's the matter with you!? Don' five hundred dollars of your own lawful money mean nothing to you? Ain't you got no head for business?

Gitlow: No! The head I got is for safekeeping, and—besides—

> (**Purlie** lifts **Ol' Cap'n's** bull whip down from its peg.)

don't touch that thing, Purlie!

> (**Gitlow** races over, snatches it from him, replaces it, and pats it soothingly into place, while at the same time looking to see if **Ol' Cap'n** is coming—and all in one continuous move.)

Purlie: Why not? It touched me!

Gitlow:

> (Aghast.)

Man, ain't nothing sacred to you!?

Ol' Cap'n:

> (Calling from Off in the commissary.)

Gitlow, come in here!

Gitlow:

> (Racing off.)

Coming, Ol' Cap'n, coming!

Ol' Cap'n:

> (Offstage.)

Now! We are going to cross-examine these watermelons one more time—one watermelon—

Gitlow:

> (Offstage.)

One watermelon!

Charlie:

> (Offstage.)

One watermelon!

Ol' Cap'n: Two watermelons—

Gitlow: Two watermelons—

Charlie: Two watermelons—

> (The sound of the watermelon count-down continues in the background. **Purlie**, finding he's got a moment, comes over to reassure **Lutiebelle**.)

Purlie: Whatever you do, don't panic!

Lutiebelle:

> (Repeating after him: almost in hypnotic rote.)

Whatever you do, don't panic!

Purlie: Just walk like I taught you to walk, and talk like I taught you to talk—

Lutiebelle: Taught like I walked you to—

Purlie:

> (Shaking her shoulders.)

Lutiebelle!

Lutiebelle: Yes, Reb'n Purlie!

Purlie: Wake up!

Lutiebelle: Oh my goodness, Reb'n Purlie—was I sleep?

Purlie: Alert!

Lutiebelle: Alert!—

Purlie: Wide awake!—

Lutiebelle: Wide awake!—

Purlie: Up on your toes!

Lutiebelle:

>*(Starting to rise on toes.)*

Up on your—

Purlie: No. No, that's just a figure of speech. Now! You remember what I told you—?

Lutiebelle: No, sir. Can't say I do, sir.

Purlie: Well—first: chit-chat—small-talk!

Lutiebelle: Yessir—how small?

Purlie: Pass the time of day—you remember? The first thing I taught you on the train?

Lutiebelle: On the train— Oh! "Delighted to remake your acquaintance, I am sure."

Purlie: That's it—that's it exactly! Now. Suppose he was to say to you:

>*(**Purlie** imitates **Ol' Cap'n**.)*

"I bet you don't remember when you wasn't kneehigh to a grasshopper and Ol' Cap'n took you by the hand, and led you down on your first trip to the cotton patch?"

Lutiebelle: Just like you told me on the train?

Purlie: Yes!

Lutiebelle: "I must confess—that much of my past life is vague and hazy."

Purlie:

>*(Imitating.)*

Doggone my hide—you're the cutest li'l ol' piece of brown skin sugar I ever did see!

Lutiebelle: Oh, thank you, Reb'n Purlie!

Purlie: I ain't exactly me, saying that—it's Ol' Cap'n.

>*(Continues imitation.)*

And this is my land, and my cotton patch, and my commissary, and my bull whip—still here, just like you left us. And what might be your name, li'l gal?

Lutiebelle:

>*(Warming to the game.)*

Beatrice Judson, sir.

Purlie: And what is your daddy's name, li'l gal?

Lutiebelle: Horace Judson, sir.

Purlie: And what did they teach you up in that college, li'l gal?

Lutiebelle: It was my major education, Ol' Cap'n.—

Purlie: You mean you majored in education.

>*(Resumes imitation.)*

Well—nothing wrong with Negras getting an education, I always say— But then again, ain't nothing right with it, either. Cousin Bee—heh, heh, heh—you don't mind if I call you Cousin Bee, do you, honey?

Lutiebelle: Oh, sir, I'd be delighted!

Purlie: Don't! Don't be delighted until he puts the money in your hands.
> *(Resumes imitation.)*

And where did you say your Maw worked at?

Lutiebelle: In North Carolina.

Purlie: Where is your maw at now?

Lutiebelle: She's at the cemetery: she died.

Purlie: And how much is the inheritance?

Lutiebelle: Five hundred dollars for the next of kin.

Purlie:
> *(Delighted at her progress.)*

Wonderful, just—just—wonderful!
> *(Enjoying his own imitation now.)*
>
> **(Ol' Cap'n** enters from the commissary, followed by **Gitlow. Lutiebelle** sees **Ol' Cap'n,** but **Purlie** is so wrapped up in his own performance he does not.)

Say, maybe you could teach a old dog like me some new tricks.
> *(He tries to get a rise out of **Lutiebelle** but she is frozen in terror.* **Ol' Cap'n** becomes aware of **Purlie's** presence, and approaches.)

By swickety—a gal like you could doggone well change a joker's luck if she had a mind to—see what I mean?
> **(Purlie** hunches what he expects to be an invisible **Gitlow** in the ribs. His blow lands upon **Ol' Cap'n** with such force, he falls onto a pile of sacks of chicken feed.)

Ol' Cap'n:
> *(Sputtering.)*

What! What in the name of—
> **(Gitlow** and **Purlie** scramble to help him to his feet.)

Purlie: My compliments, sir—are only exceeded by my humblest apologies. And allow me, if you please, to present my Aunt Henrietta's daughter, whom you remember so well: Beatrice Judson—or as we call her—Cousin Bee.

Ol' Cap'n:
> *(He is so taken by what he sees he forgets his anger.)*

Well, I'll be switched!

Purlie: Come, Cousin Bee. Say "howdo" to the man.

Lutiebelle: How do to the man. I mean—
> *(Takes time to correct herself, then.)*

Delighted to remake your acquaintance, I'm sure.

Ol' Cap'n: What's that? What's that she's saying?

Purlie: College, sir.

Ol' Cap'n: College?

Purlie: That's all she ever talks.

Ol' Cap'n: You mean Henrietta's little ol' button-eyed pickaninny was in college? Well bust my eyes wide open! Just LOOK at that!

(Gets closer, but she edges away.)
You remember me, honey. I'm still the Ol' Cap'n round here.
Lutiebelle: Oh, sir, it would not be the same without you being the Ol' Cap'n around here.
Ol' Cap'n: You don't say! Say, I'll bet you don't remember a long time ago when—
Lutiebelle: When I wasn't but knee high to a hoppergrass, and you took me by the hand, and led me on my very first trip to the cotton patch.
Ol' Cap'n:
> *(Ecstatic.)*
You mean you remember that!
Lutiebelle: Alert, wide awake, and up on my toes—if you please, sir!
> *(Rises up on her toes.)*
Ol' Cap'n:
> *(Moving in.)*
Doggone my hide. You're the cutest li'l ol' piece of brown sugar I ever did see—
Lutiebelle:
> *(Escaping.)*
And this is your land, and your cotton patch, and your commissary, and your bull whip—
Ol' Cap'n: What's that?
Lutiebelle: Just a figure of speech or two—
Ol' Cap'n: Well, Beatrice—you wouldn't mind if Ol' Cap'n was to call you Cousin Bee?
Lutiebelle: Oh, positively not, not!—since my mother's name was Henrietta Judson; my father's name was Horace Judson—
Ol' Cap'n: But most of all, I remember that little ol' dog of yours—"Spicey," wasn't it?
Lutiebelle: Oh, we wasn't much for eating dogs, sir—
Ol' Cap'n: No, no! Spicey was the name—wasn't it?
> **(Lutiebelle** *looking to* **Purlie** *for help, but* **Purlie** *cannot help. He looks to* **Gitlow,** *who also cannot remember.)*
Lutiebelle: You, er, really think we really called him "Spicey"?
Ol' Cap'n: Not him—her!
Purlie: HER!
Lutiebelle: Oh, her! Her! I am most happy to recollect that I do.
Ol' Cap'n: You do! You don't say you do!
Lutiebelle: I did, as I recall it, have a fond remembrance of you and "Spicey," since you-all went so well together—and at the same time!
Ol' Cap'n: You do? Well hush my mouth, eh, Git?
Gitlow: Hush your mouth indeed, sir.
Lutiebelle: Cose soon it is my sworn and true confession that I disremembers so many things out of my early pastime that mostly you are hazy and vaguey!
Ol' Cap'n: Oh, am I now!
Lutiebelle: Oh, yes, and sir—indeedy.

Ol' Cap'n: Doggone my hide, eh, Git?

Gitlow: Doggone your hide indeed, suh.

Lutiebelle: You see of coursely I have spount—

Purlie: Spent—

Lutiebelle: Spunt so much of my time among the college that hardly all of my ancient maidenhead—

Purlie: Hood.

Lutiebelle: Is a thing of the past!

Ol' Cap'n: You don't say!

Lutiebelle: But yes, and most precisely.

Ol' Cap'n: Tell me, Li'l Bee—what did they teach you up at that college?

Lutiebelle: Well, mostly they taught me an education, but in between I learned a lot, too.

Ol' Cap'n: Is that a fact?

Lutiebelle: Reading, writing, 'rithmetic—oh, my Lord—just sitting out on the rectangular every evening after four o'clock home work and you have your regular headache—

Ol' Cap'n: You know something, I been after these Negras down here for years: Go to school, I'd say, first chance you get—take a coupla courses in advanced cotton picking. But you think they'd listen to me? No sireebob. By swickety! A gal like you could doggone well change a joker's luck if she was a mind to.

(Gives **Gitlow** a broad wink and digs him in his ribs. **Gitlow** almost falls.)

See what I mean?

Lutiebelle: Oh, most indo I deed.

Ol' Cap'n: Look—anything! Ask me anything! Whatever you want—name it and it's yours!

Lutiebelle: You mean—really, really, really?

Ol' Cap'n: Ain't a man in Cotchipee County can beat my time when I see something I want—name it!

(Indicates with a sweep the contents of the commissary.)

Some roasted peanuts; a bottle of soda water; a piece of peppermint candy?

Lutiebelle: Thank you, sir, but if it's all the same to you I'd rather have my money.

Ol' Cap'n:

(As if shot.)

Your WHAT!

Lutiebelle:

(Frightened but determined to forge ahead under her own steam.)

Now I'm gonna tell you like it was, Your Honor: You see, Reb'n Purlie and Uncle Gitlow had one aunty between them, name of Harrietta—

Purlie: Henrietta!

Lutiebelle: Henrietta—who used to cook for this rich ol' white lady up in North Carolina years ago; and last year this ol' lady died—brain tumor—

Purlie: Bright's disease!

Lutiebelle: Bright's disease—leaving five hundred dollars to every servant who

ever worked on her place, including Henrietta. But Henrietta had already died, herself: largely from smallpox—
Purlie: No!
Lutiebelle: Smally from large pox?
Purlie: Influenza!
Lutiebelle: Influenza—and since Henrietta's husband Harris—
Purlie: Horace!
Lutiebelle: Horace—was already dead from heart trouble—
Purlie: Gunshot wounds!—
Lutiebelle:
> *(Exploding.)*

His heart stopped beating, didn't it?!
Purlie: Yes, but—
Lutiebelle: Precisely, Reb'n Purlie, precisely!
> *(Turning back to **Ol' Cap'n**.)*

Since, therefore and where-in-as Cousin Bee, her daughter, was first-in-line-for-next-of-kinfolks, the five hundred dollars left in your care and keep by Aunt Henrietta, and which you have been saving just for me all these lonesome years—
Ol' Cap'n: I ain't been saving no damn sucha thing!
Purlie:
> *(Stepping swiftly into the breach.)*

Oh, come out from behind your modesty, sir!
Ol' Cap'n: What!
Purlie: Your kindness, sir; your thoughtfulness, sir; your unflagging consideration for the welfare of your darkies, sir: have rung like the clean clear call of the clarion from Maine to Mexico. Your constant love for them is both hallmark and high water of the true gentility of the dear old South.
Ol' Cap'n: Gitlow, Gitlow—go get Charlie. I want him to hear this.
> *(**Gitlow** exits Upstage Center.)*

Go on, boy, go on!
Purlie: And as for your faithful ol' darkies themselves, sir—why, down in the quarters, sir, your name stands second only to God Himself Almighty.
Ol' Cap'n: You don't mean to tell me!
Purlie: Therefore, as a humble token of their high esteem and their deep and abiding affection, especially for saving that five hundred dollar inheritance for Cousin Bee, they have asked me to present to you . . . this plaque!
> *(**Purlie** unveils a "sheepskin scroll" from his inside coat pocket. **Ol' Cap'n** reaches for it, but **Purlie** draws it away. **Charlie** appears in the doorway Upstage Center followed by **Gitlow**.)*

Which bears the following citation to wit, and I quote: "Whereas Ol' Cap'n has kindly allowed us to remain on his land, and pick his cotton, and tend his cattle, and drive his mules, and whereas Ol' Cap'n still lets us have our hominy grits and fat back on credit and whereas Ol' Cap'n never resorts to bull whip except as a blessing or benediction, therefore be it resolved, that Ol' Cap'n Cotchipee be cited as the best friend the Negro has ever had, and officially proclaimed Great White Father of the Year!"

Ol' Cap'n:
> *(Stunned.)*

I can't believe it—I can't believe it!
> *(Sees* **Charlie***.)*

Charlie, boy—did you hear it? Did you hear it, Charlie, my boy—GREAT WHITE FATHER OF THE YEAR!

Purlie:
> *(Like a professional undertaker.)*

Let me be the first to congratulate you, sir.
> *(They shake hands solemnly.)*

Ol' Cap'n: Thank you, Purlie.

Lutiebelle: And me.
> *(They shake hands solemnly.)*

Ol' Cap'n: Thank you, Cousin Bee.

Gitlow: And me, too, Ol' Cap'n.

Ol' Cap'n:
> *(On the verge of tears, as they shake hands.)*

Gitlow—Gitlow. I know this is some of your doings—my old friend.
> *(He turns expectantly to* **Charlie***.)*

Well, boy—
> *(***Charlie** *is trapped.)*

ain't you gonna congratulate your father?

Charlie: Yessir.
> *(Shakes his hand.)*

Ol' Cap'n: This—is the happiest day of my life. My darkies—my Negras—my own—
> *(Chokes up; unable to continue.)*

Purlie: Hear, hear!

Gitlow and **Lutiebelle:** Hear, hear!
> *(***Charlie** *tries to sneak off again, but* **Ol' Cap'n** *sees him.)*

Ol' Cap'n: I am just too overcome to talk. Come back here, boy.
> *(***Charlie** *comes back and stands in intense discomfort.)*

Silent—speechless—dumb, my friends. Never in all the glorious hoary and ancient annals of all Dixie—never before—
> *(Chokes up with tears; blows nose with big red handkerchief, and pulls himself together.)*

My friends, in the holy scripture—and I could cite you chapter and verse if I was a mind to—"In the beginning God created white folks and He created black folks," and in the name of all that's white and holy, let's keep it that way. And to hell with Abraham Lincoln and Martin Luther King!

Purlie: I am moved, Ol' Cap'n—

Gitlow and **Lutiebelle:** Uhn!

Purlie: Moved beyond my jurisdiction; as for example, I have upon my person a certificate of legal tender duly affixed and so notarized to said itemized effect—
> *(Hands over an official-looking document.)*

a writ of Habeas Corpus.

Ol' Cap'n:
> *(Taking the document.)*

Habeas who?

Purlie: Habeas Corpus. It means I can have the body.

Ol' Cap'n: Body—what body?

Purlie: The body of the cash—the five hundred dollars—that they sent you to hold in trust for Cousin Bee.

Ol' Cap'n:
> *(Pauses to study the eager faces in the room; then)*

Charlie—

Charlie: Yessir.

Ol' Cap'n: Bring me—five hundred dollars—will you?
> *(**Charlie** starts for safe.)*

No, no, no—not that old stuff. Fresh money, clean money out of my private stock out back. Nothin's too good for my Negras.

Charlie: Yessir—yessir!
> *(Starts out, stops.)*

And Paw?

Ol' Cap'n: Yes, son?

Charlie: All I got to say is "Yessir!"
> *(Crosses to cash register.)*

Ol' Cap'n: Just wait—wait till I tell the Senator: "Great White Father of the Year."

Charlie:
> *(Returns with roll of bills which he hands to his father.)*

Here you are, Paw.

Ol' Cap'n: Thank you, boy.
> *(Enter **Idella**, followed by the **Sheriff** and the **Deputy**.)*

Idella: Here everybody is, back in the office.

Ol' Cap'n:
> *(Overjoyed to see them.)*

Just in time, Sheriff, for the greatest day of my life. Gentlemen—something has happened here today, between me and my Negras, makes me proud to call myself a Confederate: I have just been named Great White Father of the Year.
> *(To **Purlie**.)*

Right?

Purlie: Right. And now if you'll just—

Sheriff and **Deputy:** Great White Father of the Year! Congratulations!
> *(They shake hands warmly.)*

Ol' Cap'n: True, there are places in this world where the darky is rebellious, running hog wild, rising up and sitting down where he ain't wanted, acting sassy in jail, getting plumb out of hand, totally forgetting his place and his manners—but not in Cotchipee County!
> *(To **Purlie**.)*

Right?

Purlie: Right! And now perhaps we could get back to the business at hand.

Ol' Cap'n:
> (Finishing his count.)

All right—five hundred dollars.
> (**Purlie** impulsively reaches for the money, but **Ol' Cap'n** snatches it back.)

Just a moment. There's still one small formality: a receipt.

Purlie: A receipt? All right, I'll—

Ol' Cap'n: Not you— You!
> (Thrusts a printed form toward **Lutiebelle**.)

. . . just for the record.
> (Offers her a fountain pen.)

Sign here. Your full and legal name—right here on the dotted line.

Purlie:
> (Reaching for the pen.)

I'll do it—I have her power of attorney.

Lutiebelle:
> (Beating **Purlie** to the pen.)

It's all right, Reb'n Purlie, I can write.
> (Takes pen and signs paper with a flourish.)

Ol' Cap'n:
> (Takes up paper and reads the signature.)

Sheriff, I want this woman arrested!

Purlie: Arrested?! For what?

Ol' Cap'n: She came into my presence, together with him—
> (Indicates **Purlie**.)

and with him—
> (Indicates **Gitlow**.)

And they all swore to me that she is Beatrice Judson.

Purlie: She IS Beatrice Judson!

Ol' Cap'n:
> (Pouncing.)

Then how come she to sign her name: Lutiebelle Gussiemae Jenkins!

Purlie: Uhn-uhn!

Gitlow: Uhn-uhn!

Lutiebelle: Uhn-uhn!

Gitlow:
> (Starting off suddenly.)

Is somebody calling my name out there—

Ol' Cap'n: Come back here, Gitlow—
> (**Gitlow** halts in his tracks.)

You'll go out of that door when the Sheriff takes you out. And that goes for all of you.
> (The **Sheriff** starts forward.)

Just a minute, Sheriff. Before you take 'em away there's something I've got to do.
> (Crosses to where the whip is hung.)

Gitlow:
> *(Horrified at the thought of the whip.)*

I'll make it up to you in cotton, Ol' Cap'n—

Ol' Cap'n: Shut up, Gitlow.
> *(Takes whip down, and starts to uncoil it.)*

Something I started twenty years ago with this bull whip—
> *(Fastening his eyes on **Purlie**.)*

Something I intend to finish.

Gitlow:
> *(Drops to his knees and begins to sing.)*

"Gone are the days—"

Ol' Cap'n:
> *(Turning to **Gitlow**.)*

Dammit! I told you to shut up!
> *(Turning back to **Purlie**.)*

I'm gonna teach you to try to make a damn fool outta white folks; all right, boy, drop them britches.

Purlie: The hell you preach!

Ol' Cap'n: What's that you said?

Lutiebelle: He said, "The hell you preach!"

Charlie: Paw, wait, listen—!

Ol' Cap'n: I thought I told you to shut up!
> *(Back to **Purlie**.)*

Boy, I'm gonna teach you to mind what I say!
> *(**Purlie** doesn't move. **Ol' Cap'n** takes a vicious cut at him with the bull whip, and **Purlie**, leaping back to get out of the way, falls into the arms of the **Sheriff**.)*

Sheriff: I distinctly heard that gentleman order you to drop your britches.
> *(Spins **Purlie** around, sets him up, and swings with all his might. **Purlie** easily ducks and dances away.)*

Deputy: Save a little taste for me, Sheriff!
> *(The **Sheriff** swings again; and, again, **Purlie** dances away. He swings still again, but to no avail.)*

Sheriff:
> *(Aggravated.)*

Hold still, dammit!
> *(Swings again, and once more **Purlie** ducks away.)*

Confound it, boy! You trying to make me hurt myself?

Deputy: What's the matter, Sheriff—can't you find him?!
> *(Laughs.)*

Sheriff:
> *(Desperate.)*

Now, you listen to me, boy! Either you stand up like a man, so I can knock you down, or—

Lutiebelle:
> *(Stepping between the **Sheriff** and **Purlie**.)*

Don't you dare!

Sheriff: What!

Lutiebelle: Insultin' Reb'n Purlie, and him a man of the cloth!

> *(Grabs his gun arm and bites it.)*

Sheriff: Owwww!

> *(She kicks him in the shin.)*

Owwwwwww!

> *(The Deputy charges in to the rescue. He attempts to grab Lutiebelle, but she eludes him and steps down hard on his corns.)*

Deputy: Owwwwwwwwww!

Purlie:

> *(Going for the Deputy.)*

Keep your hands off her, you hypothetical baboon, keep your hands OFF her!

> *(Grabs the Deputy, spins him around and knocks him across the room, starts to follow, but the Sheriff grabs him and pins his arms behind him.)*

Charlie:

> *(Breaks loose from Idella, snatching at the Sheriff.)*

You let him go, dammit, let him go!

> *(With one arm the Sheriff pushes Charlie away.)*

Sheriff:

> *(Still holding Purlie's arms pinned back.)*

All right, Dep, he's all yours. Throw him your fast ball—high, tight and inside!

Deputy: Glad to oblige you, Sheriff!

> *(He draws back like a big league baseball pitcher.)*

Charlie:

> *(Rushing into the breech.)*

Stop! Stop—stop in the name of the—

> *(The Deputy swings from the floor, Purlie ducks and rolls his head sharply to one side. Charlie runs full into the force of the blow. Collapsing heavily.)*

Idella—aaaaaaa!

Ol' Cap'n:

> *(Rushing to him.)*

Charlie—!

Idella: Charlie—!

> *(**Purlie**, taking advantage of the confusion, snatches **Lutiebelle** by the arms and dashes with her out the back door.)*

Ol' Cap'n: After them, you idiots, after them!

Sheriff:

> *(To the Deputy.)*

After them, you idiot!

> *(They both run after Purlie and Lutiebelle.)*
>
> *(**Ol' Cap'n** and **Idella** are kneeling beside the prostrate **Charlie**. Gitlow, after a moment, comes into the picture.)*

Ol' Cap'n: His eyes, Idella, his eyes! Where are his eyes?

Idella: Gitlow, fetch me the asaphoetida, Ol' Cap'n, you rub his hands.

Gitlow: Yess'm.

Idella:
(*Slapping his face.*)
Charlie, honey, wake up—wake up! It's me, Idella.
(**Ol' Cap'n** *is too disorganized to be of any assistance.* **Gitlow** *has returned with a bottle which he hands to* **Idella**. *He then kneels and starts rubbing* **Charlie's** *hands.*)
Gitlow: Mr. Charlie, wake up—
(*With* **Gitlow** *and* **Idella's** *help,* **Charlie** *slowly rises to his feet. Still unsteady, his eyes glazed and vacant.*)
Ol 'Cap'n:
(*Snapping his fingers in front of his eyes.*)
It's me, Charlie, me— It's your daddy, boy! Speak to me—talk to me—say something to me!
Charlie:
(*Snaps suddenly into speech—but still out on his feet.*)
Fourscore and seven years ago, our fathers brought forth—
Ol' Cap'n: Shut up!

Curtain

SCENE 2

Time: *Two days later.*
Scene: *Back at the shack, outside in the yard area.*
At Rise: **Missy** *is discovered, busy working on some potted plants. She is preoccupied, but we feel some restlessness, some anticipation in the manner in which she works.* **Purlie** *enters.*

Purlie:
(*The great prophet intones his sorrows.*)
Toll the bell—Big Bethel; toll the big, black, ex-liberty bell; tell Freedom there's death in the family.
Missy: Purlie—
Purlie: All these wings and they still won't let me fly!
Missy: Where you been these last two days, Purlie? We been lookin' for you. All this plotting and planning—risking your dad-blasted neck like a crazy man! And for what—FOR WHAT!
(**Idella** *enters.*)
Oh, come in, Miz Idella.
Idella: Is anybody here seen Charlie Cotchipee this morning?
Missy: No, we haven't.
Purlie: Is something wrong, Miz Idella?
Idella: He left home this morning right after breakfast—here it is after lunch and I ain't seen him since. I can't find Charlie—first time in forty-five years I been working up there in that house I ever misplaced anything! You don't suppose he'd run away from home and not take me—?

Missy: Oh, no, Miz Idella! Not li'l Charlie Cotchipee.

Idella: Well, I guess I'd better be getting back. If you should see him—

Missy: Miz Idella, we all want to thank you for keeping Purlie out of jail so kindly.

> *(Hands her flowers.)*

Idella: Oh, that was nothing; I just told that ol' man if he didn't stop all that foolishness about chain gangs and stuff, I would resign from his kichen and take Charlie right along with me! But now I've lost Charlie. First time in forty-five years I ever misplaced anything!

> *(She exits.)*

Missy:

> *(Turns to **Purlie**.)*

Don't you know there's something more important in this world than having that broken down ol' ex-church of a barn to preach in?

Purlie: Yeah—like what?

Missy: Like asking Lutiebelle to marry you.

Purlie: Asking Lutiebelle to marry me?

Missy: She worships the ground you walk on. Talks about you all the time. You two could get married, settle down, like you ought to, and raise the cutest little ol' family you ever did see. And she's a cookin', po' child—she left you some of her special fritters.

Purlie: Freedom, Missy, not fritters. The crying need of this Negro day and age is not grits, but greatness; not cornbread but courage; not fat-back, but fight-back; Big Bethel is my Bethel; it belongs to me and to my people; and I intend to have it back if I have to pay for it in blood!

Missy: All right—come on in and I'll fix you some dinner.

Gitlow:

> *(Enters front door, singing.)*

"I'm comin', I'm comin'—"

Missy:

> *(Entering house.)*

Not so loud, Gitlow. You want to wake up the mule?

Gitlow: Not on his day off. "For my head is bendin' low—"

> *(**Gitlow** sits, unfolds comic section and reads.)*

Missy: Where's Lutiebelle, Gitlow?

Gitlow: "The history of the War Between the States will be continued next week." That sure is a good story—I wonder how that's gonna come out?

Missy: Grown man, deacon in the church, reading the funny-paper. And your shirt. You sneaked outta here this morning in your clean white shirt, after I told you time and time again I was saving it!

Gitlow: Saving it for what?

Missy: It's the only decent thing you got to get buried in!

> *(Exits side door.)*

Gitlow: Don't you know that arrangements for my funeral has been taken over by the white folks?

> *(To **Purlie**.)*

Besides, I got the money!

Purlie: What kinda money?

Gitlow: The five hundred dollar kinda money.

Purlie: Five hundred dollars! You mean Ol' Cap'n give the money to you?

Gitlow: "Gitlow," he said. "Ain't another man in this valley, black, white, or otherwise, I would trust to defend and protect me from the N double ACP but you."

Purlie: Is that a fact?

Gitlow: Well, now. Whatever become of you? All them gretgawdamighty plans your mouth runneth over—all that white folks' psychology?

Purlie: Gitlow! Er, Deacon Gitlow— Big Bethel is waiting!

Gitlow: So you're the good-for-nothing, raggedy ass high falute 'round here that goes for who-tied-the-bear!

Purlie: Naw, Git, man—ain't nothing to me.

Gitlow: Always so high and mighty—can't nobody on earth handle white folks but you—don't pay 'tention to Gitlow; naw—he's a Tom. Tease him— low-rate him—laugh at ol' Gitlow; he ain't nothing but a fool!

Purlie: Aw, Git, man, you got me wrong. I didn't mean nothing like that!

Gitlow: Who's the fool now, my boy—who's the fool now?

Purlie: Er—I'm the fool, Gitlow.

Gitlow: Aw, man, you can talk plainer than that.

Purlie: I'm the fool, Gitlow.

Gitlow: Uh-huh! Now go over to that window, open it wide as it will go and say it so everybody in this whole damn valley can hear you! Go on! Go on, man—I ain't got all day!

Purlie:

> (Goes to window.)

I'm the fool, Gitlow!

Gitlow: Nice. Now beg me!

Purlie: What!

Gitlow: I said if you want to see the money, beg me! Do it like you do white folks.

Purlie: I'd rather die and go to hell in a pair of gasoline drawers—

> (**Gitlow** starts to put money away.)

No, wait. Holy mackerel, dere, Massa Gitlow—hee, hee, hee. Hey! Boss, could I possible have a look at that there five hundred dollars dere, suh? Hyuh, hyuh, hyuh!

Gitlow: Man, you sure got style! You know together you and me could make the big time!

> (**Purlie** reaches for money.)

Come in and see me during office hours! As Deputy-For-The-Colored, I guess I'll just sort of step outside for a minute and let that low September sun shine down on a joker as rich as he is black!

Purlie: Gitlow—Gitlow!

> (**Gitlow** starts for side door.)

If slavery ever comes back I want to be your agent!

Gitlow: Now that was a snaggy-toothed, poverty-struck remark if I ever heard one.

PURLIE VICTORIOUS   167

Missy:

>*(Enters side door.)*

Youall wash your hands and git ready—Gitlow! Where's Lutiebelle?

Gitlow:

>*(Evasive.)*

She didn't get back yet.

Purlie: Where is Lutiebelle, Gitlow?

Missy: We know she didn't get back yet.

Gitlow: What I mean is—on our way home from church, we stopped by Ol' Cap'n's awhile, and he asked me to leave her there to help with the Sunday dinner.

Purlie: And you left her!

Missy: With that frisky ol' man?

Gitlow: For goodness' sakes, she's only waiting on table.

Purlie: The woman I love don't wait on table for nobody, especially Ol' Cap'n; I know that scoun'. I'm going and get her!

Gitlow: Wait a minute—you can't get her right now!

Purlie:

>*(Studying him.)*

What you mean, I can't get her right now?

Gitlow: Not right this minute—that'll spoil everything. Ol' Cap'n wouldn't like it.

Missy: How low can you git, Gitlow!

Gitlow: I mean she's got to stay and bring us the $500.00.

Missy: What 500 dollars?

Purlie: I thought you already had the money?

Gitlow: Well, not exactly. But he promised me faithful to send it down by Lutiebelle.

Purlie: I'm going and get Lutiebelle—

Gitlow: Wait a minute, wait a minute; you want to buy Big Bethel back or don't you?

Purlie:

>*(A glimmering of truth.)*

I hope I misunderstand you!

Gitlow: You said it yourself: It is meet that the daughters of Zion should sacrifice themselves for the cause.

Purlie:

>*(Grabbing up* **Missy's** *bat.)*

Gitlow, I'll kill you—!

Gitlow: Wait a minute, wait a minute, wait a MINUTE!

>*(The door opens suddenly, and there stands* **Lutiebelle**. *She, too, has on her Sunday best, but it is disheveled. She has a work apron over her dress, with her hat complete askew, the once proud feather now hanging over her face. In her hands she still clutches a rolling pin.)*

Missy: Lutiebelle—Lutiebelle, honey!

Lutiebelle: I think I am going to faint.

(She starts to collapse, and they rush toward her to help; but suddenly she straightens up and waves them off.)

No, I ain't, either—I'm too mad!

(She shudders in recollection.)

I was never so insulted in all my dad-blamed life!

Purlie: Lutiebelle!

Lutiebelle: Oh, excuse me, Reb'n Purlie—I know I look a mess, but—

Missy: What happened up there?

Lutiebelle:

(Boiling again.)

I'm a maid first class, Aunt Missy, and I'm proud of it!

Missy: Of course you are.

Lutiebelle: I ain't had no complaints to speak of since first I stepped into the white folks' kitchen. I'm clean; I'm honest, and I work hard—but one thing: I don't stand for no stuff from them white folks.

Purlie: Of course you don't. You don't have to—

Lutiebelle: I mean, I KNOW my job, and I DO my job—and the next ol' sweaty, ol' grimey, ol' drunkeny man puts his hands on me—so much as touch like he got no business doing—God grant me strength to kill him! Excuse me, Reb'n Purlie.

Gitlow: Well, Ol' Cap'n do get playful at times—did he send the money?

Lutiebelle: Money! What money? There ain't none!

Gitlow: What! Naw, naw! He wouldn't do that to me—not to good ol', faithful ol' Gitlow, nawsir!

Lutiebelle: The whole thing was a trick—to get you out of the house—

Gitlow: Not to ME he didn't!

Lutiebelle: So he could—sneak up behind me in the pantry!

Missy: What I tell you—what I tell you!

Lutiebelle: I know the minute I— Come grabbing on me, Reb'n Purlie; come grabbing his dirty ol' hands on me!

Purlie: He did!

Lutiebelle: And twisting me around, and—and pinching me, Reb'n Purlie!

Purlie: Pinching you—where? Where?

Lutiebelle: Must I, Reb'n Purlie—?

Purlie: I demand to know—where did he pinch you!

*(**Lutiebelle** diffidently locates a spot on her left cheek. They all examine it anxiously.)*

Missy: That's him all right!

Gitlow: Aw, Missy—

Missy: I'd know them fingerprints anywhere!

Lutiebelle: Right in the pantry—and then he, he— Oh, Reb'n Purlie, I'm so ashamed!

Purlie: What did he do? Tell me, woman, tell me: what did he do? WHAT DID HE DO?

Lutiebelle: He kissed me!

Purlie and **Missy:** No!

Lutiebelle: He kissed me—right here.
Missy:

> *(Squinting, it is a very small spot indeed.)*

Right where?

> *(****Lutiebelle**** is so broken up, she can only point to her other cheek.)*

Gitlow: Aw, for Pete's sakes.
Purlie:

> *(Almost out of control.)*

He kissed my woman, Gitlow—he kissed the woman I love!
Gitlow: So what!
Purlie: So what do you mean, "So what"? No man kisses the woman I love and lives!

> *(Gitlow laughs.)*

Go ahead, laugh! Laugh. Let's have one last look at your teeth before I knock 'em down your throat!
Gitlow: Aw, man, git off my nerves.
Purlie: I'm going up that hill, and I'm gonna call that buzzardly ol' bastard out, and I wouldn't be surprised if I didn't beat him until he died.
Lutiebelle:

> *(Suddenly not so sure.)*

Reb'n Purlie—
Gitlow:

> *(Also wondering about ****Purlie****.)*

Now looka here, Purlie—don't you be no fool, boy—you still in Georgia. If you just got to defend the honor of the woman you love, do it somewhere else.
Purlie: Kissing my woman—kissing my woman!

> *(Runs to window, flings it open and shouts out.)*

Man, I'll break your neck off!
Lutiebelle:

> *(Helping ****Gitlow**** and ****Missy**** to wrestle ****Purlie**** away from the window.)*

Please, Reb'n Purlie!
Purlie:

> *(Breaks away and goes to window and shouts again.)*

I'll stomp your eyeballs in!
Lutiebelle:

> *(They snatch him from the window again.)*

Don't, Reb'n Purlie—oh my goodness!—
Purlie:

> *(Breaks away still again and shouts from window.)*

I'll snatch your right arm outta the socket, and beat the rest of you to death!
Lutiebelle:

> *(This time they get him away, and close the window.)*

Don't talk like that, Reb'n Purlie!
Missy:

> *(Standing at the window, arms widespread to block him.)*

Have you gone crazy?

Gitlow:
>*(Still struggling with* **Purlie**.*)*

You go up that hill tonight, boy, and they'll kill you!

Purlie: Let 'em kill me, it won't be the first time.

Lutiebelle: Aunt Missy, stop him—

Gitlow: Listen, boy! This is your Deputy-For-The-Colored telling you you ain't gonna leave this house, and that's an order!

Purlie: You try and stop me!

Gitlow: Good gracious a life, what's the matter with you? The man only kissed your woman.

Purlie: Yeah! And what you suppose he'd a done to me if I'd kissed his?
>*(The one question too obvious to answer.)*

And that's exactly what I'm gonna do to him!

Lutiebelle: Please, Reb'n Purlie. I beg you on bended knees.
>*(She throws her arms around him.)*

Purlie:
>*(Holds her close.)*

For the glory and honor of the Negro National Anthem; for the glory and honor of brown-skin Negro womanhood; for the glory and honor of—
>(**Lutiebelle** *suddenly kisses him big and hard.*)

—for LUTIEBELLE!
>*(His emotions explode him out of the door which slams shut behind him.)*

Gitlow:
>*(Singing.)*

"I hear them gentle bloodhounds callin'—Old Black Joe." . . .
>(**Lutiebelle** *finds the deepest spot in* **Missy's** *shoulder to bury her head and cry, as:)*

>Curtain

Act Three
SCENE 1

Scene: *The shack.*

Time: *Later that same night.*

At Rise: *There is light only from a KEROSENE LAMP turned down low. The air of Sunday is gone from the room. The tablecloth has been changed, and things are as they were before.* **Lutiebelle** *enters Down Right.*

Lutiebelle: Is it him, Aunt Missy, is it him?

Missy: No, honey, not yet.

Lutiebelle: Oh, I could have sworn I thought it was him. What time is it?

Missy: About four in the morning from the sound of the birds. Now, why ain't you sleep after all that hot toddy I give you?

Lutiebelle: I can't sleep. The strangest thing. I keep hearing bells—

Missy: Bells?

Lutiebelle: Wedding bells. Ain't that funny? Oh, Lord, please don't let him be hurt bad, please! Where can he be, Aunt Missy?

Missy: Now don't you worry 'bout Purlie. My! You put on your pretty pink dress!

Lutiebelle: Yes, ma'am. It's the only thing I got fitting to propose in.

Missy: Oh?

Lutiebelle: I thought, to sort of show my gratitude, I'd offer him my hand in matrimony—it's all I've got.

Missy: It's a nice hand, and a nice dress—just right for matrimony.

Lutiebelle: You really think so, Aunt Missy: really, really, really?

Missy: I know so, and wherever Reb'n Purlie is this morning, you can bet your bottom dollar he knows it, too.

Lutiebelle: Ten thousand Queens of Sheba! Aunt Missy—

Missy: Yes—

Lutiebelle:
> *(Letting it out in a gush.)*

I wanted him to get mad; I wanted him to tear out up that hill; I wanted him to punch that sweaty ol' buzzard in his gizzard—You think I was wrong?

Missy: I should say not!

Lutiebelle: Course I coulda punched him myself, I reckon.

Missy: Why should you? Why shouldn't our men folks defend our honor with the white folks once in a while? They ain't got nothing else to do.

Lutiebelle: You really, really, really think so?

Missy:
> *(Shrugs.)*

Ten thousand Queens of Sheba—

Lutiebelle: Oh, my goodness, when he walks through that door, I'm just gonna—

> *(Door Down Left suddenly swings open to reveal **Gitlow**.)*

Gitlow:
> *(Entering.)*

Well, well, Lutiebelle.

Lutiebelle: Did you find him, Uncle Git?

Missy: Don't depend on Gitlow for nothing, honey—
> *(Exits to kitchen.)*

Lutiebelle: Where can he be, Uncle Gitlow, where can he be?

Gitlow: Oh—good wind like this on his tail oughta put him somewhere above Macon long 'bout now, if his shoes hold out!

Lutiebelle: You mean—running!

Gitlow: What's wrong with running? It emancipated more people than Abe Lincoln ever did.

Lutiebelle: How dare you! The finest, bravest man—

Gitlow: The finer they come, the braver they be, the deader these white folks gonna kill 'em when they catch 'em!

Missy:
> *(Entering from the kitchen.)*

Gitlow, I'll skin you!

Gitlow: All that talk about calling that man out, and whipping him—

Missy: A man is duty-bound to defend the honor of the woman he loves, and any woman worth her salt will tell you so.

Lutiebelle: Love can make you do things you really can't do—can't it, Aunt Missy?

Gitlow: Look. That man's got the president, the governor, the courthouse, and both houses of the congress—on his side!

Missy: Purlie Judson is a man the Negro woman can depend on!

Lutiebelle: An honor to his race, and a credit to his people!

Gitlow:

> *(Not to be sidetracked.)*

The army, the navy, the marines; the sheriff, the judge, the jury, the police, the F.B.I.—all on his side. Not to mention a pair of brass knucks and the hungriest dogs this side of hell! Surely youall don't expect that po' boy to go up against all that caucasiatic power empty-handed!

Missy: O, ye of little faith!

Lutiebelle: Didn't my Lord deliver Daniel?

Gitlow: Of course he did—but lions is one thing and white folks is another!

Missy: Where there's a will there's a woman—

Lutiebelle: And where there's a woman there's a way!

Gitlow:

> *(Exasperated.)*

Great Gawdamighty! All right—go ahead and have it your way. But I'll lay you six bits 'gainst half my seat on the heavenly choir, Purlie ain't been up that hill. And the minute he walks in that door—if he ever shows up again around here—I'm gonna prove it! Oh, damn—I can make better time out there talkin' to that mule.

Missy: Why not—it's one jackass to another.

> **(Gitlow** *exits to the kitchen.* **Missy** *and* **Lutiebelle** *look at each other, both determined not to give way to the very real fright they feel. There is a long, uncomfortable pause.)*

Lutiebelle: It sure is a lovely year—for this time of morning, I mean.

> *(There is a pause.)*

I can't tell you how much all this fresh air, wine-smoke, and apple-bite reminds me of Alabama.

Missy: Oh, yes—Ol' Georgia can sure smile pretty when she's of a mind to—

Purlie:

> *(Bursts in.)*

"Arise and shine for thy light has come."

Missy: Purlie—Purlie Victorious!

> *(They embrace.)*

Lutiebelle: Oh, you Reb'n Purlie you!

Purlie: "Truth and Mercy are met together, Righteousness and Peace have kissed each other!"

> *(They embrace.)*

Missy: Let me look at you—behold the man!—knee-deep in shining glory.

Great day the righteous marching! What happened to you?

Purlie: Mine enemy hath been destroyed!

Missy: What!

Purlie: I told that ol' man twenty years ago, Missy, that over his dead body, Big Bethel would rise again!

Missy: Purlie—! You mean you done—

Purlie: "Have I any pleasure that the wicked should die, saith the Lord, and not turn from his ways and live?" Lutiebelle, put on your hat and coat, and hurry!

Lutiebelle: Yessir!

Purlie: Missy, throw us some breakfast into a paper sack, and quick!

Missy: Yessir!

Purlie: Gitlow, I'm calling on you and your fellow mule to write a new page in the annals of Negro History Week.

Gitlow:

> *(Entering.)*

Well, if it ain't ol' little black riding hood, dere! How was the mean ol' peckerwolf tonight, dere, kingfish?

Missy: Tell him, Purlie boy, what you told us: how you sashayed up that hill with force and fistfight!

Gitlow: Hallelujah!

Missy: How you fit Ol' Cap'n to a halt and a standstill!

Gitlow: Talk that talk!

Missy: And left him laying in a pool of his own Confederate blood!

Gitlow: For Pete sakes, Missy—quit lying!

Missy: Don't you dare call Purlie Judson a liar!

Lutiebelle: No man calls Reb'n Purlie a liar and lives!

Gitlow: What's the matter with you people? Purlie ain't been up that hill; Purlie ain't seen Ol' Cap'n; Purlie ain't done doodley squat! And all that gabble about leaving somebody in a pool of his own Confederate blood ain't what the bull left in the barnyard!

Purlie: Five hundred dollars says it is!

> *(Draws roll of bills from his pocket, for all to see.)*

All: Five hundred dollars!

Purlie: In cool September cash!

Gitlow: Money!

> *(Lunges forward, but **Purlie** slaps his hand.)*

Purlie: And that ain't all I got—

> *(Opens bag he has brought. They look in.)*

Gitlow:

> *(Almost choking in awe.)*

Oh, my goodness, Missy—great day in the morning time—Missy—Missy!

Missy:

> *(Also impressed.)*

Gitlow, that's *it*.

Gitlow: That's *it*, Missy—that's *it!*

Missy: Of course that's *it*—ain't nothing in the world but *it*!

> (**Purlie** *slowly pulls out* **Ol' Cap'n's** *bull whip.*)

Gitlow: Ain't but one way—one way in all this world—for nobody to get that bull whip off'n Ol' Cap'n!

Missy: And that's off'n his dead body!

Gitlow: And that's the everlovin' truth, so help me.

Purlie: Here, take it—and burn it in a public place. Lutiebelle—

Lutiebelle: Yes, Reb'n Purlie.

Purlie: This money belongs to the Negro people—

Gitlow: Reb'n Purlie, my boy, I apologize from the bottom of my knees.

> (*Kneels and starts to sing.*)

"Gone are the days—"

Missy:

> (*Snatching him to his feet.*)

Get up and shut up!

Purlie:

> (*Deliberately continuing to* **Lutiebelle**.)

Take it, and wear it next to your heart.

Lutiebelle:

> (*Very conscious of the great charge laid upon her, turns her back to* **Gitlow** *and hides the money in her bosom.*)

Until death us do part.

Missy:

> (*To* **Gitlow**.)

If I ever catch you with that song in your mouth again I'll choke you with it!

Purlie: And go wake up the mule. We due in Waycross to buy Big Bethel.

Gitlow: I'm going, I'm going.

> (*Starts, but can't tear himself away.*)

Cash—five hundred dollars in cash. And a bull whip, from Ol' Cap'n Cotchipee himself— Man, I'd give a pretty piece of puddin' to know how you did it!

Missy: You go and wake up that mule!

> (*Turning back to* **Purlie**.)

Me, too! How did you do it, Purlie?

Lutiebelle: What happened when you first got there?

Purlie:

> (*Almost laughing.*)

Now wait a minute—don't rush me!

Missy: That's what I say: don't rush him—let the man talk!

Purlie: Talk! Missy, I told you. I haven't got time—

Gitlow: That's all right, Purlie, we'll listen in a hurry.

Lutiebelle: What happened when you called him out and whipped him?

Purlie: I didn't call him out and whip him!

Gitlow: What!

Missy: You didn't!

Lutiebelle: Reb'n Purlie—?

Purlie: I mean, I did call him out—
Lutiebelle:

> *(In ecstatic relief.)*

Oh— You did call him out!
Purlie: Yeah—but he didn't come.
All: What!
Purlie: So—er—I went in to get him!
All: You did! Sure enough! What happened then?
Purlie:

> *(Still seeking escape.)*

Well, like I told you—
Lutiebelle: Tell us, Reb'n Purlie—please!
Purlie:

> *(No escape.)*

Well—here was me; and there was him—twisted and bent like a pretzel!
Face twitchified like a pan of worms; eyes bugging out; sweat dreening down
like rain; tongue plumb clove to the roof of his mouth!

> *(He looks to his audience, and is impelled to go on.)*

Well—this thief! This murderer; this adulterer—this oppressor of all my
people, just a sitting there: Stonewall Jackson Cotchipee, just a sitting there.

> *(Begins to respond to his own fantasy.)*

"Go to, rich man, weep and howl, for your sorrows shall come upon you."
And-a- "Wherefore abhor yourself, and repent Ye in sackcloth and ashes!"
cause ol' Purlie is done come to get you!
Lutiebelle:

> *(Swept away.)*

Oh, my Lord!
Missy: What he do, Purlie—what he do!?
Purlie: Fell down on bended knees and cried like a baby!
Missy: Ol' Cap'n Cotchipee on his knees!?
Gitlow: Great day in the morning time!
Purlie:

> *(Warming to the task.)*

Don't beg me, white folks, it's too late. "Mercy?" What do you know about
mercy?! Did you have mercy on Ol' Uncle Tubb when he asked you not to
cheat him out of his money so hard, and you knocked him deaf in his left
ear?—Did you have mercy on Lolly's boy when he sassed you back, and you
took and dipped his head in a bucket of syrup! And twenty years ago when
little Purlie, black and manly as he could be, stood naked before you and
your bull whip and pleaded with tears in his li'l ol' eyes, did you have mercy!?
Gitlow: Naw!
Purlie: —And I'll not have mercy now!
All: Amen! Help him, Lawd! Preach it, boy, preach it!

> *(Etc.)*

Purlie: Vengeance is mine saith the Lord!

> *(Hallelujah!)*

Ye serpents; ye vipers; ye low-down sons of—!
>(Amen!)

How can ye escape the damnation of hell!

Missy: Throw it at him, boy!

Purlie: And then, bless my soul, I looked up—up from the blazing depths of my righteous indignation! And I saw tears spill over from his eyeballs; and I heard the heart be-clutching anguish of his outcry! His hands was both a-tremble; and slobber a-dribblin' down his lips!

Gitlow: Oh, my Lawd!

Purlie: And he whined and whimpered like a ol' hound dog don't want you to kick him no more!

Lutiebelle: Great goodness a mighty!

Purlie: And I commenced to ponder the meaning of this evil thing that groveled beneath my footstool—this no-good lump of nobody!—not fit to dwell on this earth beside the children of the blessed—an abomination to the Almighty and stench in the nostrils of his people! And yet—
>(Pause for effect.)

And yet—a man! A weak man; a scared man; a pitiful man; like the whole southland bogged down in sin and segregation crawling on his knees before my judgment seat—but still a MAN!

Gitlow: A man, Lawd!

Purlie: He, too, like all the South, was one of God's creatures—

Missy: Yes, Lawd!

Purlie: He, too, like all the South, could never be beyond the reach of love, hope, and redemption.

Lutiebelle: Amen!

Purlie: Somewhere for him—even for him, some father's heart was broken, some mother's tears undried.

Gitlow: Dry 'em, Lawd!

Purlie: I am my brother's keeper!

All: Yes, Lawd.

Purlie: And thinking on these things, I found myself to pause, and stumble in my great resolve—and sorrow squeezed all fury from my heart—and pity plucked all hatred from my soul—and the racing feet of an avenging anger slowed down to a halt and a standstill—and the big, black, and burly fist of my strong correction—raised on high like a stroke of God's own lightning—fell useless by my side. The book say, "Love one another."

Missy: Love one another!

Purlie: The book say, "Comfort ye one another."

Lutiebelle: Comfort ye one another.

Purlie: The book say, "Forgive ye one another."

Gitlow: Forgive Ol' Cap'n, Lord.

Purlie: Slowly I turned away—to leave this lump of human mess and misery to the infinite darkness of a hell for white folks only, when suddenly—

Missy: Suddenly, Lord.

Purlie: Suddenly I put on my brakes—Purlie Victorious Judson stopped dead in his tracks—and stood stark still, and planted his feet, and rared back, asked himself and all the powers—that—be some mighty important questions.

Lutiebelle: Yes, he did, Lawd.

Missy: And that is the truth!

Purlie: How come—I asked myself, it's always the colored folks got to do all the forgiving?

Gitlow: Man, you mighty right!

Purlie: How come the only cheek gits turned in this country is the Negro cheek!

Missy: Preach to me, boy!

Purlie: What was this, this—man—Ol' Cap'n Cotchipee—that in spite of all his sins and evils, he still had dominion over me?

Lutiebelle: Ain't that the truth!

Purlie: God made us all equal—God made us all brothers—

All: Amen, amen.

Purlie: "And hath made of one blood all nations of men for to dwell on the face of the earth."—Who changed all that!?

Gitlow:

>   *(Furious.)*

Who changed it, he said.

Purlie: Who took it and twisted it around!

Missy:

>   *(Furious.)*

Who was it, he said!

Lutiebelle:

>   *(Furious.)*

And where's that scoun' hiding?!

Purlie: So that the Declarator of Independence himself might seem to be a liar?

Gitlow: Who, that's what I want to know, who?

Purlie: That a man the color of his face—

>   *(Pointing up Cotchipee Hill.)*

could live by the sweat of a man the color of mine!

Lutiebelle: Work with him, Lawd, work with him!

Purlie: —Could live away up there in his fine, white mansion, and us down here in a shack not fitting to house the fleas upon his dogs!

Gitlow: Nothing but fleas!

Purlie: —Could wax hisself fat on the fat of the land; steaks, rice, chicken, roastineers, sweet potato pies, hot buttered biscuits and cane syrup anytime he felt like it and never hit a lick at a snake! And us got to every day git-up-and-git-with-it, sunup-to-sundown, on fatback and cornmeal hoecakes—and don't wind up owning enough ground to get buried standing up in!

Missy: Do, Lord!

Purlie: —And horses and cadillacs, bull whips and bourbon, and two for 'leven dollar seegars—and our fine young men to serve at his table; and our fine young women to serve in his bed!

Lutiebelle: Help him, Lawd.

Purlie: Who made it like this—who put the white man on top?

Gitlow: That's what I wants to know!

Purlie: Surely not the Lord God of Israel who is a just God!

Missy: Hah, Lord!

Purlie: And no respecter of persons! Who proved in the American Revolution that all men are created equal!

Gitlow: Man, I was there when he proved it!

Purlie: Endowed with Civil Rights and First Class Citizenship, Ku Klux Klan, White Citizens Council notwithstanding!

Missy: Oh, yes, he did!

Purlie: And when my mind commenced to commemorate and to reconsider all these things—

Gitlow: Watch him, Lawd!

Purlie: And I thought of the black mother in bondage—

    (Yes.)

and I thought of the black father in prison—

    (Ha, Lawd!)

And of Momma herself—Missy can tell how pretty she was—

Missy: Indeed I can!

Purlie: How she died outdoors on a dirty sheet cause the hospital doors said—"For white folks only." And of Papa, God rest his soul—who brought her tender loving body back home—and laid her to sleep in the graveyard—and cried himself to death among his children!

Missy:

    (Crying.)

Purlie, Purlie—

Purlie:

    (Really carried away.)

Then did the wrath of a righteous God possess me; and the strength of the host and of ten thousand swept into my good right arm—and I arose and I smote Ol' Cap'n a mighty blow! And the wind from my fist ripped the curtains from the eastern walls—and I felt the weight of his ol' bull whip nestling in my hands—and the fury of a good Gawd-almighty was within me; and I beat him—I whipped him—and I flogged him—and I cut him —I destroyed him!

    (Idella *enters.)*

Gitlow: Great day and the righteous marching—Whoeeeee! Man, I ain't been stirred that deep since the tree caught fire on a possum hunt and the dogs pushed Papa in the pot.

Missy: Idella, you shoulda heard him!

Idella: I did hear him—all the way across the valley. I thought he was calling hogs. Well, anyway: all hell is broke loose at the big house. Purlie, you better get outta here. Ol' Cap'n is on the phone to the sheriff.

Missy: Ol' Cap'n Cotchipee is dead.

Idella: The hell you preach.

All: What!

Idella: Ol' Cap'n ain't no more dead than I am.

Lutiebelle: That's a mighty tacky thing to say about your ex-fellow man.

Missy: Mighty tacky.

Lutiebelle: Reb'n Purlie just got through preaching 'bout it. How he marched up Cotchipee hill—

Gitlow:

> *(Showing the bull whip.)*

And took Ol' Cap'n by the bull whip—

Missy: And beat that ol' buzzard to death!

Idella: That is the biggest lie since the devil learned to talk!

Lutiebelle: I am not leaving this room till somebody apologizes to Reb'n Purlie V. Judson, the gentleman of my intended.

Idella: Purlie Judson! Are you gonna stand there sitting on your behind, and preach these people into believing you spent the night up at the big house whipping Ol' Cap'n to death when all the time you was breaking into the commissary!

Missy: Breaking into the commissary!

Gitlow: Something is rotten in the cotton!

Purlie: It's all right, Miz Idella—I'll take it from there—

Missy: It is not all right—!

Purlie: While it is true that, maybe, I did not go up that hill just word for word, and call that ol' man out, and beat him to death so much on the dotted line—!

Missy:

> *(Snatching up the paper bag.)*

I'm goin' to take back my lunch!

Purlie: Missy! Wait a minute!

Lutiebelle: You know what, Aunt Missy?

Missy: Yes, honey?

Lutiebelle: Sometimes I just wish I could drop dead for a while.

Purlie: Wait, Lutiebelle, give me a chance to—

Lutiebelle: Here's your money!—

> *(Puts roll into **Purlie's** hand.)*

And that goes for every other great big ol' handsome man in the whole world!

Purlie: What you want me to do? Go up that hill by myself and get my brains knocked out?

Missy: It's little enough for the woman you love!

Lutiebelle: Why'd you have to preach all them wonderful things that wasn't so?

Gitlow: And why'd you have to go and change your mind?

Purlie: I didn't mean for them not to be so: it was a—a parable! A prophecy! Believe me! I ain't never in all my life told a lie I didn't mean to make come true, some day! Lutiebelle—!

Idella: Purlie: unless you want to give heartbreak a headache, you better run!

Purlie: Run—run for what!

Missy: You want Ol' Cap'n to catch you here!?

Purlie: Confound Ol' Cap'n! Dad-blast Ol' Cap'n! Damn, damn, damn, and double-damn Ol' Cap'n!

(The front door swings open and in walks **Ol' Cap'n** *steaming with anger.)*

Ol' Cap'n:

(Controlling himself with great difficulty.)

Somebody—I say somebody—is calling my name!

Gitlow: Ol' Cap'n, you just in time to settle a argument: is Rudolph Valentino still dead?

Ol' Cap'n: Shut up!

Gitlow:

(To **Missy.***)*

See—I told you.

Ol' Cap'n: One thing I have not allowed in my cotton patch since am-I-born-to-die! And that's stealin'! Somebody broke into my commissary tonight—took two cans of sardines, a box of soda crackers, my bull whip!—

(Picks up whip from table.)

And five hundred dollars in cash. And, boy—

(Walking over to **Purlie.***)*

I want it back!

Lutiebelle: Stealing ain't all that black and white.

Missy: And we certainly wasn't the ones that started it!

Gitlow: Who stole me from Africa in the first place?

Lutiebelle: Who kept me in slavery from 1619 to 1863, working me to the bone without no social security?

Purlie: And tonight—just because I went up that hill, and disembezzled my own inheritance that you stole from me—!

Ol' Cap'n:

(Livid.)

I have had a belly full of your black African sass—!

(The door bursts open again; this time it is the **Sheriff** *who comes in with pistol drawn.)*

Sheriff: All right, everybody, drop that gun!

Purlie: Drop what gun?

Ol' Cap'n: So there you are, you idiot—what kept you so long?

Sheriff: Like you told us to do on the phone, suh, we was taking a good, long, slow snoop 'round and 'bout the commissary looking for clues! And dog-gone if one didn't, just a short while ago, stumble smack into our hands!

Ol' Cap'n: What!

Sheriff: We caught the culprit red-handed—bring in the prisoner, Dep!

Deputy: Glad to oblige you, Sheriff.

(Enter **Deputy,** *dragging* **Charlie,** *who has his hands cuffed behind him; wears heavy leg shackles, and has a large white gag stuck into his mouth.)*

Sheriff: Southern justice strikes again!

Ol' Cap'n: Charlie!—oh, no!

Idella: Charlie, my baby!

Ol' Cap'n: Release him, you idiots! Release him at once!

(Everybody pitches in to set **Charlie** *free.)*

What have they done to you, my boy?

Idella: What have they done to you!

Charlie:

> *(Free from the gag.)*

Hello, Paw—Idella—Purlie—

Ol' Cap'n: I'll have your thick, stupid necks for this!

Sheriff: It was you give the orders, suh!

Ol' Cap'n: Not my son, you idiot!

Deputy: It was him broke into the commissary.

Ol' Cap'n: What!

Sheriff: It was him stole the five hundred dollars—he confessed!

Ol' Cap'n: Steal? A Cotchipee? Suh, that is biologically impossible!

> *(To **Charlie**.)*

Charlie, my boy. Tell them the truth—tell them who stole the money. It was Purlie, wasn't it, boy?

Charlie: Well, as a matter of fact, Paw—it was mostly me that broke in and took the money, I'd say. In fact it WAS me!

Ol' Cap'n: No!

Charlie: It was the only thing I could do to save your life, Paw.

Ol' Cap'n: Save my life! Idella, he's delirious—!

Charlie: When Purlie come up that hill after you last night, I seen him, and lucky for you I did. The look he had on his face against you was not a Christian thing to behold! It was terrible! I had to get into that commissary, right then and there, open that safe, and pay him his inheritance—even then I had to beg him to spare your life!

Ol' Cap'n:

> *(To **Purlie**.)*

You spare my life, boy? How dare you?

> *(To **Charlie**.)*

Charlie, my son, I know you never recovered from the shock of losing your mother—almost before you were born. But don't worry—it was Purlie who stole that money and I'm going to prove it.

> *(Starts to take out gun. **Gitlow** grabs gun.)*

Gitlow, my old friend, arrest this boy, Gitlow! As Deputy-For-The-Colored— I order you to arrest this boy for stealing!

Gitlow:

> *(With a brand new meaning.)*

"Gone are the days—"

> *(Still twirls pistol safely out of **Ol' Cap'n's** reach.)*

Purlie: "Stealin," is it? Well, I'm gonna really give you something to arrest me for.

> *(Snatches bull whip.)*

Ol' Cap'n: Have a care, boy: I'm still a white man.

Purlie: Congratulations! Twenty years ago, I told you this bull whip was gonna change hands one of these days!

Missy: Purlie, wait—!

Purlie: Stay out of my struggle for power!

Missy: You can't do wrong just because it's right!

Gitlow: Never kick a man when he's down except in self-defense!

Lutiebelle: And no matter what you are, and always will be—the hero of Cotchipee Hill.

Purlie: Am I?

Lutiebelle: Ten thousand queens!

Purlie: I bow to the will of the Negro people.

    *(Throws whip away. Back to **Ol' Cap'n**.)*

But one thing, Ol' Cap'n, I am released of you—the entire Negro people is released of you! No more shouting hallelujah! every time you sneeze, nor jumping jackass every time you whistle "Dixie"! We gonna love you if you let us and laugh as we leave if you don't. We want our cut of the Constitution, and we want it now: and not with no teaspoon, white folks—throw it at us with a shovel!

Ol' Cap'n: Charlie, my boy—my own, lily-white, Anglo-Saxon, semi-confederate son. I know you never recovered from the shock of losing your mother, almost before you were born. But don't worry: there is still time to take these insolent, messy cotton-picking ingrates down a peg—and prove by word and deed that God is still a white man. Tell 'em! Boy, tell 'em!

Charlie: Tell 'em what, Paw?

Ol' Cap'n: Tell 'em what you and me have done together. Nobody here would believe me. Tell 'em how you went to Waycross, Saturday night, in my name—

Charlie: Yes, sir—I did.

Ol' Cap'n: Tell 'em how you spoke to Ol' Man Pelham in my name—

Charlie: Yes, sir—I spoke to him.

Ol' Cap'n: And paid him cash for that ol' barn they used to call Big Bethel!

Charlie: Yes, sir; that's what I did, all right.

Ol' Cap'n: And to register the deed in the courthouse in my name—

Charlie: Yes, sir, that's exactly what you told me to do—

Ol' Cap'n: Then—ain't but one thing left to do with that ramshackle dung-soaked monstrosity—that's burn the damn thing down.

    (Laughs aloud in his triumph.)

Charlie: But, Paw—

Ol' Cap'n: First thing, though—let me see the deed: I wouldn't want to destroy nothing that didn't—legally—belong to me.

    *(Snatches deed from **Charlie's** hand. Begins to mumble as he reads it.)*

Idella: Twenty years of being more than a mother to you!

Charlie: Wait, Idella, wait. I did go to Waycross, like Paw said; I did buy the barn—excuse me, Purlie: the church—like he said; and I registered the deed at the courthouse like he told me—but not in Paw's name—

Ol' Cap'n:

    (Startled by something he sees on the deed.)

What's this?

Charlie:

    *(To **Idella**.)*

I registered the deed in the name of—

PURLIE VICTORIOUS   183

Ol' Cap'n:
> *(Reading, incredulous.)*

"Purlie Victorious Judson—" No!

Idella: PURLIE VICTORIOUS Judson?

Ol' Cap'n:
> *(Choking on the words.)*

Purlie Victorious Judsssss—aaaarrrrgggghhhhh!
> *(The horror of it strikes him absolutely still.)*

Charlie:
> *(Taking the deed from **Ol' Cap'n's** limp hand.)*

It was the only thing I could do to save your life.
> *(Offering deed to **Purlie**.)*

Well, Purlie, here it is.

Purlie:
> *(Counting out the five hundred dollars.)*

You did a good job, Charlie—I'm much obliged!

Charlie:
> *(Refuses money; still holds out deeds to **Purlie**.)*

Thank you, Purlie, but—

Purlie: Big Bethel is my Bethel, Charlie: it's my responsibility. Go on, take it.

Charlie: No, no! I couldn't take your money, Purlie—

Idella: Don't be a fool, boy—business is business.
> *(She takes the deed from **Charlie** and gives it to **Purlie**, while at the same time taking the money from **Purlie**.)*

Charlie: Idella—I can't do that!

Idella: I can! I'll keep it for you.

Charlie: Well—all right. But only, if—if—

Idella: Only if what?

Charlie:
> *(To **Purlie**.)*

Would you let me be a member of your church?

Missy: You?

Gitlow: Li'l Charlie Cotchipee!

Lutiebelle: A member of Big Bethel?

Charlie: May I? That is—that is, if you don't mind—as soon as you get it started?

Purlie: Man, we're already started: the doors of Big Bethel, Church of the New Freedom for all Mankind, are hereby declared "Open for business!"

Gitlow: Brother Pastor, I move we accept Brother Charlie Cotchipee as our first candidate for membership to Big Bethel on a integrated basis—

Missy: I second that motion!

Purlie: You have heard the motion. Are you ready for the question?

All:
> *(Except **Ol' Cap'n**.)*

Question!

Purlie: Those in favor will signify by saying "Aye."
> *(Everybody, except **Ol' Cap'n**, crowds around **Charlie**, saying "Aye"*

over and over, in such a crescendo of welcome that **Purlie** *has to ride over the noise.)*

Those opposed?

(Looks at **Ol' Cap'n**, *who is still standing, as if frozen, as we last saw him. He does not answer.)*

Those opposed will signify by saying—

(He stops . . . all eyes focus on **Ol' Cap'n** *now, still standing in quiet, frozen-like immobility. There is a moment of silence, an unspoken suspicion in everybody's face. Finally,* **Gitlow** *goes over and touches* **Ol' Cap'n**, *still standing rigid. Still he does not move.* **Gitlow** *feels his pulse, listens to his heart, and lifts up his eyelids. Nothing.)*

Gitlow: The first man I ever seen in all this world to drop dead standing up!

Blackout

EPILOGUE

Time: *Immediately following.*
Scene: *We are at Big Bethel at funeral services for* **Ol' Cap'n.**
At Rise: *We cannot see the coffin. We hear the ringing of the CHURCH BELL as we come out of the blackout.* **Purlie** *is in the pulpit.*

Purlie: And toll the bell, Big Bethel, toll the bell! Dearly beloved, recently bereaved, and friends, we welcome you to Big Bethel, Church of the New Freedom: part Baptist; part Methodist; part Catholic—with the merriness of Christmas and the happiness of Hanukkah; and to the first integrated funeral in the sovereign, segregated state of Georgia. Let there be no merriments in these buryments! Though you are dead, Ol' Cap'n, and in hell, I suspect—as post-mortal guest of honor, at our expense: it is not too late to repent. We still need togetherness; we still need each otherness—with faith in the futureness of our cause. Let us, therefore, stifle the rifle of conflict, shatter the scatter of discord, smuggle the struggle, tickle the pickle, and grapple the apple of peace!

Gitlow: This funeral has been brought to you as a public service.

Purlie: Take up his bones. For he who was my skin's enemy, was brave enough to die standing for what he believed. . . . And it is the wish of his family—and his friends—that he be buried likewise—

(The **Pallbearers** *enter, carrying* **Ol' Cap'n's** *ornate coffin just as he would have wished: standing up! It is draped in a Confederate flag; and his hat, his bull whip, and his pistol, have been fastened to the lid in appropriate places.)*

Gently, gently. Put kindness in your fingers. He was a man—despite his own example. Take up his bones.

(The **Pallbearers** *slowly carry the upright coffin across the stage.)*

Tonight, my friends—I find, in being black, a thing of beauty: a joy; a strength; a secret cup of gladness; a native land in neither time nor place—

a native land in every Negro face; Be loyal to yourselves: your skin; your hair; your lips, your southern speech, your laughing kindness—are Negro kingdoms, vast as any other! Accept in full the sweetness of your blackness—not wishing to be red, nor white, nor yellow: nor any other race, or face, but this. Farewell, my deep and Africanic brothers, be brave, keep freedom in the family, do what you can for the white folks, and write me in care of the post office. Now, may the Constitution of the United States go with you; the Declaration of Independence stand by you; the Bill of Rights protect you; and the State Commission Against Discrimination keep the eyes of the law upon you, henceforth, now and forever. Amen.

Curtain

Copies of this play, in individual paper covered acting editions, are available from Samuel French, Inc., 25 W. 45th St., New York, N. Y. or 7623 Sunset Blvd., Hollywood, Calif. or in Canada Samuel French, (Canada) Ltd., 26 Grenville St., Toronto, Canada.

A ONE-ACT PLAY

FUNNYHOUSE OF A NEGRO

by Adrienne Kennedy

Adrienne Kennedy *(1931-   )*

One of the most arresting and vivid of the new black playwrights, Adrienne Kennedy, whose work has been described as "introspective" and "grimly imaginative," was born in Pittsburgh, Pennsylvania. She spent most of her early life in Cleveland, Ohio, where her mother was a school teacher and her father was a social worker. Upon graduation from high school she attended The Ohio State University at Columbus where she found a situation so hostile to the needs of black students that she became largely indifferent to her academic pursuits. Changing her major several times, she was finally graduated with a degree in education. As a child, the author tells us, she felt "small, ugly, and inferior. . . ." The only time that she felt at ease was when she was alone and writing. She wrote incessantly, she says, from the time that she was eleven. In 1969 Adrienne Kennedy left New York to live and work in London. She states that she "had always been attracted to the great tradition of English writers and the European way of life." She is now back in the United States.

Miss Kennedy has written two novels, and has tried her hand at poetry and short fiction. Her plays include *Funnyhouse of a Negro* (1962), *The Owl Answers* (1963), *A Lesson in a Dead Language* (1964), *A Rat's Mass* (1965), and *A Beast's Story (1966)*. She has adapted two of John Lennon's works for the theater, *In His Own Write* and *A Spaniard in the Works,* performed in London at the National Theatre at the Old Vic, in 1967, under the title *THE LENNON PLAY.* She won critical acclaim for two one-act plays, *Cities in Bezique,* produced by the New York Shakespeare Festival in 1969. *Funnyhouse of a Negro* won an Obie Distinguished Play Award in 1964. Miss Kennedy has received two Rockefeller grants and, in 1968, a Guggenheim Award in creative writing for the theater. A new play, *Sun,* commissioned in London by the Royal Court's experimental theater "Upstairs at the Court," is scheduled for production in the near future.

189

INTRODUCTION

Eschewing realism and naturalism for the surrealistic and expressionistic modes of the presentation of her ideas, Adrienne Kennedy's *Funnyhouse of a Negro* is avant garde theater, hallucinatory and ironic—somewhat like Genet. Although she cites Tennessee Williams as among those who have most strongly influenced her thinking about the theater, she cites Edward Albee as representing a major turning point in her career. Mr. Albee was the first to give Miss Kennedy the encouragement and recognition that she needed when she was a member of his Playwriting Workshop at the Circle in the Square. And it was at the Workshop that *Funnyhouse* got its first non-professional presentation.

Funnyhouse of a Negro opened off Broadway at the East End Theater January 14, 1964, under the aegis of the Theatre 1964, headed by Edward Albee, Richard Barr, and Clinton Wilder. Billie Allen, Ellen Holly, Cynthia Belgrave, and Gus Williams were in the leading roles. Of the play, Richard Watts, Jr. could say, "It leaves no doubt that Edward Albee and his associates in Theatre 1964 have found in Miss Kennedy an original dramatist whose voice demanded to be heard." But the play was clearly ahead of its time. When closing threatened after only 22 performances, its run was briefly extended by money advanced by Isabel Eberstadt, Ogden Nash's daughter.

Miss Kennedy is unquestionably a writer of considerable penetration with a decided gift for poetic characterization and dialogue and with a deft sense of theater values and experimental dramaturgy. A grimly imaginative and self-searching play, *Funnyhouse of a Negro* is sheer theater in which the mind and spiritual conflicts of a young black woman are brilliantly and painfully explored.

A short work in one act—it takes only some fifty minutes to play—*Funnyhouse of a Negro* is an agonizing picture of the inner torment of a young student who cannot bear the pressures of being black in America. The play gives expression to an hour of anguish in the mind of a sensitive Negro girl, Sarah, whose dreams lead to madness and eventual suicide. The characters include Queen Victoria, the Duchess of Hapsburg, Patrice Lumumba, and Jesus. The title of the play comes from an amusement park in Cleveland where there was a Funnyhouse with two big white laughing figures bobbing back and forth on each side of the entrance. "My brother and I used to hang around there a lot," the author tells us. "It always seemed to me that the white world was doing this, ridiculing the Negro." In the play on either side of the stage are a white landlady and a white boy (Raymond) made up to look like the amusement park figures. All the characters onstage except the girl and the father (Patrice Lumumba) are in white face and represent various sides of the heroine, as the contrapuntal repetitions in the dialogue from character to character indicate.

Where method is involved, Miss Kennedy in her plays is not concerned, in the traditional sense, with plot, character, or event, but with impressions and images. "All the images remain," she says, and her plays abound in what can be called "overlay" with imagistic fragments of memory, and echoes that appear and fade away only to recur and finally exist as a montage of inconclusive images. The play is a brilliant and purposively troubled orchestration of repeated motifs and symbols that emerges as a theatrical tapestry that is ornately rich and imaginative in the intricacy of its ultimate design.

The play is replete with death symbols, and its prolonged nightmare quality suggests the death of the psyche as rendered through the fragmented fantasies of the protagonist, preoccupied as she is with the myriad problems of love and identity, her relationships with the parental figures in her life, the world of color and its meaning, the nature of truth, and her relation to God. The setting, which is expressionistic and suggestive rather than literal, reflects various levels of the leading character's consciousness: it includes the Funnyhouse, the Queen's chamber, the student's room in a brownstone boarding house on New York's West Side, the chandelier ballroom of the Duchess of Hapsburg, and the jungle.

Attention should be paid to the bird symbolism—the ravens, the white doves, the owl—the flower symbols, and the central symbol of the falling kinky hair. The owl is, of course, the wise, solitary bird who cries out in the night "Who-o-o. . . ." The big questions for the Negro in his American solitude and isolation are "Who?" or "What am I?" "What is my destiny?" "In what course lies the proper road for self-discovery and self-development?" Assimilation, integration, religion, black nationalism, the new African nationalism, and Pan-Africanism are commented upon directly and indirectly in the play. The central image or symbol of the falling kinky hair, among other things, can be seen as the demonstration of externally induced self-hatred and a resultant will to self-destruction. The student's suicide at the end of the play can be seen as the result of her inability to accept her blackness and all that it implies. Incoherent and chaotic on the surface, *Funnyhouse of a Negro* is a symbolic dream play of subtle depth and intricacy that upon study reveals itself as a highly coherent work of art.

Funnyhouse of a Negro

CHARACTERS

Sarah, *Negro*
Duchess of Hapsburg, *One of Herselves*
Queen Victoria, *One of Herselves*
Patrice Lumumba, *One of Herselves*
Jesus, *One of Herselves*
The Mother
Landlady, *Funnylady*
Raymond, *Funnyman*

Beginning: *Before the closed curtain a woman dressed in a white nightgown walks across the stage carrying before her a bald head. She moves as one in a trance and is mumbling something inaudible to herself. She appears faceless, wearing a yellow whitish mask over her face, with no apparent eyes. Her hair is wild, straight and black and falls to her waist. As she moves, holding her hands before her, she gives the effect of one in a dream. She crosses the stage from right to left. Before she has barely vanished, the curtain opens. It is a white satin curtain of a cheap material and a ghastly white, a material that brings to mind the interior of a cheap casket; parts of it are frayed and it looks as if it has been gnawed by rats.*

The scene: Two women are sitting in what appears to be a queen's chamber. It is set in the middle of the stage in a strong white light, while the rest of the stage is in strong unnatural blackness. The quality of the white light is unreal and ugly. The queen's chamber consists of a dark monumental bed resembling an ebony tomb, a low dark chandelier with candles and wine-colored walls. Flying about are great black ravens. **Queen Victoria** is standing before her bed, holding a small mirror in her hand. On the white pillow of her bed is a dark indistinguishable object. The **Duchess of Hapsburg** is standing at the foot of her bed. Her back is to us as is the Queen's. Throughout the entire scene they do not move. Both women are dressed in royal gowns of white, a white similar to the white of the curtain, the material cheap satin. Their headpieces are white and of a net that falls over their faces. From beneath both their headpieces springs a headful of wild kinky hair. Although in this scene we do not see their faces, they look exactly alike and will wear masks or be made up to appear a whitish yellow. It is an alabaster face, the skin drawn tightly over the high cheekbones, great dark eyes that seem gouged out of the head, a high forehead, a full red mouth and a head of frizzy hair. If the characters do not wear a mask, the face must be highly powdered and possess a hard expressionless quality and a stillness as in the fact of death.

(We hear a knocking.)

Victoria:

(Listening to the knocking.)

It is my father. He is arriving again for the night.

(The **Duchess** makes no reply.)

He comes through the jungle to find me. He never tires of his journey.

Duchess: How dare he enter the castle, he who is the darkest of them all, the darkest one. My mother looked like a white woman, hair as straight as any white woman's. And at least I am yellow, but he is black, the blackest one of them all. I hoped he was dead. Yet he still comes through the jungle to find me.

(The knocking is louder.)

Victoria: He never tires of the journey, does he, Duchess?

(Looking at herself in the mirror.)

Duchess: How dare he enter the castle of Queen Victoria Regina, Monarch of England. It is because of him that my mother died. The wild black beast put his hands on her. She died.

Victoria: Why does he keep returning? He keeps returning forever, coming back ever and keeps coming back forever. He is my father.

Duchess: He is a black Negro.

Victoria: He is my father. I am tied to the black Negro. He came when I was a child in the south, before I was born he haunted my conception, diseased by birth.

Duchess: Killed my mother.

Victoria: My mother was the light. She was the lightest one. She looked like a white woman.

Duchess: We are tied to him unless, of course, he should die.

Victoria: But he is dead.

Duchess: And he keeps returning.

(The knocking is louder.)

                                                                    Blackout

The lights go out in the chamber. Onto the stage from the left comes the figure in the white nightgown carrying the bald head. This time we hear her speak.

Mother: Black man, black man, I never should have let a black man put his hands on me. The wild black beast raped me and now my skull is shining.

(She disappears to the right. Now the light is focused on a single white square wall that is to the left of the stage that is suspended and stands alone, of about five feet in dimension and width. It stands with the *narrow part facing the audience. A character steps through. She is a faceless dark character with a hangman's rope about her neck and red blood on the part that would be her face. She is the* **Negro**. *On first glance she might be a young person but at a closer look the impression of an ancient character is given. The most noticeable aspect of her looks is her wild kinky hair, part of which is missing. It is a ragged head with a crown which the* **Negro** *carries in her hand. She is dressed in black. She steps slowly through the wall, stands still before it and begins her monologue.)*

Negro: Part of the time I live with Raymond, part of the time with God, Prince Charles and Albert Saxe Coburg. I live in my room. It is a small room on the top floor of a brownstone in the West Nineties in New York, a room filled with my dark old volumes, a narrow bed and on the wall old photographs of castles and monarchs of England. It is also Victoria's chamber, Queen Victoria Regina's. Partly because it is consumed by a gigantic plaster statue of Queen Victoria, who is my idol, and partly for other reasons; three steps that I contrived out of boards lead to the statue which I have placed opposite the door as I enter the room. It is a sitting figure, a replica of one in London, and a thing of astonishing whiteness. I found it in a dusty shop on Morningside Heights. Raymond says it is a thing of terror, possessing the quality of nightmares, suggesting large and probable deaths. And of course he is right. When I am the Duchess of Hapsburg, I sit opposite Victoria in my headpiece and we talk. The other time I wear the dress of a student, dark clothes and dark stockings. Victoria always wants me to tell her of whiteness. She wants me to tell her of a royal world where everything and everyone is white and there are no unfortunate black ones. For as we of royal blood know, black is evil and has been from the beginning. Even before my mother's hair started to fall out. Before she was raped by a wild black beast. Black was evil.

When I am not the Duchess of Hapsburg I am myself. As for myself, I long to become even a more pallid Negro than I am now, pallid like Negroes on the covers of American Negro magazines; soulless, educated and irreligious. I want to possess no moral value, particularly value as to my being. I want not to be. I ask nothing except anonymity.

I am an English major, as my mother was when she went to school in Atlanta. My father majored in social work. I am graduated from a city college and have occasional work in libraries, but mostly spend my days preoccupied with the placement and geometric position of words on paper. I write poetry, filling white page after white page with imitations of Edith Sitwell. It is my dream to live in rooms with European antiques and my Queen Victoria, photographs of Roman ruins, walls of books, a piano, oriental carpets, and to eat my meals on a white glass table. I will visit my friends' apartments which will contain books, photographs of Roman ruins, pianos and oriental carpets. My friends will be white. I need them as an embankment to keep me from reflecting too much upon the fact that I am a Negro. For, like all educated Negroes—out of life and death essential—I find it necessary to maintain a stark fortress against recognition of myself. My white friends like myself will be shrewd, intellectual and anxious for death. Anyone's death. I will mistrust them, as I do myself. But if I had not wavered in my opinion of myself then my hair would never have fallen out. And if my hair hadn't fallen out, I wouldn't have bludgeoned my father's head with an ebony mask.

In appearance I am good-looking in a boring way, no glaring Negroid features, medium nose, medium mouth and pale yellow skin. My one defect is that I have a head of frizzy hair, unmistakably Negro kinky hair; and is indisguisable. I would like to lie and say I love Raymond. But I do not. He is a poet and is Jewish. He is very interested in Negroes.

(The **Negro** *stands by the wall and throughout her following speech, the following characters come through the wall, disappearing off into the varying directions in the darkened night of the stage—***Duchess, Queen Victoria, Jesus, Patrice Lumumba. Jesus** *is a hunchback, yellow-skinned dwarf, dressed in white rags and sandals.* **Patrice Lumumba** *is a black man. His head appears to be split in two with blood and tissue in eyes. He carries an ebony mask.)*

The characters are myself; the Duchess of Hapsburg, Queen Victoria Regina, Jesus, Patrice Lumumba. The rooms are my rooms; a Hapsburg chamber, a chamber in a Victorian castle, the hotel where I killed my father, the jungle. These are the places myselves exist in. I know no places. That is I cannot believe in places. To believe in places is to know hope and to know the emotion of hope is to know beauty. It links us across a horizon and connects us to the world. I find there are no places, only my funny-house. Streets are rooms, cities are rooms, eternal rooms. I try to create a space for myselves in cities. New York, the midwest, a southern town but it becomes a lie. I try to give myselves a logical relationship but that too is a lie. For relationships was one of my last religions. I clung loyally to the lie of relationships, again and again seeking to establish a connection between my characters. Jesus is Victoria's son. Mother loved my father before her hair fell out. A loving relationship exists between myself and Jesus but they are lies. You will assume I am trifling with you, teasing your intellect, dealing in subtleties, denying connection then suddenly at a point reveal a startling heartbreaking connection. You are wrong. For the days are past when there are places and characters with connections with themes as in stories you pick up on the shelves of public libraries.

Too, there is no theme. No statements, I might borrow a statement, struggle to fabricate a theme, borrow one from my contemporaries, renew one from the master, hawkishly scan other stories searching for statements, consider the theme then deceive myself that I held such a statement within me, refusing to accept the fact that a statement has to come from an ordered force. I might try to join horizontal elements such as dots on a horizontal line, or create a centrifugal force, or create causes and effects so that they would equal a quantity but it would be a lie. For the statement is the characters and the characters are myself.

Blackout

Then to the right front of the stage comes the white light. It goes to a suspended stairway. At the foot of it stands the **Landlady**. *She is a tall, thin woman dressed in a black hat with red and appears to be talking to someone in a suggested open doorway in a corridor of a rooming house. She laughs like a mad character in a funnyhouse throughout her speech.*

Landlady:

(Looking up the stairway.)

Ever since her father hung himself in a Harlem hotel when Patrice Lumumba was murdered, she hides in her room. Each night she repeats; he keeps returning. How dare he enter the castle walls, he who is the darkest of them all, the darkest one. My mother looked like a white woman, hair as straight as any white woman's. And I am yellow but he, he is black, the blackest one of them all. I hoped he was dead. Yet still he comes through the jungle.

I tell her: Sarah, honey, the man hung himself. It's not your blame. But, no, she stares at me: No, Mrs. Conrad, he did not hang himself, that is only the way they understand it, they do, but the truth is that I bludgeoned his head with an ebony skull that he carries about with him. Wherever he goes, he carries out black masks and heads.

She's suffering so till her hair has fallen out. But then she did always hide herself in that room with the walls of books and her statues. I always did know she thought she was somebody else, a Queen or something, somebody else.

Blackout

Funnyman's *place. The next scene is enacted with the* **Duchess** *and* **Raymond**. **Raymond's** *place is suggested as being above the* **Negro's** *room, and is etched in with a prop of blinds and a bed . . . behind the blinds are mirrors and when the blinds are opened and closed by* **Raymond**, *this is revealed.* **Raymond** *turns out to be the* **funnyman** *of the funnyhouse. He is tall, white and ghostly thin and dressed in a black shirt and black trousers in attire suggesting an artist. Throughout his dialogue he laughs. The* **Duchess** *is partially disrobed and it is implied from their attitudes of physical intimacy—he is standing and she is sitting before him clinging to his leg. During the scene,* **Raymond** *keeps opening and closing the blinds. His face has black sores on it and he is wearing a black hat. Throughout the scene he strikes her as in affection when he speaks to her.*

Duchess:

(Carrying a red paper bag.)

My father is arriving, and what am I to do?

(*Raymond* walks about the place opening the blinds and laughing.)

Funnyman: He is arriving from Africa, is he not?

Duchess: Yes, yes, he is arriving from Africa.

Funnyman: I always knew your father was African.

Duchess: He is an African who lives in the jungle. He is an African who has always lived in the jungle. Yes, he is a nigger who is an African, who is a missionary teacher and is now dedicating his life to the erection of a Christian mission in the middle of the jungle. He is a black man.

Funnyman: He is a black man who shot himself when they murdered Patrice Lumumba.

Duchess:
(*Goes on wildly.*)
Yes, my father is a black man who went to Africa years ago as a missionary teacher, got mixed up in politics, was reviled and is now devoting his foolish life to the erection of a Christian mission in the middle of the jungle in one of those newly freed countries. Hide me.
(*Clinging to his knees.*)
Hide me here so the nigger will not find me.

Funnyman:
(*Laughing.*)
Your father is in the jungle dedicating his life to the erection of a Christian mission.

Duchess: Hide me here so the jungle will not find me. Hide me.

Funnyman: Isn't it cruel of you?

Duchess: Hide me from the jungle.

Funnyman: Isn't it cruel?

Duchess: No, no.

Funnyman: Isn't it cruel of you?

Duchess: No.
(*She screams and opens her red paper bag and draws from it her fallen hair. It is a great mass of dark wild. She holds it up to him. He appears not to understand. He stares at it.*)
It is my hair.
(*He continues to stare at her.*)
When I awakened this morning it had fallen out, not all of it but a mass from the crown of my head that lay on the center of my pillow. I rose and in the greyish winter morning light of my room I stood staring at my hair, dazed by my sleeplessness, still shaken by nightmares of my mother. Was it true, yes, it was my hair. In the mirror I saw that, although my hair remained on both sides, clearly on the crown and at my temples my scalp was bare.
(*She removes her black crown and shows him the top of her head.*)

Raymond (Funnyman):
(*Staring at her.*)
Why would your hair fall out? Is it because you are cruel? How could a black father haunt you so.

Duchess: He haunted my very conception. He was a black wild beast who raped my mother.

FUNNYHOUSE OF A NEGRO 197

Raymond (Funnyman): He is a black Negro.
> *(Laughing.)*

Duchess: Ever since I can remember he's been in a nigger pose of agony. He is the wilderness. He speaks niggerly, grovelling about wanting to touch me with his black hand.

Funnyman: How tormented and cruel you are.

Duchess:
> *(As if not comprehending.)*

Yes, yes, the man's dark, very dark skinned. He is the darkest, my father is the darkest, my mother is the lightest. I am between. But my father is the darkest. My father is a nigger who drives me to misery. Any time spent with him evolves itself into suffering. He is a black man and the wilderness.

Funnyman: How tormented and cruel you are.

Duchess: He is a nigger.

Funnyman: And your mother, where is she?

Duchess: She is in the asylum. In the asylum bald. Her father was a white man. And she is the asylum.

> *(He takes her in his arms. She responds wildly.)*

Blackout

*Knocking is heard, it continues, then somewhere near the center of stage a figure appears in the darkness, a large dark faceless **Man** carrying a mask in his hand.*

Man: It begins with the disaster of my hair. I awaken. My hair has fallen out, not all of it, but a mass from the crown of my head that lies on the center of my white pillow. I arise and in the greyish winter morning light of my room I stand staring at my hair, dazed by sleeplessness, still shaken by nightmares of my mother. Is it true? Yes. It is my hair. In the mirror I see that although my hair remains on both sides, clearly on the crown and at my temples my scalp is bare. And in my sleep I had been visited by my bald crazy mother who comes to me crying, calling me to her bedside. She lies on the bed watching the strands of her own hair fall out. Her hair fell out after she married and she spent her days lying on the bed watching the strands fall from her scalp, covering the bedspread until she was bald and admitted to the hospital. Black man, black man, my mother says I never should have let a black man put his hands on me. She comes to me, her bald skull shining. Black diseases, Sarah, she says. Black diseases. I run. She follows me, her bald skull shining. That is the beginning.

> *(Several **Women** with white nightgowns on, waistlength black hair, all identical, emerge from the sides of the stage and run into the darkness, toward him shouting—black man, black man. They are carrying bald heads.)*

Blackout

Queen's Chamber. *Her hair is in a small pile on the bed and in a small pile on the floor, several other piles of hair are scattered about her and her white gown is covered with fallen out hair.*

Queen Victoria *acts out the following scene: She awakens (in pantomime) and discovers her hair has fallen. It is on her pillow. She arises and stands at the side of the bed with her back towards us staring at her hair. She opens the red paper bag that she is carrying and takes out her hair, attempting to place it back on her head (for unlike* **Victoria**, *she does not wear her headpiece now). Suddenly the women in white gowns come running from the rear of the stage carrying their skulls before them screaming.*

(The unidentified man returns out of the darkness and speaks. He carries the mask.)

Man (Patrice Lumumba): I am a nigger of two generations. I am Patrice Lumumba. I am a nigger of two generations. I am the black shadow that haunted my mother's conception. I belong to the generation born at the turn of the century and the generation born before the depression. At present I reside in New York City in a brownstone in the West Nineties. I am an English major at a city college. My nigger father majored in social work, so did my mother. I am a student and have occasional work in libraries. But mostly I spend my vile days preoccupied with the placement and geometric position of words on paper. I write poetry filling white page after white page with imitations of Sitwell. It is my vile dream to live in rooms with European antiques and my statues of Queen Victoria, photographs of Roman ruins, walls of books, a piano and oriental carpets and to eat my meals on a white glass table. It is also my nigger dreams for my friends to eat their meals on white glass tables and to live in rooms with European antiques, photographs of Roman ruins, pianos and oriental carpets. My friends will be white. I need them as an embankment to keep me from reflecting too much upon the fact that I am Patrice Lumumba who haunted my mother's conception. They are necessary for me to maintain recognition against myself. My white friends, like myself, will be shrewd intellectuals and anxious for death. Anyone's death. I will despise them as I do myself. For if I did not despise myself then my hair would not have fallen and if my hair had not fallen then I would not have bludgeoned my father's face with the ebony mask.

(Then another wall is dropped, larger than the first one was. This one is near the front of the stage facing thus. Throughout the following monologue the characters **Duchess, Victoria, Jesus** *go back and forth. As they go in their backs are to us but the* **Negro** *faces us speaking.)*

Negro: I always dreamed of a day when my mother would smile at me. My father—his mother wanted him to be Christ. From the beginning in the lamp of their dark room she said—I want you to be Jesus, to walk in Genesis and save the race. You must return to Africa, find revelation in the midst of golden savannas, nim and white frankopenny trees, white stallions roaming under a blue sky, you must walk with a white dove and heal the race, heal the misery, take us off the cross. She stared at him anguished in the kerosene light . . . at dawn he watched her rise, kill a hen for him to eat at breakfast, then go to work down at the big house till dusk, till she died.

His father told him the race was no damn good. He hated his father and adores his mother. His mother didn't want him to marry my mother and sent a dead chicken to the wedding. I DON'T want you marrying that child, she wrote, she's not good enough for you, I want you to go to Africa. When they first married they lived in New York.

Then they went to Africa where my mother fell out of love with my father. She didn't want him to save the black race and spent her days combing her hair. She would not let him touch her in their wedding bed and called him black. He is black of skin with dark eyes and a great dark square brow. Then in Africa he started to drink and came home drunk one night and raped my mother. The child from the union is me. I clung to my mother. Long after she went to the asylum I wove long dreams of her beauty, her straight hair and fair skin and gray eyes, so identical to mine. How it anguished him. I turned from him, nailing him to the cross, he said, dragging him through grass and nailing him on a cross until he bled. He pleaded with me to help him find Genesis, search for Genesis in the minds of golden savannas, nim and white frankopenny trees and white stallions roaming under a blue sky, help him search for the white dove; he wanted the black man to make a pure statement, he wanted the black man to rise from colonialism. But I sat in the room with my mother, sat by her bedside and helped her comb her straight black hair and wove long dreams of her beauty. She had long since began to curse the place and spoke of herself trapped in blackness. She preferred the company of night owls. Only at night did she rise, walking in the garden among the trees with the owls. When I spoke to her she saw I was a black man's child and she preferred speaking to owls. Nights my father came from his school in the village struggling to embrace me. But I fled and hid under my mother's bed while she screamed of remorse. Her hair was falling badly and after a while we had to return to this country.

He tried to hang himself once. After my mother went to the asylum he had hallucinations, his mother threw a dead chicken at him, his father laughed and said the race was no damn good, my mother appeared in her nightgown screaming she had trapped herself in blackness. No white doves flew. He had left Africa and was again in New York. We lived in Harlem and no white doves flew. Sarah, Sarah, he would say to me, the soldiers are coming and a cross they are placing high on a tree and are dragging me through the grass and nailing me upon the cross. My blood is gushing. I wanted to live in Genesis in the midst of golden savannas, nim and white frankopenny trees and white stallions roaming under a blue sky. I wanted to walk with a white dove. I wanted to be a Christian. Now I am Judas, I betrayed my mother. I sent your mother to the asylum. I created a yellow child who hates me. And he tried to hang himself in a Harlem hotel.

Blackout

(A bald head is dropped on a string. We hear laughing.)

Duchess's Place: *The next scene is done in the* **Duchess of Hapsburg's** *place which is a chandelier ballroom with snow falling, a black and white marble floor, a bench decorated with white flowers, all of this can be made of obviously fake materials as they would be in a funny-house. The* **Duchess** *is wearing a white dress and as in the previous scene a white headpiece with her kinky hair springing out from under it. In the scene are the* **Duchess** *and* **Jesus**. **Jesus** *enters the room which is at first dark, then suddenly brilliant, he starts to cry out at the* **Duchess** *who is seated on a bench under the chandelier, and pulls his hair from the red paper bag holding it up for the* **Duchess** *to see.*

Jesus: My hair!
> *(The* **Duchess** *does not speak,* **Jesus** *again screams.)*

My hair.
> *(Holding the hair up, waiting for a reaction from the* **Duchess**.*)*

Duchess:
> *(As if oblivious.)*

I have something I must show you.
> *(She goes quickly to shutters and darkens the room, returning standing before* **Jesus**. *She then slowly removes her headpiece and from under it takes a mass of her hair.)*

When I awakened I found it fallen out, not all of it but a mass that lay on my white pillow. I could see, although my hair hung down at the sides, clearly on my white scalp it was missing.
> *(Her baldness is identical to* **Jesus's**.*)*

Blackout

The light comes back up. They are both sitting on the bench examining each other's hair, running it through their fingers, then slowly the **Duchess** *disappears behind the shutters and returns with a long red comb. She sits on the bench next to* **Jesus** *and starts to comb her remaining hair over her baldness. This is done slowly.* **Jesus** *then takes the comb and proceeds to do the same to the* **Duchess of Hapsburg's** *hair. After they finish they place the* **Duchess's** *headpiece back on and we can see the strands of their hair falling to the floor.* **Jesus** *then lays down across the bench while the* **Duchess** *walks back and forth, the knocking does not cease. They speak in unison as the* **Duchess** *walks and* **Jesus** *lays on the bench in the falling snow, staring at the ceiling.*

Duchess and Jesus:
> *(Their hair is falling more now, they are both hideous.)*

My father isn't going to let us alone.

(Knocking.)

Our father isn't going to let us alone, our father is the darkest of us all, my mother was the fairest, I am in between, but my father is the darkest of them all. He is a black man. Our father is the darkest of them all. He is a black man. My father is a dead man.

(Then they suddenly look up at each other and scream, the lights go to their heads and we see that they are totally bald. There is a knocking. Lights go to the stairs and the **Landlady**.*)*

Landlady: He wrote to her saying he loved her and asked for forgiveness. He begged her to take him off the cross. (He had dreamed she would.) Stop them from tormenting him, the one with the chicken and his cursing father. Her mother's hair fell out, the race's hair fell out because he left Africa, he said. He had tried to save them. She must embrace him. He said his existence depended on her embrace. He wrote her from Africa where he is creating his Christian center in the jungle and that is why he came here. I know that he wanted her to return there with him and not desert the race. He came to see her once before he tried to hang himself, appearing in the corridor of my apartment. I had let him in. I found him sitting on a bench in the hallway. He put out his hand to her, tried to take her in his arms, crying out—Forgiveness, Sarah. Is it that you will never forgive me for being black? I know you were a child of torment. But forgiveness. That was before his breakdown. Then, he wrote her and repeated that his mother hoped he would be Christ but he failed. He had married his mother because he could not resist the light. Yet, his mother from the beginning in the kerosene lamp of their dark rooms in Georgia said—I want you to be Jesus, to walk in Genesis and save the race, return to Africa, find revelation in the black. He went away.

But Easter morning, she got to feeling badly and went into Harlem to see him; the streets were filled with vendors selling lillies. He had checked out of that hotel. When she arrived back at my brownstone he was here, dressed badly, rather drunk. I had let him in again. He sat on a bench in the dark hallway, put out his hand to her, trying to take her in his arms, crying out—Forgiveness, Sarah. Forgiveness for my being black, Sarah. I know you are a child of torment. I know on dark winter afternoons you sat alone, weaving stories of your mother's beauty. But, Sarah, answer me, don't turn away, Sarah. Forgive my blackness. She would not answer. He put out his hand to her. She ran past him on the stairs, left him there with his hands out to me, repeating his past, saying his mother hoped he would be Christ. From the beginning in the kerosene lamp of their dark rooms, she said—Wally, I want you to be Jesus, to walk in Genesis and save the race. You must return to Africa, Wally, find revelation in the midst of golden savannas, nim and white frankopenny trees and white stallions roaming under a blue sky. Wally, you must find the white dove and heal the pain of the race, heal the misery of the black man, Wally, take us off the cross, Wally. In the kerosene light she stared at him anguished from her old Negro face . . . but she ran past him leaving him. And now he is dead, she says, now he is dead. He left Africa and now Patrice Lumumba is dead.

*(The next scene is enacted back in the **Duchess of Hapsburg's** place. **Jesus** is still in the **Duchess's** chamber, apparently he has fallen asleep and we see him as he awakes with the **Duchess** by his side, and sits here as in a trance. He rises terrified and speaks.)*

Jesus: Through my apocalypses and my raging sermons I have tried so to escape him, through God Almighty I have tried to escape being black.

(He then appears to rouse himself from his thoughts and calls.)

Duchess, Duchess.

*(He looks about for her, there is no answer. He gets up slowly, walks back into the darkness and there we see that she is hanging on the chandelier, her bald head suddenly drops to the floor and she falls upon **Jesus**. He screams.)*

I am going to Africa and kill this black man named Patrice Lumumba. Why? Because all my life I believed my Holy Father to be God, but now I know that my father is a black man. I have no fear for whatever I do, I will do in the name of God, I will do in the name of Albert Saxe Godburg, in the name of Victoria, Queen Victoria Regina, the monarch of England, I will.

Blackout

Next scene. In the jungle, red run, flying things, wild black grass. The effect of the jungle is that it, unlike the other scenes, is over the entire stage. In time this is the longest scene in the play and is played the slowest as the slow, almost standstill stages of a dream. By lighting the desired effect would be—suddenly the jungle has overgrown the chambers and all the other places with a violence and a dark brightness, a grim yellowness.

Jesus is the first to appear in the center of the jungle darkness. Unlike in previous scenes, he has a nimbus above his head. As they each successively appear, they all too have nimbuses atop their heads in a manner to suggest that they are saviours.

Jesus: I always believed my father to be God.

*(Suddenly they all appear in various parts of the jungle. **Patrice Lumumba,** the **Duchess, Victoria,** wandering about speaking at once. Their speeches are mixed and repeated by one another.)*

All: He never tires of the journey, he who is the darkest one, the darkest one of them all. My mother looked like a white woman, hair as straight as any white woman's. I am yellow but he is black, the darkest of us all. How I hoped he was dead, yet he never tires of the journey. It was because of him that my mother died because she let a black man put his hands on her. Why does he keep returning? He keeps returning forever, keeps returning and returning and he is my father. He is a black Negro. They told me my father

FUNNYHOUSE OF A NEGRO 203

was God and my father is black. He is my father. I am tied to a black Negro. He returned when I lived in the south back in the twenties, when I was a child, he returned. Before I was born at the turn of the century, he haunted my conception, diseased my birth . . . killed my mother. He killed the light. My mother was the lightest one. I am bound to him unless, of course, he should die.

But he is dead.

And he keeps returning. Then he is not dead.

Then he is not dead.

Yes, he is dead, but dead he comes knocking at my door.

> (This is repeated several times, finally reaching a loud pitch and then all rushing about the grass. They stop and stand perfectly still. All speaking tensely at various times in a chant.)

I see him. The black ugly thing is sitting in his hallway, surrounded by his ebony masks, surrounded by the blackness of himself. My mother comes into the room. He is there with his hand out to me, groveling, saying—Forgiveness, Sarah, is it that you will never forgive me for being black.

Forgiveness, Sarah. I know you are a nigger of torment.

Why? Christ would not rape anyone.

You will never forgive me for being black.

Wild beast. Why did you rape my mother? Black beast, Christ would not rape anyone.

He is in grief from that black anguished face of his. Then at once the room will grow bright and my mother will come toward me smiling while I stand before his face and bludgeon him with an ebony head.

Forgiveness, Sarah, I know you are a nigger of torment.

> Silence—Victory: Then they suddenly begin to laugh and shout as though they are in. They continue for some minutes running about laughing and shouting.

Blackout

Another wall drops. There is a white plaster of **Queen Victoria** *which represents the* **Negro's** *room in the brownstone, the room appears near the staircases highly lit and small. The main prop is the statue but a bed could be suggested. The figure of* **Victoria** *is a sitting figure, one of astonishing repulsive whiteness, possessing the quality of nightmares and terror.* **Sarah's** *room could be further suggested by dusty volumes of books and old yellowed walls.*

> *The Negro,* **Sarah**, *is standing perfectly still, we hear the knocking, the lights come on quickly, her father's black figures with bludgeoned hands rush upon her, the lights black and we see her hanging in the room.*

> *Lights come on the laughing* **Landlady**. *And at the same time remain on the hanging figure of the* **Negro**.

Landlady: The poor bitch has hung herself.

(**Funnyman, Raymond,** *appears from his room at the commotion.*)

Landlady: The poor bitch has hung herself.

Raymond:

(Observing her hanging figure.)

She was a funny little liar.

Landlady:

(Informing him.)

Her father hung himself in a Harlem hotel when Patrice Lumumba died.

Raymond: She was a funny little liar.

Landlady: Her father hung himself in a Harlem hotel when Patrice Lumumba died.

Raymond: Her father never hung himself in a Harlem hotel when Patrice Lumumba was murdered.

I know the man. He is a doctor, married to a white whore. He lives in the city in a room with European antiques, photographs of Roman ruins, walls of books and oriental carpets. Her father is a nigger who eats his meals on a white glass table.

End

DUTCHMAN

by LeRoi Jones

LeRoi Jones *(1934-   )*

LeRoi Jones, who can be described as the instigator of the new revolutionary black theater, and as an originating force in the development of new black thought and literature, generally, was born in Newark, New Jersey. His father was a postal supervisor and his mother a social worker. As a boy in Newark, he thought of entering the ministry, the most respected profession in the community. Upon graduation from Barringer High School, he began his college work at the Newark Campus of Rutgers University where he remained for only one year because he felt like an outsider. His college work was completed at Howard University in Washington, D.C., where he received the B.A. degree in English in 1954. After a stint in the Air Force (1954-1957) which took him to Puerto Rico, Africa, the Middle East, and Europe, he continued his studies at Columbia and the New School for Social Research where he received the M.A. degree in German Literature. He has taught at several universities including the New School and Columbia. A writer of great versatility, he is a poet, novelist, essayist, musicologist, critic, writer of short stories, an editor, as well as a dramatist.

Jones's progress in the arts and in his social and political thinking represents a movement from the liberal integrationist stance of his early East Village days in New York to that of his present militant black revolutionist position. This development can be traced in his poetry, in his works on music, in his social essays, and in his fiction, but it is perhaps nowhere so clearly evidenced as in his work for the theater. His plays include a number of brief, incisive works such as *Baptism, The 8th Ditch, Home on the Range,* and *Arm Yrself or Harm Yrself,* and the more important plays of 1964 and after, including *Dutchman, The Slave, The Toilet, Black Mass* and *The Slave Ship.*

In 1965, Jones left the downtown theater in New York to center his attention upon Harlem where he founded the Black Arts Repertory Theater and School in a brownstone house on 130th Street, off Lenox Avenue. Here he revived *Dutchman* for black audiences and presented two new one acters, *J-e-l-l-o* and *Experimental Death Unit #1*. Engaged in a controversy that involved the Harlem Youth Unlimited Opportunities and Associated Community Teams, the anti-poverty program known as HARYOU-ACT, the Black Arts Theater came under attack for its policy of not admitting white patrons. Jones defended his position on the grounds of limited seating capacity—the theater could only seat ninety people—and his desire to provide black theater to black people by black artists in black Harlem. The Black Arts Theater survived only seven months; Jones moved from New York to Newark where he became the founder of the Spirit House Movers and Players, and continued his work in the militant wing of the civil rights movement. Jones was represented in 1969 by *Great Goodness of Life: A Coon Show*, an off-Broadway production that was part of *Black Quartet*, a program of four one-act plays which also included works by Ben Caldwell, Ed Bullins, and Ron Milner.

INTRODUCTION

Charles Gordone, among others, has correctly asserted that LeRoi Jones has done more than any single black playwright or poet to stimulate writing in the theater by black writers. Through his example in the off-Broadway productions of his plays, in the achievement in the Black Arts Theater in Harlem and the Spirit House Movers and Players in Newark, Jones has provided a series of brilliant and provocative works reflecting his conception of a revolutionary theater which he sees as a positive force for change. "(All their faces turned into the lights and you work on them black nigger magic, and cleansed them at having seen the ugliness. And if the beautiful see themselves, they will love themselves.) We are preaching virtue again, but by that we mean NOW, toward what seems the most constructive use of the word." And: "We will scream and cry, murder, run through the streets in agony, if it means some soul will be moved, moved to actual life understanding of what the world is, and what it ought to be. We are preaching virtue and feeling, and a natural sense of the self in the world. All men live in the world, and the world ought to be the place for them to live."

One of the most talented, Jones also is unmistakably one of the most controversial of the new black playwrights. His plays have won him much praise. Howard Taubman of the *New York Times* speaks of him as "One of the angriest writers to storm the theatre—and one of the most gifted." They have also brought upon his head such epithets as racist, demagogue, and propagandist. He has been alternately acclaimed as "great" and "awful," "divine" and "dirty," "genius" and "madman." Meantime, Jones has gone on his considered way, unperturbed by unsympathetic criticism, as he proceeds to expose the moral decay inherent in the racist and other negative connotations of our society, and to provide his audiences with an unremitting "glimpse of the anger, passion and rage—past, present and future—of the black man." At the same time, in highly imaginative constructs, he uniformly asserts the dignity of the black man's search for identity and a viable heritage in the American and in the world scheme of things. And in doing this he seems to have founded a notable school of young black playwrights which might be called the "tribe of Brother LeRoi."

Despite his early rejoinders to this notion, Jones as a playwright often works in terms of parables, symbolist techniques, allegory, and myth. Although he is decidedly concerned with ideas, he is thus manifestly considerate of the demands of the theater and the demands of the imaginative and aesthetic experience. His first major play, *Dutchman*, considered by many to be his best work up to this point, provides us with an excellent example of these facts. *Dutchman*, presented earlier at the Village South Theater, received its first professional production under the auspices of Theater 1964 Playwright's Unit Workshop of Richard Barr, Clinton Wilder, and Edward Albee (sponsors of Adrienne Kennedy), at the Cherry Lane Theater on March 24, 1964, under the direction of Edward Parone, with Robert Hooks and Jennifer West in the leading roles. And, as has been the case with all of his plays, it gave rise to heated critical debate.

Philip Roth complained about the motivation of the characters, judging this, it would seem, according to the canons of doctrinaire psychological realism. But Henry Popkin could more soundly assert that *Dutchman* involves "the encounter not of two conventional characters, but two archetypes—the respectable Negro square and the white Bohemian," while a *Newsweek* review could say that "it is the mythic dimension, as well as its complex poetic texture which raises *Dutchman* so far above sociology."

Thus *Dutchman* on one level depicts the strange encounter between a black man and a white woman on a New York subway car, their conversation as she erotically tempts him, and his eventual death when, upon his rejection of her, she murders him. But the symbolic and mythic overtones are given from the outset and have to be accounted for in order to comprehend the higher frequencies of the meanings of this densely textured short play which takes only about forty minutes to present. Here we can begin with the title which Richard Watts, Jr., called "inscrutable," but which irresistably suggests the Dutch Man-of-War, "The Treasurer," a slaveship, that brought the first "negars," twenty in number, to the Jamestown colonies in 1619. It also suggests the legends of the Flying Dutchman and the Wandering Jew. A decided aura of strangeness and a departure from the specifications of the literal are provided by Jones's stage directions for the play. The action takes place in "the flying underbelly of the city," in "the subway heaped in modern myth." It is summer and "steaming hot." "Dim lights and darkness" whistle against the glass and the loud scream of the train is heard. Thus the subway is an urban inferno, and the careening train can also be seen as the middle-passage of a modern slaveship symbolizing the black man's status and experience in contemporary American life.

Then there are the characters, the meaning of which are to be evolved from their dialogue and their actions. The antagonist is Lula (Lena the Hyena —the famous woman poet), a beautiful but sluttish white woman of thirty who is described as a liar and has been pictured as "the Anglo-Saxon bitch-goddess," "a siren," and "a complete catalogue and storehouse of scornful Bohemianism," who is an "all-round vicious combination of inviting nymphomania and castrating rejection." The protagonist is the twenty-year-old Clay, who at the outset of the action is a self-respecting, middle class, young Ivy-League black man in the process of defining himself. In the conflict that ensues one aspect of Jones's allegory becomes evident when Lula, after peering at Clay through the subway window, enters the train eating apples, and provocatively seats herself beside him. She is a tainted Eve, and the play will be a revelation of the corruption and inevitable destruction of Clay—a black Adam—at her hands. Lula is later referred to as Snow White—a fairy tale figure—"Mirror, mirror on the wall,/Who's the fairest one of all?" Thus she assumes the role of mythic white womanhood, and of white America as a whole, and the racist presuppositions that inevitably lead to what Jones conceives as the castration of the black man in our society.

Lula's omniscience in her approach to Clay is of importance: it is the presumed omniscience of white America which purports to know the Negro, more fully than he knows himself. But her knowledge of the young man is, ironically, profound. "You look like you have been trying to grow a beard. That's exactly what you look like. You look like you live in New Jersey with your parents and are trying to grow a beard." She continues to taunt him. "You look like you've been reading Chinese poetry and drinking lukewarm, sugarless tea. . . . You look like death eating a soda cracker." And when she tells him that his friend is a "tall, skinny black boy with a phony English accent," and that he is on his way to his house for a party, Clay is amazed. He is also amazed by her assertion, "You're a murderer Clay and you know it. You know damned well what I mean." Clay's response is "I do?" To which Lula responds ambiguously, "So we'll pretend that the air is light and full of perfume." And Clay, sniffing at her blouse, says, "It is." But at an earlier point in her baiting, she asks, "And what did you think you were? Who do you think you are now?" When he replies "Well, in college I thought I was Baudelaire. But I've slowed down since then," Lula retorts: "I bet you never once thought you were a black nigger," and almost shrieks, "A black Baudelaire." Later she says, "The black Baudelaire! Yes!" And then: "My Christ. My Christ." An oblique statement follows: "May the people accept you as a ghost of the future. And love you, that you may not kill them when you can."

In the course of the first scene Lula is in turn perversely interested in taunting and baiting the young man, and absent-minded and withdrawn in his presence. Sluttishly coquettish at the end of the scene, she says: ". . . we'll pretend that the people cannot see you . . . And that you are free of your own history. And I am free of my history. We'll pretend that we are both anonymous beauties smashing along through the city's entrails," and she cries out loudly, "GROOVE!"

But according to Jones's conceit the transcending of history is not part of Lula's intention, for according to Jones, and probably according to actuality, this is a metaphysical impossibility. Earlier, for instance, as has been noted, Lula is at pains to remind Clay that he is a *black nigger*. She taunts him ambiguously about his dress. "Boy, those narrow-shoulder clothes come from a tradition you ought to feel oppressed by. . . . What right do you have to be wearing a three-button suit and a striped tie? Your grandfather was a slave, he didn't go to Harvard."

Meantime, in the opening of the second scene, Lula and Clay talk about the party that they will attend, after which, as Lula fantasizes, they will "go down the street late at night eating apples and winding very deliberately towards my house." Lula significantly describes her house as a tenement. "Wouldn't live anywhere else," she says, "Reminds me specifically of my novel form of insanity." Her house is described as a "dark house." "We will have fun in the dark house, high up above the street and the ignorant cowboys." And she proposes that in the dark living room which will probably seem like Juliet's tomb to Clay, they will talk endlessly. When Clay asks, "About what?" Lula replies menacingly. "About what? About your manhood, what do you think? What do you think we have been talking about all this time?" Slow in sizing up the situation, Clay replies, "Well, I didn't know it was that. That's for sure. Every other thing in the world but that." But that is exactly what in large part the play is about, the black man's manhood and his castration in America. For in the progress of the play, as Susan Sontag says, "poked and prodded by Lula Clay strips down to his true self; he stops being nice, well-spoken, reasonable, and assumes his full Negro identity; that is, he announced the homicidal rage towards whites that Negroes bear in their hearts, whether they act on it or not." At one point, speaking of the imagined rendez-vous, Lula says, "You'll say to me very close to my face, many, many times, you'll say, even whisper, that you love me." Clay answers, "Maybe I will." To which she says, "And you'll be lying."

What incites her scorn is Clay's refusal, as the *Newsweek* review points out "to fit into her erotic and rebellious dream, to play the figure of dark passion and nihilistic protest," to be what Eldridge Cleaver calls, "the supersexual menial." She, in a frenzied speech, makes a significant remark, "Apples and long walks with deathless intelligent lovers. But you mix it up. Look out the window all the time. Turning pages. Change, change, change. Till, shit, I don't know you. Wouldn't, for that matter. I bet you're even too serious to be psychoanalyzed." Later she calls Clay "an escaped nigger." Her scorn turning into fury, she begins a frenetic and insinuating dance challenging Clay to join in. "Let's rub bellies on the train. The nasty. The nasty. Do the gritty grind. . . . Grind till you lose your mind." "Clay! You middle-class black bastard . . . you liver-lipped white man. . . . Dance with me. . . ." And she screams, "Clay, you got to break out. Don't sit there dying the way they want you to die."

Goading him to the point of explosion, she calls him "Uncle Tom" and "Thomas Woolly-head." Then, in contrast to his earlier manner of tolerant wariness, Clay bursts into a long tirade in which he asserts his manhood, and his individuality. "Don't you tell me anything! If I'm a middle-class fake white man . . . let me be. . . . I'll rip your lousy breasts off! Let me be who I feel like being. Uncle Tom, Thomas. Whoever." And he proceeds at fever pitch to demolish her pretense of knowing the black man. She listens coldly until he finishes and, as he prepares to leave the train, stabs him to death. She then orders the hitherto indifferent passengers, whom she has just aroused and alerted, to throw his body off the train. This they do and disperse at the next station. Lula settles down alone in the train and writes something in a notebook, and another young black man carrying books enters the train. Lula gives him the same slow look that she gave Clay. The drama is about to repeat itself.

In an interview that appeared in the *Literary Times* (Chicago) in 1967, LeRoi Jones provides a kind of footnote to the meaning of his play. When asked: "Why does the main character in the play stand by and take the worst kind of abuse when all he has to do is leave the scene?" Jones replied, "When he does try to leave is when he is killed. When he tries to leave, she kills him. . . . He figures that he can hang around and go through all of this and maybe he might get a little piece. And that, in a sense, is the middle-class Negro's problem in America. He's seduced by it, by what it seems to be. . . . Then when he really says what he feels, and tries to leave (when the intellectual denounces the society and says 'I have nothing to do with you any more'), that's when he's killed." And to provide a footnote to a footnote, in the same interview, when asked to respond to the underground quip that "LeRoi Jones is the black James Baldwin," Jones in part replied, "Jimmy Baldwin and I, because we differ in our social attitudes, are very different men and different writers. I think Jimmy still feels that there is a chance for a rapprochment with America, that somehow the American white man can be made reasonable. I don't happen to believe this, but Jimmy Baldwin and I are brothers."

Dutchman

For Thomas Everett Russ, American pioneer,
and Anna Cherry Brock Russ, his wife

CHARACTERS

Clay, *twenty-year-old Negro*
Lula, *thirty-year-old white woman*
Riders of Coach, *white and black*
Young Negro
Conductor

In the flying underbelly of the city. Steaming hot, and summer on top, outside. Underground. The subway heaped in modern myth.

Opening scene is a man sitting in a subway car, holding a magazine but looking vacantly just above its wilting pages. Occasionally he looks blankly toward the window on his right. Dim lights and darkness whistling by against the glass. (Or paste the lights, as admitted props, right on the subway windows. Have them move, even dim and flicker. But give the sense of speed. Also stations, whether the train is stopped or the glitter and activity of these stations merely flashes by the windows.)

The man is sitting alone. That is, only his seat is visible, though the rest of the car is outfitted as a complete subway car. But only his seat is shown. There might be, for a time, as the play begins, a loud scream of the actual train. And it can recur throughout the play, or continue on a lower key once the dialogue starts.

The train slows after a time, pulling to a brief stop at one of the stations. The man looks idly up, until he sees a woman's face staring at him through the window; when it realizes that the man has noticed the face, it begins very premeditatedly to smile. The man smiles too, for a moment, without a trace of self-consciousness. Almost an instinctive though undesirable response. Then a kind of awkwardness or embarrassment sets in, and the man makes to look away, is further embarrassed, so he brings back his eyes to where the face was, but by now the train is moving again, and the face would seem to be left behind by the way the man turns his head to look back through the other windows at the slowly fading platform. He smiles then; more

DUTCHMAN   215

comfortably confident, hoping perhaps that his memory of this brief encounter will be pleasant. And then he is idle again.

SCENE 1

Train roars. Lights flash outside the windows.

Lula enters from the rear of the car in bright, skimpy summer clothes and sandals. She carries a net bag full of paper books, fruit, and other anonymous articles. She is wearing sunglasses, which she pushes up on her forehead from time to time. Lula is a tall, slender, beautiful woman with long red hair hanging straight down her back, wearing only loud lipstick in somebody's good taste. She is eating an apple, very daintily. Coming down the car toward Clay.

She stops beside Clay's seat and hangs languidly from the strap, still managing to eat the apple. It is apparent that she is going to sit in the seat next to Clay, and that she is only waiting for him to notice her before she sits.

Clay sits as before, looking just beyond his magazine, now and again pulling the magazine slowly back and forth in front of his face in a hopeless effort to fan himself. Then he sees the woman hanging there beside him and he looks up into her face, smiling quizzically.

Lula: Hello.
Clay: Uh, hi're you?
Lula: I'm going to sit down. . . . O.K.?
Clay: Sure.
Lula:
> *(Swings down onto the seat, pushing her legs straight out as if she is very weary.)*

Oooof! Too much weight.
Clay: Ha, doesn't look like much to me.
> *(Leaning back against the window, a little surprised and maybe stiff.)*

Lula: It's so anyway.
> *(And she moves her toes in the sandals, then pulls her right leg up on the left knee, better to inspect the bottoms of the sandals and the back of her heel. She appears for a second not to notice that Clay is sitting next to her or that she has spoken to him just a second before. Clay looks at the magazine, then out the black window. As he does this, she turns very quickly toward him.)*

Weren't you staring at me through the window?
Clay:
> *(Wheeling around and very much stiffened.)*

What?
Lula: Weren't you staring at me through the window? At the last stop?
Clay: Staring at you? What do you mean?

Lula: Don't you know what staring means?

Clay: I saw you through the window . . . if that's what it means. I don't know if I was staring. Seems to me you were staring through the window at me.

Lula: I was. But only after I'd turned around and saw you staring through that window down in the vicinity of my ass and legs.

Clay: Really?

Lula: Really. I guess you were just taking those idle potshots. Nothing else to do. Run your mind over people's flesh.

Clay: Oh boy. Wow, now I admit I was looking in your direction. But the rest of that weight is yours.

Lula: I suppose.

Clay: Staring through train windows is weird business. Much weirder than staring very sedately at abstract asses.

Lula: That's why I came looking through the window . . . so you'd have more than that to go on. I even smiled at you.

Clay: That's right.

Lula: I even got into this train, going some other way than mine. Walked down the aisle . . . searching you out.

Clay: Really? That's pretty funny.

Lula: That's pretty funny. . . . God, you're dull.

Clay: Well, I'm sorry, lady, but I really wasn't prepared for party talk.

Lula: No, you're not. What are you prepared for?

(Wrapping the apple core in a Kleenex and dropping it on the floor.)

Clay:

(Takes her conversation as pure sex talk. He turns to confront her squarely with this idea.)

I'm prepared for anything. How about you?

Lula:

(Laughing loudly and cutting it off abruptly.)

What do you think you're doing?

Clay: What?

Lula: You think I want to pick you up, get you to take me somewhere and screw me, huh?

Clay: Is that the way I look?

Lula: You look like you been trying to grow a beard. That's exactly what you look like. You look like you live in New Jersey with your parents and are trying to grow a beard. That's what. You look like you've been reading Chinese poetry and drinking lukewarm sugarless tea.

(Laughs, uncrossing and recrossing her legs.)

You look like death eating a soda cracker.

Clay:

(Cocking his head from one side to the other, embarrassed and trying to make some comeback, but also intrigued by what the woman is saying . . . even the sharp city coarseness of her voice, which is still a kind of gentle sidewalk throb.)

Really? I look like all that?

DUTCHMAN 217

Lula: Not all of it.

(She feints a seriousness to cover an actual somber tone.)

I lie a lot.

(Smiling.)

It helps me control the world.

Clay:

(Relieved and laughing louder than the humor.)

Yeah, I bet.

Lula: But it's true, most of it, right? Jersey? Your bumpy neck?

Clay: How'd you know all that? Huh? Really, I mean about Jersey . . . and even the beard. I met you before? You know Warren Enright?

Lula: You tried to make it with your sister when you were ten.

(Clay leans back hard against the back of the seat, his eyes opening now, still trying to look amused.)

But I succeeded a few weeks ago.

(She starts to laugh again.)

Clay: What're you talking about? Warren tell you that? You're a friend of Georgia's?

Lula: I told you I lie. I don't know your sister. I don't know Warren Enright.

Clay: You mean you're just picking these things out of the air?

Lula: Is Warren Enright a tall skinny black black boy with a phony English accent?

Clay: I figured you knew him.

Lula: But I don't. I just figured you would know somebody like that.

(Laughs.)

Clay: Yeah, yeah.

Lula: You're probably on your way to his house now.

Clay: That's right.

Lula:

(Putting her hand on Clay's closest knee, drawing it from the knee up to the thigh's hinge, then removing it, watching his face very closely, and continuing to laugh, perhaps more gently than before.)

Dull, dull, dull. I bet you think I'm exciting.

Clay: You're O.K.

Lula: Am I exciting you now?

Clay: Right. That's not what's supposed to happen?

Lula: How do I know?

(She returns her hand, without moving it, then takes it away and plunges it in her bag to draw out an apple.)

You want this?

Clay: Sure.

Lula:

(She gets one out of the bag for herself.)

Eating apples together is always the first step. Or walking up uninhabited Seventh Avenue in the twenties on weekends.

(Bites and giggles, glancing at Clay and speaking in loose sing-song.)

Can get you involved . . . boy! Get us involved. Um-huh.

(Mock seriousness.)
Would you like to get involved with me, Mister Man?
Clay:
*(Trying to be as flippant as **Lula**, whacking happily at the apple.)*
Sure. Why not? A beautiful woman like you. Huh, I'd be a fool not too.
Lula: And I bet you're sure you know what you're talking about.
(Taking him a little roughly by the wrist, so he cannot eat the apple, then shaking the wrist.)
I bet you're sure of almost everything anybody ever asked you about . . . right?
(Shaking his wrist harder.)
Right?
Clay: Yeah, right. . . . Wow, you're pretty strong, you know? Whatta you, a lady wrestler or something?
Lula: What's wrong with lady wrestlers? And don't answer because you never knew any. Huh.
(Cynically.)
That's for sure. They don't have any lady wrestlers in that part of Jersey. That's for sure.
Clay: Hey, you still haven't told me how you know so much about me.
Lula: I told you I didn't know anything about you . . . you're a well-known type.
Clay: Really?
Lula: Or at least I know the type very well. And your skinny English friend too.
Clay: Anonymously?
Lula:
(Settles back in seat, single-mindedly finishing her apple and humming snatches of rhythm and blues song.)
What?
Clay: Without knowing us specifically?
Lula: Oh boy.
*(Looking quickly at **Clay**.)*
What a face. You know, you could be a handsome man.
Clay: I can't argue with you.
Lula:
(Vague, off-center response.)
What?
Clay:
(Raising his voice, thinking the train noise has drowned part of his sentence.)
I can't argue with you.
Lula: My hair is turning gray. A gray hair for each year and type I've come through.
Clay: Why do you want to sound so old?
Lula: But it's always gentle when it starts.
(Attention drifting.)

Hugged against tenements, day or night.

Clay: What?

Lula:

> *(Refocusing.)*

Hey, why don't you take me to that party you're going to?

Clay: You must be a friend of Warren's to know about the party.

Lula: Wouldn't you like to take me to the party?

> *(Imitates clinging vine.)*

Oh, come on, ask me to your party.

Clay: Of course I'll ask you to come with me to the party. And I'll bet you're a friend of Warren's.

Lula: Why not be a friend of Warren's? Why not?

> *(Taking his arm.)*

Have you asked me yet?

Clay: How can I ask you when I don't know your name?

Lula: Are you talking to my name?

Clay: What is it, a secret?

Lula: I'm Lena the Hyena.

Clay: The famous woman poet?

Lula: Poetess! The same!

Clay: Well, you know so much about me . . . what's my name?

Lula: Morris the Hyena.

Clay: The famous woman poet?

Lula: The same.

> *(Laughing and going into her bag.)*

You want another apple?

Clay: Can't make it lady. I only have to keep one doctor away a day.

Lula: I bet your name is . . . something like . . . uh, Gerald or Walter. Huh?

Clay: God, no.

Lula: Lloyd, Norman? One of those hopeless colored names creeping out of New Jersey. Leonard? Gag. . . .

Clay: Like Warren?

Lula: Definitely. Just exactly like Warren. Or Everett.

Clay: Gag. . . .

Lula: Well, for sure, it's not Willie.

Clay: It's Clay.

Lula: Clay? Really? Clay what?

Clay: Take your pick. Jackson, Johnson, or Williams.

Lula: Oh, really? Good for you. But it's got to be Williams. You're too pretentious to be a Jackson or Johnson.

Clay: Thass right.

Lula: But Clay's O.K.

Clay: So's Lena.

Lula: It's Lula.

Clay: Oh?

Lula: Lula the Hyena.

Clay: Very good.

Lula:

(*Starts laughing again.*)

Now you say to me, "Lula, Lula, why don't you go to this party with me tonight?" It's your turn, and let those be your lines.

Clay: Lula, why don't you go to this party with me tonight, Huh?

Lula: Say my name twice before you ask, and no huh's.

Clay: Lula, Lula, why don't you go to this party with me tonight?

Lula: I'd like to go, Clay, but how can you ask me to go when you barely know me?

Clay: That is strange, isn't it?

Lula: What kind of reaction is that? You're supposed to say, "Aw, come on, we'll get to know each other better at the party."

Clay: That's pretty corny.

Lula: What are you into anyway?

(*Looking at him half sullenly but still amused.*)

What thing are you playing at, Mister? Mister Clay Williams?

(*Grabs his thigh, up near the crotch.*)

What are *you* thinking about?

Clay: Watch it now, you're gonna excite me for real.

Lula:

(*Taking her hand away and throwing her apple core through the window.*)

I bet.

(*She slumps in the seat and is heavily silent.*)

Clay: I thought you knew everything about me? What happened?

(**Lula** *looks at him, then looks slowly away, then over where the other aisle would be. Noise of the train. She reaches in her bag and pulls out one of the paper books. She puts it on her leg and thumbs the pages listlessly.* **Clay** *cocks his head to see the title of the book. Noise of the train.* **Lula** *flips pages and her eyes drift. Both remain silent.*)

Are you going to the party with me, Lula?

Lula:

(*Bored and not even looking.*)

I don't even know you.

Clay: You said you know my type.

Lula:

(*Strangely irritated.*)

Don't get smart with me, Buster. I know you like the palm of my hand.

Clay: The one you eat the apples with?

Lula: Yeh. And the one I open doors late Saturday evening with. That's my door. Up at the top of the stairs. Five flights. Above a lot of Italians and lying Americans. And scrape carrots with. Also . . .

(*Looks at him.*)

the same hand I unbutton my dress with, or let my skirt fall down. Same hand. Lover.

Clay: Are you angry about anything? Did I say something wrong?

Lula: Everything you say is wrong.

(Mock smile.)

That's what makes you so attractive. Ha. In that funnybook jacket with all the buttons.

(More animate, taking hold of his jacket.)

What've you got that jacket and tie on in all this heat for? And why're you wearing a jacket and tie like that? Did your people ever burn witches or start revolutions over the price of tea? Boy, those narrow-shoulder clothes come from a tradition you ought to feel oppressed by. A three-button suit. What right do you have to be wearing a three-button suit and striped tie? Your grandfather was a slave, he didn't go to Harvard.

Clay: My grandfather was a night watchman.

Lula: And you went to a colored college where everybody thought they were Averell Harriman.

Clay: All except me.

Lula: And who did you think you were? Who do you think you are now?

Clay:

(Laughs as if to make light of the whole trend of the conversation.)

Well, in college I thought I was Baudelaire. But I've slowed down since.

Lula: I bet you never once thought you were a black nigger.

(Mock serious, then she howls with laughter. **Clay** *is stunned after initial reaction, he quickly tries to appreciate the humor.* **Lula** *almost shrieks.)*

A black Baudelaire.

Clay: That's right.

Lula: Boy, are you corny. I take back what I said before. Everything you say is not wrong. It's perfect. You should be on television.

Clay: You act like you're on television already.

Lula: That's because I'm an actress.

Clay: I thought so.

Lula: Well, you're wrong. I'm no actress. I told you I always lie. I'm nothing, honey, and don't you ever forget it.

(Lighter.)

Although my mother was a Communist. The only person in my family ever to amount to anything.

Clay: My mother was a Republican.

Lula: And your father voted for the man rather than the party.

Clay: Right!

Lula: Yea for him. Yea, yea for him.

Clay: Yea!

Lula: And yea for America where he is free to vote for the mediocrity of his choice! Yea!

Clay: Yea!

Lula: And yea for both your parents who even though they differ about so crucial a matter as the body politic still forged a union of love and sacrifice that was destined to flower at the birth of the noble Clay ... what's your middle name?

Clay: Clay.

Lula: A union of love and sacrifice that was destined to flower at the birth of the noble Clay Clay Williams. Yea! And most of all yea yea for you, Clay Clay. The Black Baudelaire! Yes!

(And with knifelike cynicism.)

My Christ. My Christ.

Clay: Thank you, ma'am.

Lula: May the people accept you as a ghost of the future. And love you, that you might not kill them when you can.

Clay: What?

Lula: You're a murderer, Clay, and you know it.

(Her voice darkening with significance.)

You know goddamn well what I mean.

Clay: I do?

Lula: So we'll pretend the air is light and full of perfume.

Clay:

(Sniffing at her blouse.)

It is.

Lula: And we'll pretend the people cannot see you. That is, the citizens. And that you are free of your own history. And I am free of my history. We'll pretend that we are both anonymous beauties smashing along through the city's entrails.

(She yells as loud as she can.)

GROOVE!

Blackout

SCENE 2

*Scene is the same as before, though now there are other seats visible in the car. And throughout the scene other people get on the subway. There are maybe one or two seated in the car as the scene opens, though neither **Clay** nor **Lula** notices them. **Clay's** tie is open. **Lula** is hugging his arm.*

Clay: The party!

Lula: I know it'll be something good. You can come in with me, looking casual and significant. I'll be strange, haughty, and silent, and walk with long slow strides.

Clay: Right.

Lula: When you get drunk, pat me once, very lovingly on the flanks, and I'll look at you cryptically, licking my lips.

Clay: It sounds like something we can do.

Lula: You'll go around talking to young men about your mind, and to old men about your plans. If you meet a very close friend who is also with someone like me, we can stand together, sipping our drinks and exchanging codes of lust. The atmosphere will be slithering in love and half-love and very open moral decision.

Clay: Great. Great.

Lula: And everyone will pretend they don't know your name, and then . . .

    (She pauses heavily.)

later, when they have to, they'll claim a friendship that denies your sterling character.

Clay:

    (Kissing her neck and fingers.)

And then what?

Lula: Then? Well, then we'll go down the street, late night, eating apples and winding very deliberately toward my house.

Clay: Deliberately?

Lula: I mean, we'll look in all the shopwindows, and make fun of the queers. Maybe we'll meet a Jewish Buddhist and flatten his conceits over some very pretentious coffee.

Clay: In honor of whose God?

Lula: Mine.

Clay: Who is . . . ?

Lula: Me . . . and you?

Clay: A corporate Godhead.

Lula: Exactly. Exactly.

    (Notices one of the other people entering.)

Clay: Go on with the chronicle. Then what happens to us?

Lula:

    (A mild depression, but she still makes her description triumphant and increasingly direct.)

To my house, of course.

Clay: Of course.

Lula: And up the narrow steps of the tenement.

Clay: You live in a tenement?

Lula: Wouldn't live anywhere else. Reminds me specifically of my novel form of insanity.

Clay: Up the tenement stairs.

Lula: And with my apple-eating hand I push open the door and lead you, my tender big-eyed prey, into my . . . God, what can I call it . . . into my hovel.

Clay: Then what happens?

Lula: After the dancing and games, after the long drinks and long walks, the real fun begins.

Clay: Ah, the real fun.

    (Embarrassed, in spite of himself.)

Which is . . . ?

Lula:

    (Laughs at him.)

Real fun in the dark house. Hah! Real fun in the dark house, high up above the street and the ignorant cowboys. I lead you in, holding your wet hand gently in my hand . . .

Clay: Which is not wet?

Lula: Which is dry as ashes.

Clay: And cold?

Lula: Don't think you'll get out of your responsibility that way. It's not cold at all. You Fascist! Into my dark living room. Where we'll sit and talk end-lessly, endlessly.

Clay: About what?

Lula: About what? About your manhood, what do you think? What do you think we've been talking about all this time?

Clay: Well, I didn't know it was that. That's for sure. Every other thing in the world but that.

      (Notices another person entering, looks quickly, almost involuntarily up and down the car, seeing the other people in the car.)

Hey, I didn't even notice when those people got on.

Lula: Yeah, I know.

Clay: Man, this subway is slow.

Lula: Yeah, I know.

Clay: Well, go on. We were talking about my manhood.

Lula: We still are. All the time.

Clay: We were in your living room.

Lula: My dark living room. Talking endlessly.

Clay: About my manhood.

Lula: I'll make you a map of it. Just as soon as we get to my house.

Clay: Well, that's great.

Lula: One of the things we do while we talk. And screw.

Clay:
      (Trying to make his smile broader and less shaky.)
We finally got there.

Lula: And you'll call my rooms black as a grave. You'll say, "This place is like Juliet's tomb."

Clay:
      (Laughs.)
I might.

Lula: I know. You've probably said it before.

Clay: And is that all? The whole grand tour?

Lula: Not all. You'll say to me very close to my face, many, many times, you'll say, even whisper, that you love me.

Clay: Maybe I will.

Lula: And you'll be lying.

Clay: I wouldn't lie about something like that.

Lula: Hah. It's the only kind of thing you will lie about. Especially if you think it'll keep me alive.

Clay: Keep you alive? I don't understand.

Lula:

> (Bursting out laughing, but too shrilly.)

Don't understand? Well, don't look at me. It's the path I take, that's all. Where both feet take me when I set them down. One in front of the other.

Clay: Morbid. Morbid. You sure you're not an actress? All that self-aggrandizement.

Lula: Well, I told you I wasn't an actress . . . but I also told you I lie all the time. Draw your own conclusions.

Clay: Morbid. Morbid. You sure you're not an actress? All scribed? There's no more?

Lula: I've told you all I know. Or almost all.

Clay: There's no funny parts?

Lula: I thought it was all funny.

Clay: But you mean peculiar, not ha-ha.

Lula: You don't know what I mean.

Clay: Well, tell me the almost part then. You said almost all. What else? I want the whole story.

Lula:

> (Searching aimlessly through her bag. She begins to talk breathlessly, with a light and silly tone.)

All stories are whole stories. All of 'em. Our whole story . . . nothing but change. How could things go on like that forever? Huh?

> (Slaps him on the shoulder, begins finding things in her bag, taking them out and throwing them over her shoulder into the aisle.)

Except I do go on as I do. Apples and long walks with deathless intelligent lovers. But you mix it up. Look out the window, all the time. Turning pages. Change change change. Till, shit, I don't know you. Wouldn't, for that matter. You're too serious. I bet you're even too serious to be psychoanalyzed. Like all those Jewish poets from Yonkers, who leave their mothers looking for other mothers, or others' mothers, on whose baggy tits they lay their fumbling heads. Their poems are always funny, and all about sex.

Clay: They sound great. Like movies.

Lula: But you change.

> (Blankly.)

And things work on you till you hate them.

> (More people come into the train. They come closer to the couple, some of them not sitting, but swinging drearily on the straps, staring at the two with uncertain interest.)

Clay: Wow. All these people, so suddenly. They must all come from the same place.

Lula: Right. That they do.

Clay: Oh? You know about them too?

Lula: Oh yeah. About them more than I know about you. Do they frighten you?

Clay: Frighten me? Why should they frighten me?

Lula: 'Cause you're an escaped nigger.

Clay: Yeah?

Lula: 'Cause you crawled through the wire and made tracks to my side.

Clay: Wire?

Lula: Don't they have wire around plantations?

Clay: You must be Jewish. All you can think about is wire. Plantations didn't have any wire. Plantations were big open whitewashed places like heaven, and everybody on 'em was grooved to be there. Just strummin' and hummin' all day.

Lula: Yes, yes.

Clay: And that's how the blues was born.

Lula: Yes, yes. And that's how the blues was born.

(Begins to make up a song that becomes quickly hysterical. As she sings she rises from her seat, still throwing things out of her bag into the aisle, beginning a rhythmical shudder and twistlike wiggle, which she continues up and down the aisle, bumping into many of the standing people and tripping over the feet of those sitting. Each time she runs into a person she lets out a very vicious piece of profanity, wiggling and stepping all the time.)

And that's how the blues was born. Yes. Yes. Son of a bitch, get out of the way. Yes. Quack. Yes. Yes. And that's how the blues was born. Ten little niggers sitting on a limb, but none of them ever looked like him.

(Points to **Clay,** *returns toward the seat, with her hands extended for him to rise and dance with her.)*

And that's how the blues was born. Yes. Come on, Clay. Let's do the nasty. Rub bellies. Rub bellies.

Clay:

(Waves his hands to refuse. He is embarrassed, but determined to get a kick out of the proceedings.)

Hey, what was in those apples? Mirror, mirror on the wall, who's the fairest one of all? Snow White, baby, and don't you forget it.

Lula:

(Grabbing for his hands, which he draws away.)

Come on, Clay. Let's rub bellies on the train. The nasty. The nasty. Do the gritty grind, like your ol' rag-head mammy. Grind till you lose your mind. Shake it, shake it, shake it, shake it! OOOOweeee! Come on, Clay. Let's do the choo-choo train shuffle, the navel scratcher.

Clay: Hey, you coming on like the lady who smoked up her grass skirt.

Lula:

(Becoming annoyed that he will not dance, and becoming more animated as if to embarrass him still further.)

Come on, Clay . . . let's do the thing. Uhh! Uhh! Clay! Clay! You middle-class black bastard. Forget your social-working mother for a few seconds and let's knock stomachs. Clay, you liver-lipped white man. You would-be Christian. You ain't no nigger, you're just a dirty white man. Get up, Clay. Dance with me, Clay.

Clay: Lula! Sit down, now. Be cool.

Lula:

> *(Mocking him, in wild dance.)*

Be cool. Be cool. That's all you know . . . shaking that wildroot cream-oil on your knotty head, jackets buttoning up to your chin, so full of white man's words. Christ. God. Get up and scream at these people. Like scream meaningless shit in these hopeless faces.

> *(She screams at people in train, still dancing.)*

Red trains cough Jewish underwear for keeps! Expanding smells of silence. Gravy snot whistling like sea birds. Clay. Clay, you got to break out. Don't sit there dying the way they want you to die. Get up.

Clay: Oh, sit the fuck down.

> *(He moves to restrain her.)*

Sit down, goddamn it.

Lula:

> *(Twisting out of his reach.)*

Screw yourself, Uncle Tom. Thomas Woolly-head.

> *(Begins to dance a kind of jig, mocking* **Clay** *with loud forced humor.)*

There is Uncle Tom . . . I mean, Uncle Thomas Woolly-Head. With old white matted mane. He hobbles on his wooden cane. Old Tom. Old Tom. Let the white man hump his ol' mama, and he jes' shuffle off in the woods and hide his gentle gray head. Ol' Thomas Woolly-Head.

> *(Some of the other riders are laughing now. A drunk gets up and joins* **Lula** *in her dance, singing, as best he can, her "song."* **Clay** *gets up out of his seat and visibly scans the faces of the other riders.)*

Clay: Lula! Lula!

> *(She is dancing and turning, still shouting as loud as she can. The drunk too is shouting, and waving his hands wildly.)*

Lula . . . you dumb bitch. Why don't you stop it?

> *(He rushes half stumbling from his seat, and grabs one of her flailing arms.)*

Lula: Let me go! You black son of a bitch.

> *(She struggles against him.)*

Let me go! Help!

> *(***Clay*** *is dragging her towards her seat, and the drunk seeks to interfere. He grabs* **Clay** *around the shoulders and begins wrestling with him.* **Clay** *clubs the drunk to the floor without releasing* **Lula**, *who is still screaming.* **Clay** *finally gets her to the seat and throws her into it.)*

Clay: Now you shut the hell up.

> *(Grabbing her shoulders.)*

Just shut up. You don't know what you're talking about. You don't know anything. So just keep your stupid mouth closed.

Lula: You're afraid of white people. And your father was. Uncle Tom Big Lip!

Clay:

> *(Slaps her as hard as he can, across the mouth.* **Lula**'s *head bangs against the back of the seat. When she raises it again,* **Clay** *slaps her again.)*

Now shut up and let me talk.

(He turns toward the other riders, some of whom are sitting on the edge of their seats. The drunk is on one knee, rubbing his head, and singing softly the same song. He shuts up too when he sees **Clay** *watching him. The others go back to newspapers or stare out the windows.)*

Shit, you don't have any sense, Lula, nor feelings either. I could murder you now. Such a tiny ugly throat. I could squeeze it flat, and watch you turn blue, on a humble. For dull kicks. And all these weak-faced ofays squatting around here, staring over their papers at me. Murder them too. Even if they expected it. That man there . . .

(Points to well-dressed man.)

I could rip that *Times* right out of his hand, as skinny and middle-classed as I am, I could rip that paper out of his hand and just as easily rip out his throat. It takes no great effort. For what? To kill you soft idiots? You don't understand anything but luxury.

Lula: You fool!

Clay:

(Pushing her against the seat.)

I'm not telling you again, Tallulah Bankhead! Luxury. In your face and your fingers. You telling me what I ought to do.

(Sudden scream frightening the whole coach.)

Well, don't! Don't you tell me anything! If I'm a middle-class fake white man . . . let me be. And let me be in the way I want.

(Through his teeth.)

I'll rip your lousy breasts off! Let me be who I feel like being. Uncle Tom. Thomas. Whoever. It's none of your business. You don't know anything except what's there for you to see. An act. Lies. Device. Not the pure heart, the pumping black heart. You don't ever know that. And I sit here, in this buttoned-up suit, to keep myself from cutting all your throats. I mean wantonly. You great liberated whore! You fuck some black man, and right away you're an expert on black people. What a lotta shit that is. The only thing you know is that you come if he bangs you hard enough. And that's all. The belly rub? You wanted to do the belly rub? Shit, you don't even know how. You don't know how. That ol' dipty-dip shit you do, rolling your ass like an elephant. That's not my kind of belly rub. Belly rub is not Queens. Belly rub is dark places, with big hats and overcoats held up with one arm. Belly rub hates you. Old bald-headed four-eyed ofays popping their fingers . . . and don't know yet what they're doing. They say, "I love Bessie Smith." And don't even understand that Bessie Smith is saying, "Kiss my ass, kiss my black unruly ass." Before love, suffering, desire, anything you can explain, she's saying, and very plainly, "Kiss my black ass." And if you don't know that, it's you that's doing the kissing.

Charlie Parker? Charlie Parker. All the hip white boys scream for Bird. And Bird saying, "Up your ass, feebleminded ofay! Up your ass." And they sit there talking about the tortured genius of Charlie Parker. Bird would've played not a note of music if he just walked up to East Sixty-seventh Street and killed the first ten white people he saw. Not a note! And I'm the great would-be poet. Yes. That's right! Poet. Some kind of bastard literature . . . all it needs is a simple knife thrust. Just let me bleed you, you loud whore, and one poem vanished. A whole people of neurotics, struggling to keep from being sane. And the only thing that would cure the neurosis would be your murder. Simple as that. I mean if I murdered you, then other white people would begin to understand me. You understand? No. I guess not. If Bessie Smith had killed some white people she wouldn't have needed that music. She could have talked very straight and plain about the world. No metaphors. No grunts. No wiggles in the dark of her soul. Just straight two and two are four. Money. Power. Luxury. Like that. All of them. Crazy niggers turning their backs on sanity. When all it needs is that simple act. Murder. Just murder! Would make us all sane.

> *(Suddenly weary.)*

Ahhh. Shit. But who needs it? I'd rather be a fool. Insane. Safe with my words, and no deaths, and clean, hard thoughts, urging me to new conquests. My people's madness. Hah! That's a laugh. My people. They don't need me to claim them. They got legs and arms of their own. Personal sanities. Mirrors. They don't need all those words. They don't need any defense. But listen, though, one more thing. And you tell this to your father, who's probably the kind of man who needs to know at once. So he can plan ahead. Tell him not to preach so much rationalism and cold logic to these niggers. Let them alone. Let them sing curses at you in code and see your filth as simple lack of style. Don't make the mistake, through some irresponsible surge of Christian charity, of talking too much about the advantages of Western rationalism, or the great intellectual legacy of the white man, or maybe they'll begin to listen. And then, maybe one day, you'll find they actually do understand exactly what you are talking about, all these fantasy people. All these blues people. And on that day, as sure as shit, when you really believe you can "accept" them into your fold, as half-white trusties late of the subject peoples. With no more blues, except the very old ones, and not a watermelon in sight, the great missionary heart will have triumphed, and all of those ex-coons will be stand-up Western men, with eyes for clean hard useful lives, sober, pious and sane, and they'll murder you. They'll murder you, and have very rational explanations. Very much like your own. They'll cut your throats, and drag you out to the edge of your cities so the flesh can fall away from your bones, in sanitary isolation.

Lula:

> *(Her voice takes on a different, more businesslike quality.)*

I've heard enough.

Clay:

> *(Reaching for his books.)*

I bet you have. I guess I better collect my stuff and get off this train. Looks like we won't be acting out that little pageant you outlined before.

Lula: No. We won't. You're right about that, at least.

> *(She turns to look quickly around the rest of the car.)*

All right!

> *(The others respond.)*

Clay:
(*Bending across the girl to retrieve his belongings.*)
Sorry, baby, I don't think we could make it.
(*As he is bending over her, the girls brings up a small knife and plunges it into **Clay**'s chest. Twice. He slumps across her knees, his mouth working stupidly.*)

Lula: Sorry is right.
(*Turning to the others in the car who have already gotten up from their seats.*)
Sorry is the rightest thing you've said. Get this man off me! Hurry, now!
(*The others come and drag **Clay**'s body down the aisle.*)
Open the door and throw his body out.
(*They throw him off.*)
And all of you get off at the next stop.
(***Lula** busies herself straightening her things. Getting everything in order. She takes out a note book and makes a quick scribbling note. Drops it in her bag. The train apparently stops and all the others get off, leaving her alone in the coach.*
*Very soon a young Negro of about twenty comes into the coach, with a couple of books under his arm. He sits a few seats in back of **Lula**. When he is seated she turns and gives him a long slow look. He looks up from his book and drops the books on his lap. Then an old Negro conductor comes into the car, doing a sort of restrained soft shoe, and half mumbling the words of some song. He looks at the young man, briefly, with a quick greeting.*)

Conductor: Hey, brother!
Young Man: Hey.
(*The conductor continues down the aisle with his little dance and the mumbled song. **Lula** turns to stare at him and follows his movements down the aisle. The conductor tips his hat when he reaches her seat, and continues out the car.*)

Curtain

Blues for Mister Charlie

by James Baldwin

James Baldwin *(1924-   )*

Spoken of by admiring critics as a "dark, avenging angel" and "the voice of the black revolution," James Baldwin, one of the most powerful and influential black writers on the contemporary American and international scenes, was born in Harlem, the first of nine children. Baldwin's early life was far from easy. His father, a lay minister in the Holy Roller Church, who at times worked in a bottling factory, was a religious fanatic. His mother was a gentle, stoic woman with a vein of iron, who, when she could, worked in domestic service. For many years the family was on relief. Because of his position in the family, the responsibility of looking after his brothers and sisters fell upon the young Baldwin. Although he fulfilled these responsibilities dutifully and with love, he could later say, "My childhood was awful . . . then, I hadn't made any clear connection between the fact of color and the fact of my childhood. My childhood was awful in the way many childhoods are. Because we were poor. . . . There were too many of us."

At a later time, Baldwin could note that his father's religion, which deeply affected him, was his way of getting back at white folks for their oppression of black folks. "He had his God. And God would judge them. God would punish them. He wanted to kill them and he couldn't kill them. So he hoped God would. And he hoped that all his life . . . ." Baldwin himself was a boy preacher in a store-front church from the age of fourteen to seventeen, when he left home and worked at several odd jobs before becoming a writer.

His experiences at P.S. 29, Frederick Douglass Junior High School, and De Witt Clinton High School, from which he graduated in 1942, confirmed his love of books and literature, and fired his determination to become a writer. He wrote all the time, plays, poetry, short stories. "For me," he was to say, "writing was an act of love. It was an attempt not to get the world's attention—it was an attempt to be loved. It seemed a way to save myself and to save my family. It came out of despair. And it seemed the only way to another world."

In 1948 Baldwin, disgusted with the racial situation in America, left the United States for Europe where he was to stay for nearly ten years, living mainly in Paris. On his determination to become an expatriate he says, "If I'd been born in Mississippi, I might have come to New York. But being born in New York, there's no place you can go. You have to go out. *Out* of the country. And I went out of the country and I never intended to come back here. Ever. *Ever.*" In Paris Baldwin was befriended by Richard Wright, the well known Negro novelist and writer, the author of *Native Son* and *Black Boy*; but the friendship ended in bitterness. When he returned to the United States in 1957, he said it was because he did not wish to follow the example of Richard Wright who lived in limbo.

Baldwin's successful first novel, *Go Tell It On the Mountain*, was completed in Switzerland and published in New York in 1953. Other novels followed: *Giovanni's Room* (1956), *Another Country* (1962), and *Tell Me How Long the Train's Been Gone* (1968). A collection of short stories, *Going to Meet the Man* appeared in 1966. Among the author's celebrated collections of essays *Notes of a Native Son* (1955) dealt with his European sojourn; and there are *Nobody Knows My Name* (1961), and *The Fire Next Time* (1963). Where the theater is concerned Baldwin has written two immensely moving plays, *The Amen Corner* and *Blues for Mr. Charlie* that ran simultaneously on the West Coast and in New York during the 1963-64 season. There is also an adaptation of *Giovanni's Room*, which never reached Broadway, but found a sensitive presentation at The Actors Studio Workshop in 1957, with the Turkish actor, Engin Gezzar, in the leading role.

INTRODUCTION

Blues for Mister Charlie, produced by The Actors Studio, opened at the ANTA Theatre on April 23, 1964. It was staged by Burgess Meredith and designed by Feder. The large cast included Pat Hingle, Rip Torn, Al Freeman, Jr., Diana Sands, Ann Wedgeworth, Rosetta Le Noir, Percy Rodriguez, and the author's brother, David Baldwin. In this play which calls the black man to battle at the same time that it sings the blues for "Mister Charlie," the black man's name for the white man, James Baldwin, as his biographer, Fern Marja Eckman puts it, "set down with smoking vehemence just what his characters, black and white really think and feel and do about prejudice in the United States. His harsh conflicts, crude invective, and dissonant rhythms were like a Morse code, alerting America to disaster." But critical reception of the play was mixed. Howard Taubman, writing in the *New York Times*, hailed it as "a play with fires of fury in its belly, tears of anguish in its eyes, and a roar of protest in its throat," in which the author "speaks fiercely of the Negro's anguish and passion . . . and brings eloquence and conviction to one of the momentous themes of our era."

But other reviews were less enthusiastic. Concurring, for the most part, on its social significance, many critics regarded the play as a flawed work of art. Impressionistic in style, moving backward and forward in time, punctuated by set speeches of varying emotional intensity, directed specifically to the audience, the play met with the criticism that it was at times cumbersome and confusing in its structure. Indeed, Mrs. Eckman is most perceptive when she speaks of *Blues for Mister Charlie* as "Greek tragedy with a syncopated beat," surrounded by "the inchoate jungle of Baldwin's emotions, with only an occasional shaft of light to illuminate the darkness." However, the play reads well, which suggests that Baldwin may not have been completely successful in the translation of his talents as essayist and novelist to the drama.

But Baldwin was certain that the story he had to tell in *Blues for Mister Charlie* had to take the form of a play. He felt that the actors would embellish his words more effectively than the reader could take them from the printed page to the mind. Prior to its opening the author declared, "I'm not concerned with the success or failure of the play. I want to shock people; I want to wake them up; I want to make them think; I want to trick them into an experience which I think is important." This he certainly succeeded in doing for, as Mrs. Eckman says, "The blazing hatred racism kindles in Negroes, whether accurately gauged or overstated by Baldwin, confounded the integrated audiences and, in a sense, resegregated them: most of the Negroes responded to the murderous lines with the laughter of recognition and catharsis, but many of the whites reacted with unsheathed antagonism."

Dedicated to the memory of Medgar Evers, and his widow and his children and to the memory of the dead children of Birmingham, *Blues for Mister Charlie* is very distantly based upon the case of Emmett Till—the Negro youth who was murdered in Mississippi in 1955. The murderer was acquitted and later admitted his guilt. In the play the murderer's guilt is clear from the start, and so is the acquittal the jury will give. But the play in construction and presentation is anything but simple. Presented without scenery and depending wholly on effecive lighting against a massive black curtain, the action takes place on a multiple set, the skeleton of which outlines the Negro church in the first two acts, and in the third act the Courthouse. During the first two acts the dome of the Courthouse and the American flag are dominant. In the final act the steeple of the church and the cross dominate.

According to the author's introduction, "The play takes place in Plaguetown, U. S. A., now. The plague is race, the plague is our concept of Christianity: and this raging plague has the power to destroy every human relationship." What follows is a dynamic morality play that offers a bitterly brilliant anatomy of twentieth-century American racial conflict. The play is a study of contrast and conflict and yet one of subtle and sometimes vicious interaction. WHITETOWN and BLACKTOWN stand bitterly divided. "The attention will be on one at a time," Baldwin asserts, "but the audience will always know the other is present. The play destroys private life and the theory or mythology of race supremacy. When the Negro is unfolding the story, he will be up front on the stage and WHITETOWN will be in the back. And when it's time for the whites to speak, the Negroes will be in the back." Significantly, in the third act the whites and blacks move back and forth across the separating aisle. Thus their world becomes one.

Baldwin, despite the dissenting critics and according to his own testimony, has not been concerned with the writing within the rubric of the well-made play, with decorous concerns for realism, exposition, plot, climax and denouement. His concern seems to be centered, as I have suggested, in presenting a contemporary morality play of seething indignation and rage. Hence the play can be seen as the critics viewed it, as a sermon or a rhapsody, or as harking back to the exhortatory presentations of the Federal Theater in the thirties, with combinations of German Expressionism, proletarian "agitprop," and stark melodrama. And the conception of the play as a modern morality play diminishes the pronouncements of those critics who castigated the work on the grounds that the characters are essentially stereotypes. Abstraction is basic to the notion of the morality play, and although the characters, general and main, can be seen essentially as allegorical figures, they are deftly individualized and humanized in Baldwin's rendering of his ideas.

In outline, then, the play deals with the murder of a young black man, Richard, at the hands of a white shopowner, Lyle Britten, whose only response is "I've killed men before." Richard has come back to his home in the deep South after reaching the top and the bottom in New York. A rising singing star, a favorite at the Apollo in Harlem, his nemesis has been success, white women, and drugs. He returns, "a busted musician," to the house of his father, the Reverend Meridian Henry, who is the local leader of the civil rights movement. Trying to pull himself together, he is a bag of hostility, belligerently defiant of the racial ways of the South and the North, trying to redeem himself through his reawakened love for Juanita.

The play opens just after the murder is committed with Lyle picking up the boy's body and dropping it into the weeds beside the railroad tracks just outside the town, as he chants: "And may every nigger like this nigger end like this nigger—face down in the weeds." The scene then shifts to BLACKTOWN, the church where there are sounds of mourning. A week has passed. Students carrying civil rights placards enter, they have been engaged in a brutal encounter with the whites, and Lorenzo delivers a bitter diatribe against religion and nonviolent protest. Meridian expresses his faith in Parnell to help him to bring his son's murderer to trial. Parnell, the rich newspaper editor, a white liberal, has been Meridian's personal friend and ally for years, but some of the younger people are skeptical about his intentions. He appears briefly to tell his friends of a warrant's being issued for Lyle's arrest. When he leaves, Meridian speaks: "I wonder if they'll convict him?" To which Juanita, who loved Richard, cries out: "Convict him. Convict him. You're asking for heaven on earth. After all, they haven't even *arrested* him yet. And anyway—why should they convict him? Why him? He's no worse than all the others. He's an honorable tribesman and, he's defended with blood, the honor and purity of his tribe!" The scene shifts to Lyle and WHITETOWN.

Juanita's speech just given is important, for in a basic sense tribalism, as Max Lerner points out, is what the play is all about. For is not Baldwin saying, as Lerner puts it, that "the whites in a Southern town are not persons, they are part of a tribe, hate with tribal hate, and exact tribal loyalties, tribal obedience, tribal vengeance. The Negroes start with silence and sufferance and bi-racial committees and with the motto 'God is love.' They too have to draw their lines tighter, and they end up with tribal tightness and exclusiveness."

In a subsequent scene that is a flashback to Richard before the murder, the young man is seen in his room singing. At the end of his song, his grandmother, Mother Henry, enters and there is an interesting exchange which reveals much of Richard's background and the growth of his attitudes. He speaks of his mother's death and his father's actions at the time of her death. He speaks of his hatred of whites. And we get this snatch of dialog:

> **Mother Henry:** Richard, you can't start walking around believing that all the suffering in the world is caused by white folks!
> **Richard:** I can't? Don't tell me I can't. I'm going to treat everyone of them as though they were responsible for all the crimes that ever happened in the history of the world—oh, yes! They're responsible for all the misery I've ever seen and that's good enough for me. It's because my Daddy's got no power that my Mama's dead. And he ain' got no power because he's *black*. And the only way that the black man's going to get any power is to drive all the white men into the sea.

This scene serves as the basis for Richard's action in the course of the play. Pushed beyond endurance, he moves, on his return to the South, beyond civility, beyond his *place* in that society, provokes his killer, and invites his death. The centrality of Richard's position in the play and his attitudes in his confrontation with the white world led many critics to assume that Baldwin hated all whites and was perversely preaching hatred of all whites. This is a palpable misreading of Baldwin's intentions. Baldwin himself says on this matter, "It was very important for me, to have Richard Henry as offensive and brash and stupid as he is. Sure he had no right to talk to anyone like *that*. I know *that*. But do you have a right to shoot him? That's the question." Beyond this, the general context of Baldwin's work should make it clear that an unequivocal hatred of white America is not basic to his statements. In *My Dungeon Shook: Letter to My Nephew on the One Hundredth Anniversary of the Emancipation*, for instance, Baldwin writes, "Integration means that we, with love, shall force our brothers to see themselves as they are, to cease fleeing from reality, and begin to change it."

But anger at the South and at white America as a whole is manifestly a potent force in *Blues for Mr. Charlie*. And it is possible that Baldwin's mounting fury, his laudable indignation at the assassination of Medgar Evers, the bombing of the Birmingham children, and the murder of Emmet Till erupted into a position suggesting that meaningful communication between blacks and whites had, indeed, come to a serious impasse. Certainly he is in his play—and in no uncertain terms—renouncing the effectiveness of passive resistance and the non-violent aspects of the civil rights movement. The point to be made, however, is that Richard may be his author's personna, but he is not necessarily his total spokesman.

To push this analysis forward, Richard's father, the Reverend Meridian Henry, is a kind of Martin Luther King, Jr., who is forced to wonder after the murder of his son if he was not fundamentally wrong in urging his people not to arm. In the course of the action he comes to learn that his lifelong and boasted friendship with the rich white liberal, Parnell James, is basically unfounded. But there can be no question of the fact that the interchange between Meridian Henry and Parnell are among the most probing in the play. And this is for the simple reason that the story deals as much with Parnell's tragedy as it does with the tragedy of the blacks. It is also the tragedy of the murderer, Lyle Britten, and the poor white community that he represents. Lyle is depicted as a fairly bearable man when his racial rages are not aroused. Parnell depicts a torture ridden white man who had once loved a black girl whom he can never forget. At the end of the play, after having betrayed his black friends, he penitently asks Juanita if he can march with the blacks. "Can I walk with you?" The girl answers, "We can walk in the same direction. . . . Come. Don't look like that. Let's go on."

This conclusion, however, has to be juxtaposed with the scene of the murder—interlocked with the courtroom scene—in which Lyle seeks out Richard to demand an apology for his behavior in his store. But just prior to this episode, Meridian demands of Lyle: "What was the last thing my son said to you—before you shot him down—like a dog?" To which the white man replies,

> **Lyle:** Like a dog! You a smart nigger, ain't you?
> **Meridian:** What was the last thing he said? Did he beg for his life?
> **Lyle:** *That* nigger! He was too smart for that! He must have thought he was white. And I gave him every chance—to live—
> **Meridian:** And he refused them all.

With Lyle's word, "Do you know what that nigger said to me?" the action centers upon the climactic confrontation between Richard and Lyle, the upshot of which contains these lines:

> **Richard:** Why don't you go home? And let me go home? Do we need all of this shit? Can't we live without it?
> **Lyle:** Boy, are you drunk?
> **Richard:** No, I ain't drunk. I'm just tired. Tired of all of this fighting. What are you trying to prove? What am I trying to prove?
> **Lyle:** I'm trying to give you a break. You too dumb to take it.
> **Richard:** I'm hip. You been trying to give me a break for a great, long time. But there's only one break I want. And you won't give me that.

Lyle: What kind of break do you want, boy?

Richard: For you to go home. And let me go home. I got things to do. I got—lots of things to do!

Lyle: I got things to do, too. I'd like to get home, too.

Richard: Then why are we standing here? Can't we walk? Let me walk, white man! Let me walk!

Lyle: We can walk, just as soon as we get our business settled.

Richard: It's settled. You a man and I'm a man. Let's walk.

Lyle: Nigger, you was born down here. Ain't you never said sir to a white man?

Richard: No. The only person I ever said sir to was my Daddy.

Lyle: Are you going to apologize to me?

Richard: No.

Lyle: Do you want to live?

Richard: Yes.

Lyle: Then you know what to do, then, don't you?

Richard: Go home. Go home.

Then, facing Lyle's gun, having reached as it were a point of no return, Richard savagely insults Lyle in a passage containing the deepest sexual connotations. This passage which shocked many led the *Village Voice* to protest, "I can't think of any motive but psychic sadism for Baldwin's harping on the traditional theme of Negro sexual prowess versus the white man's limited potency." But Susan Sontag could say, "Only by tapping the sexual insecurity that grips most educated white Americans, could Baldwin's virulent rhetoric have seemed so reasonable."

Although many critics asserted that Baldwin loaded his dice in favor of his black characters, and that his white characters were mainly stereotypes, Max Lerner is correct, I think, when he claims that Baldwin treats both racial communities fairly. He notes for instance that in the trial scene every witness—black as well as white—lies under oath, "lest he break the solid phalanx of his race." The picture that Baldwin draws, as Lerner says, is bleak: "the whites, mean and narrow and hate-ridden, their women sex-starved hysterics, their men killing . . . out of twisted impulse to follow the code and to prove . . . [their] manhood." The Negroes are, according to this critic treated realistically but, understandably, with greater love. But the major symbolism in the conclusion of the play centers around the Reverend Meridian Henry who, after a funeral sermon at the end of the second act that rocks the church as he urges his children to "Learn to walk again like men," reveals, in the end, that Richard's gun is in his father's pulpit under his Bible.

A remarkably stirring work, this play seemingly so complex and convoluted in its design, reflects in its entirety the convolutions in the historical and contemporary implications of black-white relations in this country as a whole as well as in the deep South.

Blues for Mister Charlie

Dedication: To the memory of Medgar Evers, and his widow and his children and to the memory of the dead children of Birmingham.

CHARACTERS

Meridian Henry, a *Negro minister*
Tom, Ken, Arthur, Juanita, Lorenzo, Pete, *Negro students*
Mother Henry, *Meridian Henry's mother*
Lyle Britten, *a white store-owner*
Jo Britten, *Lyle's wife*
Parnell James, *editor of the local newspaper*
Richard, *Meridian Henry's son*
Papa D., *owner of a juke joint*
Hazel, Lillian, Susan, Ralph, Ellis, Rev. Phelps, George,
    white townspeople
The State
Counsel for the Bereaved
Congregation of Rev. Henry's church, Pallbearers,
    Blacktown, Whitetown

NOTES FOR BLUES

This play has been on my mind—has been bugging me—for several years. It is unlike anything else I've ever attempted in that I remember vividly the first time it occurred to me; for in fact, it did not occur to me, but to Elia Kazan. Kazan asked me at the end of 1958 if I would be interested in working in the Theatre. It was a generous offer, but I did not react with great enthusiasm because I did not then, and don't now, have much respect for what goes on in the American Theatre. I am not convinced that it *is* a Theatre; it seems to me a series, merely, of commercial speculations, stale, repetitious, and timid. I certainly didn't see much future for me in that frame-work, and I was profoundly unwilling to risk my morale and my talent—my life—in endeavors which could only increase a level of frustration already dangerously high.

Nevertheless, the germ of the play persisted. It is based, very distantly indeed, on the case of Emmett Till—the Negro youth who was murdered in

Mississippi in 1955. The murderer in this case was acquitted. (His brother, who helped him do the deed, is now a deputy sheriff in Rulesville, Mississippi.) After his acquittal, he recounted the facts of the murder—for one cannot refer to his performance as a confession—to William Bradford Huie, who wrote it all down in an article called "Wolf Whistle." I do not know why the case pressed on my mind so hard—but it would not let me go. I absolutely dreaded committing myself to writing a play—there were enough people around already telling me that I couldn't write novels—but I began to see that my fear of the form masked a much deeper fear. That fear was that I would never be able to draw a valid portrait of the murderer. In life, obviously, such people baffle and terrify me and, with one part of my mind at least, I hate them and would be willing to kill them. Yet, with another part of my mind, I am aware that no man is a villain in his own eyes. Something in the man knows—*must* know—that what he is doing is evil; but in order to accept the knowledge the man would have to change. What is ghastly and really almost hopeless in our racial situation now is that the crimes we have committed are so great and so unspeakable that the acceptance of this knowledge would lead, literally, to madness. The human being, then, in order to protect himself, closes his eyes, compulsively repeats his crimes, and enters a spiritual darkness which no one can describe.

But if it is true, and I believe it is, that all men are brothers, then we have the duty to try to understand this wretched man; and while we probably cannot hope to liberate him, begin working toward the liberation of his children. For we, the American people, have created him, he is our servant; it is we who put the cattle-prodder in his hands, and we are responsible for the crimes that he commits. It is we who have locked him in the prison of his color. It is we who have persuaded him that Negroes are worthless human beings, and that it is his sacred duty, as a white man, to protect the honor and purity of his tribe. It is we who have forbidden him, on pain of exclusion from the tribe, to accept his beginnings, when he and black people loved each other, and rejoice in them, and use them; it is we who have made it mandatory—honorable—that white father should deny black son. These are grave crimes indeed, and we have committed them and continue to commit them in order to make money.

The play then, for me, takes place in Plaguetown, U.S.A., now. The plague is race, the plague is our concept of Christianity: and this raging plague has the power to destroy every human relationship. I once took a short trip with Medgar Evers to the back-woods of Mississippi. He was investigating the murder of a Negro man by a white storekeeper which had taken place months before. Many people talked to Medgar that night, in dark cabins, with their lights out, in whispers; and we had been followed for many miles out of Jackson, Mississippi, not by a lunatic with a gun, but by state troopers. I will never forget that night, as I will never forget Medgar—who took me to the plane the next day. We promised to see each other soon. When he died, something entered into me which I cannot describe, but it was then that I resolved that nothing under heaven would prevent me from getting this play done. We are walking in terrible darkness here, and this is one man's attempt to bear witness to the reality and the power of light.

James Baldwin
New York, April, 1964

Act One

Multiple set, the skeleton of which, in the first two acts, is the Negro church, and, in the third act, the courthouse. The church and the courthouse are on opposite sides of a southern street; the audience should always be aware, during the first two acts, of the dome of the courthouse and the American flag. During the final act, the audience should always be aware of the steeple of the church, and the cross.

The church is divided by an aisle. The street door upstage faces the audience. The pulpit is downstage, at an angle, so that the minister is simultaneously addressing the congregation and the audience. In the third act, the pulpit is replaced by the witness stand.

This aisle also functions as the division between **Whitetown** *and* **Blacktown***. The action among the blacks takes place on one side of the stage, the action among the whites on the opposite side of the stage—which is to be remembered during the third act, which takes place, of course, in a segregated courtroom.*

This means that **Richard***'s room,* **Lyle***'s store,* **Papa D.***'s joint,* **Jo***'s kitchen, etc., are to exist principally by suggestion, for these shouldn't be allowed to obliterate the skeleton, or, more accurately, perhaps, the frame-work, suggested above.*

For the murder scene, the aisle functions as a gulf. The stage should be built out, so that the audience reacts to the enormity of this gulf, and so that **Richard***, when he falls, falls out of sight of the audience, like a stone, into the pit.*

In the darkness we hear a shot.

Lights up slowly on **Lyle***, staring down at the ground. He looks around him, bends slowly and picks up* **Richard***'s body as though it were a sack. He carries him upstage, drops him.*

Lyle: And may every nigger like this nigger end like this nigger—face down in the weeds!
   (Exits.)
   *(***Blacktown:*** The church. A sound of mourning begins.* **Meridian, Tom, Ken** *and* **Arthur***.)*
Meridian: No, no, no! You have to say it like you mean it—the way they really say it: nigger, nigger, nigger! *Nigger!* Tom, the way *you* saying it, it sounds like you just *might* want to make friends. And that's not the way they sound out there. Remember all that's happened. Remember we having a funeral here—tomorrow night. Remember why. Go on, hit it again.

Tom: You dirty nigger, you no-good black bastard, what you doing down here, anyway?

Meridian: That's much better. Much, much better. Go on.

Tom: Hey, boy, where's your mother? I bet she's lying up in bed, just a-pumping away, ain't she, boy?

Meridian: *That's* the way they sound!

Tom: Hey, boy, how much does your mother charge? How much does your sister charge?

Ken: How much does your *wife* charge?

Meridian: Now you got it. You really got it now. That's them. Keep walking, Arthur. *Keep walking!*

Tom: You get your ass off these streets from around here, boy, or we going to do some cutting—we're going to cut that big, black thing off of you, you hear?

Meridian: Why you all standing around there like that? Go on and get you a nigger. Go on!

    (*A scuffle.*)

Meridian: All right. All right! Come on, now. Come on.

    (**Ken** *steps forward and spits in* **Arthur***'s face.*)

Arthur: You black s.o.b., what the hell do you think you're doing? Your mother—!

Meridian: Hey, hold it! Hold it! Hold it!

    (**Meridian** *wipes the boy's face. They are all trembling.*)

    (**Mother Henry** *enters.*)

Mother Henry: Here they come. And it looks like they had a time.

    (**Juanita, Lorenzo, Pete, Jimmy,** *all Negro, carry placards, enter, exhausted and dishevelled, wounded;* **Pete** *is weeping. The placards bear such legends as* Freedom Now, We Want The Murderer, One Man, One Vote, *etc.*)

Juanita: We shall overcome!

Lorenzo: We shall not be moved!

    (*Laughs.*)

We were moved tonight, though. Some of us has been moved to *tears*.

Meridian: Juanita, what happened?

Juanita: Oh, just another hometown Saturday night.

Meridian: Come on, Pete, come on, old buddy. Stop it. Stop it.

Lorenzo: I don't blame him. I do not blame the cat. You feel like a damn fool standing up there, letting them white mothers beat on your ass—shoot, if I had my way, just once—stop crying, Pete, goddammit!

Juanita: Lorenzo, you're in church.

Lorenzo: Yeah. Well, I wish to God I was in an arsenal. I'm sorry, Meridian, Mother Henry—I don't mean that for you. I don't understand you. I don't understand Meridian here. It was his son, it was your grandson, Mother Henry, that got killed, butchered! Just last week, and yet, here you sit—in this—this—the house of this damn almighty God who don't care what happens to nobody, unless, of course, they're white. Mother Henry, I got a lot of respect for you and all that, and for Meridian, too, but that white man's

God is *white*. It's that damn white God that's been lynching us and burning us and castrating us and raping our women and robbing us of everything that makes a man a man for all these hundreds of years. Now, why we sitting around here, in *His* house? If I could get my hands on Him, I'd pull Him out of heaven and drag Him through this town at the end of a rope.

Meridian: No, you wouldn't.

Lorenzo: I wouldn't? Yes, I would. Oh, yes, I would.

Juanita: And then you wouldn't be any better than they are.

Lorenzo: I don't want to be better than they are, why should I be better than they are? And better at what? Better at being a doormat, better at being a corpse? Sometimes I just don't know. We've been demonstrating—*non-violently*—for more than a year now and all that's happened is that now they'll let us into that crummy library downtown which was obsolete in 1897 and where nobody goes anyway; who in this town reads books? For that we paid I don't know how many thousands of dollars in fines, Jerome is still in the hospital, and we all know that Ruthie is never again going to be the swinging little chick she used to be. Big deal. Now we're picketing that great movie palace downtown where I wouldn't go on a bet; I can live without Yul Brynner and Doris Day, thank you very much. And we *still* can't get licensed to be electricians or plumbers, we still can't walk through the park, our kids still can't use the swimming pool in town. We still can't vote, we can't even get registered. Is it worth it? And these people trying to kill us, too? And we ain't even got no guns. The cops ain't going to protect us. They call up the people and tell them where we are and say, "Go get them! They ain't going to do nothing to you—they just dumb niggers!"

Meridian: Did they arrest anybody tonight?

Pete: No, they got their hands full now, trying to explain what Richard's body was doing in them weeds.

Lorenzo: It was wild. You know, all the time we was ducking them bricks and praying to *God* we'd get home before somebody got killed—

> *(Laughs.)*

I had a jingle going through my mind, like if I was a white man, dig? and I had to wake up every morning singing to myself, "Look at the happy nigger, he doesn't give a damn, thank God I'm not a nigger—"

Together: "*—Good Lord, perhaps I am!*"

Juanita: You've gone crazy, Lorenzo. They've done it. You have been unfitted for the struggle.

Meridian: I cannot rest until they bring my son's murderer to trial. That man who killed my son.

Lorenzo: But he killed a nigger before, as I know all of you know. Nothing never happened. Sheriff just shovelled the body into the ground and forgot about it.

Meridian: Parnell will help me.

Pete: Meridian, you know that *Mister* Parnell ain't going to let them arrest his ass-hole buddy. I'm sorry, Mother Henry!

Mother Henry: That's all right, son.

Meridian: But I think that Parnell has proven to be a pretty good friend to all of us. He's the only white man in this town who's every *really* stuck his neck out in order to do—to do right. He's *fought* to bring about this trial—I can't tell you how hard he's fought. If it weren't for him, there'd be much less hope.

Lorenzo: I guess I'm just not as nice as you are. I don't trust as many people as you trust.

Meridian: We can't afford to become too distrustful, Lorenzo.

Lorenzo: We can't afford to be too trusting, either. See, when a white man's a *good* white man, he's good because he wants *you* to be good. Well, sometimes I just might want to be *bad*. I got as much right to be bad as anybody else.

Meridian: No, you don't.

Lorenzo: Why not?

Meridian: Because you know better.

(*Parnell enters.*)

Parnell: Hello, my friends. I bring glad tidings of great joy. Is that the way the phrase goes, Meridian?

Juanita: Parnell!

Parnell: I can't stay. I just came to tell you that a warrant's being issued for Lyle's arrest.

Juanita: They're going to arrest him? Big Lyle Britten? I'd love to know how you managed *that*.

Parnell: Well, Juanita, I am not a *good* man, but I have my little ways.

Juanita: And a whole lot of folks in this town, baby, are not going to be talking to you no more, for days and days and *days*.

Parnell: I hope that you all will. I may have no other company. I think I should go to Lyle's house to warn him. After all, I brought it about and he *is* a friend of mine—and then I have to get the announcement into my paper.

Juanita: So it *is* true.

Parnell: Oh, yes. It's true.

Meridian: When is he being arrested?

Parnell: Monday morning. Will you be up later, Meridian? I'll drop by if you are—if I may.

Meridian: Yes. I'll be up.

Parnell: All right, then. I'll trundle by. Good night all. I'm sorry I've got to run.

Meridian: Good night.

Juanita: Thank you, Parnell.

Parnell: Don't thank me, dear Juanita. I only acted—as I believed I had to act. See you later, Meridian.

(*Parnell exits.*)

Meridian: I wonder if they'll convict him.

Juanita: Convict him. Convict him. You're asking for heaven on earth. After all, they haven't even *arrested* him yet. And, anyway—why *should* they convict him? Why him? He's no worse than all the others. He's an honorable tribesman and he's defended, with blood, the honor and purity of his tribe!

(Whitetown: Lyle holds his infant son up above his head.)

Lyle: Hey old pisser. You hear me, sir? I expect you to control your bladder like a *gentleman* whenever your Papa's got you on his knee.

(Jo enters.)

He got a mighty big bladder, too, for such a little fellow.

Jo: I'll tell the world he didn't steal it.

Lyle: You mighty sassy tonight.

(Hands her the child.)

Ain't that right, old pisser? Don't you reckon your Mama's getting kind of sassy? And what do you reckon I should do about it?

(Jo in changing the child's diapers.)

Jo: You tell your Daddy he can start sleeping in his own bed nights instead of coming grunting in here in the wee small hours of the morning.

Lyle: And you tell your Mama if she was getting her sleep like she should be, so she can be alert every instant to your needs, little fellow, she wouldn't *know* what time I come—*grunting* in.

Jo: I got to be alert to *your* needs, too. I think.

Lyle: Don't you go starting to imagine things. I just been over to the store. That's all.

Jo: Till three and four o'clock in the morning?

Lyle: Well, I got plans for the store, I think I'm going to try to start branching out, you know, and I been—making plans.

Jo: You thinking of branching out *now*? Why, Lyle, you know we ain't *hardly* doing no business *now*. Weren't for the country folks come to town every Saturday, I don't know *where* we'd be. This ain't no time to be branching *out*. We hardly holding *on*.

Lyle: Shoot, the niggers'll be coming back, don't you worry. They'll get over this foolishness presently. They already weary of having to drive forty-fifty miles across the state line to get their groceries—a lot of them ain't even got cars.

Jo: Those that don't have cars have *friends* with cars.

Lyle: Well, friends get weary, too. Joel come in the store a couple of days ago—

Jo: Papa D.? He don't count. You can always wrap him around your little finger.

Lyle: Listen, will you? He come in the store a couple of days ago to buy a sack of flour and he *told* me, he say, The niggers is *tired* running all over creation to put some food on the table. Ain't nobody going to keep on driving no forty-fifty miles to buy no sack of flour—what you mean when you say Joel don't count?

Jo: I don't mean nothing. But there's something wrong with anybody when his own people don't think much of him.

Lyle: Joel's got good sense, is all. I think more of him than I think of a lot of white men, that's a fact. And he knows what's right for his people, too.

Jo:

(Puts son in crib.)

Well. Selling a sack of flour once a week ain't going to send this little one through college, neither.

    (A pause.)

In what direction were you planning to branch out?

Lyle: I was thinking of trying to make the store more—well, more colorful. Folks like color—

Jo: You mean, niggers like color.

Lyle: Dammit, Jo, I ain't in business just to sell to niggers! Listen to me, can't you? I thought I'd dress it up, get a new front, put some neon signs in— and, you know, we got more space in there than we use. Well, why don't we open up a line of ladies' clothes? Nothing too fancy, but I bet you it would bring in a lot more business.

Jo: I don't know. Most of the ladies I know buy their clothes at Benton's, on Decatur Street.

Lyle: The niggers don't—anyway, we could sell them the same thing. The white ladies, I mean—

Jo: No. It wouldn't be the same.

Lyle: Why not? A dress is a dress.

Jo: But it sounds better if you say you got it on Decatur Street! At Benton's. Anyway—where would you get the money for this branching out?

Lyle: I can get a loan from the bank. I'll get old Parnell to co-sign with me, or have him get one of his rich friends to co-sign with me.

Jo: Parnell called earlier—you weren't at the store today.

Lyle: What do you mean, I wasn't at the store?

Jo: Because Parnell called earlier and said he tried to get you at the store and that there wasn't any answer.

Lyle: There wasn't any business. I took a walk.

Jo: He said he's got bad news for you.

Lyle: What kind of bad news?

Jo: He didn't say. He's coming by here this evening to give it to you himself.

Lyle: What do you think it is?

Jo: I guess they're going to arrest you?

Lyle: No, they ain't. They ain't gone crazy.

Jo: I think they might. We had so much trouble in this town lately and it's been in all the northern newspapers—and now, this—this dead boy—

Lyle: They ain't got no case.

Jo: No. But you was the last person to see that crazy boy—alive. And now everybody's got to thinking again—about that other time.

Lyle: That was self defense. The Sheriff said so himself. Hell, I ain't no mur- derer. They're just some things I don't believe is right.

Jo: Nobody never heard no more about the poor little girl—his wife.

Lyle: No. She just disappeared.

Jo: You never heard no more about her at all?

Lyle: How would I hear about her more than anybody else? No, she just took off—I believe she had people in Detroit somewhere. I reckon that's where she went.

BLUES FOR MISTER CHARLIE   249

Jo: I felt sorry for her. She looked so lost those last few times I saw her, wandering around town—and she was so young. She was a pretty little thing.
Lyle: She looked like a pickaninny to me. Like she was too young to be married. I reckon she *was* too young for him.
Jo: It happened in the store.
Lyle: Yes.
Jo: How people talked! That's what scares me now.
Lyle: Talk don't matter. I hope you didn't believe what you heard.
Jo: A lot of people did. I reckon a lot of people still do.
Lyle: *You* don't believe it?
Jo: No.

> *(A pause.)*

You know—Monday morning—we'll be married one whole year!
Lyle: Well, can't nobody talk about *us*. That little one there ain't but two months old.

> *(The door bell rings.)*

Jo: That's Parnell.

> *(Exits.)*

> *(**Lyle** walks up and down, looks into the crib. **Jo** and **Parnell** enter.)*

Lyle: It's about time you showed your face in here, you old rascal! You been so busy over there with the niggers, you ain't got time for white folks no more. You sure you ain't got some nigger wench over there on the other side of town? Because, I declare—!
Parnell: I apologize for your husband, Mrs. Britten, I really do. In fact, I'm afraid I must deplore your taste in men. If I had only seen you first, dear lady, and if you had found me charming, how much suffering I might have prevented! You got anything in this house to drink? Don't tell me you haven't, we'll both need one. Sit down.
Lyle: Bring on the booze, old lady.

> *(**Jo** brings ice, glasses, etc.; pours drinks.)*

What you been doing with yourself?
Parnell: Well, I seem to have switched territories. I haven't been defending colored people this week, I've been defending you. I've just left the Chief of Police.
Lyle: How is the old bastard?
Parnell: He seems fine. But he really *is* an old bastard. Lyle—he's issuing a warrant for your arrest.
Lyle: He's going to arrest *me*? You mean, he believes I killed that boy?
Parnell: The question of what he believes doesn't enter into it. This case presents several very particular circumstances and these circumstances force him to arrest you. I think we can take it for granted that he wouldn't arrest you if he could think of some way not to. He wouldn't arrest anybody except blind beggars and old colored women if he could think of some way not to —he's bird-brained and chicken-hearted and big-assed. The charge is murder.
Jo: Murder!
Lyle: Murder?
Parnell: Murder.

Lyle: I ain't no murderer. You know that.

Parnell: I also know that somebody killed the boy. Somebody put two slugs in his belly and dumped his body in the weeds beside the railroad track just outside of town. Somebody did all that. We pay several eminent, bird-brained, chicken-hearted, big-assed people quite a lot of money to discourage such activity. They never do, in fact, discourage it, but, still—we must find the somebody who killed that boy. And you, my friend, according to the testimony of Joel Davis, otherwise known as Papa D., were the last person to see the boy alive. It is also known that you didn't like him—to say the least.

Lyle: Nobody liked him.

Parnell: Ah. But it isn't nobody that killed him. *Somebody* killed him. We must find the somebody. And since you were the last person to see him alive, we must arrest you in order to clear you—or convict you.

Lyle: They'll never convict me.

Parnell: As to that, you may be right. But you *are* going to be arrested.

Lyle: When?

Parnell: Monday morning. Of course, you can always flee to Mexico.

Lyle: Why should I run away?

Parnell: I wasn't suggesting that you should run away. If you did, I should urge your wife to divorce you at once, and marry me.

Jo: Ah, if that don't get him out of town in a hurry, I don't know what will! The man's giving you your chance, honey. You going to take it?

Lyle: Stop talking foolishness. It looks bad for me, I guess. I swear, I don't know what's come over the folks in this town!

Parnell: It doesn't look good. In fact, if the boy had been white, it would look very, *very* bad, and your behind would be in the jail house now. What do you mean, you don't understand what's come over the people in this town?

Lyle: Raising so much fuss about a nigger—and a northern nigger at that.

Parnell: He was born here. He's Reverend Meridian Henry's son.

Lyle: Well, he's been gone so long, he might as well have been a northern nigger. Went North and got ruined and come back here to make trouble—and they tell me he was a dope fiend, too. What's all this fuss about? He probably got killed by some other nigger—they do it all the time—but ain't nobody even thought about arresting one of *them*. Has niggers suddenly got to be *holy* in this town?

Parnell: Oh, Lyle, I'm not here to discuss the sanctity of niggers. I just came to tell you that a warrant's being issued for your arrest. *You* may think that a colored boy who gets ruined in the North and then comes home to try to pull himself together deserves to die—*I* don't.

Lyle: You sound like you think I got something against colored folks—but I don't. I never have, not in all my life. But I'll be damned if I'll mix with them. That's all. I don't believe in it, and that's *all*. I don't want no big buck nigger lying up next to Josephine and that's where all this will lead to and you know it as well as I do! I'm against it and I'll do anything I have to do to stop it, yes, I will!

Parnell: Suppose *he*—my godson there—decides to marry a Chinese girl. You know, there are an awful lot of Chinese girls in the world—I bet you didn't know that. Well, there are. Let's just say that he grows up and looks around at all the pure white women, and—saving your presence, ma'am—they make him want to puke and he decides to marry a pure Chinese girl instead. What would you do? Shoot him in order to prevent it? Or would you shoot her?

Lyle: Parnell, you're my buddy. You've *always* been my buddy. You know more about me than anybody else in the world. What's come over you? You —you ain't going to turn against me, are you?

Parnell: No. No, I'll never turn against you. I'm just trying to make you think.

Lyle: I notice you didn't marry no Chinese girl. You just never got married at all. Women been trying to saddle old Parnell for I don't know how long— I don't know what you got, old buddy, but I'll be damned if you don't know how to use it! What about this present one—Loretta—you reckon you going to marry her?

Parnell: I doubt it.

Jo: Parnell, you're just awful. Awful!

Parnell: I think I'm doing her a favor. She can do much better than me. I'm just a broken-down newspaper editor—the editor of a newspaper which *nobody* reads—in a dim, grim backwater.

Lyle: I thought you liked it here.

Parnell: I don't like it here. But I love it here. Or maybe I don't. I don't know. I must go.

Lyle: What's your hurry? Why don't you stay and have pot-luck with us?

Parnell: Loretta is waiting. I must have pot-luck with *her.* And then I have errands on the other side of town.

Lyle: What they saying over there? I reckon they praying day and night for my ass to be put in a sling, ain't they? Shoot, I don't care.

Parnell: Don't. Life's much simpler that way. Anyway, Papa D.'s the only one doing a whole lot of talking.

Jo: I told you he wasn't no good, Lyle, I told you!

Lyle: I don't know what's got into him! And we been knowing each other all these years! He must be getting old. You go back and tell him I said he's got it all *confused*—about me and that boy. Tell him you talked to me and that *I* said he must have made some mistake.

Parnell: I'll drop in tomorrow, if I may. Good night, Jo, and thank you. Good night, Lyle.

Lyle: Good night, old buddy.

Jo: I'll see you to the door.

   (**Jo** and **Parnell** *exit.* **Lyle** *walks up and down.*)

Lyle: Well! *Ain't* that something! But they'll never convict me. Never in this world.

   (*Looks into crib.*)

Ain't that right, old pisser?

   (**Blacktown:** *The church, as before.*)

Lorenzo: And when they bring him to trial, I'm going to be there every day

—right across the street in that courthouse—where they been dealing death out to us for all these years.

Mother Henry: I used to hate them, too, son. But I don't hate them no more. They too pitiful.

Meridian: No witnesses.

Juanita: Meridian. Ah, Meridian.

Mother Henry: You remember that song he used to like so much?

Meridian: I sing because I'm happy.

Juanita: I sing because I'm free.

Pete: For his eye is on the sparrow—

Lorenzo: And I know he watches—me.

(Music, very faint.)

Juanita: There was another song he liked—a song about a prison and the light from a train that shone on the prisoners every night at midnight. I can hear him now: Lord, you wake up in the morning. You hear the ding-dong ring—

Mother Henry: He had a beautiful voice.

Lorenzo: Well, he was pretty tough up there in New York—till he got busted.

Meridian: And came running home.

Mother Henry: Don't blame yourself, honey. Don't blame yourself!

Juanita: You go a-marching to the table, you see the same old thing—

Jimmy: All! I'm going to tell you: knife, a fork, and a pan—

(Music stronger.)

Pete: And if you say a thing about it—

Lorenzo: You are in trouble with the man.

(Lights dim in the church. We discover **Richard***, standing in his room, singing. This number is meant to make vivid the* **Richard** *who was much loved on the Apollo Theatre stage in Harlem, the* **Richard** *who was a rising New York star.)*

Meridian: No witnesses!

(Near the end of the song, **Mother Henry** *enters, carrying a tray with milk, sandwiches, and cake.)*

Richard: You treating me like royalty, old lady—I ain't royalty. I'm just a raggedy-assed, out-of-work, busted musician. But I sure can sing, can't I?

Mother Henry: You better learn some respect, you know that neither me nor your father wants that kind of language in this house. Sit down and eat, you got to get your strength back.

Richard: What for? What am I supposed to do with it?

Mother Henry: You stop that kind of talk.

Richard: Stop that kind of talk, we don't want that kind of talk! Nobody cares what people feel or what they think or what they do—but stop that kind of talk!

Mother Henry: Richard!

Richard: All right. All right.

(Throws himself on the bed, begins eating in a kind of fury.)

What I can't get over is—what in the world am I doing *here?* Way down here in the ass-hole of the world, the deep, black, funky South.

Mother Henry: You were born here. You got folks here. And you ain't got no manners and you *won't* learn no sense and so you naturally got yourself in trouble and had to come to your folks. You lucky it wasn't no worse, the way you go on. You want some more milk?

Richard: No, old lady. Sit down.

Mother Henry: I ain't got time to be fooling with you.

(But she sits down.)

What you got on your mind?

Richard: I don't know. How do you stand it?

Mother Henry: Stand what? You?

Richard: Living down here with all these nowhere people.

Mother Henry: From what I'm told and from what I see, the people you've been among don't seem to be any better.

Richard: You mean old Aunt Edna? She's all right, she just ain't very bright, is all.

Mother Henry: I am not talking about Edna. I'm talking about all them other folks you got messed up with. Look like you'd have had better sense. You hear me?

Richard: I hear you.

Mother Henry: That all you got to say?

Richard: It's easy for you to talk, Grandmama, you don't know nothing about New York City, or what can happen to you up there!

Mother Henry: I know what can happen to you anywhere in this world. And I know right from wrong. We tried to raise you so you'd know right from wrong, too.

Richard: We don't see things the same way, Grandmama. I don't know if I really *know* right from wrong—I'd like to, I always dig people the most who know *anything*, especially right from wrong!

Mother Henry: You've had yourself a little trouble, Richard, like we all do, and you a little tired, like we all get. You'll be all right. You a young man. Only, just try not to go so much, try to calm down a little. Your Daddy loves you. You his only son.

Richard: That's a good reason, Grandmama. Let me tell you about New York. You ain't never been North, have you?

Mother Henry: Your Daddy used to tell me a little about it every time he come back from visiting you all up there.

Richard: Daddy don't know nothing about New York. He just come up for a few days and went right on back. That ain't the way to get to know New York. No ma'am. He *never* saw New York. Finally, I realized he wasn't never *going* to see it—you know, there's a whole lot of things Daddy's never seen? I've seen more than he has.

Mother Henry: All young folks thinks that.

Richard: Did *you*? When you were young? Did you think you knew more than your mother and father? But I bet you really did, you a pretty shrewd old lady, quiet as it's kept.

Mother Henry: No, I didn't think that. But I thought I could find *out* more, because *they* were born in slavery, but *I* was born free.

Richard: *Did* you find out more?

Mother Henry: I found out what I had to find out—to take care of my husband and raise my children in the fear of God.

Richard: You know I don't believe in God, Grandmama.

Mother Henry: You don't know what you talking about. Ain't no way possible for you not to believe in God. It ain't up to you.

Richard: Who's it up to, then?

Mother Henry: It's up to the life in you—the life in you. *That* knows where it comes from, *that* believes in God. You doubt me, you just try holding your breath long enough to die.

Richard: You pretty smart, ain't you?

    (A pause.)

I convinced Daddy that I'd be better off in New York—and Edna, she convinced him too, she said it wasn't as tight for a black man up there as it is down here. Well, that's a crock, Grandmama, believe me when I tell you. At first I thought it was true, hell, I was just a green country boy and they ain't got no signs up, dig, saying you can't go here or you can't go there. No, you got to find that out all by your lonesome. But—for awhile—I thought everything was swinging and Edna, she's so dizzy she thinks everything is *always* swinging, so there we were—like *swinging.*

Mother Henry: I know Edna got lost somewhere. But, Richard—why didn't *you* come back? You knew your Daddy wanted you back, your Daddy and me both.

Richard: I didn't want to come back here like a whipped dog. One whipped dog running to another whipped dog. No, I didn't want that. I wanted to make my Daddy proud of me—because, the day I left here, I sure as hell wasn't proud of *him.*

Mother Henry: Be careful, son. Be careful. Your Daddy's a fine man. Your Daddy loves you.

Richard: I know, Grandmama. But I just wish, that day that Mama died, he'd took a pistol and gone through that damn white man's hotel and shot every son of a bitch in the place. That's right. I wish he'd shot them dead. I been dreaming of that day ever since I left here. I been dreaming of my Mama falling down the steps of that hotel. *My* Mama. I never believed she fell. I *always* believed that some white man pushed her down those steps. And I know that Daddy thought so, too. But he wasn't there, he didn't know, he couldn't say nothing, he couldn't *do* nothing. I'll never forget the way he looked—whipped, whipped, whipped, whipped!

Mother Henry: She fell, Richard, she *fell.* The stairs were wet and slippery and she *fell.*

Richard: My mother *fell* down the steps of that damn white hotel? My mother was *pushed*—you remember yourself how them white bastards was always sniffing around my mother, *always* around her—because she was pretty and *black!*

Mother Henry: Richard, you can't start walking around believing that all the suffering in the world is caused by white folks!

Richard: I can't? Don't tell me I can't. I'm going to treat everyone of them as though they were responsible for all the crimes that ever happened in the history of the world—oh, yes! They're responsible for all the misery I've ever seen, and that's good enough for me. It's because my Daddy's got no power that my Mama's dead. And he ain't got no power because he's *black*. And the only way the black man's going to *get* any power is to drive all the white men into the sea.

Mother Henry: You're going to make yourself sick. You're going to make yourself sick with hatred.

Richard: No, I'm not. I'm going to make myself well. I'm going to make myself *well* with hatred—what do you think of that?

Mother Henry: It can't be done. It can never be done. Hatred is a poison, Richard.

Richard: Not for me. I'm going to learn how to drink it—a little every day in the morning, and then a booster shot late at night. I'm going to remember everything. I'm going to keep it right here, at the very top of my mind. I'm going to remember Mama, and Daddy's face that day, and Aunt Edna and all her sad little deals and all those boys and girls in Harlem and all them pimps and whores and gangsters and all them cops. And I'm going to remember all the dope that's flowed through my veins. I'm going to remember everything—the jails I been in and the cops that beat me and how long a time I spent screaming and stinking in my own dirt, trying to break my habit. I'm going to remember all that, and I'll get well. I'll get well.

Mother Henry: Oh, Richard. Richard. Richard.

Richard: Don't Richard *me*. I tell you, I'm going to get *well*.

> (He takes a small, sawed-off pistol from his pocket.)

Mother Henry: Richard, what are you doing with that gun?

Richard: I'm carrying it around with me, that's what I'm doing with it. This gun goes everywhere I go.

Mother Henry: How long have you had it?

Richard: I've had it a long, long time.

Mother Henry: Richard—you never—?

Richard: No. Not yet. But I will when I have to. I'll sure as hell take one of the bastards with me.

Mother Henry: Hand me that gun. Please.

Richard: I can't. This is all that the man understands. He don't understand nothing else. *Nothing else!*

Mother Henry: Richard—your father—think of your father—

Richard: Don't tell him! You hear me?

> (A pause.)

Don't tell him!

Mother Henry: Richard. Please.

Richard: Take the tray away, old lady. I ain't hungry no more.

> (After a moment, **Mother Henry** takes the tray and exits. **Richard** stretches out on the bed.)

Juanita:

> (Off.)

Meridian? Mother Henry? Anybody home in this house?

(Enters.)

Oh! Excuse me.

Richard: I think they might be over at the church. I reckon Grandmama went over there to pray for my soul.

Juanita: Grandmama?

Richard: Who are you? Don't I know you?

Juanita: Yes. I think you might.

Richard: Is your name Juanita?

Juanita: If your name is Richard.

Richard: I'll be damned.

Juanita: Ain't you a mess? So you finally decided to come back here—come here, let me hug you! Why, you ain't hardly changed at all—you just a little taller but you sure didn't gain much weight.

Richard: And I bet you the same old tomboy. You sure got the same loud voice—used to be able to hear you clear across this town.

Juanita: Well, it's a mighty small town, Richard, that's what you always said —and the reason my voice got so loud so early, was that I started screaming for help right quick.

*(**Pete** enters.)*

Do you know Pete Spivey? He's someone come on the scene since you been gone. He's going to school down here, you should pardon the expression.

Richard: How do you do, man? Where you from?

Pete: I'm from a little place just outside Mobile.

Richard: Why didn't you go North, man? If you was going to make a *move.* *That's* the place. You get lost up there and I guarantee you some swinging little chick is sure to find you.

Juanita: We'll let that pass. Are you together? Are you ready to meet the day?

Richard: I am *always* together, little sister. Tell me what you got on your mind.

Pete: We thought we'd just walk around town a little and maybe stop and have a couple of drinks somewhere. Or we can drive. I got a car.

Richard: I didn't think I'd never see you no more, Juanita. You been here all this time?

Juanita: I sure have, sugar. Just waiting for you to come home.

Richard: Don't let this chick upset you, Pete. All we ever did was climb trees together.

Pete: She's had me climbing a few trees, too. But we weren't doing it together.

*(**Papa D.'s Juke Joint:** Juke box music, loud. Less frantic than Richard's song. Couples dancing, all very young, doing very lively variations of the "Twist," the "Wobble," etc. **Papa D.** at the counter. It is now early evening. **Juanita, Pete** and **Richard** enter.)*

Juanita: How you making it, Papa D.? We brought someone to see you—you recognize him?

Papa D.: It seems to me I know your face, young man. Yes, I'm *sure* I know your face. Now, wait a minute, don't tell me—you ain't Shirelee Anderson's boy, are you?

Richard: No. I remember Shirelee Anderson, but we ain't no kin.

Pete: Try again, Papa D.

Papa D.: You your father's boy. I just recognized that smile—you Reverend Henry's son. Well, how you doing? It's nice to have you back with us. You going to stay awhile?

Richard: Yes sir. I think I'll be around for awhile.

Papa D.: Yeah, I remember you little old string bean of a boy, full of the devil. How long you been gone from here?

Richard: Almost eight years now. I left in September—it'll be eight years next month.

Papa D.: Yeah—how's your Daddy? And your Grandmother? I ain't seen them for awhile.

Pete: Ain't you been going to church, Papa D.?

Papa D.: Well, you know how it is. I try, God *knows* I try!

Richard: They fine, Papa D.

Papa D.: You all don't want nothing to eat?

Richard: We'll think about it.

    (They sit down.)

Pete: Old Papa D. got something on everybody, don't he?

Juanita: You better believe it.

Richard: He's kind of a Tom, ain't he?

Pete: Yeah. He *talks* about Mister Charlie, and he *says* he's with us—us kids —but he ain't going to do nothing to offend him. You know, he's still trading with Lyle Britten?

Richard: Who's Lyle Britten?

Pete: Peckerwood, owns a store nearby. And man, you ain't *seen* a peckerwood until you've seen Lyle Britten. Niggers been trading in his store for years, man, I wouldn't be surprised but if the cat was rich—but that man still expects you to step off the sidewalk when he comes along. So we been getting people to stop buying there.

Juanita: He shot a colored man a few years back, shot him dead, and wasn't nothing never said, much less done, about it.

Pete: Lyle had been carrying on with this man's wife, dig, and, naturally, Old Bill—his name was Bill Walker, everybody called him Old Bill—wanted to put a stop to it.

Juanita: She was a pretty little thing—real little and real black.

Richard: She still around here?

Pete: No. She disappeared. She went North somewhere.

Richard: Jive mothers. They can rape and kill our women and we can't do nothing. But if we touch one of their dried-up, pale-assed women, we get our nuts cut off. You remember that chick I was telling you about earlier, lives in Greenwich Village in New York?

Pete: What about her?

Richard: She's *white*, man. I got a whole *gang* of white chicks in New York. That's *right*. And they can't get enough of what little Richard's got—and I give it to them, too, baby, believe me. You say black people ain't got no dignity? Man, you ought to watch a white woman when she wants you to give her a little bit. They will do anything, baby *anything!* Wait—I got some pictures. That's the one lives in the Village. *Ain't* she fine? I'd hate to tell you where I've had that long yellow hair. And, dig this one, this is Sandy, her old man works on Wall Street—

Pete: We're making Juanita nervous.

Juanita: Don't worry about *me.* I've been a big girl for a *long* time Besides, I'm studying abnormal psychology. So please feel free. Which one is this? What does *her* father do?

Richard: That's Sylvia. I don't know what her father does. She's a model. She's loaded with loot.

Pete: You take money from her?

Richard: I take their money and they love it. Anyway, they ain't got nothing else to do with it. Every one of them's got some piss-assed, faggoty white boy on a string somewhere. They go home and marry him, dig, when they can't make it with me no more—but when they want some *loving,* funky, down-home, bring-it-on-here-and-put-it-on-the-table style—

Juanita: They sound very sad. It must be very sad for you, too.

Richard: Well, I want *them* to be sad, baby, I want to screw up *their* minds *forever.* But why should *I* be so sad? Hell, I was swinging, I just about had it made. I had me some fine chicks and a fine pad and my car, and, hell, I was on my way! But then—then I screwed up.

Juanita: We heard you were sick.

Richard: Who told you I was sick?

Juanita: Your father. Your grandmother. They didn't say what the sickness was.

    (Papa D. passes their table.)

Richard: Hey, Papa D., come on over here. I want to show you something.

    (Papa D. comes over.)

Hey, look at these, man, look! Ain't they some fine chicks? And you know who *each one* of them calls: *Baby! Oh, baby?* That's right. You looking at the man.

Papa D.: Where'd you steal those pictures, boy?

Richard:
    (Laughs.)
Steal them! Man, I ain't got to steal girls' pictures. I'm telling you the truth!

Papa D.: Put them pictures away. I thought you had good sense.

    (He goes back to the counter.)

Richard: Ain't that a bitch. He's scared because I'm carrying around pictures of white girls. That's the trouble with niggers. They all scared of the man.

Juanita: Well, I'm *not* scared of the man. But there's just no point in running around, asking—

Pete: —to be lynched.

Richard: Well, okay. I'll put my pictures away, then. I sure don't want to upset nobody.

Pete: Excuse me. I'll be back.

    (Exits.)

Richard: You want to dance?

Juanita: No. Not now.

Richard: You want something to eat?

Juanita: No. Richard?

Richard: Yeah?

Juanita: Were you *very* sick?

Richard: What d'you want to know for?

Juanita: Like that. Because I used to be your girl friend.

Richard: You was more like a boy than a girl, though. I couldn't go nowhere without you. You were determined to get your neck broken.

Juanita: Well, I've changed. I'm now much more like a girl than I am like a boy.

Richard: You didn't turn out too bad, considering what you had to start with.

Juanita: Thank you. I guess.

Richard: How come you ain't married by now? Pete, now, he seems real fond of you.

Juanita: He *is* fond of me, we're friends. But I'm not in any hurry to get married—not now. And not here. I'm not sure I'm going to stay here. I've been working very hard, but next year I think I'll leave.

Richard: Where would you go?

Juanita: I don't know. I had always intended to go North to law school and then come back down here to practice law—God knows this town could stand it. But, now, I don't know.

Richard: It's rough, huh?

Juanita: It's not that so much. It *is* rough—are you all right? Do you want to go?

Richard: No, no. I'm all right. Go on.

    (A pause.)

I'm all *right*. Go *on*.

Juanita: It's rough because you can't help being scared. I don't want to die— what was the matter with you, Richard, what were you sick with?

Richard: It wasn't serious. And I'm better now.

Juanita: Well, no, that's just it. You're not really better.

Richard: How do you mean?

Juanita: I watch you—

Richard: *Why* do you watch me?

Juanita: I care about you.

Richard: You care about me! I thought you could hold your liquor better than that, girl.

Juanita: It's not liquor. Don't you believe that anyone can care about you?

Richard: Care about me! Do you know how many times chicks have told me that? That they *cared* about me?

Juanita: Well. This isn't one of those times.

Richard: I was a junkie.

Juanita: A what?

Richard: A junkie, a dope addict, a hop-head, a mainliner—a dope fiend! My arms and my legs, too, are full of holes!

Juanita: I asked you to tell *me*, not the world.

Richard: Where'd Pete go?

Juanita: He's dancing.

Richard: You want to dance?

Juanita: In a minute.

Richard: I got hooked about five years ago. See, I couldn't stand these chicks I was making it with, and I was working real hard at my music, and, man, I was lonely. You come off a gig, you be tired, and you'd already taken as much shit as you could stand from the managers and the people in the room you were working and you'd be off to make some down scene with some pasty white-faced bitch. And so you'd make the scene and somehow you'd wake up in the morning and the chick would be beside you, alive and well, and dying to make the scene again and somehow you'd managed not to strangle her, you hadn't beaten her to death. Like you wanted to. And you get out of there and you carrying this pain around inside all day and all night long. No way to beat it—no *way*. No matter how you turned, no matter what you did—no *way*. But when I started getting high, I was cool, and it didn't bother me. And I wasn't lonely then, it was all right. And the chicks—I could handle them, they couldn't reach me. And I didn't know I was hooked—until I was *hooked*. Then I started getting into trouble and I lost a lot of gigs and I had to sell my car and I lost my pad and most of the chicks, they split, naturally—but not all of them—and then I got busted and I made that trip down to Lexington and—here I am. Way *down* upon the Swanee River. But I'm going to be all right. You can bet on it.

Juanita: I'd like to do better than that. I'd like to see to it.

Richard: How?

Juanita: Well, like I used to. I won't let you go anywhere without me.

Richard: You *still* determined to break your neck.

Juanita: Well, it's a neck-breaking time. I wouldn't like to appear to be above the battle.

Richard: Do you have any idea of what you might be letting yourself in for?

Juanita: No. But you said you were lonely. And I'm lonely, too.

> (**Lyle** *enters, goes to the counter. His appearance causes a change in the atmosphere, but no one appears to stop whatever they are doing.*)

Lyle: Joel, how about letting me have some change for cigarettes? I got a kind of long drive ahead of me, and I'm out.

Papa D.: Howdy, Mister Lyle, how you been? Folks ain't been seeing much of you lately.

Lyle:
> (*Laughs.*)

That's the truth. But I reckon old friends just stays old friends. Ain't that right?

Papa D.: That's right, Mister Lyle.

Juanita: That's Lyle Britten. The one we were talking about before.

Richard: I wonder what he'd do if I walked into a white place.

Juanita: Don't worry about it. Just stay out of white places—believe me!

Richard:
> (*Laughs.*)

Let's TCB—that means taking care of business. Let's see if I can dance.

(They rise, dance. Perhaps she is teaching him the "Fight," or he is teaching her the "Pony"; they are enjoying each other. **Lyle** *gets his change, gets cigarettes out of the machine, crosses to the counter, pauses there to watch the dancers.)*

Lyle: Joel, you know I ain't never going to be able to dance like that.

Papa D.: Ain't nothing to it. You just got to be supple, that's all. I can yet do it.

(Does a grotesque sketch of the "Twist.")

Lyle: Okay, Joel, you got it. Be seeing you now.

Papa D.: Good night, Mister Lyle.

(On **Lyle**'s *way out, he jostles* **Juanita.** **Richard** *stops, holding* **Juanita** *at the waist.* **Richard** *and* **Lyle** *stare at each other.)*

Lyle: Pardon me.

Richard: Consider yourself pardoned.

Lyle: You new around here?

Papa D.: He just come to town a couple of days ago, Mister Lyle.

Richard: Yeah, I just come to town a couple of days ago, Mister Lyle.

Lyle: Well. I sure hope your stay'll be a pleasant one.

(Exits.)

Pete: Man, are you *anxious* to leave this world? Because he wouldn't think nothing of helping you out of it.

Richard: Yeah. Well, I wouldn't think nothing of helping him out of it, neither. Come on, baby, record's going to waste—let's TCB.

(They dance.)

So you care about me, do you? Ain't that a bitch?

(The Church: Pete *and* **Juanita,** *a little apart from the others.)*

Pete: Why have you been avoiding me? Don't answer that. You started going away from me as soon as Richard came to this town. Now listen, Richard's dead but you still won't turn to me. I don't want to ask you for more than you can give, but why have you locked me out? I *know*—you liked me. We had nice times together.

Juanita: We did. I *do* like you. Pete, I don't know. I wish you wouldn't ask me now. I wish *nobody* would ask me for anything now!

Pete: Is it because of Richard? Because if that's what it is, I'll wait—I'll wait until you know inside you that Richard's dead, but you're alive, and you're *supposed* to live, and I love you.

Juanita: When Richard came, he—*hit*—me in someplace where I'd never been touched before. I don't mean—just physically. He took all my attention—the deepest attention, maybe, that one person can give another. He needed me and he made a difference for me in this terrible world—do you see what I mean? And—it's funny—when I was with him, I didn't think of the future, I didn't dare. I didn't know if I could be strong enough to give him what he needed for as long as he would need it. It only lasted four or five days, Pete —four or five days, like a storm, like lightning! And what I saw during that storm I'll always see. Before that—I thought I knew who I was. But now I know that there are more things in me than I'll ever understand—and if I can't be faithful to myself, I'm afraid to promise I'll be faithful to one man!

Pete: I need you. I'll be faithful. That helps. You'll see.

Juanita: So many people need so much!

Pete: So do you. So do I, Juanita. You take all my attention. My deepest attention.

Juanita: You probably see things that I think are hidden. You probably think I'm a fool—or worse.

Pete: No. I think there's a lot of love in you, Juanita,. If you'll let me help you, we can give it to the world. You can't give it to the world until you find a person who can help you—love the world.

Juanita: I've discovered that. The world is a loveless place.

Pete: Not yet—

(The lights of a car flash in their faces. Silence. They all listen tensely as the light of another car approach, then pass; they watch the lights disappear. The telephone rings in the office. **Mother Henry** *goes off to answer it. They listen to the murmur of* **Mother Henry**'*s voice.* **Mother Henry** *enters.)*

Mother Henry: That was Freddy Roberts. He say about two-thirty his dog started to barking and woke him up and he let the dog out on the porch and the dog run under the porch and there was two white men *under* Freddy's porch, fooling around with his gas pipes. Freddy thinks the dog bit one of them. He ran inside to get him his rifle but the rifle jammed and the men got away. He wanted to warn us, maybe they might come prowling around here.

Lorenzo: Only we ain't got no rifles.

Juanita: It was the dog that woke him up? I'll bet they come back and kill that dog!

Jimmy: What was they doing under the man's house, messing around with his gas pipes, at that hour of the morning?

Pete: They was fixing to blow up his house. They *might* be under your house, or *this* house, right now.

Lorenzo: The real question is why two white men feel safe enough to come to a black neighborhood after dark in the first place. If a couple of them get their heads blown off, they won't feel so goddamn courageous!

Juanita: I better call home.

(Exits into office.)

Pete: Will you have your mother call my house?

Lorenzo: And have *his* mother call *my* house?

Jimmy: And tell all the people that don't have rifles or dogs to stay off their porches!

Lorenzo: Tell them to fall on their knees and use their Bibles as breast-plates! Because I know that each and every one of them got *Bibles!*

*(**Meridian** has walked to the church door, stands looking off.)*

Lorenzo: Don't they, Meridian?

Mother Henry: Hush.

(We hear **Juanita**'*s voice, off. Then silence falls. Lights dim on the students until they are in silhouette. Lights up on* **Meridian**. *We hear* **Richard**'*s guitar, very lonely, far away.)*

(A car door slams. The voices of young people saying good night. **Richard** *appears, dressed as we last saw him.)*

Richard: Hello, Daddy. You still up?

Meridian: Yeah. Couldn't sleep. How was your day?

Richard: It was all right. I'd forgotten what nights down here were like. You never see the stars in the city—and all these funny country sounds—

Meridian: Crickets. And all kinds of bugs and worms, running around, busy, shaking all the bushes.

Richard: Lord, if I'd stayed here, I guess I might have married old Juanita by now, and we'd have a couple of kids and I'd be sitting around like this *every* night. What a wild thought.

Meridian: You can still marry Juanita. Maybe she's been waiting for you.

Richard: Have you ever thought of marrying again?

Meridian: I've thought of it.

Richard: Did you ever think of marrying Juanita?

Meridian: Why do you ask me that?

Richard: Because I'd like to know.

Meridian: Why would you like to know?

Richard: Why would you like to hide it? I'd like to know because I'm a man now, Daddy, and I can ask you to tell me the truth. I'm making up for lost time. Maybe you should try to make up for lost time too.

Meridian: Yes. I've thought of marrying Juanita. But I've never spoken of it to her.

Richard: That's the truth?

Meridian: Yes.

Richard: Why didn't you tell me the truth way back there? Why didn't you tell me my mother was murdered? She was pushed down them steps.

Meridian: Richard, your mother's dead. People die in all kinds of ways. They die when their time comes to die. Your mother loved you and she was gone —there was nothing more I could do for her. I had to think of you. I didn't want you to be—poisoned—by useless and terrible suspicions. I didn't want to wreck your life. I knew your life was going to be hard enough. So, I let you go. I didn't want you to grow up in this town.

Richard: But there was something else in it, too, Daddy. You didn't want me to look at you and be ashamed of you. And you didn't know what was in my eyes, you couldn't stand it, I could tell from the way you looked at me sometimes. That was it, wasn't it?

Meridian: I thought it was better. I suppose I thought it was all over for me, anyway. And I thought I owed it to your mother and to girls like your mother, to try—try to change, to purify this town, where she was born, and where we'd been so happy, and which she loved so much. I was wrong, I guess. I was wrong.

Richard: You've just been a public man, Daddy, haven't you? Since that day? You haven't been a private man at all.

Meridian: No. I haven't. Try to forgive me.

Richard: There's nothing to forgive. I've been down the road a little bit. I know what happened. I'm going to try again, Daddy.

*(A pause. **Richard** takes out the gun.)*

Here. Grandmama saw this this morning and she got all upset. So I'll let you hold it for me. You keep it till I ask you for it, okay? But when I ask you for it, you got to give it to me. Okay?

Meridian:

(Takes the gun.)

Okay. I'm proud of how you've come through—all you've had to bear.

Richard: I'm going to get some sleep. You coming over to the house now?

Meridian: Not yet.

Richard: Good night. Say, Daddy?

Meridian: Yeah?

Richard: You kind of like the idea of me and Juanita getting together?

Meridian: Yeah. I think it's a fine idea.

Richard: Well, I'm going to sleep on it, then. Good night.

Meridian: Good night.

*(**Richard** exits. After **Richard**'s exit, the lights come up on the students.)*

Juanita: Lord it's gone and started raining.

Pete: And you worried about your hair.

Juanita: I am *not* worried about my hair. I'm thinking of wearing it the way God arranged it in the first place.

Lorenzo: Now, now, Mau-Mau.

Pete: This chick is going through some weird changes.

Meridian: That's understandable. We all are.

Jimmy: Well, we'll see you sometime tomorrow. It promises to be a kind of *active* day.

Meridian: Yes, we've got some active days ahead of us. You all better get some sleep.

Juanita: How're you getting home, Jimmy?

Jimmy: Pete's driving us all home.

Juanita: And then—are you going to drive all the way to your house alone, Pete?

Pete: You're jumpy tonight. I'll stay at Lorenzo's house.

Lorenzo: You can call your house from there.

Mother Henry: You get some sleep, too, Meridian, it's past three o'clock in the morning. Don't you stay over here much longer.

Meridian: No, I won't. Good night, all.

Mother Henry: Good night, children. See you in the morning, God willing.

*(They exit. **Meridian** walks to the pulpit, puts his hand on the Bible. **Parnell** enters.)*

Parnell: I hear it was real bad tonight.

Meridian: Not as bad as it's going to get. Maybe I was wrong not to let the people arm.

Parnell: If the Negroes were armed, it's the Negroes who'd be slaughtered. You know that.

Meridian: They're slaughtered anyway. And I don't know that. I thought I knew it—but now I'm not so sure.

Parnell: What's come over you? What's going to happen to the people in this town, this church—if you go to pieces?

Meridian: Maybe they'll find a leader who can lead them someplace.

Parnell: Somebody with a gun?

    (**Meridian** *is silent.*)

Is that what you mean?

Meridian: I'm a Christian. I've been a Christian all my life, like my Mama and Daddy before me and like their Mama and Daddy before them. Of course, if you go back far enough, you get to a point *before* Christ, if you see what I mean, B.C.—and at that point, I've been thinking, black people weren't raised to turn the other cheek, and in the hope of heaven. No, then they didn't have to take low. Before Christ. They walked around just as good as anybody else, and when they died, they didn't go to heaven, they went to join their ancestors. My son's dead, but he's not gone to join his ancestors. He was a sinner, so he must have gone to hell—if we're going to believe what the Bible says. Is that such an improvement, such a mighty advance over B.C.? I've been thinking, I've had to think—would I have *been* such a Christian if I hadn't been born black? Maybe I *had* to become a Christian in order to have any dignity at all. Since I wasn't a man in men's eyes, then I could be a man in the eyes of God. But that didn't protect my wife. She's dead, too soon, we don't really know how. That didn't protect my son— he's dead, we know how too well. That hasn't changed this town—this town, where you couldn't find a white Christian at high noon on Sunday! The eyes of God—maybe those eyes are blind—I never let myself think of that before.

Parnell: Meridian, you can't be the man who gives the signal for the holocaust.

Meridian: Must I be the man who watches while his people are beaten, chained, starved, clubbed, butchered?

Parnell: You used to say that your people were all the people in the world— all the people God ever made, or would make. You said your race was the human race.

Meridian: The human race!

Parnell: I've never seen you like this before. There's something in your tone I've never heard before—rage—maybe hatred—

Meridian: You've heard it before. You just never recognized it before. You've heard it in all those blues and spirituals and gospel songs you claim to love so much.

Parnell: I was talking about *you*—not your history. I have a history, too. And don't be so sure I've never heard that sound. Maybe I've never heard anything else. Perhaps my life is also hard to bear.

Meridian: I watched you all this week up at the Police Chief's office with me. And you know how to handle him because you're sure you're better than he is. But you both have more in common with each other than either of you have with me. And, for both of you—I watched this, I never watched it before—it was just a black boy that was dead, and that was a problem. He saw the problem one way, you saw it another way. But it wasn't a *man* that was dead, not my son—you held yourselves away from *that!*

Parnell: I may have sounded—cold. It was not because I felt cold. There was no other way to sound, Meridian. I took the only tone which—it seemed to me—could accomplish what we wanted. And I *do* know the Chief of Police better than you—because I'm white. And I can make him listen to me—because I'm white. I don't know if I think I'm so much better than he is. I know what we have done—and do. But you must have mercy on us. We have no other hope.

Meridian: You have never shown us any mercy at all.

Parnell: Meridian, give me credit for knowing you're in pain. We are two men, two friends—in spite of all that could divide us. We have come too far together, there is too much at stake, for you to become black now, for me to become white. Don't accuse me. Don't accuse me. *I* didn't do it.

Meridian: So was my son—innocent.

Parnell: Meridian—when I asked for mercy a moment ago—I meant—please —please try to understand that it is not so easy to leap over fences, to give things up—all right, to surrender privilege! But if you were among the privileged you would know what I mean. It's not a matter of trying to hold *on;* the things, the privilege—are part of you, are *who* you are. It's in the *gut.*

Meridian: Then where's the point of this struggle, where's the hope? If Mister Charlie can't change—

Parnell: Who's Mister Charlie?

Meridian: You're Mister Charlie. *All* white men are Mister Charlie!

Parnell: You sound more and more like your son, do you know that? A lot of the colored people here didn't approve of him, but he said things they longed to say—said right out loud, for all the world to hear, how much he despised white people!

Meridian: He didn't say things *I* longed to say. Maybe it was because he was my son. I didn't care *what* he felt about white people. I just wanted him to live, to have his own life. There's something you don't understand about being black, Parnell. If you're a black man, with a black son, you have to forget all about white people and concentrate on trying to save your child. That's why I let him stay up North. I was wrong, I failed. Lyle walked him up the road and killed him.

Parnell: We don't *know* Lyle killed him. And Lyle denies it.

Meridian: Of course, he denies it—what do you mean, we don't *know* Lyle killed him?

Parnell: We *don't* know—all we can say is that it looks that way. And circumstantial evidence is a tricky thing.

Meridian: *When* it involves a white man killing a black man—if Lyle didn't kill him, Parnell, who did?

Parnell: I don't *know.* But we don't know that Lyle did it.

Meridian: Lyle doesn't deny that he killed Old Bill.

Parnell: No.

Meridian: And we know how Lyle feels about colored people.

Parnell: Well, yes. From your point of view. But—from another point of view —Lyle hasn't got anything *against* colored people. He just—

Meridian: He just doesn't think they're human.

Parnell: Well, even *that's* not true. He doesn't think they're *not* human—after all, I know him, he's hot-tempered and he's far from being the brightest man in the world—but he's not mean, he's not cruel. He's a poor white man. The poor whites have been just as victimized in this part of the world as the blacks have ever been!

Meridian: For God's sake spare me the historical view! Lyle's responsible for Richard's death.

Parnell: But, Meridian, we can't, even in our own minds, *decide* that he's guilty. We have to operate the way justice *always* has to operate and give him the benefit of the doubt.

Meridian: *What* doubt?

Parnell: Don't you see, Meridian, that now you're operating the way white people in this town operate whenever a colored man's on trial?

Meridian: When was the last time one of us was on *trial* here, Parnell?

Parnell: That *can't* have anything to do with it, it *can't*. We must forget about all—*all* the past injustice. We have to start from scratch, or do our best to start from scratch. It isn't vengeance we're after. Is it?

Meridian: I don't want vengeance. I don't want to be paid back—anyway, I couldn't be. I just want Lyle to be made to know that what he did was evil. I just want this town to be forced to face the evil that it countenances and to turn from evil and do good. That's why I've stayed in this town so long!

Parnell: But if Lyle didn't do it? Lyle is a friend of mine—a strange friend, but a friend. I love him. I know how he suffers.

Meridian: *How* does he suffer?

Parnell: He suffers—from being in the dark—from having things inside him that he can't name and can't face and can't control. He's not a wicked man. I know he's not. I've known him almost all his life! The face he turns to you, Meridian, isn't the face he turns to me.

Meridian: Is the face he turns to you more real than the face he turns to me? *You* go ask him if he killed my son.

Parnell: They're going to ask him that in court. That's why I fought to bring about this trial. And he'll say no.

Meridian: I don't care what he says in court. You go ask him. If he's your friend, he'll tell you the truth.

Parnell: No. No, he may not. He's—he's maybe a little afraid of me.

Meridian: If you're *his* friend, you'll know whether he's telling you the truth or not. Go ask him.

Parnell: I can't do it. I'm his friend. I can't betray him.

Meridian: But you can betray *me*? You *are* a white man, aren't you? Just another white man—after all?

Parnell: Even if he says yes, it won't make any difference. The jury will never convict him.

Meridian: Is that why you fought to bring about the trial? I don't care what the jury does. I know he won't say yes to them. He won't say yes to me. But he might say yes to you. You say we don't know. Well, I've got a right to know. And I've got the right to ask you to find out—since you're the only

man who *can* find out. And *I've* got to find out—whether we've been friends all these years, or whether I've just been your favorite Uncle Tom.
Parnell: You know better than that.
Meridian: I don't know, Parnell, any longer—any of the things I used to know. Maybe I never knew them. I'm tired. Go home.
Parnell: You don't trust me anymore, do you, Meridian?
Meridian: Maybe I never trusted you. I don't know. Maybe I never trusted myself. Go home. Leave me alone. I must look back at my record.
Parnell: Meridian—what you ask—I don't know if I can do it for you.
Meridian: I don't want you to do it for me. I want you to do it for you. Good night.
Parnell: Good night.
　　　(**Parnell** *exits.* **Meridian** *comes downstage. It is dawn.*)
Meridian: My record! Would God—would *God*—would God I had died for thee—my son, my son!

Curtain

Act Two

Whitetown: *The kitchen of* **Lyle***'s house. Sunday morning. Church bells. A group of white people, all ages, men and women.*
Jo *and an older woman,* **Hazel,** *have just taken a cake out of the oven.* **Hazel** *sets it out to cool.*

Hazel: It's a shame—having to rush everything this way. But it can't be helped.
Jo: Yes. I'm just so upset. I can't help it. I know it's silly. I know they can't do nothing to Lyle.
Hazel: Girl, you just put all those negative thoughts right out of your mind. We're going to have your little anniversary celebration *tonight* instead of *tomorrow* night because we have reason to believe that *tomorrow* night your husband might be called away on business. Now, you think about it that way. Don't you go around here with a great long face, trying to demoralize your guests. I won't have it. You too young and pretty for that.
Lillian: Hallelujah! I *do* believe that I have finally mastered this recipe.
Susan: Oh, good! Let me see.
Lillian: I've only tried it once before, and it's real hard. You've got to time it just right.
Susan: I have tried it and tried it and it never comes out! But yours is wonderful! We're going to eat tonight, folks!
Ralph: You supposed to be cooking something, too, ain't you?
Susan: I'm cooking our contribution later, at our own house. We got enough women here already, messing up Jo's kitchen.

Jo: I'm just so glad you all come by I don't know what to do. Just go ahead and mess up that kitchen, I got lots of time to clean it.

Ellis: Susan's done learned how to cook, huh?

Ralph: Oh, yeah, she's a right fine cook. All you got to do is look at me. I never weighed this much in my life.

Ellis: Old Lyle done gained weight in this year, too. Nothing like steady home cooking, I guess, ha-ha! It really don't seem like it was a year ago you two got married. Declare, I never thought Lyle was going to jump up and do that thing. But old Jo, here, she hooked him.

Rev. Phelps: Well, I said the words over them, and if I ever saw a happy man in my life, it was Big Lyle Britten that day. Both of them—there was just a light shining out of them.

George: I'd propose a toast to them, if it wasn't so early on a Sunday, and if the Reverend wasn't here.

Rev. Phelps: Ain't nothing wrong with toasting happy people, no matter what the day or hour.

Ellis: You heard the Reverend! You got anything in this house we can drink to your happiness in, Mrs. Britten?

Jo: I'm pretty sure we do. It's a pity Lyle ain't up yet. He ain't never slept through this much racket before.

Ellis: No ma'am, he ain't never been what you'd call a heavy sleeper. Not before he passed out, ha-ha! We used to have us some times together, him and me, before he got him some sense and got married.

George: Let him sleep easy. He ain't got no reason not to.

Jo: Lyle's always got his eye on the ball, you know—and he's just been at that store, night after night after night, drawing up plans and taking inventory and I don't know what all—because, come fall, he's planning to branch out and have a brand new store, just about. You all won't recognize the place, I guarantee you!

Ellis: Lyle's just like his Daddy. You can't beat him. The harder a thing is, well, the surer you can be that old Lyle Britten will do it. Why, Lyle's Daddy never got old—*never!* He was drinking and running after women—and getting them, too!—until just before they put him in his grave. I could tell you stories about the old man, boy—of course, I can't tell them now, on a Sunday morning, in front of all these women!

Jo: Here you are, gentlemen. I hope you all drink bourbon.

Ralph: Listen to her!

George: Ladies! Would you all like to join us in a morning toast to the happy and beloved and loving couple, Mr. and Mrs. Lyle Britten, on the day immediately preceding their first wedding anniversary?

Ellis: The bridegroom ain't here because he's weary from all his duties, both public and private. Ha-ha! But he's a good man, and he's done a lot for us, and I know you all know what I'm talking about, and I just feel like we should honor him and his lovely young wife. Ladies! Come on Reverend Phelps says it's all right.

Susan: Not too much for me, Ralph.

Lillian: I don't think I've ever had a drink at this hour of a Sunday morning, and in the presence of my pastor!

(They pour, drink, and sing "For He's a Jolly Good Fellow.")

Hazel: Now you've started her to crying, naturally. Here, honey, you better have a little drink yourself.

Jo: You all have been *so* wonderful. I can't imagine how Lyle can go on sleeping. Thank you, Hazel. Here's to all of you.

(Drinks.)

Listen. They're singing over there now.

(They listen.)

Hazel: Sometimes they can sound so nice. Used to take my breath away when I was a girl.

Ellis: What's happened to this town? It was peaceful here, we all got along, we didn't have no trouble.

George: Oh, we had a little trouble from time to time, but it didn't amount to a hill of beans. Niggers was all right then, you could always get you a nigger to help you catch a nigger.

Lillian: That's right. They had their ways, we had ours, and everything went along the way God intended.

Jo: I've never been scared in this town before—never. They was all like my own people. I never knew of anyone to mistreat a colored person—have you? And they certainly didn't *act* mistreated. But now, when I walk through this town—I'm scared—like I don't know what's going to happen next. How come the colored people to hate us so much, all of a sudden? We *give* them everything they've got!

Rev. Phelps: Their minds have been turned. They have turned away from God. They're a simple people—warm-hearted and good-natured. But they are very easily led, and now they are harkening to the counsel of these degenerate Communist race-mixers. And they don't know what terrible harm they can bring on themselves—and on us all.

Jo: You can't tell what they're thinking. Why, colored folks you been knowing all your life—you're almost afraid to hire them, almost afraid to *talk* to them —you don't know what they're thinking.

Ellis: *I* know what they're thinking.

Susan: We're not much better off than the Communist countries—that's what Ralph says. *They* live in fear. They don't want us to teach God in our schools —you send your child to school and you don't know *what* kind of Godless atheist is going to be filling the little one's mind with all *kinds* of filth. And he's going to believe it, of course, kids don't know no better. And now they tell us we got to send our kids to school with niggers—why, everybody *knows* that ain't going to work, won't nobody get no education, white *or* black. Niggers can't learn like white folks, they ain't got the same *interests*.

Ellis: They got one interest. And it's just below the belly button.

George:

(Laughs.)

You know them yellow niggers? Boy, ain't they the worst kind? Their own folks don't want them, don't nobody want them, and you *can't* do nothing with them—you might be able to scare a black nigger, but you can't do nothing with a yellow nigger.

Rev. Phelps: That's because he's a mongrel. And a mongrel is the lowest creation in the animal kingdom.

Ellis: Mrs. Britten, you're married and all the women in this room are married and I know you've seen your husband without no clothes on—but have you seen a nigger without no clothes on? No, I guess you haven't. Well, he ain't like a white man, Mrs. Britten.

George: That's right.

Ellis: Mrs. Britten, if you was to be raped by an orang-outang out of the jungle or a *stallion,* couldn't do you no worse than a nigger. You wouldn't be no more good for nobody. I've *seen* it.

George: That's *right.*

Ralph: That's why we men have got to be so vigilant. I tell you, I have to be away a lot nights, you know—and I bought Susan a gun and I taught her how to use it, too.

Susan: And I'm a pretty good shot now, too. Ralph says he's real proud of me.

Ralph: She's just like a pioneer woman.

Hazel: I'm so glad Esther's not here to see this. She'd die of shame. She was the sweetest colored woman—you remember her. She just about raised us, used to sing us to sleep at night, and she could tell just the most beautiful stories—the kind of stories that could scare you and make you laugh and make you cry, you know? Oh, she was wonderful. I don't remember a cross word or an evil expression all the time she was with us. She was always the same. And I believe she knew more about me than my own mother and father knew. I just told her everything. Then, one of her sons got killed—he went bad, just like this boy they having a funeral for here tonight—and she got sick. I nursed her, I bathed that woman's body with my own hands. And she told me once, she said, "Miss Hazel, you are just like an angel of light." She said, "My own couldn't have done more for me than you have done." She was a wonderful old woman.

Jo: I believe I hear Lyle stirring.

Susan: Mrs. Britten, somebody else is coming to call on you. My! It's that Parnell James! I wonder if he's sober this morning. He never *looks* sober.

Ellis: He never acts it, either.

   (**Parnell** enters.)

Parnell: Good morning, good people! Good morning, Reverend Phelps! How good it is to see brethren—and sistren—walking together. Or, in this case, standing together—something like that, anyway; my Bible's a little rusty. Is church over already? Or are you having it here? Good morning, Jo.

Jo: Good morning, Parnell. Sit down, I'll pour you a cup of coffee.

George: You look like you could use it.

Rev. Phelps: We were all just leaving.

Parnell: Please don't leave on my account, Reverend Phelps. Just go on as you were, praying or singing, just as the spirit may move you. I *would* love that cup of coffee, Jo.

Ellis: You been up all night?

Parnell: Is that the way I look? Yes, I *have* been up all night.

Ellis: Tom-catting around, I'll bet. Getting drunk and fooling with all the women.

Parnell: Ah, you flatter me. And in games of chance, my friends, you have no future at all. I'm sure you always lose at poker. So *stop betting.* I was not tom-catting. I was at home, working.

George: You been over the way this morning? You been at the nigger funeral?

Parnell: The funeral takes place this evening. And, yes, I will be there. Would you care to come along? Leaving your baseball bat at home, of course.

Jo: We heard the singing—

Parnell: Darkies are always singing. You people know that. What made you think it was a funeral?

Jo: Parnell! You are the limit! Would anybody else like a little more coffee? It's still good and hot.

Ellis: We heard that a nigger got killed. That's why we thought it was a funeral.

George: They bury their dead over the way, don't they?

Parnell: They do when the dogs leave enough to bury, yes.

    (A pause.)

Ellis: Dogs?

Parnell: Yes—you know. Teeth. Barking. Lots of noise.

Ellis: A lot of people in this town, Parnell, would like to know exactly where you stand, on a lot of things.

Parnell: That's exactly where I stand. On a lot of things. Why don't you read my paper?

Lillian: I wouldn't filthy my hands with that Communist sheet!

Parnell: Ah? But the father of your faith, the cornerstone of that church of which you are so precious an adornment, was a communist, possibly the first. He may have done some tom-catting. We *know* he did some drinking. And he knew a lot of—loose ladies and drunkards. It's all in the Bible, isn't it, Reverend Phelps?

Rev. Phelps: I won't be drawn into your blasphemous banter. Ellis is only asking what many of us want to know—are you with us or against us? And he's telling you what we all feel. We've put up with your irresponsibility long enough. We won't tolerate it any longer. Do I make myself clear?

Parnell: Not at all. If you're threatening me, be specific. First of all, what's this irresponsibility that you won't tolerate? And if you aren't going to tolerate it, what *are* you going to do? Dip me in tar and feathers? Boil me in oil? Castrate me? Burn me? Cover yourselves in white sheets and come and burn crosses in front of my house? Come on, Reverend Phelps, don't stand there with your mouth open, it makes you even more repulsive than you are with it closed, and all your foul, graveyard breath comes rushing out, and it makes me want to vomit. Out with it, boy! What's on your mind?

Ellis: You got away with a lot of things in this town, Parnell, for a long time, because your father was a big man here.

Parnell: One at a time. I was addressing your spiritual leader.

Susan: He's *worse* than a nigger.

Parnell: I take that as a compliment. I'm sure no man will ever say as much for you. Reverend Phelps?

Rev. Phelps: I think I speak for us all—for *myself* and for us all, when I say that our situation down here has become much too serious for flippancy and cynicism. When things were more in order here, we didn't really mind your attitude, and your paper didn't matter to us, we never read it, anyway.

Ellis: We knew you were just a spoiled rich boy, with too much time on his hands that he didn't know what to do with.

Rev. Phelps: And so you started this paper and tried to make yourself interesting with all these subversive attitudes. I honestly thought that you would grow out of it.

George: Or go North.

Rev. Phelps: I know these attitudes were not your father's attitudes, or your mother's. I was very often invited to your home when they were alive—

Parnell: How well I remember! What attitudes are you speaking of?

Hazel: Race-mixing!

Parnell: *Race-mixing!* Ladies and gentlemen, do you think anybody gives a good goddamn who you sleep with? You can go down to the swamps and couple with the snakes, for all I care, or for all anybody else cares. You may find that the snakes don't want you, but that's a problem for you and the snakes to work out, and it might prove astonishingly simple—the working out of the problem, I mean. I've never said a word about race-mixing. I've talked about social justice.

Lillian: That sounds Communistic to me!

Parnell: It means that if I have a hundred dollars, and I'm black, and you have a hundred dollars, and you're white, I should be able to get as much value for *my* hundred dollars—my black hundred dollars—as you get for your *white* hundred dollars. It also means that I should have an equal opportunity to *earn* that hundred dollars—

Ellis: Niggers can get work just as well as a white man can. Hell, *some* niggers make *more* money than me.

Parnell: Some niggers are smarter than you, Ellis. Much smarter. And much nicer. And niggers *can't* get work just as well as a white man can, and you know it.

Ellis: What's stopping them? They got hands.

Parnell: Ellis, you don't really work with your *hands*—you're a salesman in a shoe store. And your boss wouldn't give that job to a nigger.

George: Well, goddammit, white men come before niggers! They *got* to!

Parnell: Why?

(**Lyle** enters.)

Lyle: What's all this commotion going on in my house?

Jo: Oh, Lyle, good morning! Some folks just dropped in to see you.

Lyle: It sounded like they was about to come to blows. Good morning,

Reverend Phelps, I'm glad to see you here. I'm sorry I wasn't up, but I guess my wife might have told you, I've not been sleeping well nights. When I *do* go to sleep, she just lets me sleep on.

Rev. Phelps: Don't you apologize, son—we understand. We only came by to let you know that we're with you and every white person in this town is with you.

Jo: Isn't that nice of them, Lyle? They've been here quite a spell, and we've had *such* a nice time.

Lyle: Well, that *is* mighty nice of you, Reverend, and all of you—hey there, Ellis! Old George! And Ralph and Susan—how's married life suit you? Guess it suits you all right, ain't nobody seen you in months, ha-ha! Mrs. Proctor, Mrs. Barker, how you all? Hey! Old Parnell! What you doing up so early?

Parnell: I was on my way to church, but they seemed to be having the meeting here. So I joined the worshippers.

Lyle: On your way to church, that's a good one. Bet you ain't been to bed yet.

Parnell: No, I haven't.

Lyle: You folks don't mind if I have a little breakfast? Jo, bring me something to eat! Susan, you look mighty plump and rosy, you ain't keeping no secrets from us, are you?

Susan: I don't think so, Lyle.

Lyle: I don't know, you got that look—like a real ripe peach, just right for eating. You ain't been slack in your duty, have you, Ralph? Look at the way she's blushing! I guess you all right, boy.

Ellis: You know what time they coming for you tomorrow?

Lyle: Sometime in the morning, I reckon. I don't know.

Rev. Phelps: I saw the Chief of Police the other day. He really doesn't want to do it, but his hands are tied. It's orders from higher up, from the North.

Lyle: Shoot, I know old Frank don't want to arrest me. I understand. I ain't worried. I know the people in this town is with me. I got nothing to worry about.

Ellis: They trying to force us to put niggers on the jury—that's what I hear. Claim it won't be a fair trial if we don't.

Hazel: Did you *ever* hear anything like that in your *life*?

Lyle: Where they going to find the niggers?

Ellis: Oh, I bet your buddy, Parnell, has got that all figured out.

Lyle: How about it, Parnell? You going to find some niggers for them to put on that jury?

Parnell: It's not up to me. But I might recommend a couple.

George: And how they going to get to court? You going to protect them?

Parnell: The police will protect them. Or the State troopers—

George: That's a good one!

Parnell: Or Federal marshals.

George: Look here, you really think there should be niggers on that jury?

Parnell: Of course I do, and so would you, if you had any sense. For one thing, they're forty-four percent of the population of this town.

Ellis: But they don't vote. Not most of them.

Parnell: Well. That's also a matter of interest to the Federal government. Why *don't* they vote? They got hands.

Ellis: You claim Lyle's your buddy—

Parnell: Lyle *is* my buddy. That's why I want him to have a fair trial.

Hazel: I can't listen to no more of this, I'm sorry, I just can't. Honey, I'll see you all tonight, you hear?

Rev. Phelps: We're all going to go now. We just wanted to see how you were, and let you know that you could count on us.

Lyle: I sure appreciate it, Reverend, believe me, I do. You make me feel much better. Even if a man knows he ain't done no wrong, still, it's a kind of troublesome spot to be in. Wasn't for my good Jo, here, I don't know what I'd do. Good morning, Mrs. Barker. Mrs. Proctor. So long, George, it's been good to see you. Ralph, you take good care of Susan, you hear? And name the first one after me—you might have to bring it on up to the jail house so I can see it.

Susan: Don't think like that. Everything's going to be all right.

Lyle: You're sure?

Susan: I guarantee it. Why they couldn't—*couldn't*—do anything to you!

Lyle: Then I believe it. I believe *you*.

Susan: You keep right on believing.

Ellis: Remember what we said, Parnell.

Parnell: So long, Ellis. See you next Halloween.

Lyle: Let's get together, boy, soon as this mess is over.

Ellis: You bet. This mess is just about over now—we ain't going to let them prolong it. And I know just the thing'll knock all this clear out of your mind, this, and everything else, ha-ha! Bye-bye, Mrs. Britten.

Jo: Goodbye. And thanks for coming!

(**Hazel, Lillian, Susan, Ralph, Ellis, Reverend Phelps** and **George** exit.)

Lyle: They're nice people.

Jo: Yes. They are.

Parnell: They certainly think a lot of you.

Lyle: You ain't jealous, are you, boy? No. We've all had the same kind of trouble—it's the kind of trouble you wouldn't know about, Parnell, because you've never had to worry about making your living. But me! I been doing hard work from the time I was a puppy. Like my Mama and Daddy before me, God rest their souls, and their Mama and Daddy before them. They wore themselves out on the land—the land never give them nothing. Nothing but an empty belly and some skinny kids. I'm the only one growed up to be a man. That's because I take after my Daddy—he was skinny as a piece of wire, but he was hard as any rock. And stubborn! Lord, you ain't never seen nobody so stubborn. He should have been born sooner. Had he been born sooner, when this was still a free country, and a man could really *make* some money, I'd have been born rich as you, Parnell, maybe even richer. I tell you—the old man struggled. He worked harder than any nigger. But he left me this store.

Jo: You reckon we going to be able to leave it to the little one?

Lyle: We're going to leave him more than that. That little one ain't going to have nothing to worry about. I'm going to leave him as rich as old Parnell here, and he's going to be educated, too, better than his Daddy; better, even, than Parnell!

Parnell: You going to send him to school in Switzerland?

Lyle: *You* went there for a while, didn't you?

Jo: That's where Parnell picked up all his wild ideas.

Parnell: Yes. Be careful. There were a couple of African princes studying in the school I went to—they did a lot more studying than I did, I must say.

Lyle: African princes, huh? What were they like? Big and black, I bet, elephant tusks hanging around their necks.

Parnell: Some of them wore a little ivory, on a chain—silver chain. They were a little *better* than most of us—the Swiss girls certainly thought so.

Lyle: The *Swiss* girls? You mean they didn't have no women of their own?

Parnell: Lots of them. Swiss women, Danish women, English women, French women, Finns, Russians, even a couple of Americans.

Jo: I don't believe you. Or else they was just trying to act like foreigners. I can't stand people who try to act like something they're not.

Parnell: They were just trying to act like women—poor things. And the Africans were men, no one had ever told them that they weren't.

Lyle: You mean there weren't no African women around at *all*? Weren't the Swiss people kind of upset at having all these niggers around with no women?

Parnell: They didn't seem to be upset. They seemed delighted. The niggers had an awful lot of money. And there weren't many African girls around because African girls aren't educated the way American girls are.

Jo: The American girls didn't *mind* going out with the Africans?

Parnell: Not at all. It appears that the Africans were excellent dancers.

Lyle: I won't never send no daughter of mine to Switzerland.

Parnell: Well, what about your son? *He* might grow fond of some little African princess.

Lyle: Well, that's different. I don't care about that, long as he leaves her over there.

Jo: It's *not* different—how can you say that? White men ain't got no more business fooling around with black women than—

Lyle: Girl, will you stop getting yourself into an uproar? Men is different from women—they ain't as delicate. Man can do a lot of things a woman can't do, you know that.

Parnell: You've heard the expression, sowing wild oats? Well, all the men we know sowed a lot of wild oats before they finally settled down and got married.

Lyle: That's right. Men *have* to do it. They ain't like women. Parnell is *still* sowing his wild oats—I sowed mine.

Jo: And a woman that wants to be a decent woman just has to—*wait*—until the men get tired of going to bed with—harlots!—and decide to settle down?

Parnell: Well, it sounds very unjust, I know, but that's the way it's always been. I *suppose* the decent women were waiting—though nobody seems to know *exactly* how they spent the time.

BLUES FOR MISTER CHARLIE   277

Jo: Parnell!

Parnell: Well, there *are* some who waited too long.

Jo: Men ought to be ashamed. How can you blame a woman if she—goes wrong? If a decent woman can't find a decent man—why—it must happen all the time—they get tired of waiting.

Lyle: Not if they been raised right, no sir, that's what my Daddy said, and I've never known it to fail. And look at you—*you* didn't get tired of waiting. Ain't nobody in this town ever been able to say a word against you. Man, I was so scared when I finally asked this girl to marry me. I was afraid she'd turn me out of the house. Because I had been pretty wild. Parnell can tell you.

Jo: I had heard.

Lyle: But she didn't. I looked at her, it seemed almost like it was the first time—you know, the first time you really *look* at a woman?—and I thought, I'll be damned if I don't believe I can make it with her. I believe I can. And she looked at me like she loved me. It was in her eyes. And it was just like somebody had lifted a great big load off my heart.

Jo: You shouldn't be saying these things in front of Parnell.

Lyle: Why not? I ain't got no secrets from Parnell—he knows about men and women. Look at her blush! Like I told you. Women is more delicate than men.

(He touches her face lightly.)

I know you kind of upset, sugar. But don't you be nervous. Everything's going to be all right, and we're going to be happy again, you'll see.

Jo: I hope so, Lyle.

Lyle: I'm going to take me a bath and put some clothes on. Parnell, you sit right there, you hear? I won't be but a minute.

(Exits.)

Jo: What a funny man he is! It don't do no good at all to get mad at him, you might as well get mad at that baby in there. Parnell? Can I ask you something?

Parnell: Certainly.

Jo: Is it true that Lyle has no secrets from you?

Parnell: He said that neither of you had any secrets from me.

Jo: Oh, don't play. Lyle don't know a thing about women—what they're really like, to themselves. Men don't know. But I want to ask you a serious question. Will you answer it?

Parnell: If I can.

Jo: That means you won't answer it. But I'll ask it, anyway. Parnell—was Lyle —is it true what people said? That he was having an affair with Old Bill's wife and that's why he shot Old Bill?

Parnell: Why are you asking me that?

Jo: Because I have to know! It's true, isn't it? He had an affair with Old Bill's wife—and he had affairs with lots of colored women in this town. It's *true*. Isn't it?

Parnell: What does it matter who he slept with before he married you, Jo? I know he had a—lot of prostitutes. Maybe some of them were colored. When he was drunk, he wouldn't have been particular.

Jo: He's never talked to you about it?

Parnell: Why would he?

Jo: Men talk about things like that.

Parnell: Men often joke about things like that. But, Jo—what one man tells another man, his friend—can't be told to women.

Jo: Men certainly stick together. I wish women did. All right. You can't talk about Lyle. But tell me this. Have *you* ever had an affair with a colored girl? I don't mean a—a *night*. I mean, did she mean something to you, did you like her, did you—love her? Could you have married her—I mean, just like you would marry a white woman?

Parnell: Jo—

Jo: Oh! Tell me the truth, Parnell!

Parnell: I loved a colored girl, yes. I think I loved her. But I was only eighteen and she was only seventeen. I was still a virgin. I don't know if she was, but I think she was. A lot of the other kids in school used to drive over to niggertown at night to try and find black women. Sometimes they bought them, sometimes they frightened them, sometimes they raped them. And they were proud of it, they talked about it all the time. I couldn't do that. Those kids made me ashamed of my own body, ashamed of everything I felt, ashamed of being white—

Jo: Ashamed of being white.

Parnell: Yes.

Jo: How did you meet—this colored girl?

Parnell: Her mother worked for us. She used to come, sometimes, to pick up her mother. Sometimes she had to wait. I came in once and found her in the library, she was reading Stendhal. *The Red and The Black.* I had just read it and we talked about it. She was funny—very bright and solemn and very proud—and she was *scared,* scared of me, but much too proud to show it. Oh, she was funny. But she was bright.

Jo: What did she look like?

Parnell: She was the color of gingerbread when it's just come out of the oven. I used to call her Ginger—later. Her name was really Pearl. She had black hair, very black, kind of short, and she dressed it very carefully. Later, I used to tease her about the way she took care of her hair. There's a girl in this town now who reminds me of her. Oh, I loved her!

Jo: What happened?

Parnell: I used to look at her, the way she moved, so beautiful and free, and I'd wonder if at night, when she might be on her way home from someplace, any of those boys at school had said ugly things to her. And then I thought that I wasn't any better than they were, because I thought my own thoughts were pretty awful. And I wondered what she thought of me. But I didn't dare to ask. I got so I could hardly think of anyone but her. I got sick wanting to take her in my arms, to take her in my arms and love her and protect her from all those other people who wanted to destroy her. She wrote a little poetry, sometimes she'd show it to me, but she really wanted to be a painter.

Jo: What happened?

Parnell: Nothing happened. We got so we told each other everything. She was going to be a painter, I was going to be a writer. It was our secret. Nobody in the world knew about her *inside,* what she was like, and how she dreamed, but me. And nobody in the world knew about *me* inside, what I wanted, and how I dreamed, but her. But we couldn't look ahead, we didn't dare. We talked about going North, but I was still in school, and she was still in school. We couldn't be seen anywhere together—it would have given her too bad a name. I used to see her sometimes in the movies, with various colored boys. She didn't seem to have any special one. They'd be sitting in the balcony, in the colored section, and I'd be sitting downstairs in the white section. She couldn't come down to me, I couldn't go up to her. We'd meet some nights, late, out in the country, but—I didn't want to take her in the bushes, and I couldn't take her anywhere else. One day we were sitting in the library, we were kissing, and her mother came in. That was the day I found out how much black people can hate white people.

Jo: What did her mother do?

Parnell: She didn't say a word. She just looked at me. She just looked at me. I could see what was happening in her mind. She knew that there wasn't any point in complaining to my mother or my father. It would just make her daughter look bad. She didn't dare tell her husband. If he tried to do anything, he'd be killed. There wasn't anything she could do about me. I was just another horny white kid trying to get into a black girl's pants. She looked at me as though she were wishing with all her heart that she could raise her hand and wipe me off the face of the earth. I'll never forget that look. I still see it. She walked over to Pearl and I thought she was going to slap her. But she didn't. She took her by the hand, very sadly, and all she said was, "I'm ready to go now. Come on." And she took Pearl out of the room.

Jo: Did you ever see her again?

Parnell: No. Her mother sent her away.

Jo: But you forgot her? You must have had lots of other girls right quick, right after that.

Parnell: I never forgot her.

Jo: Do you think of her—even when you're with Loretta?

Parnell: Not all of the time, Jo. But some of the time—yes.

Jo: And if you found her again?

Parnell: If I found her again—yes, I'd marry her. I'd give her the children I've always wanted to have.

Jo: Oh, Parnell! If you felt that way about her, if you've felt it all this time!

Parnell: Yes. I know. I'm a renegade white man.

Jo: Then Lyle could have felt that way about Old Bill's wife—about Willa Mae. I know that's not the way he feels about me. And if he felt that way— he could have shot Old Bill—to keep him quiet!

Parnell: Jo!

Jo: Yes! And if he could have shot Old Bill to keep him quiet—he could have killed that boy. He could have killed that boy. And if he did—well—

that *is* murder, isn't it? It's just nothing but murder, even if the boy *was* black. Oh, Parnell! Parnell!

Parnell: Jo, please. Please, Jo. Be quiet.

Lyle:

> *(Off.)*

What's all that racket in there?

Parnell: I'm telling your wife the story of my life.

Lyle:

> *(Off.)*

Sounds pretty goddamn active.

Parnell: You've never asked him, have you, Jo?

Jo: No. No. No.

Parnell: Well, *I* asked him—

Jo: When?

Parnell: Well, I didn't really *ask* him. But he said he didn't do it, that it wasn't true. You heard him. He wouldn't lie to me.

Jo: No. He wouldn't lie to you. They say some of the niggers have guns—did you hear that?

Parnell: Yes. I've heard it. But it's not true.

Jo: *They* wouldn't lie to you, either? I've just had too much time to worry, I guess—brood and worry. Lyle's away so often nights—he spends so much time at that store. I don't know what he does there. And when he comes home, he's just dead—and he drops right off to sleep.

> *(**Lyle** enters, carrying the child.)*

Hi, honey. What a transformation. You look like you used to look when you come courting.

Lyle: I sure didn't come courting carrying no baby. He was awake, just singing away, and carrying on with his toes. He acts like he think he's got a whole lot of candy attached to the end of his legs. Here. It's about time for him to eat, ain't it? How come you looking at me like that? Why you being so nice to me, all of a sudden?

Parnell: I've been lecturing her on the duties of a wife.

Lyle: That so? Well, come on, boy, let's you and me walk down the road a piece. Believe I'll buy you a drink. You ain't ashamed to be seen with me, I hope?

Parnell: No, I'm not ashamed to be seen with you.

Jo: You going to be home for supper?

Lyle: Yeah, sugar. Come on, Parnell.

Jo: You come, too, Parnell, you and Loretta, if you're free. We'd love to have you.

Parnell: We'll try to make it. So long, Jo.

Jo: So long.

> *(They exit. **Jo** walks to the window. Turns back into the room, smiles down at the baby. Sings.)*

Hush, little baby, don't say a word,
Mama's going to buy you a mocking bird—

BLUES FOR MISTER CHARLIE   281

But you don't want no mocking bird right now, do you? I know what you want. You want something to eat. All right, Mama's going to feed you.

(Sits, slowly begins to unbutton her blouse. Sings.)

If that mocking bird don't sing,

Mama's going to buy you a diamond ring.

*(**Lyle's store:** Early evening. Both **Lyle** and **Parnell** are a little drunk.)*

Lyle: Didn't you ever get like that? Sure, you must have got like that sometimes—just restless! You got everything you need and you can't complain about nothing—and yet, look like, you just can't be satisfied. Didn't you ever get like that? I swear, men is mighty strange! I'm kind of restless now.

Parnell: What's the matter with you? You worried about the trial?

Lyle: No, I ain't worried about the trial. I ain't even mad at you, Parnell. Some folks think I should be, but I ain't mad at you. They don't know you like I know you. I ain't fooled by all your wild ideas. We both white and we both from around here, and we been buddies all our lives. That's all that counts. I know you ain't going to let nothing happen to me.

Parnell: That's good to hear.

Lyle: After all the trouble started in this town—but before that crazy boy got himself killed, soon after he got here and started raising all that hell—I started thinking about her, about Willa Mae, more and more and more. She was too young for him. Old Bill, he was sixty if he was a day, he wasn't doing her no good. Yet and still, the first time I took Willa Mae, I had to fight her. I swear I did. Maybe she was frightened. But I never had to fight her again. No. It was good, boy, let me tell you, and she liked it as much as me. Hey! You still with me?

Parnell: I'm still with you. Go on.

Lyle: What's the last thing I said?

Parnell: That she liked it as much as you—which I find hard to believe.

Lyle: Ha-ha! I'm telling you. I never had it for nobody bad as I had it for her.

Parnell: When did Old Bill find out?

Lyle: Old Bill? He wouldn't never have thought nothing if people hadn't started poisoning his mind. People started talking just because my Daddy wasn't well and she was up at the house so much because somebody had to look after him. First they said she was carrying on with *him*. Hell, my Daddy would sure have been willing, but he was far from able. He was really wore out by that time and he just wanted rest. Then people started to saying that it was me.

Parnell: Old Bill ever talk to you about it?

Lyle: How was he going to talk to me about it? Hell, we was right good friends. Many's the time I helped Old Bill out when his cash was low. I used to load Willa Mae up with things from the kitchen just to make sure they didn't go hungry.

Parnell: Old Bill never mentioned it to you? Never? He never gave you any reason to think he knew about it?

Lyle: Well, I don't know what was going on in his *mind*, Parnell. You can't never see what's in anybody else's *mind*—you know that. He didn't act no different. Hell, like I say, she was young enough to be his granddaughter damn near, so I figured he thought it might be a pretty good arrangement—me doing *his* work, ha-ha! because *he* damn sure couldn't do it no more, and helping him to stay alive.

Parnell: Then why was he so mad at you the last time you saw him?

Lyle: Like I said, he accused me of cheating him. And I ain't never cheated a black man in my life. I hate to say it, because we've always been good friends, but sometimes I think it might have been Joel—Papa D.—who told him that. Old Bill wasn't too good at figuring.

Parnell: Why would Papa D. tell him a thing like that?

Lyle: I think he might have been a little jealous.

Parnell: Jealous? You mean, of you and Willa Mae?

Lyle: Yeah. He ain't really an old man, you know. But I'm sure he didn't mean—for things to turn out like they did.

(*A pause.*)

I can still see him—the way he looked when he come into this store.

Parnell: The way *who* looked when he came into this store?

Lyle: Why—Old Bill. He looked crazy. Like he wanted to kill me. He *did* want to kill me. Crazy nigger.

Parnell: I thought you meant the other one. But the other one didn't die in the store.

Lyle: Old Bill didn't die in the store. He died over yonder, in the road.

Parnell: I thought you were talking about Richard Henry.

Lyle: That crazy boy. Yeah, he come in here. I don't know what was the matter with him, he hadn't see me but one time in his life before. And I treated him like—like I would have treated *any* man.

Parnell: I heard about it. It was in Papa D.'s joint. He was surrounded by niggers—or *you* were—

Lyle: He was dancing with one of them crazy young ones—the real pretty nigger girl—what's her name?

Parnell: Juanita.

Lyle: That's the one.

(*Juke box music, soft. Voices. Laughter.*)

Yeah. He looked at me like he wanted to kill me. And he insulted my wife. And I hadn't never done him no harm.

(*As above, a little stronger.*)

But I been thinking about it. And you know what I think? Hey! You gone to sleep?

Parnell: No. I'm thinking.

Lyle: What you thinking about?

Parnell: Us. You and me.

Lyle: And what do you think about us—you and me? What's the point of thinking about us, anyway? We've been buddies all our lives—we can't stop being buddies now.

Parnell: That's right, buddy. What were you about to say?

Lyle: Oh. I think a lot of the niggers in this town, especially the young ones, is turned bad. And I believe they was egging him on.

(*A pause. The music stops.*)

He come in here one Monday afternoon. Everybody heard about it, it was all over this town quicker'n a jack-rabbit gets his nuts off. You just missed it. You'd just walked out of here.

>   (**Lyle** *rises, walks to the doors and opens them. Sunlight fills the room. He slams the screen door shut; we see the road.*)

Jo:

>   *(Off.)*

Lyle, you want to help me bring this baby carriage inside? It's getting kind of hot out here now.

Parnell: Let me.

>   (**Lyle** *and* **Parnell** *bring in the baby carriage.* **Jo** *enters.*)

Jo: My, it's hot! Wish we'd gone for a ride or something. Declare to goodness, we ain't got no reason to be sitting around this store. Ain't nobody coming in here—not to *buy* anything, anyway.

Parnell: I'll buy some bubble gum.

Jo: You know you don't chew bubble gum.

Parnell: Well, then I'll buy some cigarettes.

Jo: Two cartons, or three? It's all right, Parnell, the Britten family's going to make it somehow.

Lyle: Couple of niggers coming down the road, Maybe they'll drop in for a Coke.

>   *(Exits, into back of store.)*

Jo: Why, no, they won't. Our Cokes is *poisoned.* I get up every morning before daybreak and drop the arsenic in myself.

Parnell: Well, then, I won't have a Coke. See you, Jo. So long, Lyle!

Lyle:

>   *(Off.)*

Be seeing you!

>   (**Parnell** *exits. Silence for a few seconds. Then we hear* **Lyle** *hammering in the back.* **Jo** *picks up a magazine, begins to read. Voices.* **Richard** *and* **Lorenzo** *appear in the road.*)

Richard: Hey, you want a Coke? I'm thirsty.

Lorenzo: Let's go on a little further.

Richard: Man, we been walking for *days,* my mouth is as dry as that damn dusty road. Come on, have a Coke with me, won't take but a minute.

Lorenzo: We don't trade in there. Come on—

Richard: Oh! Is this the place? Hell, I'd like to get another look at the peckerwood, ain't going to give him but a dime. I want to get his face fixed in my *mind,* so there won't be no time wasted when the time comes, you dig?

>   *(Enters the store.)*

Hey, Mrs. Ofay Ednolbay Ydalay! You got any Coca Cola for sale?

Jo: What?

Richard: Coke! Me and my man been toting barges and lifting bales, that's right, we been slaving, and we need a little cool. Liquid. Refreshment. Yeah, and you can take that hammer, too.

Jo: Boy, what do you want?

Richard: A Coca Cola, ma'am. Please ma'am.

Jo: They right in the box there.

Richard: Thank you kindly.

(Takes two Cokes, opens them.)

Oh, this is fine, *fine.* Did you put them in this box with your own little dainty dish-pan hands? Sure makes them taste *sweet.*

Jo: Are you talking to me?

Richard: No ma'am, just feel like talking to myself from time to time, makes the time pass faster.

(At screen door.)

Hey, Lorenzo, I got you a Coke.

Lorenzo: I don't want it. Come on out of there.

Jo: That will be twenty cents.

Richard: *Twenty* cents? All right. Don't you know how to say please? All the women *I* know say please—of course, they ain't as pretty as you. I ain't got twenty cents, ma'am. All I got is—twenty dollars!

Jo: You ain't got nothing smaller?

Richard: No ma'am. You see, I don't never carry on me more cash than I can afford to *lose.*

Jo: Lyle!

*(**Lyle** enters, carrying the hammer.)*

You got any change?

Lyle: Change for twenty? No, you know I ain't got it.

Richard: You all got this big, fine store and all—and you ain't got change for *twenty* dollars?

Lyle: It's early in the day, boy.

Richard: It ain't that early. I thought white folks was rich at *every* hour of the day.

Lyle: Now, if you looking for trouble, you just might get it. That boy outside —ain't he got twenty cents?

Richard: That boy outside is about twenty-four years old, and he ain't got twenty cents. Ain't no need to ask him.

Lyle:

(At the door.)

Boy! You got twenty cents?

Lorenzo: Come on out of there, Richard! I'm tired of hanging around here!

Lyle: Boy, didn't you hear what I asked you?

Lorenzo: Mister Britten, I ain't *in* the store, and I ain't *bought* nothing in the store, and so I ain't *got* to tell you whether or not I got twenty cents!

Richard: Maybe your wife could run home and get some change. You *got* some change at home, I know. Don't you?

Lyle: I don't stand for nobody to talk about my wife.

Richard: I only said you was a lucky man to have so fine a *wife.* I said maybe she could run *home* and look and see if there was any change—in the *home.*

Lyle: I seen you before some place. You that crazy nigger. You ain't from around here.

Richard: You *know* you seen me. And you remember where. And when. I was born right here, in this town. I'm Reverend Meridian Henry's son.

Lyle: You say that like you thought your Daddy's name was some kind of protection. He ain't no protection against *me*—him, nor that boy outside, neither.

Richard: I don't need no protection, do I? Not in my own home town, in the good old USA. I just dropped by to sip on a Coke in a simple country store—and come to find out the joker ain't got enough bread to change twenty dollars. Stud ain't got *nothing*—you people been spoofing the public, man.

Lyle: You put them Cokes down and get out of here.

Richard: I ain't finished yet. And I ain't changed my bill yet.

Lyle: Well, I ain't going to change that bill, and you ain't going to finish them Cokes. You get your black ass out of here—go on! If you got any sense, you'll get your black ass out of this town.

Richard: You don't own this town, you white mother-fucker. You don't *even* own twenty dollars. Don't you raise that hammer. I'll take it and beat your skull to jelly.

Jo: Lyle! Don't you fight that boy! He's crazy! I'm going to call the Sheriff!
>   (*Starts toward the back, returns to counter.*)

The baby! Lyle! Watch out for the baby!

Richard: A baby, huh? How many times did you have to try for it, you no-good, ball-less peckerwood? I'm surprised you could even get it up—look at the way you sweating now.
>   (**Lyle** *raises the hammer.* **Richard** *grabs his arm, forcing it back. They struggle.*)

Jo: Lyle! The baby!

Lorenzo: Richard!
>   (*He comes into the store.*)

Jo: Please get that boy out of here, get that boy out of here—he's going to get himself killed.
>   (**Richard** *knocks the hammer from* **Lyle**'s *hand, and knocks* **Lyle** *down. The hammer spins across the room.* **Lorenzo** *picks it up.*)

Lorenzo: I don't think your husband's going to kill no more black men. Not today, Mrs. Britten. Come on, Richard. Let's go.
>   (**Lyle** *looks up at them.*)

Lyle: It took two of you. Remember that.

Lorenzo: I didn't lay a hand on you, Mister Britten. You just ain't no match for—a *boy*. Not without your gun you ain't. Come on, Richard.

Jo: You'll go to jail for this! You'll go to jail! For years!

Lorenzo: We've been in jail for years. I'll leave your hammer over at Papa D.'s joint—don't look like you're going to be doing no more work today.

Richard:
>   (*Laughs.*)

Look at the mighty peckerwood! On his *ass*, baby—and his woman watching! Now, who you think is the better man? Ha-ha! The master race! You let me in that tired white chick's drawers, she'll know who's the master! Ha-ha-ha!
>   (*Exits.* **Richard**'s *laughter continues in the dark.* **Lyle** *and* **Parnell** *as before.*)

Lyle: Niggers was laughing at me for days. Everywhere I went.

Parnell: You never did call the Sheriff.

Lyle: No.

(**Parnell** *fills their glasses. We hear singing.*)

Parnell: It's almost time for his funeral.

Lyle: And may every nigger like that nigger end like that nigger—face down in the weeds!

(*A pause.*)

Parnell: Was he lying face down?

Lyle: Hell, yeah, he was face down. Said so in the papers.

Parnell: Is that what the papers said? I don't remember.

Lyle: Yeah, that's what the papers said.

Parnell: I guess they had to turn him over—to make sure it was him.

Lyle: I reckon.

(*Laughs.*)

Yeah. I reckon.

Parnell: You and me are buddies, huh?

Lyle: *Yeah,* we're buddies—to the end!

Parnell: I always wondered why you wanted to be my buddy. A lot of poor guys hate rich guys. I always wondered why you weren't like that.

Lyle: I ain't like that. Hell, Parnell, you're smarter than me. I know it. I used to wonder what made you smarter than me. I got to be your buddy so I could find out. Because, hell, you didn't seem so different in *other* ways—in spite of all your *ideas.* Two things we always had in common—liquor and poon-tang. We couldn't get enough of neither one. Of course, your liquor might have been a little better. But I doubt if the other could have been any better!

Parnell: Did you find out what made me smarter?

Lyle: Yeah. You richer!

Parnell: I'm richer! That's all you got to tell me—about Richard Henry?

Lyle: Ain't nothing more to tell. Wait till after the trial. You won't have to ask me no more questions then!

Parnell: I've got to get to the funeral.

Lyle: Don't run off. Don't leave me here alone.

Parnell: You're supposed to be home for supper.

Lyle: Supper can wait. Have another drink with me—be my buddy. Don't leave me here alone. Listen to them! Singing and praying! Singing and praying and laughing behind a man's back!

(*The singing continues in the dark.* **Blacktown:** *The church, packed.* **Meridian** *in the pulpit, the bier just below him.*)

Meridian: My heart is heavier tonight than it has ever been before. I raise my voice to you tonight out of a sorrow and a wonder I have never felt before. Not only I, my Lord, am in this case. Everyone under the sound of my voice, and many more souls than that, feel as I feel, and tremble as I tremble, and bleed as I bleed. It is not that the days are dark—we have known dark days. It is not only that the blood runs down and no man helps us; it is not only that our children are destroyed before our eyes. It is not only that our lives, from day to day and every hour of each day, are menaced by the people among whom you have set us down. We have borne all these things, my Lord, and we have done what the prophets of old could not do, we have sung the Lord's song in a strange land. In a strange land! What was the sin committed by our forefathers in the time that has vanished on the other side of the flood, which has had to be expiated by chains, by the lash, by hunger and thirst, by slaughter, by fire, by the rope, by the knife, and for so many generations, on these wild shores, in this strange land? Our offense must have been mighty, our crime immeasurable. But it is not the past which makes our hearts so heavy. It is the present. Lord, where is our hope? Who, or what, shall touch the hearts of this headlong and unthinking people and turn them back from destruction? When will they hear the words of John? *I know thy works, that thou art neither cold nor hot: I would that thou wert cold or hot. So, then because thou art lukewarm and neither cold nor hot, I will spew thee out of my mouth. Because thou sayest, I am rich and increased with goods, and have need of nothing; and knowest not that thou are wretched and miserable and poor and blind and naked.* Now, when the children come, my Lord, and ask which road to follow, my tongue stammers and my heart fails. I will not abandon the land—this strange land, which is my home. But can I ask the children forever to sustain the cruelty inflicted on them by those who have been their masters, and who are now, in very truth, their kinfolk, their brothers and their sisters and their parents? What hope is there for a people who deny their deeds and disown their kinsmen and who do so in the name of purity and love, in the name of Jesus Christ? What a light, my Lord, is needed to conquer so mighty a darkness! This darkness rules in us, and grows, in black and white alike. I have set my face against the darkness, I will not let it conquer me, even though it will, I know, one day, destroy this body. But, my Lord, what of the children? What shall I tell the children? I must be with you, Lord, like Jacob, and wrestle with you until the light appears—I will not let you go until you give me a sign! A sign that in the terrible Sahara of our time a fountain may spring, the fountain of a true morality, and bring us closer, oh, my Lord, to that peace on earth desired by so few throughout so many ages. Let not our suffering endure forever. Teach us to trust the great gift of life and learn to love one another and dare to walk the earth like men. Amen.

Mother Henry: Let's file up, children, and say goodbye.

*(Song: "Great Getting-Up Morning." **Meridian** steps down from the pulpit. **Meridian, Lorenzo, Jimmy** and **Pete** shoulder the bier. A disheveled **Parnell** enters. The **Congregation** and the **Pallbearers** file past him. **Juanita** stops.)*

Juanita: What's the matter, Parnell? You look sick.

Parnell: I tried to come sooner. I couldn't get away. Lyle wouldn't let me go.

Juanita: Were you trying to beat a confession out of him? But you look as though he's been trying to beat a confession out of you. Poor Parnell!

Parnell: Poor Lyle! He'll never confess. Never. Poor devil!

Juanita: Poor devil! You weep for Lyle. You're luckier than I am. I can't weep in front of others. I can't say goodbye in front of others. Others don't know what it is you're saying goodbye to.

Parnell: You loved him.

Juanita: Yes.

Parnell: I didn't know.

Juanita: Ah, you're so lucky, Parnell. I know you didn't know. Tell me, where do you live, Parnell? How can you not know all of the things you do not know?

Parnell: Why are you hitting out at me? I never thought you cared that much about me. But—oh, Juanita! There are so many things I've never been able to say!

Juanita: There are so many things you've never been able to hear.

Parnell: And—you've tried to tell me some of those things?

Juanita: I used to watch you roaring through this town like a St. George thirsty for dragons. And I wanted to let you know you haven't got to do all that; dragons aren't hard to find, they're everywhere. And nobody wants you to be St. George. We just want you to be Parnell. But, of course, that's much harder.

Parnell: Are we friends, Juanita? Please say that we're friends.

Juanita: Friends is not exactly what you mean, Parnell. Tell the truth.

Parnell: Yes. I've always wanted more than that, from you. But I was afraid you would misunderstand me. That you would feel that I was only trying to exploit you. In another way.

Juanita: You've been a grown man for a long time now, Parnell. You ought to trust yourself more than that.

Parnell: I've been a grown man far too long—ever to have dared to dream of offering myself to you.

Juanita: Your age was never the question, Parnell.

Parnell: Was there ever any question at all?

Juanita: Yes. Yes. Yes, once there was.

Parnell: And there isn't—there can't be—anymore?

Juanita: No. That train has gone. One day, I'll recover. I'm sure that I'll recover. And I'll see the world again—the marvelous world. And I'll have learned from Richard—how to love. I must. I can't let him die for nothing.

> *Juke box music, loud. The lights change, spot on* **Parnell**'s *face.* **Juanita** *steps across the aisle.* **Richard** *appears. They dance.* **Parnell** *watches.*

Curtain

Act Three

Two months later. The courtroom.

The courtroom is extremely high, domed, a blinding white emphasized by a dull, somehow ominous gold. The judge's stand is center stage, and at a height. Sloping down from this place on either side, are the

black and white **Townspeople:** *the* **Jury; Photographers** *and* **Journalists** *from all over the world; microphones and TV cameras. All windows open: one should be aware of masses of people outside and one should sometimes hear their voices—their roar—as well as singing from the church. The church is directly across the street from the courthouse, and the steeple and cross are visible throughout the act. Each witness, when called, is revealed behind scrim and passes through two or three tableaux before moving down the aisle to the witness stand. The witness stand is downstage, in the same place, and at the same angle as the pulpit in Acts I and II.*
Before the curtain rises, song: "I Said I Wasn't Going To Tell Nobody, But I Couldn't Keep It To Myself."
The **Judge**'s *gavel breaks across the singing, and the curtain rises.*

Clerk:
>*(Calling.)*

Mrs. Josephine Gladys Britten!
>*(***Jo***, serving coffee at a church social. She passes out coffee to invisible guests.)*

Jo: Am I going to spend the rest of my life serving coffee to strangers in, church basements? Am I?—Yes! Reverend Phelps was truly noble! As *usual!* —Reverend Phelps has been married for more than twenty years. Don't let those thoughts into your citadel. You must remember that the mind is a citadel and you can keep out all troubling thoughts!—My! Mrs. Evans! you are certainly a sight for sore eyes! I don't know how you manage to look so unruffled and *cool* and *young!* With all those *children.* And Mr. Evans. How are you tonight?—She has a baby just about every year. I don't know how she stands it. Mr. Evans don't look like that kind of man. You sure can't tell a book by its cover. Lord! I wish I was in my own home and these were *my* guests and my husband was somewhere in the room. I'm getting old! Old! Old maid! *Maid!*—Oh! Mr. Arpino! You taken time out from your engineering to come visit here with us? It sure is a pleasure to have you!—My! He is big! and dark! Like a Greek! or a Spaniard! Some people say he might have a touch of nigger blood. I don't believe that. He's just—*foreign.* That's all. He needs a hair cut. I wonder if he's got hair like that all *over* his body? Remember that your mind is a citadel. A citadel. Oh, Lord, I'm tired of serving coffee in church basements! I want, I want—Why, good evening, Ellis! And Mr. Lyle Britten! We sure don't see either of *you* very often! Why, Mr. Britten! You know you don't mean that! You come over here just to see little old *me?* Why, you just go right ahead and drink that coffee, I do believe you need to be sobered up!
>*(The light changes.)*

Reverend Phelps:
>*(Voice.)*

Do you, Josephine Gladys Miles, take this man, Lyle Britten, Jr., as your lawfully wedded husband, to have and to hold, to love and to cherish, in sickness and in health, till death do you part?

Jo: I do. I *do!* Oh, Lyle. I'll make you the best wife any man ever had. I *will.* Love me. Please love me. Look at me! *Look* at me. He *wanted* me. He wanted me. He *wanted* me! I am—Mrs. Josephine Gladys Britten!

> *(The light changes again, and Jo takes the stand. We hear the baby crying.)*

Blacktown: Man, that's the southern white lady you supposed to be willing to risk death for!

Whitetown: You know, this is a kind of hanging in reverse? Niggers out here to watch us being hanged!

The State: What is your relationship to the accused?

Jo: I am his wife.

The State: Will you please tell us, in your own words, of your first meeting with the deceased, Richard Henry?

Whitetown: Don't be afraid. Just tell the truth.

Blacktown: Here we go—down the river!

Jo: Well, I was in the store, sitting at the counter, and pretty soon this colored boy comes in, loud, and talking in just the most awful way. I didn't recognize him, I just knew he wasn't one of *our* colored people. His language was something awful, awful!

The State: He was insulting? Was he insulting, Mrs. Britten?

Jo: He said all kind of things, dirty things, like, like—well—just like I might have been a colored girl, that's what it sounded like to me. Just like some little colored girl he might have met on a street corner and wanted—wanted to—for a night! And I was scared. I hadn't seen a colored boy act like him before. He acted like he was drunk or crazy or maybe he was under the influence of that dope. I never knew nobody to be *drunk* and act like him. His eyes was just going and he acted like he had a fire in his belly. But I tried to be calm because I didn't want to upset Lyle, you know—Lyle's mighty quick-tempered—and he was working in the back of the store, he was hammering—

The State: Go on, Mrs. Britten. What happened then?

Jo: Well, he—that boy—wanted to buy him two Cokes because he had a friend outside—

The State: He brought a friend? He did not come there alone? Did this other boy enter the store?

Jo: No, not then he didn't—I—

Blacktown: Come on bitch. We *know* what you going to say. Get it over with.

Jo: I—I give him the two Cokes, and he—tried to grab my hands and pull me to him, and—I—I—he pushed himself up against me, real close and hard —and, oh, he was just like an animal, I could—smell him! And he tried to kiss me, he kept whispering these awful, filthy things and I got scared, I yelled for Lyle! Then Lyle come running out of the back—and when the boy seen I wasn't alone in the store, he yelled for this other boy outside and this other boy come rushing in and they both jumped on Lyle and knocked him down.

The State: What made you decide not to report this incident—this unprovoked assault—to the proper authorities, Mrs. Britten?

Jo: We've had so much trouble in this town!

The State: What sort of trouble, Mrs. Britten?

Jo: Why, with the colored people! We've got all these northern agitators coming through here all the time, and stirring them up so that you can't hardly sleep nights!

The State: Then you, as a responsible citizen of this town, were doing your best to keep down trouble? Even though you had been so brutally assaulted by a deranged northern Negro dope addict?

Jo: Yes. I didn't want to stir up no more trouble. I *made* Lyle keep quiet about it. I thought it would all blow over. I knew the boy's Daddy was a preacher and that he would talk to the boy about the way he was behaving. It was all over town in a second, anyway! And look like all the colored people was on the side of that crazy boy. And Lyle's always been real good to colored people!

(Laughter from **Blacktown**.*)*

The State: On the evening that the alleged crime was committed—or, rather, the morning—very early on the morning of the 24th of August—where were you and your husband, Mrs. Britten?

Jo: We were home. The next day we heard that the boy was missing.

Counsel for the Bereaved: Doesn't an attempt at sexual assault seem a rather strange thing to do, considering that your store is a public place, with people continually going in and out; that, furthermore, it is located on a public road which people use, on foot and in automobiles, all of the time; and considering that your husband, who has the reputation of being a violent man, and who is, in your own words, "mighty quick tempered," was working in the back room?

Jo: He didn't know Lyle was back there.

Counsel for the Bereaved: But he knew that someone was back there, for, according to your testimony, "He was hammering."

Jo: Well, I told you the boy was crazy. He had to be crazy. Or he was on. that dope.

Blacktown: You ever hear of a junkie trying to rape anybody?

Jo: *I didn't say rape!*

Counsel for the Bereaved: Were you struggling in Mr. Henry's arms when your husband came out of the back room, carrying his hammer in his hand?

Jo: No. I was free then.

Counsel for the Bereaved: Therefore, your husband had only *your* word for the alleged attempted assault! *You* told him that Richard Henry had attempted to assault you? Had made sexual advances to you? Please answer, Mrs. Britten!

Jo: Yes. I had—I had to—tell him. I'm his wife!

Counsel for the Bereaved: And a most loyal one. You told your husband that Richard Henry had attempted to assault you and then begged him to do nothing about it?

Jo: That's right.

Counsel for the Bereaved: And though he was under the impression that his wife had been nearly raped by a Negro, he agreed to forgive and forget and do nothing about it? He agreed neither to call the law, nor to take the law into his own hands?

Jo: Yes.

Counsel for the Bereaved: Extraordinary. Mrs. Britten, you are aware that Richard Henry met his death sometime between the hours of two and five o'clock on the morning of Monday, August 24th?

Jo: Yes.

Counsel for the Bereaved: In an earlier statement, several months ago, you stated that your husband had spent that night at the store. You now state that he came in before one o'clock and went to sleep at once. What accounts for this discrepancy?

Jo: It's natural. I made a mistake about the time. I got it mixed up with another night. He spent so many nights at that store!

Judge: The witness may step down.

*(**Jo** leaves the stand.)*

Clerk:

(Calls.)

Mr. Joel Davis!

*(We hear a shot. **Papa D.** is facing **Lyle**.)*

Lyle: Why'd you run down there this morning, shooting your mouth off about me and Willa Mae? Why? You been bringing her up here and taking her back all this time, what got into you this morning? Huh? You jealous, old man? Why you come running back here to tell me everything he said? To tell me how he cursed me out? Have you lost your mind? And we been knowing each other all this time. I don't understand you. She ain't the only girl you done brought here for me. Nigger, do you hear me talking to you?

Papa D.: I didn't think you'd shoot him, Mr. Lyle.

Lyle: I'll shoot any nigger talks to me like that. It was self defense, you hear me? He come in here and tried to kill me. You hear me?

Papa D.: Yes. Yes sir. I hear you, Mr. Lyle.

Lyle: That's right. You don't say the right thing, nigger, I'll blow your brains out, too.

Papa D.: Yes sir, Mr. Lyle.

*(Juke box music. **Papa D.** takes the stand.)*

Whitetown: He's worked hard and saved his money and ain't never had no trouble—why can't they all be like that?

Blacktown: Hey, Papa D.! You can't be walking around here without no handkerchief! You might catch cold—after all *these* years!

Papa D.: Mr. Lyle Britten—he is an *oppressor*. That is the only word for that man. He ain't never give the colored man no kind of chance. I have tried to reason with that man for *years*. I say, Mr. Lyle, look around you. Don't you see that most white folks have changed their way of thinking about us colored folks? I say, Mr. Lyle, we ain't slaves no more and white folks is ready to let us have our chance. Now, why don't you just come on up to where *most* of your people are? and we can make the South a fine place for all of us to live in. That's what I say—and I tried to keep him from being so *hard* on the colored—because I sure do love my people. And I was the closest thing to Mr. Lyle, couldn't nobody else reason with him. But he was *hard*—hard and stubborn. He say, "My folks lived and died this way, and this is the way I'm going to live and die." When he was like that couldn't do nothing with him. I know. I've known him since he was born.

Whitetown: He's always been real good to you. You were friends.

Blacktown: You loved him! Tell the truth, mother—tell the truth!

Papa D.: Yes, we were friends. And, yes, I loved him—in my way. Just like he loved me—in his way.

Blacktown: You knew he was going to kill that boy—didn't you? If you knew it, why didn't you stop him?

Papa D.: Oh. Ain't none of this easy. What it was, both Mr. Lyle Britten and me, we both love money. And I did a whole lot of things for him, for a long while. Once I had to help him cover up a killing—colored man—I was in too deep myself by that time—you understand? I know you all understand.

Blacktown: Did he kill that boy?

Papa D.: He come into my joint the night that boy died. The boy was alone, standing at the juke box. We'd been talking—

    (**Richard**, *in the juke box light.*)

If you think you've found all that, Richard—if you think you going to be well now, and you found you somebody who loves you—well, then, I would make tracks out of here. I would—

Richard: It's funny, Papa D. I feel like I'm beginning to understand my life—for the first time. I can look back—and it doesn't hurt me like it used to. I want to get Juanita out of here. This is no place for her. They're going to kill her—if she stays here!

Papa D.: You talk to Juanita about this yet?

Richard: No. I haven't talked to nobody about it yet. I just decided it. I guess I'm deciding it now. That's why I'm talking about it now—to you—to see if you'll laugh at me. Do you think she'll laugh at me?

Papa D.: No. She won't laugh.

Richard: I know I can do it. I know I can do it!

Papa D.: That boy had good sense. He was wild, but he had good sense. And I couldn't blame him too much for being so wild, it seemed to me I knew how he felt.

Richard: Papa D., I been in pain and darkness all my life. All my life. And this is the first time in my life I've ever felt—maybe it isn't all like that. Maybe there's more to it than that.

Papa D.: Lyle Britten come to the door—

    (**Lyle** *enters.*)

He come to the door and he say—

Lyle: You ready for me now, boy? Howdy, Papa D.

Papa D.: Howdy, Mr. Lyle, how's the world been treating you?

Lyle: I can't complain. You ready, boy?

Richard: No. I ain't ready. I got a record to play and a drink to finish.

Lyle: You about ready to close, ain't you, Joel?

Papa D.: Just about, Mr. Lyle.

Richard: I got a record to play.

    (Drops coin: juke box music, loud.)

And a drink to finish.

Papa D.: He played his record. Lyle Britten never moved from the door. And they just stood there, the two of them, looking at each other. When the record was just about over, the boy come to the bar—he swallowed down the last of his drink.

Richard: What do I owe you, Papa D.?

Papa D.: Oh, you pay me tomorrow. I'm closed now.

Richard: What do I owe you, Papa D.? I'm not sure I can pay you tomorrow.

Papa D.: Give me two dollars.

Richard: Here you go. Good night, Papa D. I'm ready, Charlie.

    (Exits.)

Papa D.: Good night, Richard. Go on home now. Good night, Mr. Lyle. Mr. Lyle!

Lyle: Good night, Joel. You get you some sleep, you hear?

    (Exits.)

Papa D.: Mr. Lyle! Richard! And I never saw that boy again. Lyle killed him. He killed him. I know it, just like I know I'm sitting in this chair. Just like he shot Old Bill and wasn't nothing never, never, never done about it!

Judge: The witness may step down.

    *(**Papa D.** leaves the stand.)*

Clerk:

    (Calls.)

Mr. Lorenzo Shannon!

    *(We hear a long, loud, animal cry, lonely and terrified: it is **Pete**, screaming. We discover **Lorenzo** and **Pete**, in jail. Night. From far away, we hear students humming, moaning, singing: "I Woke Up This Morning With My Mind Stayed On Freedom.")*

Pete:

    (Stammering.)

Lorenzo? Lorenzo. I was dreaming—dreaming—dreaming. I was back in that courtyard and Big Jim Byrd's boys was beating us and beating us and beating us—and Big Jim Byrd was laughing. And Anna Mae Taylor was on her knees, she was trying to pray. She say, "Oh Lord, Lord, Lord, come and help us," and they kept beating on her and beating on her and I saw blood coming down her neck and they put the prods to her, and, oh, Lorenzo! People was just running around, just crying and moaning and you look to the right and you see somebody go down and you look to the left and you see somebody go down and they was kicking that woman, and I say, "That woman's going to have a baby, don't you kick that woman!" and they say, "No, she ain't going to have no baby," and they knocked me down and they got that prod up between my legs and they say, "You ain't going to be having no babies, neither, nigger!" And then they put that prod to my head—ah!—*ah!* —to my *head!* Lorenzo! I can't see right! What have they done to my head?

Lorenzo! Lorenzo, am I going to die? Lorenzo—they going to kill us all, ain't they? They mean to kill us all—

Lorenzo: Be quiet. Be quiet. They going to come and beat us some more if you don't be quiet.

Pete: Where's Juanita? Did they get Juanita?

Lorenzo: I believe Juanita's all right. Go to sleep, Pete. Go to sleep. I won't let you dream. I'll hold you.

(**Lorenzo** *takes the stand.*)

The State: Did you accompany your late and great friend, Richard Henry, on the morning of August 17, to the store which is owned and run by Mr. and Mrs. Lyle Britten?

Lorenzo: We hadn't planned to go there—but we got to walking and talking and we found ourselves there. And it didn't happen like she said. He picked the Cokes out of the box himself, he came to the door with the Cokes in his hand, she hadn't even moved, she was still behind the counter, he never touched that dried out little peckerwood!

Whitetown: Get that nigger! Who does that nigger think he is!

Blacktown: Speak, Lorenzo! Go, my man!

The State: You cannot expect this courtroom to believe that so serious a battle was precipitated by the question of twenty cents! There was some other reason. What was this reason? Had he—and you—been drinking?

Lorenzo: It was early in the day, Cap'n. We ain't rich enough to drink in the daytime.

The State: Or *smoking,* perhaps? Perhaps your friend had just had his quota of heroin for the day, and was feeling jolly—in a mood to *prove* to you what he had already suggested with those filthy photographs of himself and naked white women!

Lorenzo: I never saw no photographs. White women are a problem for white men. We had not been drinking. All we was smoking was that goddamn tobacco that made *you* rich because we picked it for you for nothing, and carried it to market for you for nothing. And I *know* ain't no heroin in this town because none of you mothers need it. You was *born* frozen. Richard was better than that. I'd rather die than be like you, Cap'n, but I'd be *proud* to be like Richard. That's all I can tell you, Mr. Boss-Man. But I know he wasn't trying to rape nobody. Rape!

The State: Your Honor, will you instruct the witness that he is under oath, that this is a court of law, and that it is a serious matter to be held in contempt of court!

Lorenzo: More serious than the chain gang? *I* know I'm under oath. If there was any reason, it was just that Richard couldn't stand white people. *Couldn't stand white people!* And, now, do you want me to tell you all that I know about *that?* Do you think you could stand it? You'd cut my tongue out before you'd let me tell you all that I know about *that!*

Counsel for the Bereaved: You are a student here?

Lorenzo: In my spare time. I just come off the chain gang a couple of days ago. I was trespassing in the white waiting room of the bus station.

Counsel for the Bereaved: What are you studying—in your spare time—Mr. Shannon?

Lorenzo: History.

Counsel for the Bereaved: To your knowledge—during his stay in this town—was the late Mr. Richard Henry still addicted to narcotics?

Lorenzo: No. He'd kicked his habit. He'd paid his dues. He was just trying to live. And he almost made it.

Counsel for the Bereaved: You were very close to him?

Lorenzo: Yes.

Counsel for the Bereaved: To your knowledge—was he carrying about obscene photographs of himself and naked white women?

Lorenzo: To my knowledge—and I would know—no. The only times he ever opened a popular magazine was to look at the Jazz Poll. No. They been asking me about photographs they say he was carrying and they been asking me about a gun I never saw. No. It wasn't like that. He was a beautiful cat, and they killed him. That's all. That's *all*

Judge: The witness may step down.

Lorenzo: Well! I thank you kindly. *Suh!*

 (**Lorenzo** *leaves the stand.*)

Clerk:

 (*Calls.*)

Miss Juanita Harmon!

 (**Juanita** *rises from bed; early Sunday morning.*)

Juanita: He lay beside me on that bed like a rock. As heavy as a rock—like he'd fallen—fallen from a high place—fallen so far and landed so heavy, he seemed almost to be sinking out of sight—with one knee pointing to heaven. My God. He covered me like that. He wasn't at all like I thought he was. He fell on—fell on me—like life and death. My God. His chest, his belly, the rising and the falling, the moans. How he clung, how he struggled—life and death! Life and death! Why did it all seem to me like tears? That he came to me, clung to me, plunged into me, sobbing, howling, bleeding, somewhere inside his chest, his belly, and it all came out, came pouring out, like tears! My God, the smell, the touch, the taste, the sound, of anguish! Richard! Why couldn't I have held you closer? Held you, held you, borne you, given you life again? Have made you be born again! Oh, Richard. The teeth that gleamed, oh! when you smiled, the spit flying when you cursed, the teeth stinging when you bit—your breath, your hands, your weight, my God, when you moved in me! Where shall I go now, what shall I do? Oh. Oh. Oh. Mama was frightened. Frightened because little Juanita brought her first real lover to this house. I suppose God does for Mama what Richard did for me. Juanita! I don't care! I don't care! Yes, I want a lover made of flesh and blood, of flesh and blood, like me, I don't want to be God's mother! He can *have* His icy, snow-white heaven! If He is somewhere around this fearful planet, if I ever see Him, I will spit in His face! In God's face! How *dare* He presume to judge a living soul! A living soul. Mama is afraid I'm pregnant. Mama is afraid of so much. I'm not afraid. I hope I'm pregnant. I *hope* I am! One more illegitimate black baby—that's right, you jive mothers! And I am going to raise my baby to be a man. A *man,* you dig? Oh, let me be pregnant, let me be pregnant, don't let it all be gone! A man. Juanita. A man. Oh, my God, there are no more. For me. Did this happen to Mama sometime? Did she have a man sometime who vanished like smoke? And left her to get through this world as best she could? Is that why she married my father? Did this happen to Mother Henry? Is this how we all get to be mothers—so soon? of helpless men—because all the other men perish? No. No. No. What is this world like? I will end up taking care of some man, some day. Help me do it with love. Pete. Meridian. Parnell. We have been the mothers for them all. It must be dreadful to be Parnell. There is no flesh he can touch. All of it is bloody. Incest everywhere. Ha-ha! You're going crazy, Juanita. Oh, Lord, don't let me go mad. Let me be pregnant! Let me be pregnant!

(**Juanita** *takes the stand. One arm is in a sling.*)

Blacktown: Look! You should have seen her when she *first* come out of jail! Why we always got to love *them?* How come it's *us* always go to do the loving? Because you *black,* mother! Everybody knows we *strong* on loving! Except when it comes to our women.

Whitetown: Black slut! What happened to her arm? Somebody had to twist it, I reckon. She looks like she might be a right pretty little girl—why is she messing up her life this way?

The State: Miss Harmon, you have testified that you were friendly with the mother of the deceased. How old were you when she died?

Juanita: I was sixteen.

The State: Sixteen! You are older than the deceased?

Juanita: By two years.

The State: At the time of his mother's death, were you and Richard Henry considering marriage?

Juanita: No. Of course not.

The State: The question of marriage did not come up until just before he died?

Juanita: Yes.

The State: But between the time that Richard Henry left this town and returned, you had naturally attracted other boy friends?

Blacktown: Why don't you come right out and ask her if she's a virgin, man? Save you time.

Whitetown: She probably pregnant right now—and don't know who the father is. That's the way they are.

The State: The departure of the boy and the death of the mother must have left all of you extremely lonely?

Juanita: It can't be said to have made us any happier.

The State: Reverend Henry missed his wife, you missed your playmate. His grief and your common concern for the boy must have drawn you closer together?

Blacktown: Oh, man! Get to *that!*

Whitetown: That's right. What about that liver-lipped preacher?

The State: Miss Harmon, you describe yourself as a student. Where have you spent the last few weeks?

Juanita: In jail! I was arrested for—

The State: I am not concerned with the reasons for your arrest. How much time, all told, have you spent in jail?

Juanita: It would be hard to say—a long time.

The State: Excellent preparation for your future! Is it not true, Miss Harmon, that before the late Richard Henry returned to this town, you were considering marriage with another so-called student, Pete Spivey? Can you seriously expect this court to believe anything you now say concerning Richard Henry? Would you not say the same thing, and for the same reason, concerning the father? Concerning Pete Spivey? And how many others!

Whitetown: That's the way they are. It's not their fault. That's what they want us to integrate with.

Blacktown: These people are sick. Sick. Sick people's been known to be made well by a little shedding of blood.

Juanita: I am not responsible for your imagination.

The State: What do you know of the fight which took place between Richard Henry and Lyle Britten, at Mr. Britten's store?

Juanita: I was not a witness to that fight.

The State: But you had seen Richard Henry before the fight? Was he sober?

Juanita: Yes.

The State: Can you swear to that?

Juanita: Yes, I can swear to it.

The State: And you saw him after the fight? Was he sober then?

Juanita: Yes. He was sober then.

> (*Courtroom in silhouette.*)

I heard about the fight at the end of the day—when I got home. And I went running to Reverend Henry's house. And I met him on the porch—just sitting there.

The State: You met whom?

Juanita: I met—Richard.

> (*We discover* **Meridian**.)

Meridian: Hello, Juanita. Don't look like that.

Juanita: Meridian, what happened today? Where's Richard?

Meridian: He's all right now. He's sleeping. We better send him away. Lyle's dangerous. You know that.

> (*Takes* **Juanita** *in his arms; then holds her at arm's length.*)

You'll go with him. Won't you?

Juanita: Meridian—oh, my God.

Meridian: Juanita, tell me something I have to know. I'll never ask it again.

Juanita: Yes, Meridian—

Meridian: Before he came—I wasn't just making it all up, was I? There was something at least—beginning—something dimly possible—wasn't there? I thought about you so much—and it was so wonderful each time I saw you—and I started hoping as I haven't let myself hope, oh, for a long time. I knew you were much younger, and I'd known you since you were a child.

But I thought that maybe that didn't matter, after all—we got on so well together. I wasn't making it all up, was I?

Juanita: No. You weren't making it up—not all of it, anyway, there was something there. We were lonely. You were hoping. I was hoping, too—oh, Meridian! Of all the people on God's earth I would rather die than hurt!

Meridian: Hush, Juanita. I know that. I just wanted to be told that I hadn't lost my mind. I've lost so much. I think there's something wrong in being—what I've become—something really wrong. I mean, I think there's something wrong with allowing oneself to become so lonely. I think that I was proud that I could bear it. Each day became a kind of test—to see if I could bear it. And there were many days when I couldn't bear it—when I walked up and down and howled and lusted and cursed and prayed—just like any man. And I've been—I haven't been as celibate as I've seemed. But my confidence—my confidence—was destroyed back there when I pulled back that rug they had her covered with and I saw that little face on that broken neck. There wasn't any blood—just water. She was soaked. Oh, my God. My God. And I haven't trusted myself with a woman since. I keep seeing her the last time I saw her, whether I'm awake or asleep. That's why I let you get away from me. It wasn't my son that did it. It was me. And so much the better for you. And him. And I've held it all in since then—what fearful choices we must make! In order not to commit murder, in order not to become too monstrous, in order to be some kind of example to my only son. Come. Let me be an example now. And kiss you on the forehead and wish you well.

Juanita: Meridian. Meridian. Will it always be like this? Will life always be like this? Must we always suffer so?

Meridian: I don't know, Juanita. I know that we must bear what we must bear. Don't cry, Juanita. Don't cry. Let's go on.

(Exits.)

Juanita: By and by Richard woke up and I was there. And we tried to make plans to go, but he said he wasn't going to run no more from white folks—never no more!—but was going to stay and be a man—a *man!*—right here. And I couldn't *make* him see differently. I knew what he meant, I knew how he felt, but I didn't want him to die! And by the time I persuaded him to take *me* away, to take *me* away from this terrible place, it was too late. Lyle killed him! Lyle killed him! Like they been killing all our men, for years, for generations! Our husbands, our fathers, our brothers, our sons!

Judge: The witness may step down.

*(**Juanita** leaves the stand. **Mother Henry** helps her to her seat.)*

This court is adjourned until ten o'clock tomorrow morning.

*(Chaos and cacophony. The courtroom begins to empty. **Reporters** rush to phone booths and to witnesses. Light bulbs flash. We hear snatches of the **Journalists'** reports, in their various languages. Singing from the church. Blackout. The next and last day of the trial. Even more crowded and tense.)*

Clerk:

(Calls.)

Mrs. Wilhelmina Henry!

(**Mother Henry**, *in street clothes, walks down the aisle, takes the stand.*)

The State: You are Mrs. Wilhelmina Henry?

Mother Henry: Yes.

The State: Mrs. Henry, you—and your husband, until he died—lived in this town all your lives and never had any trouble. We've always gotten on well down here.

Mother Henry: No white man never called my husband Mister, neither, not as long as he lived. Ain't no white man never called *me* Mrs. Henry before today. I had to get a grandson killed for that.

The State: Mrs. Henry, your grief elicits my entire sympathy, and the sympathy of every white man in this town. But is it not true, Mrs. Henry, that your grandson arrived in this town armed? He was carrying a gun and, apparently, had carried a gun for years.

Mother Henry: I don't know where you got that story, or why you keep harping on it. *I* never saw no gun.

The State: You are under oath, Mrs. Henry.

Mother Henry: I don't need you to tell me I'm under oath. I been under oath all my life. And I tell you, I never saw no gun.

The State: Mrs. Henry, did you ever see your grandson behaving strangely— as though he were under the influence of strong drugs?

Mother Henry: No. Not since he was six and they pulled out his tonsils. They gave him ether. *He* didn't act as strange as his Mama and Daddy. He just went on to sleep. But they like to had a fit.

(**Richard**'s song.)

I remember the day he was born. His mother had a hard time holding him and a hard time getting him here. But here he come, in the wintertime, late and big and loud. And my boy looked down into his little son's face and he said, "God give us a son. God's give us a son. Lord, help us to raise him to be a good strong man."

Judge: The witness may step down.

Clerk:

(*Calls.*)

Reverend Meridian Henry!

(*Blackout.* **Meridian**, *in Sunday School. The class itself, predominantly adolescent girls, is in silhouette.*)

Meridian: —And here is the prophet, Solomon, the son of David, looking down through the ages, and speaking of Christ's love for His church.

(*Reads.*)

How fair is thy love, my sister, my spouse! How much better is thy love than wine! and the smell of thine ointments than all spices!

(*Pause. The silhouette of girls vanishes.*)

Oh, that it were one man, speaking to one woman!

(*Blackout.* **Meridian** *takes the stand.*)

Blacktown: I wonder how he feels now about all that turn-the-other-cheek jazz. His son sure didn't go for it.

Whitetown: That's the father. Claims to be a preacher. He brought this on himself. He's been raising trouble in this town for a long time.

BLUES FOR MISTER CHARLIE   301

The State: You are Reverend Meridian Henry?

Meridian: That is correct.

The State: And you are the father of the late Richard Henry?

Meridian: Yes.

The State: You are a minister?

Meridian: A Christian minister—yes.

The State: And you raised your son according to the precepts of the Christian church?

Meridian: I tried. But both my son and I had profound reservations concerning the behavior of Christians. He wondered why they treated black people as they do. And I was unable to give him—a satisfactory answer.

The State: But certainly you—as a Christian minister—did not encourage your son to go armed?

Meridian: The question never came up. He was not armed.

The State: He was not armed?

Meridian: No.

The State: You never saw him with a gun? Or with any other weapon?

Meridian: No.

The State: Reverend Henry—are you in a position to swear that your son never carried arms?

Meridian: Yes. I can swear to it. The only time the subject was ever mentioned he told me that he was stronger than white people and he could live without a gun.

Blacktown: I bet he didn't say how.

Whitetown: That liver-lipped nigger is lying. He's lying!

The State: Perhaps the difficulties your son had in accepting the Christian faith is due to your use of the pulpit as a forum for irresponsible notions concerning social equality, Reverend Henry. Perhaps the failure of the son is due to the failure of the father.

Meridian: I am afraid that the gentleman flatters himself. I do not wish to see Negroes become the equal of their murderers. I wish us to become equal to ourselves. To become a people so free in themselves that they will have no need to—fear—others—and have no need to murder others.

The State: You are not in the pulpit now. I am suggesting that you are responsible—directly responsible—for your son's tragic fate.

Meridian: I know more about that than you do. But you cannot consider my son's death to have been tragic. For you, it would have been tragic if he had lived.

The State: With such a father, it is remarkable that the son lived as long as he did.

Meridian: Remarkable, too, that the father lived!

The State: Reverend Henry—you have been a widower for how many years?

Meridian: I have been a widower for nearly eight years.

The State: You are a young man still?

Meridian: Are you asking me my age? I am not young.

The State: You are not old. It must have demanded great discipline—

Meridian: To live among you? Yes.

The State: What is your relationship to the young, so-called student, Miss Juanita Harmon?

Meridian: I am her old friend. I had hoped to become her father-in-law.

The State: You are nothing more than old friends?

Whitetown: That's right. Get it out of him. Get the truth out of him.

Blacktown: Leave the man *something*. Leave him something!

The State: You have been celibate since the death of your wife?

Blacktown: He never said he was a monk, you jive mother!

Whitetown: Make him tell us all about it. *All* about it.

Meridian: Celibate? How does my celibacy concern you?

The State: Your Honor, will you instruct the witness that he is on the witness stand, not I, and that he must answer the questions put to him!

Meridian: *The questions put to him!* All right. Do you accept this answer? I am a man. A *man!* I tried to help my son become a man. But manhood is a dangerous pursuit, here. And that pursuit undid him because of *your* guns, *your* hoses, *your* dogs, *your* judges, *your* law-makers, *your* folly, *your* pride, *your* cruelty, *your* cowardice, *your* money, *your* chain gangs, and *your* churches! Did you think it would endure forever? that we would pay for *your* ease forever?

Blacktown: Speak, my man! Amen! Amen! Amen! Amen!

Whitetown: Stirring up hate! Stirring up hate! A *preacher*—stirring up hate!

Meridian: Yes! I *am* responsible for the death of my son. I—hoped—I prayed —I struggled—so that the world would be different by the time he was a man than it had been when he was born. And I thought that—then—when he looked at me—he would think that I—his father—had helped to change it.

The State: What about those photographs your son carried about with him? Those photographs of himself and naked white women?

Blacktown: Man! Would I love to look in *your* wallet!

Whitetown: Make him tell us about it, make him tell us *all* about it!

Meridian: Photographs? My son and naked white women? He never mentioned them to me.

The State: You were closer than most fathers and sons?

Meridian: I never took a poll on most fathers and sons.

The State: You never discussed women?

Meridian: We talked about his mother. She was a woman. We talked about Miss Harmon. *She* is a woman. But we never talked about dirty pictures. We didn't need that.

The State: Reverend Henry, you have made us all aware that your love for your son transcends your respect for the truth or your devotion to the church. But—luckily for the truth—it is a matter of public record that your son was so dangerously deranged that it was found necessary, for his own sake, to incarcerate him. It was at the end of that incarceration that he returned to this town. We know that his life in the North was riotous—he brought that riot into this town. The evidence is overwhelming. And yet, you, a Christian minister, dare to bring us this tissue of lies in defense of a known pimp, dope addict, and rapist! You are yourself so eaten up by race hatred that no word of yours can be believed.

Meridian: Your judgment of myself and my motives cannot concern me at all. I have lived with that judgment far too long. The truth cannot be heard in this dreadful place. But I will tell you again what I know. I know why my son became a dope addict. I know better than you will ever know, even if I should explain it to you for all eternity, how I am responsible for that. But I know my son was not a pimp. He respected women far too much for that. And I know he was not a rapist. Rape is hard work—and, frankly, I don't think that the alleged object was my son's type at all!

The State: And you are a minister?

Meridian: I think I may be beginning to become one.

Judge: The witness may step down.

(**Meridian** *leaves the stand.*)

Clerk:

(*Calls.*)

Mr. Parnell James!

(**Parnell** *in his bedroom, dressed in a bathrobe. Night.*)

Parnell: She says I called somebody else's name. What name could I have called? And she won't repeat the name. Well. That's enough to freeze the blood and arrest the holy, the liberating orgasm! Christ, how weary I am of this dull calisthenic called love—with no love in it! What name could I have called? I hope it was—a *white* girl's name, anyway! Ha-ha! How still she became! And I hardly realized it, I was too far away—and then it was too late. And she was just looking at me. Jesus! To have somebody just looking at you—just looking at you—like that—at such a moment! It makes you feel —like you woke up and found yourself in bed with your mother! I tried to find out what was wrong—poor girl! But there's nothing you can say at a moment like that—really nothing. You're caught. Well, haven't I kept telling her that there's no future for her with me? There's no future for me with anybody! But that's all right. What name could I have called? I haven't been with anybody else for a long time, a long time. She says I haven't been with her, either. I guess she's right. I've just been using her. Using her as an anchor—to hold me here, in this house, this bed—so I won't find myself on the other side of town, ruining my reputation. *What* reputation? They all know. I swear they all *know.* Know what? What's there to know? So you get drunk and you fool around a little. Come on, Parnell. There's more to it than that. That's the reason you draw blanks whenever you get drunk. Everything comes out. Everything. They see what you don't dare to see. What name could I have called? Richard would say that you've got—black fever! Yeah, and he'd be wrong—that long, loud, black mother. I wonder if she's asleep yet—or just lying there, looking at the walls. Poor girl! All your life you've been made sick, stunned, dizzy, oh, Lord! driven half mad by blackness. Blackness in front of your eyes. Boys and girls, men and women—you've bowed down in front of them all! And then hated yourself. Hated yourself for debasing yourself? Out with it, Parnell! The nigger-lover! Black boys and girls! I've wanted my hands full of them, wanted to drown them, laughing and dancing and making love—making love—wow!—and be transformed,

formed, liberated out of this grey-white envelope. Jesus! I've always been afraid. Afraid of what I saw in their eyes? They don't love me, certainly. You don't love them, either! Sick with a disease only white men catch. Blackness. What is it like to be black? To look out on the world from that place? I give nothing! How dare she say that! My girl, if you knew what I've given! Ah. Come off it, Parnell. To whom have you given? What name did I call? What name did I call?

(*Blackout.* **Parnell** and **Lyle**. *Hunting on* **Parnell's** *land.*)

Lyle: You think it's a good idea, then? You think she won't say no?

Parnell: Well, you're the one who's got to go through it. You've got to ask for Miss Josephine's hand in marriage. And then you've got to live with her —for the rest of your life. Watch that gun. I've never seen you so jumpy. I might say it was a good idea if I thought she'd say no. But I think she'll say yes.

Lyle: Why would she say yes to me?

Parnell: I think she's drawn to you. It isn't hard to be—drawn to you. Don't you know that?

Lyle: No. When I was young, I used to come here sometimes—with my Daddy. He didn't like your Daddy a-tall! We used to steal your game, Parnell—you didn't know that, did you?

Parnell: I think I knew it.

Lyle: We shot at the game and your Daddy's overseers shot at us. But we got what we came after. They never got us!

Parnell: You're talking an awful lot today. You nervous about Miss Josephine?

Lyle: Wait a minute. You think I ought to marry Jo?

Parnell: I don't know who anybody should marry. Do you want to marry Jo?

Lyle: Well—I got to marry somebody. I got to have some kids. And Jo is— clean!..

(**Parnell** *sights, shoots.*)

Parnell: Goddamn

Lyle: Missed it. Ha-ha!

Parnell: It's probably somebody's mother.

Lyle: Watch.

(*Sights, shoots.*)

Ha-ha!

Parnell: Bravo!

Lyle: I knew it! Had my name written on it, just as pretty as you please!

(*Exits, returns with his bird.*)

See? My Daddy taught me well. It was sport for you. It was life for us.

Parnell: I reckon you shot somebody's baby.

Lyle: I tell you—I can't go on like this. There comes a time in a man's life when he's got to have a little—peace.

Parnell: You mean calm. Tranquillity.

Lyle: Yeah. I didn't mean it like it sounded. You thought I meant—no. I'm tired of—

Parnell: Poon-tang.

Lyle: How'd you know? You tired of it, too? Hell. Yeah. I want kids.

Parnell: Well, then—marry the girl.

Lyle: She ain't a girl no more. It might be her last chance, too. But, I swear, Parnell, she might be the only virgin left in this town. The only *white* virgin. I can vouch for the fact ain't many black ones.

Parnell: You've been active, I know. Any kids?

Lyle: None that I know of. Ha-ha!

Parnell: Do you think Jo might be upset—by the talk about you and Old Bill? She's real respectable, you know. She's a *librarian.*

Lyle: No. Them things happen every day. You think I ought to marry her? You really think she'll say yes?

Parnell: She'll say yes. She'd better. I wish you luck. Name the first one after me.

Lyle: No. You be the godfather. And my best man. I'm going to name the first one after my Daddy—because he taught me more about hunting on your land than *you* know. I'll give him your middle name. I'll call him Lyle Parnell Britten, Jr.!

Parnell: If the girl says yes.

Lyle: Well, if she says no, ain't no problem, is there? We know where to go when the going gets rough, don't we, old buddy?

Parnell: Do we? Look! Mine?

Lyle: What'll you bet?

Parnell: The price of your wedding rings.

Lyle: You're on. Mine? *Mine!*

    (*Blackout.* **Parnell** *walks down the aisle, takes the stand.*)

Whitetown: Here comes the nigger-lover!

But I bet you one thing—he knows more about the truth in this case than anybody else.

He ought to—he's with them all the time.

It's sad when a man turns against his own people!

Blacktown: Let's see how the Negro's friend comes through!

They been waiting for *him*—they going to tear his behind *up!*

I don't trust him. I *never* trusted him!

Why? Because he's *white,* that's why!

The State: You were acquainted with the late Richard Henry?

Parnell: Of course. His father and I have been friends all our lives.

The State: Close friends?

Parnell: Yes. Very close.

The State: And what is your relationship to the alleged murderer, Mr. Lyle Britten?

Parnell: We, also, have been friends all our lives.

The State: Close friends?

Parnell: Yes.

The State: As close as the friendship between yourself and the dead boy's father?

Parnell: I would say so—it was a very different relationship.

The State: Different in what respect, Mr. James?

Parnell: Well, we had different things to talk about. We did different things together.

The State: What sort of different things?

Parnell: Well—hunting, for example—things like that.

The State: You never went hunting with Reverend Henry?

Parnell: No. He didn't like to hunt.

The State: He told you so? He told you that he didn't like to hunt?

Parnell: The question never came up. We led very different lives.

The State: I am gratified to hear it. Is it not true, Mr. James, that it is impossible for any two people to go on a hunting trip together if either of them has any reason at all to distrust the other?

Parnell: Well, of course that would have to be true. But it's never talked about—it's just understood.

The State: We can conclude, then, that you were willing to trust Lyle Britten with your life but did not feel the same trust in Reverend Henry?

Parnell: Sir, you may not draw any such conclusion! I have told you that Reverend Henry and I led very different lives!

The State: But you have been friends all your lives. Reverend Henry is also a southern boy—he, also, I am sure, knows and loves this land, has gone swimming and fishing in her streams and rivers, and stalked game in her forests. And yet, close as you are, you have never allowed yourself to be alone with Reverend Henry when Reverend Henry had a gun. Doesn't this suggest some *lack*—in your vaunted friendship?

Parnell: Your suggestion is unwarranted and unworthy. As a soldier, I have often been alone with Negroes with guns, and it certainly never caused me any uneasiness.

The State: But you were fighting a common enemy then. What was your impression of the late Richard Henry?

Parnell: I liked him. He was very outspoken and perhaps tactless, but a very valuable person.

The State: How would you describe his effect on this town? Among his own people? Among the whites?

Parnell: His effect? He was pretty well liked.

The State: That does not answer my question.

Parnell: His effect was—kind of unsettling, I suppose. After all, he had lived in the North a long time, he wasn't used to—the way we do things down here.

The State: He was accustomed to the way things are done in the North—where he learned to carry arms, to take dope, and to couple with white women!

Parnell: I cannot testify to any of that, sir. I can only repeat that he reacted with great intensity to the racial situation in this town, and his effect on the town was, to that extent, unsettling.

The State: Did he not encourage the Negroes of this town to arm?

Parnell: Not to my knowledge, sir, no. And, in any case, they are not armed.

The State: You are in a position to reassure us on this point?

Parnell: My friends do not lie.

The State: You are remarkably fortunate. You are aware of the attitude of the late Richard Henry toward white women? You saw the photographs he carried about with him?

Parnell: We never discussed women. I never saw the photographs.

The State: But you knew of their existence?

Parnell: They were not obscene. They were simply snapshots of people he had known in the North.

The State: Snapshots of white women?

Parnell: Yes.

The State: You are the first witness to admit the existence of these photographs, Mr. James.

Parnell: It is very likely that the other witnesses never saw them. The boy had been discouraged, very early on, from mentioning them or showing them about.

The State: Discouraged by whom?

Parnell: Why—by—me.

The State: But you never saw the photographs—

Parnell: I told him I didn't want to see them and that it would be dangerous to carry them about.

The State: He showed these photographs to you, but to no one else?

Parnell: That would seem to be the case, yes.

The State: What was his motive in taking you into his confidence?

Parnell: Bravado. He wanted me to know that he had white friends in the North, that—he had been happy—in the North.

The State: You did not tell his father? You did not warn your close friend?

Parnell: I am sure that Richard never mentioned these photographs to his father. He would have been too ashamed. Those women were beneath him.

The State: A white woman who surrenders to a colored man is beneath all human consideration. She has wantonly and deliberately defiled the temple of the Holy Ghost. It is clear to me that the effect of such a boy on this town was irresponsible and incendiary to the greatest degree. Did you not find your close friendship with Reverend Henry somewhat strained by the son's attempt to rape the wife of your other close friend, Lyle Britten?

Parnell: This attempt was never mentioned before—before today.

The State: You are as close as you claim to the Britten family and knew nothing of this attempted rape? How do you explain that?

Parnell: I cannot explain it.

The State: This is a court of law, Mr. James, and we will have the truth!

Whitetown: Make him tell the truth!

Blacktown: Make him tell the truth!

The State: How can you be the close friend you claim to be of the Britten family and not have known of so grave an event?

Parnell: I—I knew of a fight. It was understood that the boy had gone to Mr. Britten's store looking for a fight. I—I cannot explain *that*, either.

The State: Who told you of the fight?

Parnell: Why—Mr. Britten.

The State: And did not tell you that Richard Henry had attempted to assault his wife? Come, Mr. James!

Parnell: We were all very much upset. Perhaps he was not as coherent as he might have been—perhaps I failed to listen closely. It was my assumption that Mrs. Britten had misconstrued the boy's actions—he had been in the North a long time, his manner was very free and bold.

The State: Mrs. Britten has testified that Richard Henry grabbed her and pulled her to him and tried to kiss her. How can those actions be misconstrued?

Parnell: Those actions are—quite explicit.

The State: Thank you, Mr. James. That is all.

Judge: The witness may step down.

> **(Parnell** *leaves the stand.)*

Blacktown: What do you think of our fine friend *now?* He didn't do it to us rough and hard. No, he was real gentle. I hardly felt a thing. Did you? You can't never go against the word of a white lady, man, not even if you're white. Can't be done. He was sad. *Sad!*

Whitetown: It took him long enough! He did his best not to say it—can you imagine! So her story was true—after all! I hope he's learned his lesson. We been trying to tell him—for years!

Clerk:

> *(Calls.)*

Mr. Lyle Britten!

> **(Lyle,** *in the woods.)*

Lyle: I wonder what he'll grow up to look like. Of course, it might be a girl. I reckon I wouldn't mind—just keep on trying till I get me a boy, ha-ha! Old Miss Josephine is something, ain't she? I really struck oil when I come across her. She's a nice woman. And she's *my* woman—I ain't got to worry about *that* a-tall! You're making big changes in your life, Lyle, and you got to be ready to take on this extra responsibility. Shoot, I'm ready. I know what I'm doing. And I'm going to work harder than I've ever worked before in my life to make Jo happy—and keep her happy—and raise our children to be fine men and women. Lord, you know I'm not a praying man. I've done a lot of wrong things in my life and I ain't never going to be perfect. I know You know that. I know You understand that. But, Lord, hear me today and help me to do what I'm supposed to do. I want to be as strong as my Mama and Daddy and raise my children like they raised me. That's what I want, oh Lord. In a few years I'll be walking here, showing my son these trees and this water and this sky. He'll have his hand in my hand, and I'll show him the world. Isn't that a funny thing! He don't even exist yet— he's just an egg in his mother's belly. I bet you couldn't even find him with a microscope—and I put him there—and he's coming out soon—with fingers and toes and eyes—and by and by, he'll learn to walk and talk—and I reckon I'll have to spank him sometime—if he's anything like me, I know I will. Isn't that something! My son! Hurry up and get here, so I can hug you in my arms and give you a good start on your long journey!

(Blackout. **Lyle** *with* **Papa D**. *Drunk. Music and dancing.)*

Lyle: You remember them days when Willa Mae was around? My mind's been going back to them days. You remember? She was a hot little piece, I just had to have some of that, I just *had* to. Half the time she didn't wear no stockings, just had them brown, round legs just moving. I couldn't keep my eyes off her legs when she didn't wear no stockings. And you know what she told me? You know what she told me? She said there wasn't a nigger alive could be as good to her as me. That's right. She said she'd like to *see* the nigger could do her like I done her. You hear me, boy? That's something, ain't it? Boy—she'd just come into a room sometimes and my old pecker would stand up at attention. You ain't jealous, are you, Joel, Ha-ha! You never did hear from her no more, did you? No, I reckon you didn't. Shoot, I got to get on home. I'm a family man now, I got—great responsibilities! Yeah. Be seeing you, Joel. You don't want to close up and walk a-ways with me, do you? No, I reckon you better not. They having fun. Sure wish I could be more like you all. Bye-bye!

> *(Blackout. As* **Lyle** *approaches the witness stand, the lights in the courtroom dim. We hear voices from the church, singing a lament. The lights come up.)*

Judge: Gentlemen of the jury, have you reached a verdict?

Foreman: We have, Your Honor.

Judge: Will the prisoner please rise?

> *(***Lyle*** *rises.)*

Do you find the defendant, Mr. Lyle Britten, guilty or not guilty?

Foreman: Not guilty, Your Honor.

> *(Cheering in* **Whitetown**. *Silence in* **Blacktown**. *The stage is taken over by* **Reporters, Photographers, Witnesses, Townspeople. Lyle** *is con-gratulated and embraced.* **Blacktown** *files out silently, not looking back.* **Whitetown** *files out jubilantly, and yet with a certain reluctance. Presently, the stage is empty, except for* **Lyle, Jo, Mother Henry, Meridian, Parnell, Juanita,** *and* **Lorenzo**.)*

Jo: Let's get out of here and go home. We've been here just for days. I wouldn't care if I *never* saw the insides of a courtroom again! Let's go home, sugar. We got something to celebrate!

Juanita: We, too, must go—to another celebration. We're having a prayer meeting on the City Hall steps.

Lorenzo: Prayer meeting!

Lyle: Well, it was touch and go there for awhile, Parnell, but you sure come through. I knew you would.

Jo: Let's go, Lyle. The baby's hungry.

Meridian: Perhaps now you can ask him to tell you the truth. He's got nothing to lose now. They can't try him again.

Lyle: Wasn't much sense in trying me now, this time, was there, Reverend? These people have been knowing me and my good Jo here all our lives, they ain't going to doubt us. And you people—you people—ought to have better sense and more things to do than running around stirring up all this hate and trouble. *That's* how your son got himself killed. He listened to crazy niggers like you!

Meridian: Did you kill him?

Lyle: They just asked me that in court, didn't they? And they just decided I didn't, didn't they? Well, that's good enough for me and all those white people and so it damn sure better be good enough for you!

Parnell: That's no answer. It's not good enough for me.

Lyle: What do you mean, that's no answer? Why isn't it an answer? Why isn't it good enough for you? You know, when you were up on the stand right now, you acted like you doubted my Jo's word. You got no right to doubt Jo's word. You ain't no better than she is! You ain't no better than me!

Parnell: I am aware of that. God knows I have been made aware of that—for the first time in my life. But, as you and I will never be the same again—since our comedy is finished, since I have failed you so badly—let me say this. I did not doubt Jo's word. I knew that she was lying and that you had made her lie. That was a terrible thing to do to her. It was a terrible thing that I just did to you. I really don't know if what I did to Meridian was as awful as what I did to you. I don't expect forgiveness, Meridian. I only hope that all of us will suffer past this agony and horror.

Lyle: What's the matter with you? Have you forgotten you a white man? A white man! My Daddy told me not to *never* forget I was a white man! Here I been knowing you all my life—and now I'm ashamed of you. Ashamed of you! Get on over to niggertown! I'm going home with my good wife.

Meridian: What was the last thing my son said to you—before you shot him down—like a dog?

Lyle: Like a dog! You a smart nigger, ain't you?

Meridian: What was the last thing he said? Did he beg you for his life?

Lyle: *That* nigger! He was too smart for that! He was too full of himself for that! He must have thought he was white. And I gave him every chance—every chance—to live!

Meridian: And he refused them all.

Lyle: Do you know what that nigger said to me?

> *(The light changes, so that everyone but* **Lyle** *is in silhouette.* **Richard** *appears, dressed as we last saw him, on the road outside* **Papa D.'s** *joint.)*

Richard: I'm ready. Here I am. You asked me if I was ready, didn't you? What's on your mind, white man?

Lyle: Boy, I always treated you with respect. I don't know what's the matter with you, or what makes you act the way you do—but you owe me an apology and I come out here tonight to get it. I mean, I ain't going away without it.

Richard: I owe *you* an apology! That's a wild idea. What am I apologizing for?

Lyle: You know, you mighty lucky to still be walking around.

Richard: So are you. White man.

BLUES FOR MISTER CHARLIE   311

Lyle: I'd like you to apologize for your behavior in my store that day. Now, I think I'm being pretty reasonable, ain't I?

Richard: You got anything to write on? I'll write you an IOU.

Lyle: Keep it up. You going to be laughing out of the other side of your mouth pretty soon.

Richard: Why don't you go home? And let me go home? Do we need all this shit? Can't we live without it?

Lyle: Boy, are you drunk?

Richard: No, I ain't drunk. I'm just tired. Tired of all this fighting. What are you trying to prove? What am *I* trying to prove?

Lyle: I'm trying to give you a break. You too dumb to take it.

Richard: I'm hip. You been trying to give me a break for a great, long time. But there's only one break I want. And you won't give me that.

Lyle: What kind of break do you want, boy?

Richard: For you to go home. And let me go home. I got things to do. I got— lots of things to do!

Lyle: I got things to do, too. I'd like to get home, too.

Richard: Then why are we standing here? Can't we walk? Let me walk, white man! Let me walk!

Lyle: We can walk, just as soon as we get our business settled.

Richard: It's settled. You a man and I'm a man. Let's walk.

Lyle: Nigger, you was born down here. Ain't you never said sir to a white man?

Richard: No. The only person I ever said sir to was my Daddy.

Lyle: Are you going to apologize to me?

Richard: No.

Lyle: Do you want to live?

Richard: Yes.

Lyle: Then you know what to do, then, don't you?

Richard: Go home. Go home.

Lyle: You facing my gun.

> *(Produces it.)*

Now, in just a minute, we can both go home.

Richard: You sick mother! Why can't you leave me alone? White man! I don't want nothing from you. You ain't got nothing to give me. You can't eat because none of your sad-assed chicks can cook. You can't talk because won't nobody talk to you. You can't dance because you've got nobody to dance with—don't you know I've watched you all my life? *All my life?* And I know your women, don't you think I don't—better than you!

> *(**Lyle** shoots, once.)*

Why have you spent so much time trying to kill me? Why are you always trying to cut off *my* cock? You worried about it? Why?

> *(**Lyle** shoots again.)*

Okay. Okay. Keep your old lady home, you hear?

Don't let her near no nigger. She might get to like it. You might get to like it, too. Wow!

> *(**Richard** falls.)*

Juanita! Daddy! *Mama!*

    (Singing from the church. Spot on **Lyle***.)*

Lyle: I had to kill him. I'm a white man! Can't nobody talk that way to *me!* I had to go and get my pick-up truck and load him in it—I had to carry him on my back—and carry him out to the high weeds. And I dumped him in the weeds, face down. And then I come on home, to my good Jo here.

Jo: Come on, Lyle. We got to get on home. We got to get the little one home now.

Lyle: And I ain't sorry. I want you to know that I ain't sorry!

Jo: Come on, Lyle. Come on. He's hungry. I got to feed him.

    (Jo *and* **Lyle** *exit.)*

Mother Henry: We got to go now, children. The children is already started to march.

Lorenzo: Prayer!

Meridian: You know, for us, it all began with the Bible and the gun. Maybe it will end with the Bible and the gun.

Juanita: What did you do with the gun, Meridian?

Parnell: You have the gun—Richard's gun?

Meridian: Yes. In the pulpit. Under the Bible. Like the pilgrims of old.

    (Exits.)

Mother Henry: Come on, children.

    (Singing. **Pete** *enters.)*

Pete:

    (Stammers.)

Are you ready, Juanita? Shall we go now?

Juanita: Yes.

Lorenzo: Come here, Pete. Stay close to me.

    (They go to the church door. The singing swells.)

Parnell: Well.

Juanita: Well. Yes, Lord!

Parnell: Can I join you on the march, Juanita? Can I walk with you?

Juanita: Well, we can walk in the same direction, Parnell. Come. Don't look like that. Let's go on on.

    (Exits. After a moment, **Parnell** *follows.)*

                                                        Curtain

The End

TWO PLAYS

Happy Ending
and Day of Absence

by Douglas Turner Ward

Douglas Turner Ward (1931-   )

Douglas Turner Ward, the eminent black actor and playwright, was born on a sugarcane and rice plantation at Burnside, Louisiana, where his parents worked as field hands. When he was eight his family moved to New Orleans where his father became a day laborer and his mother a seamstress, and where his parents today own their own tailoring business. At New Orleans Douglas Turner Ward attended a Negro Catholic High School. He spent one year at Wilberforce University in Ohio, and another at the University of Michigan. In 1948 he left college "to find out about the world." He headed for Harlem, where he lived for a while, and for three years he worked as a journalist. He soon found himself involved in some of the "more or less civil rights groups of those days, the early 1950's" and was asked by one group to write a skit for an entertainment. "That was it," he says, "I knew what I wanted to do." He continued to write, and took up acting as a member of Paul Mann's Actors Workshop not only to learn the craft of acting but also in order to learn more about plays and playwriting.

His acting career began in the off-Broadway Circle in the Square production of Eugene O'Neill's *The Iceman Cometh* (1956). He then played opposite Diana Sands in *A Land Beyond the River* (1957). He was featured in the New York City Center production of *Lost in the Stars* (1957). He served as understudy to Sidney Poitier in *A Raisin In The Sun,* and assumed the leading role opposite Claudia McNeil in the national tour. He also appeared on Broadway in *One Flew Over the Cuckoo's Nest* (1963), with Kirk Douglas. He was in the off-Broadway production of Genet's *The Blacks* and Athol Fugard's *Blood Knot.* He was featured in the Shakespeare Festival production of *Coriolanus* (1965), and he has made numerous television appearances.

Day of Absence and *Happy Ending,* Douglas Turner Ward's first plays to reach the professional stage, were produced by Robert Hooks, the stage

317

and film actor, at the St. Marks Playhouse in 1965, with Douglas Turner, (the author's stage name) and Robert Hooks assuming leading roles in each of the plays. As a result of these works, the author-actor won the off-Broadway Vernon Rice Drama Award for playwriting and an Obie Award for acting. Douglas Turner Ward is co-director with Robert Hooks of the Negro Ensemble Company, an important repertory group that resides at the St. Marks Playhouse. The group launched its first successful season in 1968. Ward's first full length play, The Reckoning, dealing with the confrontation of two evil men, a Negro pimp and a Southern governor, was produced independently by the author under the direction of Robert Hooks, in 1969.

INTRODUCTION

In 1965, during a forum on "What Negro Playwrights Are Saying," Douglas Turner Ward remarked that there were not enough plays by black writers to make the plural subject viable. Some months later the production of his two plays, Happy Ending and Day of Absence, became the third time plays by a new black playwright ran long enough to be considered a success in theater terms (the other two were A Raisin in the Sun and Dutchman), which means that they ran for over a year and made their investment back. Now, five years later, he is the artistic director of The Negro Ensemble Company which, Ward says, is "an example of Negroes controlling their own possibilities," and there are enough plays by Negro playwrights to fill a number of books and this—one is likely to conclude—is only the beginning.

Happy Ending and Day of Absence opened at the St. Marks Playhouse, off-Broadway, on November 15, 1965. The plays were produced by Robert Hooks with Juanita Poitier and Doris Kuller as associate producers, and were staged by Philip Meister, with Esther Rolle, Frances Foster, Robert Hooks, and the author, under his stage name Douglas Turner, featured in the first work; and with Lonne Elder, Arthur French, Robert Hooks, Barbara Ann Teer, and Douglas Turner in the leading roles in the second. Although Douglas Turner Ward's work has the sting of sharp and sophisticated humor, it is not propelled by the violence and fury so characteristic of the work of LeRoi Jones, James Baldwin or Ed Bullins. "I don't consider myself less angry than others in dealing with Negro conditions," Ward asserts in regard to this question, "but I realize the nature of anger has nothing to do with my work except as I transmit it into a play that works. Hate is debilitating and can't be a working emotion for an artist."

Douglas Turner Ward, as Doris E. Abramson points out, is a writer in direct descent from Langston Hughes. "How delighted the older writer must have been with the situations in Ward's two plays . . . ," she says quite correctly. "They are as bizarre and as telling as situations dreamed up by Hughes for his newspaper column and his short stories." Like Hughes, Ward uses sardonic humor and caustic laughter to attack the shrewdly observed ways of white folk and is, underneath it all, broodingly bitter at the oppression and exploitation of black folk by white folk in the American scheme of things. And this also brings him into a relation with Ossie Davis. A brilliant polemicist, decidedly committed to social change—if not an avowed proponent of the black revolutionary theater—he is a writer with a brisk and fertile imagination, a keen ear for language, that leads to the writing of sharp and authentic ethnic dialogue. In the plays before us we have exemplary evidence of his ability to work in the realistic and expressionistic modes of theater presentation.

Happy Ending is a realistic comedy, with rich, satirical overtones. The entire action takes place in the kitchen of a Harlem tenement apartment of Ellie and Vi, two sisters in their thirties or early forties, who work as domestics, as maid and laundress, for a wealthy white family, the Harrisons. As the curtain rises, the sisters, who have just come in from work, are discovered sitting at the kitchen table the picture of dejection, weeping noiselessly, passing a handkerchief back and forth, daubing their eyes. The opening dialogue and business is enticing.

> **Ellie:** Let me have your handkerchief, Vi . . .
> (**Vi** *hands it to her absently.* **Ellie** *daubs her eyes, then rests hankie on table. It lies there until* **Vi** *motions for it to be handed back.)*
> **Vi:** What we go'n do, Ellie?
> **Ellie:** Don' know. . . . Don't seem like there's much more we kin do. . . .
> **Vi:** This time it really might happen. . . .
> **Ellie:** I know. . . .
> **Vi:** Persons kin go but just so far. . . .
> **Ellie:** Lord, this may be the limit. . . .
> **Vi:** End of the line. . . .
> **Ellie:** Hear us, Savior!
> **Vi:** . . . Think it might help if I prayed a novena to him first thing tomorrow morning?
> **Ellie:** . . . Certainly couldn't do no harm. . . .

At this point Junie, a handsome, well dressed young man in his early twenties, enters. Junie, a mild militant, something of a hipster, and decidedly a ladies' man, is being reared by the older women, who are his aunts. After some bantering dialogue, upon discovery of the gloomy tears of his aunts, he asks: "What'sa matter . . . ? What's up? . . . Tell me, I wanta know! Everything was fine this morning. Som'um musta happened since. Come on, what is it?" Inordinately protective, not wanting to worry or upset him, they reluctantly tell that it is a question of their bosses, the Harrisons, who are going to be divorced because Mr. Harrison caught his wife in bed with another man. Junie greets this news cynically: "That's all? . . . I'm surprised I didn't read headlines 'bout a double murder and one suicide. . . . But I forgot!—that's our colored folks' method of cleaning up little gummy problems like that— that is MINUS the suicide bit."

When his aunts deplore his heartlessness: *"They's breaking up their* home, Junie!" "And the chillun?" The boy glibly replies: "Delicate li'l' boobies will receive nice fat allowances to ease the pain until they grow up to take over the world." The aunts, insist that the situation is "disastrous," "tragicull 'n' and unfair!" Junie can only continue to view their "boohooing" with cynicism. And as they proceed to describe their behavior in the presence of their bosses, Junie charges the ladies with being nothing less than imbeciles. "Crying your heart out," he declaims indignantly, " 'cause Massa and mistress are goin' break up housekeeping!" And, as the sisters sit stunned, he proceeds:

> Here we are—Africa rising to its place in the sun wit' prime ministers and other dignitaries taking seats around the international conference table—us here fighting for our rights like never before, changing the whole image, dumping stereotypes behind us and replacing 'em wit' new images of dignity and dimension—and I come home and find my own aunts, sisters of my mother, daughters of my grandpa who never took crap off no cracker even though he did live on a plantation—DROWNING themselves in tears jist 'cause boss man is gonna kick boss lady out on her nose . . . ! ! ! Maybe *Gone With the Wind* was accurate! Maybe we just can't help 'Miss Scarrrrrrrlet-ing' and 'Oh Lawdying' every time mistress white gets a splinter in her pinky. That's what *I'm* talking about.

And he goes on:

> So you work every day in their kitchen, Ellie, and every Thursday you wash their stinky clothes, Vi. But that don't mean they're paying you to bleed from their scratches! . . . Look—don't get me wrong—I'm not blaming you for being domestics. It's an honorable job. It's the only kind available sometimes, and it carries no stigma in itself—but that's all it is, A JOB! An exchange of work for pay. BAD PAY AT THAT! Which is all the more reason why you shouldn't give a damn whether the Harrisons kick, kill, or mangle each other!

When in disgust he declares that he is going out for a walk, his aunt sharply calls him back and as the play proceeds, he is dramatically made aware of the facts of his own life and those of his aunts. There is much fun and no little venom as the aunts reveal how, although they are underpaid and overworked, they manage to live high on the hog through what they consider their fringe benefits, which is a revelation of how they feed and dress their relatives and furnish their homes at the expense of the Harrisons. The pay is bad. "You right, Junie," Ellie says. "money I git in my pay envelope ain't worth the time 'n' the headache. . . . But—*God Helps Those Who Help Themselves.*" After this discourse, Junie asks his aunt to pass the handkerchief, and joins them at the table, a moist-faced trio, where they are later joined by Arthur, Ellie's husband. But when their despair seems complete, the phone rings and they learn that the Harrisons have made up and need Ellie to come over to baby sit while they celebrate their reunion. The family comes to jubilant life and have their own celebration.

The ironies evidenced in this play are manifold and the admixture of laughter and venom should not go unnoticed. Junie, unquestionably is a clod and a parasite. Ward is wielding a double-edged sword in this play which is considerably more than an extended vaudeville sketch as some critics regarded it. The whites are vicious and parasitically dependent upon the blacks for their existence. The blacks must counter parasitism with parasitism in order to survive. The matriarchal nature of black society is also, in this play, demonstrably underscored and demonstrably, although subtly, deplored.

Happy Ending, a play written from the inside, is decidedly black. Its arrangements are essentially fine. And as Ward has said, "it may be upsetting to some, it's seen from a particular point of view, which doesn't try to explain or apologize." Within its boundaries, it contains a rich share of social criticism.

The second of Douglas Turner Ward's plays given here, *Day of Absence: A Satirical Fantasy,* is an expressionistic situational satire, brilliantly conceived and mordantly comic in its vision. Another piece of social criticism, it engages upon the situation in which on a sultry day in a somnolent Southern town all of the Negroes suddenly disappear. Performed on a bare stage with "the actors shifting in and out and freezing into immobility as focuses change and blackouts occur," the play is described as "a reverse minstrel show," with the cast of 14 Negro actors performing in white face and blonde wigs. The only exceptions are the Announcer, who is white, and Rastus, who is "a Negro thespian in pure native black." Thus the play bears certain resemblances to Genet's *The Blacks.* But the play is an original invention in which the author points up the interdependence of the races in the South and by inference in the nation as a whole, and bitterly satirizes the South's intransigence in its refusal to see the Negro as a dignified human being.

Ward's central conceit is a compellingly clever one: the sudden and mysterious disappearance of the blacks from a small Southern town, the consequent consternation of the whites who go out to find them, and the deepening crisis as the economy of the populace grinds to a halt. The play opens and closes with Clem and Luke sitting lazily under a sign which reads "Store." These characters, who in terms of the minstrel tradition, can be seen as end men, set the stage for the action as they come to realize that there are no "Nigras" stirring in the streets. Then there follows a series of sketches which dramatize the far-reaching effects of the situation underlying the satire.

Within this framework, the black cast proceeds to give searing impersonations of a variety of Southern white stereotypes. There are the young housewife who is helpless without her black mammy-maid, the policeman who is unable to keep up his quota of two jailed "Nigras" a day. There is the Club Woman who is concerned with the lily-white images of Dixie femininity. She says in part:

> **Club Woman:** Food poisoning, severe indigestitis, chronic diarrhea, advanced diaper chafings and a plethora of unsanitary household

disasters to life, limb and property!...As a representative of the Federation of Ladies' Clubs, I must sadly report that unless the trend is reversed, a complete breakdown in family unity is imminent....Remember—it has always been pure, delicate, lily-white images of Dixie femininity which provided backbone, inspiration and ideology for our male warriors in their defense against the on-rushing black horde. If our gallant men are drained of this worship and idolatry—God knows! The cause won't be worth a Confederate nickel!

The Industrialist bewails the loss of a cheap labor supply: "With the Nigra absent, men are waiting for the machines to be cleaned, floors to be swept, crates lifted, equipment delivered and bathrooms to be deodorized." The Businessman complains that "The volume of goods moving 'cross counters has slowed down to a trickle—almost negligible. Customers are not only not purchasing—but the absence of handymen, porters, sweepers, stock-movers, deliverers and miscellaneous dirty-work doers is disrupting the smooth harmony of marketing."

A Courier rushes in to announce the disappearance of the Mayor's brother-in-law, who is also the Vice Mayor. The Mayor expresses the fear that the Negroes might be holding him as a hostage. But the Courier demolishes this theory when he explains that "Besides him—investigations reveal that dozens of more prominent citizens—two City Council members, the chairman of the Junior Chamber of Commerce, our City College All-Southern half-back, the chairlady of the Daughters of the Confederate Rebellion, Miss Cotton-Sack Festival of the Year and numerous other miscellaneous nobodies—are all absent wit'out leave. Dangerous evidence points to the conclusion that they have been infiltrating!"

> **Mayor:** Infiltrating?
> **Courier:** Passing all along!
> **Mayor:** ??? PASSING ALL ALONG???
> **Courier:** Secret Nigras all the while!
> **Mayor:** NAW!

The Club Woman keels over in a faint, and the other characters begin to eye each other suspiciously.

An Announcer, who acts henceforth in the play as a kind of interlocutor, comes into prominence as the Mayor declares that despite his commitment to States Rights outside help will have to be called upon for the town's deliverance. Assorted characters perform a kind of minstrel "walk round," in the shape of pickets bearing signs with such inscriptions as "CINDY LOU UNFAIR TO BABY JOE" and "WHY DIDN'T YOU TELL US—YOUR DEFILED WIFE AND TWO ABSENT MONGRELS."

In the newscast that follows the Announcer interviews a number of persons including Mr. Clan, Mrs. Handy Anna Aide, the city's Social Welfare Commissioner, the Reverend Reb Pious and finally the Mayor, the Honorable Henry R. E. Lee. These interviews are scathingly satiric. The Klansman insists upon the God-given right to tell the Nigras when to git. The Welfare Department and its "Nigra Git-A-Job" movement is lampooned. Pious has this counsel for the delinquent Nigras, "I say to you without rancor or vengeance, quoting a phrase of one of your greatest prophets, Booker T. Washington: 'Return your buckets to where they lay and all will be forgiven.' " The Mayor it turns out has appealed to the President, the Governor, the NAACP and other "Nigra" conspirators to help get to the bottom of "this vanishing act." And it is when the Mayor finally goes on the air his eyes rolling and his forehead perspiring, to make a nationwide appeal alternatingly threatening, imploring, and cajoling "his Nigras" to return from wherever they may be, that the satirical intent of *Day of Absence* reaches its peak. As lures in his appeal, he waves before them the cloths with which they wash cars, the brushes with which they shine shoes, and an unemptied waste basket, and cries out "Don't these things mean anything to y'all? By God are your memories so short?! Is there nothing sacred to ya?"

The play closes with Clem and Luke in the same situation discovered in the opening of the play, except that they are huddled over dazedly, trance-like. They remain so for a long time. Finally a black man drifts on stage, shuffling slowly. This figure is Rastus, who is described as "Stepin Fetchit, Willie Best, Nicodemus, B. McQueen and all the rest rolled into one." Clem and Luke are slowly aroused and stir to fascinated delight as they recognize Rastus.

> **Clem:** It is him, Luke! It is him!
> **Luke:** Rastus?
> **Rastus:** Yas. . . . sah?

And then we have the closing lines of the play, trenchant and foreboding:

> **Luke:**
> *(Eyes sweeping around in all directions.)*
> Well. . . . There's the others, Clem. . . . Back jist like they useta be. . . . Everything's same as always. . . .
> **Clem:** ??? . . . Is it . . . Luke . . . !

Happy Ending

CHARACTERS

Ellie
Vi
Junie
Arthur

Time: *The present, an early weekday evening around five or six p.m.*
Place: *The spotless kitchen of a Harlem tenement apartment. At stage left is a closed door providing entry to the outside hallway. On the opposite side of the stage is another door leading into the interior of the railroad flat. Sandwiched between this door and a window facing the brick walls of the apartment's inner shaft is a giant, dazzling white refrigerator. Positioned center-stage is a gleaming, porcelain-topped oval table. Directly behind is a modern stove-range. To the left of the stove, another window looks out upon a backyard court. The window is flanked on its left by a kitchen sink. Adjacent to the refrigerator, upstage-right, a bathroom door completes the setting.*

As curtain rises waning rays of daylight can be seen streaming through the courtyard window. Two handsome women, both in their late thirties or early forties, are sitting at opposite ends of the kitchen table. They are dressed as if recently entered from work. Hats and coats are still worn, handbags lie on floor propped against legs of respective chairs. They remain in dejected poses, weeping noiselessly.

Ellie: Let me have your handkerchief, Vi. . . .
    (Vi hands it to her absently. Ellie daubs eyes, then rests hankie on table. It lies there until Vi motions for it to be handed back.)
Vi: What we go'n' do, Ellie?
Ellie: Don' know. . . . Don't seem like there's much more we kin do. . . .
Vi: This time it really might happen. . . .
Ellie: I know. . . .
Vi: Persons kin go but just so far. . . .
Ellie: Lord, this may be the limit. . . .
Vi: End of the line. . . .
Ellie: Hear us, Savior!
Vi: . . . Think it might help if I prayed a novena to him first thing tomorrow morning?
Ellie . . . Certainly couldn't do no harm. . . .

(They lapse into silence once again, passing hankie back and forth on request. Suddenly, **Junie,** *a tall, slender, sharply handsome, tastefully dressed youth in his early twenties, bursts upon the scene, rushing through hallway door.)*

Junie:

(Rapidly crossing, shedding coat in transit.)

Hey, Vi, Ellie . . .

(Exits through interior door, talking offstage.)

Ellie, do I have any more pleated shirts clean . . . ? Gotta make fast impression on new chick tonight. . . .

(Thrusting head back into view.)

One of them foxy, black "Four-Hundred" debutantes, you dig! All class and manners, but nothing underneath but a luscious, V-8 chassis!—Which is A-O-reeet wit' me since that's all I'm after. You hear me talking to ya! Now, tell me what I say! Hah, hah, hah!

(Withdraws head back offstage.)

. . . Sure got them petty tyrants straight at the unemployment office today.

(Dripping contempt.)

Wanted me to snatchup one of them jive jobs they try to palm off on ya. I told 'em no, thanks!—SHOVE IT!

(Reentering, busily buttoning elegantly pleated shirt.)

If they can't find me something in my field, up to my standards, forget it! . . . Damn, act like they paying you money out their own pockets. . . . Whatcha got to eat, Ellie? . . . I'm scarfy as a bear. In fact—with little salt 'n' pepper, I could devour one of you—or both between a double-decker!

(Descends upon them to illustrate playfully. Pulls up short on noticing their tears for the first time.)

Hey? . . . What'sa matter . . . ? What's up?

(They fail to respond.)

Is it the kids?

(They shake their heads negatively.)

Somebody sick down home?

(Fearfully.)

Nothing's wrong wit' mother?!!!

(They shake heads again.)

Roy or Jim in jail? . . . Arthur or Ben lose their jobs?

(Another double headshake.)

Tell me, I wanta know! Everything was fine this morning. Som'um musta happened since. Come on, what is it?!

Ellie: Should we tell him, Vi?

Vi: I don't know. . . . No use gitting him worried and upset. . . .

Ellie:

(Sighing heavily.)

Maybe we better. He's got to find out sooner or later.

Junie: What are you crying for?

Ellie: . . . Our bosses—Mr. and Mrs. Harrison, Junie. . . .

Junie: ??? Mr. and Mrs. Harrison . . . ?

(Suddenly relieved, amused and sardonic.)

What happened? They escaped from a car wreck—UNHURT?

Ellie:

(Failing to grasp sarcasm.)

No.

Junie:

(Returning to shirt-buttoning.)

Did you just git disappointing news flashes they go'n' live forever?

Vi:

(Also misreading him.)

No, Junie.

Junie: Well, what then? . . . I don't get it.

Ellie: They's getting a divorce. . . .

Junie: ??? A what—?

Vi: A divorce.

Junie: ??? Why?

Ellie: 'Cause Mr. Harrison caught her wit' a man.

Junie: Well, it's not the first time 'cording to you.

Ellie: The other times wasn't wit' his best friend.

Junie: His best friend?! WHEEE! Boy, she really did it up this time. . . . Her previous excursions were restricted to his casual acquaintances! . . . But why the hell should he be so upset? He's put up wit' all the rest. This only means she's gitting closer to home. Maybe next time it'll be him, ha, ha, ha. . . .

Ellie:

(Reprimandingly.)

It's no joke, Junie.

Junie:

(Exiting into bathroom.)

How'd it happen?

Ellie:

(Flaring at the memory.)

Just walked in and caught 'em in his own bedroom!

Vi:

(Even more outraged.)

Was that dirty dog, Mr. Heller, lives on the 19th floor of the same building!

Ellie:

(Anger mounting.)

I warned her to be careful when she first started messing with him. I told her Mr. Harrison was really gon' kick her out if he found out, but she'd have the snake sneak in sometimes soon as Mr. Harrison left! Even had nerve to invite him to chaperone his wife back later in the evening for a li'l' after-dinner snack!

Junie:

(Reentering merrily.)

What's a little exchange of pleasantries among rich friends, bosom buddies? Now, all Harrison has to do is return the favor and even things up.

Vi: She really cooked her goose this time.

Junie: Good for her.

Ellie: Good . . . ?

Junie: Sure—what'd she 'spect? To wait 'till she hauled some cat into bed right next to her old man befo' he got the message?

Vi: They is getting a *divorce,* Junie!

Junie:

> *(Sauntering over to fruit bowl atop refrigerator.)*

That's all? . . . I'm surprised I didn't read headlines 'bout a double murder and one suicide. . . . But I forgot—that's our colored folk's method of clearing up little gummy problems like that—that is, MINUS the suicide bit.

Ellie: *They's breaking up their home, Junie!*

Junie:

> *(Biting into apple selected from bowl.)*

They'll learn to live wit' it. . . . Might even git to like the idea.

Vi: And the chillun?

Junie: Delicate li'l' boobies will receive nice fat allowances to ease the pain until they grow up to take over the world.

Ellie: ??? Is that all you feel at a time like this, boy?

Vi: Disastrous, that's what it is!

Ellie: Tragicull 'n' unfair!

Junie: Is this what you boohooing 'bout?!!!

Ellie: Could you think of anything worser?

Junie: But, why?!

> *(Exits into interior.)*

Ellie: 'Cause this time we KNOW HE MEANS BUSINESS, JUNIE! Ain't no false alarm like them other times. We were there, right there! . . . Had a feeling somp'um was go'n' happen soon as I answered the door and let Mr. Heller in! Like chilly pneumonia on top a breeze. . . . Miss Harrison tole me she didn't wanta be disturbed for the rest of the afternoon. Well, she was disturbed all right! They musta fell asleep 'cause Mr. Harrison even got home late and still caught 'em. . . .

Junie:

> *(Returns with tie, etc., to continue dressing.)*

Couldn't you have interrupted their togetherness and sounded a timely danger warning?

Ellie: We didn't hear him. I was in the kitchen, Vi down in basement ironing. I didn't know Mr. Harrison had come in 'till I heard screaming from the bedroom. But soon as I did, I called Vi and me and her tipped down the hall and heard Mr. Harrison order Mr. Heller to put his clothes back on and stop considering hisself a friend for the rest of his life! " 'N' you—slut! Pack up and git out soon as you find a suitable apartment." . . . Then he invited me and Vi into the room and told us he was divorcing her. . . . That man was hurt, Junie, hurt deep! Could see it in his eyes. . . . Like a little boy, so sad he made you wanta grab hold his head and rock him in your arms like a baby.

Vi: Miss Harrison looked a sight herself, po' thing! Like a li'l' girl caught stealing crackers out the cookie jar.

Ellie: I almost crowned ole back-stabber Heller! Come brushing up 'gainst *me* on his way out!

Junie:

> *(Almost cracking up with laughter.)*

Shoulda pinned medal on him as he flew by. Escaping wit' head still on shoulder and no bullet-holes dotting through his chest.

Ellie:

> *(Once again taking him literally.)*

The skunk really left us all too high and dry for that, Junie. . . . Oh, don't think it wouldn't broke your heart, too, nephew. . . . Sneaky rascal gone, rest of us in sorrow, tears pouring down our faces 'n' me and Vi jist begging and begging. . . .

> *(As if to **Harrisons**.)*

"Y'all please think twice befo' you do anything you'll be sorry for. You love each other—and who's in better position than Vi and me to know how much you love each other—"

> *(**Junie** ceases dressing to listen closely.)*

Vi: 'Course she love him, just can't help herself.

Ellie: "—When two hearts love each other as much as we know y'all do, they better take whole lots of time befo' doing something so awful as breaking up a marriage—even if it ain't hunert-percent perfect. Think about your reputation and the scandal this will cause Mr. Harrison. Jist 'bout kill your po' mother—her wit' her blood pressure, artritis, gout, heart tickle 'n' everything. But most of all, don't orphan the kids! Kids come first. Dear li'l' angels! Just innocents looking on gitting hurt in ways they can't understand."

Junie:

> *(Incredulous.)*

You told 'em this, Ellie?

Ellie: Love conquers all, Junie!

Junie: Wit' your assistance, Vi?

Vi: As much as I could deliver, Junie.

Junie: And what impression did your tender concern have on the bereaved couple?

Ellie: Mr. Harrison said he understood 'n' appreciated our feelings and was very grateful for our kindly advice—but he was sorry, his mind was made up. She'd gone too far and he couldn't forgive her—not EVER! . . . We might judge him a harsh, vindicty man, he said, but he couldn't bring hisself to do it. Even apologized to us for being so cruel.

Junie:

> *(Continuing his slow boil.)*

You accepted his apology, Vi?

Vi: I should say not. I pleaded wit' him agin to think it over for sake of home, family and good name!

Junie: Well of all the goddam things I ever heard!

Ellie:
(Heartened by his misread support.)
I'm telling ya!

Vi: I knew it was go'n' happen if she kept on like she did!

Ellie: Just wouldn't listen!

Junie: It's a disgrace!

Ellie: Ain't the word!

Vi: Lot worse than that!

Junie: Did you both plop down on your knees begging him to give her another chance?

Vi: No!—But we woulda if we'd thought about it! Why didn't we, Ellie?!

Ellie: Things happened so fast—

Junie: Never have I been so humiliated in all my life—

Vi:
(Self-disgusted by their glaring omission.)
No excuse not thinking 'bout it, Ellie!

Ellie: Certainly ain't.

Junie: What about your pride—!?

Vi: You right! Musta been false pride kept us from dropping to our knees!

Junie: Acting like imbeciles! Crying your heart out 'cause Massa and Mistress are go'n' break up housekeeping!!! Maybe I oughta go beat up the adulterous rat crawling in between the sheets!!!
(Pacing up and down in angry indignation as they sit stunned.)
Here we are—Africa rising to its place in the sun wit' prime ministers and other dignitaries taking seats around the international conference table—us here fighting for our rights like never before, changing the whole image, dumping stereotypes behind us and replacing 'em wit' new images of dignity and dimension—and I come home and find my own aunts, sisters of my mother, daughters of my grandpa who never took crap off no cracker even though he did live on a plantation—DROWNING themselves in tears jist 'cause boss man is gonna kick bosslady out on her nose . . . !!! Maybe *Gone with the Wind* was accurate! Maybe we jist can't help "Miss Scarrrrrlet-ing" and "Oh Lawdying" every time mistress white gets a splinter in her pinky. That's what *I'm* talking about.

Vi: Ain't you got no feelings, boy?

Junie: Feelings?!!! . . . So you work every day in their kitchen, Ellie, and every Thursday you wash their stinky clothes, Vi. But that don't mean they're paying you to bleed from their scratches! . . . Look—don't get me wrong— I'm not blaming you for being domestics. It's an honorable job. It's the only kind available sometimes, and it carries no stigma in itself—but that's all it is, A JOB! An exchange of work for pay! BAD PAY AT THAT! Which is all the more reason why you shouldn't give a damn whether the Harrisons kick, kill or mangle each other!

Ellie: You gotta care, Junie—

Junie: "Breaking up home and family!"—Why, I've seen both of you ditch two husbands apiece and itching to send third ones packing if they don't toe the line. You don't even cry over that!

Ellie: Don't have time to—

Junie: Boy, if some gray cat was peeping in on you, he'da sprinted back home and wrote five Uncle Tom Cabins and ten Old Black Joes!

Ellie: Wait a minute, now—

Junie: I never heard you shedding such tragic tears when your own li'l' crumbcrushers suffered through fatherless periods! All you grumbled was "good riddance, they better off wit'out the sonsabitches!" . . . Maybe Harrison tots will make out just as well. They got puny li'l' advantages of millions of dollars and slightly less parched skins!

Vi: Show some tenderness, boy. Ain't human not to trouble over our bosses' sorrows—

Junie: That's what shames me. I gave you credit for more integrity. Didn't figger you had chalk streaks in ya. You oughta be shamed for *yourselves!*

Ellie: And done what?

Junie: NOTHING!—Shoulda told 'em their sticky mess is their own mud puddle. You neutrals. Just work there. Aren't interested in what they do!

Ellie: That wouldn't be expressing our deepest sentiments—

Junie: I'm ashamed you even had any "sentiments!" . . . Look, it's hopeless, I'm not getting anywhere trying to make you understand. . . . I'm going out for a whiff of fresh air!

> *(Rushes to exit.)*

Ellie: COME BACK HERE, BOY!

Junie:

> *(Stopping at door.)*

What? To watch you blubber over Massa?? No, thanks!

Ellie: I said come here, you hear me talking to you!

Vi: You still ain't too big to git yourself slapped down!

Ellie: Your ma gave us right any time we saw fit!

> *(He returns reluctantly. Stands aside. An uneasy silence prevails. They commence a sweet, sly, needling attack.)*

. . . Better git yourself somp'um to eat.

> *(Rises, taking off coat.)*

Junie:

> *(Sulking.)*

I lost my appetite.

Ellie:

> *(Hanging coat up.)*

What you want?

Junie: I told you I'm not hungry anymore.

Vi: *We* made you lose your appetite . . . ?

> *(He doesn't reply.)*

Ellie: What did you crave befo' you lost it?

Junie: Any thing you had cooked. Didn't have anything special in mind. . . .

Ellie:

> *(Off-handedly.)*

Steak? . . . T-Bone? . . . Porterhouse? . . . Filet . . . ?

Junie: No. . . . I didn't particularly have steak in mind.

Vi: Been eating too many lately, huh?

> *(Stands at table exchanging goods from **Ellie**'s shopping bag into her own.)*

Junie: Just kinda tired of 'em, that's all.

Ellie: How 'bout some chicken then . . . ? Roast beef? . . . Lobster? . . . Squab? Duck, or something?

Junie:

> *(Nettled.)*

All I wanted was some food, Ellie! . . . In fact, I really had a hankering for some plain ole collard greens, neck bones or ham hocks. . . .

Ellie: Good eatin', boy. Glad to hear that. Means that high-class digestion hasn't spoiled your taste buds yet. . . . But if you want that rich, choice food, you welcome to it—

Junie: I know that, Ellie!

Ellie: It's in the freezer for you, go and look.

Junie: I don't hafta, Ellie, I know—

Ellie: Go look anyway.

Junie:

> *(Goes and opens refrigerator door.)*

It's there, Ellie, I didn't need look.

Vi: Come here for a second, Junie, got something on your pants leg.

> *(He obeys. She picks a piece of lint off trousers, then rubs material admiringly.)*

Pants to your suit, ain't they? . . . Sure is a fine suit to be trotting off to the unemployment office. . . . Which one 'r the other you gon' wear tonight when you try to con that girl out her virginity—if she still got it?—The gray one? Brown one? The tweed? Or maybe you go'n' git sporty and strut that snazzy plaid jacket and them tight light pants? If not—which jacket and which pants?

Ellie: Slept good last night, nephew? Or maybe you gitting tired of that foam rubber mattress and sheep-fur blanket?

Vi: How do them fine college queens and snooty office girls like the furniture they half-see when you sneak 'em in here late at night? Surprised to see such fancy stuff in a beat-up ole flat, ain't they? But it helps you put 'em at ease, don't it? I bet even those sweet li'l' white ones are impressed by your class?

Junie:

> *(Indignantly.)*

That's not fair, Vi—

Ellie: When last time you bought any food in this house, boy?

Junie: Ellie, you know—

Ellie: When, Junie?

Junie: Not since I been here, but—

Vi: And your last piece of clothes?

Junie:

> *(More indignant.)*

I bought some underwear last week, Vi!

Vi: I mean clothes you wear on top, Junie. Shirts, pants, jackets, coats?

Junie:

> *(Squirming.)*

You—you know I haven't, Vi—

Ellie:

> *(Resits.)*

Buy anything else in your room besides that tiny, midget frame for your ma's picture?

Junie: All right. I know I'm indebted to ya. You don't have to rub it in. I'll make it up to you when I git on my feet and *fulfill* my potential. . . . But that's not the point!

Ellie: You ain't indebted to us, Junie.

Junie: Yes, I am, I know it, I thank you for it.

Ellie: Don't hafta thank us—

Junie: But that's not the issue! Despite your benevolence, I refuse to let you blackmail my principle, slapping me in the face wit' how good you been to me during my temporary outta work period! I'm talking to you now, 'bout something above our personal relationship. Pride—Race—Dignity—

Ellie: What's go'n' happen to me and Vi's dignity if Mr. Harrison throws Mrs. Harrison out on her nose as you put it?

Junie: Git another job! You not dependent on them. You young, healthy, in the prime of life. . . . In fact—I've always wondered why you stagnate as domestics when you're trained and qualified to do something better and more dignified.

Ellie: Glad you brought that up. Know why I'm not breaking my back as a practical nurse and Vi's not frying hair—'cept on the side? . . . 'Cause the work's too hard, the money ain't worth it and there's not much room for advancement—

Junie: Where kin you advance as a domestic? From kitchen to closet?!

> (**Vi** *has moved to fridge to deposit meats etc.*)

Ellie:

> *(Refusing to be provoked, continuing evenly.)*

Besides, when I started working for the Harrisons, Junie, Mr. Harrison vowed that he would support me for life if I stayed with 'em until his daughter Sandy, his oldest child, reached ten years old.

Junie: Bully for him! He'll build ya a little cottage backa the penthouse garage!

Ellie:

> *(Still unruffled.)*

Mr. Harrison is strictly a man of his word, Junie. Which means that even if I left one day after Sandy made ten, he owes me some money every week or every month as long as I live. . . . Sandy is *nine*, Junie, EN-EYE-EN-EE! If I don't last another year, the deal is off.

Junie: Don't need no handouts! Even hearing you say you want any, makes me shame!

Ellie: Done used that word quite a lot, boy. You shamed of us? . . . Well, git slapped in the face wit' this? How shame you go'n' be when you hafta git outta here and hustle yourself a job?—ANY JOB?!!!

Junie: Huh?

Ellie: How shame you go'n' be when you start gitting raggedy and all them foxy girls are no longer impressed 'bout how slick, smooth and pretty you look? When you stop being one 'r the best-dressed black boys in New York City?

Junie: Don't get you, Ellie?

Ellie: I know you went to college for a coupler years, boy, but I thought you still had some sense, or I woulda told you. . . .

Vi:

    (Standing at **Junie's** *right as* **Ellie** *sits to his left.)*

Every time you bite into one of them big tender juicy steaks and chaw it down into your belly, ever think where it's coming from?

Ellie: The Harrisons.

Vi: Every time you lay one of them young gals down in that plush soft bed of yours and hear her sigh in luxury, ever think 'bout who you owe it to?

Ellie: The Harrisons.

Vi: When you swoop down home to that rundown house you ma and pa rent, latch eyes on all that fine furniture there, you ever think who's responsible?

Ellie: The Harrisons.

Vi: You ain't bought a suit or piece of clothes in five years and none of the other four men in this family have. . . . Why not?

Ellie: Mr. Harrison.

Vi: Junie, you is a fine, choice hunk of chocolate pigmeat, pretty as a new-minted penny and slick 'nuff to suck sugar outta gingerbread wit'out it losing its flavor—but the Harrisons ain't hardly elected you no favorite pin-up boy to introduce to Santa Claus. Took a heap of pow'ful coaxing to win you such splendid sponsorship and wealthy commissions, 'cause waiting for the Harrisons to voluntarily *donate* their Christian charity is one sure way of landing head-first in the poor-house dungeon. . . . Who runs the Harrisons' house, Junie?

    (Moves to sit at table.)

Junie: ???. . . Ellie . . . I guess . . . ?

Ellie: *From top to bottom.* I cook the food, scrub the floor, open the doors, serve the tables, answer the phones, dust the furniture, raise the children, lay out the clothes, greet the guests, fix the drinks and dump the garbage— all for bad pay as you said. . . . You right, Junie, money I git in my envelope ain't worth the time 'n' the headache. . . . But—*God Helps Those Who Help Themselves.* . . . I also ORDER the food, estimate the credit, PAY the bills and BALANCE the budget. Which means that each steak I order for them, befo' butcher carves cow, I done reserved TWO for myself. Miss Harrison wouldn't know how much steak cost and Mr. Harrison so loaded, he writes me a check wit'out even looking. . . . Every once in a full moon they git so good-hearted and tell me take some left-overs home, but by that time my freezer and pantry is already fuller than theirs. . . . Every one of them high price suits I lay on you haven't been worn more than once and some of 'em not at all. You lucky to be same size as Mr. Harrison, Junie. He don't know how much clothes he got in his wardrobe, which is why *yours* is as big as *his*. Jim, Roy, Arthur and Ben can't even fit into the man's clothes, but that still don't stop 'em from cutting, shortening, altering and stretching 'em to fit. Roy almost ruined his feet trying to wear the man's shoes. . . . Now, I've had a perfect record keeping y'all elegantly dressed and stylishly-fashion-plated—'cept that time Mr. Harrison caught me off-guard asking: "Ellie, where's my brown suit?" "In the cleaners," I told him and had to snatch it off your hanger and smuggle it back—temporarily.

Vi: If y'all warn't so lucky and *Mrs. Harrison* so tacky flashy Ellie and I would also be best dressed domestics of the year.

Ellie: Which, if you didn't notice, is what your Aunt Doris was—rest her soul —when we laid her in her grave, decked out in the costliest, ritziest, most expensive nightgown the good Lord ever waited to feast his eyes on. . . . As for furniture, we could move out his whole house in one day if we had to.

Vi: Which is what we did when they moved from the old penthouse and we hired us a moving van to haul 'nuff pieces to furnish both our own apartments and still had enough to ship a living room set down home to your ma. Mr. Harrison told us to donate the stuff to charity. We did—US!

Ellie: Add all *our* bills I add on to *their* bills—Jim even tried to git me to sneak in his car note, but that was going too far—all the deluxe plane tickets your ma jets up here on every year, weekly prescriptions filled on their tab, tons of laundry cleaned along wit' theirs and a thousand other services and I'm earning me quite a bonus along with my bad pay. It's the BONUS that counts, Junie. Total it up for nine years and I'd be losing money on any other job. Now Vi and I, after cutting cane, picking rice and shucking corn befo' we could braid our hair in pigtails, figure we just gitting back what's owed us. . . . But, if Mr. Harrison boots Mrs. Harrison out on her tocus, the party's over. He's not go'n' need us. Miss Harrison ain't got a copper cent of her own. Anyway, the set-up won't be as ripe for picking. My bonus is suddenly cut off and out the window go my pension.

Vi: Suppose we did git us another job wit' one 'r them penny-pinching old misers hiding behind cupboards watching whether you stealing sugar cubes? Wit' our fringe benefits choked off, we'd fall down so quick to a style of living we ain't been used to for a long time, it would make your head swim. I don't think we could stand it. . . . Could you?

Ellie: So when me and Vi saw our pigeons scampering out the window for good today, tears started flowing like rain. The first tear trickle out my eyes had a roast in it.

Vi: Mine was a chicken.

Ellie: Second had a crate of eggs.

Vi: Mine a whole pig.

Ellie: Third an oriental rug.

Vi: A continental couch.

Ellie: An overcoat for Arthur.

Vi: A bathrobe for Ben.

Ellie: My gas, electric and telephone bills in it.

Vi: Three months' rent, Lord!

Ellie: The faster the stream started gushing, the faster them nightmares crowded my eyes until I coulda flooded 'em 'nuff water to swim in. Every time I pleaded "Think of your love!—"

Vi: She meant think 'bout our bills.

Ellie: Every time I begged "Don't crack up the home!—"

Vi: It meant please keep *ours* cemented together!

Ellie: "Don't victim the chillun!—"

Vi: By all means insure the happiness of *our* li'l' darlings!

Ellie: They didn't know 'bout these eyeball visions—they only see what they see 'n' hear what they hear—and that's okey-doke wit' me—but I was gitting these watery pictures in my mind 'n' feeling a giant-size sickness in my gut! Few seconds longer and I woulda been down on my knees wit'out even thinking 'bout it!

Vi: If I didn't beat ya to the floor!

Ellie: Junie—maybe we shoulda given a little more thought to that—watcha-macallit?—"image" of yours. Maybe we did dishonor Africa, embarrass the NAACP, are hopelessly behind time and scandalously outdated. But we didn't have too much time to think. . . . Now that you know the whole truth, you have a right to disown us. We hardly worthy of your respect. . . . But when I thought 'bout that new topcoat wit' the velvet-trimmed collar I just packed to bring you . . .

    (Tears begin to re-form.)

. . . coupler new cashmere sweaters, brand-new slacks, a shiny new attache case for your appointments, and a scrumptous new collapsible swimming pool I promised your ma for her backyard—I couldn't help but cry.

    *(***Vi** has joined her in a double torrent.)*

Junie:

    (Who has been standing stoically throughout, says) . . .

Vi?

Vi: . . . What?

Junie: . . . Pass me the handkerchief. . . .

    (He receives it and joins the table—a moist-faced trio. Arthur, Ellie's husband, walks in, finding them thus.)

Arthur:

    (Beelining for bathroom.)

Even', everybody. . . .

    (Hearing no response, stops before entering john.)

Hey, what's the matter? What you three looking like somebody died for?

Ellie: It's the Harrisons, Arthur. Mr. Harrison gitting a divorce.

Arthur: Aww, not ag'in!

Vi: He really means it this time, Arthur.

Arthur: . . . He does?

Ellie: Yes, Jesus.

Arthur: You sure?

Vi: Caught her dead to rights.

Arthur:

> *(Indignant.)*

But he can't do that!

Vi: He is.

Arthur: What 'bout us?!

Junie: What you think we grieving 'bout?

Arthur: Well, just don't sit there! What we go'n' do?

Ellie: Done it, didn't work.

Arthur: Not at all.

Ellie: Nope.

Arthur: Not even a little bit?

Ellie: Not one lousy inch.

Arthur:

> *(Crestfallen.)*

Make room for me.

> *(They provide space. He sits, completing the depressed quartet.)*

Junie:

> *(Suddenly jolted with an idea.)*

Ellie! Wait! Why don't you tell him to take her on a private ocean cruise, just the two of 'em, so they kin recapture the thrill for one another!

Ellie: He did that already, until somebody told him she was cuddling up with the ship stoker in the engine room.

Junie:

> *(Undaunted.)*

Advise him to spend less time wit' his business and more with her. She wouldn't need look outside for satisfaction!

Ellie: Tried that too, but his business like to fell apart and he caught her making eyes at the messenger bringing him the news.

Junie:

> *(Desperate.)*

Convince him she's sick! It's not her fault, he should send her to a psychiatrist!

Ellie: Already did . . . till he found out she was doing more than talking on on the couch.

Junie: What 'bout a twenty-four hour guard on her? That won't give her so many opportunities?!

Ellie: What about guards? They men, too.

Junie:

> *(In angry frustration.)*

Well, damn, git her a chastity belt and lock her up!

Ellie: Locks, also, have been known to be picked.

Arthur:
> *(Inspired by a brilliant solution.)*

WAIT! I got it! I got it! . . . Tell him you know of some steady-ready goofer dust . . . or jooger-mooger saltpeter to cool her down. And you'll slip it in her food every day!

Ellie: Wouldn't work. . . . Way her glands function, probably jazz her up like a Spanish fly.

Vi: Let's face it, it's all over. We just gotta tuck in our belts, stare the future square in the eye and git ready for a depression. It's not go'n' do us no good to whine over spilt clabber. . . . You jist better start scrounging 'round for that job, Junie. Befo' you git chance to sneeze, we will have had it. And call up—NO! Write your ma and tell her not to come up this year.

Ellie: Arthur, best you scrape up another job to moonlight wit' the one you got. We facing some scuffling days 'head us.

Vi: Well. . . . I better git out of here and go warn my own crew 'bout Satan's retribution. . . . Well . . . it was good while it lasted, Ellie. . . . .

Ellie: Real good.
> *(They glance at each other and another deluge starts. The phone interrupts, but no one bothers to answer. Finally, Arthur rises and exits in the direction of peals. During his absence, the disconsolate trio remains silent.)*

Arthur:
> *(Reentering slowly, treading each step with the deliberateness of a man fearful of cracking eggs.)*

That—was—Mr. Harrison—he said—thank both of you for desperately trying to—shock him to his senses—pry open his eyes to the light—and rescue his house from collapsing—he and Mrs. Harrison, after stren'ous consideration, are gonna stick it out together!
> *(A stunned moment of absolute silence prevails, finally broken by an ear-splitting, exultant whoop which erupts simultaneously from each member of the quartet. They spring to feet, embracing and prancing around the room, crying through laughter. Arthur simmers down first, shhushes to recapture their attention.)*

ELLIE . . . Ellie. Mr. Harrison requests if it's not too much trouble, he'd like for you to come over and stay wit' Sandy and Snookie while he and Mrs. Harrison go out and celebrate their reunion and it's too late to git a baby-sitter.

Ellie: If it's all right?!!! . . . Tell him I'm climbing on a broomstick, then shuttling to a jet!
> *(**Arthur** starts to exit.)*

Wait a minute! Waaaait a minute! Hold on!—I must be crazy! Don't tell him that. . . . Tell him he knows very well it's after my working hours and I'm not paid to baby-sit and since I've already made plans for the evening, I'll be glad to do it for double-overtime, two extra days' pay and triple-time off to recuperate from the imposition. . . . And, Arthur! . . . Kinda suggest that *you is* a little peeved 'cause he's interrupting me from taking care of something important for you. He might toss in a day for your suffering.

Arthur: He'll swear he was snatching you away from my death-bed, guarding my door 'gainst Lucifer busting through!

> *(Exits.)*

Ellie: I'd better throw on some more clothes.

> *(Exits.)*

Junie: Vi, what you s'pose grandpa would say 'bout his chillun if he got a breathing-spell in between dodging pitchforks and sidestepping the fiery flames?

Vi: Shame on you, boy, Papa ain't near'bouts doing no ducking 'n' dodging. Why, he's right up there plunked down safe, snuggled up tight beside the good Lord's righteous throne.

Arthur:

> *(Reentering.)*

He was real sorry. "If it wasn't such a special occasion, he wouldn't bother us!"

> *(They guffaw heartily.)*

Junie: This IS a special occasion! . . .

> *(Grandly.)*

Arthur, break out a flagon of the latest champagne Ellie brought us.

Arthur: At your service, massa Junie.

Junie: The nineteen-forty-seven! That was a good year. Not the fifty, which was bad!

Arthur: No kidding?!

> *(**Arthur** moves to refrigerator. **Ellie** returns, ready to depart.)*

Junie: Wait for a drink, auntie. We've gotta celebrate OUR resurrection. A Toast of Deliverance.

> *(**Arthur** presents **Junie** with champagne, points out '47 label, then gets goblets from shelf. **Junie** pours, they lift goblets.)*

First! . . . To the victors and the vanquished, top-dog and the bottom-dog! Sometimes it's hard to tell which is which . . . !

Vi: If nothing else, boy, education did teach you how to sling around some GAB.

Arthur: Ain't hardly the way I heard the slinging described.

> *(They all laugh.)*

Junie: Second! . . . To my two cagey aunts. May they continue to prevail in times of distress!

Arthur: May they!

Junie: . . . Third! . . . To the Harrisons! . . . May they endure forever in marital bliss! Cheers to 'em!

> *(All cheer. After finishing drink, **Ellie** moves to exit through hallway door. **Junie** stops her.)*

Oh, Ellie . . . why don't you start fattening Mr. Harrison up? Please slip some more potatoes and starch onto his menu. I've gained a few pounds and the clothes are gitting a little tight. Don't you think it's time for him to plumpen up a bit, stick on a little weight?

Ellie: Would ten pounds do?

Junie: Perfect!

> *(Another round of laughter. Again she moves to exit.)*

. . . AND ELLIE! . . . Kinda hint 'round to him that fashions is changing. I wouldn't want him to fall behind in the latest styles. . . .

Vi:

> *(Lifting goblet, along with **Arthur** and **Ellie**, in a final toast.)*

There's hope, Junie. You'll make it, boy, you'll make it. . . .

> *(Laughter rings as lights fade.)*

CURTAIN

A SATIRICAL FANTASY

Day of Absence

CHARACTERS
Clem
Luke
John
Mary
First Operator
Second Operator
Third Operator
Supervisor
Jackson
Mayor
First Citizen
Second Citizen
Third Citizen
Industrialist
Businessman
Clubwoman
Courier
Announcer
Clan
Aide
Pious
Doll Woman
Brush Man
Mop Man
Rastus

The time is now. Play opens in unnamed Southern town of medium population on a somnolent cracker morning—meaning no matter the early tempera-
ture, it's gonna get hot. The hamlet is just beginning to rouse itself from the
sleepy lassitude of night.

NOTES ON PRODUCTION
No scenery is necessary—only actors shifting in and out on an almost bare
stage and freezing into immobility as focuses change or blackouts occur.
    Play is conceived for performance by a Negro cast, a reverse minstrel
show done in white-face. Logically, it might also be performed by whites—

at their own risk. If any producer is faced with choosing between opposite hues, author strongly suggests: "Go 'long wit' the blacks—besides all else, they need the work more."

If acted by the latter, race members are urged to go for broke, yet cautioned not to ham it up too broadly. In fact—it just might be more effective if they aspire for serious tragedy. Only qualification needed for Caucasian casting is that the company fit a uniform pattern—insipid white; also played in white-face.

Before any horrifying discrimination doubts arise, I hasten to add that a bonafide white actor should be cast as the Announcer in all productions, likewise a Negro thespian in pure native black as Rastus. This will truly subvert any charge that the production is unintegrated.

All props, except essential items (chairs, brooms, rags, mop, debris) should be imaginary (phones, switchboard, mikes, eating utensils, food, etc.). Actors should indicate their presence through mime.

The cast of characters develops as the play progresses. In the interest of economical casting, actors should double or triple in roles wherever possible.

PRODUCTION CONCEPT

This is a red-white-and-blue play—meaning the entire production should be designed around the basic color scheme of our patriotic trinity. *Lighting* should illustrate, highlight and detail time, action and mood. Opening scenes stage-lit with white rays of morning, transforming to panic reds of afternoon, flowing into ominous blues of evening. *Costuming* should be orchestrated around the same color scheme. In addition, subsidiary usage of grays, khakis, yellows, pinks, and combinated patterns of stars-and-bars should be employed. Some actors (Announcer and Rastus excepted, of course) might wear white shoes or sneakers, and some women characters clothed in knee-length frocks might wear white stockings. Blonde wigs, both for males and females, can be used in selected instances. *Makeup* should have uniform consistency, with individual touches thrown in to enhance personal identity.

SAMPLE MODELS OF MAKEUP AND COSTUMING

Mary: Kewpie-doll face, ruby-red lips painted to valentine-pursing, moon-shaped rouge circles implanted on each cheek, blond wig of fat-flowing ringlets, dazzling ankle-length snow-white nightie.

Mayor: Seersucker white ensemble, ten-gallon hat, red string-tie and blue belt.

Clem: Khaki pants, bareheaded and blond.

Luke: Blue work-jeans, strawhatted.

Club Woman: Yellow dress patterned with *symbols of Dixie, gray hat.*

Clan: A veritable, riotous advertisement of red-white-and-blue combinations with stars-and-bars tossed in.

Pious: White ministerial garb with *black* cleric's collar topping his snow-white shirt.

Operators: All in red with different color wigs.

All other characters should be carefully defined through costuming which typify their identity.

Scene: *Street.*
Time: *Early morning.*

Clem:

(*Sitting under a sign suspended by invisible wires and bold-printed with the lettering: "STORE."*)
'Morning, Luke. . . .

Luke:

(*Sitting a few paces away under an identical sign.*)
'Morning, Clem. . . .

Clem: Go'n' be a hot day

Luke: Looks that way. . . .

Clem: Might rain though. . . .

Luke: Might.

Clem: Hope it does. . . .

Luke: Me, too. . . .

Clem: Farmers could use a little wet spell for a change. . . . How's the Missis?

Luke: Same.

Clem: 'N' the kids?

Luke: Them, too. . . . How's yourns?

Clem: Fine, thank you. . . .

(*They both lapse into drowsy silence waving lethargically from time to time at imaginary passersby.*)
Hi, Joe. . . .

Luke: Joe. . . .

Clem: . . . How'd it go yesterday, Luke?

Luke: Fair.

Clem: Same wit' me. . . . Business don't seem to git no better or no worse. Guess we in a rut, Luke, don't it 'pear that way to you?—Morning, ma'am.

Luke: Morning. . . .

Clem: Tried display, sales, advertisement, stamps—everything, yet merchandising stumbles 'round in the same old groove. . . . But—that's better than plunging downwards, I reckon.

Luke: Guess it is.

Clem: Morning, Bret. How's the family? . . . That's good.

Luke: Bret—

Clem: Morning, Sue.

Luke: How do, Sue.

Clem:

(*Staring after her.*). .
. . . Fine hunk of woman.

Luke: Sure is.

Clem: Wonder if it's any good?

Luke: Bet it is.

Clem: Sure like to find out!

Luke: So would I.

Clem: You ever try?

Luke: Never did. . . .

Clem: Morning, Gus. . . .

Luke: Howdy, Gus.

Clem: Fine, thank you.

> *(They lapse into silence again.* **Clem** *rouses himself slowly, begins to look around quizzically.)*

Luke . . . ?

Luke: Huh?

Clem: Do you . . . er, er—feel anything—funny . . . ?

Luke: Like what?

Clem: Like . . . er—something—strange?

Luke: I dunno . . . haven't thought about it.

Clem: I mean . . . like something's wrong—outta place, unusual?

Luke: I don't know. . . . What you got in mind?

Clem: Nothing . . . just that—just that—like somp'ums outta kilter. I got a funny feeling somp'ums not up to snuff. Can't figger out what it is . . .

Luke: Maybe it's in your haid?

Clem: No, not like that. . . . Like somp'ums happened—or happening—gone haywire, loony.

Luke: Well, don't worry 'bout it, it'll pass.

Clem: Guess you right.

> *(Attempts return to somnolence but doesn't succeed.)*

. . . I'm sorry, Luke, but you sure you don't feel nothing peculiar . . . ?

Luke:

> *(Slightly irked.)*

Toss it out your mind, Clem! We got a long day ahead of us. If something's wrong, you'll know 'bout it in due time. No use worrying about it 'till it comes and if it's coming, it will. Now, relax!

Clem: All right, you right. . . . Hi, Margie. . . .

Luke: Marge.

Clem:

> *(Unable to control himself.)*

Luke, I don't give a damn what you say. Somp'ums topsy-turvy, I just know it!

Luke:

> *(Increasingly irritated.)*

Now look here, Clem—it's a bright day, it looks like it's go'n' git hotter. You say the wife and kids are fine and the business is no better or no worse? Well, what else could be wrong? . . . If somp'ums go'n' happen, it's go'n' happen anyway and there ain't a damn fool thing you kin do to stop it! So you ain't helping me, yourself or nobody else by thinking 'bout it. It's not go'n' be no better or no worse when it gits here. It'll come to you when it gits ready to come and it's go'n' be the same whether you worry about it or not. So stop letting it upset you!

> *(***Luke*** *settles back in his chair.* **Clem** *does likewise.* **Luke** *shuts his eyes.*

After a few moments, they reopen. He forces them shut again. They reopen in greater curiosity. Finally, he rises slowly to an upright position in the chair, looks around frowningly. Turns slowly to **Clem**.)

. . . Clem? . . . You know something? . . . Somp'um is peculiar . . .

Clem:

(Vindicated.)

I knew it, Luke! I just knew it! Ever since we been sitting here, I been having that feeling!

(Scene is blacked out abruptly. Lights rise on another section of the stage where a young couple lie in bed under an invisible-wire-suspension-sign lettered: "HOME." Loud insistent sounds of baby yells are heard. **John**, *the husband, turns over trying to ignore the cries,* **Mary**, *the wife, is undisturbed.* **John's** *efforts are futile, the cries continue until they cannot be denied. He bolts upright, jumps out of bed and disappears off-stage. Returns quickly and tries to rouse* **Mary**.)

John: Mary . . .

(Nudges her, pushes her, yells into her ear, but she fails to respond.)

Mary, get up. . . Get up!

Mary: Ummm . . .

(Shrugs away, still sleeping.)

John: GET UP!

Mary: UMMMMMMMMMM!

John: Don't you hear the baby bawling! . . . NOW GET UP!

Mary:

(Mumbling drowsily.)

. . . What baby . . . whose baby . . . ?

John: Yours!

Mary: Mine? That's ridiculous. . . . what'd you say . . . ? Somebody's baby bawling? . . . How could that be so?

(Hearing screams.)

Who's crying? Somebody's crying! . . . What's crying? . . . WHERE'S LULA?!

John: I don't know. You better get up.

Mary: That's outrageous! . . . What time is it?

John: Late 'nuff! Now rise up!

Mary: You must be joking. . . . I'm sure I still have four or five hours sleep in store—even more after that head-splittin' blow-out last night . . .

(Tumbles back under covers.)

John: Nobody told you to gulp those last six bourbons—

Mary: Don't tell me how many bourbons to swallow, not after you guzzled the whole stinking bar! . . . Get up? . . . You must be cracked. . . . Where's Lula? She must be here, she always is . . .

John: Well, she ain't here yet, so get up and muzzle that brat before she does drive me cuckoo!

Mary:

(Springing upright, finally realizing gravity of situation.)

Whaddaya mean Lula's not here? She's always here, she must be here. . . .

Where else kin she be? She supposed to be. . . . She just can't *not* be here—
CALL HER!

(Blackout as **John** *rushes offstage. Scene shifts to a trio of Telephone Operators perched on stools before imaginary switchboards. Chaos and bedlam are taking place to the sound of buzzes.* **Production Note:** *Effect of following dialogue should simulate rising pandemonium.)*

First Operator: The line is busy—
Second Operator: Line is busy—
Third Operator: Is busy—
First Operator: Doing best we can—
Second Operator: Having difficulty—
Third Operator: Soon as possible—
First Operator: Just one moment—
Second Operator: Would you hold on—
Third Operator: Awful sorry, madam—
First Operator: Would you hold on, please—
Second Operator: Just a second, please—
Third Operator: Please hold on, please—
First Operator: The line is busy—
Second Operator: The line is busy—
Third Operator: The line is busy—
First Operator: Doing best we can—
Second Operator: Hold on please—
Third Operator: Can't make connections—
First Operator: Unable to put it in—
Second Operator: Won't plug through—
Third Operator: Sorry madam—
First Operator: If you wait a moment—
Second Operator: Doing best we can—
Third Operator: Sorry—
First Operator: One moment—
Second Operator: Just a second—
Third Operator: Hold on—
First Operator: Yes—
Second Operator: STOP IT!—
Third Operator: HOW DO I KNOW—
First Operator: YOU ANOTHER ONE!
Second Operator: HOLD ON DAMMIT!
Third Operator: UP YOURS, TOO!
First Operator: THE LINE IS BUSY—
Second Operator: THE LINE IS BUSY—
Third Operator: THE LINE IS BUSY—

(The switchboard clamors a cacophony of buzzes as **Operators** *plug connections with the frenzy of a Chaplain movie. Their replies degenerate into a babble of gibberish. At the height of frenzy, the* **Supervisor** *appears.)*

Supervisor: WHAT'S THE SNARL-UP???!!!

First Operator: Everybody calling at the same time, ma'am!

Second Operator: Board can't handle it!

Third Operator: Like everybody in big New York City is trying to squeeze a call through to li'l' ole us!

Supervisor: God! . . . Somp'um terrible musta happened! . . . Buzz the emergency frequency hookup to the Mayor's office and find out what the hell's going on!

> *(Scene blacks out quickly to **Clem** and **Luke**.)*

Clem:

> *(Something slowly dawning on him.)*

Luke . . . ?

Luke: Yes, Clem?

Clem:

> *(Eyes roving around in puzzlement.)*

Luke . . . ?

Luke:

> *(Irked.)*

I said what, Clem!

Clem: Luke . . . ? Where—where is—the—the—?

Luke: THE WHAT?!

Clem: Nigras . . . ?

Luke: ?????What . . . ?

Clem: Nigras. . . . Where is the Nigras, where is they, Luke . . . ? ALL THE NIGRAS! . . . I don't see no Nigras . . . ?!

Luke: Whatcha mean . . . ?

Clem:

> *(Agitatedly.)*

Luke, there ain't a darky in sight. . . . And if you remember, we ain't spied a nappy hair all morning. . . . The Nigras, Luke! We ain't laid eyes on nary a coon this whole morning!!!

Luke: You must be crazy or something, Clem!

Clem: Think about it, Luke, we been sitting here for an hour or more—try and recollect if you remember seeing jist *one* go by?!!!

Luke:

> *(Confused.)*

. . . I don't recall. . . But . . . but there musta been some. . . . The heat musta got you, Clem! How in hell could that be so?!!!

Clem:

> *(Triumphantly.)*

Just think, Luke! . . . Look around ya. . . . Now, every morning mosta people walkin' 'long this street is colored. They's strolling by going to work, they's waiting for the buses, they's sweeping sidewalks, cleaning stores, starting to shine shoes and wetting the mops—right?! . . . Well, look around you, Luke—where is they?

> *(Luke paces up and down, checking.)*

I told you, Luke, they ain't nowheres to be seen.

Luke: ???? . . . This . . . this . . . some kind of holiday for 'em—or something?
Clem: I don't know, Luke . . . but . . . but what I do know is they ain't here 'n' we haven't seen a solitary one. . . . It's scaryfying. Luke . . . !
Luke: Well . . . maybe they's jist standing 'n' walking and shining on other streets.—Let's go look!

> (Scene blacks out to **John** and **Mary**. Baby cries are as insistent as ever.)

Mary:

> (At end of patience.)

SMOTHER IT!
John:

> (Beyond his.)

That's a hell of a thing to say 'bout your own child! You should know what to do to hush her up!
Mary: Why don't you try?!
John: You had her!
Mary: You shared in borning her?!
John: Possibly not!
Mary: Why, you lousy—!
John: What good is a mother who can't shut up her own daughter?!
Mary: I told you she yells louder every time I try to lay hands on her.—Where's Lula? Didn't you call her?!
John: I told you I can't get the call through!
Mary: Try ag'in—
John: It's no use! I tried numerous times and can't even git through to the switchboard. You've got to quiet her down yourself.

> (Firmly.)

Now, go in there and clam her up 'fore I lose my patience!

> (**Mary** exits. Soon, we hear the yells increase. She rushes back in.)

Mary: She won't let me touch her, just screams louder!
John: Probably wet 'n' soppy!
Mary: Yes! Stinks something awful! Phooooey! I can't stand that filth and odor!
John: That's why she's screaming! Needs her didee changed.—Go change it!
Mary: How you 'spect me to when I don't know how?! Suppose I faint?!
John: Well let her blast away. I'm getting outta here.
Mary: You can't leave me here like this!
John: Just watch me! . . . See this nice split-level cottage, peachy furniture, multi-colored teevee, hi-fi set 'n' the rest? . . . Well, how you think I scraped 'em together while you curled up on your fat li'l' fanny? . . . By gitting outta here—not only *on time* . . . but EARLIER!—Beating a frantic crew of nice young executives to the punch—gitting there fustest with the mostest brown-nosing you ever saw! Now if I goof one day—just ONE DAY!—You reckon I'd stay ahead? NO! . . . There'd be a wolf-pack trampling over my prostrate body, racing to replace my smiling face against the boss' left rump! . . . NO, MAM! I'm zooming outta here on time, just as I always have and what's more—you go'n' fix me some breakfast, I'M HUNGRY!
Mary: But—

John: No buts about it!
> *(Flash blackout as he gags on a mouthful of coffee.)*

What you trying to do, STRANGLE ME!!!
> *(Jumps up and starts putting on jacket.)*

Mary:
> *(Sarcastically.)*

What did you expect?

John:
> *(In biting fury.)*

That you could possibly boil a pot of water, toast a few slices of bread and fry a coupler eggs! . . . It was a mistaken assumption!

Mary: So they aren't as good as Lula's!

John: That is an overstatement. Your efforts don't result in anything that could possibly be digested by man, mammal, or insect! . . . When I married you, I thought I was fairly acquainted with your faults and weaknesses—I chalked em up to human imperfection. . . . But now I know I was being extremely generous, over-optimistic and phenomenally deluded!—You have no idea how useless you really are!

Mary: Then why'd you marry me?!

John: Decoration!

Mary: You shoulda married Lula!

John: I might've if it wasn't 'gainst the segregation law! . . . But for the sake of my home, my child and my sanity, I will even take a chance in sacrificing my slippery grip on the status pole and drive by her shanty to find out whether she or someone like her kin come over here and prevent some ultimate disaster.
> *(Storms toward door, stopping abruptly at exit.)*

Are you sure you kin make it to the bathroom wit'out Lula backing you up?!!!
> *(Blackout. Scene shifts to Mayor's office where a cluttered desk stands center amid papered debris.)*

Mayor:
> *(Striding determinedly toward desk, stopping midways, bellowing.)*

WOODFENCE! . . . WOODFENCE! . . . WOODFENCE!
> *(Receiving no reply, completes distance to desk.)*

JACKSON! . . . JACKSON!

Jackson:
> *(Entering worriedly.)*

Yes, sir . . . ?

Mayor: Where's Vice-Mayor Woodfence, that no-good brother-in-law of mine?!

Jackson: Hasn't come in yet, sir.

Mayor: HASN'T COME IN?!!! . . . Damn bastard! Knows we have a crucial conference. Soon as he staggers through that door, tell him to shoot in here!
> *(Angrily focusing on his disorderly desk and littered surroundings.)*

And git Mandy here to straighten up this mess—Rufus too! You know he shoulda been waiting to knock dust off my shoes soon as I step in. Get 'em in here! . . . What's the matter wit' them lazy Nigras? . . . Already had to dress myself because of JC, fix my own coffee without MayBelle, drive myself to work 'counta Bubber, feel my old Hag's tits after Sapphi—NEVER MIND!—Git 'em in here—QUICK!

Jackson:

(Meekly.)

They aren't . . . they aren't here, sir . . .

Mayor: Whaddaya mean they aren't here? Find out where they at. We got important business, man! You can't run a town wit' laxity like this. Can't allow things to git snafued jist because a bunch of lazy Nigras been out gitting drunk and living it up all night! Discipline, man, discipline!

Jackson: That's what I'm trying to tell you, sir . . . they didn't come in, can't be found . . . none of 'em.

Mayor: Ridiculous, boy! Scare 'em up and tell 'em scoot here in a hurry befo' I git mad and fire the whole goddamn lot of 'em!

Jackson: But we can't find 'em, sir.

Mayor: Hogwash! Can't nobody in this office do anything right?! Do I hafta handle every piddling little matter myself?! Git me their numbers, I'll have 'em here befo' you kin shout to—

(Three men burst into room in various states of undress.)

One: Henry—they vanished!

Two: Disappeared into thin air!

Three: Gone wit'out a trace!

Two: Not a one on the street!

Three: In the house!

One: On the job!

Mayor: Wait a minute!! . . . Hold your water! Calm down—!

One: But they've gone, Henry—GONE! All of 'em!

Mayor: What the hell you talking 'bout? Who's gone—?

One: The Nigras, Henry! They gone!

Mayor: Gone? . . . Gone where?

Two: That's what we trying to tell ya—they just disappeared! The Nigras have disappeared, swallowed up, vanished! All of 'em! Every last one!

Mayor: Have everybody 'round here gone batty? . . . That's impossible, how could the Nigras vanish?

Three: Beats me, but it's happened!

Mayor: You mean a whole town of Nigras just evaporate like this—poof!— Overnight?

One: Right!

Mayor: Y'all must be drunk! Why, half this town is colored. How could they just sneak out!

Two: Don't ask me, but there ain't one in sight!

Mayor: Simmer down 'n' put it to me easy-like.

One: Well . . . I first suspected somp'um smelly when Sarah Jo didn't show up this morning and I couldn't reach her—

Two: Dorothy Jane didn't 'rive at my house—

Three: Georgia Mae wasn't at mine neither—and SHE sleeps in!

One: When I reached the office, I realized I hadn't seen nary one Nigra all morning! Nobody else had either—wait a minute—Henry, have you?!

Mayor: ???Now that you mention it . . . no, I haven't . . .

One: They gone, Henry. . . . Not a one on the street, not a one in our homes, not a single, last living one to be found nowheres in town. What we gon' do?!

Mayor:

> *(Thinking.)*

Keep heads on your shoulders 'n' put clothes on your back. . . . They can't be far. . . . Must be 'round somewheres. . . . Probably playing hide 'n' seek, that's it! . . . JACKSON!

Jackson: Yessir?

Mayor: Immediately mobilize our Citizens Emergency Distress Committee!—Order a fleet of sound trucks to patrol streets urging the population to remain calm—situation's not as bad as it looks—everything's under control! Then have another squadron of squawk buggies drive slowly through all Nigra alleys, ordering them to come out wherever they are. If that don't git 'em organize a vigilante search-squad to flush 'em outta hiding! But most important of all, track down that lazy goldbricker, Woodfence and tell him to git on top of the situation! By God, we'll find 'em even if we hafta dig 'em outta the ground!

> *(Blackout. Scene shifts back to John and Mary a few hours later. A funereal solemnity pervades their mood. John stands behind Mary who sits, in a scene duplicating the famous "American Gothic" painting.)*

John: . . . Walked up to the shack, knocked on door, didn't git no answer. Hollered "LULA? LULA . . .?—Not a thing. Went 'round the side, peeped in window—nobody stirred. Next door—nobody there. Crossed other side of street and banged on five or six other doors—not a colored person could be found! Not a man, neither woman or child—not even a little black dog could be seen, smelt or heard for blocks around. . . . They've gone, Mary.

Mary: What does it all mean, John?

John: I don't know, Mary . . .

Mary: I always had Lula, John. She never missed a day at my side. . . . That's why I couldn't accept your wedding proposal until I was sure you'd welcome me and her together as a package. How am I gonna git through the day? My baby don't know *me,* I ain't acquainted wit' *it.* I've never lifted cover off pot, swung a mop or broom, dunked a dish or even pushed a dustrag. I'm lost wit'out Lula, I need her, John, I need her.

> *(Begins to weep softly. John pats her consolingly.)*

John: Courage, honey. . . . Everybody in town is facing the same dilemma. We mustn't crack up . . .

> *(Blackout. Scene shifts back to Mayor's office later in day. Atmosphere and tone resembles a wartime headquarters at the front. Mayor is poring over huge map.)*

Industrialist: Half the day is gone already, Henry. On behalf of the factory owners of this town, you've got to bail us out! Seventy-five percent of all production is paralyzed. With the Nigra absent, men are waiting for machines to be cleaned, floors to be swept, crates lifted, equipment delivered and bathrooms to be deodorized. Why, restrooms and toilets are so filthy until they not only cannot be sat in, but it's virtually impossible to get within hailing distance because of the stench!

Mayor: Keep your shirt on, Jeb—

Businessman: Business is even in worse condition, Henry. The volume of goods moving 'cross counters has slowed down to a trickle—almost negligible. Customers are not only not purchasing—but the absence of handymen, porters, sweepers, stock-movers, deliverers and miscellaneous dirty-work doers is disrupting the smooth harmony of marketing!

Club Woman: Food poisoning, severe indigestitis, chronic diarrhea, advanced diaper chafings and a plethora of unsanitary household disasters dangerous to life, limb and property! . . . As a representative of the Federation of Ladies' Clubs, I must sadly report that unless the trend is reversed, a complete breakdown in family unity is imminent. . . . Just as homosexuality and debauchery signalled the fall of Greece and Rome, the downgrading of Southern Bellesdom might very well prophesy the collapse of our indigenous institutions. . . . Remember—it has always been pure, delicate, lily-white images of Dixie femininity which provided backbone, inspiration and ideology for our male warriors in their defense against the on-rushing black horde. If our gallant men are drained of this worship and idolatry—God knows! The cause won't be worth a Confederate nickel!

Mayor: Stop this panicky defeatism, y'all hear me! All machinery at my disposal is being utilized. I assure you wit' great confidence the damage will soon repair itself.—Cheerful progress reports are expected any moment now. —Wait! See, here's Jackson. . . . Well, Jackson?

Jackson:

(Entering.)

As of now, sir, all efforts are fruitless. Neither hide nor hair of them has been located. We have not unearthed a single one in our shack-to-shack search. Not a single one has heeded our appeal. Scoured every crick and cranny inside their hovels, turning furniture upside down and inside out, breaking down walls and tearing through ceilings. We made determined efforts to discover where 'bouts of our faithful uncle Toms and informers— but even they have vanished without a trace. . . . Searching squads are on the verge of panic and hysteria, sir, wit' hotheads among 'em campaigning for scorched earth policies. Nigras on a whole lack cellars, but there's rising sentiment favoring burning to find out whether they're underground— DUG IN!

Mayor: Absolutely counter such foolhardy suggestions! Suppose they are tombed in? We'd only accelerate the gravity of the situation using incendiary tactics! Besides, when they're rounded up where will we put 'em if we've already burned up their shacks—IN OUR OWN BEDROOMS?!!!

Jackson: I agree, sir, but the mood of the crowd is becoming irrational. In anger and frustration, they's forgetting their original purpose was to FIND the Nigras!

Mayor: At all costs! Stamp out all burning proposals! Must prevent extremist

notions from gaining ascendancy. Git wit' it. . . . Wait—'n' for Jehovah's
sake, find out where the hell is that trifling slacker, WOODFENCE!
Courier:
> (Rushing in.)

Mr. Mayor! Mr. Mayor! . . . We've found some! We've found some!
Mayor:
> (Excitedly.)

Where?!
Courier: In the—in the—
> (Can't catch breath.)

Mayor:
> (Impatiently.)

Where, man? Where?!!!
Courier: In the colored wing of the city hospital!
Mayor: The hos—? The hospital! I shoulda known! How could those help-
less, crippled, cut and shot Nigras disappear from a hospital! Shoulda thought
of that! . . . Tell me more, man!
Courier: I—I didn't wait, sir. . . . I—I ran in to report soon as I heard—
Mayor: WELL GIT BACK ON THE PHONE, YOU IDIOT, DON'T YOU KNOW
WHAT THIS MEANS!
Courier: Yes, sir.
> (Races out.)

Mayor: Now we gitting somewhere! . . . Gentlemen, if one sole Nigra is
among us, we're well on the road to rehabilitation! Those Nigras in the
hospital must know somp'um 'bout the others where'bouts. . . . Scat back
to your colleagues, boost up their morale and inform 'em that things will
zip back to normal in a jiffy!
> (They start to file out, then pause to observe the **Courier** reentering
> dazedly.)

Well . . . ? Well, man . . . ? WHAT'S THE MATTER WIT' YOU, NINNY, TELL
ME WHAT ELSE WAS SAID?!
Courier: They all . . . they all . . . they all in a—in a—a coma, sir . . .
Mayor: They all in a what . . . ?
Courier: In a coma, sir . . .
Mayor: Talk sense, man! . . . Whaddaya mean, they all in a coma?
Courier: Doctor says every last one of the Nigras are jist laying in bed . . .
STILL . . . not moving . . . neither live or dead . . . laying up there in a coma
. . . every last one of 'em . . .
Mayor:
> (Sputters, then grabs phone.)

Get me Confederate Memorial. . . . Put me through to the Staff Chief. . . .
YES, this is the Mayor. . . . Sam? . . . What's this I hear? . . . But how could
they be in a coma, Sam? . . . You don't know! Well, what the hell you think
the city's paying you for! . . . You've got 'nuff damn hacks and quacks there
to find out! . . . How could it be somp'um unknown? You mean Nigras know
somp'um 'bout drugs your damn butchers don't?! . . . Well, what the crap
good are they! . . . All right, all right, I'll be calm. . . . Now, tell me. . . .

352   DOUGLAS TURNER WARD

Uh huh, uh huh. . . . Well, can't you give 'em some injections or somp'um . . . ?—You did . . . uh huh . . . DID YOU TRY A LI'L' ROUGH TREAT-MENT?—that too, huh. . . . All right, Sam, keep trying. . . .

(Puts phone down delicately, continuing absently.)

Can't wake 'em up. Just lay there. Them that's sick won't git no sicker, them that's half-well won't git no better, babies that's due won't be born and them that's come won't show no life. Nigras wit' cuts won't bleed and them which need blood won't be transfused. . . . He say dying Nigras is even refusing to pass away!

(Is silently perplexed for a moment, then suddenly breaks into action.)

JACKSON?! . . . Call up the police—THE JAIL! Find out what's going on there! Them Nigras are captives! If there's one place we got darkies under control, it's there! Them sonsabitches too onery to act right either for colored or white!

*(**Jackson** exits. The **Courier** follows.)*

Keep your fingers crossed, citizens, them Nigras in jail are the most important Nigras we got!

*(All hands are raised conspicuously aloft, fingers prominently ex-ed. Seconds tick by. Soon **Jackson** returns crestfallen.)*

Jackson: Sheriff Bull says they don't know whether they still on premises or not. When they went to rouse Nigra jailbirds this morning, cell-block doors refused to swing open. Tried everything—even exploded dynamite charges—but it just wouldn't budge. . . . Then they hoisted guards up to peep through barred windows, but couldn't see good 'nuff to tell whether Nigras was inside or not. Finally, gitting desperate, they power-hosed the cells wit' water but had to cease 'cause Sheriff Bull said he didn't wanta jeopardize drowning the Nigras since it might spoil his chance of shipping a record load of cotton pickers to the State Penitentiary for cotton-snatching jubilee. . . . Anyway—they ain't heard a Nigra-squeak all day.

Mayor: ???That so . . . ? WHAT 'BOUT TRAINS 'N' BUSSES PASSING THROUGH? There must be some dinges riding through?

Jackson: We checked . . . not a one on board.

Mayor: Did you hear whether any other towns lost their Nigras?

Jackson: Things are status-quo everywhere else.

Mayor:

(Angrily.)

Then what the hell they picking on us for!

Courier:

(Rushing in.)

MR. MAYOR! Your sister jist called—HYSTERICAL! She says Vice-Mayor Woodfence went to bed wit her last night, but when she woke up this morning he was gone! Been missing all day!

Mayor: ???Could Nigras be holding brother-in-law Woodfence hostage?!

Courier: No, sir. Besides him—investigations reveal that dozens of more prominent citizens—two City Council members, the chairman of the Junior Chamber of Commerce, our City College All-Southern half-back, the chair-lady of the Daughters of the Confederate Rebellion, Miss Cotton-Sack Festival of the Year and numerous other miscellaneous nobodies—are all absent wit'out leave. Dangerous evidence points to the conclusion that they have been infiltrating!

Mayor: Infiltrating???

Courier: Passing all along!

Mayor: ???PASSING ALL ALONG???

Courier: Secret Nigras all the while!

Mayor: NAW!

> (**Club Woman** *keels over in faint.* **Jackson, Businessman** *and* **Industrialist** *begin to eye each other suspiciously.*)

Courier: Yessir!

Mayor: PASSING???

Courier: Yessir!

Mayor: SECRET NIG—!???

Courier: Yessir!

Mayor:

> (*Momentarily stunned to silence.*)

The dirty mongrelizers! . . . Gentlemen, this is a grave predicament indeed. . . . It pains me to surrender priority to our states' right credo, but it is my solemn task and frightening duty to inform you that we have no other recourse but to seek outside help for deliverance.

> (*Blackout. Lights re-rise on Huntley-Brinkley-Murrow-Sevareid-Cronkite-Reasoner-type* **Announcer** *grasping a hand-held microphone [imaginary] a few hours later. He is vigorously, excitedly mouthing his commentary, but no sound escapes his lips. . . . During this dumb, wordless section of his broadcast, a bedraggled assortment of figures marching with picket signs occupy his attention. On their picket signs are inscribed various appeals and slogans. "CINDY LOU UNFAIR TO BABY JOE" . . . "CAP'N SAM MISS BIG BOY" . . . "RETURN LI'L' BLUE TO MARSE JIM" . . . "INFORMATION REQUESTED 'BOUT MAMMY GAIL" . . . "BOSS NATHAN PROTEST TO FAST LEROY." Trailing behind the marchers, forcibly isolated, is a woman dressed in widow-black holding a placard which reads: "WHY DIDN'T YOU TELL US—YOUR DEFILED WIFE AND TWO ABSENT MONGRELS."*)

Announcer:

> (*Who has been silently mouthing his delivery during the picketing procession, is suddenly heard as if caught in the midst of commentary.*)

. . . Factories standing idle from the loss of non-essential workers. Stores shuttered from the absconding of uncrucial personnel. Uncollected garbage threatening pestilence and pollution. . . . Also, each second somewheres in this former utopia below the Mason and Dixon, dozens of decrepit old men and women usually tended by faithful nurses and servants are popping off like flies—abandoned by sons, daughters and grandchildren whose refusal to provide their doddering relatives with bedpans and other soothing necessities result in their hasty, nasty, messy corpus delicties. . . . But most critically affected of all by this complete drought of Afro-American resources are policemen and other public safety guardians denied their daily quota of Negro arrests. One officer known affectionately as "TWO-A-DAY-PETE" because of his unblemished record of TWO Negro headwhippings per day has already been carted off to the County Insane Asylum—straight-jacketed, screaming and biting, unable to withstand the shock of having his spotless slate sullied by interruption. . . . It is feared that similar attacks are soon expected among municipal judges prevented for the first time in years of distinguished bench-sitting from sentencing one single Negro to a hoose-gow or pokey. . . . Ladies and gentlemen, as you trudge in from the joys and headaches of workday chores and dusk begins to descend on this sleepy Southern hamlet, we REPEAT—today—before early morning dew had dried upon magnolia blossoms, your comrade citizens of this lovely Dixie village awoke to the realization that some—pardon me! Not some—but ALL OF THEIR NEGROES were missing. . . . Absent, vamoosed, departed, at bay, fugitive, away, gone and so-far unretrieved. . . . In order to dispel your incredulity, gauge the temper of your suffering compatriots and just possibly prepare you for the likelihood of an equally nightmarish eventuality, we have gathered a cross-section of this city's most distinguished leaders for exclusive interviews. . . . First, Mr. Council Clan, grand-dragoon of this area's most active civic organizations and staunch bell-wether of the political opposition. . . . Mr. Clan, how do you ACCOUNT for this incredible disappearance?

Clan: A PLOT, plain and simple, that's what it is, as plain as the corns on your feet!

Announcer: Whom would you consider responsible?

Clan: I could go on all night.

Announcer: Cite a few?

Clan: Too numerous.

Announcer: Just one?

Clan: Name names when time comes.

Announcer: Could you be referring to native Negroes?

Clan: Ever try quaranteening lepers from their spots?

Announcer: Their organizations?

Clan: Could you slice a nose off a mouth and still keep a face?

Announcer: Commies?

Clan: Would you lop off a titty from a chest and still have a breast?

Announcer: Your city government?

Clan: Now you talkin'!

Announcer: State administration?

Clan: Warming up!

Announcer: Federal?

Clan: Kin a blind man see?!

Announcer: The Court?

Clan: Is a pig clean?!

Announcer: Clergy?

Clan: Do a polecat stink?!

Announcer: Well, Mr. Clan, with this massive complicity, how do you think the plot could've been prevented from succeeding?

Clan: If I'da been in office, it never woulda happened.

Announcer: Then you're laying major blame at the doorstep of the present administration?

Clan: Damn tooting!

Announcer: But from your oft-expressed views, Mr. Clan, shouldn't you and your followers be delighted at the turn of events? After all—isn't it one of the main policies of your society to *drive* Negroes away? *Drive* 'em back where they came from?

Clan: DRIVVVE, BOY! DRIIIIVVVE! That's right! . . . When we say so and not befo'. Ain't supposed to do nothing 'til we tell 'em. Got to stay put until we exercise our God-given right to tell 'em when to git!

Announcer: But why argue if they've merely jumped the gun? Why not rejoice at this premature purging of undesirables?

Clan: The time ain't ripe yet, boy. . . . The time ain't ripe yet.

Announcer: Thank you for being so informative, Mr. Clan—Mrs. Aide? Mrs. Aide? Over here, Mrs. Aide. . . . Ladies and gentlemen, this city's Social Welfare Commissioner, Mrs. Handy Anna Aide. . . . Mrs. Aide, with all your Negroes *AWOL*, haven't developments alleviated the staggering demands made upon your Welfare Department? Reduction of relief requests, elimination of case loads, removal of chronic welfare dependents, et cetera?

Aide: Quite the contrary. Disruption of our pilot projects among Nigras saddles our white community with extreme hardship. . . . You see, historically, our agencies have always been foremost contributors to the Nigra Git-A-Job movement. We pioneered in enforcing social welfare theories which oppose coddling the fakers. We strenuously believe in helping Nigras help themselves by participating in meaningful labor. "Relief is Out, Work is In," is our motto. We place them as maids, cooks, butlers, and breast-feeders, cesspool-diggers, wash-basin maintainers, shoe-shine boys, and so on—mostly on a volunteer self-work basis.

Announcer: Hired at prevailing salaried rates, of course?

Aide: God forbid! Money is unimportant. Would only make 'em worse. Our main goal is to improve their ethical behavior. "Rehabilitation Through Positive Participation" is another motto of ours. All unwed mothers, loose-living malingering fathers, bastard children and shiftless grandparents are kept occupied through constructive muscle-therapy. This provides the Nigra with less opportunity to indulge his pleasure-loving amoral inclinations.

Announcer: They volunteer to participate in these pilot projects?

Aide: Heavens no! They're notorious shirkers. When I said the program is voluntary, I meant white citizens in overwhelming majorities do the volunteering. Placing their homes, offices, appliances and persons at our disposal for use in "Operation Uplift." . . . We would never dare place such a decision in the hands of the Nigra. It would never get off the ground! . . . No, they have no choice in the matter. "Work or Starve" is the slogan we use to stimulate Nigra awareness of what's good for survival.

Announcer: Thank you, Mrs. Aide, and good luck. . . . Rev? . . . Rev? . . . Ladies and gentlemen, this city's foremost spiritual guidance counselor, Reverend Reb Pious. . . . How does it look to you, Reb Pious?

Pious:

(Continuing to gaze skyward.)

It's in *His* hands, son, it's in *His* hand.

Announcer: How would you assess the disappearance, from a moral standpoint?

Pious: An immoral act, son, morally wrong and ethically indefensible. A perversion of Christian principles to be condemned from every pulpit of this nation.

Announcer: Can you account for its occurrence after the many decades of the Church's missionary activity among them?

Pious: It's basically a reversion of the Nigra to his deep-rooted primitivism. . . . Now, at last, you can inderstand the difficulties of the Church in attempting to anchor God's kingdom among ungratefuls. It's a constant, unrelenting, no-holds-barred struggle against Satan to wrestle away souls locked in his possession for countless centuries! Despite all our aid, guidance, solace and protection, Old BeezleBub still retains tenacious grips upon the Nigras, childish loyalty—comparable to the lure of bright flames to an infant.

Announcer: But actual physical departure, Reb Pious? How do you explain that?

Pious: Voodoo, my son, voodoo. . . . With Satan's assist, they have probably employed some heathen magic which we cultivated, sophisticated Christians know absolutely nothing about. However, before long we are confident about counteracting this evil witch-doctory and triumphing in our Holy Savior's name. At this perilous juncture, true believers of all denominations are participating in joint, 'round-the-clock observances, offering prayers for our Master's swiftest intercession. I'm optimistic about the outcome of his intervention. . . . Which prompts me—if I may, sir—to offer these words of counsel to our delinquent Nigras. . . . I say to you without rancor or vengeance, quoting a phrase of one of your greatest prophets, Booker T. Washington: "Return your buckets to where they lay and all will be forgiven."

Announcer: A very inspirational appeal, Reb Pious. I'm certain they will find the tug of its magnetic sincerity irresistible. Thank you, Reb Pious. . . . All in all—as you have witnessed, ladies and gentlemen—this town symbolizes the face of disaster. Suffering as severe a prostration as any city wrecked, ravaged, and devastated by the holocaust of war. A vital, lively, throbbing organism brought to a screeching halt by the strange enigma of the missing Negroes. . . . We take you now to offices of the one man into whose hands has been thrust the final responsibility of rescuing this shuddering metropolis from the precipice of destruction. . . . We give you the honorable Mayor, Henry R. E. Lee. . . . Hello, Mayor Lee.

Mayor:

(Jovially.)

Hello, Jack.

Announcer: Mayor Lee, we have just concluded interviews with some of your city's leading spokesmen. If I may say so, sir, they don't sound too encouraging about the situation.

Mayor: Nonsense, Jack! The situation's well-in-hand as it could be under the circumstances. Couldn't be better in hand. Underneath every dark cloud, Jack, there's always a ray of sunlight, ha, ha, ha.

Announcer: Have you discovered one, sir?

Mayor: Well, Jack, I'll tell you. . . . Of course we've been faced wit' a little crisis, but look at it like this—we've faced 'em befo': Sherman marched through Georgia—ONCE! Lincoln freed the slaves—MOMENTARILY! Carpet-baggers even put Nigras in the Governor's mansion, state legislature, Congress and the Senate of the United States. But what happened?—Ole Dixie bounced right on back up. . . . At this moment the Supreme Court's trying to put Nigras in our schools and the Nigra has got it in his haid to put hisself everywhere. . . . But what you 'spect go'n' happen?—Ole Dixie will kangaroo back even higher. Southern courage, fortitude, chivalry and superiority always wins out. . . . SHUCKS! We'll have us some Nigras befo' daylight is gone!

Announcer: Mr. Mayor, I hate to introduce this note, but in an earlier interview, one of your chief opponents, Mr. Clan, hinted at your own complicity in the affair—

Mayor: A LOT OF POPPYCOCK! Clan is politicking! I've beaten him four times outta four and I'll beat him four more times outta four! This is no time for partisan politics! What we need now is level-headedness and across-the-board unity. This typical, rash, mealy-mouth, shooting-off-at-the-lip of Clan and his ilk proves their insincerity and voters will remember that in the next election! Won't you, voters?!

(Has risen to the height of his campaign oratory.)

Announcer: Mr. Mayor! . . . Mr. Mayor! . . . Please—

Mayor: . . . I tell you, I promise you—

Announcer: PLEASE, MR. MAYOR!

Mayor: Huh? . . . Oh—yes, carry on.

Announcer: Mr. Mayor, your cheerfulness and infectious good spirits lead me to conclude that startling new developments warrant fresh-found optimism. What concrete, declassified information do you have to support your claim that Negroes will reappear before nightfall?

Mayor: Because we are presently awaiting the pay-off of a masterful five-point supra-recovery program which can't help but reap us a bonanza of Nigras 'fore sundown! . . . First: Exhaustive efforts to pinpoint the where'bouts of our own missing darkies continue to zero in on the bullseye. . . . Second: The President of the United States, following an emergency cabinet meeting, has designated us the prime disaster area of the century—National Guard is already on the way. . . . Third: In an unusual, but bold maneuver, we have appealed to the NAACP 'n' all other Nigra conspirators to help us git to the bottom of the vanishing act. . . . Fourth: We have exercised our non-reciprocal option and requested that all fraternal southern states express their solidarity by lending us some of their Nigras temporarily on credit. . . . Fifth and foremost: We have already gotten consent of the Governor to round up all stray, excess and incorrigible Nigras to be shipped to us under escort of the State Militia. . . . That's why we've stifled pessimism and are brimming wit' confidence that this full-scale concerted mobilization will ring down a jackpot of jigaboos 'fore light vanishes from sky!—

Announcer: Congratulations! What happens if it fails?

Mayor: Don't even think THAT! Absolutely no reason to suspect it will. . . . *(Peers over shoulder, then whispers confidentially while placing hand over mouth by* **Announcer's** *imaginary mike.)*
. . . But speculating on the dark side of your question—if we don't turn up some by nightfall, it may be all over. The harm has already been done. You see the South has always been glued together by the uninterrupted presence of its darkies. No telling how unstuck we might git if things keep on like they have.—Wait a minute, it musta paid off already! Mission accomplished 'cause here's Jackson head a time wit' the word. . . . Well, Jackson, what's new?

Jackson: Situation on the home front remains static, sir—can't uncover scent or shadow. The NAACP and all other Nigra front groups 'n' plotters deny any knowledge or connection wit' the missing Nigras. Maintained this even after appearing befo' a Senate Emergency Investigating Committee which sub-poenaed 'em to Washington post haste and threw 'em in jail for contempt. A handful of Nigras who agreed to make spectacular appeals for ours to come back to us, have themselves mysteriously disappeared. But, worst news of all, sir, is our sister cities and counties, inside and outside the state, have changed their minds, fallen back on their promises and refused to lend us any Nigras, claiming they don't have 'nuff for themselves.

Mayor: What 'bout Nigras promised by the Governor?!

Jackson: Jailbirds and vagrants escorted here from chain-gangs and other reservations either revolted and escaped enroute or else vanished mysteri-ously on approaching our city limits. . . . Deterioration rapidly escalates, sir. Estimates predict we kin hold out only one more hour before overtaken by anarchistic turmoil. . . . Some citizens seeking haven elsewheres have already fled, but on last report were being forcibly turned back by armed sentinels in other cities who wanted no parts of 'em—claiming they carried a jinx.

Mayor: That bad, huh?

Jackson: Worse, sir . . . we've received at least five reports of plots on your life.

Mayor: What?!—We've gotta act quickly then!

Jackson: Run out of ideas, sir.

Mayor: Think harder, boy!

Jackson: Don't have much time, sir. One measly hour, then all hell go'n' break loose.

Mayor: Gotta think of something drastic, Jackson!

Jackson: I'm dry, sir.

Mayor: Jackson! Is there any planes outta here in the next hour?

Jackson: All transportation's been knocked out, sir.

Mayor: I thought so!

Jackson: What were you contemplating, sir?

Mayor: Don't ask me what I was contemplating! I'm still boss 'round here! Don't forgit it!

Jackson: Sorry, sir.

Mayor: . . . Hold the wire! . . . Wait a minute . . . ! Waaaaait a minute—

HAPPY ENDING AND DAY OF ABSENCE 359

GODAMNIT! All this time crapping 'round, diddling and fotsing wit' puny li'l' solutions—all the while neglecting our ace in the hole, our trump card! Most potent weapon for digging Nigras outta the woodpile!!! All the while right befo' our eyes! . . . Ass! Why didn't you remind me?!!!

Jackson: What is it, sir?

Mayor: . . . ME—THAT'S WHAT! ME! A personal appeal from ME! *Directly to them!* . . . Although we wouldn't let 'em march to the polls and express their affection for me through the ballot box, we've always known I'm held highest in their esteem. A direct address from their beloved Mayor! . . . If they's anywheres close within the sound of my voice, they'll shape up! Or let us know by a sign they's ready to!

Jackson: You sure *that'll* turn the trick, sir?

Mayor: As sure as my ancestors befo' me who knew that when they puckered their lips to whistle, ole Sambo was gonna come a-lickety-splitting to answer the call! . . . That same chips-down blood courses through these Confederate gray veins of Henry R. E. Lee!!!

Announcer: I'm delighted to offer our network's facilities for such a crucial public interest address, sir. We'll arrange immediately for your appearance on an international hookup, placing you in the widest proximity to contact them wherever they may be.

Mayor: Thank you, I'm very grateful. . . . Jackson, re-grease the machinery and set wheels in motion. Inform townspeople what's being done. Tell 'em we're all in this together. The next hour is countdown. I demand absolute cooperation, city-wide silence and inactivity. I don't want the Nigras frightened if they's nearby. This is the most important hour in town's history. Tell 'em if one single Nigra shows up during hour of decision, victory is within sight. I'm gonna git 'em that one—maybe all! Hurry and crack to it!

> (**Announcer** *rushes out, followed by* **Jackson**. *Blackout. Scene re-opens, with* **Mayor** *seated, eyes front, spotlight illuminating him in semi-darkness. Shadowy figures stand in the background, prepared to answer phones or aid in any other manner.* **Mayor** *waits patiently until "GO!" signal is given. Then begins, his voice combining elements of confidence, tremolo and gravity.*)

Good evening. . . . Despite the fact that millions of you wonderful people throughout the nation are viewing and listening to this momentous broadcast—and I thank you for your concern and sympathy in this hour of our peril—I primarily want to concentrate my attention and address these remarks solely for the benefit of our departed Nigra friends who may be listening somewhere in our far-flung land to the sound of my voice. . . . If you are —it is with heart-felt emotion and fond memories of our happy association that I ask—"Where are you . . . ?" Your absence has left a void in the bosom of every single man, woman and child of our great city. I tell you—you don't know what it means for us to wake up in the morning and discover that your cheerful, grinning, happy-go-lucky faces are missing! . . . From the depths of my heart, I can only meekly, humbly suggest what it means to me personally. . . . You see—the one face I will never be able to erase from my memory is the face—not of my Ma, not of Pa, neither wife or child—but the image of the first woman I came to love so well when just a wee lad—the vision of the first human I laid clear sight on at childbirth—the profile—better yet, the full face of my dear old . . . Jemimah—God rest her soul. . . . Yes! My dear ole mammy, wit' her round ebony moonbeam gleaming down upon me in the crib, teeth shining, blood-red bandana standing starched, peaked and proud, gazing down upon me affectionately as she crooned me a Southern lullaby. . . . OH! It's a memorable picture I will eternally cherish in permanent treasure chambers of my heart, now and forever always. . . . Well, if this radiant image can remain so infinitely vivid to me all these many years after her unfortunate demise in the Po' folks home—THINK of the misery the rest of us must be suffering after being *freshly* denied your soothing presence?! We need ya. If you kin hear me, just contact this station 'n' I will welcome you back personally. Let me just tell you that since you eloped, nothing has been the same. How could it? You're part of us, you belong to us. Just give us a sign and we'll be contented that all is well. . . . Now if you've skipped away on a little fun-fest, we understand, ha, ha. We know you like a good time and we don't begrudge it to ya. Hell—er, er, we like a good time ourselves—who doesn't? . . . In fact, think of all the good times we've had together, huh? We've had some real fun, you and us, yesiree! . . . Nobody knows better than you and I what fun we've had together. You singing us those old Southern coon songs and dancing those Nigra jigs and us clapping, prodding 'n' spurring you on! Lots of fun, huh?! . . . OH BOY! The times we've had together. . . . If you've snucked away for a bit of fun by yourself, we'll go 'long wit' ya—long as you let us know where you at so we won't be worried about you. . . . We'll go 'long wit' you long as you don't take the joke too far. I'll admit a joke is a joke and you've played a LULU! . . . I'm warning you, we can't stand much more horsing 'round from you! Business is business 'n' fun is fun! You've had your fun so now let's get down to business! Come on back, YOU HEAR ME!!! . . . . If you been hoodwinked by agents of some foreign government, I've been authorized by the President of these United States to inform you that this liberty-loving Republic is prepared to rescue you from their clutches. Don't pay no 'tention to their siren songs and atheistic promises! You better off under our control and you know it! . . . If you been bamboozled by rabble-rousing nonsense of your own so-called leaders, we prepared to offer same protection. Just call us up! Just give us a sign! . . . Come on, give us a sign . . . give us a sign—even a teeny-weeny one . . . ??!!

    (Glances around checking on possible communications. A bevy of headshakes indicate no success. **Mayor** *returns to address with desperate fervor.)*

Now look—you don't know what you doing! If you persist in this disobedience, you know all too well the consequences! We'll track you to the end of the earth, beyond the galaxy, across the stars! We'll capture you and chastise you with all the vengeance we command! 'N' you know only too well how stern we kin be when double-crossed! The city, the state and the entire nation will crucify you for this unpardonable defiance!

    (Checks again.)

No call . . . ? No sign . . . ? Time is running out! Deadline slipping past! They gotta respond! They gotta!

(Resuming.)

Listen to me! I'm begging y'all, you've gotta come back . . . ! LOOK, GEORGE!

(Waves dirty rag aloft.)

I brought the rag you wax the car wit'. . . . Don't this bring back memories, George, of all the days you spent shining that automobile to shimmering perfection . . . ? And you, Rufus?! . . . Here's the shoe polisher and the brush! . . . 'Member, Rufus? . . . Remember the happy mornings you spent popping this rag and whisking this brush so furiously 'till it created music that was sympho-nee to the ear . . . ? And you—MANDY? . . . Here's the waste-basket you didn't dump this morning. I saved it just for you! . . . LOOK, all y'all out there . . . ?

(Signals and a three-person procession parades one after the other before the imaginary camera.)

Doll Woman:

(Brandishing a crying baby [doll] as she strolls past and exits.)

She's been crying ever since you left, Caldonia . . .

Mop Man:

(Flashing mop.)

It's been waiting in the same corner, Buster . . .

Brush Man:

(Flagging toilet brush in one hand and toilet plunger in other.)

It's been dry ever since you left, Washington . . .

Mayor:

(Jumping in on the heels of the last exit.)

Don't these things mean anything to y'all? By God! Are your memories so short?! Is there nothing sacred to ya? . . . Please come back, for my sake, please! All of you—even you questionable ones! I promise no harm will be done to you! Revenge is disallowed! We'll forgive everything! Just come on back and I'll git down on my knees—

(Immediately drops to knees.)

I'll be kneeling in the middle of Dixie Avenue to kiss the first shoe of the first one 'a you to show up. . . . *I'll smooch any other spot you request.* . . . Erase this nightmare 'n' we'll concede any demand you make, just come on back—please???!! . . . PLEEEEEEEZE?!!!

Voice:

(Shouting.)

TIME!!!

Mayor:

(Remaining on knees, frozen in a pose of supplication. After a brief, deadly silence, he whispers almost inaudibly.)

They wouldn't answer . . . they wouldn't answer . . .

(Blackout as bedlam erupts offstage. Total blackness holds during a sufficient interval where offstage sound-effects create the illusion of complete pandemonium, followed by a diminution which trails off

into an expressionistic simulation of a city coming to a strickened standstill: industrial machinery clanks to halt, traffic blares to silence, etc. . . . The stage remains dark and silent for a long moment, then lights re-arise on the **Announcer**.)

Announcer: A pitiful sight, ladies and gentlemen. Soon after his unsuccessful appeal Mayor Lee suffered a vicious pummeling from the mob and barely escaped with his life. National Guardsmen and State Militia were impotent in quelling the fury of a town venting its frustration in an orgy of destruction—a frenzy of rioting, looting and all other aberrations of a town gone berserk. . . . Then—suddenly—as if a magic wand had been waved, madness evaporated and something more frightening replaced it: Submission. . . . Even whimperings ceased. The city: exhausted, benumbed.—Slowly its occupants slinked off into shadows, and by midnight, the town was occupied exclusively by zombies. The fight and life had been drained out. . . . Pooped. . . . Hope ebbed away as completely as the beloved, absent Negroes. . . . As our crew packed gear and crept away silently, we treaded softly—as if we were stealing away from a mausoleum. . . . The Face Of A Defeated City.

(Blackout. Lights rise slowly at the sound of rooster-crowing, signalling the approach of a new day, the next morning. Scene is same as opening of play. **Clem** and **Luke** are huddled over dazedly, trancelike. They remain so for a long count. Finally, a figure drifts on stage, shuffling slowly.)

Luke:

(Gazing in silent fascination at the approaching figure.)

. . . Clem . . . ? Do you see what I see or am I dreaming . . . ?

Clem: It's a . . . a Nigra, ain't it, Luke . . . ?

Luke: Sure looks like one, Clem—but we better make sure—eyes could be playing tricks on us. . . . Does he still look like one to you, Clem?

Clem: He still does, Luke—but I'm scared to believe—

Luke: . . . Why . . . ? It looks like Rastus, Clem!

Clem: Sure does, Luke . . . but we better not jump to no hasty conclusion . . .

Luke:

(In timid softness.)

That you, Rastus . . . ?

Rastus:

(Stepin Fetchit, Willie Best, Nicodemus, B. McQueen and all the rest rolled into one.)

Why . . . howdy . . . Mr. Luke . . . Mr. Clem . . .

Clem: It is him, Luke! It is him!

Luke: Rastus?

Rastus: Yas . . . sah?

Luke: Where was you yesterday?

Rastus:

(Very, very puzzled.)

Yes . . . ter . . . day? . . . Yester . . . day . . . ? Why . . . right . . . here . . . Mr. Luke . . .

Luke: No you warn't, Rastus, don't lie to me! Where was you yestiddy?

Rastus: Why . . . I'm sure I was . . . Mr. Luke . . . Remember . . . I made . . . that . . . delivery for you . . .

Luke: That was MONDAY, Rastus, yestiddy was TUESDAY.

Rastus: Tues . . . day . . . ? You don't say. . . . Well . . . well . . . well . . .

Luke: Where was you 'n' all the other Nigras yesterday, Rastus?

Rastus: I . . . thought . . . yestiddy . . . was Monday, Mr. Luke—I coulda swore it . . . ! . . . See how . . . things . . . kin git all mixed up? . . . I coulda swore it . . .

Luke: TODAY is WEDNESDAY, Rastus. Where was you TUESDAY?

Rastus: Tuesday . . . huh? That's somp'um . . . I . . . don't . . . remember . . . missing . . . a day . . . Mr. Luke . . . but I guess you right . . .

Luke: Then where was you!!!???

Rastus: Don't rightly know, Mr. Luke. I didn't know I had skipped a day— But that jist goes to show you how time kin fly, don't it, Mr. Luke. . . . Uuh, uuh, uuh . . .

> (*He starts shuffling off, scratching head, a flicker of a smile playing across his lips.* **Clem** *and* **Luke** *gaze dumbfoundedly as he disappears.*)

Luke:
> (*Eyes sweeping around in all directions.*)

Well. . . . There's the others, Clem. . . . Back jist like they useta be. . . . Everything's same as always . . .

Clem: ??? . . . . Is it . . . Luke . . . !

> (*Slow fade.*)

Curtain

A PARABLE IN ONE ACT

The Gentleman Caller

by Ed Bullins

Ed Bullins   *(1935-   )*

Ed Bullins, one of the most influential and prolific playwrights of the contemporary black theater movement, is extremely reticent when it comes to
talking about himself, but understandably outspoken and aggressive when it
comes to talking about his notions of the black theater and its place in the
black community. Born in Philadelphia, he was educated for the most part in
the public schools of that city. Other aspects of his personal life he con-
siders irrelevant to the proper assessment of his work. One can assume that
up to this time his work is his life. We have been told, however, that he
worked at a number of odd jobs as he sought to find himself and to express
himself as a writer. He began to search out his talents by writing novels,
none of which has been published because he is dissatisfied with them.
But he also concluded that his people were not reading novels. "But when
they are in the theater, then I've got them. Or like TV. You know my ideas
could get to them. So I moved away from the prose forms and moved into
the theater. There has been black literature for years but it has been cir-
culating in a more closed type of circle, the black arts circle, the colleges.
But it hasn't been getting down to the people. And so I think this is the
reason for there being more black plays being written and seen, for more
theaters springing up."

At present, Ed Bullins is playwright-in-residence at the New Lafayette
Theater in Harlem, a resident professional company of actors, directors,
writers, and technicians founded in 1967 by Robert Macbeth, who serves as
its artistic director.

Prior to his work in New York, Bullins had ten plays produced on
the West Coast, mainly through his own efforts. In San Francisco where early
plays such as *How Do You Do* and *Clara's Ole Man* were first produced he
was cultural director of Black House, a community center, and the San

367

Francisco Headquarters of the Black Panther Party. On the West Coast he was also associated with LeRoi Jones in stage production and film making. Bullins has been writing plays since the early sixties and has some twenty titles to his credit, including *The Electronic Nigger, A Son, Come Home, Goin'a Buffalo, The Theme Is Blackness, In the Wine Time, In New England Winter, The Gentleman Caller*. His first published piece in a national publication was an essay, "The Polished Protest: Aesthetics and the Black Writer," which appeared in *Contact* in 1963. Since then he has published essays, stories, plays, and poetry in numerous magazines such as the *Negro Digest, Liberator, Black Dialogue*, and *The Drama Review*, of which he was editor for the special issue on black theater in 1968. Ed Bullins has recently published a drama anthology *New Plays from the Black Theater. Five Plays by Ed Bullins* appeared in 1969. Bullins is editor of *Black Theater Magazine*, published by The New Lafayette Theater. He is also a leading force in the Black Arts Alliance, an organization of black theater groups.

INTRODUCTION

A Black Quartet, four one act plays: *Prayer Meeting, or The First Militant Minister,* by Ben Caldwell; *The Warning—A Theme for Linda,* by Ronald Milner; *The Gentleman Caller,* by Ed Bullins; *The Great Goodness of Life (A Coon Show),* by LeRoi Jones, opened off-Broadway at Tambellini's Gate Theater, June 30, 1969. Writing for *The New York Times,* Richard F. Sheperd described this program as "An impressive bill of four one act plays, adding up to an evening that is kaleidescopic in technique and content. . . . Each reflected a different facet of the black agony; each expressed a contempt for change that is short of radical. Each set its message in a different form, and that is what made the over-all scene so striking."

Bearing certain resemblances to LeRoi Jones' *Dutchman,* Ed Bullins' *The Gentleman Caller* is a symbolistic and expressionistic work. Staged by Allie Woods, the able cast included Minnie Gentry as The Maid; Carl Bossiere as The Gentleman; Sylvia Soares, as Madame; and Frank Carey as Mr. Mann. The most lavishly staged of the plays it was grouped with, the action takes place against a satiric backdrop, a garish drawing room, decorated in white, red and black with walls adorned with American flags. Prominent in this decor is a gun rack containing rifles and shotguns, and the mountings on spikes of the stuffed heads of a blackman, an American Indian, a Vietnamese, and a Chinese—trophies of rich white America.

As playwright in residence of the New Lafayette Theater, Ed Bullins has long displayed a seasoned mastery of his craft. *The Electronic Nigger, In the Wine Time, Goin'a Buffalo* are admirable instances of his art that show his abilities in working within the realistic and naturalistic traditions. *A Gentleman Caller* is significant as an instance of his ability to work in the realm of satirical fantasy, and it enables us to see him as an articulate fabulist. For those who like subtlety, suggestion, and innuendo brought about by a unity of setting, action and dialogue, this cryptic play will compel, although the speeches that round it out at the curtain may seem too stark and simplistic. They do, though, serve the purposes of the Revolutionary Black Theater and the play as a whole gives force to Bullins' view that "We don't want to have a higher form of white art in blackface. We are working towards something entirely different and new that encompasses the soul and spirit of Black people, and that represents the whole experience of our being here in this oppressive land."

Clayton Riley, generally an admirer of Bullins' work, called *The Gentleman Caller*, "Bullins in a minor key," because it lacked the ambitious qualities that generally characterize his work, reasoning that "the play covers what, for Bullins, at least, is ground long since traveled over with a mine sweeper." This suggests Mr. Riley's preference of the naturalistic dramas over this satirical fantasy. He does though provide us with a good summary of the play when he writes: "A young black man calls on a decadent rich white lady, sits while she babbles endlessly about her traditions, her family, her 'ecclesiastical rank.' He never speaks. No one else does except the maid, a big black woman, dressed in American flags and such. The lady's husband is painted gold (she is painted silver, both roles being played by black performers). The husband is dead. The lady is going to die, and this seems clear from the beginning, because she represents the broker, the 'whitey' from whom the reparations are going to be received. And . . . down she goes in a fusillade of lead from the maid-turned-militant who subsequently 'ices' the young man, after he discovers that Mr. Mann (read *the* man, or Mr. Charlie) wears a false beard instead of a real one the young man coveted. So the true and dedicated militant sees that what he thinks the Establishment has isn't worth having, certainly isn't what he wants. So Mama has to get rid of him in true 'sustainer' fashion." I have called this a good summary, but does this statement do justice to the play?

The answer to this question must, I think, be in the negative. One reason for this is that, as in the case of all summaries, it oversimplifies. Another is that multiple interpretations are the inevitable results of symbolistic works of art. Riley assents to "a glimmer or two of his [Bullins'] excellent sense of dramatic structure and a suspenseful blending of several bizarre events." But the play remains a disappointment to this critic because every thing is "too easy."

But on the metaphorical level parallels to Jones' *Dutchman* are illuminating, and add to the complexity of the play. Madame is a more mature, more decadent Lula, with her wild singing, her hysterical laughter, and her "groovy" seductive dance. Madame (silver) is the American bitch-goddess of success, once again, the American attitude. Mr. Mann (gold) is the American dream of success. And both are moribund. The Maid, represented as a loyal heirloom, dependent upon the noblesse oblige of the whites, represents the black masses who although ostensibly servile to their masters are filled with hate and symbolically bent upon their destruction. *The Gentleman Caller,* a well dressed young man, wearing dark glasses, hiding his true identity, smoking imported cigarettes, is a mute Clay, rather than a dedicated militant, the middle class Negro who seeks identity with the Establishment, who in the interests of the Revolution must be destroyed by Mamie, the Queen Mother. When he first appears at the door the maid says: "What you messin' wit me fo, boy? . . . Is somethin' da matta." She is confused as she reads his calling card but reluctantly lets him in, leads him into the room, takes his hat and shows him a chair. Shaking her head she says to herself: "Uummm . . . don't know what the world is comin'ta dese hare days. Always somethin's else ta mess with you!" Then speaking to the visitor she says: "What you goin 'round messin' things up fo, huh?" Then (peeved): "Well, what for? I jest can't understand you's young'uns none." These important lines lead to the encounter between the mute caller and the garrulous, flirtatious Madame, and they presage the attitude of Mamie both towards Mr. and Mrs. Mann as well as towards the gentleman caller, who is not a militant, but just "messin around," "messin' things up." For as Richard F. Sheperd says "A steady change, expertly portrayed in line and gesture, transforms the original seemingly stable order of things to a startling and revolutionary climax." Indeed, the play is one that "holds the viewer [reader] from start to finish."

Finally it should be noticed that at least one critic, Daphne Kraft of the *Newark Evening News,* sees the influence of Eldridge Cleaver's *Soul on Ice* in *The Gentleman Caller,* in which Cleaver's attempt to correlate Marx's class struggle to black and white sex partnerships involves a satirical portrayal on Bullins' part of Madame as the ultrafeminine doll who hates her emasculated mate, tempts the gentleman caller, as the super-sexual menial, we should add, and is finally done in by her black Mammy, Cleaver's Practical Amazon. These parallels are interesting too, and perhaps informative. But the play stands as an autonomous work of art. A black comedy, Bullins calls it "A Parable," so fierce in its intention that it is almost impossible to laugh at.

A PARABLE IN ONE ACT

The Gentleman Caller

THE PEOPLE

The Maid
The Gentleman
Madame
Mr. Mann

SCENE 1

At Rise: *A comfortably furnished living room in a fashionable section of a northern American city. (If there be any.) Against the back wall is a gun rack with rifles and shotguns in it. Upon the wall are mounted and stuffed heads of a Blackman, an American Indian, a Vietnamese and a Chinese. The telephone rings; the* **Maid** *enters and answers the phone.*

Maid: Hello . . . Nawh . . . Madame's not takin' no calls. Sho I'm sho. Nawh . . . nawh . . . can't do that.
> *(A knock at the door.)*

Nawh, sah . . . I can't do dat. Now I gotta hang up now, man. Bye . . . bye, I said.
> *(She hangs up. Knock at door sounds again and the* **Maid** *crosses stage to door. She is in the classic image of how a Negro maid is thought to look—large, heavy, black, sometimes though seldomly smiling, mostly fussying to herself, but always in her place, at least for the moment. She opens the door. A young, well-dressed* **Man** *stands outside, somewhat blacker than she.)*

Deliveries in the rear, boy!
> *(She slams the door. Immediately there is a knock. The* **Maid** *turns back muttering and scowling and opens the door. The* **Young Man** *is standing in the same spot.)*

What you messin' wit me fo, boy? . . . Is somethin' da matta wit you?
> *(He hands her his card. She reads the piece of paper and looks confused, turning it upside down and peering at its back, and starts to close the door partially, though thinks better of the act, and recovers.)*

Well . . . I guess you should come in.
> *(She leads him into the room, takes his hat and shows him a chair. Shakes head, to herself:)*

Uummm uummm . . . don't know what the world is comin' ta dese hare days. Always somethin's else ta mess with you!
> *(Speaks to visitor.)*

What you goin' round messin' things up fo, huh?
> *(Peeved.)*

Well, what for? I jest can't understand you's young'uns none.
> *(Turns, over her shoulder.)*

I'll go tell the Missy you's here.
> *(She exits. The* **Gentleman Caller** *observes the surroundings and lights a dark cigarette. He looks for a moment at the rifle hung above the mantle. Noises off-stage.* **Madame**'s *voice is heard warbling "America."* The **Maid**'s *voice is heard mumbling, or is not heard, being lost in the mumbles, then bursts forth in a vigorous chorus of a negro spiritual. Silence.*
> *Lights brighten to glaring orange and harsh yellow, then dim to accommodate* **Madame**'s *complexion, and* **Madame** *enters.*
> *The* **Gentleman Caller** *sits with his legs crossed, smoking.*
> **Madame** *wears an expensive looking dressing gown.*
> *If the role is played by a Black woman, she should paint her body and*

face with silver paint and wear a blond wig. If a white person is used,
then it should be an effeminate white man in drag.)

Madame: So you're here at last! Well, I suspected you'd come like this. When we least expect you or are prepared. My most private leisurely moments . . . and I find you sitting with your legs crossed in my home! Blowing smoke from those terrible imported cigarettes all over my curtains and drapes!

(Frets.)

Ohhh . . . now what do you have to say for yourself and how you treat me! . . . How you treat me! . . . No respect in my own home. Come, you, now tell me. What do you have to say for yourself?

(He continues to smoke. She takes a seat across from him.)

You'll have to wait for my husband. He's in the bathroom . . . shaving! And if I were him I wouldn't hurry . . . not for you, in any case. Ohhh . . . where is everybody!

(She calls.)

Mamie . . Mamie!

(Whines.)

Ohhh . . . where is she?

*(The **Maid** enters.)*

Maid: Yas'sum.

Madame: We'll have tea. Mamie . . . Unless our gentleman caller prefers something . . .

(He shakes his head.)

. . . No, he doesn't . . . so tea will do for the two of us.

Maid: Yas'sum.

Madame: Mr. Mann will join us later.

Maid: Yas'sum, Mrs. Mann.

*(**Maid** exits. **Madame** appears relieved, more relaxed.)*

Madame: What a blessing Mamie is.

(Broad smile.)

I don't know what I'd do without her.

(Warming up.)

She's been with the family for years. One of the truly worthwhile possessions my father left us with.

*(The **Gentleman** uncrosses and recrosses his legs. **Madame** stands, walks in back of her chair and touches the fabric.)*

She's getting old now and times are changing. . . . Yes, changing, quite a bit . . . And Mamie's getting to be something of an inconvenience . . . but tradition, family sentiments and loyalty are so much better than what the times would declare . . . don't you think so, mister . . . mister . . .

(Nods head.)

Oh, I see; I see now.

(She walks around the room, pulling together drapes, turning on a lamp, lifting a bound book and reading the title.)

You're not very conventional, sir, are you?

(Faces him.)

Are you surprised that I call you sir? . . . And you have reason to be, for though I'm entirely orthodox, as you can see, I'm not a fool. . . . Now my husband . . . well, that's another matter. But as I said . . . you're not very conventional. Or are you too conventional but in an unsuspecting way . . . your manner, perhaps . . . for one is led to think of its being very different than something usual. Say for instance an Englishman might look very out of place in the dress of an Eskimo . . . unless, of course, he were in the Arctic, or . . . well, enough of that. You're here . . . and we're here . . . and somehow it all doesn't fit together, the way things are going, I mean, not to our reckoning, at least.

(Sits again.)

Take for instance me . . . that's right, me. Wouldn't it be thought odd if I were to sit beside you on a bus when I could more easily have found a seat alone or with someone else? Someone that's . . . well, you know what I'm getting at. Now what would people think? What would they say? And, yes, it's true that I never ride in buses but it might happen one day, so I must prepare myself, we all must prepare ourselves for the worst, don't you agree? Having seen what you believe is the worst, I know you are in sympathy, aren't you . . . So, you're not.

(Gesturing.)

Now what would they say? The people, I mean. How would I feel about how they'd think? Oh, it's just too horrid to conceive.

*(The **Maid** enters with a tray. She moves to serve **Madame**. The phone rings.)*

The guest first, Mamie, please!

Maid:

(Confusion.)

But Missy . . .

Madame:

(Warning.)

Don't question me, Mamie.

Maid: Yas'sum.

Madame: And answer that telephone, Mamie. Same message, please.

Maid: Yas'sum.

(She lifts phone.)

Now lissen, man . . . I ain't got time fo all dat foolishness, now. She don' wan'na talk ta you. She ain't gonna come and I ain't gonna call her no mo' . . . good bye!

*(She hangs up. The tea is served; the **Maid** exits.)*

Madame:

(To visitor.)

You know who that is, don't you?

(He nods. She is annoyed.)

He shouldn't be so insistent. Mamie should know by now how to handle him!

(Explaining.)

This is the trouble with keeping people with you too long. They feel that

THE GENTLEMAN CALLER   373

they can question your authority as if they had some priority. Now I knew how I wanted it all done.

> *(Becomes more angry.)*

How dare she question me! Me! How dare she?

> *(The **Maid** returns.)*

Maid:

> *(Worried and sullen.)*

Is there anything else, ma'am?

Madame: Is there anything else? You meant to say is there anything wrong, didn't you? . . . Of course there's not! What would make you think that there was anything wrong?

Maid: Why I jest thought there might . . .

Madame:

> *(Rises.)*

How dare you to think!

> *(Points to exit.)*

Excuse yourself and leave us, Mamie Lee King. . . . At once! Do you hear?

Maid:

> *(More sullen, avoids visitor's eyes.)*

'Scuse me . . . yawhl.

> *(She exits.)*

Madame:

> *(Sits.)*

How dare she take it upon herself to return? . . . And to ask questions? . . . And to think? Ohhhh . . . what are the times coming to? What are they coming to? There's only one solution. I have failed to face up to it before now. She must go.

> *(Arm at her forehead in classic anguish stance.)*

She must go!

> *(Calls.)*

Mamie! Mamie, come here at once!

> *(The **Maid** enters.)*

Maid: Yas'sum.

Madame: You are fired.

Maid: Yas'sum.

Madame: Get your things and be off at once.

Maid: Yas'sum.

> *(**Maid** turns to go.)*

Madame: Is that all you have to say?

Maid: Yas'sum.

Madame: Why?

Maid: 'Cause I didn't want to upset lil Missy anymo'.

Madame: Ohhh . . . how sweet. You're such a living doll, Mamie.

> *(To visitor.)*

Isn't that simply divine. . . . So innocent . . . so childlike and naive.

Maid: Yas'sum.

> *(Phone rings; **Maid** answers.)*

Wha? . . . Ya don' say? Nawh, I ain't gonna call her . . . wouldn't if I could. Thank ya, sah.

> *(Hangs up.)*

Madame:

> *(Inspired.)*

You know . . . you know, Mamie, dear . . . I don't think you'd better go after all.

Maid: Nawh, ma'am.

Madame: In fact, I'm thinking of giving you a two dollar a month raise . . . and . . . and . . . now listen to this, Mamie, dear . . . this is the best . . . and that new black taffeta dress I got for aunt Hattie's funeral six years ago. Well, that's yours too, dear. Isn't that thrilling for you? . . . Of course I'll have to first talk to my husband, Mr. Mann, about it first and see what he has to say . . . but you know how much his word means with me . . .

Maid: Yas'sum.

Madame:

> *(Warm.)*

And you know I wouldn't turn you out anyway, don't you, you old actress, you? Why it's right in daddy's will where we are to give you a home until that day when you lay your old grey and black head on the duckdown pillows and rise no more.

Maid: Yas'sum.

Madame: Now how could I go against daddy's wishes?

Maid: Don' know, ma'am.

Madame:

> *(Smiles.)*

Good . . . now go back to your kitchen and wait until I call you.

Maid:

> *(Stands firm.)*

Well, ma'am . . .

Madame:

> *(Surprised.)*

What is it, Mamie?

Maid:

> *(Shuffles from one foot to another.)*

. . . I guess this is as good a time as any to tell you . . .

Madame:

> *(Annoyed.)*

Tell me what, Mamie?

Maid: I'm quittin'.

Madame:

> *(Disbelief.)*

You're what?

Maid: Quittin'.

Madame: You're not?

> *(To visitor.)*

Did you hear what she said?

(He doesn't respond.)
You can't be leaving, Mamie?
Maid: I'm so too.
Madame: But you can't.
Maid: Am too.
Madame: But you can't, Mamie, dear.
Maid: Yas I can.
Madame: But what about all these years you've spent with me? With us?
Maid: I dunno, ma'am.
Madame: What about my suckling your big flabby breasts?
Maid: They dry now, ma'am.
Madame: . . . and you raised me as one of your own?
Maid: Dat's cause I's never had time fo mah own, ma'am.
Madame: And the love and respect I showed you.
      (Silence.)
And the devotion and loyalty and gratitude you have for me.
      (Silence.)
What about the will?
      (Silence.)
Daddy said that if you left that it would be against his wishes and . . .
Maid:
      (Loudly.)
Yas'sum.
Madame:
      (Pleads.)
Then . . .
Maid: I'm quittin'.
Madame:
      (Last resort.)
What about your raise and . . .
Maid: Tonight's my last night.
      (She exits.)
Madame:
      (Furious.)
The idea!
      (To visitor.)
The idea . . . just think of it!
      (**Madame** *paces about the room, mutters, looking off where the* **Maid** *disappeared. Then, stops and abruptly turns to the* **Gentleman** *and pulls open her dressing gown, revealing she has nothing beneath the gown save* **Madame**.)
Like this?
      (Expressionless, the **Gentleman** *looks at her.* **Madame** *begins a slow, unfamiliar to her, dance.)*
Like this, boy? . . . Huh? You want this, boy? You want some of this? Or should I say, sir?
      (Mocking.)

Sir . . . now how does that sound? Sir? Boy Sir? Sir Boy? Now do you want people to be going around saying "Sir, this . . . Sir, that?" Huh? Do you? How about if I said, "'Sir, come and get some of this . . . come get your goodies." How would you like that?

(Moves closer to him and less clumsy.)

Let's leave that kind of sir stuff to my old hubby. . . . That stupid clunk. We'll just be more . . .

(The Gentleman rises, turns his back and moves away from Madame, moving to the bookcase where he lifts a heavy tome. Madame covers herself, exasperated.)

Why . . . I never . . . you're not going to read . . .

(She attacks him and tries to claw the book from his hands; he shoves her to the floor.)

Why you . . . you . . .

(He waggles his finger at her as she rises and pulls the service cord. She is anxious.)

Mamie . . . Mamie . . . where are you? . . . Can't you hear me ringing for you? Where is she? She couldn't have been serious about leaving. What shall I do? Mr. Mann will help.

(Calls.)

Mr. Mann! Mr. Mann! . . . come out right away. Do you hear me? At once, Mr. Mann! Ohhh . . . what's wrong with him? . . . Why won't someone come? Mr. Mann, you have company . . . a guest . . . a guest, Mr. Mann. He's waiting for you. Been here a long time waiting, Mr. Mann.

(She sighs, picks up a cigarette from a jeweled case and lights it. Then pours herself tea, composes herself and sizes up the situation. She sits, blows out smoke and sips tea.)

So you don't want me? . . . Hmmmm . . . times have really changed, haven't they?

(Annoyed, calls.)

Mr. Mann! . . . Mr. Mann! . . .

(Disgust.)

Ohhh, that man . . . What could he be doing? . . . and for so long? Always pretending to shave. . . . He'll never be without that damn white beard of his . . .

(The Gentleman moves involuntarily. Madame notices movement.)

Say . . . what goes on . . .

(Testing.)

. . . All I said was that he'll never be without that damned beard . . .

(Guest flinches.)

. . . of his . . .

(Under her breath.)

. . . he'll have it to the day he dies . . .

(Raises voice.)

. . . Oh, I'm beginning to see . . . I see now.

(To guest.)

You wouldn't want that, would you? Not that?

THE GENTLEMAN CALLER   377

(The Gentleman smiles for the first time.)
You would?
(Hilarious.)
Oh ha ha ha . . .
(She laughs very unladylike for a full minute.)
Oh, you have to be joking. You must be . . . you just can't be serious?
(He nods.)
Oh, how marvelous! Ha ha ha . . . heee heee heee. . . . Oh, dear . . . pardon
me, Sir, while I bust a dignified gut . . . ha ha . . . And for this you came so
. . . ha ha . . . so goddamned far. Oh, my god, how diabolical history is!
(The telephone rings. Catches breath.)
That damned thing again . . . doesn't he ever sleep?
(Ignores phone, to Gentleman.)
Don't you want to tell me . . . no, you don't. But just think of it . . . with
me here thinking . . . thinking . . . that . . . ha ha ha . . . You beautiful young
man, you. . . . You've made my day . . . no . . . ha ha . . . my life . . .
complete . . . ha ha . . .
(Irritated.)
Oh, Mamie, come on and answer the phone.
(Laughs more.)
MAMIE . . . MR. MANN . . . ALL OF YOU COME HERE. . . . THIS IS SIMPLY
TOO TOO . . . JUST TOO MARVELOUS FOR WORDS . . . HA HA HA . . .
(Wipes away tears.)
They won't come yet. Still playing their roles. *But if they only knew.* Why
doesn't she get that phone?
(Rises.)
Here, let me pour you some more tea.
(Touches his hand as she pours.)
Isn't there anything else I can get you? . . . Are you comfortable enough?
(Returns to her seat.)
My my . . . well, here we are. How nice. It isn't all that stuffy, is it? Really,
we do have a certain style about us, wouldn't you admit? A style that we've
acquired down through the years . . . from practice, from tradition. From
living with certain precepts in mind. It's not all soft, our life, you know.
There's a certain rigidness of the spiritual fibers . . . a kinda mystical deter-
minism of the psyche, you might say . . . a certain attitude of predestination
. . . a preordained vision of ecclesiastical rank. Keeps one's uppers tight
behind his or her straight lip, I might say. In fact, and I shall say, for I
know; I'm an expert, a virtual veteran with a daddy who was all blood and
entrails . . . all spit, sweat and shit. But *that* husband of mine . . . *him.*
(Angry.)
Mamie, answer it, please!
(A muffled scream off. She starts, frightened.)
What was that? Did you hear that?
*(The visitor smiles. Noise off of something being dragged or moved.
Relieved.)*
But here they come now. And now we can get down to cases, heh, boy?

For this is *your* story, isn't it? Now about you, my good little laddy-buck. About you . . .

    (Breaks off. Thoroughly agitated, lifts phone. In a voice of distinction.)

Hello, the Mann residence. Hello? Hello?

    (Hangs up.)

I wonder why he won't speak to me?

    (Noise off. Exaggerated aside.)

Hark! Hark! Methinks I hear the restless native stirring.

Maid:

    (Off, coming closer. Sings.)

Now hare come de judge . . . Hare come de judge . . . yeah . . . Now ev'va body git demself together . . . cause hare come de judge.

Madame: In here, Mamie . . . in here!

    *(**Maid** enters, dragging **Mr. Mann's** dead body by the heels.)*

Maid:

    (Stepin Fetchit image.)

I'se comin', Missy . . . I'se comin' fast as I can. . . .

    (She moves remarkably slow.)

. . . Feets . . . do yo duty.

    *(**Mr. Mann** is made up much like **Mrs. Mann**, except that he has on shorts that are cut from an American flag, and he wears socks that are star spangled. **Madame** is extremely calm; she circles **Mr. Mann**, her eyes upon the **Maid**. The **Gentleman** stands, looking down at **Mr. Mann's** beard.)*

Madame:

    (Interrogator.)

And now, Miss Mamie Lee King, dear, you admit that Mr. Mann is dead?

Maid: Yas'sum.

Madame: . . . you found him dead . . . dead in the john?

Maid: Yas'sum.

Madame: . . . dead from a self-inflicted wound in the throat . . .

Maid: If you say so . . . ma'am.

Madame: . . . from a straight razor!

Maid: Yas'sum. From a straight razor.

Madame:

    (Distaste.)

Well, so much for details. . . . Now let's see what shall we do? . . . hmmm. What do you suggest, Mamie? You always keep a level head in these kinds of emergencies.

    *(The **Maid** ponders. The **Gentleman** crouches down on all fours and with much trepidation touches **Mr. Mann's** white beard, appears astounded and snatches the beard off **Mr. Mann's** face.)*

Madame: Yes, it's false . . . Surprised, huh?

Maid: Wahl, dere's only one thing to do, ma'am, as I sees it.

Madame: Good . . . like I always say . . . you can always be depended upon. . . . You good nigger, you. I don't know what Mr. Mann and I would have done without you all these years . . .

*(She turns to the **Gentleman**; the **Maid** goes to the mantle and takes a pump-action shot gun from the rifle rack. The phone begins to ring.)*
Do you know that even when I was just a little girl I never feared for Mamie was there. She was like the mountains . . . unchanging. Like time . . . limitless. Always faithful . . . always the source of inspiration. Young . . .
(Paternal.)
. . . young man, you can be proud you sprang from her loins. You can be thankful for having the very salt of the earth . . . the very blood and marrow of the universe as . . .
*(The **Maid** shoots **Madame** in the head. The body falls and the **Maid** stands over the bloody body, pumping shells into the gun's chamber and firing them into the twitching corpse.)*

Maid:
(Loads gun from shell taken from her apron pocket.)
Okay, boy, you grab him and drag him in the hallway!
*(She points gun. The **Gentleman** looks dazed and confused.)*
Don't you hear me talkin' ta ya? Boy, put down that ole piece of hair . . . it came from between mah granny's legs, anyway. Now I've taken enough of yo silly behind stuff . . . grab his feet like I said.
*(The **Gentleman** grabs **Mr. Mann's** feet and drags him off, the beard stuffed in the **Gentleman's** coat pocket. The **Maid** drags **Madame** off by the back of the collar. The telephone continues ringing. A shot is heard off, and the lights turn to red and blues. New Black music plays: Sun Ra, or Milford Graves, etc. The **Maid** returns wearing an exotic gown of her own design. Her bandana has been taken off; her au naturel hair style complements her strong Black features. She answers the phone.)*

Maid:
(Black and correct.)
Hello. Yes, you wish to speak to the madame? Yes, she is speaking.
(Pause.)
Yes, father . . . the time is now. It is time for Black people to come together. It is time for Black people to rise from their knees and come together in unity, brotherhood and Black spirituality to form a nation that will rise from our enslaved mass and meet the oppressor . . . meet the devil and conquer and destroy him.
*(Slow curtain as the **Queen Mother** speaks into the phone passionately.)*
Yes, we are rising, father. We are forming the foretold Black nation that will survive, conquer and rule under your divine guidance. We Black people are preparing for the future. We are getting ready for the long war ahead of us. DEATH TO THE ENEMIES OF THE BLACK PEOPLE!
All praises is due to the Blackman.

Blackout.

A BLACK BLACK COMEDY IN THREE ACTS

NO PLACE TO BE SOMEBODY

by Charles Gordone

Charles Gordone *(1925-   )*

Charles Gordone, an extremely promising young black playwright, won the Pulitzer Prize for drama in 1970 for his first produced play, *No Place To Be Somebody*. It was the first time the prize had ever been awarded to an off-Broadway production and the first time it was won by a black playwright. Thus he became the third black person to win a Pulitzer Prize, following Monetta J. Sleet, photographer—1969—and Gwendolyn Brooks, poet—1950. Gordone describes himself as being of Negro, French, Italian, Irish, and American-Indian descent. But "first of all," he says, "we're niggers . . . you know, we're black." Born in Elkhart, Indiana, he was educated in the public schools there until, as he puts it, when in high school he was literally "run out of town by delinquent young black boys from the other side of the tracks." His father was a garage mechanic, his mother was for a time a dancer in Harlem's Cotton Club in the Duke Ellington days, and for a time a circus performer. "Of course," Gordone says, "there were no spades in the circuses then, but she passed and became an acrobat." She later became a speech teacher in Cleveland, Ohio, and still teaches in Indiana. "She was a fine actress," Gordone says, "but my parents got religion. They became Seventh Day Adventists and strong vegetarians. I had housemaid's knee when I was seven from praying."

After leaving Indiana, he went to Los Angeles where he enrolled at U.C.L.A. But, as he says, "my head wasn't ready to study," so he joined the army. Coming out of the service and "not knowing a damn thing that I wanted to do," he entered Los Angeles City College as a music major and was slowly drawn to the drama department. In 1952 he arrived in New York and three weeks later landed a part in a Moss Hart play.

Charles Gordone, like Douglas Turner Ward and Ossie Davis, brings to his work as a playwright an extensive theatrical experience. As an actor, he was in the original production of Genet's *The Blacks* and won an award for the Best Actor of the Year off-Broadway in Luther James's all-black production of *Of Mice and Men;* he also played the title role in *The Trials of Brother Jero* by the African playwright, Wole Soyinka. He has directed many shows, including, in 1959, *Faust,* the first production of the Judson Poets' Theater. Mr. Gordone was also founder and co-chairman, with Godfrey Cambridge, of the Committee for the Employment of Negro Performers, and he was the associate producer of the film *Nothing But a Man. No Place To Be Somebody,* in addition to the Pulitzer Prize, won for him a Drama Desk Award in 1969, while the critics hailed him as the best new American playwright since Edward Albee. Mr. Gordone has three plays on tap, at which he is presently working.

INTRODUCTION

No Place To Be Somebody, A Black Black Comedy in Three Acts, was aptly described by *Time Magazine's* reviewer as "a black panther of a play," which "stalks the off-Broadway stage as if it were an urban jungle, snarling and clawing with unbridled fury at the contemporary fabric of black-white and black-black relations." A long, possibly overlong work—it takes some three hours to perform—but an unmistakably powerful and moving play, *No Place To Be Somebody* is a brilliant fantasia of rage, and fury, and fear; of insecurity, of love and hate, imaginatively presented through the means of a symphonic blending of realism, naturalism, poetry, gangster movie melodrama, comedy, surrealism, and *soul.* We are told that it took Gordone eight years to complete this play and some three years of promotion before it attracted the attention of Joseph Papp who accepted it for a workshop presentation at The Other Stage of the New York Shakespeare Festival Public Theater. The critical acclaim accorded the play was such that it was moved to the Anspacher Theater where it began its professional run on May 4, 1969.

Produced by Joseph Papp, the play was directed by Ted Cornell, with sets and lighting designed by Michael Davidson. The large mixed cast included Ron O'Neal (Gabe Gabriel), Nathan George (Johnny Williams), Walter Jones (Sweets Crane) in the leading roles, and Marge Eliot as Cora Beasely, a simple-minded but wily black nurse in search of a white lover, Ronnie Thompson as an addled young white bartender, a hipster yearning to be black, Susan G. Pearson and Lynda Wescott as prostitutes—white and black —in Johnny Williams' stable, Howard Baker, as an awkward Negro pseudo-aesthete, interested in the ballet and white "culture," and Laurie Crews as a liberal college graduate, idealistically, at first, interested in the Civil Rights Movement.

For two weeks in late 1969 and early 1970 the play enjoyed a prestigious "show case" run on Broadway sponsored by Alfred de Liagre, Jr. and Jean Dalrymple of the American National Theater and Academy at the ANTA

Theatre. It then, under the co-production of the author's wife, Jeanne Warner, and Ashton Springer, moved to the off-Broadway Promenade Theatre where it was playing when to the delight of many it won the Puliter Prize for drama.

Although few critics could belie its power and intensity, its undeniable commitment, and the richness, authenticity, and turbulence of its language, many critics were wary about Gordone's dramaturgy, or the structural aspects of his play, declaring it to be overwritten, cumbersome and in need of drastic editing. It was held to be lacking in clarity of idea and, therefore, murky so far as its basic statements were concerned. The plot was held to be episodic and implausible in incident and detail; the gangster pyrotechnics were lamented as merely melodramatic; and what Aristotelians would call *unity of effect* was felt to be dissipated by the fusion of realistic and surrealist techniques. Clayton Riley, sadly, indulges himself in most of these objections, as does his recent antagonist, Martin Gottfried, with perhaps less acidity. And Richard Watts, Jr. in a *New York Post* article "Second Best New American Play," despite a pronounced admiration for Gordone's work, declares that it suffers from the fact that in its final minutes "it turns into extreme melodrama, there are four characters lying dead on the stage from gunfire, while a fifth has committed suicide off stage." In his view the play suffers because of its melodramatic nature which precludes it from attaining the high dignity of tragedy.

In my opinion, this kind of criticism is patently and indisputably mistaken and is representative of a failure to come to grips with the metaphorical aspects of the play, and to recognize the imaginative force of accumulative detail, not intended in every instance to be taken literally, and from misconceptions on the nature of melodrama and the brilliance of the functionalism of Gordone's technique, purposively designed to provide, within old rubrics, new and freshly expressed insights on the options available to the black man on the contemporary American scene.

So far as the play as a whole is concerned, I think that Walter Kerr of the *Times* is most astute when he describes it as "complex, rich, garish, improbable, overburdened, defiant, and successful." For the purposes of our analysis, let us underscore the word *successful* and go on to hear, in part at this point, what Mr. Kerr has to say: "Mr. Gordone wishes to keep every observable, every conceivable aspect of the black-white love-hate relationship alive in his head and alive in ours, without cant, without bias, without coming to any absolute conclusion except that terrifying contraries exist simultaneously." Gordone himself says of his play, "Trouble with niggers is that they're hung up on color. Some want to be all white and others want to be all black. But the black experience isn't all black and the white world isn't all white."

So far as melodrama as a genre is concerned, we can turn to the analysis of Professor Robert W. Corrigan who points out that "all drama is built upon catastrophe (literally, a shift in direction)—any event which overturns the previously existing order or system of things. As such, catastrophe is itself devoid of moral meanings, and is equally capable of producing joy and happiness or sadness and grief depending upon the context in which it occurs. The first important characteristic of melodrama, and it is this which finally distinguishes it from all other dramatic forms, is the fact that all the significant 'catastrophic' events which occur are caused by forces outside the protagonists." Professor Corrigan suggests that the term "melodrama," because it has acquired so many negative connotations ought perhaps to be dropped and substituted by the designation "drama of disaster." "Disaster," this critic asserts, "means 'that which happens because of the stars,' and as such it is an apt metaphor for the unhappiness and suffering that come to men from without—i.e., from nature, society, or other individuals."[1] The events in "the drama of disaster," or if you will of melodrama, can be just as painful and moving as the events of tragedy, although the forms are profoundly different. "Unlike tragedy, in the drama of disaster the protagonist(s) is a victim who is acted upon; his moral quality is not essential to the event, and his suffering does not imply an inevitable related guilt—in fact, there need not be any meaningful relation between the suffering of the protagonist and the cause and nature of the event."[2] It is also observed that melodrama also defined simply as drama with music and lyrics, like its musical counterpart, opera, is a grandiose theatrical style—"the characters of melodrama conceive of themselves constantly in histrionic terms; the source of their vitality and appeal are visceral and not intellectual."[3] In this connection it can be noted that critics who applauded the play most strongly admired No Place To Be Somebody for its vigorous theatricality, its music and lyrics, as well as for its ideas and commitment.

The play is intricately designed to function on two levels: on one level, the physical action takes place in a seedy West Village bar run by a black man, Johnny Williams; on the subjective and interpretative level, the action exists in the mind of the prophetic Gabe Gabriel, a poetic and philosophical figure who serves as a writer, narrator, chorus and actor in the play itself. The physical action is presented as part of a play being written by Gabe Gabriel, a black but fair-skinned actor, who is unsuccessful in getting parts because he is too white for black roles. Gabe the raconteur is also the raisonneur; the spokesman of the author, he is also the contemplative counterpart of the rough, unprincipled, violent Johnny Williams, the central figure of his play. Each of the three acts opens with a stirring soliloquy or prologue which sets the mood for the scene, gives unity to the play, and makes eloquently salient comments on the black situation.

At the opening of the play, Gabriel is seated at his typewriter; Machine Dog, the visionary black militant, who appears on a number of occasions— seen only by Johnny Williams, therefore, representing Johnny's deeper conscience—is also in the foreground. Gabe, rising from his writing, puffing on a marijuana cigarette, addresses the audience, announcing that he will be making up the play in his head as he goes along, warning that no matter

1. Robert W. Corrigan, ed., Laurel British Drama: The Nineteenth Century (New York: Dell Publishing Co., Inc., 1967), pp. 7-8.
2. Ibid., pp. 8-9.
3. Ibid., p. 10.

how far out he goes, it is not a figment of his grassy imagination, " 'Cause it ain't!" Then, holding a Bible high above his head, he declaims:

And I heard a Voice between the banks
of the U'Lai. And it called, Gabriel! Gabriel!
Make this man understand the vision! So He came
near where I stood! And when He came, I was
frightened and fell upon my face!

The action of Gabriel's play covers a fifteen-year time span in a West Village bar owned and operated by a youngish black crook, a pimp, and hustler, Johnny Williams ("Jay Cee ag'inst the worl'!"), a victim of his background and a victim of his sense of black militance and Black Power, who in his search for a place to be somebody covets a piece of the action, dominated by the white Mafia, and, indeed, to set up his own black Mafia. Cora says of him: "Never had no papa. 'Less you call that ol' dog Sweets Crane a father. His mama was always sickly an' she did drink. Never would give it out though! Who it was did it to her. Carried that to her grave! . . . I knowed her ever since I was a l'il girl down South. You know there was always sump'n funny 'bout her. Swore Jay Cee was born with a veil over his face." And she explains, "Ev'body knows babys born with veils over they faces is s'pose to see ghosts an' raise forty-one kin's of hell."

Johnny's Bar is patronized by a strange miscellany of blacks and whites —prostitutes, gangsters, ex-cons, bohemian drifters, civil-righters, crooked politicians. The setting is organic to the meaning of the play, a kind of lower depths, it is a microcosm of the culture, the society, and the world of the people who frequent it and find sustenance in its being. Hence the play has been compared to Eugene O'Neill's *The Iceman Cometh* and William Saroyan's *The Time of Your Life*. But *No Place To Be Somebody* is its own thing. It is a black play, its hero is black, pained, anguished, raising impious battle against his version of the white power structure. Symbolically Johnny's Bar becomes another urban inferno not unlike Jones's subway in *Dutchman*. But because of the larger canvas the distress is magnified, and the saloon becomes a center of multiplied rage, conflict, violence, and death. Gordone says of his characters, "They are the dispossessed. After a few drinks, they feel like somebody for a while. It's like they're trapped in themselves and there is no exit." When asked in an interview what the statement of his play was, Gordone responded that it has to do with the question of identity and where we are today. "We're all of us looking . . . for a slot . . . to try to find out just who and what we are. Sometimes we're stumped . . . we're stumped by the obstacles that are put in our way. And, if we can, some-times we invent fantasies that somehow for the time suffice us but it never does."

As the play proceeds it becomes increasingly clear that Gabe Gabriel and his creation, Johnny Williams, are one—that they are symbolic mani-festations of two aspects of the black psyche—two aspects of contemporary black aspiration. Both, in their search for identity, are smitten by what Sweets

NO PLACE TO BE SOMEBODY 387

Crane will later define as "Charlie fever." Although Gabe is given to mocking himself as he sings, "Whiter than snow, yes! Whiter than snow! Now wash me, and I shall be Whiter than snow!", he demonstrates throughout the play an increasing awareness of his blackness, or, if you will, his basic proximity to Johnny, and later when he first eats "soul food" cooked by Sweets Crane, to the very black Sweets himself. But his growing sense of his blackness, and his intellectual ambivalence towards it, is seen in his, at first, mocking, irreverent—"funky," Johnny calls it—poetry.

Consider, simply, the many faceted dimensions of the poem he declaims in the bar (Act I, Scene I) to the amusement and amazement of his audience, on the March on Washington, led by Martin Luther King, Jr., in 1963. This wonderfully rendered bravura aria, including references to warring black ideologies, worked up in terms of a doggerel parody of "The Night Before Christmas," ends with the lines:

> Now junkies don't dilly
> You hustlers don't dally!
> Don't waste your time smokin' pot
> In some park or some alley,
> 'Cause Charlie is watchin' you!
>
> Well he would'a went that'a way
> To this very day but his th'oat
> It got too hoarse!
> When he sat down wasn't a clap ner a soun',
> Couldn't tell if he'd got to the end!
> A cracker preacher there, then said a prayer!
> Said civil rights you could not fo'ce!
> By this time I was so confused that my head was in a spin!
> Somebody else got up with a grinnin' face!
> Said to leave the place like we found it!
> Tha's when I reached in my pocket an' pulled out my packet an'
>   before everybody took a sip'a my wine!
> Then we lef' the place with ne'r a trace!
> An' we didn't leave ne'r chit'lin' behin'!

Significantly, Gabe, the nearly-white Negro, is something of a parasite. He lives on Johnny, who stakes him out to money, flinging bills at him. "Aw, take the bread, nigger." And then Johnny says, "Look'a here, Gabe. I know you think I'm up 'side the wall. You hip to the books an' all like'a that. But ser-us-ly! Why ain't they doin' you no good?" And the first scene progresses to this conclusion:

Gabe: Let's jus' say I ain't in no big rush.
Johnny: It's Charlie, ain't it?
Gabe: What about Charlie?

Johnny: It's wrote all over you! Might be foolin' some people. Cock-a-doodle-dooin' an' comin' on with yo' funky po'try. . . .

Gabe: When you git me some answers other than the one's you been handin' me, I'll git in the bed with you.

Johnny: One thing Sweets says to me, 'fore he got his time. He says . . .

Gabe: Screw it, John. When you start bringin' Sweets into the picture, I know exactly what's comin' next. The answer is still negative.

Johnny: Still wanna believe you kin sell papers an' become president, huh? Snowballs in Egypt.

Gabe: I ain't lookin' to break no law.

Johnny: They ain't no law. They kill you an' me in the name'a the law. You an' me wouldn't be where we at, if it wasn't for the law. Even the laws they write for us makes us worse off.

Gabe: From the git-go, they don't operate like Sweets anymore. Harlem's all caught up.

Johnny: Who's operatin' in Harlem?

Gabe: You cain't be thinkin' about down here! It was branchin' out'a Harlem got Sweets where he's at right now.

Johnny: Man, what you think I been doin' the ten years Sweets been in the joint? I tell you the scheme is together. Me an' him gon' git us a piece'a this town.

Gabe: An' end up on the bottom'a the East River with it tied aroun' your necks.

Johnny: Bet we'll have us a box'a crackers under each arm if we do!

Gabe: Well, I don't dig crackers that much.

Johnny: Okay, Hollywood! Keep knockin' on doors with yo' jeans at half-mast. Sellin' yo'self like some cheap-ass whore. If I know one thing about you, you ain't that good'a actor. Whitey knows right away you cain't even stan' to look at him.

If Gabe Gabriel is the raconteur, the raisonneur, and the chorus of his play, and if Johnny Williams is the protagonist and the doomed victim, Sweets Crane, another victim, is, in classic theater terms, the moriturus. A father figure and a kind of tribal god, Johnny worships him as the only father he has ever known, and as the man who has taught him all he knows. The venerable and legendary black leader of the rackets in Harlem, Sweets Crane returns to Johnny's bar after ten years in "the slammers." But he is an altered man—humiliated, unrecognized, in tatters—he is ill, broken, and dying. As he says, the doctors tell him that he has "six months to ride." As the moriturus, he is the solemn voice of wisdom and thus becomes a second raisonneur in the play, who, on the verge of death, hands down the sum of his experience to the next generation. He is also a Christ figure in his penitential wish to save Johnny by the provisions of his will, which he hopes will help Johnny to get himself straightened out, and by the actual sacrifice of his own life for him. And as he prophesies, he will die between two thieves, Maffuci and Johnny. Before the final moments of the play he eats his Last Supper of Soul Food: "I got fried chicken! Ham! Candied yams! Got me some hot chit'lin's! Blackeyed peas an' rice! Cornbread! Mustard greens an' macaroni salit! Top ev'thing off I got me a thermos full'a—full'a —lemme see now. How'd my gran'daddy used to call it? Chassy San'burg coffee! An' a big chunk'a pee-kan pie." Gabe and Maffucci both partake of this supper. Gabe, significantly enough, eating chit'lin's for the first time.

But Sweets Crane's reformation, his being "all caught up with the rackets," and his death also symbolize the death of an illusion. "Sonny Boy, git us a plan," he had urged Johnny when he went up the river, and for ten years Johnny has been dreaming feverishly of their joining in a war against the Mafia, his version of the white power structure. But Sweets defines himself and Johnny when he repentantly declares:

> You got the Charlie fever, Johnny. Tha's what you got. I gave it to you. Took yo' chile's min' an' filled it with the Charlie fever. Givin' you a education or teachin' you to dinner-pail, didn't seem to me no way for you to grow up an be respected like'a man. Way we was raised, husslin' an' usin' yo' bisquit to pull quickies was the only way we could feel like we was men. Couldn't copy Charlie's good points an' live like men. So we copied his bad points. That was the way it was with my daddy an' his daddy before him. We just pissed away our lives tryin' to be like bad Charlie. With all our fine clothes an' big cars. All it did was make us hate him all the more an' ourselves too. Then I tried to go horse-to-horse with 'em up there in the Bronx. An' ended up with a ten. All because'a the Charlie fever. I gave you the Charlie fever, Johnny. An' I'm sorry! Seems to me, the worse sickness'a man kin have is the Charlie fever.

A brilliant counterpart is given to this concept when Gabe goes into his recitative, "They's mo' to bein' black than meets the eye!"

> They's mo' to bein' black than meets the
> Eye!
> Bein' black is like the way ya walk an'
> Talk!
> It's a way'a lookin' at life!
> Bein' black, is like sayin', "Wha's happenin',
> Babee!"
> An' bein' understood!
> Bein' black has a way'a makin' ya call some-
> Body a mu-tha-fuc-kah, an' really meanin' it!
> An' namin' eva'body broth-thah, even if you don't!
> Bein' black, is eatin' chit'lins an' wah-tah-
> Melon, an' to hell with anybody, if they don't
> Like it!

. . . .
Carryin' a razor! Smokin' boo an' listenin' to
Gut-bucket jazz!
. . . .
Bein' black is gittin' down loud an' wrong! Uh-huh!
It's makin' love without no hangups! . . .
. . . .
Bein' black has a way'a makin' ya mad mos'
Of the time, hurt all the time an' havin'
So many hang-ups, the problem'a soo-side
Don't even enter yo' min'! It's buyin'
What you don't want, beggin' what you don't
Need! An' stealin' what is yo's by rights! . . .
. . . .
It's all the stuff that nobody wants but
Cain't live without!
It's the body that keeps us standin'! The
Soul that keeps us goin'! An' the spirit
That'll take us thooo!
Yes! They's mo' to bein' black than meets
The eye!

And Gabe sits down at a table, cuts into a gun on a plate before him with a knife and fork, picks up the gun, bites into it and chews and swallows, then washes it down with a Molotov cocktail and cries out: "Bru-thas an' sistahs! Will you jine me!"

Although the plot is complex and at times episodic, it is not wayward, nor is it without a recognizable design. Aside from the major trinity, with Machine Dog as an important extension of Johnny's imagination and psyche, the many other persons in the play can be seen as representing allegorical presences in various states of assimilation, accommodation, alienation, and spiritual disarray, symptomatic of the soul destroying sickness of "Charlie fever." In a mixture then of metaphor and melodrama, the play moves to its appointed end. The bar is preyed on by the Mafia. Johnny persists in his heedless search for revenge, indifferent as to whether it will lead to triumph or destruction, and the bar is finally devoured by the Mafia.

In the development of the play, there is a discernible resolution of vectors as the characters surround each other, pair off and finally provide a meaningful structural balance. The characters all, of course, relate to Johnny in varying degrees of intensity, but there are other pairings of deep importance. There are Cora and Shanty Mulligan; Dee and Evie, as they relate to Johnny and to each other; Gabe and Melvin; Gabe and Dee; and as Mr. Kerr points out, it is Gordone's habit "to press his confrontations until they become reversals, until the roles are changed." There is a subtle symmetry and design in these pairings that provide us with insights into the inner meanings of the play.

NO PLACE TO BE SOMEBODY   391

Johnny's doom has been foreshadowed many times in the course of the play, but it is made implicit in the third scene of the final act, when Machine Dog enters to say:

On yo' feet, mothah fuckah!
By the powers invested in me by the brothers
I hereby deliver to you the edick! Brother
Williams. The brothers have jus' sennunced an' condemned you to death. Now, repeat after me.
I have been chosen to be the nex' brother to live on in the hearts an' min's'a the enemy host.

And he is told that his duty will be "to ha'nt they cripple an' sore min's."

Then the final confrontation with the Mafia is built up. When Maffucci attempts to humiliate Johnny, to make him take low, Sweets defiantly and purposely intervenes, lunges at the gangster with the knife he has been eating with and plunges it into his heart as Maffucci fires at him. Johnny shoots down another gangster and turns to fire three times into Maffucci's body. The dying Sweets reminds Johnny of the will—"If—if you git out'a this. Promise you'll git straightened out. Promise."

Johnny: I—I promise.
Sweets: Swear!
Johnny: Yeah! Yeah! I swear, Sweets!
Sweets: Git-git rid'a the—the Ch-Charlie fever—

But Johnny is unrepentant. He will proceed, he tells Gabe, with his plans, and holding up the will, he says "An' he's still goin' help me do it." Gabe says: "Naw, naw! That ain't the way it's s'pose to be! . . . I ain't got no stomach for this personal war you got ag'inst the white man." Johnny declares: "It's your war too, nigger. Why can't you see that? You wanna go on believin' in this lie? We at war, Gabe! Black ag'inst white." And Gabe replies: "You're wrong, John. You're so goddam wrong."

At this point Johnny puts his gun into Gabe's hand, insisting that he feel "the cold hard steel" because he is going to have to use it, "They gon' make you do it. 'Cause we at war, Gabe. Black ag'inst white." Gabe says: "I—I don't wanna—kill—you. . . ." And Johnny snorts: "You ain't got the guts! You wanna believe you kin sell papers an' become President! You're a coward, Gabe! A lousy, yellow, screamin' faggot coward!" Enraged by this, Gabe fires at Johnny who tumbles backward and then falls forward into Gabe's arms. Thus Gabe is compelled to kill his blacker counterpart and they are finally joined in an embrace of death and love. For Machine Dog appears to the startled Gabe saying: "The Brothers call me Machine Dog! It is written: 'He that slays a true brother, he hisse'f shall howsomever be perished!' "

In the brief Epilogue, the near-white black, Gabe, now neither male nor female, with the wisdom of Tiresias, dressed as a woman in mourning, a black shawl draped over his head, addressing the audience as a mirror declares: "I must try to provoke you. . . . I am the 'Black Lady in Mourning,' but my cries will not be heard. . . . I shall mourn the death of a people dying into new life."

Regarding the play as a whole, it seems likely that Gabe Gabriel (Charles Gordone) protests too much when he says "Because I call myself a black playwright, don't git the impression I'm hung up on crap like persecution an' hatred. 'Cause I ain't! I'm gonna leave that violence jazz to them cats who are better at it than me." He continues "don't think . . . my play is about Negro self-pity. Or even that ol' 'You-owe-me-whitey party line' 'Cause it ain't. In spite of what I learned in college, it did not give me that introduction to success, equality an' wealth, that to my parents were the most logical alternatives to heaven. Anyway, like I say, I'm gonna leave that social protest jive to them cats who are better equipped than me."

In this connection, Richard L. Coe, of the *Washington Post,* in a discerning commentary on the play notes that *No Place To Be Somebody* is a richly considered deep and deeply black statement, for the basic reason that "throughout the incidents and character developments there runs the effect on the blacks of having lived hundreds of years in a white world. Whitey's crimes, in this lower depths of existence, are not the crimes they seem to be to whites." Coe reports that Gordone speaking of his work cogently observed that, "There can't be a black writer in this country worth his salt who doesn't portray the sting of racism. If he doesn't he is a fool, an idiot. . . . A man writes about what he comes from. . . . If you are going to talk about black people, include the humanity of all people, the love of all people, the will to survive and the will to live of all people against fantastic odds." This, Coe says, is what *No Place To Be Somebody* does include—"not characters in their own vacuum but people living in the swirl of others. That the play might have been less complex, less occasionally confusing cannot be denied. But this is less important than the fact that a new playwright has glimpsed drama not for its anemic self-obsession but for its rich involvement with the rest of humanity."

No Place to Be Somebody

To the memory of Sidney Bernstein,
producer of "The Blacks"

CHARACTERS

Gabe Gabriel, a *young fairskinned Negro*
Shanty Mulligan, a *young white man*
Johnny Williams, a *young Negro*
Dee Jacobson, a *young white woman*
Evie Ames, a *young Negro woman*
Cora Beasely, a *young Negro woman*
Melvin Smeltz, a *young Negro man*
Mary Lou Bolton, a *white girl*
Ellen, a *white girl*
Sweets Crane, an *elderly Negro*
Mike Maffucci, a *young white man*
Truck Driver, a *young white man*
Judge Bolton, a *middle aged white man, father of Mary Lou*
Machine Dog, a *young Negro (in Johnny's imagination)*
Sergeant Cappaletti, a *young white man*
Harry, a *Negro detective*
Louis, a *young white man*

Act One

SCENE 1

Time: *The past fifteen years*
Place: *New York City*
Setting: *Johnny's Bar*
At Rise: **Gabe** *sits near jukebox, typing. Rips page from typewriter. Balls it up, flings it angrily at audience.*

Gabe: Excuse me. Forgot you were out there. My name is Gabe. Gabe Gabriel, to be exact. I'm a writer. Didn't mean to lose my temper. Something I've been working on all my life. Not losing my temper.
(Takes out marihuana cigarette. Lights it. Inhales it. Holds smoke in.)
Right now I'm working on a play. They say if you wanna be a writer you gotta go out an' live. I don't believe that no more. Take my play for instance.

Might not believe it but I'm gonna make it all up in my head as I go along. Before I prove it to you, wanna warn you not to be thinkin' I'm tellin' you a bunch'a barefaced lies. An' no matter how far out I git, don't want you goin' out'a here with the idea what you see happenin' is all a figment of my grassy imagination. 'Cause it ain't!

(He picks up Bible from table. Raises it above his head. Without looking turns pages.)

"And I heard a Voice between the banks of the U'Lai. And it called, Gabriel! Gabriel! Make this man understand the vision! So He came near where I stood! And when He came, I was frightened and fell upon my face!"

(He closes Bible. As he exits, lights dim out, then come up on **Shanty,** at jukebox. Jazz is playing. **Shanty** takes out his drumsticks. Begins to rap on bar. **Johnny** enters. Hangs up raincoat and umbrella.)

Johnny: Cool it, Shanty.

Shanty: Man, I'm practicing.

Johnny: Damned if that bar's anyplace for it. Git on that floor there.

Shanty:

(Puts drumsticks away. Takes broom.)

Ever tell you 'bout the time I went to this jam session? Max Roach was there. Lemme sit in for him.

Johnny: Said you played jus' like a spade.

Shanty: What's wrong with that? Ol' Red Taylor said wasn't nobody could hold a beat an' steady cook it like me. Said I had "the thing!" Member one time we played "Saints." For three hours, we played it.

Johnny: Had to git a bucket'a col' water an' throw it on you to git you to quit, huh?

Shanty: One these days I'm gonna have me a boss set'a skins for my comeback. Me an' Cora was diggin' a set up on "Four-Six Street." Sump'm else ag'in. Bass drum, dis'pearin' spurs, snares, tom-toms. . . .

Johnny: Gon' steal 'em?

Shanty: I been savin' up. Gonna git me them drums. Know what I'm gonna do then? I'm gonna quit you flat. Go for that. Sheee! I ain't no lifetime apron. That's for damned sure.

Johnny: Yeah, well meantime how 'bout finishin' up on that floor? Time to open the store.

(**Dee** and **Evie** enter. Hang coats up.)

You broads let them two ripe apples git away from you, huh?

Dee: Don't look at me.

Evie: Aw, later for you an' your rich Texas trade.

Dee: Just gettin' too damned sensitive.

Evie: Sensitive my black behin'! Excuse me, I mean black ass.

(Goes to jukebox. Punches up number.)

Dee: Last night we bring those two Johns up to her pad. An' like, Jack? One with the cowboy hat? Stoned? Like out of his skull. And like out of nowhere he starts cryin'.

Evie: All weekend it was, "Nigger this an' Nigger that."

Dee: Never bothered you before. I didn't like it when he started sayin' things like, "The black son'sa bitches are gettin' to be untouchables! Takin' over the country!"

Evie: Bet he'll think twice before he says sump'm like that ag'in.

Dee: That lamp I gave her? One the senator brought me back from Russia? Evie goes an' breaks it over his head.

Johnny: What the hell'd you do that for?

Evie: Sure hated to lose that lamp.

Johnny: Wouldn't care if they b'longed to the Ku Klux Klan long's they gimme the bread.

(He goes into Dee's purse.)

Shanty: Sure had plenty of it too! When they was in here, they kept buyin' me drinks. Thought I was the boss.

Johnny: Crackers cain't 'magine Niggers runnin' nothin' but elevators an' toilets.

Dee: Leave me somethin', please.

Evie: Ain't gon' do nothin' with it nohow.

Johnny:

(Finds pair of baby shoes in Dee's purse.)
Thought I tole you to git rid'a these?

Dee: I forgot.

Johnny: Save you the trouble.

(He starts to throw them away.)

Dee: Don't you do that! You black bastard. So help me, Johnny.

Evie: Aw, let'er have them things, Nigger! Wha's the big deal?

Johnny: 'Tend to your own business, bitch. Ain't a minute off your ass for messin' it up las' night.

Evie: Excuse me. Didn't know you was starvin' to death.

Johnny:

(Goes for Evie but quickly checks himself when she reaches for her purse. He turns back to Dee.)
Look'a here, girl. I ain't gon' have no harness bulls knockin' down yo' door.

Dee: All of a sudden you worried about me.

Johnny: Jus' git rid'a that crap. Worrin' over sump'm pass, over an' done with.

(Cora enters. A wet newspaper covers her head.)

Cora: Lawd'a mercy! Now I gotta do this un'form all over ag'in. Bad as I hate to iron.

Johnny: Ironin' for them crackers. Cain't see why you cain't iron for yourself.

Cora: This ain't no maid's un'form as any fool kin see. I makes my livin' as a pract'cal nurse. I ain't nobody's maid.

Johnny: Somebody tole me they seen you wheelin' a snotty nose, blue-eyed baby th'ough Washin'ton Square the other day.

Cora: They was a Wash'ton Square lie. Onlies' baby I wheel aroun' gon' be my own.

Johnny: Hell! By the time you an' Shanty git aroun' to somethin' like that . . . you aint gon' wheel nothin' roun' but a traya black-ass coffee.

(Dee and Evie laugh.)

Cora: You cheap husslers don't hit the street, you gon' be sellin' yo' wares in'a home for the cripple an' infirm.

Evie: Gon' have to bring ass to git ass.

> (**Cora** comes off her stool. Jerks off shoe. **Evie** comes up with a switch-blade.)

Johnny: Hey! Hey! Git under the bed with that shit!

> (He races around bar. Comes between them.)

What the hell's the matter with you, Cora? Cain't you take a little joke?

Cora: Don't know why every time I come in here, I gotta be insulted by you an' these here Harlows.

> (**Evie** still has her knife out.)

Evie: Bet if that heifer messes with me, I'll carve her up like'a fat piece'a barbecue.

Johnny: Naw you won't neither. Not in here, you won't. Put it away! I said put it away.

> (**Evie** reluctantly puts knife away.)

Dee: Let's get out of here, Evie. She's always pickin' her nose about some-thin'.

Evie: She don't scare me none. Jus' smells bad, tha's all.

Dee:

> (Looks at her watch.)

Well, I gotta date, and you gotta see your headshrinker, don't you?

Johnny: Headshrinker? Damned if Evie ain't gone an' got herself a pimp.

Evie: He don't come as expensive as some pimps I know.

Dee:

> (Goes for the coats.)

Now, don't you two start up again.

> (The two women start for the street doors.)

Johnny: Make money, baby. Make that money.

Dee: That's all you ever think about. Can't you just dig me for my soul?

Johnny: Wrong color be talkin' 'bout soul.

Dee: Negroes. Think you gotta corner on soul.

Evie: Us has suffahd, das why.

> (**Dee** and **Evie** exit.)

Cora: Gimme a martini, Shangy. Gotta bad taste in my mouth.

Johnny: Make sure she pays for that drink.

Cora: I works an' I pays. I don't ask a livin' ass for nothin'.

Johnny: 'Member when you did.

Cora: I was broke. Couldn't fin' no work. 'Sides I had you to take care of! Like I p'omised yo' mama I would. 'Fore she died. Till you had to go git in trouble with that Eye-talian boy.

Johnny: Maybe I jus' got tired'a all them col'-cuts an' fuck-ups.

Cora: When you got out'a that 'form school, I was ready to take care you ag'in! But that bad Nigger Sweets Crane got holt you an' ruint ya.

Johnny: Fixed it so's I didn't have to go to that orphan-house, didn't he? Took me in, treated me like I was his own son, didn't he? Damned sight more'n you or that drunken bitch of a mama'a mine did.

Cora: Jay Cee? Might God strike you dead. Maybe I ain't yo' flesh an' blood. But yo' mama? She couldn't he'p non'a the things she did.

Johnny: Do me one favor, bitch. Leave my mama on the outside. 'Nother thing, if you cain't say nothin' boss 'bout Sweets Crane, you don't have to come in here yo' dam'self.

(He slaps her on the behind and exits to the kitchen.)

Cora: Well, fan me with a brick! Tha's one Nigro you jus' can't be civil with.

*(She sips her drink as **Shanty** finishes sweeping floor.)*

Eb'm as a chile—give him a piece'a candy, wudn't the kin' he wanted, he'd rare back an' tho'w it at you. An' he'd stan' there lookin' all slang-eyed darin' you to touch him.

*(She watches **Shanty** beat upon the bar.)*

Never had no papa. Less you call that ol' dog Sweets Crane a father. His mama was always sickly an' she did drink. Never would give it out though, who it was did it to her. Carried that to her grave!

(She downs her drink.)

I knowed her ever since I was a li'l girl down South. You know, they was always sump'm funny 'bout her. Swore Jay Cee was born with a veil over his face.

Shanty: A what?

Cora: A veil over his face. Ev'body knows babies born with veils over they faces is s'pose to see ghostes an' raise forty-one kin's 'a hell.

Shanty: Johnny? Sheee.

Cora: If I'm lyin', I'm flyin'!

Shanty: Cora, you're superstishus as hell.

Cora: Cain't he'p but be, li'l bit. My peoples all had fogey-isms. Where I come from ev'body had 'em. One kin' or 'nother.

*(**Melvin** enters, hangs up knapsack and rain jacket, takes cap off, knocks the wet from his pants. His head is almost clean-shaven.)*

Chile! you sho' don't have to worry 'bout yo' head goin' back home!

Melvin: My home, sweety, is in Saint Albans. You don't have to inform me as to where yours is.

(He goes into a soft-shoe dance and sings.)

"Where the people beat they feet on the Mississippi mud."

Cora: Now, ain't that jus' like you ig'orint Nigroes. If they cain't think'a nothin' to say, they start slippin' you into the dozens.

Johnny:

(Enters from kitchen.)

You late, Mel.

Melvin: Today was my dance class, remember? Anyway, who can get a cab in this weather?

Johnny: White folks, baby. Wheeeet folks!

Melvin: Objectively speaking, plenty of them were passed up too.

(He begins to stretch his leg muscles.)

Johnny: Dig? One these days we gon' see this on tee vee.

Melvin: You got your people mixed. The dances they do on television is ster-ictly commercial.

Johnny: What hell's wrong with that? If you gon' run 'roun' wigglin' yo' tukus, mights well git paid for it.

Melvin: I study with a great artist! He deplores that sort of thing.

Johnny: Whozis great artist you study with?

Melvin: Victor Weiner! He teaches the Chenier method.

Johnny: This Shimmy-yay method you don't wiggle the tukus?

Melvin: Why?

Johnny: Them turkeys on tee vee mus' make a whole lotta coins jus' for wigglin' they tukeruseys.

Melvin: Prostitutes. All of them.

Johnny: Pros'tutes, huh?

> *(He goes to jukebox. Punches up number. Classical music comes on.)*

Go with a little sample what you jokers is puttin' down.

Melvin: Nothing doing. To appreciate true art, one must first be familiar with it.

Cora: Talk that talk, Mel. What do Jay Cee know 'bout bein' artistic?

Johnny:

> *(Rejects the music.)*

This Wineberg you study with? He's a Jew, ain't he?

Melvin: So what?

Johnny: Gotta give it to him. Connin' spades into thinkin' they gotta be taught how to dance.

Melvin: You're just prejudiced, Johnny. That's why you have no appreciation.

Johnny: When you start teachin' him maybe I'll git me some pre-she-a-shon.

> *(A loud voice is heard offstage.)*

Voice: Inn keeper!

Gabe:

> *(Bursts in clad in army raincoat and Sou'wester. He brandishes an umbrella and briefcase.)*

Cock-a-doodle-doo!

> *(**Johnny** paws the floor with his feet.)*

"I am a ringtailed squeeler. I am that very infant that refused his milk before his eyes was opened an' called out for a bottle of old rye."

> *(They circle each other.)*

Johnny: "This is me! Johnny Earthquake. I rassle with light'nin', put a cap on thunder. Set every mammy-jammer in the graveyard on a wonder."

Gabe: "I grapple with lions! Put knots in they tails! Sleep on broken glass an' for breakfast, eat nails. I'm a ba-a-a-d mother-for-ya."

> *(**Johnny** goes behind the bar and takes down a bottle of whiskey as **Gabe** spies **Cora**.)*

Eeeeeow! I feel like swallowin' a nappy-headed woman whole!

Cora:

> *(Pushes him away playfully.)*

Better stay out'a my face, fool.

> *(**Johnny** moves around bar to center. Theatrically pours a waterglass half-full of whiskey. Sets glass before **Gabe** on table. **Gabe** removes*

coat and hat. Hands them to **Cora***. He eyes the whiskey. Sniffs. Picks up the glass.)*

A-Lawd! Gabe you ain't. . . .

*(***Gabe*** puts the glass to his lips and begins to drink.)*

Ooooo!

*(***Gabe*** is emptying the glass.)*

Ooooo!

(He finishes. Eyes crossed. Sets the glass down. Grimaces. Shakes his head. **Johnny** *and* **Shanty** *laugh.)*

I swear! Y'all is sho' crazy. Ain't neither one'a ya got good sense.

Gabe: Needed that. Needed that one bad. Gimme another one.

*(***Shanty*** reaches for the bottle.)*

Cora: Don't you do it, Shangy. Let that fool kill hisse'f. Ain't no call for you to he'p him.

Johnny: Dam, Gabe! You ain't done gone an' got alcoholic on us?

Gabe: Don't you worry yo' li'l happy head 'bout me, sir. Matter fact, I'm cuttin' myself right out'a the herd.

Johnny: Tell me sump'n, baby? Is this herd pink? An' got snoots an' grea' big ears?

Gabe: No they ain't in color. They're black with big, thick, lip-pussys.

Johnny: Man! Them ain't elephants you been hangin' out with, them's hippo-bottom'a-the-pot'a-muses!

*(***Johnny*** and* **Gabe** *give each other some skin.)*

Cora: Lawd! What in the devil an' Tom Walker you Nigroes talkin' 'bout now?

Johnny: Keep her in the dark, Gabe. Keep that mulyan in the black.

Melvin: They're talking about Gabe's audition, Cora. Gabe had an audition today.

Gabe: I said it was a herd call, Melvino Rex!

Melvin: Lots of actors there, huh?

Gabe: Actors? Actors did you say? Well, yes! Every damned black actor in town.

Cora: Well, why didn't you say so in the first place? Lawd, chile! You ought'a lean up off this stuff.

*(***Gabe*** tries to put his arm around her.)*

An' take yo' arm out from 'roun' my neck.

Melvin: How'd you make out at that audition, Gabe?

Gabe: Dig this? It was a musical! A musical about slavery.

Melvin: Slavery? Well! It's about time.

Johnny: Gabe's gon' play'a ha'f-white-house Nigger! An' they ain' no whiter, half-white-house Nigger in New Yawk than Gabe is I'll bet'a fat man.

Gabe: You jus'a-got-dat-wrong, John. Stage manager calls me over. Whispers they're auditionin' the white actors tomorrow. Baby! I refuse to see anything musical at all about slavery.

(Everyone breaks up laughing.)

Cora: Say, Gabe? How about doin' one o' them crazy po'ms 'a your'n? Ain't heard none in a long time.

Shanty: Yeah, Gabe! How 'bout it?

Melvin: Might make you feel better.

Johnny: Git under the bed with that shit! Ain't runnin' no cabaret. Fixin' to git me a summons!

Gabe: What you wanna hear?

Cora: Anythin'.

Johnny: If you jus' gotta. Knowin' you, you always jus' gotta. Make it sump'n you know.

Gabe: Dig this one.

(*All except* **Johnny** *eagerly take seats.*)

They met on the banks of the Potomac, the rich, the great and the small!

It's impossible to tell you, should'a been there an' seen it all!

They came by train, by plane, by bus an' by car!

Bicycle an' tricycle from near an' very far!

On mule an' on horseback!

With greasy bag an' kroker sack!

Buckboard an' clapboard an' goats pullin' wagons!

Tin lizzies an' buggies an' trucks so weighted down with people, you could see the backends saggin'!

Carts with motors, an' trams!

Wheelchairs an' wheelbarrels an' women pushin' prams!

Little boys on scooters! Little girls on skates!

Beatnicks, hippies an' hoboes, most of them had come by freights!

We had walked in light-footed an' barefooted, had walked all out'a our shoes! Some hopped it on crutches for days!

An' then we got the news, some black power agitators was arrested along the way!

'Course they was a lotta Cadillacs an' Buicks, rich people showin' off! I didn't pay that no min',

I jus' took comfort in the thought we needed people of every kin'!

An' if all America had been there or seen it on tee vee,

They would'a knowed we all meant business in gittin' our e-kwa-le-tee!

Well, we moved to the square with the pool in the middle!

While we waited, some strange young folk from New Yawk played a flute an' a fiddle!

Then somebody pro-nounced that reb'm somebody would pray!

An' by the settin' sun, we knelt in the dust'a that day!

Somebody else got up with a great loud voice!

Said they had on han' the speaker of our choice!

Said this black man was a black man of black deeds an' black fame!

(I'll be damned to hell, I disremember his name!)

Then a hush fell on all them people that night,

'Cause we was there for one thing, our civil right!

This black man, he rizzed up an' walked to the stan'! I could tell at a glance that he was the man!

An' he boomed out over that mickey-phone an' called for all black folk to unite an' not roam to other orguzashuns who jus' wanted

to fight white people an' git what they can in a country that would
  soon give liberty an' 'quality to every man!
If we worked long an' hard, he admitted it'd be rough!
But he said, black unity an' solidarity would be enough!
Then he rizzed up his arms an' bobbled his head!
Best as I kin I'll try to remember what he said!

  (**Gabe** *pretends he is skinning a team of mules.*)

Hya!
You, Afro-Americans!
Hya!
You, American Afros!
Hya!
You Muslims an' nay-cee-pees!
Hya!
You so-called Negroes!
Tan liberals!
Black radicals!
Hya!
You respec-rabble black boorwahzeees!
Hya!
Black Demos an' 'Publicans,
Git back on the track!
You Nash-na-lissys and Marx-a-sissies
Who all been pin-pointin' black!
Hya!
You half-white pro-fesh-nals!
Hya!
Civil rights pro-sesh-nals!
Hya!
You cursed sons-a-ham!
Don't rock no boat!
Don't cut ne'r th'oat!
Be a beacon for some black magazeen!
Come doctor!
Come lawyer!
Come teacher!
Black employer!
An' keepers of white latrines!
On Donner!
On Blitzen!
You black nick-surd-rich-ins!
On! On! With the soul kweezeen!
You inter-urbans!
Satisfied suburbans!
To you, I gotta say whoa!
What's needed to save us
Is not Some-a-Davus!

Or even Benjammer O.!
Giddy-up! Yippeee-ay! Or Kidney Poteeay!
They already got they dough!
Now, here are the bare facks,
Grab yo' selves by the bootblacks!
Leave Heroin Manderson on the side!
An' all you take notice,
You'll all git yo' lettuce!
You'll own the post office yet!
Off-springs off mixed couples
Who're more than a han'fu,
You'll make the cover of *Jet*!
We'll have invented a machine that delivers
A cream to make crackers pay the debt!
Now junkies don't dilly
You husslers don't dally!
Don't waste yo' time smokin' pot
In some park or some alley,
'Cause Charlie is watchin' you!''

Well, he would'a went that'a way
To this very day but his th'oat
It got too hoarse!
When he sat down wasn't a clap ner a soun',
Couldn't tell if he'd got to the end!
A cracker preacher there, then said a prayer!
Said civil rights you could not fo'ce!
By this time I was so confused my head was in a spin!
Somebody else got up with a grinnin' face!
Said to leave that place like we found it!
Tha's when I reached in my pocket an' pulled out my packet an' before
　　everybody took a sip'a my wine!
Then we lef' that place without ne'r trace!
An' we didn't leave ne'r chit'lin' behin'!
(*Everyone laughs and claps their hands.*)

Johnny: If you ask me, its all a big-ass waste'a time an' energy. Jus' how long you gon' keep this up? Ought'a be in some office makin'a white man's pay.

Gabe: Sheee! Think I'd rather be hawkin' neckbones on a Hundred an' Twenty-Fifth Street.

Cora: Uh-aw! Better git out'a here 'fore you two start goin' at it agin.

　　(*She gets newspaper and peers out of window.*)

An' 'fore it starts up rainin' ag'in! Lawd knows I ain't prepared for neither one.

　　(*She moves to* **Melvin** *who is stirring something in a skillet. She sniffs.*)

Shanty! If you want sump'n 'sides Mel's warmed-over chili better see you for supper.

NO PLACE TO BE SOMEBODY　　403

Gabe: Better watch it, Shanty. She's thinkin' the way to a man's heart is through his stomach.

Cora:

>*(Moves to street doors.)*

Sho' ain't no way to stay there.

>*(She exits.* **Melvin** *exits to kitchen.* **Shanty** *busys himself.* **Gabe** *sits. Looks thoughtful.* **Johnny** *tosses him some bills.)*

Gabe: What's this?

Johnny: Aw, take the bread, Nigger.

>*(***Gabe** *does not pick up the money.)*

Look'a here, Gabe. I know you think I'm all up 'side the wall. You hip to the books an' all like'a that. But ser-us-ly! Why ain't they doin' you no good?

Gabe: Let's jus' say I ain't in no big rush.

Johnny: It's Charlie, ain't it?

Gabe: What about Charlie?

Johnny: It's wrote all over you! Might be foolin' some people. Cock-a-doodle-dooin' an' comin' on with yo' funky po'try. . . .

Gabe: When you git me some answers other than the one's you been handin' me, I'll git in the bed with you.

Johnny: One thing Sweets says to me, 'fore he got his time. He says. . . .

Gabe: Screw it, John. When you start bringin' Sweets into the picture, I know exactly what's comin' next. The answer is still negative.

Johnny: Still wanna believe you kin sell papers an' become President, huh? Snowballs in Egypt.

Gabe: I ain't lookin' to break no law.

Johnny: They ain't no law. They kill you an' me in the name'a the law. You an' me wouldn't be where we at, if it wasn't for the law. Even the laws they write for us makes us worse off.

Gabe: From the git-go, they don't operate like Sweets anymore. Harlem's all caught up.

Johnny: Who's operatin' in Harlem?

Gabe: You cain't be thinkin' about down here! It was branchin' out'a Harlem got Sweets where he's at right now.

Johnny: Man, what you think I been doin' the ten years Sweets been in the joint? I tell you the scheme is together. Me an' him gon' git us a piece'a this town.

Gabe: An' end up on the bottom'a the East River with it tied aroun' your necks.

Johnny: Bet we'll have us a box'a crackers under each armpit if we do!

Gabe: Well, I don't dig crackers that much.

Johnny: Okay, Hollywood! Keep knockin' on doors with yo' jeans at half-mast. Sellin' yo'-self like some cheap-ass whore. If I know one thing about you, you ain't that good'a actor. Whitey knows right away you cain't even stan' to look at him.

>*(***Gabe** *grins, picks money up. Pockets it.)*

Blackout

SCENE 2

Time: *A week later*
Place: *The same*
Setting: *The same*
At Rise: **Gabe** *stands at center.*

Gabe: When I'm by myself like this, for days, weeks, even months at a time, it sort'a gets to me! I mean deep down inside things begin to happen. Lemme confess, sometimes I git to feelin'—like I get so vicious, I wanna go out an' commit mass murder. But don't misunderstand me. Because I call myself a black playwright, don't git the impression I'm hung up on crap like persecution an' hatred. 'Cause I ain't! I'm gonna leave that violence jazz to them cats who are better at it than me. I ain't been out of the house in over two months. Not because I been that busy, I just been too damned scared. I been imaginin' all kind'a things happenin' out there. An' they're waitin' just for me. All manner of treachery an' harm. But don't think because of it my play is about Negro self-pity. Or even that ol' "You owe me whitey party line." 'Cause it ain't. In spite of what I learned in college, it did not give me that introduction to success, equality an' wealth, that to my parents were the most logical alternatives to Heaven. Anyway, like I say, I'm gonna leave that social protest jive to them cats who are better equipped than me.
    *(Lights dim out on **Gabe** and come up on **Johnny** who is asleep on the floor. One shoe is off and an empty bottle and glass lie nearby. A telegram is pushed under the door. **Johnny** rouses himself. Puts on his shoe and goes to the door. Picks up the telegram and studies it. Someone is heard trying the street doors. He hides the telegram and opens the door. **Dee** enters. Goes behind the bar. Makes a bromo. **Johnny** takes out the telegram. Peers at it again.)*

Dee: What is it?

Johnny: Looks like a telegram from Sweets.
    (He gives her the telegram.)
Read it.
    *(**Dee** downs her Bromo.)*
Read it, I said.
    (She picks up the telegram.)

Dee: It's from Sweets all right.

Johnny: Well, what does it say?

Dee: Says he going to be released in three weeks.
    *(**Johnny** snatches telegram.)*
Makes you pretty happy, doesn't it?

Johnny: Babeee! Happy ain't the word! I am dee-ler-russ! Yeeeeoweee!

Dee:
    (Grabs her head.)
Hold it down, will ya?

NO PLACE TO BE SOMEBODY   **405**

Johnny: S'matter? Rough night?

Dee: What else?

Johnny: Go home! Cop some zees!

Dee: Just sit here for awhile! If you don't mind.

Johnny: Damndest thing. Las' night I stayed here. Burnt one on. Fell asleep right here. Had this dream. 'Bout Sweets gettin' out. Man, tha's weird! Tha's damned weird.

Dee: Today's my birthday.

Johnny: Damn! Forgot all about it.

Dee: Wish to hell I could.

Johnny: Anybody'd think you was a wrinkled up ol' mulyan.

> *(He takes money from her purse. Tosses her a few bills, stuffs the rest into his pocket.)*

Here. Go out an' buy yourself sump'n real nice.

Dee:

> *(Flinging the bills back at him.)*

I don't want anything for my birthday.

Johnny: Now, lissen. Don't you start no shit this mornin'. I'm in too good'a humor.

Dee: Johnny. Let's you and me just take off for somewhere! For a couple of weeks.

Johnny: You off your wood, girl? With Sweets gittin' out?

Dee: I gotta bad feelin'.

Johnny: I don't give'a dam what kind'a feelin' you got. Sweets was like a father to me.

Dee: So you told me. A thousand times you told me.

Johnny: I know. That bitch Evie's been puttin' ideas into your head.

Dee: That's not true. You lay off her, Johnny.

Johnny: Lissen to her, she'll have you husslin' tables at Howard Johnson's.

Dee: Might be better off.

Johnny:

> *(Slaps her.)*

Kiss me an' tell me you sorry.

> *(She kisses him.)*

Dee: Sorry.

> *(She moves to street doors.)*

Johnny: Hey, girl. Gotta celebrate your birthday some way. Tomorrow mornin'. Bring over the Sunday papers an' a bottle'a my bes' wampole. "All Day, All Night, Mary Ann!"

> *(**Dee** exits. **Johnny** peers at telegram. Goes to jukebox. Punches up number. Presently **Cora** and **Shanty** enter.)*

Cora: Jay Cee? I know it ain't none'a my business but that woman'a yours. She's out there in the car. Jus'a cryin' her eyeballs out.

Johnny:

> *(Getting his jacket, moving to street doors.)*

Hol' down the store, Shanty. Be back in'a couple'a hours.

(He exits. **Shanty** *goes to door. Locks it. Punches up number on jukebox.)*

Cora: Shangy? I been doin' some thinkin'. You heard anything from Gloria?

Shanty: Heard what?

Cora: 'Bout yo' divorce! Tha's what.

Shanty: Gloria ain't gonna give me no die-vo'ce.

Cora: Well, if she ain't that don't stop us from livin' together, do it?

Shanty: What made you change your mind?

Cora: 'Nother thing. Ever since I knowed you, you been belly-achin' 'bout gittin' you some drums.

Shanty: Gonna git 'em too.

Cora: Well, I'm willin' to do everything I kin to help you.

Shanty: You mean—you mean, you'd help me git 'em? No jive?

Cora: Then you could quit ol' Jay Cee an' go back to playin' in them night-clubs like you said you used to.

Shanty: You really mean it? You'd help me git my drums?

Cora: Ain't talkin' jus' to hear myse'f rattle.

Shanty: Mama, you are the greatest.

(He hugs her.)

Cora: Honey, hush.

Shanty: Know what I'm gonna do, Cora? Soon's I git them drums I'm gonna bring 'em in here. Set 'em up an' play the thing for Johnny.

Cora: Lawd, Shangy! I wouldn't miss that for nothin' in this worl'.

*(***Shanty*** *takes out marihuana cigarette. Wets, lights it. Smokes.)*

Lawd, Shangy. I done tole you 'bout smokin' them ol' nasty things.

(He passes the cigarette to her. She grins.)

Guess it won't hurt none once in a while.

(She inhales. Coughs.)

Shanty: I was just thinkin' about ol' Gloria. How much she hated jazz. Nigger music, she called it. Man, everytime I'd set up my skins to practice, she'd take the kids an' go over to her mother's.

(They begin to pass the cigarette back and forth.)

Dig. One night after a gig brought some cats over for a little game. Some spade cat grabs her between the legs when I wasn't lookin'.

Cora: Spent the bes' part of my life on Nigroes that wasn't no good. Had to baby an' take care all of 'em.

Shanty: Never heard the last of it. You'd think he raped her or somethin'.

Cora: Cain't hol' no job! Take yo' money an' spen' it all on likker.

Shanty: Got this job playin' the Borsh-Belt. My skins was shot! Had to borrow a set from Champ Jones.

Cora: Can't make up their min's! Jus' be a man, I says.

Shanty: Gone about a week. Come home. Shades all down. Key won't fit in the door.

Cora: Git evil. Nex' thing you know they goin' up 'side yo' head.

Shanty: She's over at her mother's. Says she gonna sue me for desershun.

Cora: I thought you was a dif'rent kind'a nigger. I'm gon' git me a white man, one that'll take care me. Or he'p me take care myse'f.

Shanty: I never did nothin' to her.

Cora: Tha's when he went up 'side my head with the ash tray.

Shanty: Said she needed some bread. Went to the bank. Cashed my check. Come back. Skins the cat loaned me are gone.

Cora: I loved him so much.

Shanty: Grabbed a broom out'a the closet. Went to work on the bitch.

Cora: Them awful things he said to me.

Shanty: Bitch never made a soun' or dropped a tear.

Cora: I cried sump'm ter'ble.

Shanty: Says I'd never see my kids ag'in or the drums neither.

Cora: Wanted children so bad! Doctor said I couldn't have none.

Shanty: Started chokin' her. Would'a killed her, if my kid hadn't jumped on my back.

Cora: Ain't hard to satisfy me. Cause Lawd knows I ain't never asked for much.

Shanty: One thing I learned, I'm gonna stay away from bitches like that. They just ain't got no soul.

> (*He gets can of spray deodorant. Opens street doors and sprays the bar.*)

Cora:

> (*Rouses herself. Wipes tears.*)

Shangy! I sho' wanna see Jay Cee's face when he sees you play them drums.

Blackout

SCENE 3

Time: *Three weeks later*
Place: *The same*
Setting: *The same*
At rise: **Melvin** *is doing his dance exercises.* **Johnny** *enters with white tablecloth and slip of paper.* **Shanty** *busys himself behind the bar.*

Johnny: Sure we need all this, Mel?

Melvin: You hired me to be a short order cook around here. That's exactly what that list is too. A short order.

Johnny: Jus' checkin'. Don't want you slippin' none'a that whut-wuzzit over on me a'gin.

Melvin: Po-tahge par-mun-teeay. Everybody else like it.

Johnny: Been some chit'lin's, you'da been sayin' sump'm.

Melvin: Chit'lin's? Sometimes I think you have the taste-buds of a slave.

> (*He snatches the slip of paper out of **Johnny**'s hands and exits as **Mary Lou Bolton** enters and goes to a table.*)

Johnny: Sump'm I kin do for you?

Mary Lou: I'd like a daiquiri, please. . . .

Johnny: Got any identification?

Mary Lou: Really!

Johnny: Mary Lou Bo——

Mary Lou: Mary Lou Bolton.

Johnny: This the school you go to?

Mary Lou: Just graduated.

Johnny:
> *(Goes behind the bar to mix drink.)*

Buddy'a mine come out'a there. . . .

Mary Lou: Elmira is an all-woman's school.

Johnny: I mean the slammers up there.

Mary Lou: Beg your pardon?

Johnny:
> *(Sets drink before her.)*

Prison.

Mary Lou: Oh yes! My father spent a lot of time up there.

Johnny: You kiddin'? Your father did?

Mary Lou:
> *(She laughs.)*

He was a criminal lawyer.

Johnny: He ain't no lawyer no more?

Mary Lou: He's a judge now.

Johnny: Must'a been a hell of a lawyer.

Mary Lou: Oh, I suppose so. . . .

Johnny: What you mean, you s'pose so?

Mary Lou: I'd rather not discuss it.

Johnny: Sorry.
> *(**Ellen** enters. Carries a civil rights placard.)*

Ellen: C'mon, Mary! Everyone's waitin' on you.

Mary Lou: Be there in a second, Ellen.
> *(She looks into her purse. **Ellen** exits.)*

What do I owe you for the drink?

Johnny: Ain't you gonna fiinsh it?

Mary Lou: I really shouldn't. But this is my first time out! Kind of nervous, you know?

Johnny: First time out?

Mary Lou: We're picketing the construction work up the street. The new hospital they're building.

Johnny: What for?

Mary Lou: Haven't you heard? The unions won't accept qualified Negroes.

Johnny: Why don't them qualified Nigroes do they own pickitin'?

Mary Lou: It's everyone's responsibility.

Johnny: You only git in the way.

Mary Lou: I'm glad all Negroes don't feel the way you do.

Johnny: You don't know how I feel.

Mary Lou:
> *(Puts a bill upon the table and prepares to leave.)*

I don't think I care to find out.

Johnny: Jus' happen to think somebody invented this civil rights jive to git a whole lotta people runnin' in the wrong direction.
Mary Lou:
(*Starts to move to street doors.* **Johnny** *catches her by the arm.*)
Would you mind?
Johnny: Know what's in that daiquiri, baby?
Mary Lou: Let me go, please.
Johnny: Jizzum juice. A triple dose of jizmistic juice. Any minute you gonna turn into a depraved sex maniac! A teenage Jeckle an' Hide. Yo' head is gon' sprout fuzzy like somebody from the Fee-gee Eye-lan's. Yo' hot tongue'll roll out'a your mouth like'a fat snake. You'll pant like'a go-rilla in heat. Yo' buzzooms will blow up like gas balloons an' the nipples will swell an' hang like ripe purple plums. Yo' behin' will begin to work like the ol' gray mare an' you'll strut aroun' flappin' yo' wings like'a raped duck. Then you'll suck me up with one mighty slurp an' fly out'a here a screamin' vampire. They'll finally subdue an' slay you on top'a the Empire State Buildin', with ray guns where you'll be attemptin' to empale yo'self astride that giant antenna. An' nobody will ever know that you, li'l Mary Lou Bolton, who jus' graduated from Elmira College, was lookin' to lay down in front of a big, black bull-dozer, to keep America safe for democracy.
Mary Lou: I think I get your point.
(**Ellen** *enters.*)
Ellen: Mary Lou! Are you coming or not? Everyone's leaving.
(**Mary Lou** *and* **Ellen** *exit.* **Ellen** *scolding.* **Cora** *enters.*)
Cora: Shangy! Movin' man's waitin'.
(**Shanty** *takes off his apron.*)
Johnny: Where you think you goin'?
Shanty: Movin' in with Cora today.
Johnny: Not on my time, you ain't! An' me 'spectin' Sweets any minute.
Cora: Wha's so 'portant 'bout that Crane Nigro Shangy's just gotta be here? Or maybe you spectin' standin' room for the 'casion?
Johnny: Ain't lettin' him off an' tha's it.
Cora: Jay Cee, why is you so bent'n boun' on breakin' up our li'l club?
Johnny: Somebody's gotta look out for Shanty if he don't.
Cora: What is you talkin' about? Shangy's free, white an' long pass twenty-one! It ain't none'a yo' business what he does outside this bucket'a blood.
Johnny: Well, bitch, I got news for you. I put him in here when none'a these other hunkies 'roun' here would hire him. Talkin' his up 'side the wall talk an' beatin' up they benches.
Cora: Wha's that gotta do with me?
Johnny: Ain't lettin' you or nobody else turn his head but so far. Jus' per-teckin' my interest.
Cora: Ain't gon' let you stan' in my way, Jay Cee. Me an' Shangy took a likin' for one 'nother from the day I walked in here an' foun' you runnin' this place. Up to now they ain't been much happiness in this worl' for neither one of us. But what li'l we got comin', figger we bes' jump on it with all fo' feet.

Johnny: That the way you feel 'bout it, Shanty?

Shanty: Man, she's gonna help me git my drums.

Johnny: She ain't gon' do nothin' but turn you into sump'm you don't wanna be.

Cora: What is you talkin' 'bout, fool?

Johnny: This black bitch is gon' turn you into a real white man, Shanty.

Shanty: What??

Cora: You kin quit this nigger today, Honey. We'll manage.

Johnny: You wanna be a white man, Shanty?

Shanty: Knock that stuff off, Johnny! I don't go for it.

Johnny: You think if you git with somebody like Cora, it'll make the whole thing complete, huh?

Cora: Hush up, Jay Cee.

Johnny: Well, it won't. She'll make you so damn white you won't be able to bang two spoons together.

Cora: I'm warnin' you, Jay Cee.

Johnny: An' play the drums? You'll never play no drums.

> (**Cora** rushes at **Johnny**. *He catches her arm and throws her to the floor.* **Shanty** *is shocked by* **Johnny**'s *cruelty. He makes a move to* **Johnny**.)

Shanty: Why you—you—you mother fucker!

> (**Johnny** *stands ready to throw a punch.* **Shanty** *checks himself. Turns away.* **Cora** *gets to her feet and goes to him. Puts her arm around him. He shuns her. Exits, slowly.*)

Cora: Tha's all right, Jay Cee honey. Tha's all right! That day ain't long off, 'fore you gon' git yours. Honey, you gon' git a hurtin' put on you. You gon' git a hurtin' put on you in the place where you do wrong.

Johnny: Better wish all that hurtin' on all them Niggers that messed up yo' min'.

> (**Cora** *exits as* **Gabe** *enters.*)

Gabe: Dam! What was all that smoke about?

Johnny: Them two ain't got sense nuff to pour piss out'a a boot if the directions was wrote on the heel.

Gabe: You just don't wanna see anybody git any enjoyment out'a life.

Johnny: Bastard's movin' in with her. You dig that?

Gabe: An' you tried to stop 'em, huh?

> (**Johnny** *doesn't answer. Takes bottle of champagne and bucket. Sets it on a table.*)

Well, I see you're gettin' ready for the big homecomin', huh?

Johnny: That's right. An' I don't want you goin' into none'a yo' high'n mighty when Sweets git here. Tell you right now he don't go for none of that giddy-up-yippee-yaye shit!

Gabe: Didn't come to stay. Lemme hold some coins! Lan'lord's on my tail.

Johnny: Good.

> (**Johnny** *grins. Spreads bills over table.* **Gabe** *picks them up.*)

Gabe: You'll git it all back soon's I git me a show.

Johnny: You keepin' a record?

(A black man enters.)
On yo' way, wine.
Sweets: S'matter, Sonny Boy? Don't you know me?
Johnny: Sweets? Is it really you?
Sweets: It's me, all right.
*(**Sweets** coughs. **Johnny** rushes forward. Embraces **Sweets**.)*
Johnny: Lock the doors, Gabe. Don't want no innerrupshuns.
*(**Gabe** locks the street doors. **Johnny** and **Sweets** box playfully.)*
Sweets: Minute there, was 'bout to go out an' come back in again.
Johnny: Reason I didn't rec'nize you at firs' was, well, I always remember you bein' 'bout as sharp as a skeeter's peter in the dead'a winter. Three hundred suits he had, Gabe. Nothin' but the fines' vines. Never seen so many kicks in one closet. Wasn't a cat in Harlem. . . .
*(**Sweets** coughs violently.)*
Dam! What you doin' 'bout that cough, Sweets?
Sweets: Little souvenir I picked up at the jute mill.
Johnny: Jute mill?
Sweets: Where they make burlap bags at.
Johnny: Pretty rough in Fedsville, huh?
*(**Sweets** coughs again.)*
Meet my man, Gabe.
*(**Gabe** and **Sweets** shake hands.)*
Gabe: Pleased to meet you, Mister Crane.
Sweets: Jus' call me Sweets.
Johnny:
(Brings bottle and two glasses.)
Sweets, some'a Pete Zerroni's bes'.
Sweets: Zerroni? You don't mean ol' big fat Pete from up there in the Bronx?
Johnny: Yeah. He's runnin' everything down here from soup to nuts! But we gon' change all that, ain't we Sweets?
*(**Johnny** struggles with cork.)*
Sweets: Sonny Boy, we wasn't much on sendin' kites. Wha's been happenin' since I been in the joint?
Johnny: Jews, Irish an' the Ginees still runnin' things as usual.
Sweets: No. I mean with you, Sonny Boy.
Johnny: Like you know I had a tough gaff gittin' my divorce. Whole thing started when I wanted her to do a little merchandizin' for me. Real Magdaleen, she was! One thing led to 'nother. Boom! Back to mama, she went. Had a helluva time gittin' her to sign this joint over to me. Went into my act. Fell down on my duece'a benders. Gave her the ol' routine. Like how the worl' been treatin' us black folk an' everything. . . .
(He pops cork. Pours. Holds his glass up. The two men clink their glasses.)
Well, look here, Sweets, here's to our li'l piece'a this town.
Sweets:
*(Looks into his glass. As **Johnny** sips.)*
Speakin'a husslers, Sonny Boy.

*(He coughs. **Gabe** goes to bar. Gets large glass and fills with champagne.)*

You runnin' any kind'a stable?

Johnny: You kiddin', Sweets?

Sweets: Pushin' or bookin'?

Johnny: Nay, that ain't my stick.

Sweets: Sonny Boy, when I was yo' age, I was into some'a ev'thing.

Johnny: Wish you wouldn't call me that, Sweets! I ain't that little boy runnin' up an' down Saint Nicklas Avenue for you no more.

Sweets: Jus' habit, Johnny. But I sort'a was hopin' you was into sump'm on yo' own, like.

Johnny: Hell! I been tryin' to stay clean. Waitin' on you, man! Like we planned.

Sweet: Well, now! Tha's—tha's what I wanna talk to you 'bout, Sonny Boy.

Johnny: Yes, sir! You still the boss, Sweets. Didn't think you wanted to git into it jus' yet. Figgered we'd have us a few drinks. Talk 'bout ol' times. . . .

Sweets: Sonny Boy!

Johnny: Sir?

Sweets: Firs' off! I gotta tell you I'm th'ough. . . .

Johnny: Whatchu say?

Sweets: Wrappin' it all up for good. . . .

Johnny: Wrappin' what up?

Sweets: The rackets.

Johnny: You gotta be jokin'.

Sweets: Never been more ser'us in all my life. . . .

Johnny: Sweets, you jus' tired.

Sweets: Don't need no res'. . . .

Johnny: Git yo'self together. . . .

Sweets: My min's made up.

Johnny: Waitin' on you this long, little more ain't gon' kill me.

Sweets: Look, Sonny Boy, it's like this . . .

Johnny: Shut up with that Sonny Boy, shit!

*(He tries to control himself. **Gabe** laughs.)*

Look, man. You ain't let the slammers psyche you out? That ain't like you. That ain't like you, at all.

*(He reaches out to touch **Sweets**. **Sweets** jerks away. **Johnny** grabs **Sweets** by the throat violently.)*

Mother fucker! I been waitin' on you for ten long-ass years. You ain't gon' cop out on me like this.

Gabe:

*(Moves to contain **Johnny**.)*

Cut it out, John! Let him alone. Cain't you see the man's sick?

*(**Johnny** hits **Gabe** in the stomach. **Gabe** doubles over. Goes to the floor.)*

Johnny: What the hell they do to you, huh?

Sweets: What'd who do to me?

Johnny: In the bastille. They did sump'm to you.

NO PLACE TO BE SOMEBODY   413

Sweets: Nothin' that wasn't already done to me.

> (**Sweets** *moves to* **Gabe**.)

You all right, young fella?

Gabe: Yeah—yeah, I—I'm okay.

Sweets:

> (*Takes wallet from* **Gabe**'s *back pocket. Puts it into his own pocket.*)

Shouldn'ta mixed in.

> (*He turns back to* **Johnny**.)

You got the Charlie fever, Johnny. Tha's what you got. I gave it to you. Took yo' chile's min' an' filled it with the Charlie fever. Givin' you a education or teachin' you to dinner-pail, didn't seem to me for no way for you to grow up and be respected like'a man. Way we was raised, husslin' an' usin' yo' bisquit to pull quickies was the only way we could feel like we was men. Couldn't copy Charlie's good points an' live like men. So we copied his bad points. That was the way it was with my daddy an' his daddy before him. We just pissed away our lives tryin' to be like bad Charlie. With all our fine clothes an' big cars. All it did was make us hate him all the more an' our-selves too. Then I tried to go horse-to-horse with 'em up there in the Bronx. An' ended up with a ten. All because'a the Charlie fever. I gave you the Charlie fever, Johnny. An' I'm sorry! Seems to me, the worse sickness'a man kin have, is the Charlie fever.

Johnny:

> (*Glares at* **Sweets**.)

Git out'a here, Sweets. Goddam you! Git out'a here. 'Fore I kill you.

> (**Sweets** *coughs and exits to the street.* **Johnny** *looks after him.*)

They did sump'm to him. White sons'a bitches. They did sump'm to him. Sweets don't give up that easy. Charlie fever. Sheeee!

Gabe: Ten years is a long time. An' the man's sick. Anyone kin see that.

Johnny: He could be fakin'. He's into sump'm! Don't want me in on it. He used to do that to me all the time. He better be fakin'.

> (*Brings his arm up to look at his watch.*)

Gabe: What? What the hell. . . .

> (*He searches frantically in his pockets.*)

I'll be goddam.

Johnny: Hell's matter with you?

Gabe: My watch! It's gone.

Johnny: Hell with your watch!

Gabe: It's gone! An' my wallet! The bread you loaned me! It's gone, too.

> (**Johnny** *begins to laugh hysterically.*)

What the hell's so goddam funny?

Johnny: It's Sweets! The bastard *is* fakin'. He snatched it!

Blackout

Act Two
SCENE 1

Time: *Two days later*
Place: *The same*
Setting: *The same*
At rise: **Gabe** sits at table. *Whiskey bottle before him. He is obviously
drunk. He begins to sing an old Protestant hymn.*

Gabe: "Whiter than snow, yes!
Whiter than snow!
Now, wash me, and I shall be
Whiter than snow!"
    (He chants.)
We moved out of that dirty-black slum!
Away from those dirty-black people!
Who live in those dirty-black hovels,
Amidst all of that garbage and filth!
Away from those dirty-black people,
Who in every way,
Prove daily
They are what they are!
Just dirty-black people!

We moved to a house with a fenced-in yard!
To a clean-white neighborhood!
It had clean-white sidewalks
And clean-white sheets
That hang from clean-white clotheslines to dry!
They were clean-white people!
Who in every way
Prove daily
They are what they are!
Just clean-white people!

Now those clean-white people thought we were
Dirty-black people!
And they treated us like we were
Dirty-black people!
But we stuck it out!
We weathered the storm!
We cleansed and bathed
And tried to be and probably were

NO PLACE TO BE SOMEBODY   **415**

Cleaner than most of those clean-white people!
    (He sings.)
"Break down every idol, cast out every foe!
Oh, wash me and I shall be whiter than snow!"
    (He speaks again.)
We went to schools that had clean-white
Rooms with clean-white teachers
Who taught us and all of the clean-white
Children how to be clean and white!
    (He laughs.)
Now, those dirty-black people across
The tracks became angry, jealous and mean!
When they saw us running or skipping or
Hopping or learning with all of those
Clean-white children!

They would catch us alone
When the clean-white children weren't there!
And kick us or slap us and spit
On our clean-white clothes!
Call us dirty-black names
And say that we wanted to be like our clean-white
Neighbors!

But in spite of the kicking, the slapping,
The spitting, we were exceedingly glad!
For we knew we weren't trying to be like
Our clean-white neighbors! Most of all,
We were certain we weren't like those
Dirty-black Niggers!
Who live in hovels, far away across the tracks!
    (He sings.)
"Whiter than snow! Oh, whiter than snow!
Please wash me, and I shall be whiter than snow!"
    (He speaks again.)
So we grew up clean and keen!
And all of our clean-white neighbors
Said we had earned the right to go
Out into the clean-white world
And be accepted as clean-white people!
But we soon learned,
The world was not clean and white!
With all of its powders and soaps!
And we learned too that no matter how
Much the world scrubbed!
The world was getting no cleaner!

Most of all!
We saw that no matter how much or how
Hard we scrubbed!
It was only making us blacker!
So back we came to that dirty-black slum!
To the hovels, the filth and the garbage!
Came back to those dirty-black people!
Away from those clean-white people!
That clean, white anti-septic world!
That scrubs and scrubs and scrubs!

But those dirty-black people!
Those dirty-black people!
Were still angry, jealous and mean!
They kicked us and slapped us and spit again
On our clothes!
Denied us!
Disowned us
And cast us out!
And we still were exceedingly glad!

For at last they knew
We were not like our clean-white neighbors!
Most of all! We were safe!
Assured at last!
We could never more be
Like those dirty-black Niggers!
Those filthy dirty-black Niggers!
Who live far away!
Far away, in hovels across the tracks!
        (He bursts into song.)
"Whiter than snow! Yes! Whiter than snow!
Oh, wash me and I shall be whiter than snow!"
(**Gabe** *is on his knees. Hands stretched up to heaven. Lights slowly*
dim out on him, and come up on bar. **Shanty** *is behind the bar.* **Mike**
Maffucci *stands at center, throwing darts into a dartboard.* **Sweets**
Crane *enters.*)

Shanty: Hit the wind, Mac. This ain't the place.
Sweets: Johnny here?
Shanty: What you want with Johnny?
Sweets: I'm a frien'a his.
Shanty: Yeah? Well, he ain't here.
Sweets: Where's me a broom an' a drop pan?
Shanty: What for?
Sweets: Need me a bucket an' some rags too.
Shanty: What do you want all that shit for?

NO PLACE TO BE SOMEBODY   417

Sweets: The floor, they don't look too good an' the windas, it could stan'. . . .

Shanty: Eighty-six, ol' timer! We ain't hirin'.

Sweets: Ain't askin f'no pay.

Shanty: What'a ya? Some kind'a nut? C'mon! Out you go. Eighty-six.

Sweets: Think you better wait til Johnny gets here. Let him put me out. Think I'll fin' what I need back here.

> (**Sweets** pushes **Shanty** roughly aside and moves to kitchen.)

Shanty:

> (Looks incredulous. Scratches his head and follows **Sweets** to kitchen. **Johnny** enters.)

Hey, Johnny! Some ol' timer just came in an'. . . .

Maffucci: How you doin, Johnny Cake?

Johnny:

> (Stops short.)

Only one cat usta call me that.

Maffucci: Gettin' warm, Johnny Cake.

Johnny:

> (Moves behind bar.)

Little snotty-nose wop kid, name Mike Maffucci.

Maffucci: On the nose.

> (Sends a dart in **Johnny's** direction. **Johnny** ducks. The dart buries into the wood of the back bar. Both men laugh. They shake hands.)

Long time no see, eh, Johnny Cake?

Johnny: What you drinkin'?

Maffucci: Little dago red. Gotta take it easy on my stomach with the hard stuff.

> (**Johnny** snaps his fingers. **Shanty** brings bottle.)

Shanty: Dig, Johnny! Some ol' goat. . . .

Johnny: Cool it, Shanty. Can't you see I'm busy? How's your ol' man, Footch?

Maffucci:

> (Makes the sign of the cross.)

My ol' man chalked out, Johnny. Heart attack. Right after you went to the nursery. You ain't still sore 'bout what happened, are you Johnny Cake?

Johnny: Bygones is bygones, Footch!

Maffucci: Glad'a hear ya say that, Johnny. Didn't know what happened to you after that. When they tole me you was runnin' this joint, had'a come over an' see ya.

> (He looks around. **Sweets** enters with broom and rags. Proceeds to sweep the floor. **Johnny** registers surprise and anger. **Shanty** starts to say something but **Johnny** puts his finger to his lips.)

How ya doin' with the place, Johnny?

Johnny: Stabbin' horses to steal blankets. Jay Cee ag'inst the worl'.

Maffucci: Joe Carneri used to say that. You ain't never forgot that huh, Johnny?

> (**Johnny** glances angrily at **Sweets.**)

Remember the first time they busted him? There was this pitchure on the front page. Joe's standin' on the courthouse steps. Cops an' reporters all aroun'. Joe's yellin' "Jay Cee ag'inst the worl'. Jay Cee ag'inst the worl'!"

Johnny: He sho' was your hero all right.

Maffucci: Too bad he had'a go an' git hit like that. Sittin' in a barber chair!

Johnny: Better'n the electric chair.

> (**Sweets** *is now dusting the chairs.*)

Maffucci: You know, Johnny Cake, that was a groovy idea for a kid! Coppin' all that scrapiron from ol' Julio an' then sellin' it back to him.

> (*He breaks up laughing.*)

Johnny: Wasn't so pretty when I tried to tell the fuzz you was in on it with me.

Maffucci: Awful sorry 'bout that, Johnny Cake.

> (**Maffucci** *puts his hand on* **Johnny***'s shoulder.* **Johnny** *knocks his hand off.* **Maffucci** *comes down on* **Johnny***'s shoulder with a karate chop.* **Johnny** *punches* **Maffucci** *in the stomach and shoves him away. Comes toward* **Maffucci** *menacingly.* **Sweets** *keeps sweeping.*)

Johnny: One thing I gotta give you Ginees credit for. Sho' know how to stick together when you wanna.

Maffucci:

> (*Backs away.*)

He was my father, Johnny. Any father would'a done the same thing. If he had the connections.

Johnny: Who tole you I was runnin' this joint, Footch?

Maffucci: To give you the works, Johnny, I'm one'a Pete Zerroni's local boys now.

> (**Sweets** *dusts near* **Maffucci***.*)

Johnny: No jive! Battin' in the big leagues, ain't you? Your ol' man was aroun', bet he'd be pretty proud'a you.

Maffucci: Would you believe, my ol' man had ideas 'bout me bein' a lawyer or a doctor?

Johnny: What you doin' for Pete?

Maffucci: Sort'a community relations like, Johnny.

Johnny:

> (*Laughs.*)

I'm one'a Pete's customers! What kind'a community relashuns you got for me?

Maffucci: Glad you opened that, Johnny Cake. Pete says you got him a little concerned.

Johnny: What is he, crazy? Ain't he got more 'portant things on his min'?

Maffucci: Way we got it, first thing ol' Sweets Crane did when he got out was come see you.

Johnny: So what? Sweets was like'a father to me.

Maffucci: So I hear. But before they shut the gate on him, he let some things drop. Like, he made a few threats. What I hear 'bout him, might be crazy enough to give 'em a try.

> (**Johnny** *laughs.*)

What, am I throwin' zingers or sump'm? What's the joke?

NO PLACE TO BE SOMEBODY   419

Johnny: Sweets came 'roun' to tell me he's all caught up.

Maffucci: Wouldn't promote me would you, Johnny Cake? For ol' time's sake, let's not you an' me go horse-to-horse 'bout nothin'.

Johnny: On the up an' up, Footch. Sweets has wrapped it all up for good. Matter'a fack, right now he's doin' odd gigs an' singin' the straight an' narrow.

Maffucci: Wanna believe you, Johnny. But just in case you an' this Sweets are thinkin' 'bout makin' a little noise Pete wants me to give you the six-to-five!

> (**Sweets** *bumps into* **Maffucci**, *spilling the wine down the front of* **Maffucci's** *suit.*)

Hey! Watch it there, pops!

Sweets: Awful sorry 'bout that, mister!

> (*Attempts to wipe* **Maffucci's** *suit with the rag.* **Maffucci** *pushes him aside.*)

Maffucci: That's okay, pops!

> (**Sweets** *continues to wipe* **Maffucci's** *vest.*)

Okay, okay, I said!

> (**Sweets** *continues with his work.*)

Well, Johnny Cake. Like to stay an' jaw with ya a little bit but you know how it is. Community relations, you know.

Johnny: Sho' preshiate you lookin' out for me, Footch!

Maffucci: Think nothin' of it, Johnny Cake. It's Pete. He don't like jigs. Says, the minute they git a little somethin', they start actin' cute. You an' me, we was like brothers. Way I see it, was like you took a dive for me once. Figure I owe ya.

Johnny: You don't owe me a damned thing, Footch.

Maffucci:

> (*Heads for the street doors. Turns back.*)

You know, Johnny Cake? Some reason I never been able to git you off my mind. After all these years. I think if you'da been a wop, you'da been a big man in the rackets.

> (*Exits.* **Sweets** *holds watch to ear.*)

Johnny: All right, now Sweets. Goddamit, wha's this game you playin'?

Shanty: Sweets??? That's Sweets Crane?

Johnny: Shut up, Shanty.

> (*Snatches the rag out of* **Sweets'** *hand. Gets broom. Gives both to* **Shanty**.)

Take this crap back to the kitchen.

> (**Shanty** *takes them to kitchen.*)

Man you either gotta be stir-buggy or you puttin' on one helluva a ack.

Sweets:

> (*Checks the watch.*)

Jus' tryin' to be helpful, Sonny Boy.

Johnny: Don't you be kickin' no more farts at me, man. Wha's with this pil'fin stuff off'a people an' makin' like'a damn lackey? You mus' be plumb kinky.

Sweets: Cain't see no point in watchin' George Raff on tee vee ev'a night. All my life I been into things. Always active.

Johnny: This what you call bein' active? An' look at you? Look like you jus' come off the Bow'ry! Ain't they no pride lef' in you?

Sweets: Pride? Sheee. Pride, Sonny Boy is sump'm I ain't got no mo' use for.

Johnny: For the las' time, ol' man. You better tell me wha's happenin' with you. Don't you make me have to kill you.

Sweets:
(Produces an envelope.)
I'm as good as dead right now!
(He hands Johnny the envelope.)

Johnny: What the hell is it?

Sweets: Guess you could call it my will.

Johnny:
(Turns it over.)
Yo' will??

Sweets: Open it up.

Johnny: Shanty!

Shanty:
(Enters.)
How ya doin', Sweets?

Johnny: Check this out, Shanty. I don't read this jive so good.

Shanty:
(Reads will.)
It's legal stuff. Says here you're gonna inherit interest in barbershops, meat markets, stores an' a whole lotta Harlem real estate. Dam!

Johnny:
(Snatches the papers out of Shanty's hands.)
You gotta be jokin'.

Sweets: I'm leavin' it all to you, Sonny Boy. My lawyers will take care ev'thing.

Johnny: How come you ain't tole me nothin' 'bout this before?

Sweets: Couldn't take no chance it gittin' out. Might'a strung me out on a tax rap too.

Johnny: You lookin' to take some kind'a back gate commute? Suicide?

Sweets:
(Coughs.)
Doctors ain't gimme but six months to ride. Didn't wanna lay it on you til they made sho'.

Johnny: Six months, huh?

Sweets: Mo' or less.

Johnny: Goddamit, Sweets. What the hell kin I say? I sho' been a real bastard. Guess it don't help none for me to say I'm sorry.

Sweets: Might he'p some if you was to turn all this into sump'm worth while an' good. Maybe the Lawd will f'give me f'the way I got it.
(Bursts into laughter and coughs.)

Johnny: Git off it, Sweets. Jus' 'cause you s'pose to chalk out on us don't mean you gotta go an' 'brace relijun.

Sweets: Figure it won't hurt none if I do.

NO PLACE TO BE SOMEBODY   421

Johnny: Shit. That good Lawd you talkin' 'bout is jus' as white as that judge who sent yo' black ass to Fedsville.

Sweets: How you know? You ever seen him? When I was down there in that prison, I reads a lot. Mos'ly the Bible. Bible tells me, the Lawd was hard to look upon. Fack is, he was so hard to look upon that nobody eva looked at him an' lived. Well, I got to figgerin' on that. An' reasons that was so, 'cause he was so black.

> *(Goes into loud laughter and coughs again.)*

Lawd knows! White's easy nuff to look at!

> *(**Johnny** throws the will upon the floor. **Sweets** goes to his knees and clutches the will.)*

What you doin', Sonny Boy? My life is in them papers!

> *(Hits **Johnny** with hat. **Johnny** reaches under the bar and comes up with a revolver. Levels it at **Sweets**.)*

Johnny: See this, Sweets? My firs' an' only pistol. You gave it to me long time ago when I was a lookout for you when you was pullin' them owl jobs in Queens. I worshipped the groun' you walked on. I thought the sun rose an' set in yo' ass. You showed me how to make thirteen straight passes without givin' up the dice. Stood behin' me an' nudged me when to play my ace. Hipped me how to make a gappers cut. How to handle myself in a pill joint. Taught me to trust no woman over six or under sixty. Turned me on to the best horse players an' number runners. Showed me how to keep my ass-pocket full'a coins without goin' to jail. Said the wors' crime I ever committed was comin' out'a my mama screamin' black. Tole me all about white folks an' what to expect from the best of them. You said as long as there was a single white man on this earth, the black man only had one free choice. That was the way he died. When you went to jail for shootin' Charlie, you said, "Sonny Boy git us a plan." Well, I got us a plan. Now, you come back here nutty an' half dead, dancin' all over me about me goin' through a change'a life. An' how you want me to help you git ready to meet yo' Lawd. Well, git ready, mother fucker. Tha's exactly what I'm gon' do. Help you to meet him.

> *(**Johnny** pulls back the hammer of the gun. **Sweets** coughs and looks at the barrel of the gun.)*

Sweets: You ain't gon' shoot me, Johnny. You cain't shoot me. They's a whole lotta you, I ain't even touched.

> *(**Sweets** exits.)*

Blackout

SCENE 2

Time: *Two weeks later*
Place: *The same*
Setting: *The same*
At rise: **Gabe** sits at a table. Glass of red wine before him, strumming

a guitar. **Melvin** *stands next to him thumbing through a playscript.* **Shanty** *is behind the bar as usual.*

Melvin: "The Tooth of a Red Tiger!" What part will you play, Gabe?

Gabe: What you tryin' to do, Mel? Jinx me? I ain't got the part yet.

Melvin: They gave you this script, didn't they?

Gabe: The part calls for a guitar player. Cain't you hear these clinkers?
    (**Melvin** *puts script on table.*)
How was your recital?

Melvin: Ugh! Don't remind me, Gabe. I have this solo in "variations and diversions." I have to do three tour jêtés? Well, ol' Mel fell! Would you believe it? I stumbled and fell! Victor, my teacher, he was there shaking! He was actually shaking.

Gabe: What the hell, Mel. Always another recital.

Melvin: I suppose you could look at it that way! Anyway, I was simply heartbroken. Gabe, do you like Carl Sandburg?

Gabe: Ain't exactly in love with him.

Melvin: I was thinking, since you do write poetry, maybe you'd like to go with me to hear some of his works. Peter Demeter is reading tomorrow night. . . .

Gabe: Got somethin' I gotta do.

Melvin: Well, maybe you'd like to hear some chamber music at the Brooklyn Academy over the weekend.

Gabe: Don't dig chamber music, Mel.

Melvin: I believe an artist should learn all he can about the other forms too.
    (*He exits to kitchen.*)

Dee:
    (*Enters and goes to the bar.*)
Squeeze the bar rag out, Shanty.
    (*She glances at* **Gabe**.)
Full of little surprises, aren't you?

Gabe: Just fakin'.
    (**Shanty** *pours her drink. She takes bottle and glass to a table. Suddenly she catches* **Gabe** *staring at her.*)

Dee: What's with the fish eyes? I gotta new wrinkle or sump'm?

Gabe: Sorry! Just thinkin'!

Dee:
    (*Downs drink.*)
You think too much! Give it a rest!

Gabe: Tell me somethin', Dee . . .

Dee: What'a ya? Writin' a book or sump'm?

Gabe: How'd you meet up with John in the first place?

Dee:
    (*Doesn't answer. Pours another drink. Presently gets to her feet. Goes to window. Peers out.*)
Got Evie to thank for that. She used to come in here a lot when the joint was really jumpin'. She'll never admit it but I think she had it for Johnny.

She's never been much of a drinker but one night she got too looped to drive. Johnny brought her home. When they came in, I was in the process of having my face lifted by a boyfriend. Johnny pulled him off.

Gabe: Stop me if I'm bein' a little too personal.

Dee: Oh, you be as personal as you like, Gabe.

Gabe: How do chicks like you an' Evie . . .

Dee: Get into the life? Is that what you're askin'? For me it was easy! Got a job as a sales girl! Rich Johns would come in propositioning the girls! One day I took one up on it, and here I am.

Gabe: Was it for the money?

Dee: What cheap paperbacks you been readin', Gabe?

Gabe: I get it! You hate your father.

Dee: That poor miserable bastard? That bum? He ain't worth hating.

Gabe: You love John?

Dee: Johnny? Johnny's not the kind of man you love. I think I pity Johnny. Don't get me wrong. I don't mean the kind of pity you'd give to my father or some bum on the street. Somebody blindfolded him. Turned him around. Somewhere inside Johnny's got something. It just come out crooked! Comes out the wrong way.

    (She takes drink and becomes theatrical.)

In a way, Johnny reminds me of a classmate of mine in high school.

Gabe: Boyhood sweetheart, huh?

Dee: Got me pregnant. Nice decent boy. Only, he was black. Went to my folks. Said, "I'll marry her." The crazy bastard. They made his life miserable. I don't have to tell you.

Gabe: Did you love this boy?

Dee: You mean, why didn't we run away together? We were too young and stupid.

Gabe: And the baby?

Dee: Oh, they got rid of it for me.

    (She almost appears to be improvising.)

Word got out somehow. My mother fled to Puerto Rico for a well needed vacation. I stayed around the house.

    (She lapses into theatrical southern dialect à la Tennessee Williams.)

For weeks I just read, listened to the radio or watched television. One night late my father came in dead drunk. Staggered into my room and got into bed with me. Week later, I came to New York.

    (She giggles.)

Funny thing. When I first got into the life, I was always thinkin' about my father. He was always comin' into my mind. Like it was him I was screwin' over and over again. Like I was takin' him away from my mother and punishin' him for lettin' her rule his life.

Gabe: You know? Just the way you're standin' there like that you remind me of somebody?

Dee:

Dame May Whitty?

Gabe: Maxine.

Dee: Who?

Gabe: Maxine.

Dee: Who's Maxine?

Gabe: Probably every woman I've ever known.

Dee: I don't usually think of you with a woman.

Gabe: Come on, Dee.

Dee: I didn't mean it like that, Gabe. I always think of you—well, sort'a like the intellectual type! For some reason people kind'a think intellectual types don't even use the toilet! So who's Maxine?

Gabe: My mother.

Dee: Talking to you is like eatin' cotton candy.

Gabe: She was the little girl who sat across from me.

Dee: In grade school?

Gabe: I stole a quarter from her. It was in her ink-well. Teacher lined us up. Searched us. The quarter rolled out of the pocket of my hightop boots. I kin still hear them kids yellin' "Our theeefer!"

Dee: Pretty humiliatin', huh?

Gabe: We sang duets together in the high school choir. Necked an' rubbed stomachs in dark alleys an' doorways. They kicked her out'a school when she got pregnant. Sent her away. They was sure I did it. Her mama was wild an' crazy. Turned tricks for a cat who owned a Cadillac. Didn't want me messin' aroun' with Maxine. Said I was a dirty Nigger an' jus' wanted Maxine's ass. When Maxine didn't make her period, her mama got drunk an' come lookin' for me with a razor. I hid out for a couple days. Heard later she slashed all the upholsterin' in her pimp's Cadillac. Ha! She was smart, Maxine was. An' Jewish too. Taught me social consciousness. Said I was a good lover. Said white boys got their virility in how much money they made an' the kind'a car they drove. Said I related better 'cause I was black an' had nothin' to offer but myself. So I quit my job. Used to hide in the closet when her folks came in from Connecticut. Listened to 'em degradin' her for livin' with an' supportin' a Nigger. Maxine got herself an Afro hair-do an' joined the Black Nationalists when I couldn't afford to get her hair straightened at Rose Meta's! Didn't really wanna marry me. Jus' wanted my baby so she could go on welfare. She's out there somewhere. Maxine is. She's out there, waitin' on me to come back to her, Maxine is.

Dee:
> *(Laughs.)*

Gabe? Gabe, are you sure you're all right?
> *(He grins.)*

You really loved Maxine, didn't you?
> *(She puts her arms around his neck.)*

Gabe: I sure wanted to . . .

Johnny:
> *(Enters.)*

What the hell's goin' on here?

Gabe: You jealous?

Johnny: Depen's on yo' intenshuns.

(**Gabe** *puts guitar into case. Picks up script. Prepares to leave.*)
Johnny: What, you done gone an' got yo'self a job an' ain't tole nobody?
Gabe: It's only an audition.
Dee: Good luck, Gabe.
Johnny: Yeah. I'm lookin' forward to gettin' a few payments back on all them loans.
    (**Gabe** *gives a razz-berry and exits.*)
You know, Dee? I been thinking. Maybe we ought'a take that trip after all.
Dee: Well now, you don't say? Sweets Crane wouldn't have anything to do with this sudden change of mind, would he?
    (*She starts to pour another drink.*)
Johnny:
    (*Snatches bottle out of her hands.*)
Take it easy on that stuff, girl! Still wanna go, don't you?
Dee: Right now I got somethin' more important on my mind.
Johnny: Dump it on me.
Dee: I want out of the life, Johnny.
Johnny: Dam! You are stoned, ain't you?
Dee: I mean it, Johnny.
Johnny: Thought you an' me had a understandin'.
Dee: There's a hell of a lot more room for a better one.
Johnny: Like what for instance.
Dee: I need some permanence.
Johnny: You mean git married?
Dee: Maybe.
Johnny: Thought you was down on all that housewife jazz.
Dee: I don't take tee vee commercials very seriously if that's what you mean.
Johnny: I gotta business here! Tough nuff time keepin' it perm'nant! Wasn't for the coins you bring in, I'd go under 'fore the week was out.
Dee: Let's build it back up, Johnny. Together. Together, Johnny.
Johnny: What the hell you know 'bout this business?
Dee: Teach me, Johnny! You could teach me.
Johnny: No good. Ain't no woman'a mine gon' be workin'. She b'long at home.
    (*She laughs.*)
Look'a here, you better go on home. Git yo'self together. We'll talk 'bout it later.
Dee: I'll tie a string around my finger.
    (*She gathers her things. Weaves to the doors.*)
Johnny: Hey, girl! You still ain't said where you wanna go.
Dee:
    (*Whirls.*)
I don't know. I hear the north pole's pretty swingin' these days.
Johnny: Keep it up. I'll break yo' damn chops yet.
Dee: Where thou goest, I will follow, Johnny baby.
Johnny: Thinkin' 'bout makin' the Bimini scene. Won't have to worry 'bout crackers doin' the bird with the long red neck. Split this weekend. You make res'vashuns.

Dee:

> (*Blows him a kiss. Bows theatrically.*)

Yah suh, Boss!

> (*She exits.*)

Johnny: Bitches. Can't please none of 'em.

Blackout

SCENE 3

Time: *A day later*
Place: *The same*
Setting: *The same*
At rise: **Melvin** *is arranging chairs and straightening tablecloths.* **Gabe** *enters.*

Melvin: What happened, Gabe? Did you get the part?

Gabe: Nah! Wasn't the right type after all.

Melvin: What type did they want?

Gabe: Whatever it was I wasn't it.

Johnny:

> (*Enters from kitchen. He is munching a sandwich.*)

Nigra type.

Melvin: What type is that?

Johnny: Whatever it is, tha's what he ain't.

Melvin: Doesn't talent have anything to do with it?

Johnny: Prop'ganda, Mel! When whitey pick one'a y'all you gotta either be a clown, a freak or a Nigra type.

Gabe: They do the same thing among themselves too.

Johnny: 'Mongst themselves, they ain't so damn choosey.

Gabe: Should'a seen the cat they did pick. Hell, I'm as black as he is.

Johnny: Gabe, ain't they no mirrors in yo' house?

Gabe: I mean black in here!

Melvin: You people are more preoccupied with color than white people are.

Johnny: They won't let us be porcupined with nothin' else.

Gabe: Don't make no difference what color I am. I'm still black.

Johnny: Yeah! But you ain't gon' git no chance to prove it. Not on no stage, you ain't. You remin' whitey'a too many things he don't wanna take'a look at. Figgers he's got nuff problems dealin' with Niggers who jus' look black, like me.

Gabe: Aw, shut the fuck up, John.

Johnny: Who you talkin' to?

Gabe: You, you bastard. I'm tellin' you to shut the fuck up. Jus' cool it with yo' shit.

Johnny: Jus' tryin' to tell you like it is, Gabe! You jus' don't b'lieve a hard head makes a sof' ass!

Melvin:
>   *(Pats **Gabe** on the back.)*

Like you told me, Gabe. Always another recital.
>   *(**Melvin** exits to kitchen. **Johnny** tosses **Gabe** some bills.)*

Gabe: No more handouts, baby.

Johnny: This ain't no handout! Want you to do me a favor.

Gabe: Yeah?

Johnny: Me an' Dee goin' on a little vacation, want you to help Shanty an' Mel with the store while we gone.

Gabe: When you leavin'?

Johnny: End'a the week. Makin' it to Bim'ni.
>   *(**Cora** and **Shanty** enter. Carry black drum cases.)*

Cora: Give us a han' here, Gabe? They's more out there in the cab.
>   *(**Gabe** exits to the street.)*

Johnny: What you bringin' this junk in here for?

Cora: We bringin' this junk in here as you call it on a purpose.

Johnny: Be damned if tha's so. Git out'a here an' Shanty let's git to work.
>   *(**Gabe** returns with another case.)*

Cora: Look'a here, Jay Cee. Me and Shangy swore when we got these here drums, we was gon' bring 'em in here for you to look at an' lissen to with yo' own eyes an' ears.

Johnny: All of a sudden I done gone deaf an' blin'. Now, git this hazarae out'a here.

Cora: Ain't gon' do ner such thing. Not till me an' Shangy has got som'a what we's set out to do.

Gabe: Sure got a pretty good start.

Cora: Shangy! What is you doin' with the broom?
>   *(**Johnny** reaches for one of the drum cases.)*

Take yo' nasty, stinkin', filthy, black han's off them drums!
>   *(**Johnny** recoils.)*

Melvin:
>   *(Comes out of the kitchen.)*

What on earth is happening?

Cora: It ain't happenin' yet.

Melvin: Well, I just never would have believed it. Isn't it wonderful?

Cora: 'Fore Shangy gits on these drums, they's sum'n you oughta know, Jay Cee.

Johnny: You runnin' the show.

Cora: Shangy is quittin' you today. Right now.

Johnny: Why the hell didn't you say that in the first place?

Cora: 'Cause you was so busy gittin' these drums out'a here. Tha's why.

Melvin: You're really going to play for us, Shanty?

Cora: Tha's his intenchun, thank you. Shangy! Will you come on over here? Gabe don't know nothin' 'bout what he's doin'.
>   *(**Shanty** hands **Johnny** the broom. Approaches the drums reluctantly.)*

Johnny: Some reason, Shangy, you don't look so happy. Now I want you to jump up there an' give ol' Jay Cee a little wham-bam-thank-ya-ma'm. Price'a the funky nitty-gritty. Like the time they said you played like'a spade. Guess I kin risk gettin' a summons on that.

Cora: Ne' min', Jay Cee. Go 'head, honey! Git yo' se'f together. Take all the time you need.

Gabe: Whale, baby.

> (**Shanty** sits upon the stool. Fumbles. Accidentally puts foot on pedal. Strikes pose. Taps cymbals. Moves to snares. Mixes. Pumps. Works. Gets loud. **Cora** fidgets. Anxious. **Shanty** fakes. Can't cover up. Becomes frustrated. Louder. Stands. Begins to beat wildly. Moves around the drums banging for all he's worth. **Cora** is ashamed. **Gabe** frowns. **Cora** grabs **Shanty**'s arm. He pushes her away. Becomes a windmill.)

Cora: Stop it, Shangy! Stop it, I said!

> (**Shanty** beats as if possessed. **Cora** is helpless. **Johnny** calmly reaches behind the bar. Gets pitcher of water. Pours it over **Shanty**'s head.)

Shanty: Ya-hoooo!

> (Leaps into the air.)

I had it! I was on it! I was into it, babee!

> (He moves around doing the pimp walk.)

Ol' Red Taylor said I had the thing. Said, "Shanty man! You got the thing!"

> (Goes to **Mel**.)

Gimme some skin, motherfucker.

> (**Mel** gives him some skin. Goes to **Gabe**.)

Gimme some skin.

> (**Gabe** doesn't put his hand out.)

Ah, fuck you, man. Didn't I hip you to my happenin's, Johnny? Didn't I show you where it's at?

Johnny: You burned, baby, you burned.

> (**Shanty** gives **Johnny** some skin.)

Cora: Shangy! I—think you better start packin' up now.

Shanty: Git away from me! You funky black bitch.

Cora: Shangy!

Shanty: Just stay away from me—you evil piece'a chunky.

Cora: You ain't got no call to say nothin' like that to me.

Shanty: Oh, no? You ain't jive timin' me, you just like Gloria.

Cora: What you sayin', Shangy?

Shanty: You don't want me to play no drums.

Cora: You wrong, Shangy.

Shanty: Thought you'd make a fool out'a me, did you? Gittin' me to bring these drums in here. You thought I'd mess it up. Well I showed you where it was at. I showed all'a you.

Cora: Shangy, you crazy! You the one suggestid that!

Shanty: Bitch, call the man. Have him come git these drums.

Cora: Come git the drums? Why, Shangy? Why?

Shanty: I don't need you to help me get my drums. I get my own drums. Dig it.

NO PLACE TO BE SOMEBODY   **429**

Cora: This chile done clean los' his min'.

Shanty: You an' me are through! Dig it? We are through. We've had it. Splitsville.

> (**Cora** *is numb.*)

Now you believe me huh, Johnny? A bucket'a cold water an' throw it on me, huh?

Johnny: To git you to quit. Come on, baby. Let's git some dry clothes on you.

> (**Johnny** *leads* **Shanty** *to the kitchen.*)

Shanty: A bucket'a cold water like the night we played "Saints" . . .

> (**Johnny** *and* **Shanty** *exit to kitchen. For a moment* **Cora** *looks up at the clock.*)

Cora: What time is it, Gabe?

Gabe: My watch was stolen . . .

Cora:

> (*Points to clock above cash register.*)

What time do that clock say?

Gabe: Quarter after three . . .

Cora: Know sump'm, Gabe? I ain't never learned how to tell time. Thirty years ol' an' I don't even know the time'a day. But when I gits up in the mornin', tha's the very firs' thing I'm gon' do. I'm gonna learn how to tell me some time.

> (*She exits.*)

Johnny:

> (*Enters from kitchen.*)

Go back there an' help Shanty, Mel! He don't feel so good.

> (**Melvin** *goes to kitchen.*)

Help me tear down this thing, Gabe.

> (**Johnny** *begins to dismantle drums.*)

Gabe: Do it your damned-self. I ain't feelin' so hot either.

> (*Exits hurriedly.*)

Johnny: Now what in hell's matter with you?

> (*Busies himself with the drums.* **Mary Lou Bolton** *enters.*)

Mary Lou: Hello . . .

Johnny:

> (*His attention is still with the drums.*)

Sump'm I kin do for you?

Mary Lou:

> (*Moves to table, sits.*)

I'd like a daiquiri, please.

Johnny:

> (*Looks up.*)

Tha's one drink I ain't never been able to make right.

Mary Lou: Simple! Just go easy with the sugar.

Johnny:

> (*Goes behind bar. Begins to mix drink. Dumps in a lot of sugar.*)

Never 'spected to see you back here ag'in.

Mary Lou: Let's just say, I don't scare so easy. By the way, what were you trying to prove anyway?

Johnny:
> *(Comes to her table and sets the drink before her.)*

I was waitin' for you to ask sump'm like that.

Mary Lou: Really?

Johnny: You sho' didn't come back here for no drink.

Mary Lou: Pretty conceited, aren't you?

Johnny: Jus' hipt to yo' kin', tha's all.

Mary Lou: "My kind," huh?

Johnny: You don't like to be kept in the dark 'bout nothin'.

Mary Lou: That's the difference between man and beast.

Johnny: I kin see you ain't learned a damned thing in that college, neither.

Maffucci:
> *(Enters with **Truck Driver** who carries case of whiskey to kitchen.)*

How you doin', Johnny Cake?

Johnny: Okay, Gumba. What'd Pete do? Demote you? Got you ridin' the truck.

Maffucci: New kinda' community relations, Johnny Cake. Ride aroun' with the boys, see if the customers are happy. You happy, Johnny Cake?

> *(**Truck Driver** comes out of kitchen, exits.)*

Johnny: Dee-leruss.

Maffucci:
> *(Spies **Mary Lou**.)*

Good, good. Makes me happy too.

> *(He moves to **Mary Lou**.)*

Say! Ain't you Judge Bolton's kid?

Mary Lou: Why, yes. Yes I am.

Maffucci:
> *(Takes her in his arms. Handles her. She resists to no avail.)*

Never forget a face. Turned out to be a real nice tomata, huh? Don't mind me, kid.

> *(He releases her.)*

Next time you see your ol' man, tell him Mike Maffucci says, "hello!"

> *(He pats her on the behind.)*

See you aroun', Johnny Cake!

Johnny:
> *(Advances.)*

Chow, Footch. Okay. How does he know yo' ol' man?

Mary Lou:
> *(Visibly shaken.)*

They were clients of his.

Johnny: They? They who? You mean Footch?

Mary Lou:
> *(Nods.)*

Something about bribing a city official. And someone was murdered.

NO PLACE TO BE SOMEBODY   431

Johnny: Mary. Does the name Pete Zerroni ring a bell?

Mary Lou: Yes! He was one of the defendants. My father won the case.

Johnny: I don't care what nobody say. Your father was a damn good lawyer.

Mary Lou: What's your interest? You know this Pete Zerroni?

Johnny: Not personal.

Mary Lou: He's not a very good person to know.

Johnny: With Pete, sometimes you ain't got no choice.

(She prepares to leave.)

Here! Lemme freshen up yo' drink.

Mary Lou: No thanks. I'm getting—I'm getting a headache.

(She moves to the street doors.)

Goodbye, mister . . .

Johnny: Johnny. Johnny Williams.

Mary Lou: Goodbye, Johnny. . . .

(She exits, leaving her purse.)

Johnny:

(Picks her purse up. Thinks for a moment. Goes to phone, dials.)

Hey, Dee? Cancel them reservashuns. Sump'm important jus' came up. Won't be able to after all. Now don't hand me no crap. Just cancel.

Blackout

Act Three

SCENE 1

Time: *Two weeks later*
Place: *The same*
Setting: *The same*
At rise: *Table at center has large Molotov cocktail. A folded newspaper leans against it. Its headline reads: "Negroes Riot!" A banner resembling the American flag dangles from a flagstand. Next to the Molotov cocktail is a plate. A large, black automatic pistol rests in it. Beside the plate is a knife and fork. A toilet is heard flushing.* **Gabe** *comes on stage zipping his pants. His attitude is ceremonial.*

Gabe: "They's mo' to bein' black than meets the
Eye!
Bein' black, is like the way ya walk an'
Talk!
It's a way'a lookin' at life!
Bein' black, is like sayin', "Wha's happenin',
Babee!"
An' bein' understood!
Bein' black has a way'a makin' ya call some-
Body a mu-tha-fuc-kah, an' really meanin' it!
An' namin' eva'body broh-thah, even if you don't!

Bein' black, is eatin' chit'lins an' wah-tah-
Melon, an' to hell with anybody, if they don't
Like it!
Bein' black has a way'a makin' ya wear bright
Colors an' knowin' what a fine hat or a good
Pair'a shoes look like an' then—an' then—
It has a way'a makin' ya finger pop! Invent a
New dance! Sing the blues! Drink good Scotch!
Smoke a big seegar while pushin' a black Cadillac
With white sidewall tires! It's conkin' yo'
Head! Wearin' a black rag to keep the wave!
Carryin' a razor! Smokin' boo an' listenin' to
Gut-bucket jazz!
Yes! They's mo' to bein' black than meets the eye!
Bein' black is gittin' down loud an' wrong! Uh-huh!
It's makin' love without no hangups! Uh-huh! Or
Gittin' sanctified an' holy an' grabbin' a han'ful'a
The sistah nex' to ya when she starts speakin' in
Tongues!
Bein' black is havin' yo' palm read! Hittin' the
Numbers! Workin' long an' hard an' gittin' the
Short end'a the stick an' no glory! It's
Knowin' they ain't no dif'rence 'tween
White trash an' white quality! Uh-huh!
Bein' black is huggin' a fat mama an' havin'
Her smell like ham-fat, hot bisquits
An' black-eyed peas!
Yes! They's mo' to bein' black than meets
The eye!
Bein' black has a way'a makin' ya mad mos'
Of the time, hurt all the time an' havin'
So many hangups, the problem'a soo-side
Don't even enter yo' min'! It's buyin'
What you don't want, beggin' what you don't
Need! An' stealin' what is yo's by rights!
Yes! They's mo' to bein' black than meets the
Eye!
It's all the stuff that nobody wants but
Cain't live without!
It's the body that keeps us standin'! The
Soul that keeps us goin'! An' the spirit
That'll take us thooo!
Yes! They's mo' to bein' black than meets
The eye!"
(**Gabe** sits at table. Cuts into gun with knife and fork. Finally picks
gun up. Bites into it. Chews and swallows. Takes drink from Molotov
cocktail. Wipes mouth.)

NO PLACE TO BE SOMEBODY   433

Bru-thas an' sistahs! Will ya jine me!

*(Blackout on **Gabe**. Lights come up on **Dee** and **Shanty**. She sits at table, bottle of whiskey in front of her. **Shanty** sits on stool reading copy of* Downbeat.)

Dee: Ain't like him to stay away from the joint like this. Can't reach him at his apartment either.

Shanty: He don't come in but about once a day. Just to check things out—

Dee: It's a woman he's with, isn't it?

Shanty: Huh?

Dee: Hello?

Shanty: What you say? Eh, *que pasa?*

Dee: He's with a woman—It's a woman he's with . . .

Shanty: Uh—it's uh—Mel's day off, Dee—gotta go clean up the kitchen . . .

Dee: Shanty, come here a second . . .

(He comes to her reluctantly.)

Thanks, huh?

(She stuffs a bill into the pocket of his apron.)

For nothing!

(He shrugs. Exits to kitchen. She goes back to drinking.)

Evie:

*(Enters. Spies **Dee**. Moves to jukebox.)*

Hey.

Dee: Hey, yourself!

(Music comes on.)

How does it feel to be on your way to good citizenship?

Evie: Yeah, huh? Imagine me doin' it to an IBM machine.

Dee: It ain't hard.

Evie: That bottle ain't doin' you a damn bit'a good.

Dee: Tha's debatable.

Evie: How 'bout a nice hot cup a'black coffee?

Dee: Uh-uh! Gotta stay here an' wait for Johnny.

Evie: Pretty soon you'll be waitin' for him flat on the floor.

Dee: Drunk or sober, it doesn't matter anyway.

Evie: Why you doin' this? Sheee! He ain't worth the powder it'd take to blow him up.

Dee: Tha's mah business.

Evie: It's my business you was up at Jack's last night.

Dee: Where'd you hear that?

Evie: Jack. He called me. Now, if you wanna kill yourself, or git killed—go right ahead! But I wanna warn you 'bout one thing. Stay out'a Jack's, you hear me? A lotta niggers in there, jus' waitin' for somebody like you! 'Nother thing! Jack's my uncle—don't want'a see him lose his license—on account'a some bitch like you!

Dee: Okay, so I was up at Jack's!

Evie: What was you lookin' for anyway? Way off yo' beat! Ain't nobody up there got your price!

Dee: I wasn't sellin'—I was buyin'.

Evie: You was what?

Dee: The biggest blackest cat you ever saw picked me up.

Evie: You just lookin' to git yourself hurt, girl.

Dee: Oh, he was polite. Too polite. Took me to his room. Smelled like that greasy Pomade an' hair straitener you smell sometimes on those pretties in the subway. An' when he put on his silk stocking-cap—I just about cracked. Kept the light on so he could watch.

Evie: Git yourself together, girl. Drunk as you are—you liable to tell Johnny 'bout this an' he'd have to kill you.

Dee: When it got good to him he started singin', "Black an' white together —black an' white together!" An' the toilet down the hall was flushing over and over again.

Evie: Bitch, did you hear what I said?

Dee: No! I ain't goin' anyplace! I'm stayin' right here . . .

    (She sits at table. Goes into purse. Takes out can of shoe polish.)

If I have to stage a sit-in to do it.

    (She puts mirror before her. Begins to apply polish to her face.)

Evie: Girl, what are you doin' . . .

Dee:

    *(Knocks **Evie**'s hand away.)*

Take your hands off me, you stinkin' cunt! Dirty, black sow!

Evie:

    *(Slaps **Dee** viciously.)*

All right, you crazy, uptight, drunken whore! Sure as shit you go'n end up in Bellevue or git your ass sliced up an' thrown to the rats in some alley . . .

    *(**Johnny** enters. **Dee** sing-songs him.)*

Dee: Where you been keepin' yo'se'f, Johnneee, babeee!

Johnny: Git that crap off your face an' git the hell out'a here!

Dee:

    (Snaps her fingers.)

I's black an' I's proud!

Evie: Listen here, Johnny! This girl is in trouble!

Johnny: She's free, white an' always right!

    *(**Dee** laughs. He goes to her, wipes the black from her face, forcing her to relent. **Dee** begins to weep. He is almost tender with her.)*

Evie: She ain't free a'you—Dee, if you got an ounce a sense in yo' head you'll git on up and come on out with me now.

Dee: Hit the wind, sugar! Git on back to your stupid analyst an' your fuckin' IBM machine! Hit da win', sugar.

    *(**Evie** shakes her head, moves quickly to the door.)*

Johnny: Hey! Pussy!

I know what's eatin' yo ass. You don't like it' cause I went for her an' not you! Tha's it, ain't it?

Evie:

    *(Moves quickly to the two of them. Takes **Dee** by the shoulders. Pulls*

NO PLACE TO BE SOMEBODY   435

*her up and draws her to her roughly. Plants a hard kiss upon **Dee's** mouth. She shoves **Dee** into the arms of **Johnny** who quickly puts **Dee** aside. He faces **Evie** furiously. **Shanty** enters.)*

Darlin', you way off base. I've known Niggers like you all my life! Think everything's a game. I wouldn't piss on you if yo'.ass was on fire. Lef' to me, I'd give you a needle—let you sit in the corner like little Jackie Horner, jerkin' off all by yourself!

> *(**Johnny** raises his hand. **Evie** beats him to the punch, clubs him with her forefinger between the legs. He winces and doubles over. **Evie** exits quickly. **Dee** laughs hysterically. **Mary Lou Bolton** enters. **Dee** is lying on the floor.)*

Mary Lou: Johnny, I . . .

Johnny: Stay where you at, Mary.

Mary Lou: Johnny, maybe I'd better . . .

Dee: Well, well, well. And just might who you be, Miss Baby Cakes?

Mary Lou: Johnny!

Johnny: I said stay where you at!

Dee:

> *(Struggles to her feet. Gathers her belongings.)*

Baby Cakes, let me give you the best advice you ever had in your whole little life. Run away from here fast. Run for your life.

> *(She goes into her purse. Comes up with baby shoes. Drops them on the floor. Exits.)*

Mary Lou: Who is she, Johnny?

Johnny: Some chick with a problem.

Mary Lou: She—she looked . . .

Johnny: She was wiped out.

Mary Lou:

> *(Picks up the baby shoes.)*

Who do these belong to . . .

Johnny:

> *(Snatches them out of her hands and throws them into the waste basket.)*

Don't ask me! Never had no kid'a mine if tha's what you're thinkin'!

Mary Lou: I don't think you'll be seeing me anymore, Johnny.

Johnny: Why the hell not, Mary?

Mary Lou: Are you in any trouble, Johnny?

Johnny: Trouble? What kind'a trouble?

Mary Lou: My father! Someone called him about us!

Johnny: What about?

Mary Lou: Whoever it was said if he didn't stop me from seeing you, they would.

> *(He grins.)*

Are you in some kind of trouble?

Johnny: That depen's, Mary. Take off, Shanty!

Shanty: Man, I still got . . .

Johnny: I said, take off!

(Shanty takes off apron. Gets hat. Exits. Johnny locks doors behind him.)
'Member when we was talkin' 'bout Pete Zerroni?

Mary Lou: Yes . . .

Johnny: Pete don't like it if a Nigger's got a place'a business in his ter'tory.

Mary Lou: You gotta be kidding.

Johnny: Ain't you learned nothin' from all that civil rights?

Mary Lou: What proof do you have?

Johnny: Baby, this ain't no ord'nary type 'scrimunshun. They give you the signal. You ignore it! Place burns down.

Mary Lou: But why don't they want me to see you?

Johnny: Your ol' man was Zerroni's lawyer! Think maybe I might try to work you. . . .

Mary Lou: Work me?

Johnny: Yo' ol' man might have somethin' on Zerroni an' his boys in his records or files.

Mary Lou: That's silly! It could never be used as any real evidence.

Johnny: Sho' could make it hot for a whole lotta people if the D.A. happened to get a few tips.

Mary Lou: What are you getting at?

Johnny: Nothin'. You wanted to know why they didn't want you to see me, didn't you? 'Les yo' ol' man's prege'dice.

Mary Lou: He knows I've dated Negroes before.
    (She thinks for a moment.)
You really believe if you got this information it would keep Zerroni off your back?

Johnny: Well, they still don't know who killed Rep'senative Mahoney. . . .

Mary Lou: Well, you know I couldn't do anything like that. I mean take that information. My father would never forgive me.

Johnny: Like I say. Tha's the only reason I kin figger why they don't want you to be seein' me.

Mary Lou: Anyway, he keeps that sort of thing locked in a safe! In his office.

Johnny:
    (Comes to her. Takes her by the hand and pulls her to him. He kisses her gently. She responds.)
Queer, ain't it? Yo' ol' man's a judge. Sworn to uphol' justice. We cain't even go to him for help.

Mary Lou: I'll speak to him about it, Johnny.

Johnny: Don't you do that, Mary. Don't you do nothin' like that.

Mary Lou: But why, Johnny? He could probably help you.

Johnny: For all we know, he might be in with Zerroni.

Mary Lou: Don't you say that.

Johnny: Funny, after that rotten bunch'a Ginees got off he got to be judge right away.

Mary Lou: I think I'd better leave now.

Johnny: Why'd you come back here, Mary? Make like you wanted a daiquiri? Think I'd be a sucker for some white missionary pussy?

NO PLACE TO BE SOMEBODY · 437

Mary Lou: That is a terrible thing to say.

Johnny: You don't give a damned about civil rights. What about my civil rights? Don't I git any?

Mary Lou: There are ways to stop Zerroni. There are people we can go to for help.

Johnny: Yeah? An' they'll go over to Zerroni's an' picket!

Mary Lou: That's not funny.

Johnny: You liberal-ass white people kill me! All the time know more 'bout wha's bes' for Niggers'n Niggers do.

Mary Lou: You don't have to make the world any worse.

Johnny: Never had no chance to make it no better neither.

> (There is pounding on street doors. **Johnny** unlocks them. **Mary Lou** rushes out as **Gabe** hurries in.)

Gabe: Git your coat, John. Quick!

Johnny: What the hell for?

Gabe: It's Dee! She's dead.

Johnny: Dead?

Gabe: Can't figger how they got my number. She slit her wrists. Why'd they call me?

Johnny: Where is she?

Gabe: The ladies' room, Hotel Theresa.

Blackout

SCENE 2

Time: *Three days later*
Place: *The same*
Setting: *The same*
At rise: *Music from jukebox is going full blast.* **Shanty** *is seated on a barstool. Beats upon another.*

Shanty: Aw, blow it, baby! Workout! Yeah! I hear ya! Swing it! Work yo' show!

> (**Johnny** and **Gabe** enter dressed in suits. **Gabe** as usual carries briefcase.)

Johnny: Goddamit, Shanty! Git under the bed with that shit. Ain't you got no respect for the dead?

> (Pulls cord out of socket. **Shanty** puts sticks away. **Melvin** comes out of kitchen.)

Melvin: How was the funeral?

Gabe: How is any funeral, Mel?

Johnny:

> (Goes behind bar. Mixes drinks.)

Every damned whore in town showed up! Think they'd have a little respeck an' stay home!

Melvin: Was her people there?

Gabe: Only us!

Shanty:

> *(Picks up newspaper.)*

Paper sure gave you hell, Johnny!

Johnny: Who the hell asked ya?

> *(He comes around bar.)*

Comin' on like some bitch in'a cheap-ass movie! Writin' all that jive on the shithouse wall with lipstick!

Shanty: I always liked Dee! Good tipper.

Johnny:

> *(Bangs on bar.)*

Anybody'd think I killed her! Blamin' me for everything! Hell, I never did nothin' to her!

Gabe: Nothin' for her neither!

Cora:

> *(Enters. Dressed to kill. Wears white rose corsage.)*

Hello, ev'body.

Gabe: Hello, Cora. . . .

Cora: Wha's ev'body lookin' so down in the mouth about? Like you jus' come from a funeral.

Johnny: Is that yo' idea of some kind'a damn joke?

Melvin: Ain't you heard, Cora?

Cora: Heard what?

Melvin: It's been in all the papers! Johnny's friend, Dee. She committed suicide a couple of days ago.

Cora: Lawd have mercy! I'm so sorry! I—I haven't exactly been keepin' up with the news lately! You see I—I jus' got married this morning.

Melvin: Married? I hope you'll be very happy, Cora.

Gabe: Congratulations, Cora.

Cora: Oh, thank you! Thank you so much.

Johnny: Must'a been a whirlwin' co'tship.

Cora: Ack'shully, I been knowin' him f'quite some time! He's a heart speshlis' I met at the hospital.

Johnny: From the looks of you, he mus' be a pretty good'n.

Cora: He's jus' aroun' the corner gittin' the car checked over! It's a good distance to Kwee-beck.

Gabe: Quebec?

Cora: Our honeymoon! Wants me to meet his peoples! Cause they's French, you know. Jay Cee?

> *(She goes to* **Johnny.***)*

Johnny: What?

Cora: Awful sorry 'bout what happened.

Johnny: Yeah! Sure, Cora!

Cora: Sump'm ter'ble must'a happen to drive her to do a thing like that!

Johnny: Good luck with the married bag, huh?

Cora: Why thank you, Jay Cee! Thank you. You know me an' you knowed each other a lotta years. Some reason, I could never do nothin' to suit you. No matter how hard I tried. Some times you make me so mad I ha'f wanna kill you! But I was fool 'nuff to care sump'm 'bout you anyway. 'Cause to me you always been that li'l bad boy who was lef' all alone in the worl' with nobody to take care him!

Johnny: Guess it'll always be "Jay Cee ag'inst the worl'!"

Cora:

> *(Tries to touch him. He jerks away. She looks at* **Shanty***.)*

Ain't you gon' wish me good luck too, Shangy Mulligans?

> **(Shanty** *remains silent. Stares out of the window. She shrugs. Moves to street doors.)*

Well, o-re-vo-ree, ev'body! O-re-vo-ree!

> *(She giggles.)*

Tha's French, you know! That means, "Bye y'all!"

> *(She exits happily.)*

Shanty: Se-la-goddam-vee.

Melvin: She sure was happy!

Gabe: Different too.

Johnny: Married a doctor! Ain't that a bitch? Say one thing for her! That number don't give up! She . . .

Shanty: Shut up, man!

Johnny: What you say?

Shanty: I said shut up, Nigger.

Johnny: Now, look. I know you upset 'bout Cora, but . . .

Shanty: Will you cool it! Big man! Mister hot daddy! Think you know everything in the whole goddam world, don't you? Well, lemme tell you somethin', man. You don't know a mu-tha-fuc-kun thing.

> *(He rips off his apron and flings it into* **Johnny**'*s face.)*

Here! Do you own dirty, Nigger work! I've done all I'm gonna do! Took all I'm gonna take!

> *(He pulls out his drumsticks. Boldly beats upon the bar.)*

Stood behind this bar! Let you put me down for the last time 'cause my skin is white.

> *(He beats harder upon the bar.)*

Yeah, baby. I'm white. An' I'm proud of it. Pretty an' white. Dynamite. Eh, mothahfuckah. Know what else I got that you ain't got? I got soul. You ain't got no soul. Mothahfuckah's black an ain't got no soul. If you're an example of what the white race is ag'inst, then baby, I'm gittin' with 'em. They are gonna need a cat like me. Somebody that really knows where you black sons-a-bitches are at.

> *(He picks up the butcher knife. Plunges it into the top of the bar.)*

That's what I think of this ol' piece'a kind'lin! Take it an' stick it up you black, rusty, dusty!

> *(He moves quickly to the street doors. Turns. Gives* **Johnny** *the finger and exits quickly.)*

Johnny: Well, looks like ol' Corabelle Beasely done turned Shanty into a real white man, after all. Now, what about you, Mel?

Melvin: Huh?

Johnny: Don't you wanna cuss me out an' split too?

Melvin: I ain't got nothin' against you, Johnny.

Johnny: Tha's too damn bad.

    (Tosses **Melvin** *some bills.)*

Melvin: What this for, Johnny?

Johnny: Cain't afford to keep the kitchen open no more. Business all aroun' ain't worth lickin' the lead on a pencil.

Melvin: Let me stay on, Johnny, please? Shanty's gone, I can tend bar and still do whatever short orders there are. Please, Johnny, don't let me go?

Johnny: Damned, Mel. Didn't know you liked it aroun' here that much.

Gabe: What about your dancin', Mel? You wanna work in a bar the rest of your life?

Melvin: I—I quit my dancin', Gabe. . . .

Gabe: Why'd you do that?

Melvin: Well, I—I went to this party Victor gave at his penthouse. A lot of celebrities were there. And Gabe, you just wouldn't have believed it.

Gabe: What happened?

Melvin: I'm ashamed to tell you!

Johnny: Aw, go on, Mel. We big boys.

Melvin: Well, they all got plastered! They were smoking marihuana, too! Even the women! Can you imagine? And then they started taking off their clothes.

Johnny: Didn't you know where these turkeys was at before you went?

Melvin: I don't go to parties much. I don't drink. You know that.

Johnny: Did you take your clothes off too?

Melvin: Are you kidding?

Gabe: So you left.

Melvin: They wouldn't let me leave. So I ran into that bathroom and locked that door. But they jimmied the door open.

Johnny: An' then what happened?

Melvin: They—they held me down and took all my clothes off. It was awful. I said if that's what you gotta do to be a dancer then . . .

Johnny: Mel, yo' mama must'a gave you too many hot baths when you was a baby.

Mary Lou:

    (Enters. She carries a paper bag.)

Helped my father at the office yesterday. Must have watched him dial the combination to that safe at least twenty times.

    *(***Johnny*** snatches bag. Locks doors. Comes behind bar.* **Mary Lou** *follows.)*

Didn't get a chance to hear the tapes. Glanced through some of the other stuff, though. Looks pretty explosive.

Johnny: Don't read so good, Mary. What's this stuff say?

Mary Lou: Zerroni admits that he had Joseph Mahoney killed. Maffucci did it. And here it says that he was in on several bribes . . .

Johnny: Mary, this is it. This is the stuff I need!

Mary Lou: I—I thought about it a long time. There just wasn't any other solution.

> (**Johnny** *stuffs papers back into bag.*)

Johnny, I—I . . .

> (*She peers at* **Gabe** *and* **Melvin**.)

Johnny: Go 'head! You kin say anything in front'a them.

Mary Lou: Well, it's not the kind of thing you would say in front of . . .

Johnny: Mary, I don't think it's wise for you to be seen aroun' here. I want you to lay low for awhile.

Mary Lou: I can't go home, Johnny. Daddy will know I . . .

Johnny: Ain't they some girlfri'n you kin stay with?

Mary Lou: I—I suppose so! But I thought we . . .

Gabe: What's this all about, John?

Mary Lou: It's to keep Pete Zerroni from forcing Johnny out of business. Don't you know about it?

Melvin: First time I've heard about it.

Gabe: What's your father got to do with it?

Mary Lou: He was Zerroni's lawyer.

Gabe: And you stole that material from your father?

Mary Lou: Yes, I stole that material from my father. There was nothing else we could do.

Gabe: Why you stupid naive little bitch. Don't you know what he wants that stuff for?

Mary Lou: To keep Zerroni from forcing him out of business.

Gabe: That's a lie! He wants it so he kin blackmail his way into his own dirty racket.

Mary Lou: That's not true! Tell him, Johnny.

Gabe: A black Mafia. That's what he wants.

> (**Gabe** *laughs.*)

Mary Lou: You're crazy. Johnny, are you going to stand there and . . .

Johnny: I gotta right to my own game. Just like they do.

Mary Lou: What?

Johnny: My own game!

Mary Lou: Johnny!

Gabe: What did you do it for, Mary? For love? Sheee! He hates you, you bitch. Hates everything you stand for. Nice little suffering white girl.

> (**Mary Lou** *slaps* **Gabe**. *He throws her into a chair. She begins to weep.*)

Lemme tell you something. Before he kin lay one hot hand on you, you gonna have to git out there on that street an' hussle your ass off.

> (**Gabe** *moves to* **Johnny**.)

Gimme that file, John.

> (**Johnny** *reaches under bar. Comes up with revolver. Levels it at* **Gabe**. **Melvin** *gasps. Falls to floor.*)

Johnny: I don't wanna kill you, Gabe. This is the one break I been waitin' on. It ain't much but it's gon' have to do.

Gabe: You kill me that file ain't gonna do you no good anyway. I'm tellin' you. Gimme that file.

(**Johnny** *finally lowers gun.* **Gabe** *puts bag into briefcase. Starts to move to street doors.* **Maffucci** *and* **Judge Bolton** *enter.*)

Bolton: Get in the car, Mary Lou.

Mary Lou: Daddy, I . . .

Bolton: I said get in the car!

    (**Mary Lou** *rushes out followed by* **Maffucci**.)

You know what I'm here for, Williams.

Johnny: Just like that, huh?

Bolton: Just like that.

    (**Maffucci** *reenters.*)

Johnny: I wanna talk to Pete Zerroni.

Maffucci: Pete ain't got nothin' to say to you, Johnny Cake.

Bolton: Those notes belong to me. Not to Zerroni.

Johnny: I ain't budgin' til I see Pete, personal. He's got to come here an' go horse to horse with me. Ain't gon' wait too long neither. 'Lections comin' up. Li'l phone call to the D.A. could make him very happy 'bout his future.

    (**Maffucci** *suddenly pulls gun on* **Johnny**.)

Bolton: Put that away, you fool!

    (**Maffucci** *returns gun to shoulder holster.*)

Johnny: Footch, don't think Pete or the Judge here wanna see me git hit jus' yet.

Bolton: What is it, Williams? Money?

    (*Produces an envelope.*)

Johnny: You ofays sho' think money's the root'a all evil, don't you, Judge?

Maffucci: Let's go, Frank. We're just wastin' time.

Bolton: Williams, you'd better listen to me and listen good. You're in dangerous trouble. If you don't hand over that material, I'm not going to be responsible for what happens to you.

Johnny: An' I sho' ain't gon' be responsible for what happens to you neither, Judge.

    (*Both* **Johnny** *and the* **Judge** *laugh.* **Bolton** *starts to exit.*)

Judge?

    (**Bolton** *turns.* **Johnny** *tosses him* **Mary Lou**'s *purse.* **Bolton** *exits.*)

Maffucci: Johnny Cake?

Johnny: What?

Maffucci: Right now, your life ain't worth a plug nickel.

Johnny: Footch?

    (*Puts his thumbnail under his upper teeth and flicks it at* **Maffucci**. **Maffucci** *exits.*)

Johnny: Gabe-ree-el. How come you didn't hand over the file?

Gabe: I couldn't! When I saw those two bastards together, I just couldn't bring myself to do it!

    (**Gabe** *removes bag from briefcase. Hands it to* **Johnny**.)

Johnny: Mel, take this over to the drugstore. Get copies made, quick! Move!

    (**Melvin** *exits quickly.*)

Gabe: You know they're gonna git you.

Johnny: Gabe, we was got the day we was born! Where you been? Jus' bein' black ain't never been no real reason for livin'.

Gabe: If I thought that I'd probably go crazy or commit suicide.

Blackout

SCENE 3

Time: *A day later*
Place: *The same*
Setting: *The same*
At rise: **Johnny** *is seated upon a barstool, checking his gun.* **Gabe** *exits to kitchen.* **Machine Dog** *appears wearing a shabby military uniform.*

Machine Dog: I don't work at the garage no more, brother.

Johnny: You jive. You don't know nothin' else.

Machine Dog: They's other work to be done. They's other mo' important things to be worked on and fixed. Like my black brothers. They needs fixin' bad. Tha's when I got to thinkin' a you, Brother Williams.

Johnny: Yea, well you can just kick them farts at somebody else.

Machine Dog: On yo' feet, mothahfuckah!

*(**Johnny** comes to his feet militarily. **Machine Dog** presents a Nazi-like salute.)*

By the powers invested in me by the brothers I hereby deliver to you the edick!

*(**Johnny** and **Machine Dog** give each other some skin. **Machine Dog** goes back to his salute.)*

Brother Williams. The brothers have jus' sennunced an' condemned you to death. Now, repeat after me. I have been chosen to be the nex' brother to live on in the hearts an' min's'a the enemy host.

Johnny: I have been chosen to be the nex' brother to live on in the hearts an' min's'a the enemy host.

Machine Dog: My duty will be to ha'nt they cripple an' sore min's.

Johnny: My duty will be to ha'nt they cripple an' sore min's.

Machine Dog: I will cling to the innermos' closets'a they brains an' agonize them.

Johnny: I will cling to the innermos' closets'a they brains an' agonize them.

Machine Dog:
(Breaks his salute and gives an aside.)
Maniacks though they is already!
(He goes back into his salute.)
The more they will try to cas' me out, the mo' they torment will be.

Johnny: The more they will try to cast me out, the more they torment will be!

Machine Dog: Se la an' ayman!

*(**Machine Dog** shakes **Johnny**'s hand.)*

444   CHARLES GORDONE

You will have plen'y'a he'p, Brother Williams. All them brothers that went before you an' all them tha's comin' after you.

Johnny: I gladly accept the condemnashun, Gen'ral Sheen. Tell the brothers I won't let 'em down. Tell 'em I look forward to meetin' 'em all in par'dise.

Machine Dog: Se la! An' ayman!

> (They salute each other.)

Johnny: Se la an' ay-man!

> (**Machine Dog** goes into kitchen as **Judge Bolton** and two plainclothesmen, **Cappaletti** and **Harry**, enter.)

Bolton: This is the man, Al!

> (**Cappaletti** flashes his badge.)

Cappaletti: Cappaletti. Vice squad.

Johnny: Big deal!

Cappaletti: Judge Bolton, here. His daughter was picked up this afternoon.

Johnny: So what?

Cappaletti: She tried to solicit this officer here.

Johnny: What's that got to do with me?

Cappaletti: Said she was workin' for you.

Johnny: Tha's a lie. Tha's a goddam lie. Lemme hear her say that to my face.

Cappaletti: Plenty of time for that.

Johnny: What the hell you tryin' to pull, Bolton?

Cappaletti: Now, why would the Judge wanna pull anything on you, Johnny?

Johnny: He—he don't want his daughter seein' me. 'Cause I'm a Nigger. I'll lay odds she don't know nothin' about this.

Cappaletti: Go get Miss Bolton, Harry.

> (**Harry** moves to street doors.)

Johnny: Hurry, Harry!

> (**Harry** grins. Exits.)

Cappaletti: By the way. Ain't you the guy this girl killed herself about a few days ago? She was a call girl?

Johnny: Tell you like I tole them other fuzzys. What she did was her own business.

Cappaletti: Just the same you kin see how we kin believe Miss Bolton's story.

> (**Harry** leads **Mary Lou** into bar. **Cappaletti** seats her.)

Now, Miss Bolton. We'll ask you again. Who did you say you was workin' for when you was picked up?

Mary Lou: I—I . . .

Cappaletti: Speak up, Miss Bolton. We can't hear you.

Mary Lou: Daddy, I . . .

Bolton: All you have to do is identify him. Is he the man?

> (**Cappaletti** puts his hand on **Mary Lou**'s head.)

Take your hands off her!

> (**Harry** laughs.)

Mary Lou! Is he or isn't he?

Mary Lou:

> (Forces herself to face **Johnny**.)

NO PLACE TO BE SOMEBODY 445

Yes! This is the man! Johnny Williams! I was working for him!

(**Mary Lou** *rushes from bar followed by* **Harry**.)

Johnny: Dirty lyin' bitch.

Bolton: Now see here, Williams!

Cappaletti: You're gonna have to come with me, Johnny.

Johnny: What is this, a pinch? You gonna book me? I'm gonna call my lawyer!

Cappaletti: Shut up! You're not callin' nobody right now. Let's go.

Bolton: Just a minute, Al. I want a few words with him before you take him down.

Cappaletti: Okay, Frank, but make it snappy.

Bolton: Williams, I've worked too long and too hard to get where I am. I'm giving you one last chance to give back those notes and tape. If you don't, it's on the bottom of the woodpile for you. Even if I have to sacrifice my own daughter to do it. I want that file.

Johnny: Okay, Judge. Okay. You win.

(**Johnny** *goes behind bar. Brings out paperbag.* **Judge** *checks it. Nods to* **Cappaletti** *and exits.*)

Cappaletti: All right, Johnny. All of a sudden the Judge wants me to forget the whole thing. Lucky we didn't get you down to the precinct. Would have busted you up on general principles.

(**Cappaletti** *exits. Quickly* **Johnny** *puts his revolver into his back pocket. Goes behind the bar.*)

Johnny: Better split, Gabe. While the gittin's good.

Gabe: Don't think so, John. I'm gonna stick aroun'.

Johnny: Suit yo'self!

(*Doors open.* **Johnny** *goes for his gun.* **Sweets Crane** *enters. He is practically in tatters. He carries a shopping bag. Goes to table and begins to take out various articles of food. He coughs and rubs his hands together.*)

Sweets: I got fried chicken! Ham! Candied yams! Got me some hot chit'lin's! Blackeyed peas an' rice! Cornbread! Mustard greens an' macaroni salit!

(*Coughs.*)

Top ev'thing off I got me'a thermos full'a—full'a—lemme see now. How'd my gran'daddy used to call it? Chassy San'burg coffee!

(*Laughs.*)

An' a big chunk'a pee-kan pie. Y'all fellas is welcomed to join me.

Johnny: Wouldn't touch it if it was blessed by the pope!

Sweets: Well, now tha's a dam shame. 'Member when I couldn't pull you away from my cookin'.

Gabe: You don't mind if I join him, do you, John?

Johnny: Be my guest.

Sweets: He'p yo'se'f, young fella. They's plen'y here. Have some'a these here chit'lin's!

Gabe: Ain't never had none before.

Sweets: Then let this be the day you start.

(**Gabe** *takes a sniff.*)

Go 'head! Go 'head! You don't eat the smell.

Gabe: Lemme ask you sump'm, Sweets?

Sweets: Hope I kin answer it.

Gabe: How come you took my watch an' wallet?

Sweets: Son, all my life I been one kind'a thief or 'nother. It's jus' in me. 'Course I don't have to steal. But I steals for the pure enjoyment of it. Jus' the other day I stole a rat'la from a baby.

> *(Laughs.)*

When you steals for fun it don't matter who you steals from!

> *(Goes into his pocket. Comes up with* **Gabe**'s *watch and wallet.)*

Gabe: It's all here!

Sweets: 'Co'se it is! Gave the baby back his rat'la too.

Johnny: You ain't gon' make the white man's heaven this way.

Sweets: The Lawd died 'tween two thieves.

Maffucci:

> *(Enters with* **Louie**.*)*

Wouldn't listen to me, would you, Johnny Cake?

Johnny: What Pete say? Give a jig a half'a chance . . .

Sweets: This the fella work for big fat Pete, Sonny Boy?

Maffucci: What's it to ya, Pops? You an' this other joker better get the hell out'a here before you catch cold.

Sweets: I ain't never got up from a meal in my life 'fore I was finished . . .

Maffucci: Look, Pops! Don't make me have to . . .

> *(Glances at food.)*

What's that? Macaroni salad you got there?

Sweets: Matter fack it is!

Maffucci:

> *(Dips into it.)*

Ummm! Not bad. Who made it?

Sweets: I did.

Maffucci: No kiddin'? Knew it didn't taste like dela-ga-tes. Mama used to make macaroni salad.

Sweets: Have'a piece'a my fried chicken to go with it.

Johnny: If Zerroni could see you now, Footch.

Maffucci: How's that, Johnny Cake?

Johnny: Tha's the great Sweets Crane you eatin' with.

Maffucci: Pops, here? He's Sweets Crane?

Sweets: What's lef' of me.

Maffucci: You'd'a made out better as a cook, Pops. Mama couldn't beat that macaroni salad!

Sweets:

> *(Produces* **Maffucci**'s *watch.)*

I think this b'longs to you.

Maffucci: My watch! Gees! I been lookin' all over for it. Pops, you copped my watch.

> *(Laughs.)*

How come you're givin' it back? This watch is worth a lotta bread.

Sweets: Figger you need it wors'n I do.

Maffucci: Say, Johnny Cake, you sure Pops here is Sweets Crane?

Johnny: You don't know how much I wish he wasn't.

Maffucci: Too bad Johnny didn't learn a lesson after what happened to you, Pops. Gotta give him credit though. Takes a lotta balls to try to put the bleed on Pete Zerroni.

Sweets: You was tryin' to blackmail ol' big fat Pete, Sonny Boy?

Johnny: What the hell. Couldn't pull it off. Don't matter much now.

Maffucci: That's where you're wrong, Johnny Cake. Matters a helluva lot to me. Pete now, he's willin' to forget the whole thing. Says the trick is not to take you jigs too serious. I can't do nothin' like that, Johnny. Don't look good on my record.

Johnny: What you gonna do about it, Footch?

> (**Maffucci** *quickly pulls his gun. Levels it at* **Johnny**. *Backs to street doors. Locks them. Pulls shades. Takes a large sign from his pocket. It reads, "CLOSED." He puts it on the bar in front of* **Johnny**.)

The sign in both hands, Johnny Cake.

> (**Johnny** *slowly picks up sign.*)

Pops, you an' that other joker stay put!

> (**Maffucci** *nods to* **Louie** *who moves behind* **Sweets** *and* **Gabe**. **Johnny** *starts to tear sign.*)

Ah-ah! I want you to lick that sign an' paste it right up there on the door. Start lickin', Johnny Cake!

> (**Johnny** *begins to wet sign with his tongue.*)

That's it! Wet it up a little more! That's enough! Now start walkin' real careful like!

> (**Johnny** *moves to door with sign.*)

Now, paste it up there!

> (**Johnny** *does so.*)

Now, back up! Real slow!

> (**Johnny** *backs up.* **Maffucci** *seats* **Johnny** *on a barstool.*)

Sweets: You don't have to do that, Sonny Boy.

> (*Goes to the door with knife he has been eating with.*)

You don't have to do nothin' like that.

> (*He pulls the sign from the window and tears it up.*)

Maffucci: What are you doin', Pops? Look, if you don't want hi-call-it to get hit . . .

Johnny: Keep out'a this, Sweets. This is my game.

Sweets: Not any more, it ain't. You don't have to do nothin' like that.

> (*Advances to* **Maffucci**.)

Maffucci: What'a ya, crazy, Pops? Put that ax away.

Johnny: Lay out of it, Sweets. Lay out of it, I said!

Maffucci: I'm warnin' you, Pops! Take another step an' . . .

> (**Sweets** *lunges at* **Maffucci** *as* **Maffucci** *fires. Knife penetrates* **Maffucci's** *heart.* **Johnny** *kills* **Louie**. *Whirls and fires three shots into* **Maffucci**. *Rushes to* **Sweets**.)

Johnny: Goddamit, Sweets! I tole you I could handle it!

Gabe: I'll call a doctor!

Sweets: Fuck a doctor! Cain't you see I'm dead?

    (Coughs. Winces in pain.)

Lissen to me, Sonny Boy! You—you gotta promise me one thing . . .

Johnny: What is it, Sweets?

Sweets: The—the will! It's here in—in my pocket.

    *(**Johnny** finds will.)*

If—if you git out'a this. Promise you'll git straightened out.

    *(He grabs **Johnny**'s arm.)*

Promise!

Johnny: I—I promise.

Sweets: Swear!

Johnny: Yeah! Yeah! I swear, Sweets!

Sweets: Git—git rid'a the—the Ch-Charlie fever—

    *(**Sweets** goes limp.)*

Gabe: He did it for you, John . . .

Johnny: Look, Gabe. We gotta git our story together. When the fuzz gits here we gotta have us a story.

Gabe: We tell 'em the truth, John . . .

Johnny: What you say?

Gabe: We tell the police the truth!

Johnny: Shit. The truth is I'm alive! I got a copy'a that file an' Sweets' will.

Gabe: But you tole Sweets you was gonna throw them ideas out'a your head.

Johnny: Come on, man, you didn't think I meant that shit, did you?

Gabe: With his last dyin' breath, you gave that ol' man your word. You swore.

Johnny: What good is anybody's word to that ol' bastard? He's dead an' cain't remember.

Gabe: You are mad.

Johnny: I'm goin' ahead with my plans.

    (He holds up will.)

An' he's still gon' help me do it.

Gabe: Naw, naw! That ain't the way it's s'pose to be!

Johnny: You in this as deep as I am. Its our word ag'inst these dead turkeys. You gave me back that file, remember?

Gabe: That's where I got off. I ain't got no stomach for this personal war you got ag'inst the white man.

Johnny: It's your war too, Nigger. Why cain't you see that? You wanna go on believin' in the lie? We at war, Gabe! Black ag'inst white.

Gabe: You're wrong, John. You're so goddam wrong.

    *(**Johnny** picks up gun. Puts it into **Gabe**'s hand.)*

Johnny: Take this gun in yo' han'. Feel that col' hard steel. Bet you ain't never held a heater in yo' han' like that in yo' life. Well, you gon' have to, Gabe. They gon' make you do it. 'Cause we at war, Gabe. Black ag'inst white.

Gabe: I—I don't wanna—kill—you . . .

NO PLACE TO BE SOMEBODY   **449**

Johnny: You ain't got the guts! You wanna believe you kin sell papers an' become President! You're a coward, Gabe! A lousy, yellow, screamin' faggot coward!

> *(Enraged,* **Gabe** *fires at* **Johnny.** **Johnny** *tumbles backward and then forward into* **Gabe's** *arms.* **Gabe** *eases* **Johnny** *to the floor.* **Johnny** *goes limp.* **Gabe** *weeps softly.* **Machine Dog** *enters.)*

Gabe:

> *(Startled.)*

Who're you? Where did you come from?

Machine Dog: The brothers call me Machine Dog! It is written: "He that slays a true brother, he hisse'f shall howsomever be perished!"

Gabe: He made me kill him! He . . .

> *(During* **Machine Dog's** *speech,* **Gabe** *takes gun. Wipes it off. Places it in* **Johnny's** *hand. Covers* **Johnny** *with tablecloth. Exits.)*

Machine Dog: Hush yo' lyin', trait-ious tongue! Ver'ly, ver'ly, I says into you! You has kilt all them li'l innusunt cherbs'a the ghetto! Them li'l rams who been hatin' 'thorty eb'm from the cradle! All them holy de-lin-cunts who been the true creators'a unsolved thef's an' killin's! You has slewn an' slaughtered them young goateed billygoats who been dedcated to that sanctified an' precious art'a lootin' the destruction'a private public poverty! You has hung an' lynched the black angels'a color who went by that high code'a rooftops an' been baptised in the stink of urine scented hallways! You has burnt an' melted down a million switchblade knives an' razors an' broke preshus bottles'a communion upon the empty white-paved streets'a the enemy host! An' lef' the brothers thirsty an' col' to bang the doors'a the guilty white samaritan! You has crushed the very life fum black an' profane souls! Hordes'a un-re-gen-rants! An' smashed the spirit an' holy ghost fum rollers an' dancers who founded they faith on black, human sufferin'! Burnt an' tortured souls who knew th'ough the power of love that they trials an' trib'lashuns could not be leg'slated away by no co't, no congruss, not eb'm God Hisse'f! You has scortched an' scalded them black Moheekans an' stuffed them in the very stoves they cooked on! Se la! An' ay-man!

> *Blackout*

SCENE 4

> **Gabe** *enters dressed as a woman in mourning. A black shawl is draped over his head.*

Gabe: Like my costume? You like it? You don't like it! I know what I am by what I see in your faces. You are my mirrors. But unlike a metallic reflection, you will not hold my image for very long. Your capacity for attention is very short. Therefore, I must try to provoke you. Provoke your attention. Change my part over and over again. I am rehearsing at the moment. For tomorrow, I will go out amongst you, "The Black Lady in Mourning." I will weep, I will wail, and I will mourn. But my cries will not be heard. No one will wipe away my bitter tears. My black anguish will fall upon deaf ears. I will mourn a passing! Yes. The passing and the ending of a people dying. Of a people dying into that new life. A people whose identity could only be measured by the struggle, the dehumanization, the degradation they suffered. Or allowed themselves to suffer perhaps. I will mourn the ending of those years. I will mourn the death of a people dying. Of a people dying into that new life.

Blackout
The End